INTEREST RATE MODELLING

WILEY SERIES IN FINANCIAL ENGINEERING

INTEREST RATE MODELLING

Jessica James and Nick Webber

JOHN WILEY & SONS, LTD

Chichester • New York • Weinheim • Brisbane • Singapore • Toronto

Other Wiley Editorial Offices

John Wiley & Sons, Inc., 605 Third Avenue,
New York, NY 10158-0012, USA

Wiley-VCH Verlag GmbH, Pappelallee 3
D-69469 Weinheim, Germany

John Wiley & Sons Ltd, 33 Park Road, Milton,
Queensland 4064, Australia

John Wiley & Sons (Asia) Pte Ltd, 2 Clementi Loop #02-01,
Jin Xing Distripark, Singapore 129809

John Wiley & Sons (Canada) Ltd, 22 Worcester Road,
Rexdale, Ontario M9W 1L1, Canada

Library of Congress Cataloging-in-Publication Data

James, Jessica.
　Interest rate modelling / Jessica James and Nick Webber.
　　p. cm. — (Wiley series in financial engineering)
　Includes bibliographical references and index.
　ISBN 0–471–97523–0 (cloth : alk. paper)
　1. Interest rates—Mathematical models. I. Webber, Nick. II. Title. III. Series.

HG1621.J35 2000
332.8′2—dc21　　　　　　　　　　　　　　　　　　99–087500

British Library Cataloguing in Publication Data

A catalogue record for this book is available from the British Library

ISBN 0–471–97523–0

Typeset in 9.5/11.5pt Times by Laser Words, Madras, India
Printed and bound in Great Britain by Biddles Ltd, Guildford and King's Lynn
This book is printed on acid-free paper responsibly manufactured from sustainable forestry,
in which at least two trees are planted for each one used for paper production.

To Ken Zetie

For J A L

Contents

Foreword

In the last 25 years the history of finance has undergone one of its most radical transformations. The turning point, not surprisingly, can be placed *circa* 1973, with the
publication of Black and Scholes' seminal paper, and with Merton's work. The idea
underpinning their risk-neutral valuation framework was not necessarily the most original, path-breaking or innovative of the century. It produced, nonetheless, a watershed:
the 'dismal science' (or, rather, its applied hand-maid, finance) was for the first time
capable of producing predictions (about prices) of accuracy comparable with that attainable in the hard physical sciences. At the risk of simplifying matters, one can say that
up until 1973 the task of determining the fair price of an asset (the bread-and-butter of
asset pricing theory) was mainly tackled by means of the so-called equilibrium approach.
This, in turn, required the specification of a whole array of theoretical constructs such
as the representative market agent, the utility function, the axioms of preference or the
market price of risk. All these quantities promised, in principle, to provide an answer to
some very fundamental questions in finance, but, to say the least, did not recommend
themselves for ease of measurability. The results obtained following this route therefore
often gave a conceptually rich and powerful qualitative insight, but very little in the way
of robust quantitative predictions. Even Markowitz's more 'scientific' portfolio theory
would in practice stumble against the difficulty of estimating the immense (by those
days' standards, at least) correlation matrices needed to produce testable answers. The
reigning paradigm, up until 1973, was therefore that of the equilibrium economy, where
prices and interest rates would be determined endogenously by enforcing the axioms of
preference, choosing one of the many possible utility functions and imposing equilibrium amongst the market agents. The ultimate prize was enticing: the approach would
allow a true *explanation* of the prices observed in the market, rather than a mere description. The difficulties in obtaining quantitatively believable results, however, were no
less substantial.

Merton, and Black and Scholes effectively proposed a more modest research paradigm,
but, arguably, a more fruitful one: rather than explaining the prices of all the assets in
the economy, they would attempt to account for the prices of one set of assets (say, the
options) in terms of the prices of another set (the 'underlying' securities). They would
offer, in other words, *relative* rather than *absolute* pricing. The conceptual climb-down
was important, and goes some of the way towards explaining the scepticism, if not
outright hostility, with which the new approach was greeted. Perhaps the more telling

indication of this attitude can be taken to be Summer's comment, who described arbitrage theory as 'ketch-up economics'.[1] Despite this less-than-friendly initial reception, arbitrage pricing soon began to win over converts and friends, ready to trade off the enticing but elusive explanatory power of general equilibrium approaches for the predictive power of the new arbitrage technique.

The shift in emphasis from an explanation of the price formation process in the whole economy (general-equilibrium pricing theory) towards the achievement of relative (arbitrage) pricing was to have deep and lasting consequences. If we fast-forward to, approximately, the mid-to-late 1990s, the reader of a standard textbook in option pricing theory might well have been forgiven for asking if anybody still alive remembered what general equilibrium meant. At most one would find a cursory mention of the market price of risk, more often than not in the context of the Radon–Nikodým derivative and of the change of measure associated with Cameron–Girsanov's theorem. In other words, the only reason for introducing the market price of risk seemed to be to show how to get rid of it. Virtually all option pricing seemed to have been reduced to the important but special case of complete markets, where pure no-arbitrage arguments are sufficient to collapse the infinity of possible martingale measures to a single one. Given this state of affairs, practitioners became very lazy in distinguishing between risk neutrality, absence of arbitrage, absence of risk aversion, et cetera. These subtle concepts, however, become crucial when markets can no longer be assumed to be complete, for instance when there might not be traded instruments capable, even in principle, of reproducing exactly the option payoff.

To appreciate the 'mental short-cut' that the complete-market/relative-pricing paradigm allowed, one can start by noting that one does *not* need risk-neutral investors for the Black and Scholes formula to apply.[2] Whatever their risk-aversion, it will not enter their appraisal of the value of the option because the variance of returns of the *option plus the replicating portfolio* can be made exactly zero. Whenever one is dealing with a diffusive process for an underlying tradable asset, and one constructs a tree, or performs a Monte Carlo simulation, to price a simple option, one should therefore have, in the back of one's mind, a 'parallel' tree or simulation, in which the accompanying replicating hedge is evolved. Strictly speaking, it is only the *combined* portfolio (option plus replicating strategy) that will have zero variance, but one often takes a short-cut: one dispenses with the construction of the 'parallel' tree, recognises that the variance of return of the option *by itself* is now anything but zero, but still obtains the correct result by 'pretending' that the risk aversion of the investor (rather than the variance of the overall portfolio) is zero. The advantage is that one can now dispense altogether with the parallel tree built 'in the back of one's mind' containing the perfect hedges.

When, however, the specification of the option payoff is such that a perfect hedge cannot be put in place, this convenient sleight of hand is no longer possible. A partial hedge might still be possible, but one cannot rest assured that one will be able to match exactly the option payoff on a path-by-path basis. The variance of the portfolio now

---

[1] Quoted in Nicholas Dunbar, *Inventing Money*, John Wiley (1999). The 'real' economy, according to Summer, would be about how tomatoes end up in the ketch-up sauce.

[2] Some of these observations have been taken and adapted from my *Volatility and Correlation*, John Wiley (1999).

becomes crucial, together with the risk aversion of the investor. Valuing the option by itself (without the partially hedging strategy one has chosen) no longer makes sense, since there no longer exists the perfectly hedging portfolio 'somewhere in the back of one's mind'. At the same time, since there is no such thing as *the* perfect hedging strategy, there is no single hedging portfolio: the trader will obtain one overall variance of return for every partial hedge he might dream up.

As a consequence, invoking absence of arbitrage does not, in general, by itself lead to a unique option price. This identification constitutes a very special case, which applies only when a perfectly replicating strategy can be put together. The power of this complete-market assumption, however, is such that it has been unquestionably enforced in fields well removed from the original Black and Scholes setting. This intellectual attitude has been responsible for some peculiar choices in option modelling: jump processes, for instance, have, until recently, been very much out of favour, on the grounds that, for a random jump amplitude, the financial markets are incomplete. At the same time, risk-neutral replication has almost been invariably accepted without questioning in the case of diffusive processes where the user can only delta hedge. In reality we know that the volatility of the diffusion is neither deterministic, nor known a priori. One can empirically observe that the variance of the replicating portfolio in the presence of a relatively mild mis-match between the realised and the assumed volatility can be much larger than the variance obtained in the case of a jump process if the derivative contract to replicate is vega-hedged using just a couple of plain-vanilla options. The complete-market blinkers, and a relatively arbitrary set of decisions about what constitutes a complete market, have, in this and other cases, proved a hindrance to realistic and effective option modelling.

Should we ditch the complete-market/risk-neutral valuation paradigm? Certainly not: *pace* Summer's, it has been one of the most fruitful research programmes ever to have appeared in finance. What should be realised is that, as option contracts become increasingly complex, the margins for pricing error thinner, and the range of underlying instruments wider, this cosy view of the world is proving increasingly strained. This is exactly where Jessica James and Nick Webber's new book provides a much-needed 'holistic' approach to interest rate modelling: the traditional complete-market arbitrage pricing approach is covered in detail, both from the perspective of short-rate models and using the more modern martingale approach. The general equilibrium approach, however, is given a no less important treatment as well, and such concepts as the price kernel (rarely, if ever, to be found in books on derivatives) are clearly and thoroughly treated. Similarly, I cannot think of any other book where one can find, at the same time, a discussion of the IS–LM Phillips model and of the Brace–Gatarek–Musiela approach. The authors' intention has been not to produce an encyclopaedia of interest rate modelling. Rather, they have given a first, and important, contribution towards a much-needed synthesis between the 'explanatory view' (where the term structure of rates has to be determined endogenously) and the 'descriptive school' (which takes the market prices as an exogenous given). As is always the case with a truly new book, it is easy to point out how things might have been done differently (and, the critic always believes, better). Personally, I might have chosen to give a different emphasis to the various parts of the book, and my choice of what to include might have been somewhat different. Nonetheless, I truly believe that Jessica and Nick's new book has something very important to say, and sincerely hope that more work will be produced in the footsteps of their exciting new book.

Riccardo Rebonato

Head of Market Risk and of the Quantitative Research Centre for the NatWest Group and Visiting Lecturer at Oxford University

London, 19 January 2000

Preface

This book arose from two sources: a series of doctoral lectures given at Aarhus Business School in October 1998 where one of the authors was on sabbatical from the University of Warwick, and practitioner seminars given by both authors over a number of years. The doctoral course attempted to bring together all the main strands of thought in interest rate modelling and implementation, and to provoke fresh research ideas as a consequence of this meshing of concepts. This book attempts to achieve a related objective. It aims to bring to the reader a broad coverage of the main concepts in interest rate modelling and implementation, filtered by the authors' practical familiarity with the area, so that he or she is able to begin to implement models for real or to move on to undertake research in the area. The book is intended to be suitable for use on Masters and Doctoral courses, and may serve as a reference text for more advanced undergraduate and MBA courses.

Those in the field will be able to use this book to assist in understanding and implementing virtually any interest rate model. Practitioners will find advanced implementation and calibration methods and a very full review of existing term structure models. Academics will find expositions of the theoretical underpinnings and discussions on research issues. Much of the material in this book has been previously published only in academic or finance industry journals, or may only have been available in working paper form. There has been a need to make it accessible to a wider audience.

This book is no substitute for practical experience on the trading floor. Valuation of deals has two sides: the mathematics and coding behind the theoretical price calculation, and the practical trading and hedging of the deal. The latter is not part of this book, and indeed is difficult to learn anywhere else than on the job. The judging of bid–offer spreads, liquidity issues, precise dealing times and trickery by fellow dealers will be just as important, in practice, as the speed of a Monte Carlo simulation.

The content reflects the main divisions in the field. Part I is an introduction and an overview of modelling and modelling techniques. It gives an intuitive description of the theoretical background to interest rate modelling, as well as an overview of interest rate instruments in the market. Part II concentrates on interest rate models themselves. All the main categories of model are considered, and popular models are discussed in some detail. Exceptionally, random field models and jump models are described and implementations are illustrated. In Part III we discuss implementation, including recent developments in applications of Monte Carlo methods, lattice methods, and PDE based methods. Part IV looks at estimation problems including using GMM and ML. Calibrating to the yield curve is discussed in detail. We discuss PCA and other implementation issues.

Thanks are due to the participants on the Aarhus Doctoral course, with special thanks to Lynda McCarthy, and to the Aarhus Business School for hosting the course. Staff at the Business School including Tom Engsted, Mette Norgaard, Peter Honore and Jesper Lund are responsible for arranging for the course to happen, and for ensuring it ran smoothly.

Students on the Doctoral programme and on Masters programmes at the University of Warwick have contributed to weeding out errors in the text. Special thanks are due to Grace Kuan and Meng-Lan Yueh, and to Jukka Ahokas for his suggestions and his Latex expertise. Thanks are also due to Abhay Abhyankar, Peter Honore and Martin Hansen of SimCorp A/S, Lynda McCarthy, Peter Mikkelsen, Mark Wong and Cedric Scholtes of the Bank of England for their insightful comments on various portions of the manuscript. Remaining errors are the authors' responsibility.

We would like to thank Tony Steele for the encouragement he has shown to this endeavour from the start, and Warwick Business School for its flexibility in enabling the manuscript to be completed to schedule.

The authors are most grateful to their respective families for their tolerance during the process of writing this book. Without their forbearance and understanding it would not have been possible.

The book was mainly written in Scientific Word, without which the whole enterprise would have been much more difficult.

Portions of Chapter 2, Chapter 16 and Chapter 19 are based on working papers from the University of Warwick ([538], [422], [343], [344]).

PART I

INTRODUCTION TO INTEREST RATE MODELLING

This first part examines fundamental ideas and concepts of interest rate modelling. The ideas introduced here are elaborated upon in later parts.

Chapter 1 is introductory, discussing and defining some basic ideas of interest rates and the markets. It may be skipped by readers already familiar with the field.

Chapter 2 attempts to put interest rate modelling into an historical context. It briefly reviews the history of interest rates, which have existed, in one form or another, as far back as records of human civilisation go.

Chapter 3 introduces interest rates, basic interest rate instruments, and general modelling features. Further features of the financial markets are discussed and simple methods of extracting interest rate data from the market prices are described. The concept of the yield curve is discussed in more detail. Some simple interest rate models are presented and compared.

In Chapter 4 the mathematical theory of underpinning interest rate modelling is introduced. Interest rate models have a statistical formulation; this chapter introduces the key ideas of martingale measure, numeraire, changes of measure, and the rest of the probabilistic framework.

Chapter 5 introduces some basic modelling tools; valuation using PDEs and simulation, estimation, and yield curve stripping. These are all discussed in much greater depth in later chapters.

More useful tools are described in Chapter 6, 'Densities and Distributions', which looks at ways of describing the probability densities produced by different models, and boundary conditions associated with the models. Different models have different boundary conditions; in some the short rate is bounded below at zero, while others allow negative rates. A few models allow the possibility of hyperinflation, where rates shoot off to highly abnormal levels. There are many recent examples of hyperinflation; there have been at least three on the north American continent. Unsurprisingly, allowing the possibility of hyperinflations turns out to significantly affect valuation of interest rate instruments.

1

Introduction to Interest Rates

This chapter looks at some basic concepts of interest rates, interest rate markets, and modelling. We start with an introduction to interest rate behaviour and then examine some key elementary ideas, including hedging. In the third section we briefly discuss the difference between historical and current data, and their relative importance. We then discuss in general terms why interest models are needed and what they might be good for.

1.1 INTEREST RATE BEHAVIOUR

Borrowing is fundamental to economic activity. It is crucially important to be able to understand and manage interest rate risk. Over time, interest rates show an extraordinary range of behaviours. In the UK in the nineteenth century long rates were very stable; short rates were around 2%–8%. In the twentieth century both long and short rates have varied from 2%–17% and have shown spells of very volatile behaviour.

Figure 1.1 shows a time series of daily observations of three-month Libor from 1988 to 1995. What can be said about this time series?

Firstly, it appears to be observations from a jump–diffusion process. Most of the time today's value of Libor is similar to yesterday's, but occasionally there are movements that are significantly larger and which seem to be jumps. For instance, in October 1990 Libor fell from just under 15% to around 13.7%.[1]

Secondly, although the level changes significantly from over 15% to roundabout 7% it does so gradually—systematically would be too strong a word—through time. There also seems to be a tendency to move between levels; from October 1989 to October 1990 rates were around 15%, at around 10%–11% from September 1991 to September 1992, and about 5%–6% from March 1993 to October 1994. Is this a real effect or is this just reading too much into the data? And is the pattern cyclical? At the start of the period rates are rising; after reaching their peak they fall back until at the end of the period they appear to be rising again. Is the pattern about to repeat?

---

[1] This fall was associated with an announcement that sterling was to join the ERM.

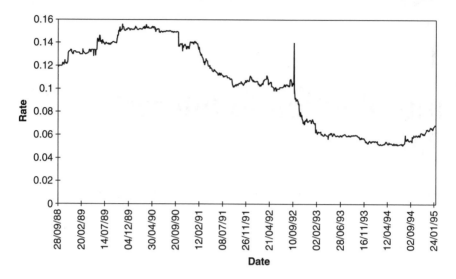

Figure 1.1   Three-month Libor, 1988–1995

Thirdly, there is an odd spike in September 1992. One's first impression is that this may be an error in the data, but it is real. Sterling was forced out of the European exchange rate mechanism in September 1992. On that day, in an attempt to defend the exchange rate, interest rates were temporarily raised, but immediately moved back when sterling left the ERM. While this spike seems extreme, it is nothing compared with what happened in the overnight rates, which traded as high as 150%.

It is clear that there is a huge range of behaviour for an interest rate model of sterling to describe and explain, but this is not the end of the matter. Figure 1.2 shows the UK bank rate (an official rate determined by the Bank of England) since its inception in 1694. Although not a market rate it nevertheless gives an impression of the overall level of rates and also of their volatility. There seem to have been three main phases.

1. An initial period of 150 years when rates remained fairly constant at 4%–5%.
2. A volatile period in the second half of the nineteenth century, up to the 1920s.
3. From the 1950s to today a second very volatile period in which rates have peaked at very high levels.

There are various historical and economic factors that explain some of the behaviour exhibited in the figure. We discuss some aspects of this in Chapters 2 and 11. For the moment we simply note that on the evidence of the figure the behaviour of interest rates may vary significantly over time. The UK has only just emerged from a period of relatively high rates; will rates over the next 10 to 20 years stay at current levels (close to 50 year lows) or will they increase to high levels once more? Many products currently being traded will still be alive in 10 or 20 years, so the question is apposite.

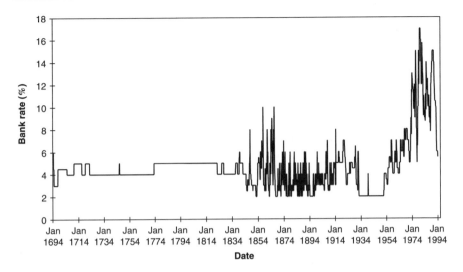

Figure 1.2 UK bank rate, 1694–1994

The occurrence not only of day-to-day fluctuations in interest rates but also of regime shifts from time to time, means that there are huge risks to be managed and controlled. Corporations with debt face a volatile and uncertain payment schedule; funds and others with bond portfolios need to manage their risk to maximise the value of their portfolios and to ensure that the portfolios meet their future obligations as cheaply as possible. There is a demand for tools to control and reduce exposure to interest rate movements. Banks design and construct products for the market place to sell to their clients, and for this they need models and tools to enable them to value and hedge the instruments they have sold.

Asking an interest rate model to cope with all the behaviours displayed in the market is likely to be too demanding. We shall see though that there are workable models that present workable solutions to the problems faced by participants in the market.

1.2 BASIC CONCEPTS

Three ideas are basic to the application of interest rate models: the ideas of present value, of marking to market, and of hedging and hedge ratios. They are elaborated upon in future chapters. For the moment we discuss the concepts in general terms.

1.2.1 Present Value

An interest rate represents a price of intertemporal substitution; given the choice between receiving x now or $1 in one year's time (for sure), what would x have to be for a representative investor to be indifferent between the alternatives? This x is the present value of one dollar received in one year's time. Ignoring default risk, the present value of a future cashflow is the value that the representative investor would accept today in exchange for the future cashflow. This is the value which would have to be invested now, at prevailing interest rates, in order to guarantee the cashflow in the future.

The cost today of receiving one dollar at time t in the future is the discount factor, δ_t, say. The continuously compounded spot interest rate $r(t)$ for time to maturity t satisfies the relationship $e^{-r(t)t} = \delta_t$. When interest rates are positive the discount factor is less than 1. The set of discount factors for all future maturities is called the discount function.

Expressing interest rates as continuously compounded rates or as discount factors is both unambiguous and mathematically tractable. In a world where future cashflows were riskless, and there were no taxes or other costs associated to trade, at any moment of time there is only one discount function, and it is dimensionless. In contrast, market interest rates are quoted in a variety of ways, and interest may be paid at different intervals, making comparisons less easy.

1.2.2   Marking to Market

The marked to market value of a financial instrument or portfolio is its value when it is benchmarked to current market prices. It is an indication of the price that the instrument or portfolio would fetch if sold on the open market, at that moment. Tracking the marked to market value through time indicates whether an instrument has lost or gained value since its inception. Marking to market portfolios is a crucially important part of performance management.

Marking to market a newly created instrument like a swap is just what happens when it is first valued. However, marking an existing instrument to market, one that is part way through its life, is a very different process. An existing swap has less time to run until maturity than it had when it was first created, and rates in the current market environment will be different to those prevailing at its inception. The marked to market value of the deal will change throughout its life, driven by changes to market rates and the diminishing time to maturity. Marking portfolios to market is a concept beloved of regulators, who imagine that this will give an accurate picture of a company's deal portfolio. While in many cases this is undoubtedly true and a useful reminder to the company of exactly where it stands with regard to its portfolio value, it is not always true that the marked to market value is a precise indication of what the portfolio would fetch if sold off. If a portfolio is large, the sell-off itself might change market rates for the worse. Regular marking to market of a large deal portfolio is an intensive use of time and resources.

When an option is bought for insurance purposes any positive value to the option is offset by the value of the loss it was purchased to protect against. In this situation not only the option value but also the value of the underlying insured risk should be marked to market. There may be little point in marking to market just the side of the deal represented by the option value, as some regulatory environments insist.

1.2.3 Hedging

Hedging is a critical part of modern trading, risk management and business. When a simple deal is hedged, a similar or identical offsetting deal is entered into, whose cashflows and potential cashflows are opposed to those of the first deal. The point is to lock in the value of the combined 'deal plus hedge' portfolio, so that thereafter its value is fixed, or earning a fixed rate of return. There are many reasons why it might be desirable to enter into hedging trades.

To Lock in Profit

If a trader puts on a deal which subsequently makes a profit, he or she may wish to ensure that the current happy situation does not disappear. To do this the trader may execute a hedging trade, which precisely cancels out the sensitivity of the deal to any further rate moves. Any cashflows which are uncertain, whose values change with changes in underlying rates, are effectively cancelled out by the hedging trade. Thus, if a deal was zero-valued at inception, and subsequently increases in value until it is worth x dollars, hedging it will ensure that this gain is not lost due to a reversal in the underlying rates which caused the gain in the first place. Of course, the hedge also precludes any further profits. It is the 'quits' answer to the choice 'double or quits'.

To Stop Out Losing Positions

In a similar way to hedging in order to lock in profits, a trader may hedge to stop out losses. If a trade is losing money, it may be hedged, ensuring that no further losses can be incurred. However, this eliminates any chances it has of reversing and coming into profit.

To Lock in Bid–Offer Spread

This is a little different from locking in a profit part way through a deal. If a complex deal is put on, the rates implicitly locked into the deal leave the buyer of the deal with a small negative value; this is the cost of entering the deal. The seller of the deal will hedge the trade at slightly different rates, obtainable in the market, and lock in a small but positive value—the profit on the deal.

To Achieve Specific Sensitivity to a Particular Market Move

A trader may have a view that market rates will change in a certain way—for example, that 10-year rates may rise relative to two-year rates. By entering into a set of trades which partially hedge each other, the trader can end up with a portfolio which will only increase value if the anticipated event occurs. Of course it will lose money if the opposite happens.

To Reduce Risk on a Portfolio

A portfolio of deals may be discovered to have a high sensitivity to a particular underlying market variable. To reduce this sensitivity, and therefore the risk on the portfolio,
a single hedging trade may be entered into which simultaneously hedges all the deals
in the portfolio that contribute to the sensitivity.

1.2.4 Hedge Ratios

The hedge ratios are a set of parameters which characterise the response of a deal to
moves in underlying variables. They are colloquially know as the 'greeks' in the market,
as they are represented by Greek letters. There are five of them; delta (δ), gamma (γ),
vega (v),[2] theta (θ) and rho (ρ).

Delta

The delta of a deal is the sensitivity of the deal value to a change in an underlying
state variable. If the deal value is P and it is sensitive to a rate r, then the delta with
respect to r is

$$\delta = \frac{\partial P}{\partial r}.$$ (1.1)

If the deal is sensitive to rates of several maturities it will have several deltas, one for
each rate. It is common for a deal or portfolio to have its sensitivities represented by a
delta ladder where its deltas are tabulated next to their respective rates.

Deltas are useful in risk management, and essential when hedging deals or deal
portfolios. Delta hedging is the process of reducing to zero the delta on the combined
hedging and deal portfolios, so that the combined portfolio value becomes insensitive to
certain (but perhaps not all) rate changes. The deal or portfolio will be delta neutral for
those rates. Delta hedging is not a 'hedge and forget' hedging strategy. The hedges must
be re-evaluated constantly and the portfolio re-hedged as necessary so that it remains
delta neutral.

Gamma

Gamma is the second derivative of the value of the deal with respect to a change in an
underlying state variable,

$$\gamma = \frac{\partial^2 P}{\partial r^2}.$$ (1.2)

It can be thought of as the delta of delta. While delta may be adjusted by buying or
selling different amounts of the underlying, gamma may only be changed by taking a
position in an option-like instrument.

---

[2] Given the status of an honorary greek by the market.

A gamma hedged portfolio is a delta hedged portfolio that also has the gamma of the combined hedging and deal portfolio equal to zero. Such a portfolio is gamma neutral. A gamma hedged portfolio will tend to require less frequent re-hedging than a portfolio that is only delta hedged.

Vega

Vega is the sensitivity of the deal or portfolio value with respect to a change in volatility. Option-like products have high values in highly volatile markets. If an option is purchased in a quiet market, subsequent increases in volatility will have the effect, all other things remaining equal, of increasing the option value.

Theta

The theta of a portfolio is the rate of change of the value of the portfolio with respect to time. It is also called time decay. For a swap, theta is non-zero because fewer cashflows with shorter maturity times are left as the deal progresses.

Delta and gamma are the most commonly used of the hedge ratios, particularly for interest rate models and products. Vega hedging is also quite frequently employed. Theta has much less theoretical interest.

Rho

The rho of a deal or portfolio is the sensitivity of the portfolio to a change in a particular interest rate. This may be useful for stock options but is redundant for interest rate products.

1.3   INTEREST RATE MARKETS

The interest rate markets today are considerably more complex than at any previous time in history. In the last 30 years a huge variety of different products have arisen and entered into general use. Many advanced concepts, discussed later in this book, have become routinely used. This section discusses some basic features of the interest rate markets.

1.3.1   Yield Curves and Term Structures

The yield curve, or term structure of interest rates, is the set of interest rates for different investment periods, or maturities. Yield curves can display a wide variety of shapes. Typically, a yield curve will slope upwards, with longer term rates being higher, although there are plenty of examples of inverted term structures where long rates are less than short rates.

In the bond markets the yield curve is found from bond data. In the money market the yield curve is derived from the prices of a variety of different types of instrument.

Cash rates provide information about the short term rates, from one week to about 18 months. These are investments or borrowings where the entire sum of interest plus principal is due at the end of the period, with no interim payments.

After cash rates come interest rate futures. These are effectively contracts to lend or borrow for a fixed, short (often three-month) period, starting on certain fixed quarterly dates. The futures rate will change as anticipated rates for that period change. Futures, in many currencies, go out to about three years. For the most liquid currencies they go out as far as four years. Futures rates provide information about the yield curve for this range of maturities.

After about the two-year point, swaps become the dominant instrument. From these it is possible to derive the yield curve until the 10- or 15-year point. After this, government bonds, if available, may be used.[3] Information about the yield curve becomes steadily more sparse as the maturity increases.

The overnight rate is often not included as it is subject to very different pressures and has a very different range of values often uncorrelated to the rest of the curve.

Libor and swap rates for maturities up to 10 years are plotted for three major currencies in Figures 1.3 and 1.4. Figure 1.4 gives rates for 7 April 1999. Figure 1.3 gives rates for five years earlier on 7 April 1994. These plots of market rates are not term structures, but they broadly indicate the level of instantaneous rates.

Rates in DEM and JPY have fallen over the five-year period, spectacularly for the yen, but dollar rates have risen at the short end and fallen at the long end. The dollar

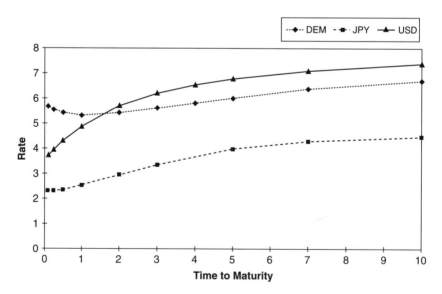

Figure 1.3 Market rates, 7 April 1994: DEM, JPY, USD

---

[3] These must be used with caution since they are usually considered to be default free. Money market instruments have default risk priced in.

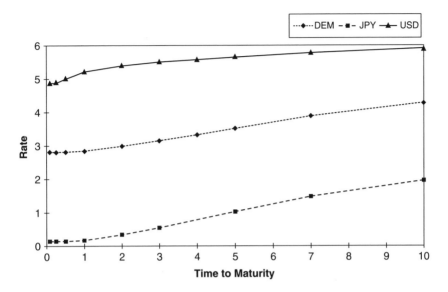

Figure 1.4   Market rates, 7 April 1999: DEM, JPY, USD

1994 curve is classically upward sloping, but the DEM curve is spoon-shaped, downward sloping at the short end before rising towards the long end. By 1999 all three curves are upwards sloping, although the dollar curve is slightly steeper at the short end than the other two.

A variety of shapes and changes need to be described by a successful term structure model.

1.3.2   Fixed and Floating Rate Borrowing

Borrowing may be at a fixed or a floating rate. In fixed rate borrowing the size of coupon payments is fixed in advance. In floating rate borrowing the coupon rate is determined from coupon to coupon by the current value of a reference market rate, such as Libor.

The existence of fixed and floating rate borrowing gave rise to the interest rate swap, now a widely used instrument but unheard of 30 years ago. Swaps were developed because different companies could borrow at different rates in different markets. If Company A is borrowing fixed for five years at $5\frac{1}{2}\%$, but could borrow floating at Libor plus $\frac{1}{2}\%$, and Company B is borrowing floating at Libor plus 1%, but could borrow fixed for five years at $6\frac{1}{2}\%$, then by agreeing to swap streams of cashflows both companies could be better off. A mediating institution would also make money.

Figure 1.5 illustrates this scenario. Company A pays Libor to the intermediary in exchange for fixed at $5\frac{3}{16}\%$. Company B pays the intermediary fixed at $5\frac{5}{16}\%$ in exchange for Libor. Net, Company A is now paying Libor plus $\frac{5}{16}\%$ instead of Libor

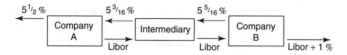

Figure 1.5   Cashflows in an intermediated swap

plus $\frac{1}{2}\%$, Company B is paying fixed at $6\frac{5}{16}\%$ instead of $6\frac{1}{2}\%$, and the intermediary receives fixed at $\frac{1}{8}\%$.

Everyone seems to be better off. Of course there is still differential credit risk; this is the reason why Company B had higher borrowing rates in the first place. It has been partly taken up by the intermediary, who accepted it in return for the money it makes on the spread.

As the swap market developed, intermediate companies looked for matched partners in the swap, but soon started to warehouse the different sides. The agreement to exchange fixed for floating has now become routine, and the spread, from being a sizeable fraction of a percent, has narrowed to a basis point. Swaps are an extremely useful market instrument which have enabled, among other things, the expansion of the UK fixed rate mortgage market.

1.3.3   Zero-Valued Instruments

A swap, and many other financial instruments, has zero value at inception. The pattern of cashflows or possible future cashflows need not be trivial, and although initially zero-valued an instrument may acquire non-zero value in the future. For example, an interest rate swap is always arranged so that at inception the present value of the stream of fixed cashflows is equal the present value of the stream of floating cashflows. To the intermediary, the swap has zero value (apart from any bid–offer spreads). After inception, as rates change, the swap will no longer be zero-valued.

The sum paid for an instrument, its price, is called the premium. The premium on a zero-valued instrument is zero.

1.3.4   Options

Most instruments are not zero valued. These include many option-like instruments. An option is the right, but not the obligation, to buy or sell an instrument (like a stock or a bond) in the future at a price agreed now. This payout is asymmetric—it is possible to receive a non-zero positive payout, if rates move in the right way, but it is not possible to have a negative payout; an option always has positive value. The most common interest rate option products are caps, floors and swaptions.

1.3.5 Exchanges

Exchanges are well established organisations for buying and selling all kinds of commodities and derivatives. They work by establishing an arena where trading may take place. In some order-driven systems, orders to buy or sell at a certain price are placed with the exchange, and when orders are matched, a trade takes place. The exchange takes the bid–offer spread, as it will buy more cheaply than it will sell, and makes money for itself. Other quote-driven systems have traders within the exchange offering to buy or sell at various prices. They do not have to wait until they are perfectly matched—they can take on one-sided trades, and wait for a match. Of course, this entails a risk. A commission is paid to the exchange by the traders.

Many exchanges use a clearing house. A clearing house facilitates the settlement of contracts and can significantly reduce a counterparty's exposure to credit risk. Those who buy and sell at the exchange have a contract not with another market counterparty, but with the clearing house. The clearing house interposes itself between the market participants. If the counterparty with whom a trade is made defaults, this does not affect the other party's contract with the clearing house.

Having a clearing house cuts out the problem of judging the credit quality of a counterparty—it is replaced by the credit quality of the clearing house, which is usually very good indeed. This high credit quality leads to fast deals and narrow bid–offer costs. Quote-driven systems are usually faster and easier to obtain deals with than order-driven systems.

In order for the exchange to be efficient, it is necessary for it to use only standard deals. Thus for a commodity, only multiples of a standard quantity may be bought or sold. Similarly, interest rate futures come in standard lots. Options are only available in certain sizes and the strike prices of the options will be standardised in some way. Exchange traded contracts can be a somewhat inflexible method of dealing. In addition, some exchanges will not accept deals over a certain size.

At all exchanges[4] a counterparty is required, before he or she may enter into a contract with the exchange, to post a sum of money to the exchange, called the initial margin. This is held by the exchange in case the deal loses money and the counterparty defaults. If the deal does start to lose money the exchange may require the counterparty to post an additional margin called the variation margin, in case the potential loss is greater than what is in the margin account. There will usually be a nuisance amount, defined as the sum by which the amount owed and the amount in the account can differ without the exchange calling for more or returning some—it would be too onerous to keep changing the margin amount every time the market moved.

Many exchange traded contracts are marked to market. A futures contract, for instance, is an agreement to make a future purchase at a price agreed today. At the end of each day's trading the contract is closed out and replaced by a fresh contract at the day's closing futures price. The difference in the prices of the two contracts is credited (debited) from the owners' margin accounts. The advantage in doing this is that if the

---

[4] Although a clearing house is often an organisation separate from the exchange, we shall refer to an exchange as if it incorporated a clearing house.

price of an underlying changes by a large amount in between entering the contract and the delivery date, rather than having to pay up a large lump sum on the delivery date, a sequence of smaller payments has been made, and at any time the counterparty on the losing side can close out the position to cut their loss.

Exchanges often settle contracts on margin. At the contract's settlement date the owner may not have to take physical delivery of the underlying. Instead the exchange settles by making a cash payment (or withdrawal) into the margin account, equal to the difference between the agreed price and the actual price on the delivery date. Some contracts require physical delivery of the underlying. All but a small proportion of these contracts are usually closed out prior to the settlement date.

1.3.6   Market Efficiency

A market is efficient if all participants, buyers and sellers, have access to all necessary price-sensitive information; prices in an efficient market are 'correct' in that they reflect all available information.[5] If the market is liquid, then prices accurately reflect true underlying values. Prices change when news arrives, but price changes will be unanticipated.

Every interest rate model used in the market assumes that the market is efficient.[6] In so far as a market fails to be efficient then an interest rate model will fail to explain prices. In practice it may sometimes occur that some participants have information before the rest of the market, but it is not possible to expect to be routinely ahead of the market in this sense. Trading models, mentioned briefly in Section 1.5, may try to second guess market behaviour and as such attempt to exploit market inefficiencies, but their success is moot.

1.4   HISTORICAL AND CURRENT DATA

An historical data set is a set of rates or prices covering some past period, for instance a set of interest rates of different maturities for the last few years. Current data is more like a snapshot; a set of prices and rates observed now. What 'current' means depends on the situation. For daily valuation purposes, the closing rates on the day may well be acceptable as 'current' for several hours. For a trader in a fast moving market, however, rates two minutes old may no longer be current.

1.4.1   Forecasting Future Rates

Current and historical data are often used to try to forecast future prices or rates. For instance, the three-month rate one month forward is sometimes used as a predictor of the three-month Libor rate in one month's time. Instruments with option properties can

---

[5] There are precise definitions of efficiency of various degrees, but the definition here catches the intuition behind the concept.

[6] A few theoretical models incorporate asymmetric information amongst market participants.

be used to obtain predictions of future realised volatilities. Cross market multicurrency products contain implied correlations that are sometimes used as predictors of future realised correlations.

Can these forecasts be accurate? Can the three-month rate one month forward actually be an accurate indicator of what the three-month rate will be in one month's time? The answer is no—there is little connection between forecast rates and volatilities and actual rates and future realised volatilities. Forecasts will be biased, in that on average the actual value of the future rate or volatility will not equal the forecast for that rate or volatility. For an intuitive explanation, consider the case of an upwardly sloping yield curve, and its implications for a rate like a three-month rate. If forward rates predict future spot rates, this yield curve is predicting that the three-month rate will initially rise and then flatten off; the forecast is that the yield curve will rise, a prediction wrong as often as it is right. The only consistent self-sustaining curve is a flat one, with all rates equal—which is rarely seen in the market.

Forecasts generally have little or no predictive power. A possible exception to this is when the market holds consistent expectations about future rates. The only recent example was as European currencies moved towards currency union. Rates across Europe were widely expected to move until they were similar to German rates. Forward rates did indeed move to align themselves with this expectation. This type of situation is however extremely rare, and in general the belief that forward rates predict the future is pure myth.

1.4.2 Historical and Current Valuation

In a liquid market, where prices are regularly updated and all quoted instruments are actually tradable, there is no confusion about which data to use for valuation. Current, liquid data must be used, and if historical data are substituted it is overwhelmingly likely that it will result in inconsistent prices that can be arbitraged against. However, in a highly illiquid market, such as an emerging market in a crisis situation, it may be that historical data are more reliable. However, such an extreme situation would have to be evaluated on an individual basis.

One calibrates by fitting to existing 'good' prices. This will include fitting to instruments that define the current term structure; bonds in the bond market, and Libor and swaps in the money markets. In the money markets one may also attempt to fit to liquid cap and swaption prices.

It is still important to look at historical data. If parameter estimates from historical and current data are systematically out of line, then one may be inclined to investigate the cause.

1.5 USES OF INTEREST RATE MODELS

How then can current market data be exploited and its information content extracted? One needs an interest rate model to provide a quantitative framework for describing interest rate movements and valuing and hedging interest rate products.

1.5.1 The Purpose of Interest Rate Models

Ultimately, the purpose of interest rate modelling is to understand interest rate behaviour. By fitting a model to available interest rate data, we would like to discover the dynamics of interest rates and the way that interest rates and derivative prices relate together, both to understand them and enable us to price and hedge interest rate products.

It would be desirable to use models to predict future movements in prices or rates. It is somewhat unfortunate, then, to realise that no interest rate model comes close to achieving this goal. Despite the enormous amount of research in banks and universities that has gone into interest rates, reflected in this book, there is no reliable method of accurately predicting tomorrow's or next week's interest rates.

Interest rate processes, while possibly less glamorous than the motion of stars in the heavens or the symmetries of elementary particles, are, in their own way, just as difficult to model. Indeed, not only are they complex by nature, they are influenced by the very models which attempt to contain them. Any model of any financial variable which allowed accurate predictions to be made would, if widely available, radically change the nature of the variable it had previously modelled, as different market participants tried to cash in.

Although the models discussed in this book cannot be used to accurately predict daily ups and downs we can certainly create models which describe distributional properties of interest rate movements. Interest rate models are generally statistically based; they do not attempt to give precise forecasts, but instead describe statistical properties like distribution width and shape, or the likelihood of reaching certain levels. By knowing the distributional properties of interest rate movements, under certain conditions, it becomes possible to find the values of interest rate derivatives as expected discounted values. Financial instruments may be reliably valued and hedged. This brings liquidity to the market, enabling the entire industry to operate.

This is not to say that people do not put effort into developing trading models that attempt to forecast future rates. Indeed, some of them may well succeed, at least for a time. But by their nature such models are not publishable; they lose their value once they become widely known. We do not discuss them in this book.

Another spin-off use for valuation models is risk management. Parameters which are modelled for pricing purposes are those which are useful for managing the risk of a portfolio, for determining its likely range of future values, and for estimating the probability of it losing more than a given amount. Valuation models are widely used for this purpose.

1.5.2 How Good are Interest Rate Models?

It is difficult to compare the performance of different models, and it is difficult to determine which model is the best in any particular circumstances. This is partly because the data which are available to test them are sparse and of poor quality. Under these circumstances a number of contrasting models may each fit the available data. Another reason is the huge variability in market conditions through time. Back-testing a model against each year of the last decade's data is likely to give very different results in each period.

One might think that testing models on available historical data would be a priority. In the markets this is not so. The priority when testing and using interest rate models is pricing and hedging. In this process the model is fitted to available current (not historical) market data. Its floating parameters are adjusted until the model prices for various liquid market instruments like swaps, caps and swaptions, or liquid bonds, match those seen in the market. This is the process of calibration. The calibrated model can then be used either in an interpolatory manner, to find prices for instruments which are similar to those used to calibrate it, or in an extrapolatory manner, to find prices for instruments which are different from those in the calibration set. The former is usually more successful, with the consequence that different models are often used for different instruments.

In the market, models are continuously being refined and tested for their efficiency in fitting current prices; they are less frequently tested for their goodness of fit to historical data. The floating parameters in a model can vary greatly from day to day with little practical consequence.

Although it is difficult to determine which model is the 'best', it is certainly possible to say what general features a good model should have.

Accurate Valuation of Simple Market Instruments

It is essential that a model gives accurate prices for liquid market instruments. Without this feature it would be useless at best, dangerous to use at worst. Traders the world over are very quick to spot when a bank (or other trading institution) is making odd prices and will pounce swiftly, buying and selling until the unfortunate bank realises that it is making a heavy loss.

Ease of Calibration to the Market

This is another important consideration when considering a choice of models. Speed and accuracy of calibration are critical in a fast moving market. The market instruments to which the model is calibrated should be liquid and easily observed.

Robustness

A robust model is highly desirable. The model should perform well in all markets it could be expected to encounter. Some models are unsuitable for some interest rate regimes — for example, a model in which movements in rates were normally distributed might become unusable at near-zero rate values. It would not be a good model to choose if one was pricing Yen swaps in 1998.

Extensibility to New Instruments

To be able to value and hedge new instruments, not previously traded, gives an institution a great advantage in the market. Many exotic instruments cannot be valued by simple models. The drive to value novel instruments is one of the foremost motivations in model development.

Stability of Floating Parameters

Of lesser importance is the ability of a model to keep its floating parameters roughly constant day to day, or varying only slowly. This is useful if data are sparse, when it would not matter so much if certain calibration instruments had not been traded for some time. This property is not so important compared with the other desirable features.

1.5.3   Position Taking

What is the 'correct' price for an instrument? Of course for a liquid instrument it is the market price, the price currently trading. However, what if one found a model whose parameters remained at roughly the same levels through time, although fluctuating from day to day? If parameter values were found to be away from their long-run levels one might be tempted to put on a position, anticipating that when parameter values returned towards their long-run levels the position would acquire positive value. In this case one believes that prices reflecting 'fundamentals'—long-run parameter values—are correct, and that current market values may occasionally get out of line.

While a model with stationary parameters would be highly prized if it was discovered, the risks attendant upon its use would be considerable. One might have to hold a losing position for some time before prices moved in the anticipated direction, and in any case the model could be incorrect. On the other hand, if the model became widely known and adopted it would lose its ability to generate profits.

1.5.4   The Uses of Interest Rate Models

Interest rate models are needed for three main purposes. These are

- *Obtaining prices and hedges*. This is the use to which traders put interest rate models. Less concerned about historical prices, the trader is focused upon accurate current valuation of different financial instruments. This is by far the largest 'user group' for interest rate models.
- *Risk management*. Risk managers use models to simulate market behaviour, with historical parameter values. This may enable them to put limits on the range of future values that a deal or portfolio of deals may have.
- *Explaining interest rate movements*. To be able to explain interest rate movements in terms of an underlying model is of great interest to academics and economists alike. It advances understanding of how economic variables relate to interest rates,

and is of critical importance when interest rate control is a key part of economic policy. It may enhance understanding of the processes, economic and otherwise, which underlie interest rate movements and regimes.

1.6 CONCLUSION

Modelling interest rates will prove to be complex and difficult. We need techniques for

- *Describing interest rate movements*. For this we need the language and tools of stochastic calculus.
- *Obtaining prices from models*. This requires sophisticated theoretical and numerical tools and techniques.
- *Estimating parameters*. Naive methods prove not to work; it is necessary to use sophisticated statistical techniques.

Much effort has been expended in modelling interest rates, but no definitive model has yet been produced, nor is one on the horizon. Interest rate behaviour is not understood. However, for practical purposes, like valuation and hedging, there are good well-founded techniques available. It is these that are the topic of this book.

2

Interest Rates in History

The latter half of the twentieth century has been a time of exceedingly turbulent interest rates. Even by the standards of the current century the decades of the 1970s, 1980s and 1990s have been extreme and atypical. This has coincided, however, with the development of the largest and most liquid interest rate markets the world has ever seen, and with the development of highly sophisticated models of interest rate dynamics.

Do today's conditions represent a permanent change in the market, or are they just a temporary aberration awaiting a future correction? There are many examples in history of idiosyncratic market conditions that have lasted for extended periods before reverting. To what extent are current models merely products of their time? Could they survive a regime shift? What would be the potential costs to banks and institutions using these models if such a shift occurred?

The first section of this chapter briefly reviews historical situations with implications for interest rate modelling today with the intention of providing a perspective on current interest rate models. The second section then looks at specific aspects of interest rate behaviour that have particular relevance for interest rate modelling.

2.1 INTEREST RATES IN MONETARY HISTORY

This section reviews some important episodes from monetary and interest rate history. It is a set of examples from which important criteria for interest rate modelling can be extracted. Starting from the ancient period and the development of coinage, we review some features of commodity money including debasement and seigniorage. Jumping to the present millennium we briefly follow the development of trade and of financial structures including the evolution of bills of exchange and deposit banking. With the introduction of paper money, at first convertible and later inconvertible, we enter the modern period.

During the last 1000 years economic historians have identified four major inflationary periods separated by periods where prices were stable or declining. We briefly describe each in turn before discussing the behaviour of interest rates in these periods.

Much of the material presented here is standard and may found in various texts on monetary history. Sources include Chown (96) [130], Homer and Sylla (91) [285],

Davies (94) [159], Cameron (89) [112] and Williams *et al.* (97) [540]. Additional material is referenced as required. Homer and Sylla (91) [285] is the source for much of the interest rate data, and see also Fischer (96) [217].

2.1.1   The Ancient Period

'Economic activity' has a very long history.[1] There is evidence of international trade dating back to 10 000 BC, which probably took the form of exchanges of goods. It is possible that money existed in this period. Hoards of shells have been discovered from the Red Sea to Switzerland whose uniformity of quality suggests a use as money. (Shells have been extensively used as money up to modern times.)

After 8000 BC, and the start of the agricultural revolution of the Neolithic era, cattle became used as a store of value and as a medium of exchange in some locations (indeed, the Latin 'pecunia', money, is supposed to derive from the word for cattle, pecus). This use persisted to Homeric times in the Eastern Mediterranean.[2] At this stage capital—in the form of cattle, seed, and agricultural equipment—became important. If conditions then are reflected by conditions encountered by anthropologists amongst similar present-day economies, loans of produce and seed would have been commonplace. Typical loans in such societies might be repaid after the harvest, with interest equal to the amount of principle; loan X, receive back $2X$ after the harvest. The implicit interest rate is not necessarily significantly onerous since the underlying is a productive asset.

By 3000 BC in Sumer metal ingots of copper or silver were used as money. There were two standards of value: grain and silver. Maximum rates of interest on grain and silver, amongst other things, were prescribed in 1800 BC by a regulatory proclamation called the Code of Hammurabi (these were $33\frac{1}{3}\%$ on grain (barley) and 20% on silver). With only one adjustment these maximums lasted for 2000 years. Homer and Sylla report ranges of interest rates charged in this period. Rates on silver vary between 10% and 40%, far higher than some categories of interest rate were to reach again until the twentieth century.

The earliest coined metal may have been issued in Lydia, in Greece, around about 700 BC, although coins may have originated prior to this in other places such as Ionia, and rapidly spread to the rest of Greece. The first coins were struck from electrum, a naturally occurring alloy of silver and gold. The silver content of electrum is highly variable. Silver coins (shekels) were minted by Croesus of Lydia (560–546 BC). Coins are stamped to guarantee the fineness of the metal used in their manufacture, and to guarantee their weight, although this may vary due to clipping or to natural wear and tear.

Coin is a convenient and useful form of money, well adapted to a largely agricultural society whose major projects are military campaigns and public works. Gold

---

[1] This account owes much to Homer and Sylla. Their references include Einzig (66) [199] and Heichelheim (58) [277].

[2] A skilled woman is valued at four oxen and a big tripod at twelve. Precious metals were also valued in oxen.

and silver are most usually used for this purpose although copper, iron and bronze have also been used. For instance, the Romans were on a copper and bronze standard, and Sweden in the sixteenth century, amongst other nations, was on a copper standard.

There was a severe economic and political crisis in Athens at the beginning of the sixth century BC. At that time default on debt was punishable by personal slavery. In 594 BC Solon revised the laws of Athens. Amongst other things he freed those enslaved for debt, and redeemed at state expense those sold abroad.

The Greek states, thanks to the campaigns of Alexander, and to local discoveries of silver and gold, usually had sufficient precious metals for coinage purposes. Shortages of precious metal often led to debasement of the coinage, or the substitution of other media or the introduction of units of account, as in, for instance, colonial America. Athens in 405 BC was suffering an acute shortage of silver as its silver mines had been captured by the Spartans. The city's gold reserves (the temple statutes) had been melted down to pay the troops. The city was forced to use copper. As reported by Aristophanes (in *The Frogs*, 405 BC):

> The noble silver drachma, that of old,
> We were so proud of, and the recent gold,
> Coins that rang true, clean-stamped and worth their weight,
> Throughout the world, have ceased to circulate.
> Instead, the purses of Athenian shoppers
> Are full of shoddy silver-plated coppers.[3]

The first international standard currency was probably the Athenian 'Owl', a coin stamped with the owl of Athena. It was current for four centuries, from about 500 BC to 100 BC, remaining unadulterated.

During the Greek and Roman periods money-lending was rife. Both states had legal maximum interest rates on loans, although these were frequently ignored. Loans were usually short term, but could be rolled over, becoming in effect floating rate debt. Interest rates were often 'conventional' rather than determined by aggregate supply and demand, although the credit status of the petitioner and the urgency of his need, then as now, would effect the rate charged. A conventional rate in Rome on silver loans was 1 ounce per pound per year, equivalent to a rate of $8\frac{1}{3}\%$. Lenders distinguished whether they were lending to private individuals, to cities or states, or to rulers. Loans to rulers and to states were riskier and carried higher interest charges than secured loans to individuals. Public debt could be secured against public revenues, but this did not prevent default. Rates were generally in the range 6%–10%, although usurious rates were normally much higher than these (Homer and Sylla).

In both Greece and Rome rates at the beginning of their periods were high. They declined steadily, only to rise again towards the end of their periods. In Greece rates were available at between 10% and 18% in the fifth and sixth centuries BC. By the second century BC rates had fallen to 6%–9% before rising to 8%–9% by the first century AD. In Rome in the fifth and fourth centuries BC rates were around the traditional level of

---

[3] Penguin classics edition, 1964, translated by David Barrett.

$8\frac{1}{3}\%$. These fell to 4%–6% at the end of the first century BC, rising to over 12% by the third and fourth centuries AD.

There were a series of debasements and financial crises in the closing centuries of the Roman era. For instance Gallenius (253–268) coined enormous numbers of highly debased double denarii. Inflation in this period was as high as that in Germany in 1923.

2.1.2   Western Europe at the Beginning of the Second Millennium

In Western Europe financial history pauses during the dark ages. In Eastern Europe Byzantium flourished. Its currency, the nomisma (or solidus), retained its standard from its introduction in 309 until its debasement in 1092. In Western Europe after the degeneration of the Western Roman Empire the economy of England reverted to a largely pre-market type; no coins were minted for two hundred years. In England, only at the time of Offa (757–796) did the economy recover to the extent that a network of market towns began to re-emerge. Concomitant with this came a renewed demand for coinage as an exchange medium. As economies recovered, capital again became significant and the demand for loans of capital resumed. The English economy was re-monetarised under Offa (Jones (93) [326]). Towards the end of the millennium England was subject to massive drains of silver to meet the demands of northern invaders. The source of the silver used to pay this tribute, the Danegeld, has been much discussed (Jones (91) [325]), but seems to have emerged from a growing trade with Europe.

The Carolingian system of coinage was introduced by Pepin the Short (751–768), and popularised by his son Charlemagne. Based on a pound of silver divided into 240 pennies, each penny would have a silver content of 24 grains. At this time the Byzantium gold solidus was worth about twelve pence, so twelve pence were referred to as a solidus. The system could be regarded as the first European currency union. The Carolingian system remained nominally supported throughout Europe for five or six centuries, but outside of England the coinage rapidly became debased. English pence retained their silver content largely unchanged until the fourteenth century. A penny under Offa could contain anywhere between 18 and 27 grains (apparently through unskilled minting rather than through other motives). William I fixed the content at 22.5 grains where it remained until 1346 when Edward III reduced it to 20 grains (with slight reductions in 1279 and 1344). During these centuries the English penny was a quality coin, and a standard of value in Europe.

A weight reduction in 1346 was prompted by a desire to simultaneously circulate both gold and silver coins. The size and volume of trade by this time required the introduction of coins of greater value than one penny. Gold is an obvious medium to introduce alongside silver where it can be used to mint high value coins much lighter than silver coins would have to be. In a bimetallic system of coinage care must be taken to ensure that the exchange rate between gold and silver is correct. In the ancient world a bimetallic ratio of twelve was standard. By the mid-fourteenth century the ratio was still close to twelve. This was to rise to about fifteen by the eighteenth century. During the present century the price of gold in terms of silver has increased markedly.

If two countries maintain different bimetallic ratios then an arbitrage occurs; gold will flow between the two countries in one direction and silver in the other until one country is denuded of its stocks of the cheaper metal. In practice ratios could and did vary because of the cost and risk of transporting bullion to effect the arbitrage. When Edward III introduced a gold florin in 1344 (in imitation of the Florentine gold florin, a worthy coin circulating since 1252) he did so at a ratio of 14.81—far too high. Silver in England was cheap (in terms of gold) so silver left the country. The florin was almost immediately withdrawn and replaced by the gold noble at a ratio of 11.9—this time slightly too low. The correction of 1346 gave a ratio of 12.44. A further correction was required in 1355 to give a ratio of 12.00. The ratio was achieved by reducing the silver content of the penny to 18 grains.[4]

In England during the twelfth century good credit personal loans would earn interest of two pence per pound per week, equivalent to an annual rate of $43\frac{1}{3}\%$ a year. Elsewhere in Europe rates for commercial loans were much less; in the Netherlands rates of 10%–16% are reported.

2.1.3   The Inflations of the Second Millennium

Many historians and economists have noted and studied the various inflationary periods in Europe during the last one thousand years, for example Goldstone (91) [254], [255] and Schwartz (73) [481]. Tallman (93) [512] also gives a review. Fischer (96) [217] examines these inflationary periods and gives a great many references. Since the twelfth century there have been four major inflationary periods separated by periods when prices have been relatively stable and may even have declined.[5]

The first inflationary period runs from about 1180 to 1350. From 1400 to 1470 prices were relatively stable, coinciding with the period of the Renaissance. The second inflationary period started about 1500 and continued to 1650. It was followed by a relatively stable period from 1660 to 1730 coinciding with the period known as the Age of Enlightenment. The third period ran from approximately 1730 to 1820, and was followed by the relative stability of the Victorian Era, from 1820 to 1900. The final great inflationary period has been running during the twentieth century.

We briefly discuss these inflationary periods, and the financial innovations associated with them, before commenting on the behaviour of interest rates in the second millennium.

The Commercial Revolution

The first inflationary period coincides with the commercial revolution in Europe. Population in Europe had been steadily increasing since the ninth and tenth centuries, and

---

[4] Henry III had tried to introduce a gold penny in 1257 at a ratio of 10. These coins were immediately melted down for export of their gold content.

[5] Much of this work has only been made possible by the economic historians who have compiled many historical time series. The key British price index is due to Phelps Brown and Hopkins (56) [438].

continued to rise until the mid-thirteenth century. Society was moving away from an essentially feudal model. The demands of trade were becoming more sophisticated. A network of trade fairs became established in Champagne in the second half of the twelfth century. Merchants from Italy could trade with those of France and the North. These trade fairs—essentially international trade exhibitions where import and export contracts could be agreed—required new regulatory and financial structures. Feudal rulers were not providing them, so merchants devised them for themselves. They were supported by the princes of the regions in which the fairs were held since the fairs brought revenue and status. The rulers guaranteed safe passage to merchants, and provided security at the fairs. The 'peace of the fair' prevailed during which merchants were immune to prosecution from offences committed outside the fair. The fairs had a strong internal arbitration system. A merchant refusing to abide by a decision might bring the 'interdict of the fair' down upon his city; all merchants from his city would be banned from the fair.

Financial arrangements based on credit were normal. Debts were settled at the end of each fair, and credit was frequently extended across fairs by means of bills of exchange. The embryonic form of modern bills of exchange were essentially credit instruments that allowed debts incurred at one fair to be settled in another currency at a specified future fair. Although nominally associated with commodity trades, bills of exchange were frequently used to circumvent the churches' interdict on lending at interest. Bills of exchange could be netted-off, and thus their use considerably reduced the need to send bullion from one location to another in settlement of debts. Bullion convoys could be smaller, and could be timed to coincide with embassies or other official journeys when advantage could be taken of an armed escort. In fact, bills of exchange were frequently settled by bank transfers in the developing banking system.

In the north around the Baltic another trade federation was evolving. The Hanseatic League, formally established in 1367, but operational for many years previously, was a customs union and trade association that at its height included 200 cities. The commercial power of the League was enormous. The League obtained favourable trading terms in England. An area in London (the 'Stalhof', or Steelyard) won self-government by 1281 for its resident traders.

The increase in commercial activity and the use of bills of exchange revolutionised the money supply. Not only was the effective quantity of money increased, so was its velocity. These statements are difficult to verify, but see Mayhew (95) [383].

Great banking houses were established, based in Italy but with offices throughout the cities of Europe. European deposit banking started in Venice and Genoa in the twelfth century. Originally these acted purely as safe deposits but soon extended to allowing transfers between accounts. These banks were not permitted to loan their deposits (although 'overdraft facilities' were granted to favoured clients). Soon, however, private banks began to trade bills of exchange as a natural consequence of the desire to net out trade transactions.

The end of the commercial revolution may be conveniently dated at 1294, the beginning of a period of warfare across Europe, although prices may not have stabilised for another 50 years. The Hundred Years War that devastated Europe was to begin in 1330.

Population, rising throughout Europe during the thirteenth century, began to decline during the fourteenth century. The Great Plague of 1348 and the recurrent plagues of the following century merely emphasised a pre-existing trend.

The Price Revolution of the Sixteenth Century

The second inflationary period occurred between 1500 and 1650. Known as the Price Revolution it has long been the source of study and speculation. Although rising prices can be observed from the beginning of the sixteenth century there is no doubt that the influx of enormous quantities of silver in the middle of the century from Spanish possessions in South America, notably the Potosi deposits, resulted in sustained increased price levels. This huge wealth, in less incompetent hands, could have turned Spain into a prosperous world superpower. Indeed, when Charles I of Spain became in 1519 Charles V of the Holy Roman Empire he controlled vast expanses of central Europe and the low countries. Instead, through mal-administration, the pursuit of fruitless wars, and ostentation, Spain was left a legacy of poverty and debt.

Motomura (94) [405] analyses Spanish currency and finances in the first half of the seventeenth century. Little of the Potosi silver seems to have remained in Europe. A proportion went directly to China,[6] and most of that which reached the Spanish monarchy—silver imports were taxed at 40%—was already pledged in debt repayment, and left Europe by way of Italy. Some of the silver went into Italian coinage.

When the silver supply began to increase dramatically in the mid-sixteenth century the price level had already been rising for several decades. The trend seems unaffected by the import levels. The money supply in England is estimated to have risen three-fold over this period, whereas the price level rose four-fold (Mayhew (95) [383]). Goldstone (91) [254] argues that the money supply was not responsible for the price revolution, attributing it instead to population and velocity effects. Population appears to be increasing throughout the period, decreasing only towards the middle of the seventeenth century.

By the mid-sixteenth century sophisticated financial structures were firmly in place. An example of the scope of possible operations occurred in 1587 when Gresham, an outstanding financial operator of the Elizabethan period, succeeded in cornering a sufficient quantity of Genoan bills of exchange that the financing of the equipping of Philip of Spain's Great Armada was delayed. This may well have contributed to the delay of the sailing of the Armada until 1588.

The Inflation of the Eighteenth Century

The third inflationary period occurred in the eighteenth century. Running from 1730 to 1820 it coincides with a great rise in deposit banking and funded state debt. For the first half of this period currencies throughout Europe were stable; there was a

---

[6] It has been speculated that subsequent interruptions in the flow of silver to China in the 1640s led to an economic crisis and to the downfall of the Ming dynasty. This view has been challenged by von Glahn (96) [535].

consistent bimetallic ratio, and paper, where issued, was fully convertible. However, as well as facilitating economic activity, banking, if poorly regulated, can pose a threat to an economy. During this period, and for a considerable time thereafter, over-issue of convertible notes provoked one crisis after another, with considerable implications for short-term interest rates.

Modern public banking could be said to have begun in 1609 with the founding of the Bank of Amsterdam (Amsterdamsche Wisselbank). It came equipped with the 'guarantee of the city' for its deposits. Coin on deposit with the Bank was called bank money. All bills over 600 florins had to be settled using bank money. Because of its relative security bank money established a premium over coin. The premium—the agio—was fixed by the Bank which guaranteed to buy and sell at 4% and 5% agio, respectively. The Bank kept a 100% reserve ratio, and charged interest on its deposits at a rate of 0.25% per six months on silver and 0.5% per six months on gold. Initially it was not permitted to issue bank notes or to loan deposits, although it later did lend deposits. Public banks in other places followed; for instance, Hamburg in 1619 and Sweden in 1658. The Bank of Sweden became the first national bank when it was taken over by the state in 1668.

In England in the early seventeenth century the Tower of London was available for use by merchants and others as a deposit for bullion. The Tower lost its reputation for safety when in 1640 Charles I seized the assets in the Tower because he had been unable to obtain a loan. (The assets were later returned when Charles was allowed a loan secured against tax revenue. Charles II later defaulted on this loan.) Merchants began to leave money on deposit with goldsmiths, for interest. Goldsmiths then lent out the deposits. Receipts of deposit were exchangeable like bank notes. There was a crisis in 1672 when Charles II stopped paying interest on deposits placed by goldsmiths at the Exchequer, bankrupting a number of them. There were runs on goldsmiths in 1674, 1678, 1682, and 1688.

Another crisis occurred after the Glorious Revolution of 1688 which brought William and Mary to the throne of England. The country was on a silver standard until this time. However, the government debt burden led to disruptions in the foreign exchange market between London and Amsterdam. Quinn (96) [445] illustrates how an FX arbitrageur, Stephan Evance, by conducting paired trades of bullion and bills of exchange, was able to arbitrage between bullion exchange rates and rates on bills of exchange. The round trip profit was (conservatively) 1%. The operations of arbitrageurs like Evance caused a crisis which led to considerable public debate at the time over the relative merits of gold and silver. After the reminting of 1696 (under Isaac Newton), although technically still under a silver standard, England was essentially bimetallic. It was to remain this way until 1821 when after the Napoleonic wars the convertibility of paper money was restored to a gold standard. The mechanisms that essentially monetarised gold were

1. The Royal Mint was obliged to buy and sell gold,
2. The Bank of England was obliged to convert banknotes, and
3. No restrictions were placed on the export or import of gold.

In parallel with these developments the Bank of England was established in 1694 with a capital of £1.2m. Its purpose was simply to be a vehicle to allow the British government to borrow (to meet the expenses of a war against France) on similar terms to the those available to other states, such as the Dutch. The British government was paying 6%–30% for short–term loans, whereas comparable rates in Holland were 3%– 4%.

Although long-term rates became and generally remained low, short-term rates reacted strongly to financial circumstances. In the two centuries following the founding of the Bank of England a succession of crises hit the financial system. The system survived, perhaps on occasion more by luck than judgement. For instance, during the crisis of 1763, with £5.3m face value of notes in circulation the Bank found its bullion reserves were down to £367 000. In the crisis of 1825 there was a severe run on country banks. There were insufficient gold coin and bank notes to satisfy demand; notes could not physically be printed quickly enough. On Saturday 17 December the Bank ran out of £5 and £10 notes, and was famously saved only when a box of £1 notes was discovered locked away in a cupboard. Fortunately a supply of notes arrived from the printers on the Sunday morning (Lord Bentinck commented that Britain had been 24 hours away from barter). There were other crisis in 1837, 1847, 1857 and 1866.

During the relative stability of the Victorian era, population continued to rise. Thanks to new discoveries in America and Australia the gold supply kept pace with money demand. Eichengreen and McLean (94) [198] investigate the nineteenth century world gold supply. The size of American and Australian gold production dominated all other sources of gold. During this period the ratio of market prices of gold and silver still fluctuated around 15.5 (Redish (95) [450]).

The Great Inflation of the Twentieth Century

The fourth inflationary period began at the start of the twentieth century and continues still. It is the first period in which inconvertible paper money has been the normal form of currency. There is no doubt that seigniorage has significantly contributed to inflation in this period. There is now no commodity-backed peg to prevent prices from escalating without bound. It is only with inconvertible currency that hyperinflations can be commonplace; when a coinage is debased creditors may still be able to insist on payment in specie.

There seem to be two main causes of excessive seigniorage; the first, and historically most important, is military expediency. Wars are expensive and seigniorage, in the short term, is easy. The second, modern, cause is welfare spending. Proposed by Keynes as a remedy for recession, public spending and the associated funding requirement is a modern cause of inflationary pressure. It is possible that this may account for some of the inflation observed in Europe in the latter half of the twentieth century.

The amount of seigniorage that may be obtained is considerable. Neumann (92) [413] estimates seigniorage in the US to be US$15bn in 1990. Excessive seigniorage can be associated with political instability (Cukierman et al. (92) [150]).

The role of inconvertible paper money   Inconvertible paper money has a very long history in China. In Europe, bank notes were first issued by the Bank of Sweden (the Sveriges Riksbank) in 1661. These were withdrawn in 1664. These notes were not issued against deposits, but such was the state of Swedish coinage (Sweden was on a copper standard at the time) that paper went to a premium to coin.

The process leading to the establishment of fiat money has been studied both theoretically and historically, for instance by Ritter (95) [455] and Selgin (94) [486]. The
usual way that inconvertible money is established is via the previous introduction of
convertible money. At a certain stage of economic development the use of commodity
money becomes costly or inconvenient and inhibits further development. Convertible
paper money is introduced, or evolves from certificates of deposits or some other instrument. Perhaps at first this is interest-bearing, but after a short period the inconvenience
and instability of interest-bearing money becomes apparent.[7] Interest bearing or no,
if not initially legal tender (used, for instance, to pay taxes) it rapidly becomes so.
Convertible money, if unabused by over-issuing, becomes established and confidence
in it as a medium and store of value is high. There is then a crisis, perhaps due to a
military threat, and to forestall an economic crisis the currency is made inconvertible.
This is usually announced as a temporary measure to be reversed at the earliest possible
moment. Because confidence in the convertible currency is high, and the government is
credible, the inconvertible currency is accepted as money. After a while the triggering
crisis is resolved, but since confidence in the currency remains high the re-establishment
of convertibility is postponed. Later convertibility may be restored, but eventually, after
further triggering crises, it will not be. The currency is now fiat.

This process has been followed in Britain, America, France, and many other
economies. It may go wrong in several ways. Often the currency will be made
inconvertible *en passant*.

1. The convertible money may be over-issued. This will lead to a banking crisis.
    Over-issue occurred in America and England, and in France under John Law.
2. The triggering crisis proves too great. External factors, such as military defeat, lead
    to economic collapse. An example is the Confederate dollar.
3. The inconvertible currency is over-issued, for example, the French assignats.

In all three cases if collapse occurs it is often preceded by hyperinflation. We review
several illustrations of the collapse—or non-collapse—of currencies when crises occur.
These are the episode of John Law and the Banque Royale in France; the assignat, also
in France, 60 years later; and the convertibility of sterling.

John Law and the Banque Royale   This remarkable Scotsman was responsible for
initiating one of the first European experiments with paper money. So devastating were
the eventual results that it was only after a further 80 years that the experiment was
repeated, and then only under desperation.

In May 1716 Law formed a bank for the purpose of taking over the national debt of
France. This was France's first public bank. Notes issued by the bank were acceptable
in payment of taxes; in other words, they were legal tender. The notes were redeemable
on demand 'into coin current at the time of issue'. Initially there was confidence in the
bank.[8] In 1719 its fortunes became linked with that of the Mississippi Company. This

---

[7] Interest-bearing money has been widely studied, both theoretically and empirically. See, for
instance, Calvo and Vegh (96) [111], Aiyagari *et al.* (96) [11], and also Gherity (93) [246].

[8] Although Law is supposed to have said a little earlier in 1715 that he had discovered that the
secret of the philosopher's stone was to make gold out of paper.

company, very similar to the South Sea Company, was granted a monopoly on trade with the East Indies. A bubble developed on its shares. Unlike an analogous situation in England with the South Sea Company, with which the Bank of England did not become involved, Law's bank, now taken over by the state and called the Banque Royale, began to heavily over-issue. Much of its note was used to buy shares in the Company of the Indies, as the Mississippi Company was now called. In 1718, when taken over by the king, the bank's note issue was 59 million livres, which the king guaranteed to redeem in specie. By December 1719 it had issued over 1 billion livres. The bank could not now meet large demands for conversion. Its notes were made inconvertible. In May 1720 when the scheme collapsed the issue was 2.6 billion livres; the issue of coin was less than half of this.

Assignats   The French Revolution was funded by assignats. First issued in December 1789, and authorised by the National Assembly, this paper money remained stable for five years before collapsing. Eventually it went the same way as its less well known namesake. (The Russian assignat was issued by Catherine the Great in 1768. Initially convertible, Catherine announced that it would always remain so. Convertibility was dropped in 1786.)

Not originally legal tender, the first issue of the French assignat was interest bearing with redemption promised within five years upon sale of confiscated church land. By July 1794 there was a circulation of 7.2 billion livres. Robespierre had maintained the value of the assignat with measures to force the circulation, but with his fall at the end of July 1794 the assignat fell too. Price indexation kept the assignat in use until February 1796 when it was finally replaced by the mandate. Paper money had run its course for the moment. Napoleon funded his campaigns not by seigniorage but taxation. Interestingly, the British war effort during the Napoleonic campaigns was mainly debt financed. Britain had a successful track record of 'tax smoothing' and did not have to radically expand its tax base. One small tax that was introduced at this time was Income Tax.

The convertibility of the pound   By 1797 England was still technically on a silver standard, although the value of the gold guinea had been fixed at 21 shillings, implying a bimetallic ratio of 15.21 (slightly too high). The government was incurring excessive borrowing because of the war effort. The Bank of England's gold reserves had fallen to £1.3m. A panic at this stage would have been uncontrollable. On Saturday 18 February farmers in Newcastle started a run on their local banks, presenting notes for conversion to gold. By Monday the local banks had stopped payments. By the end of the week, on Sunday 26 February, the Privy Council instructed the Bank to suspend convertibility. At a hastily organised meeting the following day at Mansion House merchants and bankers issued a resolution that they would continue to accept bank notes. It had 4000 signatures. At the time it was thought that suspension might last one month or two. In fact it lasted 24 years. Convertibility was resumed in 1821 at the old parity, although Britain was now officially on a gold standard.[9]

---

[9] Redish (91) [449] analyses factors contributing to the return to gold.

Convertibility was next suspended in August 1914. In fact there was no official suspension. A stock market collapse following the Austrian ultimatum on Sunday 26 July provoked a panic which saw interest rates rise from 3% to 10% within a week. During a prolonged 'bank holiday'—the August 1 bank holiday was extended up to 4 August—huge quantities of £1 bank notes were printed to replace gold coin. These were put into circulation on August 7, followed a week later by 10 shilling notes. These notes were technically convertible but in the mood of the time it was regarded as unpatriotic to exercise convertibility.

Britain returned to the international gold standard in 1925—a short-lived flirtation sustained in part by deliberate falsification of official statistics for flows of gold (Garrett (95) [242]). The Gold Standard Act of 1925 finally removed the public's right to convert bank notes.

2.1.4 Inflation and Interest Rates

One of the first acts of the incoming UK Labour government in May 1997 was to assert its financial credibility by raising short-term interest rates. This was perceived by the markets as a credible attempt to control inflation, and the long end of the yield curve dropped by an amount almost equivalent to the rise in the short rate. Reactions of this sort are often seen in the market. Factor analyses of yield curve movements normally find a shift component and a tilt component. One would like to identify these two components with the inflationary and deflationary effects of an increase in the short rate, respectively. Control of the short rate as an economic instrument has been used in the UK since the nineteenth century (for countries on the gold standard short rate control is an essential 'automatic' correction mechanism.).

During the inflationary periods there is some evidence that interest rates were higher than during the stable periods, although the effect of the inflationary periods upon interest rates is difficult to determine. The Fisher hypothesis, briefly discussed in Chapter 11, would lead one to expect that during an inflationary period interest rates would be higher, commensurate with the level of inflation. Indeed, during the twentieth century high inflation has coincided with high nominal interest rates. In previous inflations, however, the link is more tenuous.

During the Commercial Revolution rates were high, but may have declined after prices ceased to rise, from the mid-thirteenth century onwards. The pattern is different for the Price Revolution. Interest rates appear to rise during the course of the sixteenth century while prices were rising, falling back, possibly to lower levels, during the seventeenth century when prices were more stable. This pattern is consistent with the idea that inflation expectations are impounded into nominal interest rates. That this pattern is not evident for the Commercial Revolution may reflect a paucity of information, or perhaps the relatively limited demands of trade compared with later periods.

Yields on UK perpetuals during the inflation of the eighteenth century followed a similar pattern. Consols were issued in large volumes and have remained actively traded. Their yields are indicative of long-term rates, but since they can be redeemed at par their yields are unreliable when rates fall close to the coupon rate—which acts as a notional floor to their yield.[10]

The British government first issued 3% perpetual annuities in 1722. In 1749, when rates dropped from a previous high of 4.5% back to 3%, the greater part of the national debt was converted to 3% consolidated funds. Consol yields rose from relatively stable lows of 3% in the 1730s to relatively volatile highs in the range of 5% from 1800 to 1820, declining again thereafter.

The upwards movement coincides with the inflation of the eighteenth century. This is consistent with the pattern found during the Price Revolution. Despite volatile short-term rates, the Consol rate remained at roughly 3% until towards the end of the nineteenth century. In 1888 rates were very low and the government was able to convert the national debt into $2\frac{1}{2}$% Consols. Yields on Consols reached their lowest levels in 1896–1897. The yield of 2.21% has never been equalled. At the time the bank rate was down to 2% and short-term market rates were occasionally below 1%, rivalling recent Japanese rates.

With the arrival of the twentieth century rates rose dramatically, coinciding with the current inflationary period. There appears to have been a structural shift coinciding with the Great War. At this time Consol yields rose from approximately 3% to about 5% in 1920. They then declined to around 3% by the late 1940s before heading skywards to over 13% by the late 1970s. Since then the Consol rate has declined to around 7% or 8%. One possible reason for the structural break may be the severance of the link between the money supply and gold that occurred when convertibility was suspended. The markets may have accurately perceived the inflationary potential of the new arrangements, confirmed when the re-introduced gold standard broke down, and impounded these into the long rate.

Later in the century the rise in rates may have been caused and sustained by economic policies designed to secure full employment rather than optimal growth or low inflation.

2.2   CHARACTERISTICS OF INTEREST RATE BEHAVIOUR

This section identifies a number of features of importance to interest rate modelling that are apparent from monetary history. These include the incidence of hyperinflations, the long rate, and the risk-free rate. We shall use these features subsequently to help us compare modern interest rate models.

2.2.1   Hyperinflations

A hyperinflation occurs when prices denominated in a particular currency increase dramatically and continuously. Cagan (56) [110] arbitrarily defined a hyperinflation as an inflation where the monthly inflation rate exceeds 50%, but a more informal definition is a situation where interest rates are rising rapidly solely due to monetary effects, in which the real economy plays no part. Hyperinflations have occurred in Germany, Poland and Hungary, and in South America. Other examples are discussed

---

[10] Care must be taken in calculating yields from consols (Klovland (94) [337]).

below. Hyperinflation, unlike ordinary inflation, is essentially caused by over-supply of money by the state. The chief reason why this happens often seems to be a desire by the state to generate seigniorage to finance its activities when it has no other way of doing so. Expanding the money supply literally enables it to create money. Inflation will catch up, but not until later. Meanwhile the state is effectively taxing its citizens by reducing the real value of their savings and income. Once started, hyperinflation may be maintained by price indexation.

American monetary history furnishes several examples of inflations and hyperinflations. For a brief review see Russell (91) [465]. The classic book on recent American monetary history is Friedman and Schwartz (63) [231]. The American revolution was financed by the infamous Continental Currency. Since the revolution was triggered by disputes over taxation, the rebels were unable to use taxation to finance their activities. Seigniorage was the only solution. The currency rapidly hyperinflated.

At the outbreak of the American civil war each side needed to raise money to finance its war effort. The North issued Greenbacks, redeemable at any time into coupon bonds. Notes bore interest if deposited for at least 30 days. The value in gold of US$100 of Greenbacks, as a percentage of face value, dropped to 30% of par in July 1864 but rose again as confidence in eventual convertibility grew. The notes were made convertible at par into gold in June 1879. Nominal interest rates remained less than 7% during this period, despite realised inflation of 30% at times. Gherity (93) [246] examines the use of interest-bearing notes to finance this war.

In the South, the civil war was financed by seigniorage (Davis and Pecquet (90) [160] discuss some of these issues in detail). The South had a small tax base and an undeveloped civil administration. A northern blockade of ports prevented export earnings. Although the Confederate dollar hyperinflated, price levels seemed to have been relatively stable in gold denominated values.

Hyperinflation is mainly a property of inconvertible paper money. Prior to modern times an analogous process occurred with monetary debasements. There have been many examples throughout history of debasements and the consequent effect on prices. These have not received the same degree of interest in the modern literature as inconvertible currency inflations have had. Studied debasements include the Kipper und Wipper debasements of 1615–1623 in the Germanic states (Kindleberger (91) [334]), the French debasements of 1415–1423 (Sussman (93) [510]), and the Great Debasement of Henry VIII (Chown (96) [130], Davies (94) [159], et cetera.

The first recorded paper on hyperinflation occurred in China in 1190–1240 (Lui (83) [369]). The cause was excessive seigniorage due to military expenses (the cost of dealing with a Tartar invasion). The currency inevitably collapsed, although at a much more sedate pace than a modern hyperinflation.

Quite often a practical accompaniment of a hyperinflation has been the development of currency substitutes. In modern times this may be a foreign currency such as the American dollar. In previous eras it might be undebased coins, if available. There are examples of countries with more than one currency circulating simultaneously. For instance, in Russia between 1922 and 1924 the stable chervonetz circulated at the same time as the depreciating ruble. In Hungary after the Second World War the hyperinflating pengo circulated alongside the 'tax' pengo, an indexed currency used for tax purposes.

Such cases have been studied by Sturzenegger (94) [508]. He develops a model and applied it to the Argentine hyperinflations of 1989 and 1990.

2.2.2 The Long Rate

It may be argued that an effective long rate came into existence only when perpetuals were first issued. Early examples were the Venetian prestiti, the French rentes and later the English Consols. By the seventeenth century long-term annuities and perpetuities were common. A famous example is the perpetual bond bought by Elsken Jorisdochter in 1624 from the Lekdyk Bovendams Company. It was still paying interest (at $2\frac{1}{2}\%$, reduced from an original $6\frac{1}{4}\%$) three centuries later.

Prior to inconvertible paper money perpetuities were subject to default risk. For instance, the Venetian prestiti, issued as forced loans with 5% coupons, but freely tradable, survived for two centuries. It was in 1377 that the Venetian state defaulted on interest payments for the first time.

In fact a form of long-running obligation was very common in medieval times. Called a census it was essentially a form of mortgage-linked annuity; a loan secured by property that often ran for the life of the buyer or seller. Many forms of census were available, their variety resembling in scope today's swaps market. An important feature of the census was that because interest was considered as being paid out of the produce of the land upon which it was secured it was not deemed to be usurious by the church, as long as the effective interest rate was not too high.

Usury was not permitted by the church, and as time went by any lending at interest became increasingly difficult. To further the needs of trade, merchants were forced to resort to measures to sidestep the churches' prohibitions. One mechanism was the Contractus Trinius, a medieval example of a structured financial product. Instead of simply lending money, three contracts were signed:

1. A partnership agreement to include profit sharing;
2. An agreement to indemnify one partner against loss in return for a cap on his profits;
3. The sale by that partner of a floor on his profits in return for regular payments.

No individual contract infringed the usury restrictions, but taken together the arrangement was simply a straight loan with interest.

2.2.3 Risk-Free Rates

It is only in the recent historical period, since the introduction of paper money and the arrival of monetary authorities with associated seigniorage powers, that riskless debt as a concept has had any meaning. States and rulers can default on metal loans. Despite the import of huge quantities of South American silver from the Potosi mine, the Habsburg dynasty of Charles V of Spain declared itself bankrupt in 1557, and again in 1575, 1596, 1607, 1627, 1649, 1653, and 1680. Each bankruptcy led to financial panic and to the failure of creditor houses. The Fuggers lost much of their wealth this way. Spain was reduced to a copper standard. Philip the Fair of France (1285–1314) repudiated his debts, ruining his chief creditors, the Order of Knights Templar. Edward III of England (1327–1377) bankrupted the Bardi and Peruzzi companies of Florence when he defaulted in the 1340s.

Reputational effects can be important in individual cases, even with 'riskless' nominal debt. The defaults of a number of American states in the 1840s is a case in point. Many of these states did eventually repay their debts in full. These were subsequently able to re-borrow come the Civil War. States which did not were not able to re-borrow.

Even with inconvertible money a government debt may still be repudiated. This may happen, for instance, if the government itself is overthrown. This happened after the French Revolution. Later, Tzarist debt was repudiated by the incoming communist government, and in England in the early years of the eighteenth century it was a general belief that the Jacobites, were they to be restored, would repudiate the national debt; see Fisher (35) [219]. Successful rebels may often feel little sympathy with the creditors of their oppressors.

2.2.4   Summary

In this review of monetary history and interest rate behaviour we have identified several structural themes.

First, periods of relatively high price inflation abound throughout history. In addition to the inflationary periods, specific examples of localised inflations are common. Before inconvertible paper money these instances were often associated with debasement of the currency. Interest rates were unaffected as long as they referred to metal loans, but effective interest rates for those having to pay with debased coin to lenders accepting payment only in specie would rise in direct proportion to the degree of the debasement. (Debasements have sometimes been accompanied by proclamations that debased coins must be accepted 'in tale' for debt repayment. These proclamations are often not effective.) Even before the introduction of fiat paper money and nominal loans, interest rates begin to anticipate inflation. Without a metal standard in the background, seigniorage on inconvertible paper has often led beyond mere high inflation to hyperinflation. During these periods interest rates may become essentially unbounded. The structural shift in long rates at the start of the twentieth century may signal the markets' awareness of the inflationary potential of inconvertible currency. All currencies eventually cease to exist; hyperinflation has been a popular way to exit with a bang rather than a whimper.

Second, as the needs of industry and the financial markets have become more sophisticated the period of loans has been increasing. Early loans were often for terms of a few months or one or two years at most. Loans could often be rolled over, becoming in effect floating rate loans. Perpetual annuities were introduced by the Greeks, and used extensively by the Venetians, as we have seen. In the UK from 1749 Consols at 3%, and at $2\frac{1}{2}\%$ after the conversion of 1888, were a standard investment vehicle. Perpetuals were also used by the Spanish Habsburgs in the fifteenth and sixteenth centuries with disastrous results. (Isabella warned her descendants in her will not to issue any more. Her advice was ignored.) Even so, with the exception of Consols the term of a loan must necessarily be finite. However, the value of the longest rate can fluctuate considerably, and empirically is more volatile than simple term structure models can explain. The long rate, in the sense of a spot rate of infinite maturity, is a fiction. The yield on even a hundred year bond is not the long rate. We shall see in a later chapter that the theoretical long rate in many interest rate models is actually a constant. Even so, term structures derived from these models may only asymptotically approach the long rate at very long maturities.

Third, the short rate seems to fluctuate about a mean value, but this mean value may itself vary through time. In the Victorian era the short rate was normally in a range from 2% to 9%. By the 1970s and 1980s short rates were moving in a range closer to 10% to 15%.

Fourth, there is no such thing as a risk-free rate. Before the invention of inconvertible paper money default was possible on metal loans. With an inconvertible currency default can occur when a currency collapses, or the government itself is replaced by one sufficiently opposed to it that it repudiates the previous government's debts. Currency collapse may happen in extreme debasement, or after hyperinflations, or after military defeat.

Fifth, we mentioned in a previous section that inflation expectations may well be impounded into the yield curve. It is a commonplace of economic theory that a rise in short-term interest rates introduced as a credible attempt at inflation reduction will result in long yields diminishing. Conversely a drop in short-term rates perceived as inflationary will result in long-term yields rising. A rise in the short rate not seen as deflationary may increase the long rate.

We shall look to see if these properties are properly accounted for by existing financial models of interest rates.

3
Introduction to Interest Rate Modelling

Having reviewed some facets of interest rate markets and the development of interest rates and interest rate instruments in history, we now turn to interest rate modelling proper.

This chapter is introductory; in the first section we look in more detail at money market instruments, showing how quoted market rates convert into cashflows. We also give Black's formulae for caps and swaptions. In the second section we introduce the notation of stochastic processes, using as examples geometric Brownian motion and the Ornstein–Ulhenbeck process. The concept of a probability space with a filtration is introduced.

In the next section we introduce three basic interest rate models, and compare them using a set of criteria we develop. The fourth section describes in broad terms the major categories of interest rate models, comparing them by the same criteria as we compared the basic models, and also by additional criteria found from our previous analysis of historical features of interest rates.

The chapter concludes with a brief survey of how the short rate emerges from several interest rate models.

3.1 YIELD CURVE BASICS

In this section we review some basic concepts of interest rate modelling. We first give idealised definitions of continuously compounded spot and forward rates. We then define the corresponding market instruments: Libor and forward rate agreements (FRAs). In subsequent sections we describe the mechanics of swaps, swaptions and caps. Finally we briefly review day bases (day count conventions or day count functions).

There are many treatments available of this fairly standard material. A good reference is Rebonato (98) [448] and see also Wilmott (99) [541] and Hull (99) [290].

3.1.1 Discount Factors, Spot and Forward Rates

Pricing financial instruments uses the concept of present or discounted value. For a riskless coupon bond all cashflows are discounted back to the current date, and the sum of these discounted cashflows is the present value of the instrument.

Let $B_t(T)$ be the value at time t of £1 received for sure at time T. $B_t(T)$ is the value at time t of a pure discount bond maturing with value 1 at time T. We may also write $P(t, T)$ or $\delta(T) = \delta_t(T)$ for this value. $\delta(T)$ is the discount factor for cashflows occurring at time T. $\{\delta_t(T) \mid t \leq T\}$ is the discount curve at time t.

Suppose a bond or a bond portfolio has riskless cashflows C_i at times $t_i, i = 1, \ldots, n$. The value P of the portfolio of cashflows is the sum of the discounted cashflows,

$$P = \sum_{i=1}^{n} C_i \delta(t_i). \tag{3.1}$$

P is the present value of the cashflow stream $\{C_i\}_{i=1,\ldots,n}$.

Given a set of pure discount bond prices, $\{B_t(T)\}_{t<T}$, the term structure of interest rates is the set of yields to maturity $r_t(T)$, $t < T$,

$$r_t(T) = -\frac{1}{T - t} \ln B_t(T), \quad t < T. \tag{3.2}$$

This is also know as the yield curve. We shall often write $\tau = T - t$ for a time to maturity. The short rate $r_t \equiv r_t(t)$ is the rate on instantaneous borrowing or lending (in the absence of a spread).[1] A sum of £1 invested in the short rate at time zero and continuously rolled over is called the accumulator account or the money market account. Its value p_t at time t is

$$p_t = \exp\left(\int_0^t r_s \, ds\right). \tag{3.3}$$

A short Libor rate, such as a three-month rate, is often used as a surrogate for the short rate, but it must not be confused with the true instantaneous short rate. In some markets the overnight rate can be used as a surrogate, but in others it may be an extremely volatile rate reflecting short-term supply and demand that does not reflect the underlying levels of interest rate.[2]

Forward rates are rates it is possible to lock into today for borrowing or lending in the future. Their values can be derived directly from pure discount bond prices. Define $f_t(T_1, T_2)$ to be the continuously compounded forward rate available at time t for borrowing at time T_1, and repaying at time T_2.

We must have

$$e^{r_t(T_2)(T_2-t)} = e^{r_t(T_1)(T_1-t)} e^{f_t(T_1,T_2)(T_2-T_1)}, \tag{3.4}$$

so that

$$f_t(T_1, T_2) = \frac{1}{(T_2 - T_1)} [r_t(T_2)(T_2 - t) - r_t(T_1)(T_1 - t)], \tag{3.5}$$

or

$$f_t(T_1, T_2) = \frac{1}{(T_2 - T_1)} \ln \frac{B_t(T_1)}{B_t(T_2)}, \tag{3.6}$$

otherwise an arbitrage would be possible.

---

[1] The instantaneous short rate is a theoretical entity which does not exist in real life. In practice intra-day cashflows within a bank do not attract interest.

[2] In particular, its correlation with rates further up the term structure may be very slight.

Instantaneous forward rates are analogous to the instantaneous short rate. The instantaneous forward rate of maturity T is

$$f_t(T) \equiv f_t(T, T) = \lim_{T_2 \to T} f_t(T, T_2). \tag{3.7}$$

It is the rate obtainable at time t for instantaneous borrowing at time T. We note the following:

1. It is assumed that all rates are riskless rates, so that there is no default risk. We do not venture into credit issues here.
2. Forward rates, as defined here, correspond to FRAs, described below.
3. Spot rates are forward rates for immediate delivery, $r_t(T) = f_t(t, T) = \lim_{T_1 \to t} f_t(T_1, T)$, and $r_t = f_t(t)$.
4. Investing at a spot rate is equivalent to rolling over at the appropriate instantaneous forward rates,

$$e^{r_t(T)(T-t)} = e^{\int_t^T f_t(s) \mathrm{d}s}. \tag{3.8}$$

5. Instantaneous forward rates can be read directly off the discount curve or the yield curve,

$$f_t(T) = -\frac{\partial}{\partial T}(\ln B_t(T)) = r_t(T) + (T-t)\frac{\partial r_t(T)}{\partial T}. \tag{3.9}$$

6. Forward rates are not the same as futures rates. An adjustment, called the convexity adjustment, is needed to convert futures prices into equivalent forward rates. We go into this in more detail in Chapter 5.

3.1.2 Simple Interest Rate Instruments

Markets have many different ways of quoting rates. There are conventional algorithms to convert quoted rates into actual cashflows. We describe Libor and FRAs and show how quoted rates corresponds to cashflows.

Libor

Write $L(t, \tau)$ for the Libor rate at time t, of tenor τ.[3] If one lends at Libor then one pays 1 at time t. At time $t + \tau$ one receives back $1 + L(t, \tau)\alpha_L(t, t + \tau)$, where $\alpha_L(t, t + \tau)$ is the day count fraction for L. $\alpha_L(t, t + \tau)$ is the proportion of L paid out at time $t + \tau$, and is computed as a fraction of a year. We discuss day bases in more detail below. For simplicity we may often set $\alpha(t, t + \tau) \equiv \tau$, a constant.

To avoid arbitrage[4] we must have

$$B_t(t + \tau) = \frac{1}{1 + L(t, \tau)\alpha_L(t, \tau)}. \tag{3.10}$$

---

[3] The tenor of an interest rate is its maturity period, the period from the point of investment to the time that interest is paid.

[4] Ignoring credit issues.

We will also use the alternative notation $L(t_{i-1}, t_i)$ for a Libor rate, which means the same as $L(t_{i-1}, t_i - t_{i-1})$. It will always be clear from the context which notation we are using.

Forward Rate Agreements (FRAs)

These are the market equivalents of the theoretical forward rates defined earlier. Write $F = F_0(t, \tau)$ for the FRA rate agreed at time 0 for time t, tenor τ. The rate F is fixed so that the premium at time 0 is 0. At time t the holder of the FRA receives

$$c = \frac{(L(t, \tau) - F) \times \alpha_L(t, \tau)}{1 + L(t, \tau)\alpha_L(t, \tau)}. \tag{3.11}$$

This quantity, which can be positive or negative, is the present value (at time t) of the difference between borrowing at Libor of tenor τ at time t and borrowing at the FRA rate F. It is as if one locked in, at time 0, to a borrowing rate of F at time t, tenor τ, since the FRA pays off the difference between what one actually has to borrow at $L(t, \tau)$, and the FRA rate. One can buy or sell FRAs, equivalent to future borrowing or lending at the FRA rate.

To avoid arbitrage the FRA rate F must be related to market Libor rates. In fact

$$1 + L(0, t + \tau)\alpha_L(0, t + \tau) = (1 + L(0, t)\alpha_L(0, t))(1 + F_0(t, \tau)\alpha_F(t, \tau)), \tag{3.12}$$

where, for instance, $t = \tau =$ three months, $L(0, t + \tau)$ is a six-month Libor rate and $L(0, t)$ is a three-month Libor rate. Since $1/(1 + L(0, t)\alpha_L(0, t)) = P(0, t)$ the FRA rate is also given by

$$F_0(t, \tau) = \frac{1}{\tau}\left(\frac{P(0, t)}{P(0, t + \tau)} - 1\right). \tag{3.13}$$

If equation (3.12) is not satisfied (in the absence of transaction costs) an arbitrage is possible. One lends at the more expensive rates, hedging by borrowing at the cheaper rates.

3.1.3 Interest Rate Swaps

A swap rate is the coupon rate, S, on fixed rate borrowing with equal present value to floating rate borrowing over the same period. The present value of borrowing a principal of 1 at a fixed rate S with coupons paid at times t_i, $i = 1, \ldots, n$, is

$$\text{Pv(fixed leg)} = \sum_{i=1}^{n} S\alpha_S(t_{i-1}, t_i)\delta(t_i) + \delta(t_n), \tag{3.14}$$

where α_S is the relevant day count fraction. The present value of the floating rate leg (the stream of floating rate cashflows) of the swap is

$$\text{Pv(floating leg)} = \sum_{i=1}^{n} L(t_{i-1}, t_i)\alpha_L(t_{i-1}, t_i)\delta(t_i) + \delta(t_n), \tag{3.15}$$

where for simplicity we are assuming that the tenors of the floating and fixed legs are the same. $L(t_{i-1}, t_i)$ is fixed at time t_{i-1} but the cashflow it determines is paid at time t_i.

It is possible to reduce (3.15) considerably. Although $L(t_{i-1}, t_i)$ is only fixed at time t_{i-1} one can find the value at $t = 0$ of a portfolio generating the amount $L(t_{i-1}, t_i)\alpha_L(t_{i-1}, t_i)$ at time t_i.

Table 3.1 shows the cashflows generated at time t and time $t + \tau$ by pure discount bonds purchased at time 0. $\delta(t)$ matures at time t with value 1. This is immediately re-invested at the contemporaneous Libor rate to yield cash of $1 + L(t, t + \tau)\alpha_L(t, t + \tau)$ at time $t + \tau$. Going short a bond maturing at $t + \tau$ leaves net cash of $L(t, t + \tau)\alpha_L(t, t + \tau)$ at time $t + \tau$ as required.

The portfolio $\delta(t) - \delta(t + \tau)$ generates $L(t, t + \tau)\alpha_L(t, t + \tau)$ at time $t + \tau$, even though L is not known until time t. Now the value of the floating leg simplifies:

$$\text{Pv(floating leg)} = \sum_{i=1}^{n} L(t_{i-1}, t_i)\alpha_L(t_{i-1}, t_i)\delta(t_i) + \delta(t_n) \qquad (3.16)$$

$$= \sum_{i=1}^{n} (\delta(t_{i-1}) - \delta(t_i)) + \delta(t_n) \qquad (3.17)$$

$$= \delta(t_0) = 1. \qquad (3.18)$$

Equating the value of the fixed and floating legs,

$$1 = \sum_{i=1}^{n} S\alpha_S(t_{i-1}, t_i)\delta(t_i) + \delta(t_n). \qquad (3.19)$$

This means that S can be interpreted as the annual coupon rate, payable at times t_i, giving a bond a market price of 1 at $t = 0$. This is just the par coupon rate, so swap rates are equivalent to par coupon rates.

Re-arranging equation (3.19) we can express the time t_n swap rate S_{t_n} in terms of discount factors

$$S_{t_n} = \frac{1 - \delta(t_n)}{\sum_{i=1}^{n} \alpha_S(t_{i-1}, t_i)\delta(t_i)}, \qquad (3.20)$$

so from a knowledge of the discount factors one immediately derives swap rates.

Table 3.1 Replicating a Libor cashflow

0	t	$t + \tau$
$\delta(t)$	1	$1 + L(t, t + \tau)\alpha_L(t, t + \tau)$
$\delta(t + \tau)$	$\dfrac{1}{1 + L(t, t + \tau)\alpha_L(t, t + \tau)}$	1
$\delta(t) - \delta(t + \tau)$	$\dfrac{L(t, t + \tau)\alpha_L(t, t + \tau)}{1 + L(t, t + \tau)\alpha_L(t, t + \tau)}$	$L(t, t + \tau)\alpha_L(t, t + \tau)$

Alternatively we can re-arrange (3.19) to express the time t_n discount factor $\delta(t_n)$ in terms of discount factors for previous times and the time t_n swap rate, S_{t_n},

$$\delta(t_n) = \frac{1 - S_{t_n} \sum_{i=1}^{n-1} \alpha_S(t_{i-1}, t_i)\delta(t_i)}{1 + S_{t_n}\alpha_S(t_{n-1}, t_n)}. \tag{3.21}$$

Equation (3.21) is useful because it helps us to bootstrap up an estimate of the term structure from a set of swap rates of increasing maturity.

3.1.4 Swaptions

A swaption is an option to enter a swap at a pre-agreed fixed rate, the exercise rate. Swaptions come in many varieties but we shall be concerned only with vanilla swaptions. In fact a vanilla swaption is equivalent to an option on a coupon bond. If one is using a one-factor term structure model, as we see later, it turns out to be easy to value an option on a coupon bond, and hence a swaption. (If one is using a two-factor model things become more difficult.)

We wish to describe the cashflows generated by swaptions. To do so we extend the notation introduced above. Suppose α_S is the day basis of a swap. At times t_i, $i = 1, \ldots, n$, the swap generates cashflows

$$p_i = \alpha_S(t_{i-1}, t_i)(L(t_{i-1}, t_i) - L_X), \tag{3.22}$$

where L_X is the rate on the fixed leg of the swap. If the swap was created some time in the past, L_X may no longer equal the current swap rate and the swap will no longer have net zero value.

Write $V = V(t, t_0, \alpha_S, n, L_X)$ for the time t value of the swap, $t \leq t_0$, and let $P(t, T)$ be the time t discount factor for time T. When $t = t_0$, V is zero if L_X has the value

$$S = S_t(t, t_n) = \frac{1 - P(t, t_n)}{\sum_{i=1}^{n} \alpha_S P(t, t_i)}, \tag{3.23}$$

which is just the current swap rate.

If $t < t_0$ we have a forward start swap. Cashflows are exchanged starting at a future time, rather than immediately. The value of the floating leg is now $P(t, t_0)$, and the value of the fixed leg is $\sum_{i=1}^{n} \alpha_S L_X P(t, t_i) + P(t, t_n)$, so the value V at time t of the forward start swap is

$$V(t, t_0, \alpha_S, n, L_X) = P(t, t_0) - \sum_{i=1}^{n} \alpha_S L_X P(t, t_i) - P(t, t_n). \tag{3.24}$$

This is zero when $L_X = S_t(t_0, t_n)$,

$$S_t(t_0, t_n) \equiv S_t(t_0, t_n, \alpha_S) = \frac{P(t, t_0) - P(t, t_n)}{\sum_{i=1}^{n} \alpha_S P(t, t_i)}. \tag{3.25}$$

$S_t(t_0, t_n)$ is the forward start swap rate at time t on a forward start swap starting at time $t_0 > t$ and maturing at time t_n, where the tenor $\tau \sim \alpha_S$ is understood and has been omitted from the notation. If t_n is clear from the context, we shall abbreviate $S_t(t_0, t_n)$ to $S_t(t_0)$.

We consider a European swaption on a (forward start) swap with exercise rate L_S, exercised at time t_0. The payoff to this swaption at time t_0 is

$$p = \max(S_{t_0} - L_S, 0) \times P, \tag{3.26}$$

where $P = \sum_{i=1}^{n} \alpha_S P(t_0, t_i)$ and S_{t_0} is the time t_0 swap rate. Equivalently, writing

$$p = \max \left(\sum_{i=1}^{n} (\alpha_S P(t_0, t_i) S_{t_0} - \alpha_S P(t_0, t_i) L_S), 0 \right) \tag{3.27}$$

makes it clear that the payoff to a swaption is the difference between the discounted cashflows on the fixed legs of swaps at the current swap rate of S_{t_0} and the swaption exercise rate L_S.

Black's Formula for Swaptions

Suppose that $t_i - t_{i-1} = \tau$ is a constant and that $\alpha_S(t_{i-1}, t_i) = \tau$, then the swap has constant tenor τ. Consider a swaption maturing at time t_0 on a swap of tenor τ and final cashflow time t_n. Let $S_t(t_0)$ be the time t forward start swap rate on a forward start swap of tenor τ starting at time t_0 with a final cashflow time t_n. At time $t < t_0$ the swaption has value v,

$$v = P(S_t(t_0)N(d_1) - L_S N(d_2)), \tag{3.28}$$

where $P = \sum_{i=1}^{n} \tau P(t_0, t_i)$, $N(d)$ is the standard normal distribution function and

$$d_1 = \frac{1}{\sigma \sqrt{t_0 - t}} \ln \frac{S_t(t_0)}{L_S} + \frac{1}{2} \sigma \sqrt{t_0 - t}, \tag{3.29}$$

$$d_2 = d_1 - \sigma \sqrt{t_0 - t}, \tag{3.30}$$

with $\sigma = \sigma(t, t_0, \tau, n, L_S)$, the Black's swaption volatility.

Black's formula assumes that the forward start swap rate $S_t(t_0)$ is the underlying state variable. If $S_t(t_0)$ were log-normal with volatility σ, then Black's formula would be 'correct'.

Swaption prices are usually quoted as the volatility σ. All other variables in Black's formula are known from either the specification of the swaption, or from current market prices. Table 3.2 gives examples of quoted swaption volatilities for GBP on 21 July 1999. The rows are labelled by the maturity period of the underlying swap, $t_n - t_0$, the columns by the time to maturity of the swaption, t_0. A slight volatility hump is visible; along several rows, for increasing times to maturity, volatilities rise slightly—peaking at about two years—before dropping away. This is a normal feature in the market.

Table 3.2   Example of swaption volatilies

Vols (%)	Time to maturity										
Length	6m	1y	2y	3y	4y	5y	6y	7y	8y	9y	10y
1y	22	22	23.5	23.5	23	22.5	21.75	21	20.5	20	19.5
2y	22	22	22.5	22.5	22.5	22	21.35	20.7	20.23	19.77	19.3
3y	22	22	22	22	22	21.5	20.95	20.4	19.97	19.53	19.1
4y	22	22	22	21.75	21.5	21	20.5	20	19.63	19.27	18.9
5y	22	22	22	21.5	21	20.5	20	19.5	19.17	18.83	18.5
6y	21.75	21.75	21.75	21.25	20.75	20	19.5	19	18.67	18.33	18
7y	21	21	21.25	21	20.25	19.5	19	18.5	18.17	17.83	17.5
8y	20.75	20.75	21	20.5	19.75	19	18.5	18	17.67	17.33	17
9y	20.25	20.25	20.5	20	19.25	18.5	18	17.5	17.17	16.83	16.5
10y	19.75	19.75	20	19.5	18.75	18	17.5	17	16.67	16.33	16

GBP swaption vols, 21-Jul-1999. Freq.: 3m–6m, DCB, act/365, act/365.

The columns also display a falling volatility, although since the underlying instrument changes as one goes down the column less can be made of this.

Figure 3.1 shows US dollar swaption volatilities plotted as a surface. The data are for 23 July 1999. This shows the same stylised structure as Table 3.2. In the time to maturity direction there is a slight hump peaking at roughly two–three years. Volatilities decline sharply at greater maturities.

Swaps and Forward Rates

We have seen that creating a portfolio worth $P(t, t_{i-1}) - P(t, t_i)$ at time $t < t_{i-1}$ gives a payoff of $L(t_{i-1}, t_i)\tau$ at time t_i, where τ is a constant tenor, so a portfolio

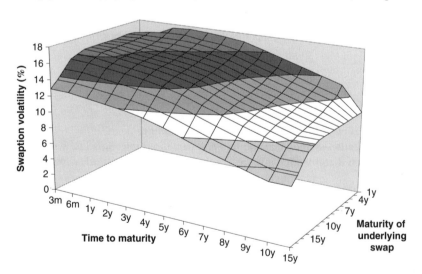

Figure 3.1   US dollar swaption volatility surface

worth $(1/\tau)(P(t, t_{i-1})/P(t, t_i) - 1)$ at time t generates $L(t_{i-1}, t_i)/P(t, t_i)$ at time t_i. But $(1/\tau)(P(t, t_{i-1})/P(t, t_i) - 1) = F_t(t_{i-1}, t_i)$, the market forward rate. We use this in equation (3.25). The forward start swap rate $S_t(t_0)$ can be expressed as:

$$S_t(t_0) = \frac{\sum_{i=1}^{n} F_t(t_{i-1}, t_i)\tau P(t, t_i)}{\sum_{i=1}^{n} \tau P(t, t_i)}. \tag{3.31}$$

Set $w_i = \tau P(t, t_i)/\sum_{i=1}^{n} \tau P(t, t_i)$, then $S_t(t_0) = \sum_{i=1}^{n} w_i F_t(t_{i-1}, t_i)$ is a weighted average of forward rates. Hence the arithmetic volatility σ_S of $S_t(t_0)$ is a weighted average of forward rate volatilities,

$$\sigma_S^2 = \sum_{i,j} w_i w_j \sigma_i \sigma_j \rho_{i,j}, \tag{3.32}$$

where σ_i is the volatility of $F_t(t_{i-1}, t_i)$, and $\rho_{i,j}$ is the correlation between $F_t(t_{i-1}, t_i)$ and $F_t(t_{j-1}, t_j)$. Hence swaption volatilities are functions of market forward rate volatilities.

3.1.5 Caps and Floors

On each date that an interest payment is due a cap pays out the difference between interest payments at a floating rate r_t, and interest payments at a fixed exercise rate r_X, when r_t is greater than r_X, on a principal of P. On each exercise date the cap pays out $p = \tau P \max(0, r_t - r_X)$, where τ is the tenor of r_t. For a floating rate borrower, buying a cap effectively caps interest payments at the rate r_X.

The floating rate r_t is usually a Libor rate, L_t, of some fixed tenor τ. We assume this from now on, writing L_{t_i} for the Libor value $L(t_i, t_{i+1})$.

An interest rate cap is a strip of individual interest rate options on r_t, called caplets. There is one caplet for each exercise date. An interest rate floor pays off $p = \tau P \max(0, r_X - r_t)$ at each exercise date, ensuring that interest is paid at a rate at least as great as r_X. A floor is a strip of individual floorlets.

Caps and floors are used by corporates in the management of interest rate risk on floating rate debt. Purchasing a cap allows the floating rate borrower to determine the maximum interest rate they will ever have to pay on the debt. A floating rate borrower who sells a floor generates capital at the cost of ensuring that interest is always paid at a rate at least that of the floor rate.

Equivalence to a Portfolio of Bond Options

Suppose a cap is composed of caplets on Libor at times t_i, $i = 1, \ldots, n$. The payoff to the caplet on L_{t_i} is made at time t_{i+1}. The payment of $\tau P \max(0, L_{t_i} - r_X)$ must be discounted back from time t_{i+1} to time t_i. The correct discount rate is the Libor rate $L(t_i, t_{i+1})$, which is known at time t_i. The value v_i at time t_i of the ith caplet is

$$v_i = \frac{\tau P \max(0, L_{t_i} - r_X)}{1 + \tau L_{t_i}}, \tag{3.33}$$

$$= \max \left(0, P - \frac{P(1 + \tau r_X)}{(1 + \tau L_{t_i})} \right). \tag{3.34}$$

But $P(1 + \tau r_X)/(1 + \tau L_{t_i})$ is the value at time t_i of a pure discount bond maturing at time t_{i+1} with value $P(1 + \tau r_X)$, so the value v_i of the ith caplet at time t_i is the value of a put maturing at time t_i with exercise price P, on a pure discount bond maturing at time t_{i+1} with value $P(1 + \tau r_X)$.[5]

Each caplet is equivalent to a bond put option. This is important because many of the simpler interest rate models we shall meet later have explicit formulae for bond option values, which means that caps[6] can be priced very easily in those models. For instance, we shall see the bond option formula of Jamshidian (89) [308] in the extended Vasicek model.

Black's Formula for Caps

Consider a cap on Libor of tenor τ with individual caplets maturing at time $t_i = t_0 + i\tau$, $i = 1, \ldots, n$. The payoff to the ith caplet at time t_{i+1} is

$$p_i = \tau \max (0, L_{t_i} - r_X), \tag{3.35}$$

where L_{t_i} is the market quoted Libor rate at time t_i, r_X is the exercise rate and the notional principal is 1. Let c_i be the value at time t of the ith caplet. The value of the cap at time $t < t_0$ is $c = \sum_{i=1}^{n} c_i$.

For an individual caplet, maturing at time t_i, Black's formula for the value of the caplet is

$$c_i = \tau P(t, t_{i+1})(F_t(t_i, t_{i+1})N(d_1) - r_X N(d_2)), \tag{3.36}$$

where $P(t, t_{i+1})$ is the time t value of the time t_{i+1} maturity pure discount bond, $F_t(t_i, t_{i+1})$ is the market forward rate,

$$d_1 = \frac{1}{\sigma_i \sqrt{t_i - t}} \ln \frac{F_t(t_i, t_{i+1})}{r_X} + \frac{1}{2} \sigma_i \sqrt{t_i - t}, \tag{3.37}$$

$$d_2 = d_1 - \sigma_i \sqrt{t_i - t}, \tag{3.38}$$

and σ_i is the Black's volatility of the ith caplet. Write $c_i = c_i(\sigma_i)$. For $c = \sum_{i=1}^{n} c_i$, the Black's cap volatility is σ such that $c = \sum_{i=1}^{n} c_i(\sigma)$. In some sense σ represents an 'average volatility' of the set of individual caplets. σ_i coincides with the actual forward rate volatility if the market forward rate is log-normal with zero drift, $df_{i,t} = \sigma_i f_{i,t} dz_{i,t}$.

Cap prices are quoted in the market in terms of the Black's volatility σ. Table 3.3 gives examples of market quoted cap volatilities for different maturity times. An ATM (at-the-money) cap is a cap whose exercise rate r_X is set equal to the value of the relevant forward start swap. The cap volatilities in Table 3.3 are called flat volatilities.

---

[5] A put is a financial instrument giving the holder the right to sell an asset at a fixed price in the future. A call is an instrument giving its owner the right to buy an asset at a predetermined price at some time in the future.

[6] And perhaps also swaptions.

Table 3.3   US dollar ATM
cap volatilities

Cap volatilities, US dollar 23 July 1999	
Maturity	ATM vols
1y	14.10%
2y	17.40%
3y	18.50%
4y	18.80%
5y	18.90%
6y	18.70%
7y	18.40%
8y	18.20%
10y	17.70%
12y	17.00%
15y	16.50%
20y	14.70%
30y	12.40%

There is a very clear volatility hump with the highest implied volatilities at four to five years. Volatilities at the long end are falling but do not seem to be tending to zero.

It is possible to buy forward start caps where the first caplet matures at a future time. With a complete set of cap and forward start cap prices it is possible in principle to back out the values c_i of each individual caplet, and hence the individual volatilities σ_i. The individual σ_i are called forward-forward volatilities. Suppose we impose a functional form

$$\sigma_i = \sigma(t_i) = \beta_0 + (\beta_1 + \beta_2 t_i)\, e^{-kt_i} \tag{3.39}$$

onto the forward-forward volatilities.[7] We can choose the values of $(\beta_0, \beta_1, \beta_2, k)$ to give a best fit to ATM prices (perhaps by a least squares criterion). Figure 3.2 shows plots of both the flat volatilities and the forward-forward volatilities obtained in this way. With these forward-forward volatilities ATM prices are recovered very closely. The forward-forward volatility curve is significantly more humped than the flat volatility curve.

If a complete set of swaption volatilities σ_S, for all different periods and times to maturity, were available, one could in principle use (3.32) to back out correlations between different pairs of forward rates. Although regularisation becomes an issue (see Chapter 19), this insight is the basis for various attempts to calibrate some types of interest rate models.

Libor in Arrears

The payoff at time t_{i+1} to an ordinary caplet is $p_i = \tau \max(0, L_{t_i} - r_X)$, where L_{t_i} is the Libor rate observed at time t_i. For a Libor in arrears caplet the payoff p_i is made

---

[7] This is a Nelson and Siegel functional form; see Chapter 15.

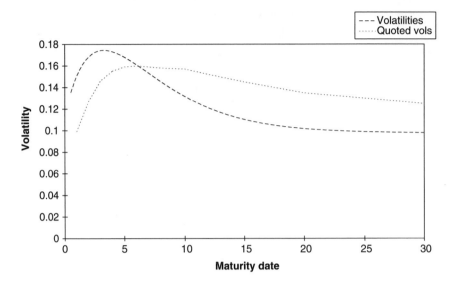

Figure 3.2 Flat and forward-forward volatilities

at time t_i, instead of time t_{i+1}. This is equivalent to a payoff of

$$\bar{p}_i = p_i(1 + \tau L_{t_i}) = \tau \max\left(0, L_{t_i}(1 - \tau r_X) + \tau L_{t_i}^2 - r_X\right) \qquad (3.40)$$

at time t_{i+1}. The discounted forward payoff is quadratic in L_{t_i}, so that an ordinary Black-like formula cannot be used. Of course, if numerical methods are being used to compute the value of a caplet it matters very little to the complexity of the calculation whether the payoff is at time t_i or at time t_{i+1}.

3.1.6 Comparison of Instruments

We have described several types of interest rate instrument. These, and others listed below, vary in the demands they place on interest rate models.

- *Short sterling futures options.* Have a short time to maturity, and are exercisable into short dated instruments.
- *Swaptions and bond options.* May have short times to maturity, and are exercisable into long dated instruments.
- *Caps.* Some caplets may have long times to maturity, but in any case are exercisable into short dated instruments.
- *Captions.* A caption may have a short time to maturity, and is exercisable into another derivative, which itself is exercisable into short and long dated underlying.

Even this short list contains instruments with very different problems. Short sterling futures options are short dated and exercise into a short interest rate. If a model is needed for these (and one is, since they are very commonly used for hedging purposes) it may only need to accurately model a short interest rate. On the other hand, a cap contains caplets which mature from times quite near the present right up to the final maturity of the cap which may be 20 years or more in the future. In this case it is essential to be able to model not only the short rate, but also longer rates up to the final cap maturity date. Correlation effects between long and short rates may also become important.

Other instruments—American options and exotics with path-dependent payoffs—give even greater problems. We will find that no one model is currently able to simultaneously and satisfactorily value and hedge all the instruments available in the market.

3.1.7 Day Bases

Calculating the cashflows, and their timing, accruing from a financial instrument such as a bond or a swap ought to be simple. Unfortunately, different countries and markets have different market conventions for calculating cashflows and timings from quoted rates. The differences are generally small in percentage terms, but can amount to significant sums when large principals are involved, and so it is important to apply the conventions correctly. The most frequently encountered of these methods of calculating the day count fraction, called day bases or day count conventions, are

- actual/365
- actual/360
- actual/actual
- 30/360.

The details of how these day bases are used, under all possible circumstances, are confusing and illogical. Exceptional situations are handled differently in different countries and markets, and the reader is referred to the ISDA annual booklet (ISDA (98) [303]) for further details. Here we restrict ourselves to describing just the principles of each method. Apart from this section we will rarely concern ourselves again with the details of day count functions.

The usual way of calculating the size of interest cashflows to a coupon bond or other instrument is

$$\text{cashflow} = \text{annual coupon} \times \text{the year fraction the cashflow relates to.} \quad (3.41)$$

Write d_1 and d_2 for the start and end dates of some calendar period. There are two aspects to calculating the year fraction of an interest rate instrument. The first is to determine the year fraction, $\alpha(d_1, d_2)$, given the dates d_1 and d_2. The second is to determine the start and end dates, d_1 and d_2.

α depends upon the day basis being used. We illustrate the day bases listed above, but variations on these themes appear constantly.

The first two methods, actual/365 and actual/360, are straightforward:

$$\text{actual/365: } \alpha(d_1, d_2) = \frac{d_2 - d_1}{365}, \quad (3.42)$$

$$\text{actual/360: } \alpha(d_1, d_2) = \frac{d_2 - d_1}{360}. \tag{3.43}$$

Actual/actual is less simple. It counts the number of whole calendar years between two dates and adds on the fractions of the year at the start and end of the period:

$$\text{actual/actual: } \alpha(d_1, d_2) = \frac{f_2 - d_1}{f_2 - f_1} + (n - 3) + \frac{d_2 - f_{n-1}}{f_n - f_{n-1}}, \tag{3.44}$$

where f_i are year end dates, and $f_1 \le d_1 \le f_2 < \cdots < f_{n-1} \le d_2 \le f_n$. If each year is assumed to have 365 days, the expression simplifies to (3.42).

30/360 is more complicated. This counts the whole number of calendar months in between d_1 and d_2 and then adds on the fractions of each month at the start and end of the period. When calculating fractions the method assumes that a year has 12 months of 30 days each. α is broadly calculated as

$$\text{30/360: } \alpha(d_1, d_2) = \frac{1}{12} \left(\frac{m_2 - d_1}{30} + (n - 3) + \frac{d_2 - m_{n-1}}{30} \right), \tag{3.45}$$

where m_i are month end dates, and $m_1 \le d_1 \le m_2 < \cdots < m_{n-1} \le d_2 \le m_n$. However, markets vary in how they treat situations where, for instance, $d_2 = m_n$ and $m_n = 31$ or $m_n = 29$. The reader is referred to specialist publications for details.

One may convert from an actual/365 rate to an actual/360 rate just by multiplying by $\frac{365}{360}$, but a conversion to and from a 30/360 rate is more complicated and arbitrary.

Use of Day Count Conventions

The section lists which conventions are used in a number of major markets.

Libor and cash rates Day count: AUD, BEF, CAD and GBP use actual/365, while most others are actual/360. Eurolibor and Euribor both use 30/360.

Start date: AUD, CAD, GBP use same day; FRF uses same day +1; most others including Eurolibor and Euribor use same day +2.

End date: many currencies use the 'modified following business day' convention. The end date is on the following business day, unless it is in a different month, in which case it is on the previous business day. But if the start date was the last business day of a month then the end date is the last business day in the corresponding month.

Swaps Floating side: uses Libor conventions. Fixed side: uses the same start date as the floating side

Day count: CAD, GBP and JPY use actual/365. USD uses actual/actual while most European currencies use 30/360.

Government bonds nearly always have the same day count as swaps.

3.2   DESCRIBING INTEREST RATE PROCESSES

In this section we introduce basic ideas of the statistical modelling of financial time series. In the first part of this section we provide an intuition for the standard notation used to specify stochastic processes. In the second part we describe the probabilistic framework that allows us to rigorously capture important concepts such as conditional expectations, and the way they change through time.

The ideas of this section pervade the entire field of interest rate modelling. They are used extensively in Chapter 4 where we describe a theoretical pricing framework.

3.2.1 State Variables and their Processes

A model is defined by its state variables and by their processes. The values taken by the set of state variables in a model completely determine the state of the system. The state variables' processes determined how they change through time.

All stock prices and interest rate processes are stochastic processes. They change randomly over time, but the manner in which they change can be modelled. It is possible to divide the changes in their values into two parts, the first is a non-random, deterministic component, called the drift of the process, and second is a 'noise' term—the random part, which we call the volatility component of the process.[8]

The Drift Component

For a stock price, the deterministic drift component might be geometric growth. With no noise the stock price S_t would satisfy the differential equation

$$\frac{\mathrm{d}S_t}{\mathrm{d}t} = \mu S_t, \tag{3.46}$$

where μ is the exponential growth rate. The solution to (3.46) is

$$S_t = S_0 e^{\mu t}, \tag{3.47}$$

where S_t is the stock price at time t, with initial value S_0 at time 0. We can write Equation (3.46) as

$$\mathrm{d}S_t = \mu S_t \, \mathrm{d}t, \tag{3.48}$$

which is to be understood to be short-hand for

$$\int \mathrm{d}S_t = \int \mu S_t \, \mathrm{d}t. \tag{3.49}$$

Interest rate processes might be expected to have a tendency to return to a mean value or range of values. A simple way of modelling this is as

$$\frac{\mathrm{d}r_t}{\mathrm{d}t} = \alpha(\mu - r_t), \quad \alpha > 0. \tag{3.50}$$

---

[8] Strictly, a process can be decomposed into a finite or bounded component and a component of infinite variation. These we refer to casually as the drift and volatility components (see Protter (90) [444]).

If $r_t < \mu$, then the left-hand side of (3.50) is positive, so r_t tends to increase. If $r_t > \mu$, r_t will tend to decrease. We can write (3.50) as

$$\mathrm{d}r_t = \alpha(\mu - r_t)\,\mathrm{d}t, \tag{3.51}$$

which is understood to be short-hand for

$$\int \mathrm{d}r_t = \int \alpha(\mu - r_t)\mathrm{d}t. \tag{3.52}$$

The solution to (3.51) is

$$r_t = \mu + (r_0 - \mu)\mathrm{e}^{-\alpha t}, \tag{3.53}$$

where at time 0, r_0 is the initial value. r_t trends towards the level μ, the mean reversion level, and α, the mean reversion rate, is the speed it goes there at.

The Volatility Component

For a financial time series without jumps, noise is assumed to be a function of a Wiener process (we consider the inclusion of jumps in a later chapter). A Wiener process is a certain standardised stochastic process. We shall usually write z_t for the value of a Wiener process at time t. For a Wiener process with value z_t at time t, its value z_T at time $T > t$, conditional on its value z_t at time t, is normally distributed, with a mean z_t and variance $T - t$. Figure 3.3 shows a set of sample paths for a simulated Wiener process. The paths of z_t are continuous, but differentiable almost nowhere.[9] z_t can be scaled, so that given z_t, σz_T is normal with mean z_t, variance $\sigma^2(T - t)$.

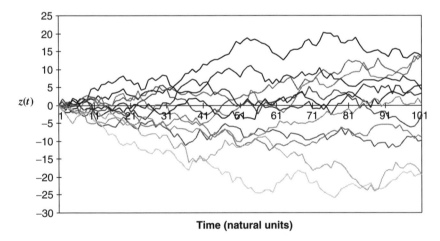

Figure 3.3 Sample paths of a Wiener process

---

[9] Sample paths are differentiable only on a set of measure zero—a set with zero probability mass.

We will need to integrate with respect to changes in z_t, in order to evaluate expressions such as $\int_0^t \sigma r_t^\gamma \, dz_s$. dz_t can be interpreted as an infinitesimal change in z_t, over an infinitesimal time dt. The concept of an infinitesimal increment in a Wiener process z_t can be made rigorous, but we do not attempt to do so here. For our purposes we will assume that infinitesimals like dt and dz_t always appear under integral signs and are, in effect, integrated away. For instance, we have (both intuitively and rigorously) $\int_0^t dz_s = z_t - z_0$. All the expressions we shall write involving infinitesimals are to be interpreted as having integral signs in front of them. For full discussions of stochastic calculus, at various degrees of abstraction, the reader is referred to Øksendal (95) [424], Karatzas and Shreve (91) [329], Protter (90) [444], Williams (91) [539], Rogers and Williams (87) [459], and others. Baxter and Rennie (96) [55] is a very readable account at a non-technical level.

In the meantime we shall heuristically interpret the symbol dz_t as a small random increment in z_t with mean 0 and variance dt.

To introduce noise to a stock price process S_t or an interest rate process r_t, we add on a term in the random increment dz_t of a Wiener process z_t. The share price process for S_t becomes, for instance,

$$dS_t = \mu S_t \, dt + \sigma S_t \, dz_t, \qquad (3.54)$$

where dz_t is scaled by σS_t, so that returns to S_t have a constant standard deviation σ. This process is called geometric Brownian motion. The process (3.54) is interpreted as being integrated:

$$\int dS_t = \int \mu S_t \, dt + \int \sigma S_t \, dz_t. \qquad (3.55)$$

The interest rate process becomes

$$dr_t = \alpha(\mu - r_t)dt + \sigma \, dz_t, \qquad (3.56)$$

which is interpreted as

$$\int dr_t = \int \alpha(\mu - r_t)dt + \int \sigma \, dz_t. \qquad (3.57)$$

The process (3.56) is called an Ornstein–Ulhenbeck process, and was the process assumed for the short rate in the very first no-arbitrage interest rate model, the Vasicek (77) [529] model.

To see what sample paths generated by the process (3.56) look like it is easy to simulate paths of r_t, for a time step Δt. We suppose we are given a value r_0 for the short rate at time 0. If we have generated a value r_t for the interest rate at time t, define

$$r_{t+\Delta t} = r_t + \alpha(\mu - r_t)\Delta t + \sigma w_t, \qquad (3.58)$$

where $w_t \sim N(0, \Delta t)$, iid, is a normal variate with mean 0 and variance Δt, with independent samplings. Note that $w_t = \sqrt{\Delta t}\, \varepsilon_t$, where $\varepsilon_t \sim N(0, 1)$, iid, is standard normal. Successively applying (3.58) we evolve a sample path up to some time horizon T_{max}. This is a naive Euler simulation. We shall examine discretisation methods in more detail in Chapter 13.

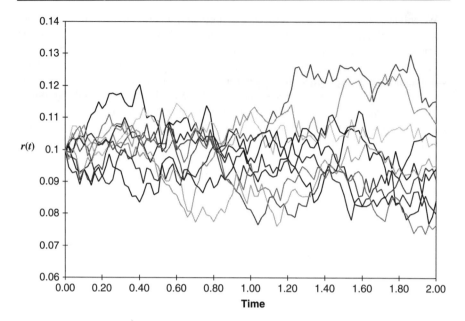

Figure 3.4   Sample paths for a Vasicek process, $\alpha = 2$, $\sigma = 0.02$, $\mu = 0.10$

Figure 3.4 shows the result of using equation (3.56), via equation (3.58), to simulate the short rate process. It is clear that these sample paths have values that lie close to the mean value μ. Comparing Figure 3.3 with Figure 3.4 the sample paths for the Ornstein–Ulhenbeck process are apparently more tightly bound to the level μ then the Wiener process. Statistics for the Vasicek process are available, as we shall see later. For the moment we note that the limiting distribution of r_t as $r_t \to \infty$ is $N(\mu, \sigma^2/2\alpha)$. The larger the value of α the faster the process reverts towards μ, and the tighter the process is bound to μ.

The parameter σ in (3.54) and (3.56) is called the volatility of the asset price and interest rate processes. σ can be estimated in two quite different ways; historical volatility is an estimate of σ derived from an historical time series, and implied volatility is a value of σ backed out from prices of derivative instruments. We will refer to volatility estimation again in later chapters.

3.2.2   A Probabilistic Framework

Prices of financial instruments are critically dependent upon the probabilities of events occurring in the markets, and of the markets' attitude to risk. A rigorous mathematical framework is required to enable us to develop a mechanism to value and hedge derivative securities. Here we present some necessary concepts. In Chapter 4 we apply these concepts to the valuation and hedging problem.

The fundamental object is the probability space $(\Omega, \mathcal{F}, Q)$. Ω is the sample space, $\mathcal{F}$ is a family of events, and Q is a probability measure.

Probability, Events and Filtrations

Ω, the sample space, can be thought of as the set of all possible histories of the world up to some maximum time horizon $T_{\max}$. For example, if the world consists of one stock S_t and one interest rate r_t observed over the time interval $t \in [0, T_{\max}]$, then $\omega \in \Omega$ represents a particular pair of paths of stock prices and rates from time 0 to time $T_{\max}$. $\omega \in \Omega$ is called a sample point. For a fixed $\omega \in \Omega$, and for $t \in [0, T_{\max}]$, write $S_t(\omega)$ and $r_t(\omega)$ for the price and rate of that particular history. At time $T_{\max}$, we are able to identify which $\omega \in \Omega$ was the actual history observed, but for $t < T_{\max}$ we have only seen price and rates up to time t, so we cannot yet identify exactly which ω we will turn out to have belonged to.

An 'event' is a subset of Ω which can be given a probability of occurring. If $A \subseteq \Omega$ is an event, then the probability of A occurring is the probability of the actual history being one of the possible histories contained in A. A could be an event like an interest rate reaching a certain level, or it could be something much more complicated—for instance the event could be path dependent. The set $A = \{\omega \in \Omega \mid S_0 = 100, 130 \leq S_{t_0} \leq 150\}$ is the event that the process S_t has value 100 at time 0, and lies in the range $[130, 150]$ at time t_0.

$\mathcal{F}$ is the set of all events, so if $A \in \mathcal{F}$, then $A \subseteq \Omega$, and the probability of A occurring can be defined. If $B \subseteq \Omega$ but $B \notin \mathcal{F}$, then B is not an event and cannot be assigned a probability.

Q is a probability measure on the sample space Ω. For $A \in \mathcal{F}$, $Q(A)$ is the probability of A occurring; that is, the probability of A containing the actual history. Technically $\mathcal{F}$ is constructed to be a σ-algebra, which means, essentially, that probabilities 'work correctly' on the events in $\mathcal{F}$.[10] If $Q(A) = 0$, then A is said to be a set of measure zero, with zero probability of occurring.[11] Q has various necessary properties:

- $Q(\Omega) = 1$, and $Q(\phi) = 0$. The probability of the actual history being contained within the set of all possible histories is equal to 1. The probability of no history occurring is zero.
- If A_1 and A_2 are events, and $A_1 \cap A_2 = \phi$, then $Q(A_1 \cup A_2) = Q(A_1) + Q(A_2)$. This means if A_1 and A_2 are independent, then the probability of either happening is the sum of the probabilities of each happening.

Filtrations   For each time t, S_t and r_t are the stock price and interest rate at time t. As time goes by, we see more and more prices and rates, and learn more and more about which $\omega \in \Omega$ is the actual history. We steadily accumulate information which enables us to distinguish between more and more events, in the sense that there are more and more sets $A \subseteq \Omega$ to which we can assign probabilities, as explained below. Suppose that at time t we can distinguish events in a set $\mathcal{F}_t$. If $t_1 < T_2 < T_{\max}$, then $\mathcal{F}_{t_1} \subseteq \mathcal{F}_{t_2} \subseteq \mathcal{F}_{T_{\max}} \equiv \mathcal{F}$.

---

[10] We shall not give a definition of a σ-algebra here; see Williams (91) [539], for instance.

[11] If A is defined by some property that the sample paths possess and $Q(A) = 1$, then one says that the property holds almost always, a.a., almost everywhere, a.e., or almost surely, a.s.

The set $\{\mathcal{F}_t\}_{t\in[0,T_{\max}]}$ is called a filtration. Having a filtration enables us to alter the probabilities we assign to future events, conditioned by what is observed to have happened already. For example, suppose that between time 0 and time t_1 an interest rate path was observed to be $r_t = f(t)$, $t \in [0, t_1]$. For some fixed interval $[a, b] \subset \mathbb{R}^+$, and $T > t_1$, define the sets

$$A = \{\omega \in \Omega \mid r_0 = f(0) \text{ and } r_T \in [a, b]\}, \tag{3.59}$$

$$A_f = \{\omega \in \Omega \mid r_t = f(t), t \in [0, t_1] \text{ and } r_T \in [a, b]\}. \tag{3.60}$$

Then if r_t has a 'sensible' process (for instance the Ornstein–Ulhenbeck process (3.56)), then $A \in \mathcal{F}_0$, but either $A_f \notin \mathcal{F}_0$, or $A_f \in \mathcal{F}_0$ and $Q(A_f) = 0$, since the probability of any particular path occurring is zero, if it has a probability at all. But $A_f \in \mathcal{F}_{t_1}$, with non-zero measure, $Q(A_f) \neq 0$. In fact $A_f \in \mathcal{F}_{t_1}$ for all possible paths f. At time t_1 we can now distinguish between all those events with different paths up to time t_1, but it is not possible to distinguish between these events before time t_1. This is illustrated in Figure 3.5. At time t_1 we know the path followed up to that time, but we do not know the full path up to time T.

Conditional expectations Given a probability space, as set out above, we can now compute useful quantities such as, for instance, the expected interest rate at time T, given that we know all that has happened up to some time $t < T$. Write this expectation as $\mathbb{E}[r_T \mid \mathcal{F}_t]$ or as $\mathbb{E}_t[r_T]$. This is the conditional expectation, conditional upon our knowledge at time t as represented by the family of events $\mathcal{F}_t$. $\mathbb{E}[r_T \mid \mathcal{F}_t]$ has a technical definition, but it is conceptually equivalent to the usual idea of conditional expectation.

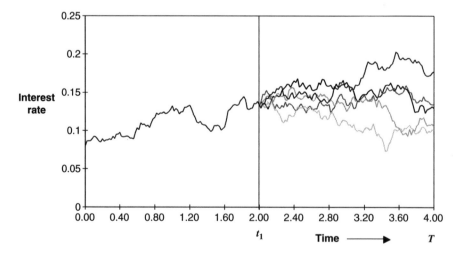

Figure 3.5 Sample paths from time t_1

Stochastic Processes and Martingales

The framework described above is quite abstract. In practice we need to be able to compute using the things we can observe in the market, such as time series of interest rates and derivative prices. It means being able to assign probabilities to all useful events. We can do this if the state variables in our model are stochastic processes.

Stochastic processes   For our purposes, a stochastic process S_t is a random variable defined on Ω for each $t \in [0, T_{\max}]$, with the property that

$$(S_t)^{-1}(a, b) \in \mathcal{F}_t, \text{ for all intervals } (a, b) \subseteq \mathbb{R}. \tag{3.61}$$

This means that $A = \{\omega \in \Omega \mid S_t(\omega) \in (a, b)\}$ is an event at time t for all intervals $(a, b) \subseteq \mathbb{R}$, and we can give a probability to this event occurring. In other words, informally, we know a.e. the distribution function of S_t for all times $t \in [0, T_{\max}]$ (see Protter (90) [444]). If a set of random variables S_t has the property (3.61) for some filtration $\mathcal{F}_t$, then S_t is adapted to $\mathcal{F}_t$.

The processes (3.54) and (3.56) defined above for geometric Brownian motion and for the Vasicek process, are both stochastic processes. In fact they are examples of special types of stochastic processes called Itō diffusions. They have no jump terms, and functions of either of them may also be well-defined stochastic processes.

Martingales   An extremely important type of stochastic process is the martingale. These are fundamental to the pricing mechanisms we will encounter in Chapter 4.

A stochastic process is a martingale if $\mathbb{E}_t[S_T] = S_t$, for all times $t \leq T$. That is, the expected value in the future conditioned on what is known now is always identical to today's value. For example, a Wiener process z_t is a martingale, by definition. A stock or share price process

$$\mathrm{d}S_t = \mu S_t \, \mathrm{d}t + \sigma S_t \, \mathrm{d}z_t \tag{3.62}$$

is not a martingale unless $\mu = 0$, because otherwise it has a drift and its expected value will move farther from its value today as time goes on.

A supermartingale is a stochastic process with the property that $\mathbb{E}_t[S_T] \leq S_t$, and a submartingale is one with the property that $\mathbb{E}_t[S_T] \geq S_t$, for all $0 \leq t \leq T \leq T_{\max}$.

3.3   INTRODUCTION TO INTEREST RATE MODELS

This section introduces some examples of elementary interest rate models. We discuss a set of possible criteria against which a model may be assessed and compare the examples by the criteria. The section gives a brief overview of how models are used in practice.

3.3.1   Types of Interest Rate Model

Any interest rate model has to have two main ingredients if it is to have any hope of practical application. It must provide a statistical description of how the state variables in the model change through time, and it must provide (if only implicitly) a procedure to price interest rate derivatives from the statistical description. Some models, such as Hull and White (93) (94) [295], [296], [297], have extremely straightforward pricing procedures. (Hull and White has an efficient lattice method, for instance; see Chapter 14.) Other models may have appealing and more realistic statistics, but be relatively intractable.

The mathematical form that the statistical description of an interest rate process takes has been touched upon in a preceding section. Such a description entails firstly identifying the state variables that the model uses, and secondly specifying the dynamics of the state variables. The models described below spring from various sources, but all are specified in this form.

The main categories of model are briefly reviewed here and discussed in detail in later chapters. The categorisation used here is one of several that could be employed (for a somewhat different alternative see Hunt and Kennedy (99) [301]) but it has the advantage of being relatively intuitive.

We divide the models into six main types, which shall be defined in due course and examined in detail in later chapters.

1. Affine yield models, for example Duffie and Kan (94) [182], (96) [183]);
2. Whole yield curve models, for example Heath, Jarrow and Morton (92) [275] and Brace *et al.* (97) [88];
3. Market models, for example Jamshidian (96) [312], (97) [313];
4. Price kernel models, for example Constantinides (92) [139], Rogers (97) [458];
5. Positive models, for example Flesaker and Hughston (96) [224] and log-r models;
6. Consol models, for example Brennan and Schwartz (79) [93];

Other types of model exist—random field models and models with jump components, for instance. We discuss these also in a later chapter, in the context of a more theoretical modelling framework. There is also a collection of non-linear models that do not fit precisely into the categories given above. These models are not widely used in practice, however.

In this section we present three elementary models. Two are affine yield models and one is a simple model with a non-linear volatility function. All three models have a single state variable—the short rate—and all three of them are inadequate for valuing or hedging sophisticated instruments. (They might be quite acceptable for simpler instruments.)

With these models, as with all models, procedures exist to extract prices from the model. Ideally a model will have explicit solutions, with explicit formulae for the values of simple instruments such as bonds or bond options. Usually, however, one must use numerical methods to find prices for any instrument other than the most simple, and for many models there may be no explicit solutions at all.

3.3.2 Examples of Basic Models

We compare three elementary models from various points of view. For all three models the underlying state variable is the short rate r_t. The models are

- Extended Vasicek (time-varying mean, Hull and White (93) [295]),

$$dr_t = \alpha(\theta(t) - r_t)dt + \sigma \, dz_t; \qquad (3.63)$$

- Extended CIR (time-varying mean, Cox, Ingersoll and Ross (85) [148], Jamshidian (95) [310]),

$$dr_t = \alpha(\theta(t) - r_t)dt + \sigma r_t^{1/2} \, dz_t; \qquad (3.64)$$

- CKLS (Chan, Karolyi, Longstaff and Sanders (92) [124]),

$$dr_t = \alpha(\mu - r_t)dt + \sigma r_t^{\gamma} \, dz_t. \qquad (3.65)$$

The extended Vasicek and extended CIR models have time-varying mean reversion levels which, through the proper choice of $\theta(t)$, enables them to fit to the current term structure. The extended CIR model has a factor of $r_t^{1/2}$ in its volatility, which can ensure that rates do not go negative. (The short rate can become negative in the extended Vasicek model.) The CKLS model has a constant mean reversion level μ but has a slightly more flexible volatility function.

We can gain some intuition for the behaviour of these models by simulating sample paths for r_t. Take a time step Δt and an initial value r_0 at time 0. Given a value r_t, at time t, set

$$r_{t+\Delta t} = r_t + \alpha(\theta(t) - r_t)\Delta t + \sigma r_t^{\gamma} \sqrt{\Delta t} \, \varepsilon_{t+\Delta t}, \qquad (3.66)$$

i.e.

$$r_{t+\Delta t} = (1 - \alpha \Delta t)r_t + \alpha \theta(t)\Delta t + \sigma r_t^{\gamma} \sqrt{\Delta t} \, \varepsilon_{t+\Delta t},$$

where $\varepsilon_{t+\Delta t} \sim N(0, 1)$. The factor of $\sqrt{\Delta t}$ ensures that (3.66) is properly simulating the Wiener process z_t.

Evolve (3.66) for N time steps. Figures 3.6 and 3.7 show simulated interest rate paths with typical values of γ and σ. They use the same set of ε_t and differ only in the values of σ and γ. The sample paths look quite similar, but there are nevertheless important differences in the scale of changes at different values of r_t. Figures 3.8 and 3.9 show the resulting frequency histograms for sample paths (A) and (B), respectively. The values of γ and σ have been chosen so that σr_t^{γ} has approximately the same range of values. It can be seen that both histograms are roughly unimodal, although the mean value for the histogram with larger γ looks lower, with values generally shifted down.

Compare Figures 3.6 and 3.8 with Figure 3.10. Figure 3.10 shows an empirical frequency histogram for sterling three-month Libor.

The histogram of three-month Libor bears no resemblance to Figures 3.8 and 3.9. It is multimodal; a plot of the time series of sterling three-month Libor given in Figure 3.11 clearly shows what appears to be a regime shift occurring in September 1992 immediately after sterling left the ERM.

We can already conclude that the simple models may not be suitable for modelling sterling three-month Libor over long time spans.

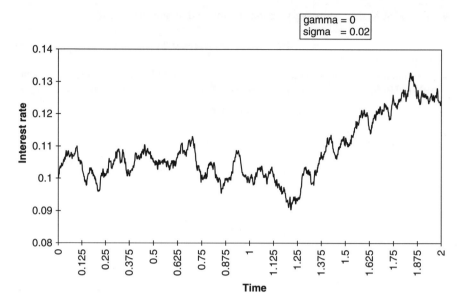

Figure 3.6   Sample path for a CKLS process (A)

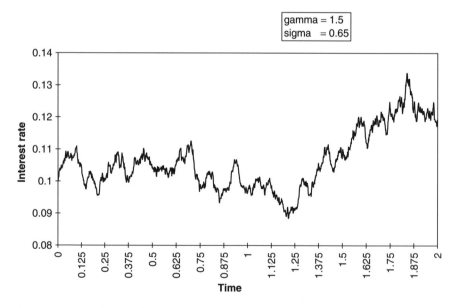

Figure 3.7   Sample path for a CKLS process (B)

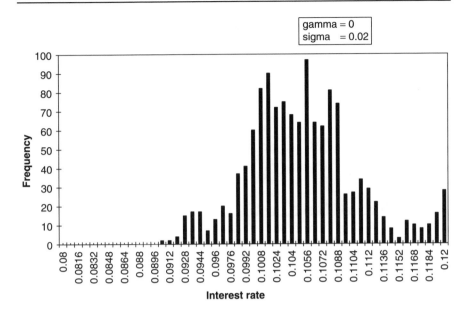

Figure 3.8 Frequency histogram of the simulated series (A)

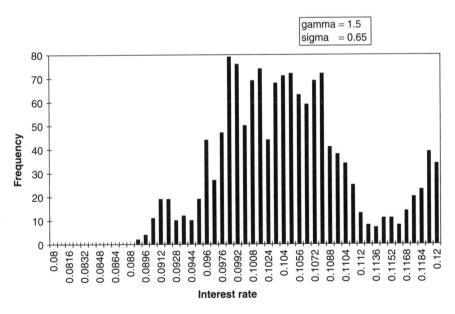

Figure 3.9 Frequency histogram of the simulated series (B)

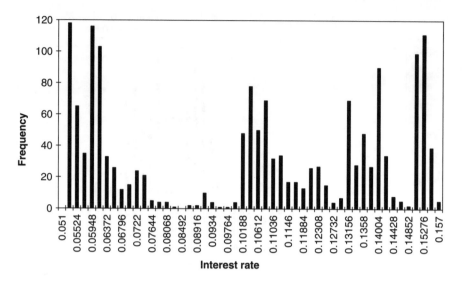

Figure 3.10   Empirical frequency histogram of UK three-month Libor, 1988–1995

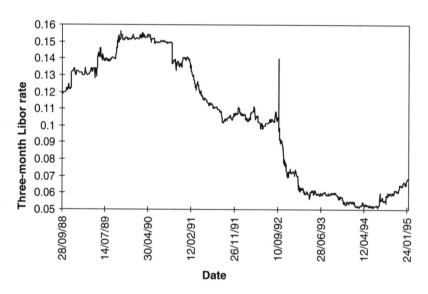

Figure 3.11   Empirical time series of UK three-month Libor, 1988–1995

3.3.3   Criteria for Model Selection

Interest rate modelling is a pragmatic as well as an academic area. Although a model may have strong theoretical properties, unless it actually *works* it is of relatively little use. Determining whether a model works or not is an ill-defined objective, but there are various desirable properties a model could possess which increase the likelihood of it being used in practice. We split these into three headings; the model should fit market data, it should have good dynamical properties, and it should be tractable.

Fitting Market Data

Interest rate models can be regarded as methods of interpolation and extrapolation. Given some set of market data, choose the parameters of the model so that (a) the model fits closely to the market data and (b) using these parameters other instruments may now be priced consistently with the market data.

In practice it is usually not possible to fit more than a few aspects of the complete set of available market data. One would like to fit

- the current yield curve,
- current caplet/bond option prices,
- the current volatility structure, for instance the term structure of ATM bond option implied volatilities.

In addition, if one wants to price some new or exotic product, one would like to produce a good match with the prices of instruments similar in kind to the new product. This may not always be possible, since similar products may not always exist, but it is highly desirable. For instance, similar liquid products may be used to hedge the new product, and it is essential for instruments in the hedge portfolio to be accurately priced by a model. Vanilla swaptions may be used to hedge unusual swaption products; in such a case one expects vanilla swaption prices to be fitted accurately by a model.

A Digression on Fitting the Yield Curve

A money market yield curve usually has between 12 and 20 points given by market rates. These will be four to six short Libor-type rates, six or seven swap rates, and four to twelve futures contracts. The idea behind fitting a model to a market yield curve is to fit it to the given points, allowing all floatable parameters to float, and see how good a fit results, for instance how large the residuals are. To a large extent this is purely a function of how many floating parameters the model contains. To be plausible, a model must have few enough parameters that a good fit is significant, and enough to ensure that a good fit is possible.

Frequently it is desirable to use a model to simulate for future yield curves, starting from an initial yield curve, usually the current one. We shall see that several models fit any initial yield curve well, for example the Heath, Jarrow and Morton (92) [275] model and the Hull and White (93) [295] model. Other models which give good approximate fits to an initial yield curve are dynamic mean models (Sørensen (94) [501], Chen (96)

[126]) and stochastic volatility models (Longstaff and Schwartz (92) [365], Fong and Vasicek (91) [226]).

Some models, for example single factor Vasicek, do not have a large range of shapes, and will provide a poor fit to some initial yield curves. Others like Cox, Ingersoll and Ross will give a good fit to most initial curves but then may produce implausible dynamics for individual rates if used for simulation. However, depending upon the desired application, this may be acceptable.

It is not always the case that one wishes to fit the entire yield curve. We might only be interested in the two to five year region. We might be concerned only with dynamics of a single rate, for example when considering short dated options on short bonds. It is also possible that we might be interested only in the price of a single type of instrument, like caps, and not be concerned with fitting other instrument prices. So models which are inadequate in some respects may still be useful for specialised purposes.

Good Dynamics

Current market prices are essentially static features. A model should also be able to fit, to some extent, the way that prices change through time. This means having the theoretical model distributions of future prices as close as possible to the distributions of actual market prices. Of course, there are problems in knowing, at any point in time, what the distributions of market prices for future times actually are. Putting this to one side, in practice one may only hope at best to match selected dynamical features. Even then, if the dynamical feature is observed under the objective measure rather than a pricing measure, one may have to estimate the prices of risk for the model, as well as the coefficients of interest. (We discuss the objective and pricing measures in Chapter 4.)

The types/types of dynamical feature that it may be thought desirable to match may include:

- the dynamics of the short rate, for instance its reversion level and rate, and its volatility;
- the dynamics of the whole yield curve, for example, the number and shape of underlying principal components (see Chapter 16);
- the dynamics of selected instruments.

'Dynamics' may be measured as moments of an historical time series.

Tractability

To be useful, any model must give computable solutions. It is no accident that some of the most popular interest rate models are those which have either explicit solutions for the values of a range of instruments, or else come equipped with good computational methods, such as lattice implementations. No model has explicit solutions for every type of instrument, so one may ask how tractable a model is for different classes of instrument. Does the model:

- have explicit solutions for 'simple' instruments such as bonds, bond options and caplets?
- have simple numerical solution methods for more complicated instruments such as swaptions, American options, and path-dependent instruments?

In many cases one still has to use the full machinery of finite difference methods or Monte Carlo methods, but even here some models may be easier to compute with than others.

Strengths and Weaknesses of Basic Models

Table 3.4 presents a rough and ready comparison of the three basic models described above. The table is largely self-explanatory, but its entries are to some extent a matter of opinion. There is latitude for interpretation over the meaning of the different categories of comparison. At best the table represents an indication of the sort of things that each model may be good or bad at compared with the other models.

None of the models performs particularly well across the full range of interest rate products. Their chief advantage is their relative tractability compared with the more complex models we shall meet later.

The extended Vasicek model can fit the initial term structure exactly, and it has a very simple lattice implementation that enables it to value and hedge a wide range of instruments (see Chapter 14). Being only a one-factor model it is unable to price instruments that manifestly depend upon two or more sources of risk, such as options on spreads.

The extended Cox, Ingersoll and Ross is also reasonably tractable, although its lattice implementation is slightly more complicated than extended Vasicek. It has a slightly

Table 3.4 Comparison of basic models

Models:	H&W(i)	CIR(i)	CKLS
Features:			
Statics			
Bond prices	Exact	Good	$\sim$
Caplet/bond options	OK[1]	OK[1]	Bad
Term structure of volatility	$\sim$[1]	$\sim$[1]	$\sim$[1]
Dynamics			
Short rate	$\sim$	$\sim$	$\sim$[2]
Yield curve	Bad[3]	Bad[3]	Bad
Tractable			
Simple	Good	OK	OK
Complex	OK	OK	OK

H&W(i): $dr_t = \alpha(\theta(t) - r_t)dt + \sigma\,dz_t$.
CIR(i): $dr_t = \alpha(\theta(t) - r_t)dt + \sigma r_t^{1/2} dz_t$.
CKLS: $dr_t = \alpha(\mu - r_t)dt + \sigma r_t^{\gamma}\, dz_t$.
[1]When $\sigma = \sigma(t)$ is a function of time.
[2]Better than H&W or CIR.
[3]The yield curve evolves unrealistically.

restricted set of term structures compared with the extended Vasicek model, stemming from the limitations that the $r_t^{1/2}$ term places on its volatility (Jarrow (88) [315]).

The Chan, Karolyi, Longstaff and Sanders model was essentially developed as a framework to carry out empirical comparisons of a set of models nested within it. It fits market data quite poorly, and it is significantly less tractable than the other two models, although it is still relatively easy to price within it using a finite difference or a Monte Carlo method.

None of the models can satisfactorily model the dynamics of either individual rates or of the yield curve as a whole.

The models can be nested into the general form:

$$dr_t = (\theta(t) + a(t)r_t)dt + \sigma(t)r_t^\gamma dz_t, \qquad (3.67)$$

where $\theta(t)$, $a(t)$ and $\sigma(t)$ are three deterministic functions of time. For CKLS, θ, a and σ are constants, and for H&W and CIR, $\gamma = 0$ or $\frac{1}{2}$. We discuss the specification (3.67) more fully in a later chapter. It appears at first sight to be quite flexible. Since up to three functions can be supplied, it should be able to fit three functions observable in the market, for instance:

- the initial term structure,
- the initial term structure of volatility,
- the time path of the short rate volatility.

Unfortunately, although the model may fit these selected features exactly at the initial time, there is no guarantee that the model will continue to provide sensible prices and volatilities as it evolves. In fact, if $\sigma(t)$ or $a(t)$ are specified so that the model fits an initial term structure of volatility, because these functions are deterministic, one characteristically finds that at later times the term structure of volatility will have evolved significantly away from reasonable values.

3.3.4 Overview of Using Interest Rate Models

A model intended to price and hedge will usually either be:

1. Tailored for some particular application or
2. An off-the-peg model adapted for in-house use.

If constructing one's own model from scratch there are several stages to go through. We suppose that a factor model is being constructed, rather than an HJM-type model, but analogous considerations apply.

First: Decide upon the state variables.

Frequently, if one has a particular application in mind, a choice of state variables may be obvious. State variables may be:[12]

---

[12] In an HJM model state variables are the components of variation in the yield curve as a whole; see Chapter 8.

1. Found directly off the yield curve, for instance, the short rate or spot rates of various maturities, or forward rates or swap rates;
2. 'Indirect' state variables, for instance, the short rate volatility, or the mean of the short rate, that cannot be directly observed;
3. 'Pure' state variables for which there is no immediate underlying intuition.

It may be preferable to choose easy to measure state variables, whose values can be observed directly and which do not have to be inferred. For instance, if the short rate process is $dr_t = \alpha(x_t - r_t)dt + \sigma_r \, dz_{r,t}$, then r_t, the short rate, might be assumed to be directly observed, but x_t, a stochastic reversion level, must be inferred, perhaps using a filtering method (see Chapter 18).

If a model is derived from an underlying economic framework, then the state variables may correspond to underlying economic processes. This is the case in Cox, Ingersoll and Ross (85) [148], Longstaff and Schwartz (92) [365], Duffie et al. (97) [187], Bakshi and Chen (96) [45] and Demmel (98) [165] models. It is not clear whether this makes it easier to identify values for the state variables; in practical applications of this type of model the underlying source of the state variables is usually ignored.

With the development of market models, almost anything can be used as a state variable—forward swap rates, the present values of annuities, et cetera—since they can be given tractable dynamics under the appropriate probability measure. This leads on to the next stage of the procedure

Second: Decide upon the dynamics of the state variables.

For instance, an interest rate might be declared to be mean reverting, $dr_t = \alpha(\mu - r_t)dt + \sigma_r \, dz_t$. Since it is hard to match to observed dynamics the choice of process will be guided by a desire either to make the model tractable, or to provide good fits to market prices. The dynamics might be specified under altered probabilities; see Chapter 4. So-called affine formulations are much more tractable than non-affine formulations. See Section 3.4.

Third: Decide upon an appropriate valuation method.

In the absence of explicit solutions there may be little choice but to use a Monte Carlo or finite difference method. However, these methods are not always available for certain models and certain instruments.

A model in which the state variables have state independent volatilities may have a lattice implementation. This is an advantage, but the cost of imposing restrictions on the form of the volatility functions may be high.

Fourth: Decide upon the parameter estimation method.

The model must still be calibrated to market prices; that is, the values of parameters in the model must be found so that market prices are recovered as closely as possible by the model. Standard techniques of calibrating to time series are the general method of moments (GMM), and the maximum likelihood method (ML).[13] These methods are

---

[13] One generally calibrates to prices in the market today, rather than to a time series. These issues are discussed further in Part IV.

described in Chapter 17. There is the problem of what to calibrate to; in the money market does one fit to caps or to swaptions, or to both, or to something else entirely? In the absence of suitable instruments to calibrate to, one may sometimes be forced to calibrate to historical data and estimate separately any prices of risk.

Models will usually need re-calibrating quite frequently. If a model were perfect and exactly explained market prices not only at an initial time, but also forever thereafter, then it would never need re-calibrating. In practice, models are far from perfect and have to be re-calibrated, perhaps daily or even more frequently.

Some models are more sensitive to changes in market prices than others. The Black, Derman and Toy model is a log-r model implemented on a lattice. It is notoriously sensitive to changes in market prices and requires frequent re-calibration. The underlying state variable is $X_t = \ln r_t$, the log of the short rate. For interest rates at normal levels, X_t is of the order -2 to -3, perhaps 40 or 50 times larger in absolute value than r_t itself. This means that, other things being equal, coefficients in the process for X_t are also likely to be much larger that those in the process for r_t, with implications for their sensitivity to market prices. There are also theoretical reasons why log-r models have stability problems as the lattice time step becomes small (see Chapter 9).

3.4   CATEGORIES OF INTEREST RATE MODEL

In this section we define the major categories of model mentioned in the previous section. We examine the models in detail in Part II. We leave the definition of other more minor categories—positive models, Consol-based models and non-linear models—to that Part. Consideration of jump models and other more general, theoretical categories are deferred until Chapter 10.

In the second part of this section we present comparisons between the categories of model based on criteria established in Section 3.3.3 and Chapter 2.

3.4.1   Descriptions of the Categories

The categories of model we define here are affine models, whole yield curve models, market models and price kernel models.

Affine Models

In affine models spot rates are affine functions of the state variables, and the state variables can be taken to be spot rates of particular maturities. To ensure these properties the dynamics of the state variables are heavily restricted. The short rate is affine in the state variables, $X_{1,t}, \ldots, X_{n,t}$, $r_t = f + g_1 X_{1,t} + \cdots + g_n X_{n,t}$, and the processes followed by the state variables are

$$dX_{i,t} = \left(\sum_{j=1}^{n} a_j X_{j,t} + b_i \right) dt + \sum_{j,k=1}^{n} \sigma_{i,j} v_{j,k} \, dz_{k,t}, \qquad (3.68)$$

where

$$v_{j,j} = \sqrt{\alpha_j + \sum_{k=1}^{n} \beta_{j,k} X_k}, \quad v_{j,k} = 0, \quad j \neq k,$$

under the pricing measure, and a_j, b_i, α_j, $\beta_{j,k}$ and $\sigma_{i,j}$ are constants.

In general one does not obtain explicit formulae (although in specific instances they may be available), but the models produce relatively simple partial differential equations, with relatively easy numerics.

Spot rates are of the form $r_t(\tau) = (1/\tau)A(\tau) + (1/\tau)B(\tau)X_t$, where A and B satisfy the differential equations:

$$-\frac{\partial A(\tau)}{\partial \tau} = -f + b'B + \frac{1}{2}B' \Sigma \operatorname{diag}(\alpha)\Sigma'B, \tag{3.69}$$

$$-\frac{\partial B(\tau)}{\partial \tau} = -g + a'B + \frac{1}{2}B' \Sigma \beta \Sigma'B, \tag{3.70}$$

where $\Sigma = \{\sigma_{i,j}\}_{i,j=1,\dots,n}$, $\beta = \{\beta_{i,j}\}_{i,j=1,\dots,n}$, and with boundary conditions $A(0) = 0$, $B(0) = 0$.

Because of their tractability affine models are heavily used. Most of the early examples of term structure models were affine. A particularly tractable type of affine model are the dynamic mean models.

Dynamic Mean Models

The process (3.68) is the general form that state variables must have in the affine framework. If the model is to be mean reverting, the form of the drift of (3.68) is constrained. Furthermore, one may wish to reparameterise a model so that one of the state variables is the short rate itself. On the assumption that the short rate is mean reverting one may further reparameterise the model so that the short rate mean reversion level is either a constant or another state variable. A dynamic mean model is an affine model where the short rate mean reversion level is time dependent, being either a deterministic function of time or a stochastic variable. The short rate volatility may also be a deterministic function of time.

There are two main types of dynamic mean model in popular use. These are the extended Vasicek/CIR models, with a deterministic mean, and the generalised Vasicek/CIR models with a stochastic mean.

Extended Vasicek/CIR   The short rate process is of the form

$$\mathrm{d}r_t = \alpha(t)(\theta(t) - r_t)\mathrm{d}t + \sigma(t)r_t^{\gamma}\,\mathrm{d}z_t, \tag{3.71}$$

where $\theta(t)$, $\alpha(t)$ and $\sigma(t)$ are deterministic function of time. When $\gamma = 0$ we have the extended Vasicek model, when $\gamma = \frac{1}{2}$ it is extended CIR. This type of model is described by, for instance, Hull and White (93) [295]. We met this type of model in Section 3.3.3 where we noted that the model is able to fit exactly the initial term structure.

Generalised Vasicek/CIR   In a generalised Vasicek/CIR model the short rate mean reversion level is a stochastic variable. One such model was described by Hull and White (94) [296], and we shall meet a variety of others in Chapter 7. Consider the following model where the two state variables are the short rate r_t and its mean reversion level x_t:

$$dr_t = \alpha(x_t - r_t)dt + \sigma_r r_t^\gamma \, dz_{r,t}, \tag{3.72}$$

$$dx_t = \beta(\mu - x_t)dt + \sigma_x x_t^\gamma \, dz_{x,t}, \tag{3.73}$$

under the EMM. $\gamma = 0$ gives a generalised Vasicek model and $\gamma = \frac{1}{2}$ is generalised CIR. The model has five parameters, $(\alpha, \beta, \mu, \sigma_r, \sigma_x, \rho_{r,x})$, where $\rho_{r,x}$ is the correlation between $z_{r,t}$ and $z_{x,t}$. Although it cannot fit an initial term structure exactly, because of its large number of parameters it can usually give a reasonable fit.

Whole Yield Curve Models

This class models the yield curve as a whole. It is usually specified quite generally in terms of the instantaneous forward rate process

$$df_t(T) = \alpha(t, T, \omega)dt + \sigma(t, T, \omega)dz_t, \quad t < T, \tag{3.74}$$

where z_t is an n-dimensional Wiener process and the dependence of the drift $\alpha(t, T, \omega)$ and volatility $\sigma(t, T, \omega)$ on the sample point ω is explicitly displayed. The process (3.74) describes changes in the entire curve, $f_t(T)$, for all $t < T$.

Because of their dependence upon ω, the drift and volatility are fully path-dependent and can depend upon previous or current forward rates.

These models were first developed by Heath, Jarrow and Morton (92) [275] (the HJM model). More recently a family of whole yield curve market models has been developed by Brace, Gatarek and Musiela (97) [88] (the BGM model). The BGM framework is log-normal, where volatilities are proportional to forward rates.

Market Models

This is a recently investigated family of model where the state variables are market quoted rates. Contributions include Brace, Gatarek and Musiela (97) [88], Sandmann and Sondermann (94) [471], Miltersen *et al.* (97) [399], *et cetera*. The motivation is to obtain Black-like formulae for the values of options. This requires log-normal state variables. The short rate cannot be log-normal, as it explodes: expected futures rates become unbounded (Hogan and Weintraub (93) [284]). The solution, proposed by Sandmann and Sondermann (91) [470] and subsequently exploited by BGM, is to use market quoted rates as state variables.

Suppose that L_t is three-month Libor and $B_t(1/4)$ is the value of the pure discount bond maturing in three months, with spot rate $r_t(1/4)$, then $(1 + L_t/4)^4 = r_t(1/4)$, and we shall see in Chapter 4 that under a certain measure P,

$$B_t(1/4) = \mathbb{E}_t^P \left[\exp\left(-\int_t^{t+1/4} r_s \, ds \right) \right] = \frac{1}{1 + L_t/4}, \tag{3.75}$$

where $\mathbb{E}^P$ is the expectations operator with respect to P. It can be shown (see Chapter 9) that L_t can safely be log-normal without problems, and that within this framework one can obtain Black-like formulae for caplet and swaption prices.

Price Kernel Models

For some measure P and some asset value p_t acting as numeraire (see Chapter 4) pure discount bond prices are given by $B_t(T) = \mathbb{E}^P_t[Z_T/Z_t]$, where $Z_t = 1/p_t$. Z_t is the price kernel with respect to P. The idea of a price kernel model is to model directly the process for Z_t under P.

When $P = Q$ is the objective measure, Z_t is the standard price kernel and has a standard economic interpretation. The process for Z_t is normally chosen for convenience, but may also be chosen on economic grounds.

The first no-arbitrage interest rate model based on the price kernel approach was Constantinides (92) [139]. Recently Rogers (97) [458] has developed and generalised the approach and Glasserman and Zhao (98) [249] have related it to the HJM model and to positive rate models.

3.4.2 Comparison of Models

We compare models according to two different sets of criteria. The first comparison is on the strengths and weaknesses of the models based on the features described in Section 3.3.3. The second comparison is based on features derived from the historical investigation of Chapter 2.

Strengths and Weaknesses of the Models

This rough and ready comparison extends the earlier comparison to the broader range of interest rate models. The same caveats apply here as there. Table 3.5 compares the major classes of model.

HJM and market models give the best results overall, but for specific applications affine yield or dynamic mean models may be more appropriate.

The choice of model is not straightforward. It depends on both the modelling objectives and on the nature of the risk to be managed. Desks with large exotics exposure and a commitment to sell anything may be more likely to implement whole yield curve models, although in any case such groups will probably implement new models as a matter of course and are likely to have their own in-house models. At the other end of the scale, simple bond or bond option trading may not require anything more sophisticated than Black's to assist the trader.

Comparison Based on Historical Criteria

In Chapter 2 we explored aspects of interest rate behaviour that recur over the centuries. We identified several aspects of this behaviour that seemed to be good features to

Table 3.5   Comparison between major categories of model

Models:	DM (i)	DM (ii)	AY	HJM	MM
Features:					
Statics					
Bond prices	Exact	OK	Good	Exact	Exact
Caplet/Bond options	~	~	~	Exact	Exact
Volatility structure	No	~	OK	Excellent	Excellent
Dynamics					
Short rate	Good	Good	OK	~	~
Yield curve	No	~	Good	Excellent	Excellent
Tractable					
Simple	Good	Good	OK	~	Good
Complex	OK	OK	OK	~	OK

DM (i): Extended dynamic mean models.
DM (ii): Generalised dynamic mean models.
AY: Affine yield models.
MM: Market models.
Exact: Can fit exactly.
~: Does not really match the feature.
No: Does not match the feature at all.

incorporate into interest rate models. There are four features that we now wish to highlight. These are

1. *The behaviour of the short rate*: Does the model have a time-varying reversion level for the short rate?
2. *The behaviour of the long rate*: Does a long rate (for example a 20-year rate) have a sufficient range of movement?
3. *Term structure tilts*: Can the long end and the short end move simultaneously and roughly equally in opposite directions?
4. *Hyperinflations*: Is there a non-vanishing chance that the short rate becomes unbounded in finite time?

Table 3.6 compares a number of models, grouped into categories, by each of these four features. (The models will be described in more detail in Part II). All of the models considered in the table assume that the term structure is default-free (Duffie and Singleton (95), (97) [189], [190] have indicated that default may be accommodated by suitably adjusting the volatility structure, but this is outside the scope of this book).

Table entries are of course a matter of opinion, and a judgement must be made as to what each feature means in the context of each model. For instance, whole yield curve models contain all the other models, but the table describes their features as they are usually implemented. Dynamic mean models can be forced to hyperinflate by making their mean reversion levels explode, but this would then destroy their ability to capture any of the other features.

It can be seen from the table that whole yield curve models capture the long rate feature, and the tilt feature, but do not give good behaviour to the short rate. Affine

Table 3.6 Comparison of models on historical criteria

Features:	S	L	S/L	H
Model:				
Whole yield curve				
HJM (92) [275], BGM (97) [88]	×	Yes	Yes	×
Sommer (96) [500]	~	Yes	Yes	~
Affine				
Duffie and Kan (96) [183]	Yes	Yes	Yes	×
Babbs and Nowman (97) [38]	Yes	Yes	Yes	×
Longstaff and Schwartz (92) [365]	Yes	×	~	×
CIR (85) [148], 'standard' model	×	×	×	×
CIR (85) [148], 'inflation' model	~	~	~	×
Dynamic mean				
Tice and Webber (97) [523]	Yes	×	~	×
Hull and White (90) [292]	Yes	×	×	~
Fong and Vasicek (91) [226]	Yes	×	~	×
Chen (96) [126]	Yes	×	~	×
Ho and Lee (86) [280]	Yes	~	×	Yes
Price kernel				
Bakshi and Chen (96) [45]	×	×	×	×
Constantinides (92) [139]	×	×	×	×
Jump models				
Babbs and Webber (94) [40]	Yes	Yes	×	×

S: short rate behaviour; L: long rate behaviour.
S/L: tilt behaviour; H: hyperinflations.
Yes: the model has this feature.
~: the feature is present but unrealistic.
×: the model does not have this feature.

models can give good behaviour to the first three features, although they cannot fit market data as well as whole yield curve models. Dynamic mean models can give very good behaviour to the short rate, but do not rank highly otherwise. The price kernel models, stemming from an economic framework, do least well of all.

Only the Ho and Lee model explodes, yet this explosion is inevitable and cannot be said to mimic hyperinflationary behaviour. The time-varying drift in Ho and Lee is usually used to enable the model to match the current term structure. If used in this way the behaviour of the short rate becomes unrealistic. Hull and White, and Sommer, can be adapted to ensure that an explosion occurs. For Hull and White the explosion is manufactured by allowing the time-dependent reversion level to become unbounded. However, this is very much an exogenous effect. We shall see in Chapter 11 how Sommer's model can be implemented to allow explosions to occur endogenously.

From the table it appears that of the models tabulated, affine models such as Duffie and Kan (94) [182], including special cases of it such as Babbs and Nowman (99) [39] or Edmister and Madan (93) [196], best fit the listed features. Unfortunately they are unable to generate endogenous hyperinflations, and so fail to be ideal by our criteria.

Interest Rate Models and Regime Shifts

We saw in Chapter 2 that the current inflationary period is different to any that have preceded it. Expected inflation is no longer tied to a slowly changing supply of commodity money. One may speculate about possible future regime shifts. There seem to be two extreme possibilities, depending upon the success of the regulatory systems and government control in restricting the growth of the money supply. The two extreme scenarios are:

1. Money supply becomes exogenously uncontrollable.
2. It becomes possible to peg, credibly, the money supply.

The first scenario admits the possibility of hyperinflation, the second represents a reversion to some future version of a commodity standard.[14] Either case represents a regime shift over the present situation where governments are able to control the money supply, but cannot credibly reliably peg either it or its growth rate.

Let us suppose that one or other of these outcomes might become realistic within the next 20 years. This time span is long enough for major changes in culture, politics, the military balance and economics to take place, and is also within the maturity span of financial instruments currently being traded.

If the first scenario is deemed possible, then current interest rate models need to take into account the possibility of hyperinflation. One might argue that the market might already price in this risk; this is certainly possible and may perhaps be observed in the failure of long-run volatilities to decline away to zero in a dignified way. Further evidence that the market may indeed already take account of the possibility of hyperinflation lies in the difficulty that empirical studies encounter when attempting to demonstrate that interest rate processes are stationary. If hyperinflation is 'priced in', then one might expect interest rate processes to possess a unit root (so that the interest rate process could have an upward trend).

If the second scenario is more likely, then it is possible that Gaussian models would not adequately model rates; if rates are low, but positive and volatile, then a Gaussian model might allow significant probabilities of nominal rates becoming negative. Furthermore, with the yield curve necessarily flatter, and the long end considerably less volatile, the range of shapes currently observed for the yield curve might decline. Two- or three-factor models of the term structure might over-fit, and the market might return to using simple one-factor models like CIR or Black, Derman and Toy (90) [73] and Black and Karasinski (91) [74]. We speculate that CIR might provide a good fit to a suitable time series of nineteenth century term structure cross-sections.

The consequences for financial institutions are debatable. If the first scenario appears likely, then currency would not provide a good store of value. Institutions could move to commodity denominated contracts, if a suitable commodity could be found.[15,16]

---

[14] In an age of electronic banking and financial control one might deem such a putative electronic standard the 'electrum' standard in commemoration of the earliest coinage medium.

[15] Schnadt and Whittaker (93) [480] investigate the feasibility of commodity money.

[16] The author Douglas Adams in one of his novels (Adams (80) [5]) has leaves used as money. A defoliation programme is initiated when the price of a ship's peanut rises to three deciduous forests.

Whether gold or silver are still suitable, or whether some other abstract commodity is preferable is moot. Long-term contracts might begin to specify delivery in specie denominated values instead of inconvertible currency. Alternatively, pricing models might need to price in the possibility of hyperinflation. Since the occurrence of a hyperinflation is analogous to a default, because a contract to deliver a hyperinflating currency is essential worthless, hyperinflation could be regarded as a credit risk. Unfortunately it would not be diversifiable, and could be global. Even if some form of indexing were possible, great care would need to be taken that banks, as creditors, did not lose out to debtors.

Notice that the anticipation of hyperinflation may serve to drive the economy onto a commodity standard, effectively 'accidentally' adopting scenario 2.

In the second scenario there is no melt-down, but banks may be over-charging for long-term business. This is an opportunity cost, and is mild compared with the consequences of the first scenario. However, it may become relevant in the future if a perception develops that a monetary peg may be achievable. The expectation of the event may itself bring down long yields and long volatilities. Banks would need to be aware of what was happening and to incorporate it into their pricing models.

3.5 THE ROLE OF THE SHORT RATE

In this final section we briefly review how the short rate emerges in some of the models we have seen.

The short rate r_t is a key interest rate in all models, even though it cannot be directly observed. The overnight interest rate is not usually considered to be a good proxy for the short rate, because the motives and needs driving overnight borrowers are very different from those of borrowers who want money for a month or more. In some markets, such as the dollar, the overnight rate (the fed funds rate) is nevertheless comparatively stable and perhaps a fair proxy for the short rate, although more than one study suggests that it should not be used because of its low correlation with other spot rates. The one- or three-month interest rate is often taken to be the best available proxy, but is obviously not ideal, as the short rate is defined to have an instantaneous holding period, compared with which three months is a long way down the yield curve. (Using a three-month rate as a proxy for the short rate introduces theoretical problems. See Honore (98) [286].) In practice, however, 'short' rates like one-, three- and six-month rates are very liquid and often used for hedging purposes along with futures contracts of comparable maturities.

The short rate is fundamental to pricing theory since it is the return to all bonds under certain altered probabilities (see Chapter 4). The way it is determined within an interest rate model is of some interest. For instance:

- r_t can be a state variable itself.
- r_t can be an affine sum of state variables, in the affine framework,

$$r_t = f + g'Y_t. \tag{3.76}$$

- r_t can be a sum of the squares of the state variables, in the squared Gaussian framework,

$$r_t = Y_t' Y_t. \tag{3.77}$$

- r_t can be the exponential of a state variable, in the log-r framework,

$$r_t = e^{Y_t}. \tag{3.78}$$

- r_t can be just the point at the short end of the forward rate curve, in HJM models.

In price kernel models the short rate turns out to be the negative of the drift of the price kernel Z_t. r_t could be a complicated function of other state variables.

r_t is the only state variable   If r_t is the only state variable, a general continuous process for it that nests a number of different models is

$$dr_t = (\theta(t) + c(t)r_t + br_t^2)dt + \sigma(t)(r_t + d)^\gamma dz_t. \tag{3.79}$$

In (3.79), d is almost always zero apart from a special case of the Duffie and Kan model, and b also is almost always zero. θ, c and σ are always non-zero, apart from the Ho and Lee model, where $c = 0$. The factor γ is always 0, $\frac{1}{2}$ or 1, as the mathematics becomes intractable otherwise. The Ait-Sahalia model includes a k/r_t term in the drift, where k is a constant.

The most common version of (3.79) is

$$dr_t = (\theta(t) + c(t)r_t)dt + \sigma(t)r_t^\gamma dz_t, \tag{3.80}$$

with $\gamma = 0$ or $\frac{1}{2}$.

r_t is not the only state variable   A factor model with pretensions to be serious may well have two or more state variables. It is often possible to reparameterise a model so that one of the state variables is the short rate r_t. How do the other state variables relate to r_t? There are two cases:

- The process for r_t is independent of the other state variables.
- The process for r_t is dependent upon the other state variables.

In the first case, the other state variables usually attempt to capture some additional feature of the term structure, like the behaviour of longer yields. Examples of this type of model are Duffie and Kan (96) [183], Brennan and Schwartz (83) [95], and Schaefer and Schwartz (84) [478]. In the second case, the mean or volatility of r_t is usually controlled by the other state variables, and becomes stochastic. Examples of this type of model are Longstaff and Schwartz (92) [365], Chen (96) [126], and Tice and Webber (97) [523].

Does the model include jumps?   There are undoubtedly jumps in interest rates, where a change in rates is much larger than a diffusion model could account for. Some models try to include these jumps, like Shirakawa (91) [492] and Ahn and Thompson (88) [7], the jump extensions of the Heath, Jarrow and Morton model. Another model which includes jumps is the factor model of Babbs and Webber (94) (95) [40], [41].

It is not always necessary to model jumps—it is often the case that a simple diffusion model is sufficient. However, for instruments where the excess kurtosis caused by jumps is a problem, they should be included if possible. We investigate jump models in Chapter 10.

4

Interest Rate Models: Theory

This chapter provides an overview of valuation for interest rate products. It is not intended to give a rigorous technical treatment—the reader is referred to the many excellent books and papers on the subject. These include general books of varying technicality such as Baxter and Rennie (96) [55], Bjork (98) [66], Dothan (90) [171], and Duffie (92) [181], as well as technical books such as Musiela and Rutkowski (97) [408]. Important technical papers include Bjork (96) [65], El-Karoui *et al.* (92a) [202], (92b) [203], and Geman *et al.* (95) [244].

Early seminal papers are Harrison and Kreps (79) [269], Harrison and Pliska (81) [270], (83) [271], Back and Pliska (91) [42], and other important and interesting papers include Bjork *et al.* (96) [71], Artzner and Delbaen (89) [27], Jamshidian (89) [308], (91) [309], (97) [313], Rady (95) [446], Rydberg (98) [468], and Stutzer (96) [509].

The chapter starts with a summary of the valuation procedure. We describe a trading scenario and state intuitively the main results of no-arbitrage and the existence of an equivalent martingale measure. We discuss the existence of an EMM in a two-period case. The concepts of a numeraire and of equivalent martingale measures are introduced and discussed and changes of numeraire are described. We finish with an example from the extended Vasicek model (see Bjork (96) [65]).

4.1 SUMMARY OF VALUATION

The theoretical valuation framework is deeply mathematical, but fortunately there is a relatively straightforward intuition behind it. Our purpose is to emphasise the intuition, not the mathematics. A rigorous treatment is demanding and subtle, and is necessary for theoretical advances in the area. We emphasise aspects relevant to practical valuation.

We shall discuss the theory and its application to European style options. The theory for American style options is similar but is complicated by the early exercise feature.

We suppose we have an instrument with a terminal cashflow of c_T at maturity time T. c_T may be random, or known for sure at time 0. For example,

- $c_T = 1$, the payoff to a pure discount bond;
- $c_T = \max(B_T(S) - X, 0)$ where X is a constant and $B_T(S)$ is the value at time T of pure discount bond maturing at time S, $T < S$. This is the payoff to a bond option.

Write v_t for the value of the option at time $t < T$, so that $v_T = c_T$. Our problem is to find v_t for $t < T$.

4.1.1 Objective Probabilities

A model has a set of state variables and specifies the processes they follow, as their values are observed from moment to moment. It implicitly specifies the densities governing the values of the state variables at future times. In the Vasicek model the short rate process is

$$dr_t = \alpha(\mu - r_t)dt + \sigma dz_t. \tag{4.1}$$

Given the value r_0 of the short rate at time 0 its value r_t at time t is conditionally normally distributed with

$$\text{mean: } \mu + (r_0 - \mu)e^{-\alpha t}, \tag{4.2}$$

$$\text{variance: } \sigma^2 \frac{1 - e^{-2\alpha t}}{2\alpha}. \tag{4.3}$$

In a world where economic agents were indifferent to risk the value of a derivative would be its expected discounted payoff at the riskless rate under this objective measure. However, the market does not price derivatives as their expected value under these real world probabilities. It is necessary to account for the market's attitude towards risk.

Formulate in Terms of a Numeraire

A numeraire is a particular asset that can be used to price relative to. If p_t is the value at time t of the numeraire, then for an asset with value v_t its value $\tilde{v}_t$ relative to the numeraire is

$$\tilde{v}_t = \frac{v_t}{p_t}. \tag{4.4}$$

A numeraire must have strictly positive value and must be self-financing (with no disbursements, for instance). There are many assets (or portfolios) that could be chosen as a numeraire. A numeraire is chosen for convenience only, and for no other reason. The choice of numeraire does not affect eventual prices in any way.

Two examples of numeraire are:

1. The money market account,

$$p_t = \exp\left(\int_0^t r_s \, ds\right); \tag{4.5}$$

this is the value at time t of 1 invested in the short rate at time 0 and continuously rolled over.

2. A pure discount bond maturing at some convenient date,

$$p_t = B_t(T), \quad t < T. \tag{4.6}$$

Other examples, as we shall see in later chapters, include the values of annuities, cash, and discretely rolled over borrowing.

Basic Fact

For any given choice of numeraire it is possible to change the objective probabilities to get a new set, 'the subjective probabilities' or 'the risk-adjusted probabilities' under which all relative prices are martingales.

Martingale? A random process $\tilde{v}_t$ is a martingale if its expected future value equals its current value:

$$\mathbb{E}_t[\tilde{v}_T] = \tilde{v}_t, \tag{4.7}$$

where $\mathbb{E}_t$ is the expectation conditional on what is known at time t. Relative prices are martingales under risk-adjusted probabilities, $\widetilde{\mathbb{E}}_t[\tilde{v}_T] = \tilde{v}_t$, where $\widetilde{\mathbb{E}}$ is the expectation under risk-adjusted probabilities.

It is beyond the scope of this book to justify this fact in detail. The interested reader is referred to the original papers of Harrison and Kreps (79) [269], Harrison and Pliska (81) [270], and to more recent books such as Baxter and Rennie (96) [55], Musiela and Rutkowski (97) [408], Bjork (98) [66] and many others. The explanation is essentially to do with consistency conditions. It must be possible construct a risk-free hedge portfolio for the instrument, under conditions of no-arbitrage, using any suitable combination of instruments in the market. In some sense all instruments must earn rates of return related by their risk.

If bonds are priced consistently with some one-factor term structure model, such as Vasicek, then any pure discount bond can be hedged by a portfolio of two others. Instantaneous returns to the pure discount bond and to the hedge must be identical, by no-arbitrage. This restricts the form of the risk-adjusted probabilities. This concept is sometimes referred to as 'arbitrage across maturities'.

Relative Prices are Martingales

How does knowing that relative prices are martingales help us to price derivatives? For the moment we use the money market account $p_t = \exp\left(\int_0^t r_s \, ds\right)$ as numeraire. If relative prices are martingales, then for all $t < T$,

$$\frac{v_t}{p_t} = \widetilde{\mathbb{E}}_t\left[\frac{v_T}{p_T}\right]. \tag{4.8}$$

The current relative price is equal to the expected value of the future relative price. At time T, the value of the (European) derivative is equal to its payoff, $v_T = c_T$, so

$$v_t = \widetilde{\mathbb{E}}_t \left[v_T \frac{p_t}{p_T} \right] = \widetilde{\mathbb{E}}_t \left[c_T \frac{p_t}{p_T} \right]. \tag{4.9}$$

When p_t is the money market account we have

$$v_t = \widetilde{\mathbb{E}}_t \left[c_T \exp \left(- \int_t^T r_s \, ds \right) \right]. \tag{4.10}$$

v_t is the expected discounted payoff under risk-adjusted probabilities. When $c_T \equiv 1$, so that the instrument is a pure discount bond, then

$$v_t = B_t(T) = \widetilde{\mathbb{E}}_t \left[\exp \left(- \int_t^T r_s \, ds \right) \right]. \tag{4.11}$$

This is wonderful, but what is $\widetilde{\mathbb{E}}$ and how can it be computed?

4.1.2 Short Rate Models and $\widetilde{\mathbb{E}}$

One simple way of proceeding is to define the risk-adjusted probabilities straight away, and not to bother with objective probabilities at all. This is essentially the approach of Duffie and Kan, Vasicek, and many other authors. For instance, Vasicek specifies the form of $\widetilde{\mathbb{E}}$ and then backs out prices consistent with it. Given the objective process

$$dr_t = \alpha(\mu - r_t)dt + \sigma dz_t, \tag{4.12}$$

for constant α, μ and σ, Vasicek declares the risk-adjusted process to be

$$dr_t = (\alpha(\mu - r_t) - \lambda\sigma)dt + \sigma d\tilde{z}_t, \tag{4.13}$$

for some constant λ, so that the risk-adjusted process is

$$dr_t = \alpha(\tilde{\mu} - r_t)dt + \sigma d\tilde{z}_t, \tag{4.14}$$

where $\tilde{\mu} = \mu - (\lambda\sigma/\alpha)$, and $\tilde{z}_t$ is a Wiener process under $\widetilde{\mathbb{E}}$. We can now price instruments by taking expectations under the risk-adjusted process, not the objective process.

λ is the market price of risk. It determines how much the drift of r_t must be adjusted in order to get from the objective to the risk-adjusted measure. Altering the drift alters the expected future value of r_t, $\mathbb{E}_t[r_T]$, scaling it so that expected future payoffs reflect the returns required by the market to hold the risk implicit in r_t. We shall see later that if S_t is a traded asset, with process $dS_t = \mu S_t \, dt + \sigma S_t \, dz_t$ then $\lambda = (\mu - r)/\sigma$. λ determines how much the drift of S_t must be scaled in units of the volatility of S_t.

Pricing Under Vasicek

Given the process (4.14) the density of $r_T \mid r_t$ is conditionally normal. This is tractable enough that it is sometimes possible to evaluate expectations directly. For example, for

pure discount bonds, $c_T \equiv 1$. From (4.11) bond prices are $B_t(T) = \widetilde{\mathbb{E}}_t \left[\exp \left(-\int_t^T r_s \, ds \right) \right]$.
If $r_s \mid r_t, s > t$, is conditionally normal, then so is $\gamma_t(T) = \int_t^T r_s \, ds$.
If a random variable X is normal, then

$$\mathbb{E}\left[e^X \right] = e^{\mathbb{E}[X] + \frac{1}{2} \text{var}[X]}. \tag{4.15}$$

In our case

$$B_t(T) = \mathbb{E}_t[\exp(-\gamma_t(T)) \mid r_t] = \exp(-\mathbb{E}_t[\gamma_t(T)] + \tfrac{1}{2}\text{var}_t[\gamma_t(T)]), \tag{4.16}$$

where the expectation and variance are conditional. Using standard methods from stochastic calculus it is possible to show that (re-parameterising in terms of time to maturity $\tau = T - t$)

$$\mathbb{E}_t[\gamma_t(\tau)] = \mu\tau + (r_t - \mu)\frac{1 - e^{-\alpha\tau}}{\alpha}, \tag{4.17}$$

$$\text{var}_t[\gamma_t(\tau)] = \frac{\sigma^2}{\alpha^2} \left(\tau - \frac{1 - e^{-\alpha\tau}}{\alpha} - \frac{1}{2}\alpha \left(\frac{1 - e^{-\alpha\tau}}{\alpha} \right)^2 \right). \tag{4.18}$$

Substituting in we find that $B_t(t + \tau) = \exp(-r_t(\tau)\tau)$ where spot rates $r_t(\tau)$ are

$$r_t(\tau) = r_\infty + (r_t - r_\infty)\frac{1 - e^{-\alpha\tau}}{\alpha\tau} + \frac{\sigma^2\tau}{4\alpha} \left(\frac{1 - e^{-\alpha\tau}}{\alpha\tau} \right)^2, \tag{4.19}$$

with $r_\infty = \mu - \left(\sigma^2/2\alpha^2 \right)$.

A special case of this is Merton's toy model. Suppose $dr_t = \mu dt + \sigma dz_t$, where μ and σ are constant. r_t and $\gamma_0(t) = \int_0^t r_s \, ds$ are both normally distributed, conditional on the value of r_0, with

$$r_t = r_0 + \mu t + \sigma z_t, \tag{4.20}$$

$$\gamma_0(t) = r_0 t + \frac{1}{2}\mu t^2 + \sigma \int_0^t z_s \, ds, \tag{4.21}$$

where $z_0 = 0$. We can compute

$$\mathbb{E}_0[\gamma_0(t)] = r_0 t + \tfrac{1}{2}\mu t^2, \tag{4.22}$$

$$\text{var}_0[\gamma_0(t)] = \tfrac{1}{3}\sigma^2 t^3. \tag{4.23}$$

Hence with $\tau = T - t$

$$B_t(r_t, T) = B_t(r_t, \tau) = \exp \left(-r_t\tau - \tfrac{1}{2}\mu\tau^2 + \tfrac{1}{6}\sigma^2\tau^3 \right) \tag{4.24}$$

and spot rates are

$$r_t(\tau) = r_t + \tfrac{1}{2}\mu\tau - \tfrac{1}{6}\sigma^2\tau^2. \tag{4.25}$$

This explicit solution is not in fact very helpful since the model itself was only constructed for illustrative purposes and is not a sensible description of interest rate behaviour.

Extended Vasicek

The extended Vasicek model is a much more relevant example. Suppose that under risk-adjusted probabilities the short rate process is $dr_t = \alpha(\theta(t) - r_t)dt + \sigma dz_t$, where $\theta(t)$ is a deterministic function of time. Consider a bond option maturing at time T_1 on a pure discount bond maturing at time $T_2 > T_1$. The payoff at time T_1 is $c_{T_1} = \max(B_{T_1}(T_2) - X, 0)$. Jamshidian (89) [308] was able to show, using arguments analogous to those above (with a different numeraire—see Section 4.4), that bond call option prices $v_t(T_1, T_2)$ in the extended Vasicek model are

$$v_t(T_1, T_2) = B_t(T_2) \, \mathrm{N}(d) - X B_t(T_1) \, \mathrm{N}(d - \sigma_p), \qquad (4.26)$$

where

$$d = \frac{1}{\sigma_P} \ln \frac{B_t(T_2)}{X B_t(T_1)} + \frac{1}{2}\sigma_p,$$

$$\sigma_p = \sigma \frac{1 - e^{-\alpha(T_2 - T_1)}}{\alpha} \left(\frac{1 - e^{-2\alpha(T_1 - t)}}{2\alpha} \right)^{\frac{1}{2}}, \qquad (4.27)$$

where $B_t(T)$ are the theoretical extended Vasicek bond prices consistent with $\theta(t)$.

Given market bond prices $B_t(T)$ one can find the $\theta(t)$ that generates these prices (under risk neutrality). Suppose we are given an initial term structure at $t = 0$ in terms of the instantaneous forward rate curve, $f(0, t)$, so that $r_0(T) = (1/T) \int_0^T f(0, u)du$. If $dr_t = \alpha(\theta(t) - r_t)dt + \sigma dz_t$, $t > 0$, then setting

$$\theta(t) = \frac{1}{\alpha} \frac{\partial f}{\partial t}(0, t) + f(0, t) + \frac{\sigma^2}{2\alpha^2}(1 - e^{-2\alpha t}), \qquad (4.28)$$

the model exactly recovers the current term structure. This means that the extended Vasicek model can in principle be calibrated to the yield curve.

4.1.3 Solving the Pricing Equation in General

If prices are given in the form

$$v_t = \widetilde{\mathbb{E}}_t \left[v_T \frac{p_t}{p_T} \right] = \widetilde{\mathbb{E}}_t \left[c_T \frac{p_t}{p_T} \right] \qquad (4.29)$$

we are left with the problem of how to solve this expectation in general. There are four main possibilities, depending on how much is known about the distribution of $c_T p_t / p_T$, and how tractable it is.

1. *Solve explicitly.* This is possible only rarely in special cases such as Vasicek and CIR where the distribution is known explicitly.
2. *Convert to a partial differential equation.* If v_t satisfies the pricing equation (4.10), then it satisfies a certain partial differential equation with boundary conditions

determined by the particular financial instrument one is pricing. For the extended Vasicek model, prices satisfy the partial differential equation

$$\frac{\partial v}{\partial t} + \alpha(\tilde{\mu} - r)\frac{\partial v}{\partial r} + \frac{1}{2}\sigma^2 \frac{\partial^2 v}{\partial r^2} = rv. \tag{4.30}$$

A model with n state variables will in general satisfy an n-factor PDE. It is usually infeasible to solve the PDE numerically if there are more than two or three factors. Sometimes approximations can be made that give simplified PDEs with explicit solutions (Schaefer and Schwartz (84) [478]).

3. *Lattice methods.* The continuous time state variable r_t is approximated by a series of discrete tractable variables, $r_t^{(n)}$, $n = 1, 2, \ldots$, where for some n, $r_t^{(n)}$ is an approximation of sufficiently small error (see Schmidt (97) [479]). These methods are convenient when they can be applied; unless the state variables are Markov the lattice will be non-recombining. Lattice methods can price American options and can also price some types of path-dependent options.

4. *Evaluate the expectation by numerical integration.* Monte Carlo methods can be used here, but they have limited use for American style options. Monte Carlo methods have to be used if the processes followed by the state variables are known, but the PDE and lattice methods cannot be used.

Each of these alternatives will be discussed in later chapters.

4.2   A THEORETICAL MARKET FRAMEWORK

In this section we set up a theoretical market framework and state how in principle derivative prices can be found.

We suppose that there is a fixed time horizon $T < \infty$, so $t \in [0, T]$,[1] and that there are d underlying Wiener processes $z_{1,t}, \ldots, z_{d,t}$ representing the risk in the economy. We select $d + 1$ assets, $P_i(t, \omega)$, $i = 0, \ldots, d$, that span the market, where, as usual, ω is a sample path so that $P_i(t, \omega)$ could be path dependent. Any other asset is a derivative. The zeroth asset is a riskless bond. We suppose that the assets $P_1, \ldots, P_d$ are stocks (although they could be anything). Asset prices have processes

$$\frac{dP_i(t)}{P_i(t)} = b_i(t, \omega)dt + \sum_{j=1}^{d} \sigma_{i,j}(t, \omega)dz_{j,t}, \tag{4.31}$$

$$P_i(0) = p_i, \quad i = 1, \ldots, d, \tag{4.32}$$

for the stocks, and

$$\frac{dP_0(t)}{P_0(t)} = r(t, \omega)dt, \tag{4.33}$$

$$P_0(0) = 1, \tag{4.34}$$

for the bond $\left(\text{so } P_0(t) = \exp\left(\int_0^t r(s)ds\right)\right)$. The interest rate r is stochastic.

---

[1] The condition is not necessary, but gives considerable technical simplications. Essentially only perpetuals are excluded from the market.

The drifts and volatilities b_i and $\sigma_{i,j}$ can be very general. In practical models they are often assumed to be quite simple, for instance constants. For notational convenience we shall often drop the explicit reference to ω shown, for instance, in equations (4.31) and (4.33).

Write

$$b(t) = (b_1(t), \ldots, b_d(t))', \tag{4.35}$$

$$\sigma(t) = \{\sigma_{i,j}(t)\}_{i,j=1,\ldots,d}, \tag{4.36}$$

for the drift vector $b(t)$ and the volatility matrix $\sigma(t)$.

r, b and σ must obey certain regularity conditions. We must be able to integrate them appropriately, to exchange the order of integration, *et cetera*, and they must have certain finite expected values. See Bjork (96) [65], for instance, for details. We shall assume that all necessary regularity conditions are satisfied. $a(t) = \sigma(t)\sigma(t)'$ must be bounded away from zero, so that σ and σ' have inverses and are bounded. a is the covariance matrix.

4.2.1 Derivative Securities

We only consider European instruments, for example pure discount bonds. A (European) derivative security is an instrument with payoff $H(T, \omega)$ at time T. H depends upon prices up to or at time T. For example, the payoff to a lookback call option on an asset S_t is

$$H(T, \omega) = \max(0, S_T(\omega) - X), \tag{4.37}$$

where

$$X = \min_{0 \le t \le T} (S_t(\omega)). \tag{4.38}$$

A (riskless) pure discount bond maturing at time T has payoff

$$H(T, \omega) \equiv 1, \tag{4.39}$$

for all ω.

4.2.2 Trading Strategies

Given assets $P_0, \ldots, P_t$, a trading strategy determines how much of each asset is owned at each time t. A trading strategy is

$$q(t, \omega) = (q_0(t, \omega), \ldots, q_d(t, \omega)), \tag{4.40}$$

where $q_i(t, \omega)$ is the amount of the ith asset owned at time t.

q must be a predictable process. It must be possible to compute $q(t, \omega)$ in terms of things known at time t_-.

Self-financing Portfolios

The value of the strategy q at time t is

$$V(q, t) = \sum_{i=0}^{d} q_i(t) P_i(t). \tag{4.41}$$

A trading strategy q is self-financing if

$$V(q, t) = V(q, 0) + \sum_{i=0}^{d} \int_0^t q_i(s) \mathrm{d}P_i(s), \tag{4.42}$$

so that

$$\mathrm{d}V(q, t) = \sum_{i=0}^{d} q_i(t) \mathrm{d}P_i(t). \tag{4.43}$$

No extra money is put in (or taken out) after the initial investment at time 0, but wealth can be switched between assets in the portfolio. It is assumed that there are no transaction costs.

Hedging Strategy

A derivative security with payoff $H(T)$ is attainable if there is a self-financing trading strategy q such that

$$V(q, T) = H(T), \tag{4.44}$$

with probability 1.

q is called the hedging strategy, or replicating strategy, for H. If all derivative securities are attainable, then the market is complete.

Arbitrage

Arbitrage is a guaranteed way of making money without risk. Arbitrage must be excluded from any theoretically viable model. In this context, an arbitrage opportunity is a self-financing trading strategy such that

1. $V(q, 0) = 0$, and
2. $\mathrm{Prob}(V(q, T) \geq 0) = 1$, and $\mathrm{Prob}(V(q, T) > 0) > 0$.

No wealth is put in at time 0, but there is a chance of the portfolio acquiring positive wealth at some future time, with no possibility of a loss.

Pricing Derivatives

Suppose $H(T)$ is attainable using either strategy q_1 or strategy q_2. If $V(q_1, 0) \neq V(q_2, 0)$ then there would exist an arbitrage opportunity (by shorting the expensive portfolio and

hedging with the cheaper portfolio). If there is no arbitrage in the economy, then the
security defined by $H(T)$ has a unique price,

$$V(H) = V(q, 0), \qquad (4.45)$$

for any self-financing trading strategy attaining H. This is 'pricing by arbitrage'.

When can no arbitrage be guaranteed and when are all $H(T)$ attainable? Answers to
these questions were given by Harrison and Kreps (79) [269], and Harrison and Pliska
(81) [270]. The method is to price assets and derivatives relative to a numeraire.

A numeraire is an asset such that

1. Its price is strictly positive, and
2. It has no dividends, *et cetera* (it is self-financing).

Suppose P_1 can be used as a numeraire. Relative prices (relative to P_1) are

$$\tilde{P}_i = \frac{P_i}{P_1}. \qquad (4.46)$$

P_0, the money market or accumulator account, is often used as numeraire. This is
sometimes convenient—sometimes not—and other assets may often be better choices.

4.2.3   Equivalent Martingale Measures

A probability measure $\widetilde{Q}$ is equivalent to Q if Q and $\widetilde{Q}$ have the same null sets, that is,
if for all $A \in \mathcal{F}$, $\widetilde{Q}(A) = 0$ if and only if $Q(A) = 0$. $\widetilde{Q}$ and Q agree upon which events
are impossible.

Q_P is a martingale measure if all relative prices (relative to P) are martingales
under Q_P,

$$\tilde{P}_i(t) = \mathbb{E}_t^{Q_P} \left[\tilde{P}_i(T) \right], \qquad (4.47)$$

for all $t \leq T$, where $\mathbb{E}^{Q_P}$ denotes the expectation operator with respect to Q_P, $\mathbb{E}^{Q_P}[f] = \int_\Omega f \, dQ_P$.

Q_P is an Equivalent Martingale Measure (EMM) relative to P if

1. Q_P is equivalent to Q; and
2. Q_P is a Martingale measure (relative to P).

Extremely Important Basic Facts

Equivalent martingale measures are crucially important because of the following facts
established by Harrison and Kreps and Harrison and Pliska. For a given numeraire P:

1. If an EMM exists, then there is no arbitrage.
2. If the EMM is unique, then all derivatives are attainable.

This is subject to certain regularity conditions and other complications, naturally. See
Bjork (96) [65] or Musiela and Rutkowski (97) [408], *et cetera*.

For a given numeraire, P, if a unique EMM exists, then all relative prices are martingales, including the price of the self-financing trading strategy of a derivative, so that

$$\widetilde{V}(q, t) = \frac{V(q, t)}{P(t)} \tag{4.48}$$

is a Q_P-martingale. If q_H is the hedging strategy for H, then for $t \leq T$

$$\frac{V(q_H, t)}{P(t)} = \mathbb{E}_t^{Q_P} \left[\frac{V(q_H, T)}{P(T)} \right], \tag{4.49}$$

so that

$$V(q_H, t) = P(t) \mathbb{E}_t^{Q_P} \left[\frac{V(q_H, T)}{P(T)} \right]$$

$$= P(t) \mathbb{E}_t^{Q_P} \left[\frac{H(T)}{P(T)} \right]. \tag{4.50}$$

The value at time t of the derivative security with payoff $H(T)$ at time T is equal to its expected value under the EMM, Q_P, where prices are relative to the numeraire P.

The choice of P is irrelevant. If P_0, the rolled over short rate, is the numeraire, then $Q_{P_0} = Q_0$ is often called *the* EMM. Using P_0 as numeraire, since

$$P_0(t) = \exp \left(\int_0^t r(s) \mathrm{d}s \right) \tag{4.51}$$

we have

$$V(q_H, t) = P_0(t) \mathbb{E}_t^{Q_0} \left[\frac{H(T)}{P_0(T)} \right]$$

$$= \exp \left(\int_0^t r(s) \mathrm{d}s \right) \mathbb{E}_t^{Q_0} \left[\exp \left(- \int_0^T r(s) \mathrm{d}s \right) H(T) \right]$$

$$= \mathbb{E}_t^{Q_0} \left[\exp \left(- \int_t^T r(s) \mathrm{d}s \right) H(T) \right] \tag{4.52}$$

The price of the derivative is the expected discounted payoff under Q_0.

4.2.4   Bond Pricing

The payoff to a pure discount bond, maturing at time T, is identically 1. The price of the bond, $B_t(T)$, under the EMM is

$$B_t(T) = \mathbb{E}_t^{Q_0} \left[\exp \left(- \int_t^T r(s) \mathrm{d}s \right) \right]. \tag{4.53}$$

This value can be computed using a number of technical devices.

1. Use Girsanov's theorem to work out the change of measure.
2. Use Itō's lemma to find the process followed by the relative price.
3. Solve the expectation. If necessary use the Feynman–Kac formula to convert the expectation into a partial differential equation, or use Monte Carlo or a lattice method.

4.2.5 Girsanov's Theorem

Suppose that z_t is a Wiener process under a measure Q. Given a process $\theta(t)$ such that

$$\mathbb{E}\left[\int_0^t |\theta(s)|^2 \, ds\right] < \infty \tag{4.54}$$

the process

$$\tilde{z}_t = z_t - \int_0^t \theta(s) ds \tag{4.55}$$

is a Wiener process under the measure $\widetilde{Q}$ defined by

$$d\widetilde{Q} = \rho dQ, \tag{4.56}$$

where

$$\rho(t) = \exp\left(\int_0^t \theta(s) dz_s - \frac{1}{2}\int_0^t |\theta(s)|^2 \, ds\right), \tag{4.57}$$

so that

$$d\rho(t) = \rho(t)\theta(t) dz_t. \tag{4.58}$$

$\rho(t)$ is called the likelihood function or the Radon–Nikodým derivative.

This means that, for example,

$$\mathbb{E}_t^{\widetilde{Q}}[X] = \int X \, d\widetilde{Q}t = \int X\rho_t \, dQ_t. \tag{4.59}$$

Given a process for the state variables in a model, perhaps under the objective measure, Girsanov's theorem is used to find the processes of the variables under the EMM, where relative prices are martingales.

4.2.6 Itō's Lemma

Suppose f is a function of a stochastic process S_t; for example, f could be the value of a call option written on a share price S_t. If

$$dS_t = \mu(t, \omega) dt + \sigma(t, \omega) dz_t, \tag{4.60}$$

then $f_t = f(S_t, t)$ follows the process

$$df_t = \left(\frac{\partial f}{\partial t} + \mu\frac{\partial f}{\partial S} + \frac{1}{2}\sigma^2\frac{\partial^2 f}{\partial S^2}\right) dt + \sigma\frac{\partial f}{\partial S} dz_t, \tag{4.61}$$

The formula generalises when $f_t = f(S_{1,t}, \ldots, S_{n,t}, t)$ depends on several processes. Suppose that $dS_{i,t} = \mu_i \, dt + \sigma_i \, dz_{i,t}$, $i = 1, \ldots, n$, for functions μ_i and σ_i. Then

$$df_t = \frac{\partial f}{\partial t} dt + \sum_{i=1}^{n} \frac{\partial f}{\partial S_i} dS_{i,t} + \frac{1}{2} \sum_{i,j=1}^{n} \frac{\partial^2 f}{\partial S_i \partial S_i} dS_{i,t} dS_{j,t} \tag{4.62}$$

$$= \left(\frac{\partial f}{\partial t} + \sum_{i=1}^{n} \mu_i \frac{\partial f}{\partial S_i} + \frac{1}{2} \sum_{i,j=1}^{n} \sigma_{i,j} \frac{\partial^2 f}{\partial S_i \partial S_i} \right) dt + \sum_{i=1}^{n} \sigma_i \frac{\partial f}{\partial S_i} dz_{i,t}, \tag{4.63}$$

where $\sigma_{i,j} = \sigma_i \sigma_j \rho_{i,j}$ and $\rho_{i,j}$ is the correlation between $z_{i,t}$ and $z_{j,t}$, $dz_{i,t} \, dz_{j,t} = {}_j \rho_{i,j} dt$. Itō's lemma looks a lot like a Taylor's series expansion,

$$\Delta f = f(S + \Delta S, t + \Delta t) - f(S, t)$$

$$= \frac{\partial f}{\partial t} \Delta t + \frac{\partial f}{\partial S} \Delta S + \frac{1}{2} \frac{\partial^2 f}{\partial S^2} (\Delta S)^2 + \cdots \tag{4.64}$$

where $\Delta S = \mu \Delta t + \sigma \Delta z$. Substituting in, setting $(\Delta z)^2 = \Delta t$ in the limit and letting other higher order terms go to zero, one obtains precisely (4.61). Without wishing to provide deeper justification, since $\mathbb{E}[(\Delta z_t)^2] = \text{var}(\Delta z_t) = \Delta t$, it is not unreasonable that $(\Delta z)^2 \to \Delta t$.

As an example, suppose $f(S_t) = S_t^2$, then

$$\frac{\partial f}{\partial t} = 0, \tag{4.65}$$

$$\frac{\partial f}{\partial S} = 2S, \tag{4.66}$$

$$\frac{\partial^2 f}{\partial S^2} = 2, \tag{4.67}$$

and

$$df_t = \left(2\mu S_t + \sigma^2 \right) dt + 2\sigma S_t dz_t \tag{4.68}$$

$$= \left(2\mu \sqrt{f_t} + \sigma^2 \right) dt + 2\sigma \sqrt{f_t} \, dz_t. \tag{4.69}$$

In this example care has to be taken in moving from (4.68) to (4.69) if S_t can become negative.

4.2.7   The Feynman–Kac Formula

Suppose that S_t follows the process

$$dS_t = \mu(t, \omega) dt + \sigma(t, \omega) dz_t \tag{4.70}$$

under the probability measure Q. Suppose V is defined as

$$V(t, S_t) = \mathbb{E}_t^Q \left[\exp \left(-\int_t^T r(s, S_s) ds \right) H(T, S_T) \right], \tag{4.71}$$

then V satisfies the differential equation

$$\frac{\partial V}{\partial t} + \mu \frac{\partial V}{\partial S} + \frac{1}{2}\sigma^2 \frac{\partial^2 V}{\partial S^2} = rV, \tag{4.72}$$

with boundary condition $V(T, S_T) = H(T, S_T)$. This is the Feynman–Kac formula. It can be generalised to the case where H is a function of more than one underlying process, S_t. For $dS_{i,t} = \mu_i dt + \sigma_i dz_{i,t}$, $i = 1, \ldots, n$, we obtain

$$\frac{\partial V}{\partial t} + \sum_{i=1}^{n} \mu_i \frac{\partial V}{\partial S_i} + \frac{1}{2}\sum_{i,j=1}^{n} \sigma_{i,j} \frac{\partial^2 V}{\partial S_i \partial S_i} = rV, \tag{4.73}$$

where $\sigma_{i,j} = \sigma_i \sigma_j \rho_{i,j}$ and $\rho_{i,j}$ is the correlation between $z_{i,t}$ and $z_{j,t}$.

Kolmogorov Backward Equation

If V is defined to be

$$V(t, S_t) = \mathbb{E}_t^Q[H(T, S_T)], \tag{4.74}$$

then V satisfies the differential equation

$$\frac{\partial V}{\partial t} + \mu \frac{\partial V}{\partial S} + \frac{1}{2}\sigma^2 \frac{\partial^2 V}{\partial S^2} = 0, \tag{4.75}$$

with boundary condition $V(T, S_T) = H(T, S_T)$. This also extends to the case when V is a function of several processes.

Pure Discount Bonds

We can apply Feynman–Kac immediately. Suppose bond prices $B_t(T)$ depend only upon the short rate r_t. Then under the EMM

$$B_t(T) = \mathbb{E}_t^{\tilde{Q}}\left[\exp\left(-\int_t^T r(s)ds\right) \cdot 1\right]. \tag{4.76}$$

Suppose that under the EMM the short rate process is

$$dr_t = \tilde{\mu}dt + \sigma d\tilde{z}_t \tag{4.77}$$

for some functions $\tilde{\mu}$ and σ. From the Feynman–Kac formula bond prices obey the partial differential equation

$$\frac{\partial B}{\partial t} + \tilde{\mu}\frac{\partial B}{\partial r} + \frac{1}{2}\sigma^2 \frac{\partial^2 B}{\partial r^2} = rB, \tag{4.78}$$

subject to the boundary condition

$$B_T(T) = 1. \tag{4.79}$$

One may now attempt to solve (4.78), either explicitly or numerically.

4.3 FUNDAMENTALS OF PRICING

This section provides some justification, in a two-period case, for the martingale pricing relationship (4.50).

A derivative security is defined by its payoff, which is a function from the state space Ω to the reals. Only a slightly restricted set of functions will be allowed as payoff functions. The restrictions are essentially to ensure that payoffs are sufficiently finite and that prices in the market are also finite.

Suppose an economy has an associated probability space $(\Omega, \mathcal{F}, P)$. We initially consider a two-period world, $t = 0, 1$. At time 0 we are in a known state, so Ω indexes the states at time 1 and P is a measure over these states. Suppose that $x : \Omega \to \mathbb{R}$, then we shall suppose that x defines the payoff to a security if $x \in L^2(\Omega)$ (that is, $\int_\Omega |x|^2 dP < \infty$). Imposing this restriction results in considerable simplifications. $L^2(\Omega)$ is a Hilbert space; it has an inner product

$$(x, y)_P = \int_\Omega xy dP = \mathbb{E}^P[xy]. \tag{4.80}$$

Since $L^2(\Omega)$ is the space of payoffs, a map $F : L^2(\Omega) \to \mathbb{R}$, assigning a value to each payoff, is a pricing function.

The existence of an inner product enables us to apply immediately the Rietz representation theorem.

4.3.1 Rietz Representation Theorem

This theorem, enabling us to make the bridge between pricing functions F and numeraires, is crucial for pricing theory.

The Rietz representation theorem *If $F : L^2(\Omega) \to \mathbb{R}$ is continuous and linear, then there exists $\pi^P \in L^2(\Omega)$ such that*

$$F(x) = \left(x, \pi^P\right)_P = \mathbb{E}^P\left[x\pi^P\right], \tag{4.81}$$

for all x in $L^2(\Omega)$. (See Royden (88) [461], et cetera)

Continuity and linearity are mathematical conditions that might not be expected to hold exactly in any real economy. For instance, if a pricing function were linear, then the price of a million of something would be exactly equal to a million times the price of one of the something. Although this is unreasonable, in general, since prices are not linear over large ranges, we are prepared to go along with this assumption as a rough approximation for prices and quantities near equilibrium.

Equation (4.81) says that the price $F(x)$ of a derivative defined by x can be represented as the expected value of x rebased by π^P. Note that $F(1_A) = \int_A \pi^P dP$, where 1_A is the indicator function for a measurable subset $A \subseteq \Omega$, so π^P is a density over Ω. Intuitively, where it is defined, $\pi^P(\omega)$ is the value of a payoff of 1 in state ω. The Rietz representation theorem tells us that, at least for a certain type of payoff and a certain type of pricing functional, an economy is determined by pure securities that pay off with value 1 in one and only one state.

In our context, π^P is called the pricing kernel with respect to P. It is very closely related to the state price deflator.

4.3.2 State Price Deflator

Suppose that P has a density f^P on Ω so that

$$dP = f^P(\omega)d\omega. \tag{4.82}$$

This is a very strong condition, but if it holds then

$$F(x) = \mathbb{E}^P\left[x\pi^P\right] = \int_\Omega x\pi^P dP = \int_\Omega x\pi^P f^P(\omega)d\omega. \tag{4.83}$$

Set $\delta^P(\omega) = \pi^P f^P(\omega)$ so that we have

$$F(x) = \int_\Omega x\delta^P d\omega. \tag{4.84}$$

δ^P goes by a variety of names. In various contexts it may be called the state price deflator, the state price density, the Arrow–Debreu security price function, the kernel density, or the Green's function. δ^P is not defined unless P has a density.

4.3.3 Change of Measure

Suppose that Q is equivalent to P. We must have

$$F(x) = \mathbb{E}^P\left[x\pi^P\right] = \mathbb{E}^Q\left[x\pi^Q\right] \tag{4.85}$$

so that

$$\int_\Omega x\pi^P dP = \int_\Omega x\pi^Q dQ. \tag{4.86}$$

The Radon–Nikodým derivative of P with respect to Q, dP/dQ, is defined to be the function one scales Q by to get P, $dP = (dP/dQ)dQ$. This is well defined if Q and P are equivalent. Since

$$\int_\Omega x\pi^P dP = \int_\Omega x\pi^P \frac{dP}{dQ}dQ = \int_\Omega x\pi^Q dQ, \tag{4.87}$$

we have

$$\frac{dP}{dQ} = \frac{\pi^Q}{\pi^P}. \tag{4.88}$$

If P and Q have densities f^P and f^Q, then

$$\frac{dP}{dQ} = \frac{f^P}{f^Q} \tag{4.89}$$

and

$$\pi^Q = \pi^P \frac{f^P}{f^Q}. \tag{4.90}$$

4.3.4 Numeraires and Equivalent Measures

Given any security y, with $y(\omega) > 0$, define a measure Q by

$$dQ = \pi^P \frac{y}{F(y)} dP. \tag{4.91}$$

In other words,

$$\frac{dP}{dQ} = \frac{F(y)}{y\pi^P} \tag{4.92}$$

and

$$\pi^Q = \frac{F(y)}{y}. \tag{4.93}$$

Then Q is a measure, it is equivalent to P, and

$$\frac{F(x)}{F(y)} = \int_\Omega \frac{x}{y} dQ = \mathbb{E}^Q \left[\frac{x}{y} \right],$$

so that Q is a martingale measure with respect to the numeraire y.

For example, suppose that $y = 1_\Omega$. Then

$$\frac{F(x)}{F(1_\Omega)} = \int_\Omega x \, dQ \tag{4.94}$$

so

$$F(x) = F(1_\Omega) \mathbb{E}^Q[x]. \tag{4.95}$$

The asset y can be thought of as a pure discount bond maturing at time 1. The martingale measure associated with y is just the forward measure. (In a two-period world the forward measure and the EMM are identical.)

4.4 VALUING BY CHANGE OF NUMERAIRE

This section extends the results of the previous section to the continuous time case. Our treatment stresses the intuition behind the mathematics. For a rigorous discussion see Musiela and Rutkowski (97) [408] or Geman *et al.* (95) [244].

Suppose that P is the equivalent martingale measure for a numeraire p_t, and Q is the equivalent martingale measure for a numeraire q_t, then

$$v_t = \mathbb{E}_t^P \left[v_T \frac{p_t}{p_T} \right]$$

$$= \mathbb{E}_t^Q \left[v_T \frac{q_t}{q_T} \right]. \tag{4.96}$$

We can easily move from one measure to another. We have

$$v_t = \mathbb{E}_t^P \left[v_T \frac{p_t}{p_T} \right] = \int_\Omega v_T \frac{p_t}{p_T} dP_t,$$

where P_t refers to P restricted to $\mathcal{F}_t$. If P and Q are equivalent, then there is a function $(dP/dQ)(t)$ such that

$$dP_t = \frac{dP}{dQ}(t) dQ_t. \tag{4.97}$$

dP/dQ is the Radon–Nikodým derivative of P with respect to Q, as in the two-period case. dP/dQ is a random variable; it is defined over measurable sets $A \in \mathcal{F}_t$. It is easy in principle to find dP/dQ; it is just the ratio of the numeraires. We have

$$v_t = \int_\Omega v_T \frac{p_t}{p_T} dP_t = \int_\Omega v_T \frac{p_t}{p_T} \frac{dP}{dQ}(t) dQ_t, \tag{4.98}$$

and also

$$v_t = \int_\Omega v_T \frac{q_t}{q_T} dQ_t. \tag{4.99}$$

Comparing the two expressions (which hold for all v_T) we conclude that

$$\frac{dP}{dQ}(t) = \frac{p_T}{p_t} \frac{q_t}{q_T}. \tag{4.100}$$

This means that

$$v_t = \mathbb{E}_t^P \left[v_T \frac{p_t}{p_T} \right] = \mathbb{E}_t^Q \left[v_T \frac{p_t}{p_T} \frac{dP}{dQ}(t) \right], \tag{4.101}$$

so that, to change measure, it is only necessary to multiply by the Radon–Nikodým derivative.

Apart from the money market account, another convenient choice of numeraire is $q_t = B_t(T)$, the pure discount bond maturing at time T. This give the forward measure for time T, F_T (Jamshidian (89) [308], Geman (89) [243], Geman et al. (95) [244]).

4.4.1 Pricing under the Forward Measure

Under the forward measure F_T,

$$v_t = \mathbb{E}_t^{F_T} \left[v_T \frac{B_t(T)}{B_T(T)} \right] = B_t(T) \mathbb{E}_t^{F_T} [v_T], \tag{4.102}$$

since $B_T(T) = 1$ and $B_t(T)$ is known at time t. Under the T-forward measure the value of a derivative is just its discounted expected payoff. Using the money market account as numeraire the value is the expected discounted payoff:

$$v_t = \mathbb{E}_t^P \left[v_T \exp \left(-\int_t^T r_s ds \right) \right], \tag{4.103}$$

Equation (4.103) is intrinsically a more complicated expression to calculate with than equation (4.102). One may have to compute correlations between the derivative payoff and the discount factor, and in any case (4.102) involves fewer integrations than (4.103). The downside of the T-forward measure is computing expectations under it. In general this might be hard, but in practice, as usual, one chooses processes for the underlying state variables to make the computation easy.

The T-forward measure may simplify calculations for instruments maturing at time T, but it can complicate matters if cashflows also occur at times other that T.

Pricing a Caplet

Let $c(t, r_t, T)$ be the value at time t of a caplet, exercise rate r_X, maturing at time T, on Libor in arrears of tenor τ, r_t. Write f_t for the forward rate at time t for time T of tenor τ. Under the forward measure:

$$c(t, T, \tau) = \tau B_t(T) \mathbb{E}_t^{F_T} [\max(0, r_T - r_X)]$$

$$= \tau B_t(T) \int \max(0, f_T - r_X) \mathrm{d}F_T, \qquad (4.104)$$

since $f_T = r_T$ at time T. Suppose that the underlying state variable is f_t, and that this rate has a log-normal process under F_T. Then

$$c(t, T, \tau) = \tau B_t(T) \int \max(0, f_T - r_X) \mathrm{d}F_T$$

$$= \tau B_t(T) \int \max(0, f_T - r_X) n(f_T \mid f_t) \mathrm{d}f_T, \qquad (4.105)$$

for some log-normal density $n(f_T \mid f_t)$. But this will have a Black's formula solution,

$$c(t, T, \tau) = \tau B_t(T)(f_t N(d) - r_X N(d - w)), \qquad (4.106)$$

for some d and w depending on the process.

Forward Rates in the Forward Measure

Under F_T, the instantaneous forward rate equals the expected future spot rate. We have

$$B_t(T) = \mathbb{E}_t^P \left[\exp\left(-\int_t^T r_s \mathrm{d}s \right) \right] \qquad (4.107)$$

under the money market measure P. Differentiating both sides:

$$-\frac{\partial}{\partial T} B_t(T) = \mathbb{E}_t^P \left[-\frac{\partial}{\partial T} \exp\left(-\int_t^T r_s \mathrm{d}s \right) \right]$$

$$= \mathbb{E}_t^P \left[\exp\left(-\int_t^T r_s \mathrm{d}s \right) r_T \right]$$

$$= B_t(T) \mathbb{E}_t^{F_T} [r_T] \qquad (4.108)$$

under the T-forward measure F_T. But then

$$f_t(T) = -\frac{1}{B_t(T)} \frac{\partial}{\partial T} B_t(T) = \mathbb{E}_t^{F_T}[r_T]. \tag{4.109}$$

The conclusion is the standard expectations hypothesis result: the current forward rate is the expected value of the future spot rate. But this result is true under the T-forward measure, not the objective measure. One frequently sees attempts to 'test' the relationship (4.109), or some modification of it, but usually an implicit assumption is made that (4.109) is under the objective measure. Such attempts are evidently mis-specified. For further discussion see Bjork (98) [66].

Computing the Change of Measure

The processes for the state variables in a model may be specified under the objective measure P. It is necessary to be able to compute their processes under other measures. If we know the process then we may be able to compute expectations explicitly. Suppose

$$dr_t = \mu(r_t, t)dt + \sigma(r_t, t)dz_t, \tag{4.110}$$

under some measure P with numeraire p_t. What is the process for r_t under another measure Q, with numeraire q_t? We know that

$$\frac{dQ}{dP}(t) = \frac{q_T}{q_t} \frac{p_t}{p_T} \tag{4.111}$$

is the Radon–Nikodým derivative. To shorten notation, set $\rho_{t,T} = (q_T/q_t)(p_t/p_T)$, for $t < T$. Girsanov's theorem (Section 4.2.5) states that if z_t is a Wiener process under P, then

$$\tilde{z}_t = z_t - \int_0^t \theta(s)ds \tag{4.112}$$

is a Wiener process under Q, where

$$d\rho_{t,T} = \rho_{t,T}\theta_T dz_T. \tag{4.113}$$

$\theta(t)$ can be computed. Conditional upon $\mathcal{F}_t$, $\rho_{t,T} = (q_T/q_t)(p_t/p_T)$ is a process in T. p_t and q_t are known at time t; p_T and q_T are unknown. But (q_T/p_T) is a martingale under P. Suppose that

$$dp_t = \mu_p dt + \sigma_p dz_t, \tag{4.114}$$

$$dq_t = \mu_q dt + \sigma_q dz_t, \tag{4.115}$$

then

$$\frac{d\rho_T}{\rho_T} = \frac{dq_T}{q_T} - \frac{dp_T}{p_T} - \frac{dq_T}{q_T}\frac{dp_T}{p_T} + \frac{dp_T}{p_T}\frac{dp_T}{p_T}$$

$$= \left(\frac{\sigma_q}{q_T} - \frac{\sigma_p}{p_T}\right) dz_T, \tag{4.116}$$

since ρ_T is a martingale under P. We conclude that $\theta(t) = (\sigma_q/q_t) - (\sigma_p/p_t)$.

4.4.2 Changing from the EMM to the T-Forward Measure

Suppose that P is the EMM under the accumulator numeraire and Q is the T-forward measure, then for $s < t < T$

$$\rho_{s,t} = \frac{q_t}{q_s} \frac{p_s}{p_t} = \frac{B_t(T)}{B_s(T)} \exp\left(-\int_s^t r_u \mathrm{d}u\right). \tag{4.117}$$

Under the measure P we have

$$\frac{\mathrm{d}B_t(T)}{B_t(T)} = r_t \mathrm{d}t + \sigma_t \mathrm{d}z_t, \tag{4.118}$$

for some volatility function σ_t. Computing the process for $\rho_t \equiv \rho_{s,t}$ (conditional on $\mathcal{F}_s$) we have

$$\frac{\mathrm{d}\rho_t}{\rho_t} = \frac{\mathrm{d}B_t(T)}{B_t(T)} - r_t \mathrm{d}t = \sigma_t \mathrm{d}z_t, \tag{4.119}$$

so that when z_t is a Wiener process under P then

$$\tilde{z}_t = z_t - \int_0^t \sigma_s \mathrm{d}s \tag{4.120}$$

is a Wiener process under Q. If under P the process for some variable X_t is

$$\mathrm{d}X_t = \mu_X \mathrm{d}t + \sigma_X \mathrm{d}z_t, \tag{4.121}$$

then under Q the process for X_t is

$$\mathrm{d}X_t = (\mu_X + \sigma_t \sigma_X)\mathrm{d}t + \sigma_X \mathrm{d}\tilde{z}_t. \tag{4.122}$$

4.5 DERIVATIVES IN THE EXTENDED VASICEK MODEL

This section has its roots in Bjork (96) [65]. Suppose that the short rate process under the accumulator EMM, Q, is

$$\mathrm{d}r_t = (\theta(t) - ar_t)\mathrm{d}t + \sigma \mathrm{d}z_t. \tag{4.123}$$

This is the extended Vasicek model. Bond prices are

$$P_t(T) = \mathbb{E}_t^Q\left[\exp\left(-\int_t^T r_s \mathrm{d}s\right)\right]. \tag{4.124}$$

Suppose a European option has payoff $H(r_T)$ at time T. Under the T-forward measure, F_T, its value at time t is

$$c_t = P_t(T)\mathbb{E}_t^{F_T}[H(r_T)]. \tag{4.125}$$

We need to discover the distribution of r_T under F_T. Under F_T we have seen that the process for r_t is

$$\mathrm{d}r_t = (\theta(t) - ar_t + \sigma_T \sigma)\mathrm{d}t + \sigma \mathrm{d}\tilde{z}_t, \tag{4.126}$$

where σ_T is the volatility of $B_t(T)$. But in the extended Vasicek model we know that

$$P_t(T) = e^{A(t,T) - B(t,T)r_t},\tag{4.127}$$

where $B(t, T) = \left(1 - e^{-a(T-t)}\right)/a$, so that

$$\frac{dP_t(T)}{P_t(T)} = r_t dt - \sigma B(t, T) dz_t,\tag{4.128}$$

and $\sigma_T = -\sigma B(t, T)$. Hence under F_T

$$dr_t = \left(\theta(t) - ar_t - \sigma^2 B(t, T)\right) dt + \sigma d\tilde{z}_t.\tag{4.129}$$

This can be solved for r_T. Re-arrange (4.129) as

$$dr_t + ar_t dt = (\theta(t) - \sigma^2 B(t, T)) dt + \sigma d\tilde{z}_t,\tag{4.130}$$

and multiply both sides by e^{at}. The left-hand side is now a total derivative. Integrate both sides between t and T and re-arrange to get

$$r_T = e^{-a(T-t)} r_t + \int_t^T e^{-a(T-s)} \left(\theta(t) - \sigma^2 B(t, T)\right) ds + \sigma \int_t^T e^{-a(T-s)} d\tilde{z}_s.\tag{4.131}$$

Stochastic integrals like $\int_t^T f(s) d\tilde{z}_s$ have the property that

$$\mathbb{E}_t \left[\int_t^T f(s) d\tilde{z}_s\right] = 0,\tag{4.132}$$

$$\text{var}_t \left[\int_t^T f(s) d\tilde{z}_s\right] = \int_t^T f^2(s) ds,\tag{4.133}$$

so r_T is Gaussian with

$$\text{variance: } \sigma^2 \int_t^T e^{-2a(T-s)} ds = \frac{\sigma^2}{2a} \left(1 - e^{-2a(T-t)}\right),\tag{4.134}$$

$$\text{mean: } \mathbb{E}_t^{F_T}[r_T] = f_t(T).\tag{4.135}$$

Hence

$$c_t = P_t(T) \mathbb{E}_t^{F_T}[H(r_T)]$$

$$= P_t(T) \int_{-\infty}^{\infty} H(z) n \left(f_t(T), \frac{\sigma^2}{2a} \left(1 - e^{-2a(T-t)}\right)\right) dz,\tag{4.136}$$

where n is the normal density function.

4.5.1 European Bond Options

The payoff to a European bond call option maturing at time T on a bond maturing at $S > T$ is

$$H(T, S) = \max(B_T(S) - X, 0).\tag{4.137}$$

Its value at time $t < T$ is $c_t(T, S)$. Bjork (96) [65] demonstrates that under the accumulator measure Q,

$$c_t(T, S) = \mathbb{E}_t^Q \left[\exp\left(-\int_t^T r_s \, ds \right) \max(B_T(S) - X, 0) \right],$$

$$= \mathbb{E}_t^Q \left[\exp\left(-\int_t^T r_s \, ds \right) B_T(S) I_{\{B_T(S) \geq X\}} \right],$$

$$- \mathbb{E}_t^Q \left[\exp\left(-\int_t^T r_s \, ds \right) X I_{\{B_T(S) \geq X\}} \right],$$

$$\equiv A - B, \tag{4.138}$$

where I_A is the indicator function. It is straightforward to evaluate A and B by a change of measure. For A, change to the S-forward measure,

$$A = B_t(S)\mathbb{E}_t^{F_S} \left[I_{\{B_T(S) \geq X\}} \right] = B_t(S) \, \text{Pr}^{F_S}[B_T(S) \geq X], \tag{4.139}$$

and for B, change to the T-forward measure,

$$B = B_t(T)X\mathbb{E}_t^{F_T} \left[I_{\{B_T(S) \geq X\}} \right] = B_t(T)X \, \text{Pr}^{F_T}[B_T(S) \geq X]. \tag{4.140}$$

These are very general results.

Under some restrictions the expectations can be computed explicitly. Bjork solves for them in the extended Vasicek model. By changing to the T-forward measure he shows that

$$\text{Pr}^{F_S}[B_T(S) \geq X] = N(d_1), \tag{4.141}$$

$$d_1 = \frac{1}{\sqrt{\sigma_Z^2}} \ln\left(\frac{Z_t}{X}\right) + \frac{1}{2}\sqrt{\sigma_Z^2}, \tag{4.142}$$

and

$$\text{Pr}^{F_T}[B_T(S) \geq X] = N(d_2), \tag{4.143}$$

$$d_2 = \frac{1}{\sqrt{\sigma_Z^2}} \ln\left(\frac{Z_t}{X}\right) - \frac{1}{2}\sqrt{\sigma_Z^2}, \tag{4.144}$$

where $Z_t = B_t(S)/B_t(T)$, with process $dZ_t = Z_t\sigma_t d\tilde{z}_t$, where $\tilde{z}_t$ is a Wiener process under F_T, and $\sigma_Z^2 = \int_t^T |\sigma_s|^2 \, ds$.

Bringing both parts together we conclude that

$$c_t(T, S) = B_t(S)N(d_1) - B_t(T)XN(d_2), \tag{4.145}$$

a standard Black-like formula. For a more rigorous treatment see Bjork (98) [66].

5

Basic Modelling Tools

This chapter investigates further important modelling tools and concepts: valuation and hedging; estimation and stripping. We show how the basic pricing PDE can be obtained using a simple hedging argument. A basic Monte Carlo method is described. Next some basic ideas of model calibration are discussed. (Estimation is covered in detail in Part IV.) The chapter closes by describing a naive yield curve stripping method.

5.1 INTRODUCTION TO VALUATION

We have identified several methods of pricing. All evaluate an expectation, explicitly or implicitly, by

1. Explicit solutions. These may involve a change of measure.
2. Numerical integration, such as Monte Carlo.
3. Converting to a PDE, and solving with appropriate boundary conditions.
   - Full blown PDE methods.
   - Approximate solutions by simplifying the PDE into something you can solve. (For example, Schaefer and Schwartz (84) [478], Rhee (99) [451].)
4. Approximating the underlying state variable, obtaining a lattice method.

We discuss in more detail the pricing PDE, deriving it by a hedging argument. We also introduce the Monte Carlo valuation method.

5.1.1 Pricing with a PDE

We have asserted that the Feynman–Kac formula gives us a PDE satisfied by the prices of derivative securities. In this section we show how to construct the PDE using a simple hedging argument. The number of factors in the PDE and the functional form of its coefficients are model-dependent features. The particular instrument we are pricing determines the boundary conditions for the PDE.

Suppose there are k state variables,

$$r_{i,t}, \quad i = 1, \ldots, k, \tag{5.1}$$

with

$$dr_{i,t} = m_i \, dt + s_i \, dz_{i,t}, \tag{5.2}$$

and with correlations $\rho_{i,j}$, so that $dz_{i,t} \, dz_{j,t} = \rho_{i,j} \, dt$. m_i and s_i could be functions of $\{r_i\}$ and of time t. For clarity we now drop the t subscript.

Suppose there are $k + 1$ traded securities,

$$B_j = B_t(\tau_j), \quad j = 0, \ldots, k. \tag{5.3}$$

We take B_j, $j = 1, \ldots, k$, to be pure discount bonds and $B_0 = c$ is the derivative we want to price. We derive the process followed by c and the PDE that c satisfies. For notational convenience set

$$c_t = \frac{\partial c}{\partial t}, \quad c_i = \frac{\partial c}{\partial r_i} \quad \text{and} \quad c_{i,j} = \frac{\partial^2 c}{\partial r_i \partial r_j}. \tag{5.4}$$

The value of $c = c(r_1, \ldots, r_k, t)$ depends on the values of the state variables. By Itō's lemma

$$dc = \sum_{i=1}^{k} c_i \, dr_i + \frac{1}{2} \sum_{i,j=1}^{k} c_{i,j} \, dr_i \, dr_j + c_t \, dt, \tag{5.5}$$

$$= \left(c_t + \sum_{i=1}^{k} c_i m_i + \frac{1}{2} \sum_{i,j=1}^{k} c_{i,j} \rho_{i,j} s_i s_j \right) dt + \sum_{i=1}^{k} c_i s_i \, dz_i. \tag{5.6}$$

Write this as $dc = \mu_c c \, dt + \Sigma_{i=1}^{k} \sigma_{c,i} c \, dz_i$ where

$$\mu_c = \frac{1}{c} \left(c_t + \sum_{i=1}^{k} c_i m_i + \frac{1}{2} \sum_{i,j=1}^{k} c_{i,j} \rho_{i,j} s_i s_j \right), \tag{5.7}$$

$$\sigma_{c,i} = \frac{c_i s_i}{c}. \tag{5.8}$$

Write

$$dB_i = \mu_i B_i \, dt + \sum_{j=1}^{k} \sigma_{i,j} B_i \, dz_j \tag{5.9}$$

for the processes followed by the B_i, $i = 0, \ldots, k$, for some functions μ_i and $\sigma_{i,j}$. Since there are k sources of risk, using the $k + 1$ assets we can construct a riskless portfolio. That is, it is possible to find quantities q_i, $i = 0, \ldots, k$, such that the portfolio containing q_i of each B_i is riskless. Its value is $\Sigma_{i=0}^{k} q_i B_i$ and

$$d \left(\sum_{i=0}^{k} q_i B_i \right) = r \left(\sum_{i=0}^{k} q_i B_i \right) dt, \tag{5.10}$$

where r is the instantaneous riskless short rate at time t, which is a function of the state variables in the model. Equation 5.10 implies that

$$\sum_{i=0}^{k} q_i \mu_i B_i = \sum_{i=0}^{k} q_i r B_i, \quad \text{that is,} \quad \sum_{i=0}^{k} q_i B_i (\mu_i - r) = 0, \tag{5.11}$$

$$\sum_{i=0}^{k} q_i \sigma_{i,j} B_i = 0, \quad j = 1, \ldots, k. \tag{5.12}$$

These two equations can be consistent only if it is possible to find λ_j, $j = 1, \ldots, k$, such that

$$B_i (\mu_i - r) = \sum_{j=1}^{k} B_i \sigma_{i,j} \lambda_j, \quad \text{for each } i = 1, \ldots, k. \tag{5.13}$$

A justification for this is given below. From (5.13) we have

$$\mu_i - r = \sum_{j=1}^{k} \sigma_{i,j} \lambda_j, \quad \text{for each } i = 1, \ldots, k. \tag{5.14}$$

Equation 5.14 is a fundamental relationship. In Chapter 8 we shall see that it extends more generally. The λ_j are the prices of risk in the model. They determine the excess return required for the bonds as multiples of their volatilities. They may depend on the state variables r_i, $i = 1, \ldots, k$, and on t, but the λ_j are independent of bond maturity times, since the choice of τ_j was arbitrary. This means that 'arbitrage across maturities' is prohibited. Bond prices are consistent with one another in the sense that no zero cost bond portfolio can guarantee positive returns.

For the derivative $c = B_0$, substitute for $\mu_c c = \mu_0 B_0$ and $\sigma_{c,i} c = \sigma_{0,j} B_0$ into Equation 5.13 with $i = 0$ and re-arrange to obtain

$$c_t + \sum_{i=1}^{k} (m_i - \lambda_i s_i) c_i + \frac{1}{2} \sum_{i,j=1}^{k} \rho_{i,j} s_i s_j c_{i,j} = rc. \tag{5.15}$$

Under our assumptions this is the general PDE followed by any security. Boundary conditions are determined by the particular instrument.

Obtaining (5.13)

Suppose that $q \in \mathbb{R}^{k+1}$, $v_j \in \mathbb{R}^{k+1}$, $j = 1, \ldots, k$, such that $q'v_j = 0$, $j = 1, \ldots, k$. This means that the $\{v_j\}$ lie in the co-space Q to q, $Q \sim \mathbb{R}^k$ (Figure 5.1).

If $\{v_j\}$ are independent then $Q = \text{span}\{v_j\}$. Suppose also that $q'w = 0$. Then $w \in Q = \text{span}\{v_j\}$, so there exist λ_j, $j = 1, \ldots, k$, such that $w = \Sigma_{j=1}^{k} \lambda_j v_j$.

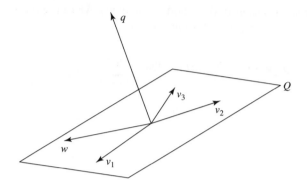

Figure 5.1 q and its co-space Q

Example: Pricing a Bond Option

In the Vasicek model there is one source of risk, the short rate r_t, whose process is $\mathrm{d}r_t = \alpha(\mu - r_t)\mathrm{d}t + \sigma\,\mathrm{d}z_t$. The PDE (5.15) is

$$c_t + (\alpha(\mu - r) - \lambda\sigma)c_r + \tfrac{1}{2}\sigma^2 c_{r,r} = rc. \tag{5.16}$$

Set $\tilde{\mu} = \mu - \lambda(\sigma/\alpha)$. The PDE can be rewritten as

$$c_t + c_r\alpha(\tilde{\mu} - r) + \tfrac{1}{2}\sigma^2 c_{r,r} = rc. \tag{5.17}$$

The same PDE would have been obtained had we started with the process

$$\mathrm{d}r_t = \alpha(\tilde{\mu} - r_t)\mathrm{d}t + \sigma\,\mathrm{d}z_t \tag{5.18}$$

and had $\lambda_i \equiv 0$. Equation 5.18 is the process for r_t under the EMM.

For a bond call option $c_t(T_1, T_2)$ the boundary condition is

$$c_t(T_1, T_2) = \max(0, B_{T_1}(T_2) - X), \tag{5.19}$$

where $B_{T_1}(T_2)$ is a function of the value of r_t,

$$B_t(\tau) = \exp(-r_t(\tau)\tau), \tag{5.20}$$

with

$$r_t(\tau) = r_\infty + (r_t - r_\infty)\frac{1 - e^{-\alpha\tau}}{\alpha\tau} + \frac{\sigma^2\tau}{4\alpha}\left(\frac{1 - e^{-\alpha\tau}}{\alpha\tau}\right)^2. \tag{5.21}$$

We saw in Chapter 4 that there is an explicit solution for $c_t(T_1, T_2)$. It can be verified that this solution satisfies the PDE (5.16) subject to the boundary condition (5.19).

With an explicit formula hedge ratios are simple to calculate and so it is simple to value and hedge caps, swaptions, and similar instruments, as long as assumptions of the model are valid.

5.1.2 Valuing an Option on a Coupon Bond

For a one-factor model Jamshidian (89) [308] demonstrated that a European option on a coupon bond is equivalent to a set of European options on individual coupons. Since a swaption is precisely an option on a coupon bond, this result has important practical consequences.

Suppose there is a coupon bond paying out cashflows $c_i > 0$ at times $T_i, i = 1, \ldots, n$. The bond matures at time T_n, with a final terminal cashflow c_n. The value $B_t(\{c_i, T_i\}, r_t)$ of the coupon bond at time t depends on the interest rate r_t.

Suppose there is an option on B_t, with exercise price X, exercisable at time $T < T_1$. A necessary condition for exercise is that

$$B_t(\{c_i, T_i\}, r_t) = \sum_{i=1}^{n} c_i B_t(T_i, r_t) > X, \tag{5.22}$$

for pure discount bond prices $B_t(T_i, r_t)$.

In a sensible model bond prices are decreasing in the interest rate r, so there is a unique critical value r^* of r such that

$$\sum_{i=1}^{n} c_i B_t(T_i, r^*) = X. \tag{5.23}$$

Set $X_i = B_t(T_i, r^*)$. The payoff to the option if exercised is

$$V = \max\left(0, \sum_{i=1}^{n} c_i B_t(T_i, r) - X\right) \tag{5.24}$$

$$= \sum_{i=1}^{n} c_i \max(0, B_t(T_i, r) - X_i), \tag{5.25}$$

so that the payoff if the bond option is exercised is identical to the payoff on a portfolio of options on the pure discount bonds $B_t(T_i)$, with exercise prices $X_i, i = 1, \ldots, n$.

Since only cashflows occur at maturity, an identical value if exercised implies identical value always, so that the option portfolio has identical value to the value of the bond option.

The argument above does not extend to models with more than one factor. However, Hunt and Kennedy showed that in a one-factor model a much broader range of non-vanilla swaptions can be valued.

Extending Jamshidian

The extension is given in Hunt and Kennedy (98) [300]. Suppose that there is a set of money market instruments comprised of vanilla swaps and swaptions with known cashflow times, $T = T_0, \ldots, T_n$. Write $U_t^i(K_i)$ for the value at time $t < T$ of a forward start swap with fixed rate K_i, starting at time $T = T_0$, and finishing at time T_i, and write $V_t^i(K_i)$ for the value at time $t < T$ of the vanilla swaption maturing at time T with strike K_i.

Consider an irregular swaption maturing at time T. The underlying instrument has cashflows c_i at time T_i, $i = 0, \ldots, n$. c_i have to be constants, but they are not restricted to positive values. Write U_t for the value of the underlying instrument U_t at times $t < T$, and V_t for the value of the swaption. The payoff to the irregular swaption at time T is $V_T = \max(0, U_T)$.

Examples of instruments that fit this situation are forward start swaptions, amortising swaptions, acreting swaptions, and roller-coaster swaptions (Hunt and Kennedy give details). For instance, a forward start swap, with principal A and fixed rate K, starting at time T_{i_0}, has cashflows

$$
c_i = \begin{cases}
0, & i < i_0, \\
-A, & i = i_0, \\
A\alpha_i K, & i_0 < i < n, \\
A(1 + \alpha_i K), & i = n,
\end{cases}
\tag{5.26}
$$

where $\alpha_i = T_i - T_{i-1}$ is the accrual factor. An amortising swap with principal A has cashflows

$$
c_i = M_i(1 + \alpha_i K) - M_{i-1},
\tag{5.27}
$$

where

$$
M_i = A \frac{\displaystyle\sum_{l=i}^{n} \alpha_l}{\displaystyle\sum_{l=1}^{n} \alpha_l}.
\tag{5.28}
$$

Hunt and Kennedy use an analogous argument to Jamshidian. Using vanilla swaps and swaptions they show how it is possible to replicate U_t. Suppose that swap and swaption values depend upon a single factor r, and that there is a unique value $r = r^*$ with $U_t(r^*) = 0$ (which will be true for 'reasonable' instruments), then Hunt and Kennedy show that it is possible to choose K_i and A_i such that

$$
U_t = \sum_{i=1}^{n} A_i U_t^i(K_i),
\tag{5.29}
$$

$$
U_t^i(K_i, r^*) = 0,
\tag{5.30}
$$

and that with these K_i and A_i we have

$$
V_t = \sum_{i=1}^{n} A_i V_t^i(K_i).
\tag{5.31}
$$

This decomposes the irregular swaption into standard swaptions which can be valued and hedged.

5.1.3 Introduction to Hedging

We discuss the principles of hedging in general, and in the case of interest rate products.

General Hedging Principles

A hedge portfolio is a self-financing portfolio that exactly replicates the cash flows to another instrument. A bank that sells an over-the-counter (OTC) product will simultaneously set up a hedge. In theory, by definition, the value of the hedged instrument is exactly the value of the hedge. In practice, when dealing costs and liquidity are very important; transaction costs make it impossible to hedge perfectly. It is usual and reasonable in such circumstances to over-hedge, passing the additional costs on to the client.

Suppose that we want to hedge an instrument whose value $V \equiv V(r_{1,t}, \ldots, r_{k,t}, t)$ depends upon k state variables, $r_{1,t}, \ldots, r_{k,t}$. To hedge this we need $k + 1$ hedging instruments, $H_0 \equiv H_0(r_1, \ldots, r_k, t), \ldots, H_k \equiv H_k(r_1, \ldots, r_k, t)$. The hedge portfolio for V has the same value as V so there are quantities $q_0, \ldots, q_k$ such that

$$V = \sum_{i=0}^{k} q_i H_i. \tag{5.32}$$

The q_i are 'predictable' so that the hedge can be constructed without making guesses about the future evolution of the state variables (see, for instance, Baxter and Rennie (96) [55]). Suppose that the $r_{i,t}$ have the processes given in Equation 5.2 (so that in particular jumps are not included). Since (5.32) is satisfied (and the q_i are predictable) we have

$$dV = \sum_{i=0}^{k} q_i \, dH_i. \tag{5.33}$$

Since the left-hand side is a hedge portfolio for V the combined portfolio is riskless, so that the coefficients of dz_j, $j = 1, \ldots, k$, on each side must be equal. Expanding out,

$$\frac{\partial V}{\partial r_j} s_j \, dz_j = \sum_{i=0}^{k} q_i \frac{\partial H_i}{\partial r_j} s_j \, dz_j, \tag{5.34}$$

so that

$$\frac{\partial V}{\partial r_j} = \sum_{i=0}^{k} q_i \frac{\partial H_i}{\partial r_j}. \tag{5.35}$$

Equations 5.32 and 5.35 are a linear system of $k + 1$ equations in $k + 1$ unknowns, q_i. Barring degeneracy this is solvable so that a hedge portfolio can be constructed. The hedge portfolio is self-financing since the combined portfolio is riskless.

Note that $q_i \equiv q_i(r_1, \ldots, r_k, t)$ vary through time. The hedge portfolio needs, theoretically, continuous re-hedging.

Delta and Gamma Hedging

The delta of an instrument with respect to some state variable is the first derivative of the value of the instrument with respect to that state variable. A delta hedge is a portfolio whose delta equals the delta of the instrument it is hedging. The hedge portfolio constructed in the previous section is automatically delta hedged. A continuously re-hedged delta hedged portfolio is a perfect hedge.

In practice it is not possible to continuously re-hedge the hedging portfolio. A practical solution is to re-hedge only when the value V of the hedged instrument changes by some predetermined amount. Treating $V \equiv V(r_1, \ldots, r_k, t)$ as if it were a function of non-stochastic variables $r_1, \ldots, r_k$ we can expand it out in a Taylor series approximation:

$$\Delta V = \sum_{j=0}^{k} \frac{\partial V}{\partial r_j} \Delta r_j + \frac{1}{2} \sum_{j,l=0}^{k} \frac{\partial^2 V}{\partial r_j \partial r_l} \Delta r_j \Delta r_l + \cdots. \tag{5.36}$$

To first order, a discretely rehedged delta hedged portfolio will require rehedging more frequently than a portfolio in which $\partial^2 V / \partial r_j \partial r_l$ is also zero.

$\partial^2 V / \partial r_j^2$ is the gamma of V with respect to r_j. A portfolio is gamma hedged if its hedging portfolio has the properties that

$$V = \sum_{i=0}^{k} q_i H_i, \tag{5.37}$$

$$\frac{\partial V}{\partial r_j} = \sum_{i=0}^{k} q_i \frac{\partial H_i}{\partial r_j}, \tag{5.38}$$

$$\frac{\partial^2 V}{\partial r_j^2} = \sum_{i=0}^{k} q_i \frac{\partial^2 H_i}{\partial r_j^2}. \tag{5.39}$$

A gamma hedged portfolio is also delta hedged. A gamma hedged portfolio requires re-hedging at less frequent intervals than a purely delta hedged portfolio. Gamma hedges are more stable and match the value of the hedged instrument better. On the other hand, they require the presence of more instruments in the hedging portfolio, and they are harder and more expensive to set up and maintain. Delta and gamma hedging are extremely popular for option portfolios.

Delta and gamma hedging require a knowledge of the first and second derivatives of the assets V and H_i with respect to the state variables. To know these requires a model.

Example: Hedging a Bond Option

In the Vasicek model the process for the short rate r_t is

$$dr_t = \alpha(\mu - r_t)dt + \sigma \, dz_t, \tag{5.40}$$

and the value of a bond option $c_t(T_1, T_2)$ is

$$c_t(T_1, T_2) = B_t(T_2)N(d) - XB_t(T_1)N(d - \sigma_p), \tag{5.41}$$

$$d = \frac{1}{\sigma_p} \ln \frac{B_t(T_2)}{B_t(T_1)} + \frac{1}{2}\sigma_p, \tag{5.42}$$

$$\sigma_p = \sigma \frac{1 - e^{-\alpha(T_2 - T_1)}}{\alpha} \left(\frac{1 - e^{2\alpha(T_2 - T_1)}}{2\alpha} \right)^{\frac{1}{2}}, \tag{5.43}$$

where

$$B_t(\tau) = e^{r_t(\tau)\tau}, \tag{5.44}$$

with

$$r_t(\tau) = r_\infty + (r_t - r_\infty)\frac{1 - e^{-\alpha\tau}}{\alpha\tau} + \frac{\sigma^2\tau}{4\alpha}\left(\frac{1 - e^{-\alpha\tau}}{\alpha\tau}\right)^2. \tag{5.45}$$

The short rate r_t is the only source of risk in the Vasicek model. The 'natural' instruments[1] to use to hedge this option are the two pure discount bonds $B_t(T_1)$ and $B_t(T_2)$. To construct a delta hedge we need to find q_1 and q_2 such that

$$q_1 B_t(T_1) + q_2 B_t(T_2) = c, \tag{5.46}$$

$$q_1 \frac{\partial B_t(T_1)}{\partial r_t} + q_2 \frac{\partial B_t(T_2)}{\partial r_t} = \frac{\partial c}{\partial r_t}. \tag{5.47}$$

Since

$$\frac{\partial c}{\partial r_t} = \frac{\partial c}{\partial B_t(T_1)} \frac{\partial B_t(T_1)}{\partial r_t} + \frac{\partial c}{\partial B_t(T_2)} \frac{\partial B_t(T_2)}{\partial r_t}, \tag{5.48}$$

it can be shown that

$$q_1 = \frac{\partial c}{\partial B_t(T_1)} = -XN(d - \sigma_p), \tag{5.49}$$

$$q_2 = \frac{\partial c}{\partial B_t(T_2)} = N(d). \tag{5.50}$$

Thus the hedge is to buy $N(d)$ units of $B_t(T_2)$, and sell (or short) $XN(d - \sigma_p)$ units of $B_t(T_1)$.

Hedging by Replication

Consider the following pair of hypothetical instruments. Each is written on three-month Libor, paying off in nine months based on the three-month Libor rate in six months, time. Set $T = 0.5$ and write L_T for the Libor rate at six months. Set $\tau = 0.25$ so that the payoff is at time $T + \tau$. Write P for a notional principal:

Option A: The payoff $H^A(T + \tau)$ at time $T + \tau$ is

$$H^A(T + \tau) = \begin{cases} 0, & L_T < 0.05, \\ \tau P \times (L_T - 0.05)^2, & 0.05 < L_T < 0.08, \\ \tau P \times 9 \times 10^{-4}, & 0.08 < L_T. \end{cases} \tag{5.51}$$

---

[1] We define natural hedging instruments below. 'Natural' does not necessarily mean 'best'.

Option B: The payoff $H^B(T + \tau)$ at time $T + \tau$ is

$$H^B(T + \tau) = \begin{cases} 0, & L_T < 0.05, \\ \tau P \times (100L_T - 5) \times 10^{-4}, & 0.05 < L_T < 0.06, \\ \tau P \times (300L_T - 14) \times 10^{-4}, & 0.06 < L_T < 0.07, \\ \tau P \times (500L_T - 31) \times 10^{-4}, & 0.07 < L_T < 0.08, \\ \tau P \times 9 \times 10^{-4}, & 0.08 < L_T. \end{cases} \quad (5.52)$$

The payoff to option B may look odd, but see Figure 5.2. The figure illustrates the payoff functions to options A and B for a normalised principal. The payoff to option B is piece-wise linear, matching the payoff to option A when $L_T = 0.05$, 0.06, 0.07 and 0.08.

Suppose that in this hypothetical market there are liquid caplets on L_T also paying off at time $T + \tau$, at strikes $X = (0.05, 0.06, 0.07, 0.08)$, and also the corresponding FRA, F_T, but no other plausible hedging instruments. Write c_i for the current value of the caplet with strike X_i, $i = 1, \ldots, 4$.

Option B can be perfectly hedged by the replicating portfolio $q^B = (1, 2, 2, -5)$, where q_i^B is the quantity c_i of the hedge portfolio. Hence the value v^B of option B is $v^B = \Sigma_{i=1}^4 q_i^B c_i$.

Option A cannot be perfectly hedged using just the caplets c_i. However, the portfolio q^B super-replicates it so that $v^A \leq v^B$. If every caplet c_i could be priced with a Black's formula with the same Black's implied volatility, so that the caplets were priced as if F_T were log-normal with constant volatility, then a formula is available to give an

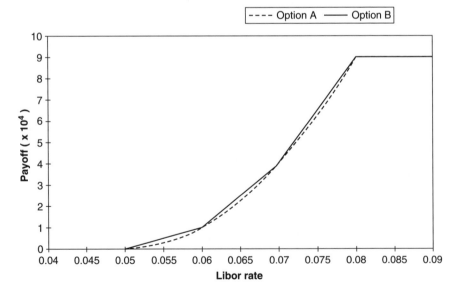

Figure 5.2   Payoffs to options A and B

exact value for v^A. Unfortunately in the presence of a volatility smile the formula does not work. Furthermore, we have no intuition from the Black's implied volatilities of the caplets as to what would be the correct volatility to put into the formula. Also, the formula would mislead us as to the amount of the FRA we might put into the hedge for option A.

Despite the fact that v^B is clearly an over-estimate of the value of option A, it reflects the value of the only valid hedging portfolio we can construct. Therefore there is some justification for pricing and hedging option A using the hedge q^B.

Choosing Hedging Instruments

The idea of a natural hedge is quite important, albeit artificial in practical terms. An instrument is a natural hedging instrument for some derivative if

- it is explicitly referred to in the definition of the derivative; for example, for a bond option the underlying bond is explicitly referred to;
- it is implicitly referred to in the definition of the derivative; for example, if a cashflow occurs at time T, for instance at the maturity date of a bond option, then the pure discount bond $B_t(T)$ is implicitly referred to.

The natural hedge—the hedge composed of natural hedging instruments—may not always be available. Pure discount bonds of the relevant maturities may not exist, and where instruments do exist they may not be liquid.

It may well be the case that there are instruments available in the market which are quite similar to the derivative itself. For instance, if the derivative is a bond option there may be bond options available of similar strike or maturity. If these are liquid, then it is often much better to use these than the natural hedge. In theory, if the model which one is using to hedge is correct, and the market is perfect, then any instrument which is sensitive to the same source of risk as a derivative may be used to hedge that derivative. However, the model will not be correct and some instruments may not be usable for one reason or another.

The solution is to hedge with instruments as similar as possible to the derivative and to top up with instruments in the natural hedge. These hedges are likely to have similar risk characteristics to the derivative being hedged, irrespective of the model or market.

Duration and Convexity

When hedging interest rate derivatives and bond portfolios in particular, the market uses duration and convexity. These concepts are equivalent to delta and gamma hedging.

The duration of an instrument B with respect to a state variable r is

$$D_r(B) = -\frac{1}{B}\frac{\partial B}{\partial r}. \tag{5.53}$$

If $B = B_t(T)$ is a pure discount bond, a conventional definition of duration is just its time to maturity. This coincides with Equation 5.53 if the yield to maturity $r_t(T)$ of

$B_t(T)$ is used as a state variable. Then

$$D_{r_t(T)}(B_t(T)) = -\frac{1}{B_t(T)}\frac{\partial}{\partial r_t(T)}\left(e^{-r_t(T)(T-t)}\right) \tag{5.54}$$

$$= T - t. \tag{5.55}$$

Using duration   Suppose we are short one unit of a bond $B_t(T)$ and want to hedge by constructing a portfolio using bonds $B_t(T_1)$ and $B_t(T_2)$. If there is a single state variable r we need to find the quantities q_1 and q_2 such that

$$q_1 B_t(T_1) + q_2 B_t(T_2) = B_t(T), \tag{5.56}$$

$$q_1\frac{\partial B_t(T_1)}{\partial r} + q_2\frac{\partial B_t(T_2)}{\partial r} = \frac{\partial B_t(T)}{\partial r}. \tag{5.57}$$

Define the weights w_i,

$$w_i = q_i\frac{B_t(T_i)}{B_t(T)}. \tag{5.58}$$

w_i is the proportion of the value of $B_t(T)$ that we invest in $B_t(T_i)$. For notational simplicity, set $D_r(T) = D_r(B_t(T))$. We do not require that the bonds are pure discount bonds. Re-arranging (5.56) and (5.57) we get

$$w_1 + w_2 = 1, \tag{5.59}$$

$$w_1 D_r(T_1) + w_2 D_r(T_2) = D_r(T). \tag{5.60}$$

Thus the duration of the hedge portfolio is the weighted average duration of its constituents, and to hedge the derivative one constructs a hedging portfolio of equal duration.

Vasicek duration   In the Vasicek model spot rates are

$$r_t(\tau) = r_\infty + (r_t - r_\infty)\frac{1 - e^{-\alpha\tau}}{\alpha\tau} + \frac{\sigma^2\tau}{4\alpha}\left(\frac{1 - e^{-\alpha\tau}}{\alpha\tau}\right)^2, \tag{5.61}$$

where r_t is the short rate and $\tau = T - t$. The state variable is the short rate r_t. The Vasicek duration is

$$D_{r_t}^V(B_t(T)) = -\frac{1}{B_t(T)}\frac{\partial}{\partial r_t}\left(e^{-r_t(T)(T-t)}\right) \tag{5.62}$$

$$= \frac{1}{B_t(T)}\frac{\partial r_t(T)}{\partial r_t}(T - t)B_t(T) \tag{5.63}$$

$$= \frac{1 - e^{-\alpha(T-t)}}{\alpha}. \tag{5.64}$$

When the bond is close to maturity, so that $T - t$ is small, $D_{r_t}^V(B_t(T)) \approx T - t$, but when $T - t$ is large, $D_{r_t}^V(B_t(T)) \approx 1/\alpha$. For shorter maturities the Vasicek duration approximates to the conventional duration, but for longer maturities it tends to a constant. This reflects the decreasing sensitivity of longer spot rates to changes in the short rate.

To see how Vasicek hedging works, consider hedging a 10-year liability with 5- and 15-year pure discount bonds. We assume that under the EMM

$$dr_t = \alpha(\mu - r_t)dt + \sigma\, dz_t, \tag{5.65}$$

where $\alpha = 0.2$, $\mu = 0.1$, $\sigma = 0.05$ and $r_t = 0.08$. We find that

Bond	Bond prices	Conventional duration	Vasicek duration	
$B_t(5)$	0.7293	5	3.1606	(5.66)
$B_t(10)$	0.5144	10	4.3233	
$B_t(15)$	0.3632	15	4.7511	

To construct a delta hedge, we need to find w_5 and $w_{15} = 1 - w_5$, such that

$$w_5 D_5 + w_{15} D_{15} = D_{10}. \tag{5.67}$$

For conventional duration we find $w_5 = w_{15} = 0.5$, but using Vasicek duration we get $w_5 = 0.27$, only about half as much.

This is a significant result. The contents of a hedge are extremely sensitive to the model one adopts. Although Vasicek is an extreme example, and its use is not generally recommended for these purposes, it demonstrates that the choice of model is very important.

Convexity Convexity hedging is equivalent to gamma hedging. Convexity is defined as

$$C_r(B) = -\frac{1}{B}\frac{\partial^2 B}{\partial r^2}, \tag{5.68}$$

where the value of B depends on the state variable r. Treating its yield to maturity as a state variable, the convexity of a pure discount bond $B_t(T)$ is

$$C_{r_t(T)}(B_t(T)) = -\frac{1}{B_t(T)}\frac{\partial}{\partial r_t(T)}\left(e^{-r_t(T)(T-t)}\right) \tag{5.69}$$

$$= (T - t)^2. \tag{5.70}$$

This is a conventional definition of convexity. Like duration, convexity is very model dependent.

We can gamma hedge a derivative by constructing a hedging portfolio whose convexity and duration are equal to those of the derivative. Three hedging instruments with durations and convexities D_i and C_i, $i = 1, 2, 3$ are needed to gamma hedge a derivative with duration D and convexity C against only two required for delta hedging.

To gamma hedge, we need to find w_1, w_2 and w_3 such that

$$w_1 + w_2 + w_3 = 1, \tag{5.71}$$

$$w_1 D_1 + w_2 D_2 + w_3 D_3 = D, \tag{5.72}$$

$$w_1 C_1 + w_2 C_2 + w_3 C_3 = C. \tag{5.73}$$

Hedging Single Products and Hedging Portfolios

The principles are the same for hedging a portfolio as for hedging single products. With a portfolio, however, there may be a certain amount of netting—where offsetting risks are taken into account—which may be done before additional hedging is needed. The simplest example of netting is where a portfolio contains two identical but opposing deals. It is unnecessary to hedge each of these separately, as they provide a hedge for each other. If the deals were similar but with different maturities, then after netting there would be residual risk left to hedge.

Some netting can be performed if the instruments in a portfolio have different but correlated underlyings, such as interest rates in related but different countries. If the correlation can be modelled and estimated, then a partial hedge can be formed by hedging one interest rate by that of another currency. This practice has obvious flaws; the hedge is not perfect and may fail even if the correlation does not change. There have been recent spectacular examples of the failure of correlation hedges.

In practice, a bank will maintain one portfolio of simple or vanilla deals, and another of exotics which may require careful active management. The middle office might manage the vanilla deals while the front office looks after the exotics.

Single and Multifactor Pricing and Hedging

With a one-factor yield curve model, it is only possible to hedge one source of risk. If a derivative is subject to two or more obvious sources of risk, then one-factor models are inadequate, and it becomes necessary to use a multifactor model. An example would be an option on a spread S_t, where

$$S_t = r_t(T_1) - r_t(T_2) \tag{5.74}$$

is the difference between spot rates of two different maturities. In a one-factor model changes in $r_t(T_1)$ and $r_t(T_2)$ are perfectly correlated. This is not the case empirically. A spread option is particularly sensitive to correlations between rates. To value and hedge spread options a two-factor yield curve model must be employed.

5.1.4   The Monte Carlo Method

We describe the Monte Carlo method in some detail in Chapter 13. Here we outline the basic method.

The value of a derivative is the expected discounted payoff under the EMM. The Monte Carlo method is a numerical way of evaluating the expectation. Given the probability density of the value of the underlying asset, it is possible to compute expected values and discount back. If the density is unknown, it is possible to approximate it by simulating the process followed by the underlying.

The Monte Carlo Method and Interest Rates

Suppose we want to value a derivative with payoff $H(T, r_T)$ at time T. The value at time $t = 0$ is

$$V_0 = \mathbb{E}_0^Q \left[\exp \left(- \int_0^T r_s \, ds \right) H(T, r_T) \right],$$ (5.75)

where $\mathbb{E}_0^Q$ is the expected value at time 0 under the EMM, Q. Suppose the process for r_t under the EMM is

$$dr_t = \mu(r_t, t)dt + \sigma(r_t, t)dz_t.$$ (5.76)

The Monte Carlo method uses a discrete approximation for this process to evolve r_t up to time T. At time T we compute $H(T, r_T)$ and discount it back along the path of interest rates. We do this many times and take the average of the discounted payoffs.

The method in more detail Divide the period $[0, T]$ into N time steps and set $\Delta_t = T/N$. Evolve r_t as

$$r_{t_{i+1}} = r_{t_i} + \mu(r_{t_i}, t_i)\Delta_t + \sigma(r_{t_i}, t)\sqrt{\Delta_t}\, z_{t_{i+1}},$$ (5.77)

for instance, where $z_t \sim N(0, 1)$ is a sequence of standard normal iid variates. Obtain a value r_T at time T.

Compute $H(T, r_T)$ and discount it back using the generated values of the short rate, r_t. Set

$$V = \exp \left(- \sum_{i=0}^{T-1} r_{t_i} \Delta_t \right) H(T, r_T).$$ (5.78)

This is the value at time 0 of the derivative under the particular sample path $r_0, \ldots, r_T$.

To find the Monte Carlo estimate compute M sample paths, finding values V_i, $i = 1, \ldots, M$, and set

$$V = \frac{1}{M} \sum_{i=1}^M V_i.$$ (5.79)

This is the Monte Carlo estimate of the value V.

The basic method is very simple to implement, but as we see in Chapter 13, a practical implementation needs to be a serious elaboration of the basic method. Some features of the method are:

1. The distribution of the simulated r_T needs to be as close as possible to the actual distribution. This means using a sensible discretisation method. If the Euler discretisation is used, a small time step Δ_t is necessary.
2. If the underlying asset for a derivative is not itself a state variable, it is usually necessary to simulate beyond the maturity of the option to get a value for the underlying.
3. It is possible to simulate many state variables at once. Multifactor models are easy to evaluate.

4. The method values path-dependent options easily.
5. The method requires many simulated paths which can take a long time to compute. It is necessary to use speed-up methods.

Limitations of the Monte Carlo method include:

1. It cannot easily value American style options or Bermudans.
2. It produces values that are probabilistic only.
3. It needs reliable sampling methods.

These limitations are discussed more fully in Chapter 13.

5.2 INTRODUCTION TO ESTIMATION

Finding good efficient methods of estimating the values of parameters occurring in interest rate models is extremely important. Given a potential interest rate model one needs to be able to evaluate it, by fitting it to market data to discover how well it performs. In Part IV we explore methods such as the general method of moments (GMM), maximum likelihood (ML), and filtering techniques. In this section we focus on concepts of estimation and the failings of naive methods.

There are three aspects to calibrating a model.

1. Fitting the model to historical data.
2. Fitting the model to current data.
3. Fitting the model to future data. In other words, assessing how well the model forecasts, and its stability and robustness.

To fit to historical or current data, as well as needing a data set, it is also necessary to decide on what aspects of the data to fit to. One needs to decide how to fit the model and how to decide if the fit is a good one or not.

We also require stable parameter values. In a calibrated model state variables can vary through time, but constants may not. Different data sets should not invalidate the model. For instance, if there is a shift in level of rates the performance of the model should not be affected.

5.2.1   Obtaining a Data Set

Market prices for both primary yield curve instruments, such as FRAs and swaps, and for derivatives such as caps and swaptions, can be used for calibration purposes.

Given a set of yield curve data—either for the money market (Libor and swap rates) or for a government bond market (bond prices)—one hopes to impute an entire yield curve. With derivative data one obtains information about volatilities and correlations.

A model can be tested by computing the model yield curve, for instance, and comparing it with the actual. Once the model is calibrated it can be used to price and hedge less liquid instruments.

Historical and Cross-sectional Data

Cross-sectional data is a set of prices or rates all observed at the same time, for instance, the yield curve at 10.00 am on 4 July. Historical data are data observed over a period of time. For instance, a time series of three-month Libor from 1975 to 1991.

To fit dynamics—the way in which rates change through time—historical data are needed, whereas fitting to current data gives a snapshot of the market's expectations of future rate movements. Historical data suffer from the flaw that it is changing through time. In the real world parameter values cannot be expected to be constants. If they are varying even slowly, then estimating with too long an historical time series will provide estimates of what the parameter values used to be instead of what they are today.

These represent two quite different approaches to calibrating a model. Calibrating to current prices is far more pertinent than calibrating to an historical time series, although in practice models are calibrated both ways—a natural belt-and-braces approach. In fact, since current prices are obtained under a risk-adjusted measure, one expects to obtain different parameters from each approach. The difference enables one to estimate the market price of risk.

5.2.2   Fitting the Model

What to fit to may depend on the purposes to which the model is being put. A desk interested in valuing OTC swaptions will want to calibrate to vanilla swaps and swaptions. An application to find cheap or rich bonds may only need current bond data.

If calibrating to a short rate time series a decision must be made as to what surrogate to use for the short rate. In the dollar market the fed funds rate may be used, but in markets without a reliable liquid overnight rate the decision is harder. A three-month rate may be less noisy than a one-week rate, but it is much farther down the yield curve.

Fitting methods are essentially statistical procedures, and in theory should only be used in conjunction with specification tests. GMM and ML methods described in Chapter 17 come equipped with a full battery of tests. In practice, a model will fail any sufficiently stringent specification test, and in any case if looking to develop a structure a practitioner does not want the data to fit too closely too often to a model.

5.2.3   Example: Calibrating the Vasicek Model

It is possible to fit Vasicek to

1. A time series of the short rate, or
2. The current term structure.

Fitting Vasicek: Dynamics

Sophisticated estimation techniques are necessary for interest rate models. It is woefully inadequate to use a naive estimation method such as ordinary least squares (OLS) regression. Even when regression may be a theoretically valid method to use, its faults in practical applications are well documented (Honore (98) [286], Ball and Torous (96) [51]).

Suppose we have a time series $\{r_t\}_{t=1,...,n}$, of short rate data. Discretise the Vasicek process

$$dr_t = \alpha(\mu - r_t)dt + \sigma\, dz_t \tag{5.80}$$

using the Euler discretisation

$$r_{t+\Delta t} = (1 - \alpha\Delta t)r_t + \alpha\mu\Delta t + \sigma\sqrt{\Delta t}\,\varepsilon_t. \tag{5.81}$$

One may attempt to calibrate by performing the regression $r_{t+\Delta t} = a + br_t + \eta_t$, where η_t is normal noise. The estimates $\hat{\alpha}$ and $\hat{\mu}$ of α and μ are

$$\hat{\alpha} = \frac{1 - b}{\Delta t}, \qquad \hat{\mu} = \frac{a}{1 - b}, \tag{5.82}$$

and $\sigma^2\Delta t = \text{var}(\eta_t)$.

Of course, these estimates are only sensible if the model is not mis-specified. If the residuals $\varepsilon_t = \eta_t/\sigma\sqrt{\Delta t}$ suffer from non-normality, heteroscedasticity or serial correlation, then the model does not fit the data and great care must be taken in interpreting any inferences from the model.

But several other things go wrong with this procedure.

1. Unless Δt is very small the estimates of $\hat{\mu}$ and in particular $\hat{\alpha}$ are significantly biased. This is because the process (5.81) is close to having a unit root (Ball and Torous (96) [51]), Honore (98) [286]).
2. OLS regression is equivalent to minimising σ, and is not equivalent to ensuring that ε_t is standard normal iid. If the process (5.81) was the data-generating process (DGP), this would not matter, but since in interest rate modelling the DGP is unknown, and existing models do not match it closely, it is unclear whether minimising σ is a valid objective or not.

Interest rate models help practitioners to decide how to hedge and value individual products worth tens or hundreds of millions of dollars. Poor decisions are extremely costly. Whereas in some economic (and indeed some financial) applications heteroscedasticity and other evidence of mis-specification is tolerated, in derivatives models even a moderate mis-specification can have striking consequences—in practical terms—for the contents of a hedge. It is essential that if residuals are not normal iid (and they almost certainly will not be) then the causes of the mis-specification should be understood and compensated for wherever possible.

Fitting Vasicek: Statics

Vasicek yield curves are of the form

$$r_t(\tau) = r_\infty + (r_t - r_\infty)\frac{1 - e^{-\alpha\tau}}{\alpha\tau} + \frac{\sigma^2\tau}{4\alpha}\left(\frac{1 - e^{-\alpha\tau}}{\alpha\tau}\right)^2, \tag{5.83}$$

where

$$r_\infty = \mu - \frac{\lambda\sigma}{\alpha} - \frac{\sigma^2}{2\alpha^2}. \tag{5.84}$$

The yield curve is parameterised by the set $\{\alpha, \sigma, r_\infty\}$, $r_t(\tau) = r_t(\tau \mid \alpha, \sigma, r_\infty)$. Suppose we observe rates $R_t = (R_{1,t}, \ldots, R_{k,t})'$, where $R_{i,t}$ is the spot rate of maturity τ_i at time t. For example, $R_{1,t}$ could be three-month Libor at time t, with $\tau_1 = 0.25$, *et cetera*. Set

$$r_t(\alpha, \sigma, r_\infty) = (r_t(\tau_1 \mid \alpha, \sigma, r_\infty), \ldots, r_t(\tau_k \mid \alpha, \sigma, r_\infty))'. \tag{5.85}$$

Calibration to the yield curve means choosing $(\alpha, \sigma, r_\infty)$ so that $r_t(\alpha, \sigma, r_\infty)$ best matches R_t. For instance, one might try to minimise

$$J(\alpha, \sigma, r_\infty) = (R_t - r_t(\alpha, \sigma, r_\infty))'(R_t - r_t(\alpha, \sigma, r_\infty)), \tag{5.86}$$

the sum of squared deviations.[2]

The yield curve is derived under risk-adjusted probabilities, so calibrating to it fits to risk-adjusted probabilities rather than objective probabilities. The parameters α, σ and r_∞ incorporate the market price of risk. The short rate time series is observed under objective probabilities, which are not adjusted by a price of risk. For the Vasicek model, if the objective process is

$$dr_t = \alpha(\mu - r_t)dt + \sigma\,dz_t, \tag{5.87}$$

then the risk-adjusted process is

$$dr_t = \alpha(\mu - r_t)dt + \sigma\,d\tilde{z}_t - \lambda\sigma dt \tag{5.88}$$

$$= \alpha(\tilde{\mu} - r_t)dt + \sigma\,d\tilde{z}_t, \tag{5.89}$$

where $\tilde{\mu} = \mu - \lambda\sigma/\alpha$ and λ is the price of risk.

To estimate a value for the price of risk, we would need to use cross-sectional data to find $\tilde{\mu}$, and historical data to find μ. Given μ and $\tilde{\mu}$ set $\lambda = \alpha(\mu - \tilde{\mu})/\sigma$.

5.2.4 Example: The CKLS Process

A number of authors (Chan *et al.* (92) [124], Honore (98) [286], Rogers (95) [457], Bliss and Smith (98) [79]) have investigated a one-factor family of interest rate models with the short rate process

$$dr_t = \alpha(\mu - r_t)dt + \sigma r_t^\gamma\,dz_t. \tag{5.90}$$

It includes a number of standard one-factor models,

$$\gamma = \begin{cases} 0, & \text{Vasicek,} \\ \frac{1}{2}, & \text{Cox, Ingersoll and Ross,} \\ 1, & \text{Brennan and Schwartz (80) [94] Courtadon (82) [145], } \textit{et cetera.} \end{cases} \tag{5.91}$$

---

[2] We shall see in Chapter 17 that this may not be an optimal criterion.

Unfortunately, none of these models nor the slightly more general formulation (5.90) fits market data *at all*. Empirical work (Chan *et al.* (92) [124], Babbs and Nowman (97) [38]) suggests $\gamma \approx 1.5$ but these results are only as good as the fit of the model to the data.

If (5.90) was considered a plausible model there are a number of reasons why one might expect that $\gamma \neq 0$. The most convincing reason would be that the model fitted market data. Failing this, allowing $\gamma \neq 0$ permits the model to fit certain aspects of market data. For instance, it can produce fat tails, and it may prevent rates from becoming negative (if this is thought to be desirable; in fact 0 may still be attainable if σ is large enough). Some values of λ give r_t important distributional properties:

$$\gamma \begin{cases} = 0, & r_t \text{ is a conditional normal distribution,} \\ = \frac{1}{2}, & r_t \text{ is a non-central } \chi^2 \text{ distribution,} \\ > 1, & \text{expected futures values are unbounded.} \end{cases} \quad (5.92)$$

5.2.5 Simulation

Simulating sample paths is a very important method for validating any estimation procedure. The three stages to the procedure are:

1. Simulate sample paths from a model with known parameter values.
2. Using the estimation method find estimates of the parameter values.
3. Test if the actual parameter values lie inside the confidence intervals of the estimated values.

It should be possible to establish whether the estimation method has certain undesirable properties. Is it

- Biased? Do estimated values vary systematically from actual values?
- Inefficient? Do estimated values have a variance larger than the smallest possible?
- Consistent? As the amount of data grow, do estimated values converge to actual values?

An estimation method with some of these undesirable properties may nevertheless be acceptable in practice. For instance, one may be prepared to use a slightly biased method if it had very low variance compared with the most efficient unbiased method. If you have very little data it may not matter if the estimation method is inconsistent.

On the whole we want to use an unbiased consistent method.

Discretising a Continuous Process

When simulating a continuous time process it is first necessary to discretise it. A naive Euler approximation to the continuous process may not be best. For example, the Euler approximation to the continuous process

$$\mathrm{d}r_t = \mu(r_t)\mathrm{d}t + \sigma(r_t)\mathrm{d}z_t \quad (5.93)$$

is

$$r_{t+1} = r_t + \mu(r_t)\Delta_t + \sigma(r_t)\sqrt{\Delta_t}\,\varepsilon_{t+1}, \tag{5.94}$$

where $\varepsilon_t \sim N(0, 1)$. The discretisation (5.94) has the same mean and same stationary variance as (5.93), but only in the limit does it have the same higher order conditional moments. The Milshtein approximation to the process (5.93) is

$$r_{t+1} = r_t + \mu(r_t)\Delta_t + \sigma(r_t)\sqrt{\Delta_t}\,\varepsilon_{t+1} + \tfrac{1}{2}\sigma(r_t)\sigma'(r_t)(\varepsilon_{t+1}^2 - 1)\Delta_t, \tag{5.95}$$

where $\sigma'(r_t)$ is the derivative of $\sigma(r_t)$ with respect to r_t. It converges faster than the Euler approximation. (Note that the additional term has expected value zero.) The Milshtein approximation may be useful for simulating stock processes but its usefulness for simulating interest rate processes is less clear. For instance, for the CIR process where $\sigma(r_t) \equiv \sigma\sqrt{r_t}$, we have $\tfrac{1}{4}\sigma^2\left(\varepsilon_{t+1}^2 - 1\right)\Delta_t \sim 10^{-5}\Delta_t$, usually a relatively minor correction.

5.2.6 Naive Estimation?

Suppose one wants to estimate the parameters of the continuous time CKLS process (5.90). Discretise the short rate process as

$$r_{t+1} = a + br_t + \sigma r_t^\gamma \sqrt{\Delta_t}\,\eta_{t+1}, \tag{5.96}$$

where $\eta_t \sim N(0, 1)$. The hardest parameter to estimate is γ. It is easy in principle to test if γ has some particular value. For the candidate value of γ perform the regression

$$r_{t+1}r_t^{-\gamma} = \hat{a}r_t^{-\gamma} + \hat{b}r_t^{1-\gamma} + \hat{\sigma}\sqrt{\Delta_t}\,\eta_{t+1}, \tag{5.97}$$

and test the hypothesis:

$$H_0 : \eta_t \sim N(0, 1), \text{ iid.} \tag{5.98}$$

If the hypothesis cannot be rejected, then neither can the hypothesis that the value of γ is the test value.

It is not possible to estimate γ as the test value that returns the best R^2 in the regression (5.97). That is equivalent to returning the value of γ that estimates the lowest value of σ, not the value that gives the 'best' time series of η_t.

Note that if (5.96) is the DGP then any of the methods we discuss in Chapter 17 will return good estimates of the parameters. In practice the DGP for interest rate time series in unknown and any model is likely to be rejected by the data. The objective is then to come up with parameter estimates that 'best fit' in the sense of determining consistent, reliable, arbitrage-free prices and hedging portfolios. To this end we seek estimated parameter values so that η_t is as close as possible to being standard normal iid. Unfortunately there is no single test to determine this, only a set of tests on different aspects of the hypothesis.

The next section discusses various tests that can—and should—be used.

5.3   STATISTICAL TESTS

We need to establish whether a series $\{\hat{\varepsilon}_t\}_{t=1,\dots,n}$ is standard normal iid. There are several properties to verify, each of which has different tests. We need to test for normality, serial correlation and heteroscedasticity. Tests are often applied to residuals obtained from regressions, but they can apply more generally. In Chapter 17 we meet the GMM and ML estimation methods and the tests associated with them. Here we may imagine that the series $\{\hat{\varepsilon}_t\}$ are the residuals from a regression, perhaps of the type (5.81).

We describe a few standard tests. For further information the reader is referred to standard books such as Campbell, Lo and MacKinlay (97) [113], Mills (90) [396], Maddala (89) [375], or Makridakis, Wheelwright and McGee (83) [377], *et cetera*.

5.3.1   Tests for Normality

We can try to confirm that the moments of $\hat{\varepsilon}_t$ are normal. Define

$$\hat{\sigma}^2 = \frac{1}{n}\sum_{t=1}^{n}\hat{\varepsilon}_t^2, \tag{5.99}$$

$$\hat{\mu}_3 = \frac{1}{n}\sum_{t=1}^{n}\hat{\varepsilon}_t^3, \tag{5.100}$$

$$\hat{\mu}_4 = \frac{1}{n}\sum_{t=1}^{n}\hat{\varepsilon}_t^4. \tag{5.101}$$

Then

$$\text{skewness} = s = \frac{\hat{\mu}_3}{\hat{\sigma}^3}, \tag{5.102}$$

$$\text{kurtosis} = k = \frac{\hat{\mu}_4}{\hat{\sigma}^4}. \tag{5.103}$$

If $\hat{\varepsilon}_t$ is normal, then $s = 0$ and $k = 3$. The Jarque–Bera statistic is

$$JB = n\left(\frac{\hat{\mu}_3^2}{6\hat{\sigma}^6} + \frac{(\hat{\mu}_4 - 3\hat{\sigma}^4)^2}{24\hat{\sigma}^8}\right) = \frac{n}{6}\left(s^2 + 2(k-3)^2\right), \tag{5.104}$$

and $JB \sim \chi^2(2)$ under the null hypothesis, $H_0 : s = 0, k = 3$. The Jarque-Bera test is simple and effective. Passing the JB test does not guarantee normality, but it rejects many time series of residuals obtained from financial estimations.

5.3.2   Tests for Serial Correlation (Autoregression)

$\hat{\varepsilon}_t$ should not be serially correlated, $\text{cov}\left(\hat{\varepsilon}_t, \hat{\varepsilon}_{t-s}\right) = 0$, $s \neq 0$. A possible cause of serial correlation is a model with too few state variables. We give two tests for serial correlation: the Durbin-Watson test and the LM test.

The Durbin–Watson Test for Serial Correlation

Compute the statistic

$$DW = \frac{\sum_{t=1}^{n} \left(\hat{\varepsilon}_t - \hat{\varepsilon}_{t-1}\right)^2}{\sum_{t=1}^{n} \hat{\varepsilon}_t^2}. \tag{5.105}$$

Then $DW \approx 2\left(1 - \mathrm{corr}\left(\hat{\varepsilon}_t, \hat{\varepsilon}_{t-1}\right)\right)$ in large samples. Tables are available to test whether it is sufficiently far from 2 to reject the null hypothesis.

The Durbin–Watson test only tests for first-order autocorrelation. When applied to residuals from OLS regression it cannot be used for systems with lagged dependent variables.

The LM test for Serial Correlation

Suppose that serial correlation results from a system

$$y_t = f(x_t, y_{t-1} \mid \varphi) + \varepsilon_t, \tag{5.106}$$

$$\varepsilon_t = \theta_1 \varepsilon_{t-1} + \ldots + \theta_p \varepsilon_{t-p} + u_t, \, u_t \sim \mathrm{N}(0, \sigma^2), \tag{5.107}$$

for some function f of lags of y_t and other variables x_t, with parameter set φ. Serial correlation is absent if $\theta_i = 0$, $i = 1, \ldots, p$, so test for the null hypothesis: $\mathrm{H}_0 : \theta_1 = \ldots = \theta_p = 0$. The steps are:

1. Estimate the parameter set φ to obtain $\hat{\varepsilon}_t$.
2. Regress $\hat{\varepsilon}_t$ on $\hat{\varepsilon}_{t-1}, \ldots, \hat{\varepsilon}_{t-p}$ and obtain the R^2.
3. The LM statistic is $LM = nR^2 \sim \chi^2(p)$, under the null hypothesis.

Instead of using the LM statistic it is also possible to use a standard F-test for $\theta_1 = \ldots = \theta_p = 0$.

Correcting for Serial Correlation

If the residuals ε_t have first-order autocorrelation, ρ, so that

$$y_t = \alpha + \beta x_t + \varepsilon_t, \tag{5.108}$$

$$\varepsilon_t = \rho \varepsilon_{t-1} + u_t, \, u_t \sim \mathrm{N}(0, \sigma^2), \tag{5.109}$$

it is possible to adjust the discrete drift function $\alpha + \beta x_t$ to get rid of it. The procedure is:

1. Regress $y_t = \alpha + \beta x_t + \varepsilon_t$ and obtain $\hat{\varepsilon}_t$.
2. Regress $\hat{\varepsilon}_t = \rho \hat{\varepsilon}_{t-1} + u_t$ to get an estimate $\hat{\rho}$ of ρ.

To remove serial correlation we can now use ρth differencing. Set

$$\nabla^\rho y_t = y_t - \rho y_{t-1}, \tag{5.110}$$

then

$$\nabla^\rho y_t = \alpha (1 - \rho) + \beta \nabla^\rho x_t + u_t. \tag{5.111}$$

The residuals are now u_t, and are not first-order autocorrelated. ρth differencing removes first-order autocorrelation. The process for y_t has an adjusted drift

$$y_t = \alpha + \beta x_t + \rho (y_{t-1} - \alpha - \beta x_{t-1}) + u_t \tag{5.112}$$

$$= \alpha + \beta x_t + \rho u_{t-1} + u_t. \tag{5.113}$$

5.3.3 Heteroscedasticity

Suppose that $\varepsilon_t \sim N(0, h_t)$. h_t should be constant for homoscedasticity. If h_t is dependent on time, then heteroscedasticity is present. If the residuals found from estimating a discrete process like (5.106) are heteroscedastic, then the following apply.

1. Parameter estimates may be biased and inefficient.
2. t-and F-tests are not valid.

We describe the Breusch–Pagan test for heteroscedasticity.

The Breusch–Pagan Test

Suppose h_t depends on the variables $z_{1,t}, \ldots, z_{k,t}$, $h_t = f(\gamma_0 + \gamma_1 z_{1,t} + \ldots + \gamma_k z_{k,t})$. $z_{i,t}$ could be anything—exogenous variables, or non-linear functions of the independent variable x_t, et cetera. The procedure is:

1. Regress $y_t = \alpha + \beta x_t + \varepsilon_t$ to obtain $\hat{\varepsilon}_t$.
2. Compute

$$\hat{u}_t = \frac{\hat{\varepsilon}_t^2}{\hat{\sigma}^2}, \quad \text{where} \quad \hat{\sigma}^2 = \frac{1}{n} \sum_{t=1}^{n} \hat{\varepsilon}_t^2. \tag{5.114}$$

3. Regress $\hat{u}_t$ on $z_{1,t}, \ldots, z_{k,t}$ and compute the Breusch–Pagan statistic $BP = \frac{1}{2} RSS$. $BP \sim \chi^2(k-1)$ under the null hypothesis $H_0 : \gamma_0 = \ldots = \gamma_k = 0$. (This is an asymptotic distribution.)

Causes of Heteroscedasticity

From the empirical observation that implied volatilities vary stochastically through time, many financial models, and models of interest rates in particular, interpret heteroscedasticity as a failure to incorporate a specific stochastic volatility state variable in the model. However, heteroscedasticity in the residuals may have several other causes.

Coefficients may be time dependent   For instance, suppose that $y_t = \alpha + \beta_t x_t + \varepsilon_t$, with $\beta_t = \beta + u_t$, where u_t is time dependent. Then

$$y_t = \alpha + \beta x_t + \eta_t, \qquad (5.115)$$

where $\eta_t = u_t x_t + \varepsilon_t$ is the new error term. η_t has time-dependent variance.

Variables may be omitted   If x_t only partly 'explains' y_t, then the regression $y_t = \alpha + \beta x_t + \varepsilon_t$ will not capture all the structure in y_t. Suppose in fact

$$y_t = \alpha + \beta x_t + \gamma z_t + \eta_t. \qquad (5.116)$$

Then $\varepsilon_t = \gamma z_t + \eta_t$ will have non-constant variance. Note that z_t is not specifically a stochastic volatility.

5.3.4   Tests for Stability

A stability test can determine whether parameters have varied through time. Specifically it is possible to test for regime shifts between two intervals of the data. Split the data set into two (or more) subperiods with sample sizes n_1 and n_2. For each sample, $i = 1, 2$, regress

$$y_t^{(i)} = \alpha^{(i)} + \beta_1^{(i)} x_{1,t}^{(i)} + \cdots + \beta_k^{(i)} x_{k,t}^{(i)} + \varepsilon_t. \qquad (5.117)$$

The null hypothesis is

$$H_0 : \alpha^{(1)} = \alpha^{(2)}, \quad \beta_1^{(1)} = \beta_1^{(2)}, \ldots, \beta_k^{(1)} = \beta_k^{(2)}. \qquad (5.118)$$

Compute

$$F = \frac{(RRSS - (RSS_1 + RSS_2))/(k + 1)}{(RSS_1 + RSS_2)/(n_1 + n_2 - 2k - 2)}. \qquad (5.119)$$

This is $F_{k+1, n_1 + n_2 - 2k - 2}$ under the null hypothesis. More sophisticated versions of these tests will be met in Chapter 17.

5.4   YIELD CURVE STRIPPING

Money market yield curves are constructed from relatively few instruments. This means that it may indeed be possible to find a curve with as many parameters as there are prices that can exactly reconstruct market prices. Instruments include Libor, futures, FRAs and swaps. The idea is to build up the yield curve from shorter maturities to longer maturities.

In this section we describe a naive bootstrapping method of fitting to a money market yield curve. The method exactly recovers money market rates but has the disadvantage, amongst others, of producing an unstable forward rate curve. We look at non-parametric techniques in detail in Chapter 15.

Table 5.1   Yen data, 9 January 1996

Libor (%)		Futures		Swaps (%)	
o/n	0.49	Mar 96	99.34	2y	1.14
1w	0.50	Jun 96	99.25	3y	1.60
1m	0.53	Sep 96	99.10	4y	2.04
2m	0.55	Dec 96	98.90	5y	2.43
3m	0.56			7y	3.01
				10y	3.36

As an example of the method we build a JPY yield curve for 9 January 1996.[3] The method is very basic and is designed to illustrate problems encountered by naive methods. For 9 January 1996 the spot date is 11 January. Market rates and prices for this date are shown in Table 5.1.

5.4.1   Constructing the Yield Curve

The method calculates discount factors at certain 'grid points'. To obtain discount factors for other times one interpolates between values at the grid points.

For Libor rates the discount factors are calculated directly. Futures are treated as if they were FRAs. A discount factor for a 'stub' date is required. Swaps are semi-semi, so that on both the fixed and floating legs cashflows are made semi-annually, and require discount factors at six-monthly intervals.

Calculating Discount Factors from Libor

Let $L(t, \tau)$ be the Libor rate at time t of tenor period τ. Libor is bought for 1 at time t and pays $1 + L(t, \tau)\alpha_L(t, t + \tau)$ at time $t + \tau$, where $\alpha_L(t, t + \tau)$ is the day count function for L. The discount factor for time τ is

$$\delta(\tau) = \frac{1}{1 + L(0, \tau)\alpha_L(0, \tau)}. \tag{5.120}$$

From the set of Libor rates we obtain the discount factors in Table 5.2. The day count is actual/360, so that $\alpha_L(0, \tau) = \tau/360$.

Calculating Discount Factors from Futures

Futures are treated as if they were FRAs. On their delivery date we suppose they deliver Libor at the rate implied by the futures price. Margin payments are ignored. The implied FRA rates are given in Table 5.3.

---

[3] With grateful thanks to Paul Doust for this illustrative curve. Any errors are our own.

Table 5.2 Discount factors from yen Libor

Maturity	τ	$L(\tau)$	$\alpha_L(0, \tau)$	$\delta(\tau)$
o/n	1	0.0049	0.00277	0.999986
1w	7	0.0050	0.01944	0.999903
1m	33	0.0053	0.09166	0.999514
2m	60	0.0055	0.16666	0.999094
3m	91	0.0056	0.25277	0.998586

Table 5.3 Implied yen FRA rates

Maturity	Price	FRA rate
20 Mar 96	99.34	0.0066
19 Jun 96	99.25	0.0075
18 Sep 96	99.10	0.0090
18 Dec 96	98.90	0.0110

To calculate discount factors from futures prices we require a discount factor for 20 March 96, the 'stub date'. To get this, we interpolate between discount factors obtained from two-month and three-month Libor.

The calculation in Table 5.4 uses geometric interpolation. (This is equivalent to using linear interpolation on the spot rates.) For the stub date $t = 69$, $\delta(t) = \delta(t_1)^k \delta(t_2)^{1-k}$, where $t_1 = 60$, $t_2 = 69$, and $k = (t_2 - t)/(t_2 - t_1) = (91 - 69)/(91 - 69) = 0.709677$. Now Table 5.5 calculates discount factors from futures prices for times up to three months beyond the maturity date of the December futures contract.

Table 5.4 Obtaining the Stub Discount Factor

Maturity	τ	$\delta(\tau)$
2m	60	0.999094
3m	91	0.998586
Stub	69	0.998940

Table 5.5 Discount factors obtained from yen futures

Start date	Factor for start date	Forward factor	Factor for end date
20 Mar	0.998940	0.998334	0.997276
19 Jun	0.997276	0.998108	0.995389
18 Sep	0.995389	0.997730	0.993129
18 Dec	0.993129	0.997227	0.990376

The forward factor is the forward discount factor $1/(1 + F(t_i, t_{i+1})\alpha_F(t_i, t_{i+1}))$. Given a discount factor $\delta(t_i)$ for the time t_i that a futures contract matures, the discount factor for the time t_{i+1} that the imputed FRA expires is just

$$\delta(t_{i+1}) = \delta(t_i) \times \frac{1}{1 + F(t_i, t_{i+1})\alpha_F(t_i, t_{i+1})}, \qquad (5.121)$$

where F is the FRA rate and $\alpha_F = 91/360$.

Calculating Discount Factors from Swaps

Yen swaps have cashflows at six-monthly intervals so discount factors are needed at six-monthly intervals. They are found in three stages.

1. Interpolate for the 6m and 12m discount factors. Using these, impute swap rates for 6m and 12m. (This is done because Libor and swaps have different day counts.)
2. Interpolate for the 18m swap rate from the 12m swap rate found in Table 5.1 and the 2y swap rate. With the 18m swap rate impute the 18m discount factor.
3. Interpolate for swap rates $2\frac{1}{2}$, $3\frac{1}{2}$, $4\frac{1}{2}$,... at six-monthly intervals from the 2y, 3y, 4y,... swap rates. From the set of swap rates compute the discount factors.

The calculations at each stage are as follow.

Discount Factors and Swap Rates for 6m and 12m

The interpolated discount factor for 6m is

$$\delta(6\text{m}) = 0.996819 = 0.997276^{1-k}0.995389^k, \qquad (5.122)$$

where $k = 22/91 = 0.241758$. The interpolated discount factor for 12m is

$$\delta(12\text{m}) = 0.992342 = 0.993129^{1-k}0.990376^k, \qquad (5.123)$$

where $k = 26/91 = 0.285714$. Swap rates for 6m and 12m are found from the formula

$$S_{t_N} = \frac{1 - \delta(t_N)}{\displaystyle\sum_{i=1}^{N} \alpha_S(t_{i-1}, t_i)\delta(t_i)}, \qquad (5.124)$$

where α_S is act/365. The swap rate for 6m is

$$S_{6\text{m}} = \frac{1 - 0.996819}{\frac{182}{365} \times 0.996819} = 0.6377\%. \qquad (5.125)$$

The swap rate for 12m is

$$S_{12\text{m}} = \frac{1 - 0.992342}{\frac{182}{365} \times 0.996819 + \frac{186}{365} \times 0.992342} = 0.7637\%, \qquad (5.126)$$

where $11/7/96 - 11/1/96 = 182$ days, and $13/1/97 - 11/7/96 = 186$ days.

The Swap Rate and Discount Factor for 18m

The interpolated swap rate for 18m, using linear interpolation, is

$$S_{18m} = \tfrac{1}{2}(S_{1y} + S_{2y}) = \tfrac{1}{2}(0.7637 + 1.1400) = 0.9519\%. \qquad (5.127)$$

The discount factor for 18m is based on the formula

$$\delta(t_i) = \frac{1 - S(t_i) \sum\limits_{j=1}^{i-1} \alpha_S(t_{j-1}, t_j)\delta(t_j)}{1 + S(t_i)\alpha_S(t_{i-1}, t_i)}, \qquad (5.128)$$

so that

$$\delta(18m) = \frac{1 - 0.009519 \times 1.002731}{1 + \frac{179}{365} \times 0.009519} = 0.985853, \qquad (5.129)$$

where $11/7/97 - 13/1/97 = 179$ days.

The remaining swap rates and discount factors are obtained by repeated application of Equation (5.128).

The full calculations are contained in Figure 5.3. Figure 5.4 shows a plot of the spot rates and forward rates produced by the method. The forward rate curve is noticeably wobbly, suggesting that there may be problems with the method.

5.4.2   Problems with the Method

The method attempts to integrate rates from three different sources, which lie on three different curves. The method makes no attempt to meld the three curves together. Figure 5.5 shows spot rates found from Libor, futures and swaps, out to two years, plotted separately.

It is clear from the figure that the three curves are not coincident to a common underlying curve. This results in characteristic steps in the yield curve when rates derived from Libor give over to rates derived from futures, and when rates from futures give over to those from swaps.

Libor rates permit discount factors to be calculated directly. But there is default risk inherent in these rates; the money market curve lies significantly above the riskless government curve because investors require higher returns to compensate for the increased risk.

An approximation was used when we treated futures as if they were FRAs. In fact an adjustment, called the convexity adjustment, is required to convert futures prices to equivalent FRAs. The adjustment is model dependent; see Section 5.5. Futures contracts, being exchange traded and marked to market, have significantly less counterparty risk than Libor.

Swaps have less default risk than Libor, in some sense, since the cashflows involved are inherently less than those for a Libor transaction; for interest rate swaps the principal may not be exchanged—on the other hand the times to maturity are much greater for swaps than for Libor. Swap rates are not available for all grid points and some

Computation of JPY yield curve, 9 January 1996.		Thanks to Paul Doust, BZW.

Summary of yield curve calculations

Days	Period	rate, %	Date	Time to maturity	Discount factor
	spot		11/01/96	0.00	1.000000
1	o/n	0.49	12/01/96	0.003	0.999986
7	1w	0.50	18/01/96	0.02	0.999903
33	1m	0.53	13/02/96	0.09	0.999514
60	2m	0.55	11/03/96	0.16	0.999084
69	stub		20/03/96	0.19	0.998940
91	Mar-96	99.34	19/06/96	0.44	0.997276
91	Jun-96	99.25	18/09/96	0.69	0.995389
91	Sep-96	99.10	18/12/96	0.94	0.993129
91	Dec-96	98.90	19/03/97	1.19	0.990376
	18m		11/07/97	1.50	0.985853
	2	1.14	12/01/98	2.01	0.977410
	2.5		13/07/98	2.50	0.966251
	3	1.60	11/01/99	3.00	0.952983
	3.5		12/07/99	3.50	0.938005
	4	2.04	11/02/00	4.09	0.921090
	4.5		11/07/00	4.50	0.903479
	5	2.43	11/01/01	5.01	0.884226
	5.5		11/07/01	5.50	0.866256
	6		11/01/02	6.01	0.847110
	6.5		11/07/02	6.50	0.827207
	7	3.01	13/01/03	7.01	0.806097
	7.5		11/07/03	7.50	0.790445
	8		12/01/04	8.01	0.774192
	8.5		12/07/04	8.51	0.757942
	9		11/01/05	9.01	0.741452
	9.5		11/07/05	9.50	0.724933
	10	3.36	11/01/06	10.01	0.708080

Calculation of stub discount factor

Period	Rate, %	Date	Weight	Discount factor
2m	0.55	11/03/96	0.290323	0.999084
3m	0.56	11/04/96	0.709677	0.998586
stub		20/03/96		0.998940

Calculation of 6-monthly spot rates

period	Date	Time to maturity	Interpolation dates: prior	next	Discount factor	Annuity	swap rate, %
spot	11/01/96	0.00			1.000000		
6m	11/07/96	0.50	19/06/96	18/09/96	0.996819	0.497044	0.6399
1yr	13/01/97	1.01	18/12/96	19/03/97	0.992342	1.002731	0.7637
18m	11/07/97	1.50			0.985853	1.486204	0.9519
2	12/01/98	2.01			0.977410	1.981603	1.1400
2.5	13/07/98	2.50			0.966251	2.463405	1.3700
3	11/01/99	3.00			0.952983	2.938591	1.6000
3.5	12/07/99	3.50			0.938005	3.406309	1.8200
4	11/01/00	4.00			0.921090	3.868116	2.0400
4.5	11/07/00	4.50			0.903479	4.318618	2.2350
5	11/01/01	5.01			0.884226	4.764364	2.4300
5.5	11/07/01	5.50			0.866256	5.193933	2.5750
6	11/01/02	6.01			0.847110	5.620969	2.7200
6.5	11/07/02	6.50			0.827207	6.031173	2.8650
7	13/01/03	7.01			0.806097	6.441951	3.0100
7.5	11/07/03	7.50			0.790445	6.829594	3.0683
8	12/01/04	8.01			0.774192	7.221993	3.1267
8.5	12/07/04	8.51			0.757942	7.599926	3.1850
9	11/01/05	9.01			0.741452	7.971668	3.2433
9.5	11/07/05	9.50			0.724933	8.331155	3.3017
10	11/01/06	10.01			0.708080	8.688105	3.3600

Figure 5.3   Summary of calculations

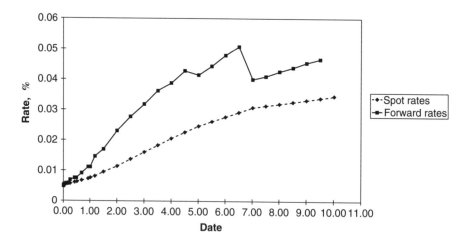

Figure 5.4   Spot rates and forward rates

form of interpolation is required. The method used linear interpolation which produces characteristic problems with forward rates calculated from the curve.

Because this bootstrapping method works up from rates of nearer maturity to rates of further maturity, a slight change in a near maturity rate can cause variations farther up the curve of spot rates found by the method. This results in oscillations in the forward rate curve. Figure 5.6 shows spot and forward rates at the short end of

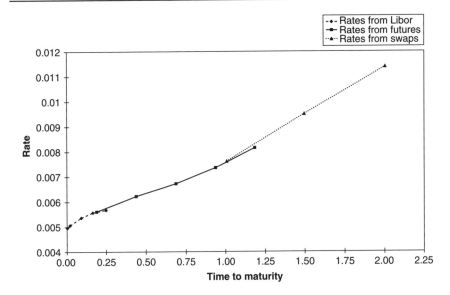

Figure 5.5 Comparison of money market curves

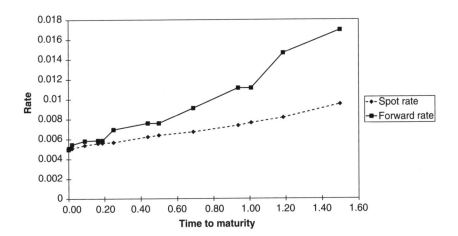

Figure 5.6 Spot and forward rates up to 18 months

the curve. Although the spot rate curve looks relatively smooth, the forward rate curve, calculated as

$$f_{t_i} = -\frac{365}{t_{i+1} - t_i} \ln\left(\frac{\delta(t_{i+1})}{\delta(t_i)}\right) \tag{5.130}$$

and reflecting the derivative of the spot rate curve, is very ragged and is clearly sensitive to slight variations in prices.

Other problems with the method are:

1. Libor rates beyond the stub date are ignored once the stub date discount factor is found.
2. Swaps are inappropriately interpolated. The linear interpolation method used produces a sawtooth in the forward rate curve. Figure 5.4 shows large dips at 5 and 7 years. This is an artifact of the interpolation. However, in some markets intermediate swaps are indeed priced as if their prices were found by linear interpolation. Of course, spreads help to smooth out the sawtooth effect.

In summary, a poor stripping method produces a characteristic symptom of a sawtooth structure in the forward rate curve. This can be seen at the transition maturities between different instruments and at knot points of an inappropriate interpolation scheme. (In fact even more dangerous is a poor stripping method that does not display this symptom.)

5.5   THE CONVEXITY ADJUSTMENT

The naive stripping method treated futures as if they were FRAs. In reality futures rates $(100 -$ the futures price) are greater than the corresponding FRA rates. The arbitrage is to short the future, and to receive fixed on the corresponding FRA. If rates rise, then margin payments on the futures contract are received immediately whereas the loss on the FRA is not crystallised until later. The converse happens if rates fall.

The amount by which the futures rate needs to be decreased is called the convexity adjustment. The convexity adjustment is determined by the market's expectations of future changes in rates, so that different interest rate models give different convexity adjustments.

For example, the Ho and Lee model assumes that rates have a constant volatility over different maturities. With continuous marking to market the Ho and Lee convexity adjustment is

$$\text{FRA} = \text{future} - \tfrac{1}{2}\sigma^2\tau^2, \tag{5.131}$$

where τ is the time to maturity of the futures contract.

Write $f(t, s, T)$ for the value at time t of the forward rate to borrow at time s to repay at T, and write $f_F(t, s, T)$ for the value at time t of the futures contract delivering the T-maturity spot rate at time s. Suppose that futures are marked to market every $1/k$ years (so if they were marked to market daily, $k = 250$, say). If all forwards have constant identical volatility σ, then Flesaker (93) [221] showed that

$$f(t, s, T) = f_F(t, s, T) + \sigma^2(s - t)(T - s) - \frac{\sigma^2}{2}\left(1 - \frac{1}{k}\right)(s - t)^2. \tag{5.132}$$

If futures are continuously settled, $k \to \infty$, then instantaneous forwards and futures (so that $s = T$) are related by

$$f(t, T) = f_F(t, T) - \frac{\sigma^2}{2}(T - t)^2, \tag{5.133}$$

which is just the Ho and Lee convexity adjustment.

5.5.1 Convexity Adjustment in General

Theoretical forward rates are computed from bond prices whereas futures rates are expected future spot rates, computed under the EMM Q. That is,

$$f(t, s, T) = \frac{1}{T - s} \ln \frac{P(t, T)}{P(t, s)}, \tag{5.134}$$

$$f_F(t, s, T) = \mathbb{E}_t^Q[r(s, T)], \tag{5.135}$$

where $P(t, T)$ is the value at time t of the T-maturity pure discount bond and $r_s(T)$ is the T-maturity spot rate at time s, $P(t, T) = e^{-r_t(T)(T-t)}$. Suppose that spot rates are affine in the short rate,

$$r(t, T) = A(t, T) + B(t, T)r_t, \tag{5.136}$$

where $r_t = r_t(t)$ is the short rate at time t, then for $t \le s \le T$

$$f(t, s, T) = \frac{A(t, T)(T - t) - A(t, s)(s - t)}{T - s} + \frac{B(t, T)(T - t) - B(t, s)(s - t)}{T - s} r_t, \tag{5.137}$$

$$f_F(t, s, T) = A(s, T) + B(s, T)\mathbb{E}_t^Q[r_s]. \tag{5.138}$$

In particular models the expectation can be computed and the convexity adjustment found.

The Extended Vasicek Convexity Adjustment

Suppose that under the EMM the short rate reverts to a time-dependent mean

$$dr_t = (\theta(t) - ar_t)dt + \sigma\, dz_t. \tag{5.139}$$

Given an initial forward rate curve $f(0, t)$ choose $\theta(t)$ to be

$$\theta(t) = \frac{\partial}{\partial t} f(0, t) + af(0, t) + \frac{\sigma^2}{2a}\left(1 - e^{-2at}\right), \tag{5.140}$$

then the model term structure exactly recovers the initial term structure given by $f(0, t)$. Spot rates are affine

$$r_t(T) = A(t, T) + B(t, T)r_t, \tag{5.141}$$

where

$$B(t, T) = \frac{1 - e^{-a(T-t)}}{a(T - t)}, \tag{5.142}$$

$$A(t, T) = -f(0, t, T) + B(t, T)f(0, t, t) - \frac{\sigma^2}{4a^3}\left(e^{-aT} - e^{-at}\right)^2\left(e^{2at} - 1\right). \tag{5.143}$$

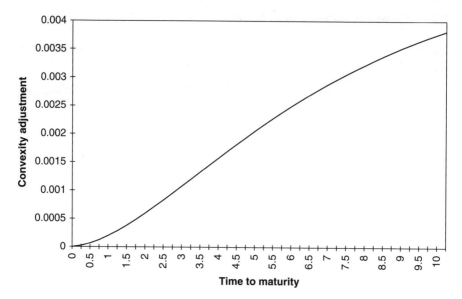

Figure 5.7   The Convexity adjustment

In this model Hull (99) [290] shows that

$$\mathbb{E}_t^Q[r_s] = f(t, s) + \frac{\sigma^2}{2a^2} \left(1 - e^{-a(s-t)}\right)^2, \qquad (5.144)$$

so that the convexity adjustment is

$$f_F(t, s, T) = f(t, s, T) + B(s, T)$$

$$\times \left[B(s, T)\left(1 - e^{-2a(s-t)}\right)(T - s) + 2aB(t, s)^2(s - t)^2\right]\frac{\sigma^2}{4a}. \qquad (5.145)$$

Figure 5.7 plots the convexity adjustment calculated from (5.145) for different maturity dates for futures contracts on three-month Libor, where $\sigma = 0.02$ and $\alpha = 0.2$. At two years the convexity adjustment is approximately five basis points while at 10 years it is a staggering 40 basis points. In practice a yield curve may only use Eurodollar futures (say) of short maturities. At longer maturities the yield curve may be constructed as a spread over Treasury yields. Hence the usefulness of the convexity adjustment—small at short maturities and not used at long maturities—is moot.

6

Densities and Distributions

This chapter considers some issues concerned with the use of the density function in interest rate modelling, and the types of distributions one might reasonably expect an interest rate model to generate. We briefly introduce the density function; both the transition density function and the stationary density are important for calibration and valuation and are discussed. Kernel functions are described and kernel methods for estimating the stationary density are discussed. We investigate the effect of imposing boundaries on interest rate models so that the density function is non-zero only on some interval. The classification of the behaviour of stochastic processes near boundaries is given and its implications discussed. We look at the impact on modelling of economic situations where interest rates are at extreme levels. Both unbounded behaviour at high levels and barriers at low levels are discussed. Finally we investigate tail densities and their application to interest rate densities.

Kernel methods are a widely used estimation technique. General books include Silverman (86) [495], Scott (92) [482] and Wand and Jones (95) [537]. Kernel methods are used by Ait-Sahalia (96a) [8], (96b) [9], Stanton (97) [502]. Boudoukh *et al.* (98) [83] use these methods to develop a general non-parametric motivated and derived interest rate model.

Our main source for much of the discussion in Section 6.3 is Karlin and Taylor (81) [330]. These probabilistic methods are extensively used by Conley *et al.* (97) [138].

Interest rate models with boundaries, implicit or explicit, are considered by Longstaff (92) [361], Black (95) [72], Rady (97) [447] and Goldstein and Keirstead (97) [253]. Fuhrer and Madigan (97) [233] consider monetary policy when rates are bounded at zero. More generally, Balduzzi *et al.* (97) [50] consider the effects of barriers in asset price processes, and Goldenberg (91) [250] finds Black formulae for options on assets with boundaries at zero.

6.1 THE DENSITY FUNCTION

Consider the short rate process

$$dr_t = \mu (r_t \mid \theta) dt + \sigma (r_t \mid \theta) dz_t \qquad (6.1)$$

for some drift μ and volatility σ depending on a parameter vector θ.

The transition density function,

$$p(s, r_s; t, r_t \mid \theta), \quad s \geq t, \tag{6.2}$$

is the likelihood that the variable r_t will move from state (t, r_t) at time t to state (s, r_s) at time $s \geq t$. The density (6.2) depends upon the parameters θ. Conditional on the state (t, r_t), the probability that r_s at time s lies between $\underline{r}$ and $\bar{r}$ is

$$\int_{\underline{r}}^{\bar{r}} p(s, r; t, r_t) \, dr. \tag{6.3}$$

The stationary or unconditional density $\psi(r)$, if it exists, is the long-run density as $s \to \infty$. It is independent of an initial state and has the property that

$$\psi(r) = \int_{-\infty}^{+\infty} \psi(x) p(s, r; t, x) dx. \tag{6.4}$$

In the general case the transition density at time t is conditional on $\mathcal{F}_t$, and may be highly path dependent. When a process is Markov things simplify considerably; the density is conditional only upon values at time t. It is this important, more tractable case that we consider here. Explicit densities for the non-Markov case are not currently exploited in interest rate modelling.

6.1.1   The Kolmogorov Forward Equation

The Kolmogorov forward equation, or Fokker–Planck partial differential equation, is the differential equation satisfied by the densities of a process. It is adjoint to the backward equation (see Øksendal (95) [424]). If $p = p(s, y; t, x \mid \theta)$ is the transition density function corresponding to the Markov process (6.1) then p satisfies the Kolmogorov forward equation

$$\frac{\partial p}{\partial s} + \frac{\partial(\mu(y)p)}{\partial y} - \frac{1}{2}\frac{\partial^2 \left(\sigma^2(y)p\right)}{\partial y^2} = 0. \tag{6.5}$$

Since the stationary density has the property that

$$\frac{\partial \psi}{\partial t} = 0, \tag{6.6}$$

it satisfies the equation

$$\frac{\partial(\mu(y)\psi(y))}{\partial y} - \frac{1}{2}\frac{\partial^2 \left(\sigma^2(y)\psi(y)\right)}{\partial y^2} = 0, \tag{6.7}$$

which may be integrated, as we see in Section 6.3.3.

Given a time series $\{r_{t_i}\}_{i=1,\ldots,N}$ we need to back out as much information as possible about the process (6.1). If we have functional forms for μ or σ, we may use estimation techniques such as the general method of moments or maximum likelihood (see Chapter 17) to try to find values for parameters θ. If functional forms are not available for either μ or σ we shall need to use non-parametric methods (Stanton (97) [502], Boudoukh *et al.* (98) [83]). Variants of these methods, for instance Ait-Sahalia (96a) [8], (96b) [9], may be used if only one of the functional forms is known.

The non-parametric methods we describe below estimate the stationary density ψ, and from ψ compute μ and σ. The Kolmogorov forward equation is used to relate ψ to the functions μ and σ. To implement this procedure it is first necessary to find the empirical stationary density, and for this kernel methods are often used.

6.2 KERNEL METHODS

In this section we introduce kernel functions. We describe how they may be used to obtain estimates of the stationary density from time series data, and illustrate the methods using UK Libor data.

6.2.1 Kernel Functions

A kernel function (Silverman (86) [495], Scott (92) [482], Wand and Jones (95) [537]) is a map $K : [-1, 1] \to \mathbb{R}$ used to express the influence a point at zero has on points u elsewhere in the interval $[-1, 1]$. A kernel function will normally be hump-shaped, taking larger values around zero and tailing off to 0 at ± 1, reflecting the greater influence that the point at zero has on nearby points compared with points farther away.

There are many possible choices of kernel function. In practice the exact choice does not usually seem to be crucial. Much the same results are usually achieved whatever the kernel function used. Table 6.1 lists some of the commoner kernel functions. Others are listed by Silverman, Wand and Jones, *et cetera*.

K is often chosen so that it is a density. Then it must integrate to 1, and its variance must be positive. In addition it is reasonable to demand (although not necessary) that the kernel be a symmetric function:

$$\text{volume:} \int_{-1}^{1} K(u)\mathrm{d}u = 1, \tag{6.8}$$

$$\text{variance:} \int_{-1}^{1} u^2 K(u)\mathrm{d}u > 0, \tag{6.9}$$

$$\text{symmetry:} \; K(u) = K(-u). \tag{6.10}$$

Table 6.1 Types of kernel function

Type	$K(u), u \in [-1, 1]$
Uniform	$\frac{1}{2}$
Epanechnikov	$\frac{3}{4}\left(1 - u^2\right)$
Quartic	$\frac{15}{16}\left(1 - u^2\right)^2$
Gaussian	$\frac{1}{\sqrt{2\pi}}\mathrm{e}^{-\frac{1}{2}u^2}, \; u \in [-\infty, \infty]$

In term structure estimation, and in other interest rate estimation procedures, a Gaussian kernel is often chosen. This is defined over the entire real line, not just the interval $[-1, 1]$.

Kernel functions are usually used in conjunction with an auxiliary variable, the bandwidth or window width h. Set $K_h(u) = (1/h)K(u/h)$. h specifies the effective width of the kernel function $K_h(u)$. When h is large, the width of the function $K_h : [-h, h] \rightarrow \mathbb{R}$ is large. It determines how much smoothing takes place. A large value of h gives a lot of smoothing, while a small value gives very little.

The choice of bandwidth is crucially important. In empirical work in interest rates a choice of h may only be made through a process of trial and error and a great deal of personal judgement. There is a 'rule of thumb' that sets

$$h = \sigma N^{-\frac{1}{5}}, \tag{6.11}$$

where N is the number of data points in the sample (see Scott, *et cetera*) and σ is a constant to be determined.[1]

6.2.2   Using Kernel Functions

Suppose that we have a Markov process r_t whose actual stationary density is $\psi(r)$. We have a time series $r_{t_i}, i = 1, \ldots, N$, of observations of r and we want to find a data driven approximation to ψ. We can approximate ψ by $\hat{\psi}$:

$$\hat{\psi}(r) = \frac{1}{N} \sum_{i=1}^{N} \frac{1}{h} K\left(\frac{r - r_{t_i}}{h}\right), \tag{6.12}$$

where $K(z)$ is a kernel function and h is the bandwidth. We will normally suppose that $K(z)$ is the Gaussian kernel $K(z) = \left(1/\sqrt{2\pi}\right) e^{-\frac{1}{2}z^2}$.

6.2.3   Libor Example

We apply (6.12) to a time series of UK Libor. Figure 6.1 shows three-month Libor from September 1988 to February 1995. We use a normal kernel with h determined by equation (6.11) and several values of σ. A large value of σ over-smooths, giving a result like Figure 6.2. Conversely, too small a value of σ over-fits. Figure 6.3 uses $\sigma = 0.01$, and is over-fitting the data.

The distributions of Figures 6.2 and 6.3 are evidently multimodal. It is clear, also, that they do not show an underlying stationary distribution. If for the moment we think of the sample path shown in Figure 6.1 as coming from a process with fast mean reversion to a time-varying mean, where the mean may be cycling from high to low values, then it is clear that we are only seeing part of a single cycle. Alternatively if the figure is thought of as showing a time series undergoing a regime shift from high to low levels, then presumably there are other regime shifts that may have occurred

---

[1] This is optimal, in a rather special sense, for fitting certain kernels to certain distributions.

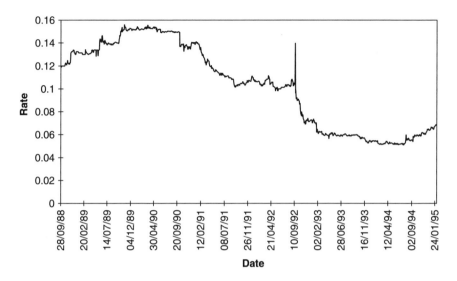

Figure 6.1   Three-month Libor, 1988–1995

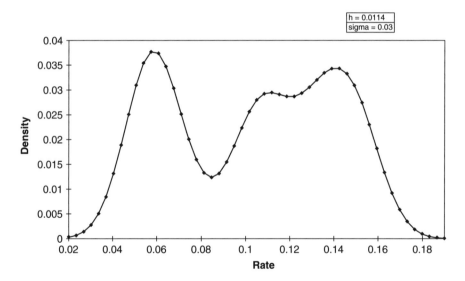

Figure 6.2   Kernel estimate of the stationary density of UK Libor, $\sigma = 0.05$

but did not. The hypothesis that we are reliably estimating a stationary distribution is clearly untenable.

For comparison, we saw the frequency histogram of the time series in Chapter 3, repeated here in Figure 6.4. By itself this is not evidence obviously in favour of a simple Gaussian term structure model.

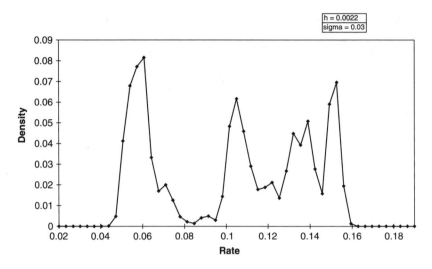

Figure 6.3   Kernel estimate of the stationary density of UK Libor, $\sigma = 0.01$

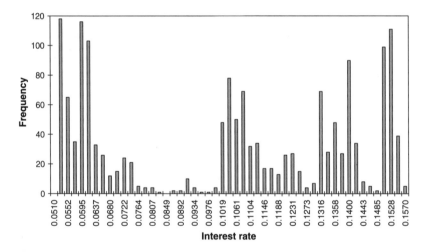

Figure 6.4   Frequency histogram of UK three-month Libor

6.2.4   Approximating the Drift and Volatility

The standard first-order approximations to $\mu\,(r_t)$ and $\sigma^2\,(r_t)$ are given by

$$\mu\,(r_t) = \frac{1}{\Delta t}\mathbb{E}^{r_t}\left[r_{t+\Delta t} - r_t\right], \qquad (6.13)$$

$$\sigma^2\,(r_t) = \frac{1}{\Delta t}\mathbb{E}^{r_t}\left[(r_{t+\Delta t} - r_t)^2\right], \qquad (6.14)$$

where $\mathbb{E}^{r_t}$ is the expectation conditional on r having the value r_t.

Equations (6.13) and (6.14) can be implemented using kernel estimates to find approximations to $\mu(r)$ and $\sigma^2(r)$. We compute these approximations at certain values $r_1, \ldots, r_M$ of r. Set

$$w_i(r_j) = \frac{K\left(\dfrac{r_j - r_{t_i}}{h}\right)}{\displaystyle\sum_{i=1}^{N} K\left(\dfrac{r_j - r_{t_i}}{h}\right)}, \quad j = 1, \ldots, M. \tag{6.15}$$

$w_i(r_j)$ represents the influence that r_{t_i} has at the point r_j, as a proportion of the total influence from all points at r_j. The approximations are

$$\tilde{\mu}(r_j) = \sum_{i=1}^{N-1} \frac{r_{t_{i+1}} - r_{t_i}}{t_{i+1} - t_i} w_i(r_j), \tag{6.16}$$

$$\tilde{\sigma}^2(r_j) = \sum_{i=1}^{N-1} \left(\frac{r_{t_{i+1}} - r_{t_i}}{t_{i+1} - t_i} - \tilde{\mu}(r_j)\right)^2 w_i(r_j). \tag{6.17}$$

The approximation to each moment is the sample moment weighted by the relative kernel density, $w_i(r_j)$.

The approximations (6.16) and (6.17) can be improved. Stanton (97) [502] uses higher order approximations to estimate μ and σ. If we observe a time series r_t at fixed intervals Δt, we may compute moments from it by sampling at different multiples of Δt, as in Table 6.2. By using estimates at several sampling frequencies, we can construct more accurate approximations to $\mu(r_t)$ and $\sigma(r_t)$.

Table 6.2 Approximations to moments

First moment	Second moment
$\mathbb{E}^{r_t}[r_{t+\Delta t} - r_t]$	$\mathbb{E}^{r_t}\left[(r_{t+\Delta t} - r_t)^2\right]$
$\mathbb{E}^{r_t}[r_{t+2\Delta t} - r_t]$	$\mathbb{E}^{r_t}\left[(r_{t+2\Delta t} - r_t)^2\right]$
$\mathbb{E}^{r_t}[r_{t+3\Delta t} - r_t]$	$\mathbb{E}^{r_t}\left[(r_{t+3\Delta t} - r_t)^2\right]$

Approximations to the Drift $\mu(r_t)$

Higher order approximations are:

Second-order

$$\mu(r_t) = \frac{1}{2\Delta t}\left(4\mathbb{E}^{r_t}[r_{t+\Delta t} - r_t] - \mathbb{E}^{r_t}[r_{t+2\Delta t} - r_t]\right), \tag{6.18}$$

Third-order

$$\mu(r_t) = \frac{1}{6\Delta t}\left(18\mathbb{E}^{r_t}[r_{t+\Delta t} - r_t] - 9\mathbb{E}^{r_t}[r_{t+2\Delta t} - r_t] + 2\mathbb{E}^{r_t}[r_{t+3\Delta t} - r_t]\right). \tag{6.19}$$

These approximations, found by expanding out the appropriate Taylor series approximations in the infinitesimal generator of r_t (see Stanton (97) [502] and Boudoukh *et al.* (98) [83]), are increasingly accurate. Without these higher order approximations, decreasing Δt would be the only way of improving the accuracy of the process. Using higher order approximations Δt can be larger thus allowing the data to be sampled less frequently. Since the sampling interval is often predetermined, a higher order approximation enables us to get the most mileage from the data available.

Approximations to the Volatility

Higher order approximations to the volatility are:

Second-order

$$\sigma^2(r_t) = \frac{1}{2\Delta t} \left\{ 4\mathbb{E}^{r_t} \left[(r_{t+\Delta t} - r_t)^2 \right] - \mathbb{E}^{r_t} \left[(r_{t+2\Delta t} - r_t)^2 \right] \right\}, \tag{6.20}$$

Third-order

$$\sigma^2(r_t) = \frac{1}{6\Delta t} \left\{ 18\mathbb{E}^{r_t} \left[(r_{t+\Delta t} - r_t)^2 \right] - 9\mathbb{E}^{r_t} \left[(r_{t+2\Delta t} - r_t)^2 \right] + 2\mathbb{E}^{r_t} \left[(r_{t+3\Delta t} - r_t)^2 \right] \right\}. \tag{6.21}$$

We may use a similar method to estimate the price of risk, $\lambda(r_t)$ (see Stanton (97) [502]).

In these approximations we need to find estimates of several expected values and variances. Just use

$$\mathbb{E}[r_{t+k\Delta t} - r_t \mid r_t = r_j] \equiv E_{k,j} = \sum_{i=1}^{N-1} (r_{t_{i+k}} - r_{t_i}) w_i(r_j), \tag{6.22}$$

$$\mathrm{var}[r_{t+k\Delta t} - r_t \mid r_t = r_j] = \sum_{i=1}^{N-1} ((r_{t_{i+k}} - r_{t_i}) - E_{k,j})^2 w_i(r_j). \tag{6.23}$$

6.2.5 Libor Example Revisited

We estimate the drift and variance of UK three-month Libor using the methods of the previous section. Figure 6.5 is the drift estimated using a high value of $\sigma = 0.05$. This drift is smooth, reverting to two levels, 6% and 12%. This is consistent with Figures 6.2 and 6.3 which show concentrations in the estimated stationary density at roughly the same levels. By contrast, Figure 6.6 shows the drift calculated with $\sigma = 0.03$. This is very different; although a reversion level at about 6% remains stable the second reversion level at about 12% is now far flatter—the process reverts much less strongly to this level.

The volatility is just as complex—it has a bimodal distribution with peaks at 10% and 14%. The behaviour is very sensitive to the chosen value of h, the window period. Figure 6.7 is over-smoothed with $\sigma = 0.05$. Figure 6.8, with $\sigma = 0.03$, is much 'peakier' but seems not yet over-fitted.

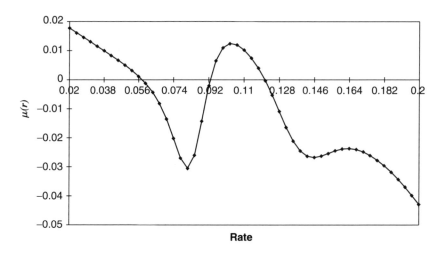

Figure 6.5   Kernel estimate of the drift of UK three-month Libor ($\sigma = 0.05$)

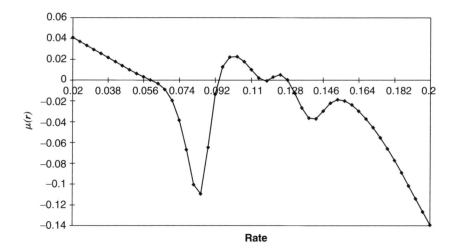

Figure 6.6   Kernel estimate of the drift of UK three-month Libor ($\sigma = 0.03$)

All these figures use a first-order approximation. There seems little point in using a higher order approximation when the estimate of the stationary density, upon which the drift and volatility estimates hinge, is suspect: garbage in — garbage out.

6.2.6   Subordinated Diffusions

Conley *et al.* (97) [138] estimate a one-factor model with irregular times between observations. Actual observations could be regular, but market time can speed up or

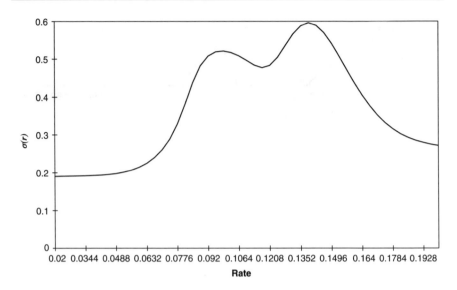

Figure 6.7 Kernel estimate of the volatility of UK three-month Libor ($\sigma = 0.05$)

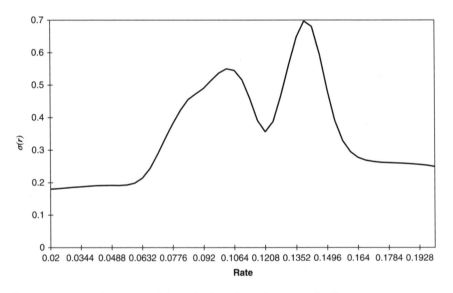

Figure 6.8 Kernel estimate of the volatility of UK three-month Libor ($\sigma = 0.03$)

slow down, for example at weekends or during holidays, so that, in effect, observations of interest rates cannot be considered to be at regular intervals.

Suppose the underlying process, r_t, is observed at times $t_i = f(i), i = 1, \ldots, N$, for some increasing function f (possible stochastic). Conley *et al.* estimate an extension of the CKLS process $dr_t = \mu(r_t)dt + \sigma r_t^\gamma dz_t$, with $\mu(r) = \sum_{i=-k}^{l} a_i r^i$, with $k = 1$, $l = 2$, and taking f to be undefined. They use GMM (see Chapter 17) with a sophisticated choice of moments.

They concluded (amongst other things) that $1.5 < \gamma < 2$, in line with the results of CKLS who estimated $\gamma \sim 1.5$. Their method avoids the usual criticisms of the Chan *et al.* (92) [124] estimation.

6.3 BOUNDARY BEHAVIOUR

In a number of models the values taken by the underlying state variables are constrained to lie in a proper subset of the real line. Positive rate models force the short rate to be positive. Other models have explicit lower, and perhaps upper, boundaries (Rady (97) [447]). In this section we investigate some theoretical and empirical aspects of boundary behaviour, and related issues, following in part Karlin and Taylor (81) [330]. In Section 6.4 we discuss how boundaries are used in actual models and their economic consequences.

A concrete example of a process confined to the interval $[a, b]$ is

$$dr_t = \alpha \frac{(\mu - r_t)}{(r_t - a)(b - r_t)} dt + \sigma(r_t - a)(b - r_t)dz_t, \qquad (6.24)$$

for $a < \mu < b$. As r_t approaches a, say, its drift is positive and becomes arbitrarily large while at the same time its volatility goes to zero. This prevents r_t from breaching the lower boundary. There is a similar effect at the top boundary.

Another example would be an extended BGM model in which the process followed by a forward rate $f_t(T)$, under some martingale measure, is

$$df_t(T) = \sigma_t(T)(\gamma(T) + f_t(T))dz_t, \qquad (6.25)$$

for a Wiener process z_t. $f_t(T)$ is bounded below by $-\gamma(T)$.

6.3.1 Processes with Boundaries

When rates are confined to regions with boundaries the behaviour of the rate close to a boundary must be specified very carefully. When rates are close to zero, which has occurred in Switzerland and Japan, different assumptions about boundary behaviour can significantly affect pricing and hedging. For instance, if rates can indeed go briefly negative in these regimes, this will cause problems, both theoretical and practical, for positive rate models.

Figure 6.9 shows the yen three-month interbank rate. Despite the low levels of interest rate over the past few years, rates nevertheless seem astonishingly volatile. From the figure it is remarkable that rates have not been able to become negative more frequently than they have.

Suppose that X_t is a diffusion process defined on an interval I where I may or may not include its end points. Write r and l for the upper and lower end points, $-\infty < l < r < \infty$, so that I is one of $[l, r]$, $(l, r]$, $[l, r)$, or (l, r).

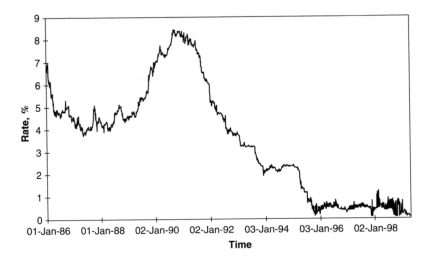

Figure 6.9 Japanese yen, three-month interbank rate

Suppose the process for X_t is

$$\mathrm{d}X_t = \mu(X_t)\mathrm{d}t + \sigma(X_t)\mathrm{d}z_t, \qquad\qquad (6.26)$$

where μ and σ are defined on the interior of the interval I, both are continuous, and $\sigma^2(X_t) > 0$. Let T_y be the first hitting time to the interest rate level y, $T_y = \inf_t\{X_t = y \mid X_0 = x\}$. Write Pr^x and $\mathbb{E}^x$ for the conditional probabilities and expectations, conditional on $X_0 = x$. We require X to be regular in the interior of I, so that for all starting points x within I, there is a non-zero probability of hitting all other points within I, within a finite time,

$$\mathrm{Pr}^x[T_y < \infty] = \mathrm{Pr}[T_y < \infty \mid X_0 = x] > 0, \quad \text{for all } x \in (l, r). \qquad (6.27)$$

An interest rate process is regular if, starting from any level of the rate, rates may rise or fall to any other level in I, with positive probability.

Examples

Consider the short rate process

$$\mathrm{d}r_t = \alpha(\mu - r_t)\mathrm{d}t + \sigma(r_t)\mathrm{d}z_t. \qquad\qquad (6.28)$$

Its behaviour at 0 depends crucially on the function $\sigma(r_t)$. The following are some examples of processes and boundaries with a variety of boundary behaviour.

- The Vasicek process with $\sigma(r_t) \equiv \sigma$, a constant, defined on $(-\infty, \infty)$.
- The Vasicek process with $\sigma(r_t) \equiv \sigma$, a constant, with r_t restricted to $[0, \infty)$. There is an explicit boundary at zero; the behaviour of r_t at zero must be specified.

- The CIR model with $\sigma(r_t) = \sigma\sqrt{r_t}$, with r_t restricted to $[0, \infty)$. Depending on the parameter values of the process (6.28) r_t may or may not be able assume the value 0 (starting from a strictly positive value).
- A log-normal model (like the continuous time limit of the Black, Derman and Toy (90) [73] model) with $\sigma(r_t) = \sigma r_t$. If r_t is initially positive it cannot leave the interval $(0, \infty)$.

6.3.2 Speed and Scale

The speed and scale of a process are important functions which simplify many calculations and which are useful in classifying the behaviour of processes near boundaries. The intuition behind the scale of a process will be given following equation (6.39). The speed of a process will be discussed after equation (6.40).

The Scale and Speed Functions

The four key functions are

$$s(x) = \exp\left(-\int^x \frac{2\mu(s)}{\sigma^2(s)}ds\right), \quad \text{the scale density,}$$

$$S(x) = \int^x s(y)dy, \quad \text{the scale function,}$$

$$m(x) = \frac{1}{\sigma^2(x)s(x)}, \quad \text{the speed density,}$$

$$M(x) = \int^x m(y)dy, \quad \text{the speed function.}$$

$$(6.29)$$

They are defined using an indefinite integral in x.

6.3.3 The Infinitesimal Generator

The infinitesimal generator A of a one-dimensional Itō process $X_t \in \mathbb{R}$ simplifies many calculations. Suppose that at time t, X_t has value x. For $f : \mathbb{R} \to \mathbb{R}$, $Af : \mathbb{R} \to \mathbb{R}$ is defined as

$$Af(x) = \lim_{\Delta t \to 0} \frac{\mathbb{E}[f(X_{t+\Delta t}) - f(x)]}{\Delta t}. \qquad (6.30)$$

This is just the rate of expected change in the process $f(X_t)$ at the point $X_t = x$, and is just the drift of $f(X_t)$ for suitably regular processes X_t and functions f. It can be shown that Af is the function

$$Af(x) = \mu(x)\frac{\partial f}{\partial x} + \frac{1}{2}\sigma^2(x)\frac{\partial^2 f}{\partial x^2}. \qquad (6.31)$$

In terms of scale and speed it is easy to show that

$$Af(x) = \frac{1}{2} \frac{1}{m(x)} \frac{\partial}{\partial x} \left(\frac{1}{s(x)} \frac{\partial f}{\partial x} \right) \tag{6.32}$$

and since $m(x) = \partial M / \partial x$,

$$Af(x) = \frac{1}{2} \frac{\partial}{\partial M} \left(\frac{\partial f}{\partial S}(x) \right). \tag{6.33}$$

This is the canonical representation of the generator A of X_t.

Suppose that $a < x < b$ in I. We would like to be able to compute various useful quantities. For instance, conditional on $X_0 = x$:

• The probability that X_t hits the level b before it hits level a,

$$u(x) = \text{Pr}^x [T_b < T_a]; \tag{6.34}$$

• The expected time before X_t hits either a or b,

$$v(x) = \mathbb{E}^x [T_a \wedge T_b]; \tag{6.35}$$

• The expected payoff at a payoff rate g, continuous and bounded, before X_t hits either a or b,

$$w(x) = \mathbb{E}^x \left[\int_0^{T_a \wedge T_b} g(X_s) ds \right]. \tag{6.36}$$

Each of these functions has an intuitive application in finance, for instance to barrier options. We are chiefly concerned with bounds for the process X_t.

The three functions u, v and w are all functions of X_t and satisfy the PDE (Karlin and Taylor (81) [330])

$$AF(x) = \mu(x) \frac{\partial F}{\partial x} + \frac{1}{2} \sigma^2(x) \frac{\partial^2 F}{\partial x^2} = G(x), \tag{6.37}$$

where the function $G(x)$ and the boundary conditions for F are specified in Table 6.3.

For instance, from (6.33), $u(x)$ satisfies

$$\frac{1}{2} \frac{\partial}{\partial M} \left(\frac{\partial u}{\partial S}(x) \right) = 0, \tag{6.38}$$

where $a < x < b$, $u(a) = 0$, $u(b) = 1$. With these boundary conditions, the solution for $u(x)$ is

$$u(x) = \frac{S(x) - S(a)}{S(b) - S(a)}. \tag{6.39}$$

Note that the choice of the constants of integration does not alter the solution.

Table 6.3 Specifications of the PDE

F	$G(x)$	Boundaries
u	0	$u(a) = 0$, $u(b) = 1$,
v	1	$v(a) = 0$, $v(b) = 0$,
w	$-g(x)$	$w(a) = 0$, $w(b) = 0$

The scale function re-scales the real line so that, in terms of equation (6.34), probabilities are proportional to relative distance. If S remains finite, approaching and including a boundary point, there will be a positive probability of reaching that boundary. A process X_t is in natural scale if $S(X_t) = X_t$. For instance, for some process X_t, $Y_t = S(X_t)$ is in natural scale.

Using similar methods it is possible to find solutions for $v(x)$ and $w(x)$. The interested reader is referred to Karlin and Taylor. For instance,

$$v(x) = 2\left\{u(x) \int_x^b (S(b) - S(y))m(y)dy + (1 - u(x)) \int_a^x (S(y) - S(a))m(y)dy\right\},$$
(6.40)

for $a = x - \varepsilon$, $b = x + \varepsilon$. For a process in natural scale, in the limit as $\varepsilon \to 0$, we find

$$\mathbb{E}^x \left[T_{x-\varepsilon} \wedge T_{x+\varepsilon}\right] = \lim_{\varepsilon \to 0} v(x) \sim \varepsilon^2 m(x).$$
(6.41)

$m(x)$ does indeed represent the speed of the process X_t in the sense that speed is related to the expected time to exit a small interval.

Scale and Speed for Standard Processes

We illustrate with some examples of speed and scale for several standard processes.

- *Standard Brownian motion.* This has $\mu = 0$ and $\sigma^2 = 1$. So $s(x) = 1$, $S(x) = x$, and $m(x) = 1$. It is in natural scale. We obtain

$$u(x) = \frac{x - a}{b - a}.$$
(6.42)

Furthermore

$$v(x) = (x - a)(b - a), \quad \text{for } a \le x \le b.$$
(6.43)

- *Brownian motion with drift.* $\mu(x) = \mu$, $\sigma^2 = 1$. Set $\lambda = -2\mu/\sigma^2$. Then $s(x) = e^{\lambda x}$, $S(x) = (1/\lambda)e^{\lambda x} + c$, where c is a constant, and

$$u(x) = \frac{e^{\lambda x} - e^{\lambda a}}{e^{\lambda b} - e^{\lambda a}}.$$
(6.44)

- *An Ornstein–Uhlenbeck process.* $dX_t = -\alpha X_t dt + \sigma dz_t$. Set $\gamma = 2\alpha/\sigma^2$. Then $s(x) = e^{\gamma x^2}$ and $m(x) = (1/\sigma^2) e^{-\gamma x^2}$.

The Interpretation of $s(x)$

Conley *et al.* (97) [138] provide an interpretation of $s(x)$. If $r_1 < r < r_2$, then we know that

$$\frac{\int_{r_1}^r s(x)dx}{\int_{r_1}^{r_2} s(x)dx} = \frac{S(r) - S(r_1)}{S(r_2) - S(r_1)} = \Pr^x \left[T_{r_2} < T_{r_1}\right]$$
(6.45)

is the probability of hitting r_2 before hitting r_1. For $r_1 = r - \varepsilon$, $r_2 = r + \varepsilon$, the probability of hitting $r - \varepsilon$ before hitting $r + \varepsilon$ is

$$
\pi_r(\varepsilon) = \frac{\displaystyle\int_{r-\varepsilon}^{r} s(x)\mathrm{d}x}{\displaystyle\int_{r-\varepsilon}^{r+\varepsilon} s(x)\mathrm{d}x}
\tag{6.46}
$$

$$
= \frac{1}{2} + \frac{\mu(r)}{2\sigma^2(r)}\varepsilon + O\left(\varepsilon^2\right).
\tag{6.47}
$$

Intuitively the quantity $\mu(r)/2\sigma^2(r)$ measures the 'pull to the right' in the neighbourhood of r. Conley *et al.* define 'volatility induced stationarity'. If as $r \to \infty$ the term $\mu(r)/2\sigma^2(r) \to 0$ faster than r^{-1}, then the short rate process is stationary, even if μ remains positive. This has the practical implication that rates may not become unbounded even if $\sigma(r) = \sigma r^\gamma$ for some $\gamma \geq 1$, as long as $\mu(r) \sim r^{-\theta}$, where $\theta > 2\gamma + 1$.

The Stationary Distribution

We are now at a stage where we can derive the stationary distribution $\psi(x)$, if it exists. The Kolmogorov forward equation for $\psi(x)$ is

$$
\frac{\partial}{\partial y}(\mu(y)\psi(y)) - \frac{1}{2}\frac{\partial^2}{\partial y^2}\left(\sigma^2(y)\psi(y)\right) = 0.
\tag{6.48}
$$

We can integrate up to obtain

$$
\psi(x) = m(x)(C_1 S(x) + C_2),
\tag{6.49}
$$

where C_1 and C_2 are constants of integration.

If a stationary distribution exists $\psi(x)$ must be a density and so satisfy the conditions

- $\psi(x) \geq 0$ on (l, r)
- $\int_l^r \psi(x)\mathrm{d}x = 1$.

For instance, for an Ornstein-Uhlenbeck process, $\mathrm{d}X_t = -\alpha X_t \mathrm{d}t + \sigma \mathrm{d}z_t$, and for $\gamma = 2\alpha/\sigma^2$. Then $m(x) = \left(1/\sigma^2\right)\mathrm{e}^{-\gamma x^2}$ and $S(x) = \int^x \mathrm{e}^{-\gamma x^2}$. The condition $\int_l^r \psi(x)\mathrm{d}x = 1$ can only be satisfied if $C_1 = 0$, so $\psi(x) = c\mathrm{e}^{-\gamma x^2}$, for a scaling parameter c, and it is a normal density.

6.3.4   Finding μ and σ from the Stationary Density

Given a time series $\left\{r_{t_i}\right\}_{i=1,\ldots,N}$ we would like, if possible, to find the drift and volatility functions of an underlying continuous time process, r_t, generating the observed discrete time series. Ait-Sahalia (96a) [8], (96b) [9] uses the observed time series to obtain an approximation to the stationary density of r_t, and from this, using (6.49), finds estimates of μ and σ.

The estimation was performed under two sets of assumptions. In the first he assumed he was given functional forms for both $\mu \equiv \mu(r \mid \theta)$ and $\sigma \equiv \sigma(r \mid \theta)$. In the second he assumed that he had a functional form only for μ. In the first case the problem is just to find the parameter vector θ. In the second if one can obtain estimates of θ from elsewhere, one can back out a non-parametric estimate of $\sigma(r)$.

Functional Forms Exist for Both μ and σ

Ait-Sahalia (96b) [9] implements the following procedure.

1. Use a kernel method to find an estimate $\tilde{\psi}(r)$ of $\psi(r)$.
2. Set $\psi(r \mid \theta) = m(r \mid \theta)c(\theta)$, where $c(\theta)$ is a normalisation function so that $\int_{-\infty}^{+\infty} \psi(r \mid \theta) = 1$.
3. Choose θ to minimise a criteria function

$$M = \min_{\theta} \mathbb{E}\left[\left(\psi(r \mid \theta) - \tilde{\psi}(r)\right)^2\right] \tag{6.50}$$

discretised as

$$\widetilde{M} = \min_{\theta} \frac{1}{n} \sum_{i=1}^{n} \left(\psi(r_i \mid \theta) - \tilde{\psi}(r_i)\right)^2. \tag{6.51}$$

Using this procedure, it is possible to find the distribution of the estimated parameters, θ, and hence to perform statistical tests on the estimates. There may be practical difficulties involved in successfully implementing this method, however; see Pritsker (98) [443].

A Functional Form Exists for $\mu(r \mid \theta)$ but not σ

Ait-Sahalia (96a) [8] describes a procedure to estimate $\sigma(r)$ non-parametrically when a functional form for μ is provided. It assumes that r_t is confined to $(0, \infty)$. Ait-Sahalia assumed that $\mu(r \mid \theta) = \alpha(\beta - r)$, so that $\theta = \{\alpha, \beta\}$. The parameters θ must be independently estimated from time series data. The method proceeds:

- Use a kernel method to find an estimate $\tilde{\psi}(r)$ of $\psi(r)$.
- From (6.48) we have

$$\int_{-\infty}^{y} \mu(u \mid \theta)\psi(u)du = \tfrac{1}{2}\sigma^2(y)\psi(y). \tag{6.52}$$

Set

$$\tilde{\sigma}^2(r) = \frac{2}{\tilde{\psi}(r)} \int_{0}^{r} \mu(u \mid \theta)\tilde{\psi}(u)du.$$

The functions $\mu(u \mid \theta)\tilde{\psi}$ and $\tilde{\sigma}^2(r)$ are under the objective measure. Ait-Sahalia then estimates a market price of risk, λ, assumed constant, by fitting to the term structure. In principle, it is now possible to price anything.

6.3.5   Speed and Scale Near Boundaries

If an interest rate process has a boundary the behaviour of the process at the boundary is crucially important: it may have serious implications for valuation and hedging. In this section we give a standard classification of boundary behaviour for continuous Markov processes and relate it to its implications for interest rate modelling.

Consider a diffusion process X_t defined on an interval I, where I may or may not include its endpoints l and r, $-\infty < l < r < \infty$. Define four functions S, Σ, M and N for each boundary. Boundaries are classified according to the values of the four functions, in particular whether they are finite or not. $s(x)$ and $m(x)$ denote the scale and speed densities as before.

Suppose that $a < b \in (l, r)$. The functions are:

$$S^b(l) = \lim_{a \to l} \int_a^b s(x)\,\mathrm{d}x, \tag{6.53}$$

$$M^b(l) = \lim_{a \to l} \int_a^b m(x)\,\mathrm{d}x, \tag{6.54}$$

$$N^b(l) = \lim_{a \to l} \int_a^b \int_y^b s(x)m(y)\,\mathrm{d}x\mathrm{d}y, \tag{6.55}$$

$$\Sigma^b(l) = \lim_{a \to l} \int_a^b \int_y^b s(y)m(x)\,\mathrm{d}x\mathrm{d}y, \tag{6.56}$$

The choice of b will be irrelevant. The definitions are given for the left-hand boundary. Definitions for the right-hand boundary are found by the obvious modifications.

Interpretation of the Functions

We are concerned only whether the functions are finite or not. Suppose that $l < a < x < b$ as usual. First we consider $S^b(l)$.

- If $S^b(l) < \infty$ for some $b \in (l, r)$, then $\lim_{a \to l} \Pr^x[T_a < T_b] > 0$ for all $a < x < b$, so that X_t can get arbitrarily close to l in finite time.
- If $S^b(l) = \infty$ for some $b \in (l, r)$, then $\lim_{a \to l} \Pr^x[T_a < T_b] = 0$ for all $a < x < b$, so that X_t cannot approach l arbitrarily closely in finite time.

If $S^b(l) < \infty$, then say that l is attracting. For a standard Brownian motion $S^b(-\infty) = \infty(= b - (-\infty))$, so that $-\infty$ is not attracting. For Brownian motion with drift $\mu < 0$,

$$S^b(-\infty) = \lim_{a \to -\infty} (\mathrm{e}^{-2\mu b} - \mathrm{e}^{-2\mu a}) = \mathrm{e}^{-2\mu b} < \infty, \tag{6.57}$$

so that $-\infty$ is attracting.

For $\Sigma^b(l)$ it can be shown that (Karlin and Taylor)

$$\lim_{a \to l} \mathbb{E}^x[T_a \wedge T_b] < \infty \Leftrightarrow \Sigma^b(l) < \infty. \tag{6.58}$$

If l is attracting and $l < x < b$, then

$$\Sigma^b(l) < \infty \Leftrightarrow \mathbb{E}^x[T_l \wedge T_b] < \infty \tag{6.59}$$

$$\Leftrightarrow \Pr^x[T_l < \infty] > 0. \tag{6.60}$$

Say that l is attainable if $\Sigma(l) < \infty$, otherwise say that l is unattainable. For Brownian motion with drift $\mu < 0$, $\Sigma^b(l) = \infty$ so that $-\infty$ is unattainable. For Brownian motion on $[0, \infty)$, with 0 absorbing, 0 is attracting and attainable since

$$\mathbb{E}^x[T_0 \wedge T_b] = x(b - x) < \infty, \quad 0 < x < \infty. \tag{6.61}$$

The two other functions can also be interpreted. $M^b(l)$ is the speed of X_t near l. $N^b(l)$ corresponds to the time it takes to reach b starting from l. If $N^b(l) = \infty$ for every b, the process starting at l cannot reach the interior of I.

A Boundary Classification

Boundaries can be classified as to how the boundary point is connected to the interior of the interval I. Table 6.4 presents a summary. At a regular boundary X_t can reach l and can return to the interior of I. At a separate boundary, l cannot be reached by X_t, unless X_t started there. If it started there, however, it never leaves. The boundary is a separate, disjoint, part of the state space.

At an exit boundary X_t can enter l but can never leave, and at an entrance boundary X_t can leave l but can never return.

Separate boundaries divide into three types, according to the values of S and M. Table 6.5 lists the possibilities. (If $S < \infty$ and $M < \infty$, then $\Sigma < \infty$ so that l is no longer separate.)

We make a few comments on different types of boundary. Karlin and Taylor present further details.

- Regular boundary ($N < \infty$, $\Sigma < \infty$). The process can enter and leave a regular boundary. The behaviour at the boundary ranges from reflected to absorbing, with

Table 6.4 A classification of boundary behaviour

Boundary classification		$L \to I$?	
		Yes, $N < \infty$	No, $N = \infty$
$I \to L$?	Yes, $\Sigma < \infty$	Regular	Exit
	No, $\Sigma = \infty$	Entrance	Separate

Table 6.5 Classification of separate boundaries

Separate boundaries	$M = \infty$	$M < \infty$
$S = \infty$, unattracting	Natural	Natural
$S < \infty$, attracting	Attracting, unattainable	n / a

'sticky' behaviour in between. If the process is permitted to jump at the boundary, it could jump back to the interior of I.

- Exit boundary ($N = \infty$, $\Sigma < \infty$). If l is an exit boundary, then

$$\lim_{b \to l} \lim_{x \to l} \Pr^x [T_b < t] = 0, \quad \forall t > 0, \tag{6.62}$$

so that if the process starts at l it can never leave l, if jumps are precluded. If jumps at l are allowed, then X_t can jump into the interior of I after waiting a finite time at l.

- Entrance boundary ($\Sigma = \infty$, $N < \infty$). The process cannot reach l from the interior of I, but it may start at l. We have

$$\lim_{a \to l} T_a \wedge T_b = T_b. \tag{6.63}$$

- Separate boundary ($\Sigma = \infty$, $N = \infty$). l cannot be reached by X_t, unless X_t started there. For processes defined on $\mathbb{R}$ the points $\pm\infty$ can be thought of as natural boundaries.

Examples

Processes commonly used models may be classified in this way. For instance:

- Geometric Brownian motion on $[0, \infty)$:

$$dX_t = \mu X_t dt + \sigma X_t dz_t, \tag{6.64}$$

$$s(x) = e^{-2\mu x/\sigma}, \tag{6.65}$$

$$m(x) = \frac{1}{\sigma x} e^{-2\mu x/\sigma}. \tag{6.66}$$

It follows that $\Sigma(0) < \infty$ and $N(0) = \infty$, so 0 is an exit boundary, and ∞ is a natural boundary.

- Ornstein–Uhlenbeck process on $(-\infty, +\infty)$:

$$dX_t = -X_t dt + dz_t, \tag{6.67}$$

$$s(x) = e^{x^2}, \tag{6.68}$$

$$m(x) = e^{-x^2}. \tag{6.69}$$

Then $\Sigma(l) = N(l) = \infty$ for $l = -\infty$, hence $l = -\infty$ is natural.

- Ornstein–Uhlenbeck process on $[0, +\infty)$: At 0, both $\Sigma(0) < \infty$ and $N(0) < \infty$ so it is a regular boundary. The behaviour of X_t at 0 must be specified.

- The CIR process, $dr_t = \alpha(\mu - r_t)dt + \sigma dz_t$, on $[0, +\infty)$:
0 is the entrance if $2\alpha/\sigma^2 > 1$ and regular if $2\alpha/\sigma^2 \leq 1$. In the latter case the behaviour of X_t at 0 must be specified.

6.4 INTEREST RATE MODELS AT EXTREME VALUES OF INTEREST RATES

Standard models like Brace, Gatarek and Musiela (97) [88], Black and Karasinski (91) [74], Hull and White (93) [295], *et cetera* are 'mid-range' models, which assume that interest rate behaviour varies uniformly as rates vary. No special behaviour is allowed at extreme values of interest rate. Intuitively, this seems somewhat unrealistic. The true behaviour of interest rates at high or low levels could be expected to be different from their 'normal' behaviour. At very high levels of rates one is likely to have an economy with high inflation where the monetary regime will be qualitatively different to one where inflation is at 'normal' levels. When rates are very low an economy may be deflating and the regime is once again likely to be different from 'normal'. This would be reflected in both the objective behaviour of interest rates, and also in the markets' perceptions of risk, so that both objective and risk-adjusted processes can be anticipated to change at extreme values of rates.

For currencies like the Brazilian real or Japanese yen, which have respectively very high and very low rates at the time of writing, mid-range models may be suspect. When rates are low, we have to decide whether a model should allow rates to go briefly negative or not; our decision will have important consequences for valuing and hedging. When rates are high, hyperinflation scenarios may become plausible with the possibility of extremely high payouts on caps and swaptions, and even the possibility of meltdown. Economic conditions are extreme in both cases, and one would not expect a mid-range model to adequately model interest rate behaviour.

For currencies like the USD, currently well served by mid-range models, extreme range models may seem to have little relevance. However, economies can change radically in a 10- or 20-year period, as we have seen in Chapter 2. There are many dollar-denominated instruments with maturities above 20 years whose valuation could potentially be effected if dollar hyperinflation within the next two decades was considered plausible by the markets.

To prevent rates from becoming negative we might consider putting a barrier at zero; Gaussian models have non-zero probabilities of negative rates. To preclude negative rates, a reflecting barrier at zero could be inserted, for instance. This would have a very significant effect upon the term structure at low rate levels (Goldstein and Keirstead (97) [253]).

If the possibility of hyperinflations were priced by the market, spot rates would be expected to rise at longer maturities, reflecting the risk of higher future interest rates. In a hyperinflation, bond prices fall to zero and payoffs to caps and swaptions rise enormously. There may be a risk that the banking system will default on the very high payments. A bank default of course means that the caplet payoff would be zero (or some recovery fraction) and therefore an effective ceiling to rates may exist. Alternatively banks, or the monetary authorities, may impose a ceiling on caplet payoffs, *et cetera*. In any case there is considerable uncertainty as to how hyperinflation could or should be incorporated into an interest rate model.

6.4.1   Interest Rates and Stationarity

A process is stationary if its distributional properties are time invariant; that is, if the joint distributions of $r_{t_1}, \ldots, r_{t_n}$ are the same as those for $r_{t_1+k}, \ldots, r_{t_n+k}$ for all k. In particular, the first and second moments should be time independent. Stationarity implies that the process has no trend, so that in a stationary interest rate model, rates may either be driftless or may stay roughly within some range. Periodic behaviour is not allowed.

Statistical tests for stationarity involve looking for unit roots within the time series—if unit roots do exist, then the series is not stationary.[2] Tests for the presence of unit roots in interest rate time series (such as El-Jahel *et al.* (97) [200], Ball and Torous (96) [51]) indicate that the hypothesis that a unit root is present cannot be ruled out. Unfortunately these tests have very low statistical power, so it is not possible to conclude whether or not interest rates have been stationary in the past.

Is it desirable for a model to be stationary? From the point of view of mathematical simplicity, undoubtedly. Stationary models are simpler. Allowing a model to be non-stationary may have some desirable consequences though. Extended Vasicek models have time-dependent reversion levels. This makes them non-stationary but also permits them to be calibrated exactly to the yield curve. However, reasonably good calibration can be achieved by a stationary generalised Vasicek model without having to put up with the potentially considerable disadvantages of non-stationarity. These include:

1. A calibrated model will not evolve consistently with the way the market evolves, so consequently
2. Models have to re-calibrated frequently.

Behaviour at extreme values can be accommodated without having to introduce non-stationarity. However, non-stationarity may not fit reality, particularly for events like hyperinflations, where the distributional properties of the process may change radically.

6.4.2   An Interest Rate Model with Hyperinflation

In Chapter 2 we saw that hyperinflations have been common throughout history. Examples include not only emerging markets but also those in North America and Europe. Hyperinflations are usually not foreseen even a few years in advance.

At a more modest level, in many currencies there have been regimes of high levels of rates alternating with periods of rates at mid-levels. Figure 6.10 shows rates in the Indonesian rupiah from 1988 to 1999. The East Asian crisis of 1997–1998 is clearly visible. Figure 6.11 shows rates in the Brazilian real for 1994–1999, and Figure 6.12 is for the Mexican peso in the period 1994–1999. The real shows the crisis in Autumn 1998 continuing through the devaluation in January 1999. The peso crisis of December

---

[2] For definitions and discussion of time series properties such as unit roots, see Enders (95) [206], Campbell, Lo and MacKinlay (97) [113], Mills (90) [396], *et cetera*.

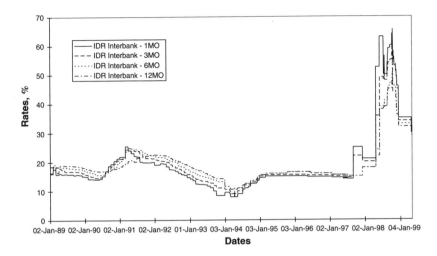

Figure 6.10   Interbank rates, Indonesian rupiah

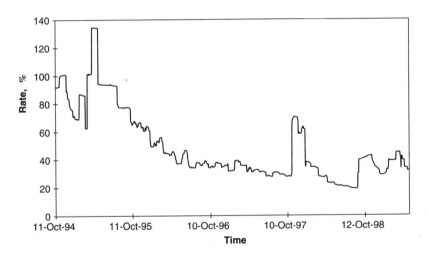

Figure 6.11   Brazilian real overnight mid-rate

1994 is very clearly visible. In both plots there is evidently a radical change of behaviour before and after triggering events.

When rates become very high:

- the market is less liquid,
- the maturity of the longest bond declines,
- borrowing is short term, at floating rates, and

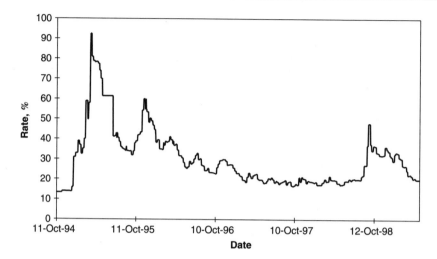

Figure 6.12   Mexican peso, 28-day Cetes, mid-rate

- indexing may be introduced, so that bond returns may be directly or indirectly linked to a price index.

Does hyperinflation need to be incorporated into a model? This, as with so many other modelling decisions, has to be a judgement call, but two properties seem necessary in a stationary model which includes hyperinflation:

- The model exhibits mean reversion when rates are at mid-levels.
- If rates get too high, they may escape to infinity.

A process for the short rate that incorporates these two properties is

$$dr_t = (De^{-\lambda_1 r_t} + Ee^{-\lambda_2 r_t} + F)dt + \sigma dz_t, \tag{6.70}$$

under the EMM. This is locally Lipschitz. The parameters $D, E, F, \lambda_1, \lambda_2$ can be chosen so that

- r_t usually reverts towards 0.1;
- There is a high negative drift at $r_t \approx 0.2$, so that rates are 'pushed down' from 0.2; and
- Rates diverge to ∞ if r_t exceeds 0.25.

We use the parameter values $(D, E, F, \lambda_1, \lambda_2) = (0.3, 2 \times 10^{-7}, -0.3, 1, 50)$, with $\sigma = 0.03$ The drift $\mu(r) = De^{-\lambda_1 r} + Ee^{-\lambda_2 r} + F$ is plotted in Figure 6.13 and can be seen to cause r_t to have the advertised properties.

A set of sample rate paths are generated in Figure 6.14. If a path fluctuates to too high a level, it is driven up and explodes. In the figure, rates are capped at 50%. If the initial value of the short rate is small enough, most paths revert.

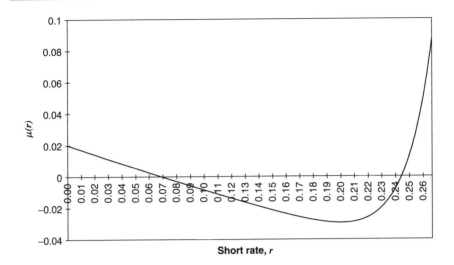

Figure 6.13   The drift of the short rate

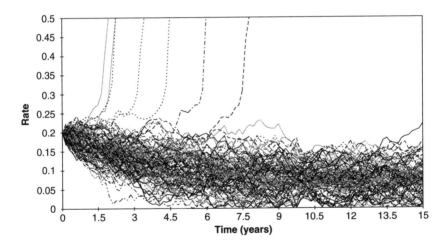

Figure 6.14   Simulated sample paths

If there is a non-vanishing probability of rates exploding, then valuation in the model may become problematical. Hogan and Weintraub (93) [284] showed that if the short rate has a log-normal process, then futures prices explode (see Chapter 9). For processes like (6.70) similar arguments may not apply since discount factors decrease at a greater rate than payoffs increase, as $r \to \infty$. Alternatively, if (6.70) holds under the objective measure and if hyperinflation risk is not priced by the market, then under the EMM the drift term may not explode.

If rates are effectively capped at relatively low levels, for example at 50%, then caplets will not be priced at overly high levels.

6.4.3   Low Rates: Boundaries at Zero

What happens at low rates? Empirical evidence, gathered from currencies like the yen, suggests that when nominal rates decline towards zero, volatility does not also go to zero. Indeed, 1998 yen data has Black implied volatilities of $\sim 60\%$ at low strikes for extended periods.

If we want to keep interest rates positive, there is a family of positive models in which process constraints implicitly give positive interest rates (see Chapter 9). Included in this general class of models are some that result from imposing positivity onto models in which rates might otherwise become negative.

- Set $r_t = f(x_t)$, for some process x_t, where $f(x) \geq 0$ for all x. For example, take $r = x^2$ or $r = e^x$ for squared Gaussian models or log-r models.
- Make 0 an unattainable boundary for r_t, as in the CIR model, where 0 is unattainable from $r_0 > 0$ for certain parameter values.
- Make 0 an attainable boundary for r_t; for example, Goldstein and Keirstead (97) [253] impose a reflecting or absorbing boundary at 0. Black (95) [72] imposes a sticky boundary at zero.

The Black model has as its premise the notion that one can always exchange the money market account for cash. Investors will always perform the exchange if r_t falls to 0, so we have

$$r_t = \max(0, r_t'), \tag{6.71}$$

where r_t' is the 'shadow' nominal rate. If r_t' hits 0 from above, investors sell the account for cash. If it hits 0 from below, they buy the account with cash. This strategy has guaranteed non-negative returns, if it can be implemented. The model has zero as a 'sticky' boundary. However, market frictions become very important at low levels of rate and there are in any case problems involved with putting on the arbitrage. There is not enough cash in a real world economy to enable investors to pursue the strategy.

In practice the 'cash under the mattress' arbitrage adopted by this model and by others cannot be justified. Only a small proportion of the money supply exists as cash; by far the greatest proportion exists as bank deposits. If the shadow rate r_t' did reach 0, there would be a run on the banks. It is unclear whether in theory the monetary authorities could maintain an incremental supply of notes and coin to keep rates positive, or whether there would be a 'speculative attack' against bank deposits. In practice it seems not unlikely that economic consequences would be enormous.

The Nature of the Boundary at Zero

We assume for the moment that rates are bounded below, and in particular that the short rate process has a boundary at zero. (It may be the case that yen data can be explained if there is a boundary just below zero.) In Section 6.3 we examined the types of boundary that might be found for diffusion processes.

In this section we are chiefly concerned with regular boundaries. Entrance and natural boundaries arise for positive interest rate models such as CIR and Black and Karasinski.

At a regular boundary it is necessary to separately specify the process behaviour away from the boundary and the behaviour at the boundary itself. For example, we define a short rate process on $[0, \infty)$. Suppose that

$$dr_t = \alpha(\mu - r_t)dt + \sigma r_t^\gamma dB_t \tag{6.72}$$

on $(0, \infty)$, with α, μ, σ, $\gamma > 0$. If $\gamma = 1$, 0 is an entrance boundary. If $\gamma = \frac{1}{2}$, and $\sigma^2 > 2\alpha\mu$, 0 is a regular boundary, and if $\gamma = 0$, 0 is a regular boundary. If 0 is regular, then the behaviour of r_t at 0 must be specified. Is zero:

- Absorbing? This seems unrealistic.
- Reflecting? This is possible and plausible.
- Something else? Any other boundary type is likely to involve something complex or even implausible, for example that the rate stays at zero for a while before jumping out.

It is worth noting that introducing a boundary condition does not of itself introduce arbitrage into the model.

Prices of Pure Discount Bonds

Once boundary conditions have been defined, their effect on prices can be investigated. Let $B(r, \tau)$ be the value of a pure discount bond with time τ to maturity when the short rate has value r. Suppose that the short rate process is

$$dr_t = \mu(r_t)dt + \sigma(r_t)dz_t \tag{6.73}$$

and is defined on $[l, \infty)$. $B = B(r, \tau)$ satisfies the usual PDE (with subscripts denoting derivatives)

$$B_\tau = -rB + \mu(r)B_r + \frac{1}{2}\sigma^2(r)B_{rr} \tag{6.74}$$

with boundary conditions $B(r, 0) = 1$ and $B(\infty, \tau) = 0$. Goldstein and Keirstead (97) [253] show that for a reflecting boundary at l,

$$\left.\frac{B_r}{s(r)}\right|_{r=l} = 0, \tag{6.75}$$

where $s(r)$ is the scale density of r, and for an absorbing boundary at l,

$$B(l, \tau) = e^{-l\tau}. \tag{6.76}$$

Goldstein and Keirstead find explicit solutions. If $dr_t = \kappa(\theta - r_t)dt + \sigma dz_t$ is a Vasicek process under the EMM, then for $l = 0$

$$B(r, \tau) = \int_0^\infty G(r, s, \tau)ds, \tag{6.77}$$

where

$$G(r, s, \tau) = \sum_j c_j e^{-\alpha_j \tau} e^{-ar + \frac{1}{2}br^2} U\left(-\lambda_j, \frac{r-d}{c}\right), \qquad (6.78)$$

where U are the parabolic cylinder functions (see Abramowitz and Stegun (65) [3]), and where

$$c_j = \frac{e^{as - \frac{1}{2}bs^2} U\left(-\lambda_j, \frac{s-d}{c}\right)}{\int_0^\infty U\left(-\lambda_j, \frac{z-d}{c}\right)^2 dz}, \qquad (6.79)$$

$$a = \frac{\kappa\theta}{\sigma^2}, \qquad (6.80)$$

$$b = \frac{\kappa}{\sigma^2}, \qquad (6.81)$$

$$c = \sqrt{\frac{1}{2b}}, \qquad (6.82)$$

$$d = \frac{a}{b} - \frac{1}{b^2\sigma^2}, \qquad (6.83)$$

$$\alpha_j = \lambda_j b\sigma^2 + \frac{a}{b} - \frac{b\sigma^2}{2} - \frac{1}{2b^2\sigma^2}, \qquad (6.84)$$

and the λ_j satisfy:

1. For a reflecting boundary,

$$acU\left(-\lambda_j, -\frac{d}{c}\right) = \frac{\partial}{\partial z} U(-\lambda_j, z)\Big|_{z=-d/c}. \qquad (6.85)$$

2. For an absorbing boundary,

$$U\left(-\lambda_j, -\frac{d}{c}\right) = 0. \qquad (6.86)$$

Goldstein and Keirstead also find solutions when r_t obeys a CIR process.

6.4.4 Effect on Pricing

Using the process (6.70) we investigate the effect of two types of boundary at zero on pricing pure discount bonds and caplets. We find strong effects, but only if the short rate is initially near the boundary. (When the initial value of the short rate is close to zero, the behaviour at high levels of r has an insignificant effect.) The two types of boundary are

- a reflecting boundary at zero, and
- a floored boundary at zero.

For a floored boundary, $r_t = \max(0, r'_t)$, where r'_t is the process without any boundary at zero.

Pure Discount Bonds

A Monte Carlo method was used to find term structures. The results are illustrated in Figure 6.15. The figure plots term structures found under each boundary assumption. If the short rate is small, the term structure is steeper at the short end with a reflecting boundary than with a floored boundary, and rises to higher levels faster. For a high short rate, there is no discernible difference between term structures from floored and reflective boundaries.

Caplet Pricing

Caplet prices at low levels of r_t might be expected to be sensitive to the behaviour of r_t near the boundary. Caplet prices were also found using a Monte Carlo method. For a three-month at-the-money (ATM) caplet, with volatility $\sigma = 0.03$, Table 6.6 summarises the results.

For Table 6.6, rates were capped at 50%. Standard errors are similar for both the reflecting and floored cases. We can see that prices differ significantly for $r_0 = 0.005$, but when short rates are even slightly higher, $r_0 \geq 0.01$, they are very similar.

We conclude that boundary conditions at zero become significant only at very low levels of rate. We are left uncertain as to the correct assumption to make for a boundary there. Some yen rates in 1998 became briefly negative, though only by 10 or 20 basis points at most, so perhaps a boundary a little below zero is appropriate. On this evidence, whether a boundary should be floored or reflecting appears an open question.

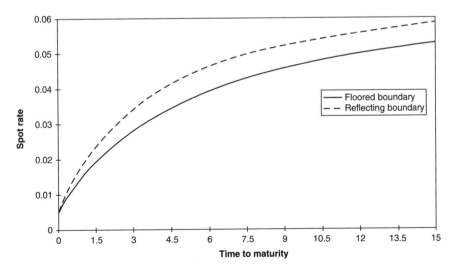

Figure 6.15   Term structures with alternative boundaries

Table 6.6   Caplet prices with different boundary conditions

r_0:	0.005	0.01	0.05	0.25
Caplet price with reflecting boundary	0.010	0.008	0.006	0.027
Caplet price with floored boundary	0.008	0.008	0.006	0.030
Standard error	0.0005	0.0006	0.0006	0.0050

Hyperinflations, by contrast, have large effects at high rate levels, even when a hyperinflation is not actually underway. However, to discover how this behaviour impacts high rate regimes, we need to model how hyperinflations start, how they keep going and what happens when they stop. This last would be very challenging given that this often involves devaluation and possibly renormalisation of the currency. We do not attempt to model these features here.

6.5   TAIL DISTRIBUTIONS

In the yen market it is often explicitly or implicitly assumed that there is indeed a boundary of some sort at zero. In fact techniques exist to establish whether or not, based on historical data, a boundary seems to be present. These techniques are based on an analysis of tail distributions.

In this section we discuss the three canonical tail distributions and empirical tests of them. We apply these tests to UK three-month Libor, concluding that the data set analysed behaved as if it were bounded for both the right and left tails. This section is based on Kuan and Webber (98) [344].

There has been some recent interest in applying extreme value theory, and the theory of tail distributions, to financial time series. Much of this has been prompted by the emergence of Value at Risk (VaR) as a market sanctioned risk management tool,[3] although the literature predates this. There is a parallel strand in the literature investigating margin requirements.

A number of markets have been investigated. Koedijk and Kool (92) [339] investigate east European FX rates, Broussard and Booth (98) [102] look at German stock index futures, Koedijk *et al.* (90) [340] explore EMS data, Huisman *et al.* (98) [289] review various FX series, Akgiray *et al.* (88) [12] test black market FX rates in Latin America, Kofman and de Vries (89) [341] write on potato futures, and Longin (96) [358] estimates tail statistics of stock market returns. Few investigations seem to have been made of interest rate data.

6.5.1   The Three Canonical Tail Distributions

The tail behaviour of a continuous distribution falls into one of three categories. We illustrate using upper tails, but there are obvious corresponding relationships for lower tails.

---

[3] See Duffie and Pan (97) [185] for a review.

One must distinguish between tail distributions and extreme value distributions. Suppose one has a sample $X_1, \ldots, X_n$ drawn from some distribution. Set $M_n = \max_{i=1,\ldots,n} X_i$. The distribution of M_n as $n \to \infty$ is called the extremal distribution. Asymptotically, the upper tails of an extremal distribution $G(x)$ must resemble those of the one of the following three types:

- Fat tails (Fréchet distribution. 'Type II'):
  For $x \leq 0$, $G(x) = 0$. For $x > 0$, $G(x) = e^{-x^{-k}}$, for some $k > 0$.
- Thin tails (Weibull distribution. 'Type III'):
  For $x > 0$, $G(x) = 1$, and for $x \leq 0$, $G(x) = e^{-(-x)^k}$, for some $k > 0$.
- Normal tails (Gumbel distribution. 'Type I'):
  $-\infty < x < \infty$, $G(x) = e^{-e^x}$.

Fat tails are fatter than normal tails and have unbounded second moments. Thin tails are thinner than normal tails and are bounded in that they have zero density above (below) some level.

The three types of asymptotic extreme value distributions can be expressed in a common form

$$U(Y; \mu, \sigma, \tau) = \exp\left[-\left(1 + \tau\left(\frac{Y-\mu}{\sigma}\right)^{-\frac{1}{\tau}}\right)\right], \qquad (6.87)$$

where μ and σ are location and scale parameters, respectively, and τ is the tail parameter. For a Fréchet distribution ($\tau > 0$) the distribution (6.87) is defined only for $Y \geq \mu - \sigma/\tau$ and is set to zero for $Y < \mu - \sigma/\tau$. When $\tau < 0$, for a Weibull distribution, the expression is defined only for $Y \leq \mu - \sigma/\tau$, and is set equal to 1 for $Y > \mu - \sigma/\tau$. The case of $\tau = 0$ is treated as a limiting value,

$$U(Y; \mu, \sigma, \tau) = \exp\left[-\exp\left(\frac{Y-\mu}{\sigma}\right)\right]. \qquad (6.88)$$

The densities $U(Y; 0, 1, \tau)$ corresponding to the distribution $U(Y; 0, 1, \tau)$, for $\tau = -0.5, 0, 0.5$, are shown in Figure 6.16. We are only interested in the right hand tails. If $\tau < 0$, $U(Y)$ has a thinner tail than the exponential distribution. If $\tau > 0$, $U(Y)$ has fatter tails. Tails for the densities $u(Y; 0, 1, \tau)$, for $\tau = -0.2, 0, 0.2$. are shown in Figure 6.17. It is apparent that the right tail of $u(Y; 0, 1, 0.2)$ is fatter than that of $u(Y; 0, 1, 0)$, which corresponds to a normal tail. $u(Y; 0, 1, -0.2)$ is thinner than a normal tail. Note that $u(Y; 0, 1, -0.2)$ is zero for $Y \geq 5$.

There is a convenient set of distributions with extreme value distributions as above. These are the generalised Pareto distributions (GPDs), $N(Y; \mu, \sigma, \tau)$,

$$N(Y; \mu, \sigma, \tau) = 1 - \left(1 + \tau\frac{Y-\mu}{\sigma}\right)^{-\frac{1}{\tau}}, \qquad Y > \mu, \qquad (6.89)$$

as $Y \to \infty$ for a Fréchet distribution, or as $Y \to \mu - \sigma/\tau$ for a Weibull distribution. It is type I for $\tau = 0$ as $Y \to \infty$. In this case equation (6.89) is interpreted as the limit

$$N(Y; \mu, \sigma, \tau) = 1 - \exp\left(-\left(\frac{Y-\mu}{\sigma}\right)\right).$$

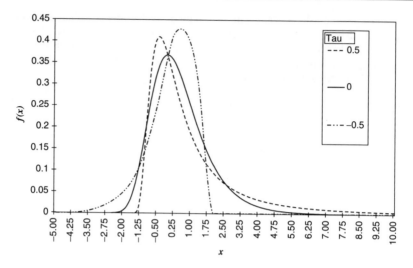

Figure 6.16   The canonical density functions

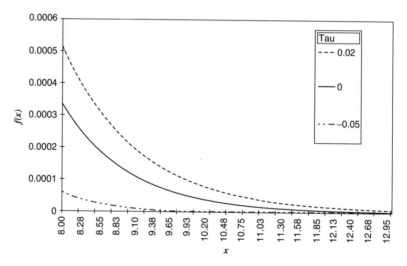

Figure 6.17   The three tail densities

If we are interested in only the tail behaviour, then the general Pareto distribution provides a useful, tractable set of examples.

6.5.2   Empirical Investigation of Tail Parameters

We describe three methods of estimating the tail parameter: Pickands' test, a direct fit test, and an excess mean fit test.

Suppose we have observed a series $\left\{ r_{t_i} \right\}_{i=1,\ldots,N}$. For Pickands' test, order the series in ascending order as

$$r_{(1)} \leq \cdots \leq r_{(N)}, \tag{6.90}$$

where $r_{(j)}$ is the jth smallest value in the set $\left\{ r_{t_i} \right\}_{i=1,\ldots,N}$. For Pickands' test we choose an integer m, where $0 < m < N/4$. Pickands' estimator is

$$\tau_p = \frac{\ln \left[r_{(m)} - r_{(2m)} \right] - \ln \left[r_{(2m)} - r_{(4m)} \right]}{\ln 2}. \tag{6.91}$$

$k_P = 1/\tau_p$ is asymptotically normally distributed (see Dekker and de Hann (89) [163]). This test assumes that the series $\left\{ r_{t_i} \right\}$ has no serial correlation, an inaccurate assumption in the case of interest rates that reduce the significance of these test results.

For some threshold parameter u, the empirical tail distribution is $F_u(\bar{r})$,

$$F_u(\bar{r}) = \Pr \left[r - u \leq \bar{r} \mid r > u \right]. \tag{6.92}$$

We may directly fit this to a generalised Pareto distribution

$$F(r \mid \mu, \sigma, \tau) = 1 - \left(1 + \tau \frac{r - \mu}{\sigma} \right)^{-1/\tau}. \tag{6.93}$$

A third test is based on the excess mean function $e(u) = \mathbb{E}\left[r - u \mid r > u \right]$. In the tail this has linear limiting behaviour:

$$e(u) \sim \frac{\tau}{\tau - 1} (1 + u). \tag{6.94}$$

Choose u_c so that $e(u)$ is linear for $u > u_c$. The parameter τ is obtained from the slope of $e(u)$.

Tails of Financial Time Series

In practice, returns to asset prices are usually found to be Fréchet. Tail behaviour is intimately linked to extreme value theory, which means it has a potential relationship to VaR. Tails analysis and extreme value theory have been applied to most markets:

- Equity (Broussard and Booth (98) [102], Longin (96) [358]).
- FX (Koedijk and Kool (92) [339], Huisman *et al.* (98) [289]).
- Commodities (Kofman and de Vries (89) [341]); the tails of these series are found to be Fréchet.
- Interest rates (Kuan and Webber (98) [344]); the tails are found to be Weibull.

The Tails of UK Three-month Libor

Kuan and Webber (98) [344] performed an analysis of the tails of UK three-month Libor. The tails were tested using Pickands' estimate, the GPD fit, and the excess mean

Table 6.7   Pickands' estimate

	Right tail		Left tail	
m	50	160	50	160
Tail parameter, τ	−1.66	−0.94	−2.66	−3.07
Variance of τ	0.48	4.01	0.11	0.07
95% c.i. (+/−)	1.36	3.92	0.65	0.53
Scale parameter	0.067	0.040	0.012	0.146

Table 6.8   GDP fit

	Right tail	Left tail
Tail parameter	−0.1216	−1.2055
Scale parameter	0.00121	0.00483
Location parameter	0.1517	0.058

Table 6.9   Mean excess estimate

	Right tail	Left tail
Slope	−0.393	0.638
Variance of slope	0.00029	3.9E-05
Tail parameter	−0.6474	−1.7624

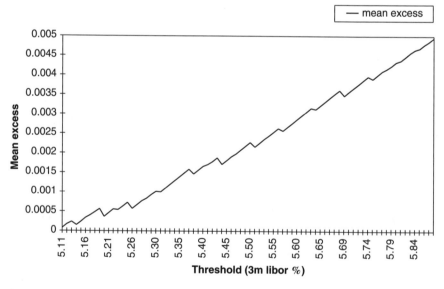

Figure 6.18   Mean excess plot, left tail

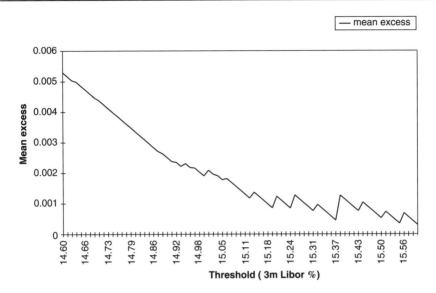

Figure 6.19 Mean excess plot, right tail

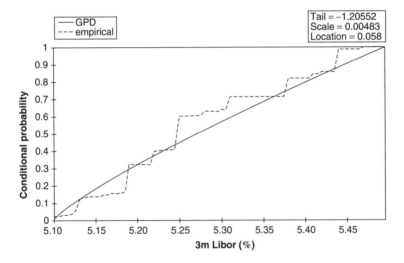

Figure 6.20 Generalised Pareto fit, left tail

fit. The results are presented in Tables 6.7, 6.8 and 6.9. Figures 6.18 and 6.19 show respectively the mean excess plots for the left and right tails, and Figures 6.20 and 6.21 show the GPD fit for each tail.

The conclusions are consistent with a negative tail parameter on both the left and right tails. Using reasonable values of τ for the right and left tails, one concludes

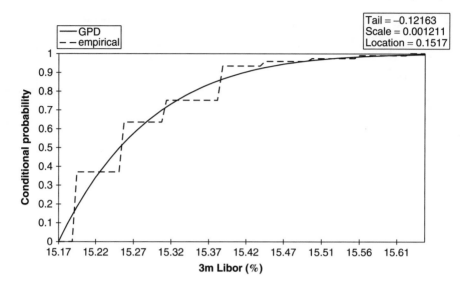

Figure 6.21   General Pareto fit, right tail

that UK Libor over the period of the test behaved as if it were bounded in a range [0.054, 0.164].

Implications

- *The stationary density.* The tails of the stationary density are not necessarily log-normal. In estimation work involving the stationary density it may be better to use the empirical tail parameter.
- *Implied volatilities.* If the volatility smile has an upward slope to one side, Fréchet tails are implied on that side. If there is a downward slope to one side, Weibull tails are implied. However, there may not be enough data in the sample to see the limiting behaviour of the underlying variable.
- *Prices.* There may be a big effect for very far in or out of the money options. If the tails are Weibull, far out of the money calls are worth zero, and far in the money calls have $\partial C/\partial K = 1$.

PART II
INTEREST RATE MODELS

Part I described concepts underlying interest rate modelling; in Part II we examine the models themselves, covering all the main categories of models used today. Historically, models have been classified as factor models (using a number of underlying factors to generate rate dynamics) or as whole yield curve models (modelling the evolution of the entire curve itself). Our emphasis is on the intuition underlying the models. We split out treatment into five chapters

- Affine models
- Heath, Jarrow and Morton (HJM) and market models
- Other interest rate models
- General interest rate models and jump models
- Economics and interest rate models

Affine models are among the most tractable type of interest rate models, and affine models of one sort or another are probably the most popular models to implement. More sophisticated applications may require the use of a whole yield curve model. Recently Brace, Gatarek and Musiela (BGM) and market models have become quite common. These models focus on the evolution of market-quoted rates themselves. They may be even easier to use than an affine model if one is simply using them as a substitute for Black's formulae; more difficult applications need less tractable methods.

Affine models are investigated in Chapter 7 and HJM and market models in Chapter 8. HJM/BGM models may yet find themselves formulated analogously to factor models. de Jong and Santa-Clara (99) [162], building on Ritchken and Sankarasubramanian (95) [454], are starting to incorporate a factor-like approach.

Positive rate models and price kernel models are amongst those explored in Chapter 9. These models have attracted a great deal of attention recently and further developments are likely.

Chapter 10 looks at some of the other more general attempts that have been made to model interest rate behaviour, including infinite factor random field models and models with jumps.

The final chapter of Part II looks more particularly at models with an economic basis of some sort. The general equilibrium framework is described, as are models based on ideas from macro-economics. It might be supposed that economic models would offer advantages over other types of model since interest rates are so deeply imbedded in an economics framework. In fact the importance of economics-based models is mainly theoretical.

7

Affine Models

In this chapter we review models of affine type. There is a vast number of factor models, many examples of which have been investigated and are used in the finance industry. The very first term structure model, Vasicek (77) [529], is an affine model, as are other popular models such as Longstaff and Schwartz (92) [365] and Hull and White (93) [295], (96) [298].

Their popularity is due both to their tractability and to their flexibility. A model like Longstaff and Schwartz has explicit solutions for bond prices and for bond option prices. It is relatively straightforward to price other instruments in this model, and it has sufficient free parameters so that it can fit most market term structures quite well (Rebonato (98) [448]).

Affine models were first investigated as a category by Brown and Schaefer (94) [104]. Duffie and Kan (94) [182], (96) [183] developed a general theory, and showed how the state variables in a general affine model might be re-interpreted as pure discount bond yields. Dai and Singleton (98) [154] have provided a classification of affine models and have established, for instance, the most general representative example of each class of affine models.

We first review the general theory of affine models, and show how the state variables are related to spot rates. In the next section we give an overview of the three main families of affine models that have appeared in the literature. Then we examine in more detail some of the better known affine models. These are the extended Vasicek and extended CIR single-factor models, the two-factor model of Longstaff and Schwartz, and the three-factor Balduzzi, Das, Foresi and Sundaram (96) [49] (BDFS) model (which contains the two-factor Fong and Vasicek model). Finally we describe the Dai and Singleton classification.

7.1 AFFINE TERM STRUCTURE MODELS

We consider a model with n state variables, $X_t = (X_{1,t}, \ldots, X_{n,t})'$. A model is affine if the pure discount bond prices $B_t(X, \tau)$ can be written in the form

$$B_t(X, \tau) = e^{a(\tau) + b(\tau)' X_t}, \tag{7.1}$$

where $\tau = T - t$ is the time to maturity of the bond, $a(\tau)$ is a scalar function of τ and $b(\tau) = (b_1(\tau), \ldots, b_n(\tau))'$ is a vector valued function of τ. Spot rates are of the form

$$r_t(\tau) = -\frac{a(\tau)}{\tau} - \frac{b(\tau)'}{\tau} X_t. \tag{7.2}$$

It turns out that imposing this particularly simple functional relationship between state variables and bond prices imposes a great deal of tractability on the model. Bond prices will be found to be solutions to a Riccati equation, which may sometimes have explicit solutions, and bond option prices may also have explicit formulae. When numerical solutions are necessary there are often easy methods available.

Taking limits as $\tau \to 0$ in (7.2) we obtain an expression for the short rate r_t,

$$r_t = f + g'X_t, \tag{7.3}$$

where f and g are constants:

$$f = -\left.\frac{\partial a(\tau)}{\partial \tau}\right|_{\tau=0}, \tag{7.4}$$

$$g = -\left.\frac{\partial b(\tau)}{\partial \tau}\right|_{\tau=0} = -\left(\left.\frac{\partial b_1(\tau)}{\partial \tau}\right|_{\tau=0}, \ldots, \left.\frac{\partial b_n(\tau)}{\partial \tau}\right|_{\tau=0}\right)', \tag{7.5}$$

since, for instance,

$$-\left.\frac{\partial a(\tau)}{\partial \tau}\right|_{\tau=0} = \lim_{\tau \to 0} -\frac{a(\tau)}{\tau}.$$

Once the processes for the vector of state variables X_t have been specified (under the EMM, say), equation (7.3) is sufficient to establish prices in the model, since $a(\tau)$ and $b(\tau)$ are determined, as we shall see below, by the process for X_t. It is not possible to allow X_t to have an arbitrary process. Duffie and Kan (96) [183] show that the process for X_t (under the EMM) must be of the form

$$dX_t = (uX_t + v)dt + \Sigma V\,dz_t, \tag{7.6}$$

where z_t is an n-dimensional Wiener process, u and Σ are constant $n \times n$ matrices, and v is a constant n-dimensional vector. V_t is a diagonal matrix of the form

$$V_t = \begin{pmatrix} \sqrt{\alpha_1 + \beta_1'X_t} & & 0 \\ & \ddots & \\ 0 & & \sqrt{\alpha_n + \beta_n'X_t} \end{pmatrix}, \tag{7.7}$$

where $\alpha_i \in \mathbb{R}$, $\beta_i \in \mathbb{R}^n$, $i = 1, \ldots, n$, are constants (with mild regularity conditions to ensure that $\alpha_i + \beta_i'X_t$, $i = 1, \ldots, n$, remain positive).

To find pure discount bond prices we need to solve for $a(\tau)$ and $b(\tau)$. Set $\alpha = (\alpha_1, \ldots, \alpha_n)'$ and let β be the $n \times n$ matrix whose columns are the vectors β_i. It is straightforward to show, by writing down the short rate process using Itō's lemma (7.3), that $a(\tau)$ and $b(\tau)$ satisfy the pair of differential equations

$$\frac{\partial a(\tau)}{\partial \tau} = -f + v'b + \frac{1}{2}b'\Sigma\mathrm{diag}(\alpha)\Sigma'b \tag{7.8}$$

and

$$\frac{\partial b(\tau)}{\partial \tau} = -g + u'b + \frac{1}{2}b'\Sigma\beta\Sigma'b, \tag{7.9}$$

with boundary conditions $a(0) = 0$ and $b(0) = 0$. $b(\tau)$ may be solved for from (7.9) and the solution substituted into (7.8) to solve for $a(\tau)$. (7.9) is a Riccati equation, with coefficients quadratic in $b(\tau)$. There are fairly easy numerical solution methods available for this type of PDE. For the commoner (and simpler) interest rate models discussed below there may be explicit solutions.

7.2 INTERPRETING THE STATE VARIABLES

An affine model is defined in terms of abstract state variables. Duffie and Kan (96) [183] showed that affine combinations of the state variables are spot rates and that as long as the model is non-degenerate it is possible to transform the set of state variables into a set of spot rates. It may then be possible for the affine model to be calibrated to spot rates of chosen maturities. This is a very convenient feature, and makes it possible to construct examples of affine models with an intuitive motivation. For instance, the set of state variables could be calibrated to a three-month, a two-year and a 10-year spot rate. Each spot rate is given a process of the form (7.6), and the correlations between the different spot rates can be arranged to reflect market correlations.

The link between spot rate processes and the processes for the state variables is given by (7.12) below. Although it is straightforward to find the spot rate processes from the processes of the state variables the converse is not so easy. It is possible to implement a workable procedure, however; see Pang and Hodges (95) [426].

To re-express an affine model in the abstract form (7.1) in terms of spot rates, choose a set of maturity times $\{\tau_i\}_{i=1,\dots,n}$ and define

$$h_{i,j} = -\frac{b_j(\tau_i)}{\tau_i}, \quad i = 1, \dots, n, \quad j = 1, \dots, n, \tag{7.10}$$

$$k_i = -\frac{a(\tau_i)}{\tau_i}, \quad i = 1, \dots, n. \tag{7.11}$$

Set $h = \{h_{i,j}\}_{i=1,\dots,n, j=1,\dots,n}$ and $k = \{k_i\}_{i=1,\dots,n}$ so that

$$r_t(\tau_i) = \{k + hX_t\}_i \tag{7.12}$$

is the τ_i maturity spot rate. We suppose that h is invertible. Set $Y_t = k + hX_t$. Then we have

$$B_t(X_t, \tau) = e^{a(\tau)+b'(\tau)X_t}$$

$$= e^{a(\tau)+b'(\tau)(h^{-1}Y_t - h^{-1}k)}$$

$$= e^{\tilde{a}(\tau)+\tilde{b}'(\tau)Y_t} \equiv B_t(Y_t, \tau), \tag{7.13}$$

where

$$\tilde{a}(\tau) = a(\tau) - b'(\tau)h^{-1}k, \tag{7.14}$$

$$\tilde{b}'(\tau) = b'(\tau)h^{-1}. \tag{7.15}$$

The representation (7.13) expresses spot rates as affine functions of the new state variables Y_t. But this is a vector of spot rates of fixed, reference maturities $\{\tau_i\}_{i=1,\ldots,n}$.

This demonstrates that an affine model can be re-parameterised so that we can take the state variables to be spot rates. The spot rates can be of any maturity as long as the matrix h is invertible. An affine model expressed in this form is called an affine yield model. Pang and Hodges (95) [426] explore these models further, finding conditions under which spot rates are guaranteed to be positive.

7.3 TYPES OF AFFINE MODEL

Commonly used affine models can be conveniently separated into three main types. This categorisation is distinct from the classification we describe in Section 7.6, which is a complete canonical mathematical classification; here we are describing models that have been investigated and used. The three categories are:

- *Gaussian affine models.* All state variables have constant volatilities.
- *CIR affine models.* All state variables have CIR-type square root volatilities.
- A *three-factor affine family.* A particular set of three-factor models, and certain restrictions to two-factor models, which have been studied by a number of authors, and which have had some practical application.

In addition, an affine model may be 'extended'; some of its parameters may be allowed to be deterministic functions of time. A number of models considered below have state variables with extended processes in this sense. A model some of whose state variables are extended may have sufficient flexibility to enable it to fit exactly a wide range of term structures, and perhaps also volatility term structures.

The drift of the state variable, $\mu(X_t) = uX_t + v$, is often specified with u a diagonal matrix with negative entries with at most a single off diagonal entry in each row, so that each component $X_{i,t}$ is mean reverting with a drift dependent on at most one other component. This is a considerable simplification, but, as we shall see, results in models that are heavily over-specified.

The canonical classification of Section 7.6 subsumes our categorisation. However, affine models that have actually been studied and used belong on the whole to one or other of our divisions. We consider each of the three categories in turn.

7.3.1 Gaussian Affine Models

Suppose that the short rate r_t is a function $r_t = f + g_1 X_{1,t} + \cdots + g_n X_{n,t}$ of state variables $X_t = (X_{1,t}, \ldots, X_{n,t})'$. The model is Gaussian affine if the processes followed by the state variables are of the form

$$\mathrm{d}X_{i,t} = (uX_t + v)\mathrm{d}t + \sigma_i \, \mathrm{d}z_{i,t}, \tag{7.16}$$

for σ_i constant, $i = 1, \ldots, n$, or, in some extended models, deterministic functions of time.

Table 7.1   Gaussian affine models

Author	n	
Vasicek (77) [529]	1	Bond options priced by Jamshidian (89) [308].
Hull and White (90) [292], (93) [295]	1	Extended Vasicek. Easy lattice implementation.
Steeley (91) [506]	2	Estimated on UK gilts.
Chen and Yang (96) [129]	3	Two of the three factors are extended Vasicek.
Beaglehole and Tenney (91) [57]	n	Solutions in the general case.
Babbs (93) [36]	n	Solutions in the general case.
Babbs and Nowman (99) [39]	n	Solutions in the general case.
Nunes (98) [421]	n	Fast approximate solutions in the general case.

Some papers exploring Gaussian affine models are listed in Table 7.1. The brief comments sketch the contribution of the paper, in the context of the development of affine models. Key papers are Hull and White (93) [295], (96) [298] and Beaglehole and Tenney (91) [57]. The Hull and White extended Vasicek model is discussed in Section 7.4.1 and its lattice implementation is described in Chapter 14. The Babbs and Nowman model is described in Section 7.5.3 and in Chapter 18.

Gaussian affine models do not have as extensive a literature as CIR affine models. This may be for the following reasons.

- They are tractable, and good numerical valuation procedures exist when there are no explicit solutions available. Thus the category may be to some extent exhausted.
- Gaussian affine models permit interest rates to become negative with non-zero probability, a possibility that may be ruled out with CIR affine models. There is an opinion in some academic quarters that negative interest rates are not possible in practice, and should be forbidden in any 'sensible' model. Such an opinion may have influenced the direction of research in this area. Some markets, where rates are very low, may indeed require the use of a positive rate model such as those of CIR affine type.

Although for Gaussian affine models there is a positive probability of negative interest rates, a number of authors (for instance Rogers (95) [457] have argued that for models fitted to 'ordinary' term structures the risk of actually getting negative rates is very low. Nevertheless we have seen in Chapter 6 that when rates in a Gaussian model are prevented from becoming negative, perhaps by imposing a reflecting barrier at zero, there may be a significant effect on bond and option prices.

Of course, if one believes that rates need not remain positive, and that the negative rates sometimes observed in the market are not spurious abnormalities, then one may be perfectly prepared to use a Gaussian affine model in any event.

7.3.2   CIR Affine Models

When the short rate r_t is a function $r_t = f + g_1 X_{1,t} + \cdots + g_n X_{n,t}$ of state variables $X_t = (X_{1,t}, \ldots, X_{n,t})'$, a model is CIR affine if all the state variables have processes of the form

$$dX_{i,t} = (uX_t + v)dt + \sigma_i \sqrt{X_{i,t}} \, dz_{i,t}, \qquad (7.17)$$

for σ_i constant, $i = 1, \ldots, n$, or deterministic functions of time. The literature on CIR affine models is much richer than that for Gaussian affine models. One-factor models are summarised in Table 7.2 and two-factor models in Table 7.3. The Longstaff and Schwartz model is described in Section 7.5.1 and placed in an economic context in Chapter 11. The general case is summarised in Table 7.4.

CIR affine models are less tractable than Gaussian affine models, but explicit solutions are available in some cases for some simpler instruments. Extended CIR affine models can fit to a wide range of term structures, but are not as general as Gaussian affine models (Jarrow (88) [315]).

7.3.3   The Three-Factor Affine Family

This family represents models that mix Gaussian and CIR type state variables. The motivation for the family seems to stem from a desire to bolt on a stochastic mean

Table 7.2   One-factor CIR affine models

Author	
CIR (85) [148]	Original general equilibrium model.
Hull and White (90) [292]	Extended CIR.
Jamshidian (95) [310]	Extended CIR.
Pelsser (96) [436]	Extended CIR with explicit solutions.
Maghsoodi (96) [376]	Extended CIR with explicit solutions.
Longstaff (90) [360]	Options on yields.
Feldman (93) [212]	Options on bond futures.

Table 7.3   Two-factor CIR affine models

Author	
Richard (78) [452]	Solves for bond prices.
Longstaff and Schwartz (92) [365]	Solutions for bond option prices.
Chen and Scott (92) [127]	Solutions for bond option prices.
Nielsen and Saa-Requejo (93) [417]	Two country Longstaff and Schwartz.

Table 7.4   General CIR affine models

Author	
Beaglehole and Tenney (91) [57]	General theory.
El-Karoui et al. (92) [203]	General theory.
Jamshidian (96) [311]	General theory and explicit solutions.
Scott (95) [483]	Explicit solutions. Empirical investigation.

or a stochastic volatility, or both, to the Vasicek model, while ensuring that volatilities remain positive. (Without extensions the Vasicek model certainly does not perform very well.) It turns out that models from this category have some tractability, and some explicit solutions are available.

The three processes (under a pricing measure) are:

1. The short rate process

$$\mathrm{d}r_t = \alpha(\mu_t - r_t)\mathrm{d}t + \sqrt{v_t}\,\mathrm{d}z_{r,t}. \tag{7.18}$$

2. The drift process

$$\mathrm{d}\mu_t = \beta(\gamma - \mu_t)\,\mathrm{d}t + \eta\mu_t^{\phi}\,\mathrm{d}z_{\mu,t}, \tag{7.19}$$

where $\phi = 0, \frac{1}{2}$.

3. The volatility process

$$\mathrm{d}v_t = \delta(\kappa - v_t)\mathrm{d}t + \lambda\sqrt{v_t}\,\mathrm{d}z_{v,t}. \tag{7.20}$$

Table 7.5 summarises some of the work done on this family. The BDFS three-factor model is described in Section 7.5.2. It nests the two-factor Fong and Vasicek model. We shall see in Section 7.6 that models with $\phi = 0$ are classified differently by the canonical classification to models with $\phi = 1/2$.

7.4 EXAMPLES OF ONE-FACTOR AFFINE MODELS

A number of widely used one-factor models have the general form

$$\mathrm{d}r_t = (\theta(t) + c(t)r_t)\mathrm{d}t + \sigma(t)r_t^{\gamma}\,\mathrm{d}z_t, \tag{7.21}$$

where $\gamma = 0$ or $1/2$ for an affine model, and $\theta(t)$, $c(t)$ and $\sigma(t)$ are deterministic functions of time.[1]

Table 7.5 The three-factor family

Author	Equations	ϕ	
Sørensen (94) [501]	(7.18) and (7.19)	0	Explicit solutions.
BDFS (96b) [49]	(7.18) and (7.19)	0	Solutions and estimates.
Fong and Vasicek (91) [226]	(7.18) and (7.20)	$\sim$	Explicit solution.
BDFS (96a) [48]	(7.18), (7.19) and (7.20)	0	Numerical solutions.
Chen (96) [126]	(7.18), (7.19) and (7.20)	$\frac{1}{2}$	Explicit solutions.
Rhee (99) [451]	(7.18), (7.19) and (7.20)	$\frac{1}{2}$	Uses a generalised drift.

---

[1] The exponent γ has the value 1 in the Courtadon (82) [145], Babbs and Webber (94) [40] and Brennan and Schwartz (79) [93] models. Market models (described in Chapter 8), where r_t is a market quoted rate, also have $\gamma = 1$. These models are stable, generating Black-like formulae for caplet prices. A log-normal short rate process is unstable (see Chapter 9).

Conventionally one supposes that the model is calibrated at time $t = 0$, and the process is defined only for $t \geq 0$. With three free functions the general model has the flexibility to fit three functions observed in the market. For instance, an initial yield curve, an initial term structure of volatility, a time path of future expected values of an interest rate of a chosen maturity, or perhaps a time path of the volatility of some interest rate.

While the general model can fit functions observed at some initial time, there are no built-in constraints which ensure that it remains a sensible representation of interest rates as they evolve. For example, the Ho and Lee (86) [280] model has a constant volatility, and a deterministic time-varying drift:

$$dr_t = \theta(t)dt + \sigma \, dz_t. \tag{7.22}$$

This can be solved explicitly for both bond prices and spot rates, giving term structures of the form

$$r_t(\tau) = r_t - \frac{1}{6}\sigma^2\tau^2 + \frac{1}{\tau}\int_t^{t+\tau} \theta(s)(T-s)ds. \tag{7.23}$$

When θ is constant this is just

$$r_t(\tau) = r_t - \frac{1}{6}\sigma^2\tau^2 + \frac{1}{2}\theta\tau. \tag{7.24}$$

Given an initial instantaneous forward rate curve, $f(0, t)$, the function $\theta(t)$ that recovers initial bond prices is

$$\theta(t) = \left.\frac{\partial f(0, t)}{\partial t}\right|_t + \sigma^2 t. \tag{7.25}$$

Unfortunately, term structures are unrealistic. The long rate becomes unbounded.

There are also explicit solutions for bond options in the Ho and Lee model. Let $c_t(T_1, T_2)$ be the value at time t of a European call option maturing at time T_1 on a pure discount bond maturing at time $T_2 \geq T_1$ with strike X. Then

$$c_t(T_1, T_2) = B_t(T_2)N(d_1) - XB_t(T_1)N(d_2), \tag{7.26}$$

where

$$d_1 = \frac{1}{\hat{\sigma}\sqrt{T_1 - t}}\ln\frac{B_t(T_2)}{XB_t(T_1)} + \frac{1}{2}\hat{\sigma}\sqrt{T_1 - t}, \tag{7.27}$$

$$d_2 = d_1 - \hat{\sigma}\sqrt{T_1 - t}, \tag{7.28}$$

$$\hat{\sigma} = \sigma(T_2 - T_1), \tag{7.29}$$

and where here $B_t(T)$ is the Ho and Lee pure discount bond price.

The Ho and Lee model was originally presented as a discrete time whole yield curve model and was the precursor to the continuous time HJM models. Equation (7.22) is the continuous time limit of the discrete time model. It has a lattice implementation, described by Ho and Lee, and despite its drawbacks is still occasionally used.[2]

---

[2] It is implemented in some commercial packages.

7.4.1   Extended Vasicek Models

This class of one-factor models has the short rate process

$$dr_t = (\theta(t) - a(t)r_t)dt + \sigma(t)dz_t. \tag{7.30}$$

This is (7.21) with $\gamma = 0$. It can be solved in principle. Set

$$K(t) = \exp\left(\int_0^t a(s)ds\right). \tag{7.31}$$

Spot rates can be shown (for instance, Rogers (95) [457]) to be

$$r_t(T) = \frac{A(t,T)}{T-t} + \frac{B(t,T)}{T-t}r_t, \tag{7.32}$$

where

$$B(t,T) = K(t)\int_t^T \frac{1}{K(u)}\,du, \tag{7.33}$$

$$A(t,T) = \int_t^T \frac{1}{K(u)}\int_t^u \left(\theta(s)K(s) - \frac{1}{K(s)}\int_t^s \sigma^2(y)K^2(y)dy\right)ds\,du. \tag{7.34}$$

Extended Vasicek models can be fitted to an initial term structure of volatility, at the same time as fitting to an initial term structure. Suppose that $\sigma_t(\tau)$ is the volatility of the $t + \tau$ maturity spot rate $r_t(\tau)$, so that

$$dr_t(\tau) = \mu_t(\tau)dt + \sigma_t(\tau)dz_t \tag{7.35}$$

for some drift function $\mu_t(\tau)$ and with $\sigma_t(0) = \sigma(t)$. In an extended Vasicek model it is easy to show that

$$\sigma_t(\tau) = \sigma(t)B(t, t + \tau)\tau, \tag{7.36}$$

where $B(t, T)$ is defined by (7.33). If calibrating the model to initial term structures $\sigma_0(\tau)$ and $r_0(\tau)$, equation (7.36) can be used to back out $B(0, T)$. $A(0, T)$ can then be found from (7.32). $a(t)$ can in principle be found from $B(t, T)$ but then $\theta(t)$ and $\sigma(t)$ cannot be uniquely identified from $A(t, T)$. Further information must be provided, or a functional form assumed for $\sigma(t)$, say.

An analysis of the general model is given by Pelsser (96) [436], amongst others. We restrict ourselves here to two special cases.

Special Case 1: a and σ are Constants

This is the extended Vasicek model of Hull and White (93) [294], [295]. r_t reverts to a time-dependent mean $\theta(t)/a$, with the process

$$dr_t = (\theta(t) - ar_t)dt + \sigma\,dz_t. \tag{7.37}$$

Defining

$$\alpha(t) = e^{-at} \left(r_0 + \int_0^t e^{as}\theta(s)ds \right) \tag{7.38}$$

for $t \geq 0$, term structures are given explicitly as

$$r_t(\tau) = A(t, \tau) + B(t, \tau)(r_t - \alpha(t)), \tag{7.39}$$

where $A(t, \tau)$ and $B(t, \tau)$ are

$$A(t, \tau) = -\frac{\sigma^2}{2a^2} \left(\tau - 2\frac{1 - e^{-a\tau}}{a\tau} + \frac{1 - e^{-2a\tau}}{2a\tau} - \frac{1}{a\tau} \int_t^T \alpha(s)ds \right), \tag{7.40}$$

$$B(t, \tau) = \frac{1 - e^{-a\tau}}{a\tau}. \tag{7.41}$$

Jamshidian (89) [308] obtained a closed form formula for the values of bond options in this framework. The price $c_t(T_1, T_2)$ of a European call option on a pure discount bond with strike X is

$$c_t(T_1, T_2) = B_t(T_2)N(d) - XB_t(T_1)N(d - \sigma_p), \tag{7.42}$$

where

$$d = \frac{1}{\sigma_p} \ln \frac{B_t(T_2)}{XB_t(T_1)} + \frac{1}{2}\sigma_p, \tag{7.43}$$

$$\sigma_p = \sigma \frac{1 - e^{-a(T_2 - T_1)}}{a} \left(\frac{1 - e^{-2a(T_1 - t)}}{2a} \right)^{\frac{1}{2}}, \tag{7.44}$$

and $B_t(T)$ are the theoretical extended Vasicek bond prices.

Given an initial term structure $B_0(T)$ and associated instantaneous forward rate curve $f(0, t)$, the $\theta(t)$ that recover these bond prices are given by

$$\theta(t) = \left. \frac{\partial f(0, t)}{\partial t} \right|_t + af(0, t) + \frac{\sigma^2}{2a}(1 - e^{-2at}). \tag{7.45}$$

Special Case 2: All Parameters are Constant

This is the Vasicek model. The short rate process is equivalent to (barring degeneracies)

$$dr_t = \alpha(\tilde{\mu} - r_t)dt + \sigma d\tilde{z}_t, \tag{7.46}$$

where α, $\tilde{\mu}$ and σ are constants. If (7.46) is the process under the EMM, then the term structures are

$$r_t(\tau) = r_\infty + (r_t - r_\infty)\frac{1 - e^{-\alpha\tau}}{\alpha\tau} + \frac{\sigma^2\tau^2}{4\alpha} \left(\frac{1 - e^{-\alpha\tau}}{\alpha\tau} \right)^2, \tag{7.47}$$

where $\tau = T - t$ as usual and

$$r_\infty = \tilde{\mu} - \frac{\sigma^2}{2\alpha^2} \qquad (7.48)$$

is the long rate. If r_t has the process

$$dr_t = \alpha(\mu - r_t)dt + \sigma\,dz_t \qquad (7.49)$$

under the objective measure, with α and μ constant, then $\tilde{\mu} = \mu - \sigma\lambda/\alpha$ for a constant price of risk λ. The long rate r_∞ is now

$$r_\infty = \mu - \frac{\sigma\lambda}{\alpha} - \frac{\sigma^2}{2\alpha^2}. \qquad (7.50)$$

7.4.2 Extended CIR Models

Extended CIR models have $\gamma = 1/2$ in equation (7.21), so the short rate process is

$$dr_t = (\theta(t) - a(t)r_t)dt + \sigma(t)r_t^{\frac{1}{2}}\,dz_t. \qquad (7.51)$$

Spot rates are affine. Writing $\tau = T - t$ we have

$$r_t(\tau) = -\frac{A(t,\tau)}{\tau} - \frac{B(t,\tau)}{\tau}r_t, \qquad (7.52)$$

where $A(t,\tau)$ and $B(t,\tau)$ satisfy the ODEs

$$\frac{\partial A(t,\tau)}{\partial t} = -\theta(t)B(t,\tau), \qquad (7.53)$$

$$\frac{\partial B(t,\tau)}{\partial t} = 1 + a(t)B(t,\tau) - \frac{1}{2}\sigma^2(t)B(t,\tau)^2, \qquad (7.54)$$

subject to the boundary conditions $A(t,0) = B(t,0) = 0$.

When θ, a and σ are constants, we have the Cox, Ingersoll and Ross (CIR) (85) [148] model. The extended case was described by Hull and White (90) [292]. Explicit solutions can be found for $A(\tau)$ and $B(\tau)$:

$$A(\tau) = -\frac{2\theta}{\sigma^2}\ln\left[\frac{\gamma e^{\frac{a\tau}{2}}}{\gamma\cosh\gamma\tau + \frac{1}{2}a\sinh\gamma\tau}\right], \qquad (7.55)$$

$$B(\tau) = \frac{\sinh\gamma\tau}{\gamma\cosh\gamma\tau + \frac{1}{2}a\sinh\gamma\tau}, \qquad (7.56)$$

where $2\gamma = \sqrt{a^2 + 2\sigma^2}$. Writing the objective short rate process as

$$dr_t = \alpha(\mu - r_t)dt + \sigma\sqrt{r_t}\,dz_t, \qquad (7.57)$$

with a market price of risk parameter λ, the value at time t of the European call option $c_t(T_t, T_2)$ with strike X is

$$
c_t(T_1, T_2) = B_t(T_2)\chi^2\left(2r_X(\phi + \psi + B(T_1, T_2)); \frac{4\alpha\mu}{\sigma^2}, \frac{2\phi^2 r_t e^{\gamma(T_1 - t)}}{\phi + \psi + B(T_1, T_2)}\right)
$$

$$
- XB_t(T_1)\chi^2\left(2r_X(\phi + \psi); \frac{4\alpha\mu}{\sigma^2}, \frac{2\phi^2 r_t e^{\gamma(T_1 - t)}}{\phi + \psi}\right). \tag{7.58}
$$

Here χ^2 is the non-central χ^2 distribution and

$$
\gamma^2 = (\alpha + \lambda)^2 + 2\sigma^2, \tag{7.59}
$$

$$
\phi = \frac{2\gamma}{\sigma^2(e^{\gamma(T_1 - t)} - 1)}, \tag{7.60}
$$

$$
\psi = \frac{\alpha + \lambda + \gamma}{\sigma^2}, \tag{7.61}
$$

$$
B(T_1, T_2) = \frac{2\left(e^{\gamma(T_2 - T_1)} - 1\right)}{(\alpha + \gamma + \lambda)\left(e^{\gamma(T_2 - T_1)} - 1\right) + 2\gamma}, \tag{7.62}
$$

and r_X is the short rate value corresponding to the exercise price X, $X = B_{T_1}(T_2 \mid r_X)$.

7.5   EXAMPLES OF n-FACTOR AFFINE MODELS

We describe the Longstaff and Schwartz and the three-factor BDFS models. Longstaff and Schwartz is a well-known two-factor model which has a great deal of flexibility, achieving good calibration to a variety of term structures. BDFS has much less tractability, not having explicit solutions even for the term structure. It contains the two-factor Fong and Vasicek model.

7.5.1   The Longstaff and Schwartz Two-Factor Model

This is an affine model derived in an economic framework (discussed further in Chapter 11). There are two underlying state variables, x_t and y_t, which have an economic interpretation described in Chapter 11 but which is unimportant to us here. The processes for x_t and y_t are

$$
dx_t = (a - bx_t)dt + c\sqrt{x_t}\,dz_{1,t}, \tag{7.63}
$$

$$
dy_t = (d - ey_t)dt + f\sqrt{y_t}\,dz_{2,t}, \tag{7.64}
$$

under the objective measure.

The short rate r_t is a linear function of x_t and y_t, and the short rate volatility v_t, defined by $dr_t\,dr_t = v_t\,dt$, also turns out to be a linear function of x_t and y_t,

$$
r_t = \alpha x_t + \beta y_t, \tag{7.65}
$$

$$
v_t = \alpha^2 x_t + \beta^2 y_t, \tag{7.66}
$$

for constants α and β. Equations (7.65) and (7.66) can be inverted and the processes for r_t and v_t written down in terms of each other:

$$
dr_t = \left((\alpha\gamma + \beta\eta) - \frac{\beta\delta - \alpha\xi}{\beta - \alpha} r_t - \frac{\xi - \delta}{\beta - \alpha} v_t \right) dt
$$

$$
+ \left(\frac{\alpha\beta r_t - \alpha v_t}{\beta - \alpha} \right)^{\frac{1}{2}} dz_{1,t} + \left(\frac{\beta v_t - \alpha\beta r_t}{\beta - \alpha} \right)^{\frac{1}{2}} dz_{2,t} \tag{7.67}
$$

and

$$
dv_t = \left((\alpha^2\gamma + \beta^2\eta) - \frac{\alpha\beta(\delta - \xi)}{\beta - \alpha} r_t - \frac{\beta\xi - \alpha\delta}{\beta - \alpha} v_t \right) dt
$$

$$
+ \left(\frac{\alpha^3\beta r_t - \alpha^3 v_t}{\beta - \alpha} \right)^{\frac{1}{2}} dz_{1,t} + \left(\frac{\beta^3 v_t - \alpha\beta^3 r_t}{\beta - \alpha} \right)^{\frac{1}{2}} dz_{2,t}, \tag{7.68}
$$

for certain constants γ, δ, η and ξ. The Longstaff and Schwartz model can be solved for the prices of pure discount bonds. In terms of r_t and v_t, pure discount bond prices are

$$
B_t(\tau, r_t, v_t) = A^{2\gamma}(\tau) B^{2\eta}(\tau) \exp(\kappa\tau + C(\tau)r_t + D(\tau)v_t) \tag{7.69}
$$

for $\tau = T - t$ and

$$
A(\tau) = \frac{2\varphi}{(\delta + \varphi)(e^{\varphi\tau} - 1) + 2\varphi}, \tag{7.70}
$$

$$
B(\tau) = \frac{2\psi}{(\upsilon + \psi)(e^{\psi\tau} - 1) + 2\psi}, \tag{7.71}
$$

$$
C(\tau) = \frac{\alpha\varphi(e^{\psi\tau} - 1)B(\tau) - \beta\psi(e^{\varphi\tau} - 1)A(\tau)}{\varphi\psi(\beta - \alpha)}, \tag{7.72}
$$

$$
D(\tau) = \frac{-\varphi(e^{\psi\tau} - 1)B(\tau) + \psi(e^{\varphi\tau} - 1)A(\tau)}{\varphi\psi(\beta - \alpha)}, \tag{7.73}
$$

with $\upsilon = \lambda + \xi$, $\varphi = \sqrt{2\alpha + \delta^2}$, $\psi = \sqrt{2\beta + \upsilon^2}$ and $\kappa = \gamma(\delta + \varphi) + \eta(\upsilon + \psi)$, where λ is a market price of risk.

Specimen term structures are shown in Figure 7.1. These curves were achieved by altering only the value of the state variable v_t and the market price of risk, λ, other parameters remaining constant. A wide range of shapes is possible, making this a fairly flexible model.

The model has six underlying parameters, α, β, γ, δ, η and ξ. The market price of risk λ appears only in combination with ξ.

There are also explicit solutions for the values of bond options. Let X be the strike price of the European call option that matures at time T. The price of the call option price $c_t(T_1, T_2)$ is

$$
c_t(T_1, T_2) = B_t(T_2)\Psi(\theta_1, \theta_2; 4\gamma, 4\eta, \omega_1, \omega_2) - XB_t(T_1)\Psi(\theta_3, \theta_4; 4\gamma, 4\eta, \omega_3, \omega_4), \tag{7.74}
$$

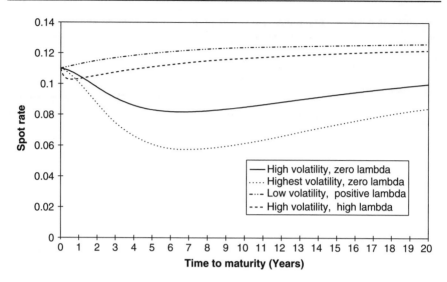

Figure 7.1   Longstaff and Schwartz specimen term structures

where $B_t(T)$ is the price of a zero coupon bond maturing at time T, and Ψ is a bivariate, non-central χ^2 distribution. The rest of the factors are defined as follows:

$$\theta_1 = \frac{4\zeta\phi^2}{\alpha(e^{\phi T_1} - 1)^2 A(T_2)}, \tag{7.75}$$

$$\theta_2 = \frac{4\zeta\psi^2}{\beta(e^{\psi T_1} - 1)^2 B(T_2)}, \tag{7.76}$$

$$\theta_3 = \frac{4\zeta\phi^2}{\alpha(e^{\phi T_1} - 1)^2 A(T_1)A(T_2 - T_1)}, \tag{7.77}$$

$$\theta_4 = \frac{4\zeta\psi^2}{\beta(e^{\psi T_1} - 1)^2 B(T_1)B(T_2 - T_1)}, \tag{7.78}$$

and

$$\omega_1 = \frac{4\phi e^{\phi T_1} A(T_2)(\beta r_t - v_t)}{\alpha(\beta - \alpha)(e^{\phi T_1} - 1)A(T_2 - T_1)}, \tag{7.79}$$

$$\omega_2 = \frac{4\psi e^{\psi T_1} B(T_2)(v_t - \alpha r_t)}{\beta(\beta - \alpha)(e^{\psi T_1} - 1)B(T_2 - T_1)}, \tag{7.80}$$

$$\omega_3 = \frac{4\phi e^{\phi T_1} A(T_1)(\beta r_t - v_t)}{\alpha(\beta - \alpha)(e^{\phi T_1} - 1)}, \tag{7.81}$$

$$\omega_4 = \frac{4\psi e^{\psi T_1} B(T_1)(v_t - \alpha r_t)}{\beta(\beta - \alpha)(e^{\psi T_1} - 1)}, \tag{7.82}$$

where

$$\zeta = \alpha(T_2 - T_1) + 2\gamma \ln A(T_2 - T_1), +2\eta \ln B(T_2 - T_1) - \ln X, \qquad (7.83)$$

$$A(\tau) = \frac{2\phi}{(\delta + \phi)(e^{\phi\tau} - 1) + 2\phi}, \qquad (7.84)$$

$$B(\tau) = \frac{2\psi}{(\xi + \psi)(e^{\psi T_1} - 1) + 2\psi}, \qquad (7.85)$$

$$\phi^2 = 2\alpha^2 + \delta^2, \qquad (7.86)$$

$$\psi^2 = 2\beta^2 + \xi^2. \qquad (7.87)$$

The existence of an explicit bond option formula, however complex, means that it is easy to calibrate to cap prices.

7.5.2   The BDFS Three-Factor Model

The Balduzzi, Das, Foresi and Sundaram (BDFS) (96) [48] model belongs to the three-factor affine family with $\phi = 0$. It is defined by the processes

$$dr_t = \kappa(\mu_t - r_t)dt + \sqrt{v_t}\,dz_{r,t}. \qquad (7.88)$$

$$d\mu_t = \alpha(\beta - \mu_t)dt + \eta\,dz_{\mu,t}, \qquad (7.89)$$

$$dv_t = a(b - v_t)dt + \phi\sqrt{v_t}\,dz_{v,t}, \qquad (7.90)$$

under the objective measure, where r_t is the short rate, μ_t is its mean and v_t is its volatility. $z_{r,t}$ and $z_{v,t}$ are correlated, with correlation coefficient ρ. All other correlations are zero. The parameters for the market prices of risk, λ_r, λ_μ and λ_v are constants.[3]

The BDFS model embeds the Fong and Vasicek model which has a constant mean, μ. BDFS described the model and solved for term structures using numerical methods. For time to maturity τ, pure discount bond prices $P(t, \tau)$ are of the form

$$P(t, \tau \mid r_t, \mu_t, v_t) = A(\tau)\exp(-B(\tau)r_t - C(\tau)\mu_t - D(\tau)v_t), \qquad (7.91)$$

where $P(t, \tau)$ satisfies the PDE

$$rP = (\kappa(\mu_t - r_t) - \lambda_r\sqrt{v_t})P_r + (\alpha(\beta - \mu_t) - \lambda_\mu\eta)P_\mu + (a(b - v_t) - \lambda_v\phi\sqrt{v_t})P_v$$

$$+ \tfrac{1}{2}v_t P_{r,r} + \tfrac{1}{2}\eta^2 P_{\mu,\mu} + \tfrac{1}{2}\phi^2 v_t P_{v,v} + \rho\phi v_t P_{r,v} - P_\tau, \qquad (7.92)$$

where subscripts on P denote differentiation. When (7.91) is substituted into (7.92) the PDE decomposes. It is easy to solve for $B(\tau)$ and $C(\tau)$, obtaining

$$B(\tau) = \frac{1 - e^{-\kappa\tau}}{\kappa}, \qquad (7.93)$$

$$C(\tau) = \frac{1 - e^{-\kappa\tau} + \dfrac{\kappa}{\alpha}e^{-\alpha\tau}(1 - e^{-\alpha\tau})}{(\alpha - \kappa)}, \qquad (7.94)$$

---

[3] In general the prices of risk could be functions of the state variables.

but explicit solutions for $A(\tau)$ and $D(\tau)$ are not known. They satisfy the ODEs

$$\lambda_r B + \tfrac{1}{2} B^2 + aD + \tfrac{1}{2}\phi^2 D^2 + \rho\phi BD + D_\tau + \lambda_v D = 0, \qquad (7.95)$$

$$-\alpha\beta\tau C + \frac{1}{2}\eta^2 C^2 - abAD - \frac{A_\tau}{A} + \lambda_\mu C = 0, \qquad (7.96)$$

where $B \equiv B(\tau)$ and $C \equiv C(\tau)$ as above, with boundary conditions $A(0) = 1$, $D(0) = 0$. Solving (7.95) and (7.96) numerically is quite possible using standard methods.

BDFS term structures are highly flexible, giving rise to hump- and spoon-shaped yield curves. Fong and Vasicek term structures are a special case. Fong and Vasicek yield curves are of comparable flexibility to the Longstaff and Schwartz model, but are evidently less flexible than those of BDFS.

In their original paper Fong and Vasicek gave solutions for spot rates in terms of confluent hypergeometric functions. These functions are not straightforward to compute rapidly[4] and this may have contributed to the mixed reception the model received in the market and the preference given to the Longstaff and Schwartz model.

We shall see in Section 7.6 that the Longstaff and Schwartz and Fong and Vasicek models, along with the two-factor Babbs and Nowman model, represent each of the three distinct categories of two-factor models.

The Chen three-factor model also has explicit solutions but once again they are in terms of functions that are difficult to compute rapidly—Bessel functions, Kummer functions and, again, confluent hypergeometric functions. The interested reader is referred to Chen (96) [126].

The lack of explicit formulae for the BDFS model makes it awkward to calibrate to market data. This is a major disadvantage. It is significantly easier to find numerical solutions for the Fong and Vasicek model because of its reduced dimensionality.

7.5.3 An n-Factor Gaussian Model

Babbs and Nowman (97) [38], (99) [39] investigate an n-factor Vasicek model. It is equivalent to the n-factor Gaussian models of Langetieg (80) [349] and Beaglehole and Tenney (91) [57].

Let $r_t = \mu - \sum_{i=1}^{n} X_{i,t}$, where

$$dX_{i,t} = -\alpha_i X_{i,t}\, dt + \sum_{j=1}^{n} \sigma_{i,j}\, dz_{j,t}, \qquad (7.97)$$

under the objective measure.[5] Suppose that each $X_{i,t}$ has a constant price of risk, λ_i. This system can be solved explicitly. Term structures are of the form

$$r_t(\tau) = A(\tau) + \sum_{i=1}^{n} A_i(\tau)X_{i,t}, \qquad (7.98)$$

---

[4] Selby and Strickland (93) [485] present a fast algorithm.

[5] Babbs and Nowman also analyse the case where parameters of the model are deterministic functions of time.

with $A_i(\tau) = -H(\alpha_i \tau)$, $A(\tau) = r_\infty - w(\tau)$, where

$$r_\infty = \mu + \sum_{i=1}^n \lambda_i \sum_{j=1}^n \frac{\sigma_{j,i}}{\alpha_j} - \frac{1}{2} \sum_{i=1}^n \left(\sum_{j=1}^n \frac{\sigma_{j,i}}{\alpha_j} \right)^2, \tag{7.99}$$

$$w(\tau) = \sum_{i=1}^n H(\alpha_i \tau) \left(\sum_{j=1}^n \lambda_j \frac{\sigma_{i,j}}{\alpha_i} - \sum_{j=1}^n \sum_{k=1}^n \frac{\sigma_{k,j}\sigma_{i,j}}{\alpha_k \alpha_i} \right)$$
$$+ \frac{1}{2} \sum_{i=1}^n \sum_{j=1}^n H((\alpha_i + \alpha_j)\tau) \sum_{k=1}^n \frac{\sigma_{i,k}\sigma_{j,k}}{\alpha_i \alpha_j}, \tag{7.100}$$

and $H(x) = (1 - e^{-x})/x$.

7.6 A GENERAL FRAMEWORK FOR AFFINE MODELS

Section 7.5 described some of the specific affine models that have been investigated and which are used in practice. The discussion was, however, largely *ad hoc*. What is needed is a general framework to enable affine models to be compared and classified. For instance, it is not clear from the presentation so far how it is possible to tell two affine models apart. By a transformation of variables, a model could be represented in two apparently different ways. So how many essentially different affine models are there? An answer to this question has been provided by Dai and Singleton (98) [154] who showed that affine models could be classified according to

1. The number of state variables, and
2. How many of the state variables appear in the volatility matrix.

They find the most general representative of each class, so that every affine model is a restriction of a general type. We shall see that this classification is extremely useful. We can place existing models in a general context, enabling us to determine when, for instance, a given model is over-specified.

This section follows the treatment of Dai and Singleton. We first present their classification and then illustrate it by reference to some of the models we have previously seen.

7.6.1 The Equivalence of Two Affine Models

Suppose that X_t is an n-dimensional vector of state variables, as in the previous section. Dai and Singleton base their classification on processes for X_t that are specified in the form

$$dX_t = \kappa(\theta - X_t)dt + \Sigma V dz_t, \tag{7.101}$$

under the objective measure P, where κ and Σ are constant $n \times n$ matrices and θ is a constant n-dimensional vector. V has the same form as before:

$$V = \begin{pmatrix} \sqrt{\alpha_1 + \beta_1' X_t} & & 0 \\ & \ddots & \\ 0 & & \sqrt{\alpha_n + \beta_n' X_t} \end{pmatrix}. \tag{7.102}$$

To convert to the process for X_t under the EMM we require a price of risk vector $\lambda = (\lambda_1, \ldots, \lambda_n)'$, assumed to be constant. For constants f and g set the short rate to be $r_t = f + g' X_t$. A model is specified by the structure

$$M = (f, g; \kappa, \theta, \Sigma, \alpha, \beta; \lambda). \tag{7.103}$$

Dai and Singleton give criteria for establishing when two models are equivalent, in the sense that they generate identical prices for all interest rate instruments. They show that two models (7.103) are equivalent if they can be transformed into one another by a sequence of operations from the following list.

1. Permuting the elements of X_t gives a model equivalent to M. That is, if π is a permutation of $\{1, \ldots, n\}$ and if M' is the model obtained by permuting the components of g, θ, α and λ by π, and similarly permuting the components of the vectors β_i, $i = 1, \ldots, n$, as well as the position of the β_i in the matrix β, then M' is equivalent to M.
2. Suppose T is a matrix that commutes with V, and T is orthogonal, $T^{-1} = T'$, then

$$M_T = (f, g; \kappa, \theta, \Sigma T', \alpha, \beta; T\lambda) \tag{7.104}$$

    is equivalent to M.
3. Suppose $T = \mathrm{diag}(T_1, \ldots, T_n)$ is diagonal and non-singular, then

$$M_T = (f, g; \kappa, \theta, \Sigma, \underline{\alpha}, \underline{\beta}; T\lambda) \tag{7.105}$$

    is equivalent to M where $\underline{\alpha}_i = T_i^2 \alpha_i$, $\underline{\beta}_i = T_i^2 \beta_i$.
4. Suppose L is a non-singular $n \times n$ matrix, and ψ is an n-dimensional vector. Then

$$M_L = (f - gL^{-1}\psi, L^{-1}g; L\kappa L^{-1}, \psi + L\theta, L, \underline{\underline{\alpha}}, \underline{\underline{\beta}}; \lambda) \tag{7.106}$$

    is equivalent to M where $\underline{\underline{\alpha}}_i = \alpha_i - \beta_i' L^{-1}\psi$, $\underline{\underline{\beta}}_i = L'^{-1}\beta_i$.

It is clear from this list that it may not always be obvious when two models are equivalent. Dai and Singleton give a canonical representative of each equivalence class, and a rule to determine which class any particular model belongs to.

7.6.2 The Classification of Affine Models

For every integer $n \geq 1$ and for each integer $0 \leq m \leq n$, Dai and Singleton show that every affine model is equivalent to a restriction of one of the form $M_m(n)$, where $M_m(n)$ is defined as

$$M_m(n) = (f, g; \kappa_m(n), \theta_m(n), I, \alpha_m(n), \beta_m(n); \lambda), \tag{7.107}$$

where
$$\kappa_m(n) = \begin{pmatrix} \kappa^{1,1} & 0 \\ \kappa^{2,1} & \kappa^{2,2} \end{pmatrix} \qquad (7.108)$$

for $\kappa^{1,1} \in \mathbb{R}^{m \times m}$, $\kappa^{2,1} \in \mathbb{R}^{(n-m) \times m}$, $\kappa^{2,2} \in \mathbb{R}^{(n-m) \times (n-m)}$, and for $m = 0$, $\kappa_0(n)$ is either lower or upper triangular, and

$$\theta_m(n) = \begin{pmatrix} \theta \\ 0 \end{pmatrix}, \qquad \text{where } \theta \in \mathbb{R}^m, 0 \in \mathbb{R}^{n-m},$$

$$\alpha_m(n) = \begin{pmatrix} 0 \\ 1 \end{pmatrix}, \qquad \text{where } 0 \in \mathbb{R}^m, 1 \in \mathbb{R}^{n-m}, \qquad (7.109)$$

$$\beta_m(n) = \begin{pmatrix} I & \beta^{1,2} \\ 0 & 0 \end{pmatrix},$$

where $I \in \mathbb{R}^{m \times m}$ is the identity matrix, and $\beta^{1,2} \in \mathbb{R}^{m \times (n-m)}$. (There are also some restrictions on the allowed values of some parameters.) This representation is not unique, but it is intuitive and easy enough to work with.

n is the number of state variables in the model and m is the number of state variables that appear in the matrix V. For n-factor models there are only $n + 1$ distinct equivalence classes.

One may count the total number of free parameters in each equivalence class of affine model. For $m > 0$ there are $n^2 + n + 1 + m$ free parameters. For $m = 0$ there are $\frac{1}{2}(n + 1)(n + 2)$ free parameters. For three-factor models, $n = 3$, and there are $13 + m$ parameters if $m > 0$, and 10 parameters for $m = 0$. For two-factor models $7 + m$ parameters if $m > 0$, and six parameters for $m = 0$, and for one-factor models $M_0(1)$ has three parameters and $M_1(1)$ has four.

g and λ are mutually determined. Between them there are only n degrees of freedom.

7.6.3 A Classification of One-Factor Models

There are two classes of one-factor model.

1. $M_0(1)$ (Vasicek):
$$dX_{1,t} = -k_{1,1} X_{1,t} \, dt + dz_{1,t}. \qquad (7.110)$$

The process has one parameter, and there are two more for f and g, making three altogether as expected.

2. $M_1(1)$ (CIR):
$$dX_{1,t} = k_{1,1}(\theta_1 - X_{1,t})dt + \sqrt{X_1} \, dz_{1,t}, \qquad (7.111)$$

The process has two parameters, and there are two more for f and g, making four altogether as expected.

7.6.4 A Classification of Two-Factor Models

There are three distinct equivalence classes of two-factor affine models. Let the two state variables be X_1 and X_2. In the notation of Dai and Singleton the three equivalence classes are represented as

1. $M_0(2)$ (Two-factor Vasicek):

$$dX_{1,t} = -k_{1,1}X_{1,t}\,dt + dz_{1,t}, \tag{7.112}$$

$$dX_{2,t} = (-k_{2,1}X_{1,t} - k_{2,2}X_{2,t})dt + dz_{2,t}. \tag{7.113}$$

The processes have three parameters, and there are three more for f and g, making six altogether as expected.

2. $M_1(2)$ (For example, Fong and Vasicek):

$$dX_{1,t} = k_{1,1}(\theta_1 - X_{1,t})dt + \sqrt{X_1}\,dz_{1,t}, \tag{7.114}$$

$$dX_{2,t} = (k_{2,1}(\theta_1 - X_{1,t}) - k_{2,2}X_{2,t})dt + (1 + \beta_{2,1}\sqrt{X_{1,t}})dz_{2,t}. \tag{7.115}$$

The processes have five parameters, plus the three more for f and g, making eight altogether.

3. $M_2(2)$ (For example, Longstaff and Schwartz):

$$dX_{1,t} = (k_{1,1}(\theta_1 - X_{1,t}) + k_{1,2}(\theta_2 - X_{2,t}))dt + \sqrt{X_{1,t}}\,dz_{t,1}, \tag{7.116}$$

$$dX_{2,t} = (k_{2,1}(\theta_1 - X_{1,t}) + k_{2,2}(\theta_2 - X_{2,t}))dt + \sqrt{X_{2,t}}\,dz_{2,t}. \tag{7.117}$$

The processes have six parameters, and there are three more for f and g, making the nine expected.

Particular models, such as Longstaff and Schwartz and Fong and Vasicek, are not usually presented in the forms given above, but they may be transformed to be in these representations. It may be found that the transformed model imposes restrictions on the parameters in the general representation; some parameters may be constrained to have particular values, or there may be dependencies between them. This means that the original model is in some sense over-specified, a fact that may not be apparent in the original specification of the model.

For instance, the Longstaff and Schwartz model has six parameters but $M_2(2)$ has nine. The Longstaff and Schwartz model imposes $f = 0$ and g is a function of other parameters in the model.

7.6.5   A Classification of Three-Factor Models

Dai and Singleton present a classification of three-factor models. There are four three-factor models. Their canonical forms are:

1. $M_0(3)$ (Three-factor Vasicek):

$$dX_{1,t} = -k_{1,1}X_{1,t}\,dt + dz_{1,t}, \tag{7.118}$$

$$dX_{2,t} = (-k_{2,1}X_{1,t} - k_{2,2}X_{2,t})dt + dz_{2,t}, \tag{7.119}$$

$$dX_{3,t} = (-k_{3,1}X_{1,t} - k_{3,2}X_{2,t} - k_{3,3}X_{3,t})dt + dz_{3,t}, \tag{7.120}$$

2. $M_1(3)$ (For example, BDFS (96a) [48]):

$$dX_{1,t} = k_{1,1}(\theta_1 - X_{1,t})dt + \sqrt{X_{1,t}}\,dz_{1,t}, \tag{7.121}$$

$$dX_{2,t} = (k_{2,1}(\theta_1 - X_{1,t}) - k_{2,2}X_{2,t} - k_{3,2}X_{3,t})dt + (1 + \beta_{2,1}\sqrt{X_{1,t}})dz_{2,t}, \tag{7.122}$$

$$dX_{3,t} = (k_{3,1}(\theta_1 - X_{1,t}) - k_{3,2}X_{2,t} - k_{3,3}X_{3,t})dt + (1 + \beta_{3,1}\sqrt{X_{1,t}})dz_{3,t}. \tag{7.123}$$

3. $M_2(3)$ (For example, Chen (96) [126]):

$$dX_{1,t} = (k_{1,1}(\theta_1 - X_{1,t}) + k_{1,2}(\theta_2 - X_{2,t}))dt + \sqrt{X_{1,t}}\,dz_{1,t}, \tag{7.124}$$

$$dX_{2,t} = (k_{2,1}(\theta_1 - X_{1,t}) + k_{2,2}(\theta_2 - X_{2,t}))dt + \sqrt{X_{2,t}}\,dz_{2,t}, \tag{7.125}$$

$$dX_{3,t} = (k_{3,1}(\theta_1 - X_{1,t}) + k_{3,2}(\theta_2 - X_{2,t}) - k_{3,3}X_{3,t})dt$$
$$+ (1 + \beta_{3,1}\sqrt{X_{1,t}} + \beta_{3,2}\sqrt{X_{2,t}})dz_{3,t}. \tag{7.126}$$

4. $M_3(3)$ (Three-factor CIR):

$$dX_{1,t} = (k_{1,1}(\theta_1 - X_{1,t}) + k_{1,2}(\theta_2 - X_{2,t}) + k_{1,3}(\theta_3 - X_{3,t}))dt + \sqrt{X_{1,t}}\,dz_{1,t}, \tag{7.127}$$

$$dX_{2,t} = (k_{2,1}(\theta_1 - X_{1,t}) + k_{2,2}(\theta_2 - X_{2,t}) + k_{2,3}(\theta_3 - X_{3,t}))dt + \sqrt{X_{2,t}}\,dz_{2,t}, \tag{7.128}$$

$$dX_{3,t} = (k_{3,1}(\theta_1 - X_{1,t}) + k_{3,2}(\theta_2 - X_{2,t}) + k_{3,3}(\theta_3 - X_{3,t}))dt + \sqrt{X_3}\,dz_{3,t}. \tag{7.129}$$

Three-factor affine models in the literature are indeed all special cases of these representative forms, although they are all over-specified. When put into the general form, parameters are not necessarily independent. For example, the BDFS (96a) [48] model can be transformed into an $M_1(3)$ model with six parameters set to zero, and one parameter set to -1 (see Dai and Singleton).

Dai and Singleton use a simulated method of moments to fit the four three-factor models to US money market data. They find that the best results were achieved by an $M_1(3)$ model.

8

Market Models and the Heath, Jarrow and Morton Framework

Market models are of increasing importance in interest rate modelling. In this chapter we describe the Heath, Jarrow and Morton (HJM) framework and its relationship to the Brace, Gatarek and Musiela (BGM) market model. We also look at models where only a discrete set of rates is presumed to exist.

In the previous chapter we met the Ho and Lee model. While the Ho and Lee model is not particularly useful in its own right, it did lead on to the widely used Heath, Jarrow and Morton model. In the HJM model an entire curve of forward rates evolves simultaneously, according to a set of volatility curves. In principle any interest rate model with a continuous forward rate curve can be embedded into an HJM model. In this chapter we consider only diffusion models, but in Chapter 10 we look at models with jump–diffusion and more general processes.

Although the HJM model is often described as a model of forward evolution, it can be re-expressed so that the evolution of a spot rate curve, or indeed of a bond price curve, is fundamental. It makes little difference to the theory, although the forward rate setting has greater elegance, but it is convenient to bear the other interpretations in mind. Empirical work, for instance, is often performed on spot rate curves—not on the forward rate curve.

They are many good accounts of the HJM modelling framework. Baxter and Rennie (96) [55] is very approachable, Bjork (96) [65], (98) [66] is very readable. Rebonato (98) [448] also gives a very good account. Our treatment, as in the book as a whole, emphasises implementation issues and practical considerations.

In this chapter we introduce the model and its mathematical framework. After an introduction to the HJM model, giving the forward rate condition for no-arbitrage, we review the types of volatility functions that have been tried out in practice. We look at valuation methods for HJM models in Chapters 13 and 14. In the second half of this chapter we investigate market models and the BGM model. Although the BGM model is contained in the HJM framework, general market models are not.

8.1   INTRODUCTION TO THE HEATH, JARROW AND MORTON MODEL

The HJM model specifies the instantaneous forward rate process as

$$\mathrm{d}f_t(T) = \alpha(t, T, \omega)\mathrm{d}t + \sigma(t, T, \omega)\mathrm{d}z_t, \quad t \leq T, \tag{8.1}$$

where z_t is an $\mathbb{R}^n$ valued Brownian motion and ω is a sample point in the sample space Ω. Because of their dependence on ω, α and σ are path-dependent. Equation 8.1 is specified under the objective measure Q. The process simultaneously evolves each forward rate $f_t(T)$. Given a non-random initial forward curve $f_0(T)$, Equation 8.1 can be integrated as

$$f_t(T) = f_0(T) + \int_0^t \alpha(s, T, \omega)\mathrm{d}s + \int_0^t \sigma(s, T, \omega)\mathrm{d}z_s. \tag{8.2}$$

From (8.1) we can write down the processes followed by spot rates and by pure discount bonds. Bond prices $B_t(T)$ and spot rates $r_t(T)$ are expressed in terms of forward rates as

$$r_t(T) = \frac{1}{T-t} \int_t^T f_t(s)\mathrm{d}s, \tag{8.3}$$

$$B_t(T) = \mathrm{e}^{-\int_t^T f_t(s)\mathrm{d}s}. \tag{8.4}$$

Using these functional relationships the spot rate process and its integrated form are

$$\mathrm{d}r_t = \mathrm{d}f_t(t) = \left(\alpha(t, t, \omega) + \frac{\partial}{\partial T}f_t(T)\bigg|_{t+}\right)\mathrm{d}t + \sigma(t, t, \omega)\mathrm{d}z_t, \tag{8.5}$$

$$r_t = f_0(t) + \int_0^t \alpha(s, t, \omega)\mathrm{d}s + \int_0^t \sigma(s, t, \omega)\mathrm{d}z_s, \tag{8.6}$$

and pure discount bond prices follow the process

$$\frac{\mathrm{d}B_t(T)}{B_t(T)} = (r_t + b(t, T))\mathrm{d}t + a(t, T)\mathrm{d}z_t, \tag{8.7}$$

under the objective measure Q, where

$$a = (a_1, \ldots, a_n)', \tag{8.8}$$

$$a_i(t, T, \omega) = -\int_t^T \sigma_i(t, s, \omega)\mathrm{d}s, \quad i = 1, \ldots, n, \tag{8.9}$$

$$b(t, T, \omega) = -\int_t^T \alpha(t, s, \omega)\mathrm{d}s + \frac{1}{2}\sum_{i=1}^n a_i^2(t, T, \omega). \tag{8.10}$$

$B_t(T)$ is not necessarily Markov; there is a possible dependency upon the past market price history via ω, so that $B_t(T)$ may be path-dependent. For clarity we will often drop an explicit reference to ω from now on, but unless stated otherwise, all functions may be path-dependent.

To rule out arbitrage, bond price drifts and volatilities must be consistent. For any set of n bonds with maturities $S = (S_1, \ldots, S_n)'$, $0 < S_1 < \cdots < S_n$, we set

$$A_S(t) = (a_i(t, S_j))_{i,j=1,\ldots,n}, \tag{8.11}$$

$$\mu_S(t) = (r_t + b(t, S_i))'_{i=1,\ldots,n}. \tag{8.12}$$

S can be regarded as the maturity times of bonds to be used in a hedge portfolio. Instruments can be hedged up to time S_1, the time when the first bond matures.

Heath, Jarrow and Morton (92) [275] showed that the market determined by (8.1) is arbitrage free only if it is possible to find n functions, $\lambda_S(t, \omega) = (\lambda_{1,S}(t, \omega), \ldots, \lambda_{n,S}(t, \omega))'$, such that

$$\mu_S(t) - r_t 1 = -A(t)\lambda_S(t), \tag{8.13}$$

where 1 is the unit vector in $\mathbb{R}^n$ and $\lambda_{i,S}$ is the market price of risk associated with $z_{i,t}$; see also Babbs (89) [35]. The left-hand side of (8.13) is $b(t, T)$ in Equation 8.7 evaluated for the given set of maturities, S.

For fixed $S = (S_1, \ldots, S_n)'$, if $A_S(t) = (a_i(t, S_j))_{i,j=1,\ldots,n}$ is non-singular, then the market is complete and any derivative security can be valued and hedged (up to time S_1).

λ_S is still dependent on the choice of the maturity set S. One would like λ_S to be independent of the choice of S; that is, for all maturity sets S, T,

$$\lambda_S(t) = \lambda_T(t), \quad 0 \le t < \min(S_1, T_1). \tag{8.14}$$

If (8.14) holds for all maturity sets S and T, then it does not matter which n bonds you hedge with in a hedging portfolio. Heath, Jarrow and Morton show that this intuitively sensible outcome holds if and only if for all maturity sets S,

$$\alpha(t, T) = \sum_{i=1}^{n} \sigma_i(t, T) \int_t^T \sigma_i(t, s) \mathrm{d}s - \sum_{i=1}^{n} \sigma_i(t, T)\lambda_{i,S}\sigma_i(t), \tag{8.15}$$

where $\alpha(t, T)$ and $\sigma_i(t, T)$, $i = 1, \ldots, n$, are the coefficient functions in the forward rate process under the objective measure Q. This follows directly from (8.13) (modulo certain technical conditions). Equation 8.15 is called the 'Forward Rate Drift Condition'; α, σ and λ_S must be mutually consistent. When (8.15) holds the price of the risk function is unique, $\lambda_S(t) \equiv \lambda(t)$. To transform to the EMM P, set $\lambda(t) \equiv 0$.

One may sometimes start a modelling exercise by writing down a set of processes under the objective measure Q. To transform to a pricing measure P one incorporates a price of risk. For HJM models setting the price of risk to zero takes us from the drift under the objective measure Q to the drift under the EMM P. In the HJM framework, the processes (8.1), (8.5), (8.7) and (8.15) are all under the objective measure Q. Separating out the price of risk $\lambda(t)$ defined by Equation 8.13 gives us the relationship (8.15) satisfied by $\alpha(t, T)$ and $\sigma(t, s)$ under Q, so setting $\lambda(t)$ to zero takes us to the relationship satisfied by the drift and volatility under the EMM P.

A consequence of this is that in the HJM framework one does not have to separately model a price of risk (unless one is calibrating to time series data). The preferred calibration method is to current cross-sectional market prices, so the price of risk is marginalised.

8.1.1   Example: Ho and Lee

Suppose $df_t(T) = \alpha(t, T)dt + \sigma(t, T)dz_t$, with $n = 1$ and $\sigma(t, T) \equiv \sigma > 0$, constant. This gives us the Ho and Lee model in continuous time. Suppose the price of risk is some arbitrary function $\lambda(t)$. If the forward rate drift condition is satisfied, so that

$$\alpha(t, T) = -\sigma\lambda(t) + \sigma^2(T - t), \quad \text{for all } T > t, \tag{8.16}$$

and other technical conditions are satisfied, then under the EMM P, setting $\lambda(t) = 0$, one finds

$$r_t = f_0(t) + \sigma^2 \frac{t^2}{2} + \sigma\tilde{z}_t, \tag{8.17}$$

$$f_t(T) = f_0(T) + \sigma^2 t\left(T - \frac{t}{2}\right) + \sigma\tilde{z}_t, \tag{8.18}$$

where $\tilde{z}_t$ is a P-Wiener process. It is clear that either r_t or $f_t(T)$ may be negative with positive probability.

Bond prices are a function of forward rates

$$B_t(T) = \exp\left(-\int_t^T f_t(s)ds\right). \tag{8.19}$$

Substituting (8.18) into (8.19) we find bond prices as functions of the current value of $\tilde{z}_t$:

$$B_t(T) = \frac{B_0(T)}{B_0(t)} \exp\left(-\frac{\sigma^2}{2} Tt(T - t) - \sigma(T - t)\tilde{z}_t\right). \tag{8.20}$$

Pricing instruments such as European call prices is now easy. The European call option $c_t(T_1, T_2)$ has payoff $c_{T_1} = \max(B_{T_1}(T_2) - X, 0)$ at time T_1. Its value at time $t < T_1$ is

$$c_t(T_1, T_2) = \tilde{\mathbb{E}}_t\left[\max(B_{T_1}(T_2) - X, 0)\frac{p_t}{p_T}\right], \tag{8.21}$$

where p_t is the accumulator account numeraire, $p_t = \exp(\int_0^t r_s ds)$. Evaluating the expectation one finds that

$$c_t(T_1, T_2) = B_t(T_2)N(d_1) - XB_t(T_1)N(d_2), \tag{8.22}$$

where

$$d_1 = \frac{1}{\sigma(T_2 - T_1)(T_1 - t)^{\frac{1}{2}}} \ln\frac{B_t(T_2)}{XB_t(T_1)} + \frac{1}{2}\sigma(T_2 - T_1)(T_1 - t)^{\frac{1}{2}}, \tag{8.23}$$

$$d_2 = d_1 - \sigma(T_2 - T_1)(T_1 - t)^{\frac{1}{2}}, \tag{8.24}$$

and $B_t(T)$ are the Ho and Lee pure discount bond prices. This is a special case of the Gaussian bond option formula given in Section 8.2.1.

8.2 VOLATILITY FUNCTIONS IN HJM

To implement an HJM model two things are needed. The first is a practical method to obtain prices from the model, and the second is the volatility functions $\sigma(t, T, \omega)$. The former problem is of great practical significance. We deal with it in the relevant chapters. The latter problem concerns us here. In practice, to avoid unnecessary complexity, it is usual, if not inevitable, for $\sigma(t, T, \omega)$ to be Markov, i.e. to depend on ω only through things observed at time t. There are four distinct approaches. Volatility functions can be specified as

1. Standard functional forms,
2. General Gaussian functions, i.e. volatility functions giving Gaussian forward rate processes,
3. Functions giving Markov spot rates,
4. Functions implied from option prices, for instance a BGM model calibrated to caps and swaptions.

The consequences of the choice of volatility specification are enormous. A Gaussian specification may lead, for simpler options, to explicit formulae. A Markov specification is likely to result in valuations using approximate trees. In the general case when $\sigma(t, T, \omega)$ is not Markov, it may be possible to value even simple options only by using difficult simulations or non-recombining trees.

We examine the first three specifications here. Principal Components Analysis (PCA), which obtains Gaussian volatilities from historical time series data and from implied covariance matrices, is discussed in Chapter 16.

Standard Functional Forms

Several standard functional forms for $\sigma(t, T, \omega)$ have been investigated. Only the first two listed below have been used much in practice. In fact a common type of implementation would use several volatility functions, one a constant, and the others of type (2) below, with various pairs of values for (σ, λ).

1. $\sigma(t, T, \omega) \equiv \sigma$, a constant.
   This is a Ho and Lee type volatility. It is tractable but unrealistic. Flesaker (93) [222] tested it on Eurodollar futures and futures option data but it was convincingly rejected.
2. $\sigma(t, T, \omega) = \sigma e^{-\lambda(T-t)}$, σ, λ constants.
   This is a Vasicek type volatility. Like the Ho and Lee volatility, it is tractable but unrealistic, although it performs better than a constant volatility (Gibson et al. (95) [248]).
3. $\sigma(t, T, \omega) = \sigma \sqrt{r_t}\, 4\delta^2 e^{\delta(T-t)}/(\phi(e^{\delta(T-t)} - 1) + 2\delta)^2$, δ, ϕ constants.
   This is a CIR volatility function. Spot rates are still Markovian with this specification.
4. Miscellaneous: $\sigma(t, T, \omega) = \sigma f$, $\sigma \sqrt{f}$, $\sigma_0 + \sigma_1(T - t)$, $(\sigma_0 + \sigma_1(T - t))f$.
   These various functional forms were compared by Amin and Morton (94) [14]. All were rejected.

Functional forms involving the forward rates $f_t(T)$ give non-Markovian spot rates, with all the problems that entails, with little or no benefit. BGM models (Section 8.3) use volatilities of the form $\sigma(t, T, \omega) = \gamma(t, T)f_t(T)$, where $\gamma(t, T)$ is implied from cap and swaption data and $f_t(T)$ is a market rate. These functions work very well.

Markov Functional Forms

Markov functional forms for $\sigma(t, T, \omega)$ are those that result in Markov spot rates. Jeffrey (94) [319], (95) [320] found sufficient and necessary conditions for Markov spot rates. Other authors such as Hull and White (93) [294], Carverhill (94) [120] and Au and Thurston (94) [30] have also investigated Markov interest rate processes and Markov versions of HJM models.

To be Markov $\sigma(t, T, \omega)$ may be a function of ω only via the short rate r_t. Jeffrey's conditions are:

1. The functions $\theta(r, t)$ and $h(t, T)$ must exist such that

$$\sigma(r_t, t, T) \int_t^T \sigma(r_t, t, s) \mathrm{d}s = \frac{\sigma(r_t, t, T)}{\sigma(r_t, t, t)} \theta(r, t) + \frac{\partial}{\partial t} \int_0^{r_t} \frac{\sigma(m, t, T)}{\sigma(m, t, t)} \mathrm{d}m$$

$$+ h(t, T) + \frac{1}{2}\sigma^2(r_t, t, t)\frac{\partial}{\partial t}\left(\frac{\sigma(r_t, t, T)}{\sigma(r_t, t, t)}\right). \quad (8.25)$$

2. A function $k(T)$ must exist such that

$$f_0(r_t, T) = \int_0^r \frac{\sigma(m, 0, T)}{\sigma(m, 0, 0)} \mathrm{d}m + k(T), \quad (8.26)$$

for $k(T) = -\int_0^T h(s, T)\mathrm{d}s$, where $h(t, T)$ is the function appearing in the first condition.

In fact $\theta(r, t) = (\partial f(r, t, T)/\partial T)|_{T=t}$ is the slope of the forward rate curve at the initial time t.

The first condition guarantees that the model is Markov as it evolves. The second condition guarantees that the initial forward rate curve is consistent with a Markov evolution. If one requires that a model should be able to fit to any initial forward rate curve, then one has the stronger conditions:

1. $\sigma(r_t, t, T) = \xi(t, T)\gamma(r_t, t)$, where $\gamma(r_t, t)$ is the short rate volatility, and
2. $\gamma^2(r_t, t) = a(t)r_t + b(t)$.

There are two cases, depending on whether σ depends on r_t or not.

1. σ is deterministic (so it does not depend on r_t).
    Then $\sigma(t, T) = \sigma(t)\exp(\xi(T) - \xi(t))$, for some function $\xi(t)$, and $\sigma(t)$ is the short rate volatility.
2. σ depends on r_t.

Then $\sigma(r_t, t, T) = c(t, T)\sqrt{a(t)r_t + b(t)}$, where $c(t, T)$ depends on $a(t)$. Initial forward rates are $f_t(r_t, T) = d(T)r_t + k(T)$, where $d(T)$ is determined by $c(t, T)$ and $a(t)$, and $k(T)$ can be freely chosen; see Jeffrey (95) [320].

An analysis of Markovian volatilities is provided by Ritchken and Sankarasubramanian (92) [453], (95) [454], and Li, Ritchken and Sankarasubramanian (95) [351] who use the functional form

$$\sigma(t, T, \omega) = \sigma(r_t, t)e^{-\int_t^T k(s)ds}, \qquad (8.27)$$

where $\sigma(r_t, t)$ is Markovian (it is the short rate volatility), and $k(t)$ is deterministic. For instance, in the Hull and White (93) [295] model, with $dr_t = (\theta(t) - a(t)r_t)dt + \sigma(t)dz_t$, the spot rate volatility function is

$$\sigma(r_t, t, T) = \sigma(t)e^{-\int_t^T a(s)ds} \qquad (8.28)$$

which is of Ritchken and Sankarasubramanian type.

Other authors have proposed and investigated Markovian functional forms. For instance, Mercurio and Moraleda (96) [392] wanted to construct a functional form that has the same hump shape as the term structure of volatility often observed in the market. They proposed the alternative functional forms

$$\sigma(r_t, t, T) = \sigma(1 + \gamma(T - t))e^{-\lambda(T-t)} \qquad (8.29)$$

and

$$\sigma(r_t, t, T) = \sigma r_t^\rho \frac{1 + \gamma T}{1 + \gamma t}e^{-\lambda(T-t)}. \qquad (8.30)$$

Each of these is in Ritchken and Sankarasubramanian form. Mercurio and Moraleda found that although they could match market volatility structures quite well with these functional forms, they had the disadvantage that as t increases, the shape of the hump is not preserved.

Markov functional forms have the advantage that they result in recombining trees, as opposed to non-recombining trees. This results in huge savings in computational complexity (see Chapter 14).

8.2.1   Bond Options in Gaussian HJM Models

When forward rate volatilities are Gaussian it is possible to obtain formulae for some simpler instruments. Suppose that $df_t(T) = \alpha(t, T)dt + \Sigma_{i=1}^n \sigma_i(t, T)dz_{i,t}$, as usual, where $\sigma_i(t, T)$, $i = 1, \ldots, n$, are Gaussian. Set $v_i(t, T) = -\int_t^T \sigma_i(t, s)ds$, $i = 1, \ldots, n$. Then Brenner and Jarrow (93) [97] and Au and Thurston (94) [29] showed that there is a Black's formula for $c_t(T_1, T_2)$,

$$c_t(T_1, T_2) = B_t(T_2)N(d) - XB_t(T_1)N(d - w), \qquad (8.31)$$

where

$$d = \frac{1}{\sqrt{w}} \ln \left(\frac{B_t(T_2)}{XB_t(T_1)} \right) + \frac{1}{2}\sqrt{w}, \tag{8.32}$$

$$w = \sum_{i=1}^{n} \int_{t}^{T_1} (v_i(u, T_2) - v_i(u, T_1))^2 du, \tag{8.33}$$

and the initial forward curve has been fitted to match the market values $B_t(T)$ of PDBs. When $n = 1$ and $\sigma_1(t, T) \equiv \sigma$, a constant, then $v = -\sigma(T - t)$ and $w = \sigma^2(T_1 - T_2)^2(T_1 - t)$, which is just the Ho and Lee bond option formula.

As another special case consider a two-factor Gaussian HJM model in which the volatility functions are

$$\sigma_1(t, T) \equiv \sigma_1, \tag{8.34}$$

$$\sigma_2(t, T) = \sigma_2 e^{-(\lambda/2)(T-t)}, \tag{8.35}$$

where λ, σ_1 and σ_2 are strictly positive constants, and the underlying Wiener processes are uncorrelated. HJM showed that the bond option value is

$$c_t(T_1, T_2) = B_t(T_1)N(d_1) - XB_t(T_2)N(d_2), \tag{8.36}$$

where

$$d_1 = \frac{1}{w} \ln \frac{B_t(T_2)}{XB_t(T_1)} + \frac{1}{2}w, \tag{8.37}$$

$$d_2 = d_1 - w, \tag{8.38}$$

$$w^2 = \sigma^2(T_2 - T_1)^2(T_1 - t) + \frac{4\sigma_2^2}{\lambda^3}(e^{-(\lambda/2)T_2} - e^{-(\lambda/2)T_1})^2(e^{\lambda T_1} - e^{\lambda t}). \tag{8.39}$$

8.2.2 Pricing Methods for HJM Models

We have just seen that when $\sigma(t, T)$ is deterministic it may be possible to obtain explicit formulae. For instance, Au and Thurston (94) [29] find an explicit formula for an option to exchange one bond with another.

When volatilities are Markovian, one can value using recombining lattices. In the general case, though, it will be necessary to use simulation methods. For particular types of volatility function, such as Gaussian volatilities, it may be possible to find 'good' simulations; see Chapter 13.

In cases where simulation techniques cannot be used, for instance for American options, one may be forced to use non-recombining, or bushy, lattices. This is a daunting prospect, although in practice enumeration algorithms may be used to step through the lattice without necessarily having to store information at all the nodes of the tree. Non-recombining lattices can also be used for European instruments where simplifications occur; because only the terminal distribution matters, short-cuts can be used.

Non-recombining lattices are described by Heath, Jarrow and Morton (90) [274] and Heath *et al.* (92) [276] and discussed in Chapter 14. McCarthy and Webber (99) [386] found it possible to accurately price in a three-factor Gaussian HJM framework using a sophisticated implementation of a non-recombining lattice.

8.3 MARKET MODELS

Market models have become very popular in the market in recent years. Practitioners who have for many years been using Black's formulae to price caps and swaptions have been able, with the advent of market models, to content themselves that they were right all along. They can now claim that they are in fact using BGM and not Black's at all. This does not mean that anyone quoting a Black's implied volatility is necessarily using a market model; it all depends on how it is being used.

Market models recover market pricing formulae by the direct modelling of market quoted rates. There are two main approaches.

1. *Derive market quoted rates from an underlying model.* For example, from an underlying Heath, Jarrow and Morton model, Brace, Gatarek and Musiela (97) [88] derive the processes followed by market quoted rates in the HJM framework. They deduce the restrictions necessary in the HJM model to ensure that market quoted rates of a chosen tenor are log-normal. With these restrictions, caplets on rates of that tenor satisfy a Black's formula.
2. *Model market rates directly.* For example, Jamshidian (96) [312], (97) [313], Musiela and Rutkowski (97) [407] or Rutkowski (97) [467]. The approach is to find a numeraire and a measure in which market quoted rates are martingales. Log-normality is imposed directly onto these processes, and Black-like formulae are obtained. A key feature of this approach is that rates other than market rates (of some tenor) may not even exist in the model.

We investigate each approach. First we review the BGM model, following the BGM paper. Then we review general market models, following Rutkowski (97) [467]. Pricing and calibration issues are discussed by Pedersen (98) [434], Mikkelsen (99) [394] and Glasserman and Zhao (98) [249].

8.3.1 Brace–Gatarek–Musiela (BGM)

This is a whole yield curve model, consistent with market pricing practice. It is straightforward to calibrate to caps and swaptions using Black-like formulae.

The underlying concept is that for a particular tenor, τ, market quoted forward rates are required to be log-normal. Because of the way forward rates add up, rates of only one tenor at a time can be log-normal. The tenor τ is fixed once and for all. If these forward rates are log-normal under the pricing measure, then Black's formulae are obtained (for the particular tenor).

BGM models are closely related to the log-r models of Sandmann and Sondermann (94) [471] and Miltersen, Sandmann and Sondermann (97) [399] examined in Chapter 9.

We set τ to be the chosen tenor. We use the following notation:

- $f(t, x)$, the instantaneous forward rate at time t, for time $t + x$;
- $L(t, x)$, the market quoted forward rate at time t for time $t + x$ of tenor τ.

The Process for $L(t, x)$

In an HJM model, under the EMM, suppose that

$$\frac{dB_t(T)}{B_t(T)} = r_t dt - \sigma(t, T - t) dz_t, \tag{8.40}$$

for some vector of bond volatilities, $\sigma(t, x)$, parameterised in time to maturity x, and a d-dimensional Wiener process z_t. We write $D(t, x) = B_t(T - t)$ for the value at time t of the PDB with time to maturity x. The process for $D(t, x)$ is

$$\frac{dD(t, x)}{D(t, x)} = (r_t - f(t, x))dt + \sigma(t, x)dz_t \tag{8.41}$$

under the EMM. The process for the forward rates $f(t, x)$ is

$$df(t, x) = \alpha(t, x)dt + \frac{\partial \sigma(t, x)}{\partial x}dz_t, \tag{8.42}$$

where

$$\alpha(t, x) = \frac{\partial f(t, x)}{\partial x} + \frac{1}{2}\frac{\partial}{\partial x}|\sigma(t, x)|^2. \tag{8.43}$$

In terms of instantaneous forward rates the market quoted forward rate is

$$1 + \tau L(t, x) = \exp\left(\int_x^{x+\tau} f(t, u)du\right), \tag{8.44}$$

so that $L(t, x)$ is the market quoted rate corresponding to the continuously compounded forward rate

$$f(t, t + x, t + x + \tau) = \frac{1}{\tau}\int_x^{x+\tau} f(t, u)du. \tag{8.45}$$

We require that $L(t, x)$ has a log-normal process,

$$dL(t, x) = \mu(t, x)dt + \gamma(t, x)L(t, x)dz_t, \tag{8.46}$$

where $\gamma(t, x)$ is a d-dimensional vector, for some drift $\mu(t, x)$. BGM show that $\mu(t, x)$ must have the form:

$$\frac{\partial}{\partial x}L(t, x) + L(t, x)\gamma(t, x)\sigma(t, x) + \frac{\tau L^2(t, x)}{1 + \tau L(t, x)}|\gamma(t, x)|^2, \tag{8.47}$$

where $\sigma(t, x)$ is related to $\gamma(t, x)$ by

$$\sigma(t, x) = \begin{cases} 0, & 0 \leq x \leq \tau, \\ \sum_{k=1}^{\lfloor \frac{x}{\tau} \rfloor} \frac{\tau L(t, x - k\tau)}{1 + \tau L(t, x - k\tau)}\gamma(t, x - k\tau), & \tau \leq x. \end{cases} \tag{8.48}$$

Expressions (8.47) and (8.48) give the conditions under which market quoted forward rates of tenor τ are log-normal in the HJM framework. Given $\sigma(t, x)$ one gets $\gamma(t, x)$ and vice versa.[1]

Valuing a Cap

BGM derive cap prices in their framework. Consider a cap with cashflows p_i at times $t_i = t_0 + i\tau$, $i = 1, \ldots, n$, where

$$p_i = \tau \max(0, L(t_{i-1}, 0) - L_X), \tag{8.49}$$

for some exercise rate L_X. The BGM value of the cap at time $t < t_0$ is

$$c(t) = \sum_{i=1}^{n} c_i(t), \tag{8.50}$$

where the value $c_i(t)$ of each caplet is given by a Black's formula

$$c_i(t) = \tau P(t, t_i)(L(t, t_{i-1} - t)N(d_1) - L_X N(d_2)), \tag{8.51}$$

where

$$d_1 = \frac{1}{\sigma_i \sqrt{t_{i-1} - t}} \ln \frac{L(t, t_{i-1} - t)}{L_X} + \frac{1}{2}\sigma_i \sqrt{t_{i-1} - t}, \tag{8.52}$$

$$d_2 = d_1 - \sigma_i \sqrt{t_{i-1} - t} \tag{8.53}$$

and

$$\sigma_i^2 = \frac{1}{t_{i-1} - t} \int_t^{t_{i-1}} |\gamma(s, t_{i-1} - s)|^2 ds. \tag{8.54}$$

With this landmark result BGM, together with Miltersen, Sandmann and Sondermann, succeeded in justifying the use of Black's formula, confounding a decade of academic snootiness.

Equation 8.51 is only the beginning of the modelling procedure. The heart of the BGM model is to calibrate the functions $\gamma(t, x)$ to observed Black's implied volatilities via (8.54).

Valuing a Swaption

Consider a payer swaption maturing at time t_0, with an exercise rate L_S, to receive the value of underlying forward payer swap. The cashflows to the underlying forward payer swap are p_i at time $t_i = t_0 + i\tau$, $i = 1, \ldots, n$, where

$$p_i = \tau(L(t_{i-1}, 0) - L_X), \tag{8.55}$$

---

[1] We ignore certain technical conditions. Brace, Gatarek and Musiela (97) [88] contains the details.

where L_X is the swap rate at time t_0, and the value v of the swaption at maturity is

$$v = \tau P \max(0, L_X - L_S),\tag{8.56}$$

$$P = \sum_{i=1}^{n} P(t, t_i).\tag{8.57}$$

The cashflows from the fixed leg of a swap at a swap rate L_S are

$$c_i = \begin{cases} \tau L_S, & i = 1, \ldots, n-1, \\ 1 + \tau L_S, & i = n. \end{cases}\tag{8.58}$$

BGM define the 'correlation function' $\Delta_{i,j}$ as

$$\Delta_{i,j} = \int_t^{t_0} \gamma(s, t_{i-1} - s)\gamma(s, t_{j-1} - s)\mathrm{d}s, \quad i, j = 1, \ldots, n,\tag{8.59}$$

and suppose it is possible to approximate $\Delta_{i,j}$ reasonably accurately as the outer product of a vector Γ_i, $i = 1, \ldots, n$, with itself:

$$\Delta_{i,j} = \Gamma_i \Gamma_j.\tag{8.60}$$

BGM then find an approximate value for the swaption at time $t < t_0$. The approximate swaption value $\tilde{v}$ is

$$\tilde{v}(t) = \sum_{i=1}^{n} v_i(t),\tag{8.61}$$

where

$$v_i(t) = \tau P(t, t_i)(L(t, t_{i-1} - t)N(h_i) - L_S N(h_i - \Gamma_i)),\tag{8.62}$$

where $h_i = -s_0 - d_i + \Gamma_i$ for

$$d_i = \sum_{j=1}^{i} \frac{\tau L(t, t_{j-1} - t)}{1 + \tau L(t, t_{j-1} - t)}\Gamma_j,\tag{8.63}$$

and s_0 solves

$$\sum_{i=1}^{n} c_i \left(\prod_{j=1}^{i} \left(1 + \tau L(t, t_{j-1} - t) \exp\left(\Gamma_j(s_0 + d_j) - \frac{1}{2}\Gamma_j^2\right)\right) \right)^{-1} = 1,\tag{8.64}$$

where c_i are given by (8.58). BGM report that the approximation is quite accurate in practice.

Mis-Matched Tenors

The formula assumes that rates of tenor τ are log-normal. If rates of tenor τ are log-normal then rates of other tenors cannot be. In practice caps and swaptions are based on rates of different tenors. Table 8.1 gives the tenors of the rates underlying caps and swaptions in several major markets.

Table 8.1 Cap and swaption tenors

Tenor, τ	Caps	Swaptions
US, UK, Japan	$\frac{1}{4}$	$\frac{1}{2}$
Germany	$\frac{1}{4}$	1

BGM are able to modify their approximate swaption formula to take this discrepancy into account. They assume that the swaption tenor is a multiple k of the cap tenor, and take the cap rate tenor to be log-normal. Caps are still priced using Black's formula. BGM obtain a modified formula for swaptions.

The Modified Swaption Formula

Suppose the swaption tenor is a multiple k of the cap tenor, for instance for USD, GBP and JPY, $k = 2$, and for DEM, $k = 4$, as illustrated in Figure 8.1.

The forward swap rate is

$$L_X^0 = \frac{P(t, t_0) - P(t, t_{kn})}{\sum_{i=1}^{n} \tau P(t, t_{ki})}. \tag{8.65}$$

The cashflows from the fixed leg of a swap at a swap rate L_S are

$$c_i^k = \begin{cases} k\tau L_S, & i = 1, \ldots, n - 1, \\ 1 + k\tau L_S, & i = n. \end{cases} \tag{8.66}$$

The modified 0approximate BGM swaption formula for the value $\hat{v}$ of the swaption is

$$\hat{v}(t) = \sum_{i=1}^{n} v_i(t), \tag{8.67}$$

where

$$v_i(t) = \tau \sum_{j=k(i-1)+1}^{ki} \left\{ P(t, t_j) L(t, t_{j-1} - t) N \left(-s_0^k - d_j + \Gamma_j \right) \right.$$

$$\left. - P(t, t_{kj}) k L_S N \left(-s_0^k - d_{kj} \right) \right\}, \tag{8.68}$$

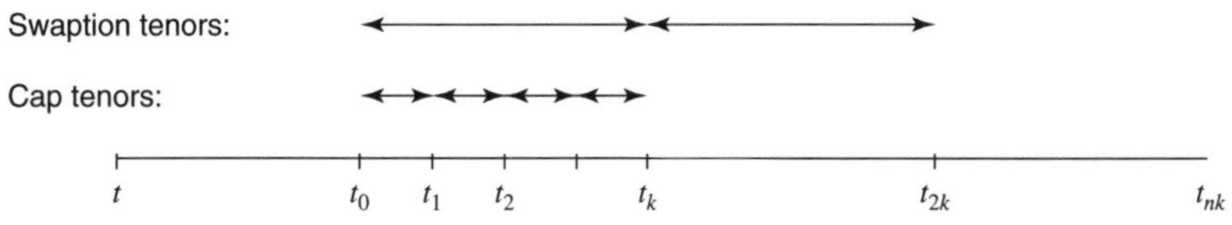

Swaption tenors:

Cap tenors:

Figure 8.1 Swaption and caplet tenors

where

$$d_i = \sum_{j=1}^{i} \frac{\tau L(t, t_{j-1} - t)}{1 + \tau L(t, t_{j-1} - t)} \Gamma_j, \tag{8.69}$$

and s_0^k solves

$$\sum_{i=1}^{n} c_i^k \left(\prod_{j=1}^{ki} \left(1 + \tau L(t, t_{j-1} - t) \exp \left(\Gamma_j \left(s_0^k + d_j \right) - \frac{1}{2} \Gamma_j^2 \right) \right) \right)^{-1} = 1, \tag{8.70}$$

Γ_i is the approximate decomposition of the 'correlation function' and c_i^k are given by (8.66).

How good are the formulae? This breaks down into two separate questions.

- *How good is the approximation?* BGM compare the approximate formula to accurate prices found by a simulation procedure. The approximation is very good (within spreads).
- *Are swaptions priced consistently with caps?* Yes, within the approximation.

Using BGM

BGM has to be calibrated to cap and swaption prices. This, of course, is usually to current prices when enough are available, but historical forward rate correlations may need to be incorporated. It is necessary to make further assumptions about the structure of $\gamma(t, x)$. For example, in their paper BGM assume that $\gamma(t, x)$ takes the form

$$\gamma(t, x) = f(t)(\gamma_1(x), \gamma_2(x)), \tag{8.71}$$

a two-factor system.

From caplets and cap prices one may read off Black's implied volatilities σ_i. A forward–forward volatility curve can be backed out using the techniques described in Chapter 3. The vector Γ_i can be approximated from swaption prices. This is sufficient information to back out $\gamma(t, x)$, suitably regularised.

Now we are ready to price anything, consistent with market cap and swaption prices, using, at worst, Monte Carlo methods.

8.4 GENERAL MARKET MODELS

Jamshidian (97) [313], (96) [312], Musiela and Rutkowski (97) [407], and Rutkowski (97) [467], building on Miltersen, Sandmann and Sondermann (97) [399] and Sandmann and Sondermann (94) [471], have developed a set of models which takes market quoted prices and rates and models them directly, without the need for rates of other maturities. We find a numeraire and a measure in which market quoted rates are martingales. Underlying instantaneous rates are irrelevant; they may not even be defined.

8.4.1   The Structure of the Model

Our treatment follows Rutkowski (97) [467] and Jamshidian (97) [313]. Suppose there is a fixed set of reset dates,

$$0 = T_0 < \cdots < T_M = T^*, \tag{8.72}$$

for a fixed terminal date T^*. The terminal measure, the T^*-forward measure, will be used as a reference measure. The reset intervals,

$$\tau_j = T_j - T_{j-1}, \tag{8.73}$$

define the tenor structure of the model. The premise is that cashflows in the market occur only on reset dates. We shall assume that there are bonds $B_t(T_j)$ for each reset date, and that caps and swaptions in the market pay off only on dates in the set of reset dates. Our initial measure is the terminal measure—the T^*-forward measure.

We would like to price caplets and caps, on fixed maturity swaps, and swaptions on fixed length swaps. The underlying instruments for these derivatives are forward Libor, fixed maturity swaps and fixed length swaps, respectively.

Libor Rates

The forward Libor rate of tenor τ, $L_\tau(t, T)$, is the market forward rate at time t for the period $[T, T + \tau]$. From our reset structure we have

$$1 + \tau_{j+1} L_{\tau_{j+1}}(t, T_j) = \frac{B_t(T_j)}{B_t(T_{j+1})} \tag{8.74}$$

or

$$L_{\tau_{j+1}}(t, T_j) = \frac{B_t(T_j) - B_t(T_{j+1})}{\tau_{j+1} B_t(T_{j+1})}. \tag{8.75}$$

We drop the τ_{j+1} subscript on $L_{\tau_{j+1}}(t, T_j)$ since it is clear from the reset structure.

Swap Rates

It is necessary to distinguish between fixed maturity and fixed length swap rates. They are distinct underlyings; an American option could be written on either.

The swap rate for a fixed maturity forward start swap, starting at time T_j and finishing at time T_M, is

$$\kappa_t^M(T_j) = \frac{B_t(T_j) - B_t(T_M)}{\tau_{j+1} B_t(T_{j+1}) + \cdots + \tau_M B_t(T_M)}. \tag{8.76}$$

The fixed maturity swap has cashflows of $\kappa_t^M(T_j) - L(t, T_{k-1})$ at times T_k, $k = j + 1, \ldots, M$.

The swap rate for a fixed length forward start swap, starting at time T_j and finishing at time T_{j+K}, is

$$\kappa_t^K(T_j) = \frac{B_t(T_j) - B_t(T_{j+K})}{\tau_{j+1} B_t(T_{j+1}) + \cdots + \tau_{j+K} B_t(T_{j+K})}, \tag{8.77}$$

so that there are cashflows of $\kappa_t^K(T_j) - L(t, T_{k-1})$ at times T_k, $k = j+1, \ldots,$ $j + K$.

Caplets

Caplets are options on $L(t, T_{j-1})$. It is convenient to use $B_t(T_j)$ as numeraire. The equivalent martingale measure, P^{T_j}, is just the T_j-forward measure. Under this measure $B_t(T_k)/B_t(T_j)$ are all martingales. Since

$$L(t, T_j) = \frac{B_t(T_j) - B_t(T_{j+1})}{\tau_{j+1} B_t(T_{j+1})}, \tag{8.78}$$

$L(t, T_j)$ is a martingale under $P^{T_{j+1}}$. To price consistently across the entire tenor structure we need to convert from the reference measure—the T^*-forward measure—to the T_j-forward measure, for each T_j. We need to identify the change of measure dP^{T_j}/dP^* and Wiener processes $z_t^{T_j}$ under P^{T_j}.

Suppose we have identified these for $P^{T_{j+1}}$; we get them for P^{T_j} recursively. To initialise we have that $P^{T_M} \equiv P^*$, by assumption. Suppose we impose log-normality on the forward Libor rates for time T_j under the T_{j+1}-forward measure,

$$dL(t, T_j) = L(t, T_j)\lambda_t(T_j)dz_t^{T_j}, \tag{8.79}$$

for some deterministic volatility $\lambda_t(T_j)$. $\lambda_t(T_j)$ could be read off from Black's implied volatilities for caplets on $L(t, T_j)$. It can be shown that (Rutkowski (97) [467], Musiela and Rutkowski (97) [407])

$$z_t^{T_j} = z_t^{T_{j+1}} - \int_0^t \gamma(u, T_j)du, \tag{8.80}$$

where

$$\gamma(t, T_j) = \frac{\tau_j L(t, T_j)}{1 + \tau_j L(t, T_j)}\lambda_t(T_j). \tag{8.81}$$

Then from Girsanov's theorem,

$$\frac{dP^{T_j}}{dP^{T_{j+1}}} = \exp\left[\int_0^{T_j} \gamma(u, T_j)dz_t^{T_{j+1}} - \frac{1}{2}\int_0^{T_j} |\gamma(u, T_j)|^2 du\right]. \tag{8.82}$$

Hence we can recursively get dP^{T_j}/dP^*. This is all the information needed to price caps in this framework. One obtains formula identical to (8.51).

Fixed Maturity Swaptions

Fixed maturity swaptions are options on $\kappa_t^M(T_j)$. For a numeraire we use

$$H_t^M(T_m) = \sum_{j=m}^M \tau_j B_t(T_j). \tag{8.83}$$

This is an annuity. With this numeraire the equivalent martingale measure, P^{S_m}, has the property that

$$\frac{B_t(T_k)}{H_t^M(T_m)} \tag{8.84}$$

are all martingales. Since

$$\kappa_t^M(T_j) = \frac{B_t(T_j) - B_t(T_M)}{\tau_{j+1}B_t(T_{j+1}) + \cdots + \tau_M B_t(T_M)}, \tag{8.85}$$

$\kappa_t^M(T_j)$ is a martingale under $P^{S_{j+1}}$.

Rutkowski gives a formula for a fixed maturity swaption. We impose log-normality on $\kappa_t^M(T_j)$ under the $P^{S_{j+1}}$-measure,

$$d\kappa_t^M(T_j) = \kappa_t^M(T_j)v_t(T_j)dz_t^{S_{j+1}}, \tag{8.86}$$

for some deterministic volatility $v_t(T_j)$. The value c_t at time t of a T_j maturity swaption, with exercise rate κ, into a fixed maturity date swap, with maturity date T_M is

$$c_t = \sum_{k=j+1}^{M} \tau_k B_t(T_k) \left(\kappa_t^M(T_j)N(d_1) - \kappa N(d_2) \right), \tag{8.87}$$

with

$$d_1 = \frac{1}{\tilde{v}_t(T_j)} \ln \frac{\kappa_t^M(T_j)}{\kappa} + \frac{1}{2}\tilde{v}(T_j), \tag{8.88}$$

$$d_2 = d_1 - \tilde{v}(T_j), \tag{8.89}$$

where

$$\tilde{v}^2(T_j) = \int_t^{T_j} |v_u(T_j)|^2 du. \tag{8.90}$$

Fixed Length Swaptions

Fixed length swaptions are options on $\kappa_t^K(T_j)$. For numeraire use the annuity

$$H_t^K(T_m) = \sum_{j=m}^{j+K} \tau_j B_t(T_j). \tag{8.91}$$

Under the equivalent martingale measure, $P^{S_{m,K}}$, the relative prices

$$\frac{B_t(T_k)}{H_t^K(T_m)} \tag{8.92}$$

are all martingales. Since

$$\kappa_t^K(T_j) = \frac{B_t(T_j) - B_t(T_{j+K})}{\tau_{j+1}B_t(T_{j+1}) + \cdots + \tau_{j+K}B_t(T_{j+K})}, \tag{8.93}$$

$\kappa_t^K(T_j)$ is a martingale under $P^{S_{j+1,K}}$. As before, we impose log-normality on $\kappa_t^K(T_j)$ under the $P^{S_{j+1,K}}$-measure,

$$d\kappa_t^K(T_j) = \kappa_t^K(T_j)v_t(T_j)dz_t^{S_{j+1,K}},\tag{8.94}$$

for some deterministic volatility $v_t(T_j)$. Rutkowski gives a Black's formula for the value c_t at time t of a T_j maturity swaption, with exercise rate κ, into a fixed length swap of length K periods:

$$c_t = \sum_{k=j+1}^{j+K} \tau_k B_t(T_k)\left(\kappa_t^K(T_j)N(d_1) - \kappa N(d_2)\right),\tag{8.95}$$

with

$$d_1 = \frac{1}{\tilde{v}_t(T_j)}\ln\frac{\kappa_t^K(T_j)}{\kappa} + \frac{1}{2}\tilde{v}(T_j),\tag{8.96}$$

$$d_2 = d_1 - \tilde{v}(T_j),\tag{8.97}$$

where

$$\tilde{v}^2(T_j) = \int_t^{T_j} |v_u(T_j)|^2 du.\tag{8.98}$$

8.4.2 Summary

Market models focus in on market quoted instruments. Instantaneous rates are not needed and need not be modelled. However, the models are not general purpose. Different models seem to be required for each type of instrument, and there seem to be compatibility problems between them. It may be hard to aggregate risk.

It seems likely that market models will be increasingly used. Already there are signs that their theory is maturing, following a route taken by other types of model. Jamshidian (99) [314] has recently described a market model in which underlying processes may be semi-martingales rather than simply diffusion processes. We expect to see a further development of these models.

9

Other Interest Rate Models

This chapter examines four remaining categories of interest rate models. We describe

- Consol models
- Price kernel models
- Positive models and
- Non-linear models.

Price kernel models and positive rate models have been of growing importance. The price kernel framework allows many interest rate models to be generated, and is amenable to direct estimation. Positive rate models ensure that interest rates remain positive. The relationship between these two categories of model and the HJM framework has been clarified by Jin and Glasserman (99) [323].

Consol models seem promising, but are less tractable than comparable affine models. Non-linear models have been investigated for a variety of reasons, but are not often used in practice because of problems with tractability.

In Chapter 18 we discuss GARCH based models due to Duan (96a) [176], (96b) [177].

9.1 CONSOL MODELS

Consol models stem from early attempts to include a long rate into an interest rate model. Affine yield models allow spot rates of long maturities to be related to the state variables of the model, but before affine models were developed it was attractive to take the Consol rate as a surrogate for the long rate, and to use the Consol rate as a state variable.

Consols are perpetual coupon bonds. Their yield to maturity is the Consol rate. Market Consols have discrete coupons and are usually callable. For modelling purposes some idealised assumptions are made. The Consol rate l_t is assumed to be the yield to maturity on a perpetual, non-callable bond, with continuous coupons paid at a constant rate c per unit time. The price B_∞ of the idealised Consol in terms of c and l_t is

$$B_\infty = \int_t^\infty c e^{-l_t s} \, ds = \frac{c}{l_t}. \tag{9.1}$$

We immediately suppose that $c = 1$.

As well as being a surrogate for a long rate, the Consol bond is traded in the market so that B_∞ is observed as a market price. Since B_∞ is a function only of the state variable l_t, it is possible to obtain an expression for the price of risk λ_t of l_t—it does not have to be estimated separately.

The first Consol models were due to Brennan and Schwartz (79) [93] and Schaefer and Schwartz (84) [478]. Interest in these models waned when Hogan (93) [283] showed that a specific form of a process assumed by Brennan and Schwartz produced an unstable model in which rates went to $+\infty$ with probability 1. Although the general framework remained valid, further work was deterred.

In a no-arbitrage framework care must be taken that the process followed by the Consol rate is compatible with the short rate process. Duffie, Ma and Yong (95) [184] found conditions for compatibility of the short rate and Consol rate processes. Delbaen (93) [164] investigated compatibility in a CIR framework. Recently several papers have appeared that explore Consol models further. Rhee (99) [451] investigated a three-factor Consol model with stochastic volatility, extending the Schaefer and Schwartz model. See also a model of Walter described by Buhler *et al.* (95) [107]. Rebonato (98) [448] describes a two-factor Consol model.

9.1.1 The Brennan and Schwartz Model

The Brennan and Schwartz (79) [93] Consol model has two state variables, l_t and r_t, with processes

$$\mathrm{d}r_t = \mu_r(r_t, l_t)\mathrm{d}t + \sigma_r(r_t, l_t)\mathrm{d}z_{r,t}, \tag{9.2}$$

$$\mathrm{d}l_t = \mu_l(r_t, l_t)\mathrm{d}t + \sigma_l(r_t, l_t)\mathrm{d}z_{l,t}, \tag{9.3}$$

under the objective measure Q. The two-factor differential equation satisfied by the prices B of derivative securities in this model is

$$rB = \frac{1}{2}\sigma_r^2\frac{\partial^2 B}{\partial r^2} + \sigma_{l,r}\frac{\partial^2 B}{\partial r\partial l} + \frac{1}{2}\sigma_l^2\frac{\partial^2 B}{\partial l^2} + (\mu_r - \lambda_r\sigma_r)\frac{\partial B}{\partial r} + (\mu_l - \lambda_l\sigma_l)\frac{\partial B}{\partial l} + \frac{\partial B}{\partial t}, \tag{9.4}$$

where $\sigma_{l,r} = \rho_{l,r}\sigma_l\sigma_r$ is the covariance between $z_{r,t}$ and $z_{l,t}$ whose correlation is $\rho_{l,r}$. λ_r and λ_l are the prices of risk for the short rate and the Consol rate, respectively, adjusting the drifts to those under the EMM. One now specifies functional forms for the drifts and volatilities, and for the short rate price of risk, λ_r. An expression can be found for the price of risk of the Consol rate.

The Price of Risk, λ_l

$B_\infty \equiv B_\infty(l_t)$ is a function of the state variable l_t. By Itō's lemma it has the process

$$\mathrm{d}B_{\infty,t} = \left(\frac{\partial B_\infty}{\partial t} + \mu_l\frac{\partial B_\infty}{\partial l} + \frac{1}{2}\sigma_l^2\frac{\partial^2 B_\infty}{\partial l^2}\right)\mathrm{d}t + \sigma_l\frac{\partial B_\infty}{\partial l}\mathrm{d}z_{l,t} \tag{9.5}$$

$$\equiv \mu_B B_{\infty,t}\,\mathrm{d}t + \sigma_B B_{\infty,t}\,\mathrm{d}z_{l,t}, \tag{9.6}$$

where $\partial B_\infty/\partial t = 1$ since B_∞ pays a continuous unit dividend. Because B_∞ is traded $\lambda_l = (\mu_B - r)/\sigma_B$. Substituting for the derivatives of $B_\infty(l_t) = 1/l_t$, one finds that

$$\lambda_l = \frac{\mu_l + rl - l^2}{\sigma_l} - \frac{\sigma_l}{l}. \tag{9.7}$$

Specific Consol Models

The functional forms chosen by Brennan and Schwartz for μ_r, σ_r, μ_l and σ_l are unstable in that both r_t and l_t rapidly go to infinity, but it is easy to find more appropriate functional forms that work. Duffie, Ma and Yong show that under certain conditions the volatility function σ_l must be compatible with the short rate process to prevent arbitrage.[1] However, the conditions are not strong, in practical terms, and do not seem to prevent the development of effective Consol rate models.

9.1.2   The Schaefer and Schwartz Model

This is a two-factor model, for once without the short rate as a factor. The factors are the Consol rate l_t and the spread s_t between the long and the short rates. The processes for the factors are

$$dl_t = \mu_l\,dt + \sigma_l\sqrt{l_t}\,dz_{l,t}, \tag{9.8}$$

$$ds_t = \alpha(\mu - s_t)dt + \sigma_s\,dz_{s,t}, \tag{9.9}$$

under the objective measure, where $z_{l,t}$ and $z_{s,t}$ are assumed to be uncorrelated (arguably an empirically plausible assumption), and for some drift μ_l. Pure discount bond prices $B_t(T)$ satisfy the PDE

$$(l_t + s_t)B = \frac{1}{2}\sigma_s^2\frac{\partial^2 B}{\partial s^2} + \frac{1}{2}\sigma_l^2 l_t\frac{\partial^2 B}{\partial l^2} + \alpha(\tilde{\mu} - s_t)\frac{\partial B}{\partial s} + \left(\sigma_l^2 - l_t s_t\right)\frac{\partial B}{\partial l} + \frac{\partial B}{\partial t}, \tag{9.10}$$

with boundary condition $B_T(T) = 1$, where $\tilde{\mu} = \mu - (\lambda_s\sigma_s/\alpha)$ is the risk-adjusted mean reversion level for s_t. Note that μ_l does not appear in the PDE (since the Consol bond is a traded security).

The PDE (9.10) cannot be solved explicitly. However, a modification of (9.10) can be. Consider the PDE

$$(l_t + s_t)B = \frac{1}{2}\sigma_s^2\frac{\partial^2 B}{\partial s^2} + \frac{1}{2}\sigma_l^2 l_t\frac{\partial^2 B}{\partial l^2} + \alpha(\tilde{\mu} - s_t)\frac{\partial B}{\partial s} + \left(\sigma_l^2 - l_t\hat{s}\right)\frac{\partial B}{\partial l} + \frac{\partial B}{\partial t}, \tag{9.11}$$

where the only difference between (9.10) and (9.11) is that s_t has been replaced by a constant $\hat{s}$ in the coefficient of $\partial B/\partial l$ in (9.11). Equation (9.11) can be solved explicitly

---

[1] Essentially because the Consol bond can be priced in the usual way as $B_\infty = \mathbb{E}_0\left[\int_0^\infty \exp\left(-\int_0^t r_s\,ds\right)dt\right]$, a function of the short rate process.

for bond prices. Solutions $B_t(l_t, s_t \mid T)$ decompose as $B_t(l_t, s_t) = P_t(s_t)Q_t(l_t)$ where P_t and Q_t satisfy the PDEs

$$\frac{1}{2}\sigma_s^2 \frac{\partial^2 P}{\partial s^2} + \alpha(\tilde{\mu} - s_t)\frac{\partial P}{\partial s} + \frac{\partial P}{\partial t} = s_t P, \tag{9.12}$$

$$\frac{1}{2}\sigma_l^2 l_t \frac{\partial^2 Q}{\partial l^2} + \left(\sigma_l^2 - l_t\hat{s}\right)\frac{\partial Q}{\partial l} + \frac{\partial Q}{\partial t} = l_t Q, \tag{9.13}$$

with boundary conditions $P_T(s_T) = Q_T(l_T) = 1$ (since $B_T(l_T, s_T) \equiv 1$). Schaefer and Schwartz find explicit solutions to these equations and compare them with solutions found to (9.10) by an ADI finite difference method (see Chapter 12). The value of $\hat{s}$ must be chosen to provide a good approximation. For moderate levels of volatility Schaefer and Schwartz report bond prices within a few basis points of their true values for maturities out to 20 years. Their results are significantly worse for higher levels of volatility.

Rhee (99) [451] adds a stochastic volatility factor onto the Schaefer and Schwartz model. He finds significantly better fits than those achieved by Schaefer and Schwartz.

9.1.3 The Rebonato Model

Rebonato (98) [448] describes a two-factor Consol model with state variables, the Consol rate l_t and the short rate r_t. The novelty of the model is that Rebonato supposes that l_t and the ratio $k_t = l_t/r_t$ have log-normal processes. With these assumptions Rebonato finds that to avoid arbitrage the Consol rate and short rate must have the processes

$$dr_t = r_t \left(\sigma_l^2 + \mu_k + l_t - r_t\right)dt + \sigma_r r_t \, dz_{r,t}, \tag{9.14}$$

$$dl_t = l_t \left(\sigma_l^2 + l_t - r_t\right)dt + \sigma_l l_t \, dz_{l,t}, \tag{9.15}$$

under the EMM where $z_{r,t}$ and $z_{l,t}$ are correlated, μ_k and σ_k are the drift and volatility of k_t, and $\sigma_r^2 = \sigma_k^2 + \sigma_l^2$.

The system does not explode. Rebonato investigates calibration and implementation issues when $\mu_k \equiv a(t) + bk_t$. He achieves good simultaneous fits to bond prices, caplet and swaption prices.

9.2 PRICE KERNEL MODELS

Price kernel models have a long tradition in economics where they arise naturally from asset pricing in an expected utility framework. Price kernels are also called state-price deflators. Their first proper application in interest rate modelling came with Constantinides' (92) [139] 'SAINTS' model which adopted a rigorous no-arbitrage framework. Since then several authors have used the price kernel framework. Zheng (93) [546] derived formulae for bond option prices in the Constantinides framework, comparing the behaviour of one- and two-factor versions. Backus and Zin (94) [43] displayed a simple discrete time version. Dillen (97) [169] developed a three-factor model of the evolution of the price kernel, based on macro considerations.

Possibly the most important applications from our viewpoint are Flesaker and Hughston (96) [224] and Rogers (97) [458]. Flesaker and Hughston developed their rational log-normal model in a price kernel framework. Rogers' potential model shows how price kernel models can be generated at will. Both these models are in continuous time, and both are quite tractable.

Jin and Glasserman (99) [323] show how HJM models arise from the price kernel framework, and how positive rate models can always be put into Flesaker–Hughston form.

In this section we describe the price kernel approach, and describe the models of Constantinides and Rogers. We defer discussion of Flesaker and Hughston to Section 9.3.1.

9.2.1 The Price Kernel Approach

The value c_t at time t of an instrument maturing at time T with value $H_T = c_T$ is

$$c_t = \mathbb{E}_t^P \left[H_T \frac{p_t}{p_T} \right] \tag{9.16}$$

under some pricing measure P where p_t is the numeraire associated with P. Under the objective measure Q the value is

$$c_t = \mathbb{E}_t^Q \left[H_T \frac{q_t}{q_T} \right] \tag{9.17}$$

for some abstract numeraire q_t defined from the Radon–Nikodým derivative. Set $Z_t = 1/q_t$, so that

$$c_t Z_t = \mathbb{E}_t^Q[H_T Z_T]. \tag{9.18}$$

Z_t is the price kernel.[2] We shall see in Chapter 11 that equation (9.18) has a natural economic interpretation; the process for Z_t turns out to be

$$dZ_t = -r_t Z_t \, dt - \theta_t Z_t \, dz_t, \tag{9.19}$$

where r_t is the short rate process and θ_t is the market price of risk. For the moment we take (9.19) to be given, without further justification.

It follows from (9.19) that an interest rate model under the objective measure, with a price of risk, is equivalent to a price kernel model. The price of risk θ_t cannot be specified arbitrarily. Set $A_t = -\int_0^t r_s Z_s \, ds$, then under certain reasonable conditions it can be shown that

$$Z_t = M_t - A_t, \tag{9.20}$$

---

[2] Sometimes $Z(t, T) = Z_T/Z_t$ is referred to as the price kernel.

where $M_t = \mathbb{E}_t[A_\infty]$. M_t is a martingale and can be uniquely represented as

$$M_t = \mu + \int_0^t Y_s \, dz_s \tag{9.21}$$

for a certain process Y_t. Jin and Glasserman show that $\theta_t = Y_t/Z_t$ is precisely the market price of risk.

Z_t corresponds to a discount factor. It has a log-normal process with negative drift, so although it is always positive its expected future value tends monotonically to zero. For a pure discount bond we have $B_t(T) = \mathbb{E}_t^Q[Z_T/Z_t]$. If P is the EMM, so that the numeraire is the accumulator account, then

$$B_t(T) = \mathbb{E}_t^P\left[e^{-\int_t^T r_s \, ds}\right] = \mathbb{E}_t^Q\left[e^{-\int_t^T r_s \, ds}\frac{dP}{dQ}(t, T)\right] \tag{9.22}$$

so that

$$Z(t, T) = \frac{Z_T}{Z_t} = e^{-\int_t^T r_s \, ds}\frac{dP}{dQ}(t, T).$$

The idea of the price kernel approach is to model the evolution of Z_t as fundamental. Having specified a process for Z_t one values instruments using (9.18). The process for Z_t can be determined from an economic context, or from considerations of the eventual form of an interest rate process, or it can be generated by a general procedure that produces processes for Z_t with the correct properties.

In an extension to the method one may alternatively specify a process for the numeraire p_t under the measure P in (9.16). Asset pricing using (9.16) in this manner is a price kernel approach under P.

9.2.2 Generating Price Kernel Models

Rogers (97) [458] notes, as we noted above, that

1. Z_t is a positive supermartingale.
2. $\mathbb{E}_t^Q[Z_T] \to 0$, a.s. t.

A process Z_t with these properties is called a potential. Potentials have been well studied and there is plenty of existing machinery. It is easy to generate examples of potentials, each of which gives an interest rate model. In any particular case the model may not be useful or even interesting, but it will be arbitrage free and it will specify the market price of risk.

One useful method of generating potentials, described by Rogers, uses the resolvent operator of a Markov process. This is related to the generator of an Itō diffusion. We digress briefly to define these two concepts before returning to see how the resolvent helps us to find interest rate models. (Rigorous treatments of these topics can be found in Øksendal (95) [424] or Karlin and Taylor (81) [330].)

The Generator of an Itō Diffusion

We met the infinitesimal generator of a one-dimensional process in Chapter 6. Now suppose that X_t is an Itō diffusion in $\mathbb{R}^n$ and that at time zero $X_0 = x$. The generator of X_t is the operator A, acting on functions $f : \mathbb{R}^n \to \mathbb{R}$, defined by

$$(Af)(x) = \lim_{t \to 0+} \frac{1}{t}(\mathbb{E}_0[f(X_t)] - f(x)), \quad x \in \mathbb{R}^n. \tag{9.23}$$

If $X_t \in \mathbb{R}^n$ has the process $dX_t = \mu(X_t)dt + \sigma(X_t)dz_t$, then for twice differentiable functions f, non-zero only on a closed and bounded subset of $\mathbb{R}^n$, the limit defining Af exists and

$$Af(x) = \sum_{i=1}^{n} \mu(x)\frac{\partial f}{\partial x_i} + \frac{1}{2} \sum_{i,j=1}^{n} (\sigma\sigma')_{i,j}(x)\frac{\partial^2 f}{\partial x_i \partial x_j}. \tag{9.24}$$

This expression is, of course, the drift of the process $f(X_t)$, conditional on $X_0 = x$.

The Resolvent Operator, R_α

For $\alpha > 0$, and for $g : \mathbb{R}^n \to \mathbb{R}$ a bounded and continuous function, the resolvent operator R_α is defined to be

$$(R_\alpha(g))(x) = \mathbb{E}_0\left[\int_0^\infty e^{-\alpha t}g(X_t)dt \mid X_0 = x\right]. \tag{9.25}$$

$R_\alpha g$ is also bounded and continuous. R_α is not defined for $\alpha = 0$. For a slightly restricted set of functions, R_α is an inverse operator to $\alpha I - A$, for the identity operator I:

1 If f is twice differentiable, then $R_\alpha(\alpha - A)f = f$.
2 If g is bounded and continuous, then $(\alpha - A)R_\alpha g = g$.

Since α can be very small, R_α is 'almost' an inverse operator to A, so that $(R_\alpha g)(X_t)$ is a function whose drift is 'almost' $-g(X_t)$.

The usefulness of the resolvent operator for our purposes is that if R_α is the resolvent of a Markov process X_t, then for suitable positive functions g, $Z_t = e^{-\alpha t}R_\alpha g(X_t)$ is a potential. Furthermore, it is easy to show that the interest rate determined by Z_t (its downward rate of drift) is

$$r_t = \frac{g(X_t)}{R_\alpha g(X_t)}. \tag{9.26}$$

This gives us an inexhaustible supply of potentials; simply choose the Markov process X_t and the positive function g, and plug into (9.26). In practice, however, (9.26) could be hard to compute. Rogers points out that it is far easier to differentiate in (9.24) than it is to integrate in (9.25). Instead of choosing X_t and g, as above, choose X_t and a non-negative function f. Set $g = (\alpha - A)f$. Then, scaling by a constant,

$$Z_t = e^{-\alpha t}\frac{R_\alpha g(X_t)}{R_\alpha g(X_0)} = e^{-\alpha t}\frac{f(X_t)}{f(X_0)} \tag{9.27}$$

and

$$r_t = \frac{g(X_t)}{f(X_t)} = \frac{(\alpha - A)f(X_t)}{f(X_t)}. \tag{9.28}$$

This actually has a direct economic interpretation: α corresponds to the discount factor for consumption preferences, X_t is the output process in the economy, and f is the marginal utility of consumption, u_c, for a utility function u (see Chapter 11).

Rogers gives several examples, of which we give two. Let X_t be the $\mathbb{R}^n$-valued Markov process $dX_t = -BX_t\,dt + dz_t$, where z_t is an n-dimensional Brownian motion and B is an $n \times n$ matrix, and let $f : \mathbb{R}^n \to \mathbb{R}^+$ be the function

$$f(x) = \exp\left(\tfrac{1}{2}(x - c)'Q(x - c)\right), \tag{9.29}$$

where $c \in \mathbb{R}^n$ is a constant and Q is an $n \times n$ positive-definite symmetric matrix. Set $\alpha = \tfrac{1}{2}\mathrm{tr}Q + \tfrac{1}{2}(Qc)^2 + \tfrac{1}{2}v'S^{-1}v$. One easily computes that

$$g(x) = (\alpha - A)f(x) = f(x)\tfrac{1}{2}\left(x - S^{-1}v\right)' S \left(x - S^{-1}v\right), \tag{9.30}$$

where

$$S = B'Q + QB - Q^2, \tag{9.31}$$

$$v = (B' - Q)Qc, \tag{9.32}$$

and that

$$r_t = \tfrac{1}{2}\left(x_t - S^{-1}v\right)' S \left(x_t - S^{-1}v\right). \tag{9.33}$$

This is a squared-Gaussian process of a type we discuss in Section 9.3.2.

Rogers and Zane (98) [460] fit a two-factor version of this and an alternative model to US and UK term structure and FX data.

The second example is more exotic. Let X_t be a one-dimensional Markov process $dX_t = -\beta X_t\,dt + dz_t$, and take $f(x) = \cosh\gamma(x + c)$ for constants γ and c. Then

$$g(x) = \alpha \cosh\gamma(x + c) - \tfrac{1}{2}\gamma^2 \cosh\gamma(x + c) - \beta\gamma x \sinh\gamma(x + c) \tag{9.34}$$

so that

$$r_t = \beta\gamma X_t \tanh\gamma(X_t + c) + \alpha - \tfrac{1}{2}\gamma^2. \tag{9.35}$$

When $c = 0$, r_t is positive if $\alpha \geq \tfrac{1}{2}\gamma^2$, so we can set $r_t = \beta\gamma X_t \tanh\gamma X_t$. When x is large, $\tanh x \sim 1$ so that r_t tends to a normal process. When x is near zero, $\tanh x \sim x$ so that r_t is approximately squared Gaussian.

9.2.3 Constantinides' 'SAINTS' Model

The Constantinides (92) [139] 'SAINTS' (for Squared Autoregressive Independent variable Nominal Term Structure) model seems to have been the first genuine price kernel model of interest rates. It is an n-factor model, although Constantinides estimates only the one factor version of it.

From a heuristic economic argument, which does not concern us here, the price kernel is defined to be

$$Z_t = \exp\left(-at + \sum_{i=1}^{N} (X_{i,t} - \alpha_i)^2\right), \tag{9.36}$$

where $X_{i,t}$, $i = 1, \ldots, N$, are Markov state variables with processes $dX_{i,t} = -\lambda_i X_{i,t}\, dt + \sigma_i\, dz_{i,t}$ under the objective measure Q, and a and α_i, $i = 1, \ldots, N$, are constants. Set $v_i = \sigma_i^2/\lambda_i$. For (9.36) to be a potential one must have

1. $v_i < 1$, so that $X_{i,t}$ is well behaved, and
2. $a - \sum_{i=1}^{N} \lambda_i \left(v_i - \frac{1}{2}\alpha_i^2/(1 - v_i)\right) > 0$, so that Z_t is a supermartingale.

If these condition are satisfied, then the model can be solved to obtain explicit formulae for pure discount bond prices and spot rates. r_t is an affine sum of squared Gaussian variables,

$$r_t = a + \sum_{i=1}^{N} \left(-b + c(X_{i,t} - d_i)^2\right), \tag{9.37}$$

for constants a, b, c and d determined from the parameters of the model. The process for r_t is obtained directly from (9.37). For example, in the one-factor case, $N = 1$, and

$$dr_t = (a - bX_t(X_t - c))dt + d(X_t - c)dz_t. \tag{9.38}$$

This has a quadratic drift function. Unless the conditions above apply, there is a positive probability of r_t becoming unbounded.

9.2.4 Fitting to the Current Term Structure

Constantinides points out that a price kernel model can be calibrated to an initial term structure. This technique is related to the method due to Dybvig, discussed in Chapter 12. Define $Z_t^f = Z_t e^{-f(t)}$, for some deterministic function $f(t)$. Then using Z_T^f as the price kernel, bond prices $B_t^f(T)$ are

$$B_t^f(T) = \mathbb{E}_t^P\left[Z_T^f\right]/Z_t^f = e^{f(T)-f(t)}B_t(T), \tag{9.39}$$

where $B_t(T)$ are bond prices under Z_t. Hence r_t^f, the short rate under Z_t^f, is given by $r_t^f = r_t + f'(t)$. Suppose that the market term structure is $\{\tilde{r}_t(T)\}_{t \leq T}$. Given a price kernel Z_t generating short rates r_t choose $f(t)$ so that

$$\tilde{r}_t(T) = r_t(T) + \frac{f(T) - f(t)}{T - t}. \tag{9.40}$$

Then the term structure $r_t^f(T)$ generated by $Z_t^f = Z_t e^{-f(t)}$ exactly fits the initial term structure: $r_t^f(T) = \tilde{r}_t(T)$.

Having calibrated the price kernel to the market yield curve, other instruments can be priced using Z_t^f with some claim to be consistent with the yield curve. This technique may have some theoretical legitimacy if $f(t)$ is close to zero everywhere. It can then be regarded as a perturbation of the price kernel Z_t. If $f(t)$ is large, then Z_t^f may differ significantly from Z_t. One may then question whether the use of Z_t is appropriate in the first place.

Note that if rates are guaranteed to be positive under the original kernel it does not follow that under Z_t^f rates will still be positive.

9.3   POSITIVE INTEREST RATE MODELS

Market rates are usually, although not always, observed to be positive. This has led to the development of several types of model whose rationale is that they guarantee the rates they generate are always positive. These models, including the rational log-normal model of Flesaker and Hughston, Jamshidian's square Gaussian models, and the log-r models (with lattice implementations due to Black, Derman and Toy, and Black and Karasinski) are the subject of this section.

Although the Black, Derman and Toy, and Black and Karasinski lattice methods are widely used in the market, this is not because they are positive models *per se*, rather that they are easy lattice methods. Positive models, for the sake of positive rates, are not widely used in the market. This may be because of difficulties with specific examples; the rational log-normal model has calibration problems, log-r models have theoretical problems (in the continuous time limit), and square Gaussian models are not fashionable.

The world is still waiting for a tractable, sound, attractive positive rate model.

9.3.1   The Positive Rate Framework

This is a price kernel model with rates guaranteed to be positive. The positive rate approach was devised by Flesaker and Hughston (96a) [223], (96b) [224] and described more fully by Musiela and Rutkowski (97) [408] and Rutkowski (97) [466]. We first describe the general formulation of the positive rates model, and then give Flesaker and Hughston's rational log-normal example.

We suppose that there is a maximum maturity horizon T^*, although we shall consider the limit as $T^* \to \infty$.

Suppose that for all $t < T < T^*$, under the T^*-forward measure (the 'terminal measure') we have a martingale $M_t(T)$ in t, with $M_0(T) = 1$. Then $M_s(T) = \mathbb{E}_s^*[M_t(T)]$ for all $s \le t \le T$, where $\mathbb{E}^*$ is the expectation operator with respect to the T^*-forward measure. Suppose we have an initial pure discount bond curve, $B_0(T)$, that has positive forward rates, so that $B_0(T_1)/B_0(T_2) < 1$ for $0 < T_2 < T_1 < T^*$. Flesaker and Hughston show that rates remain positive if and only if pure discount bond prices can be expressed in the form

$$B_t(T) = \frac{B_0(T^*) - \int_T^{T^*} M_t(s)\frac{\partial}{\partial s}B_0(s)\mathrm{d}s}{B_0(T^*) - \int_t^{T^*} M_t(s)\frac{\partial}{\partial s}B_0(s)\mathrm{d}s} \qquad (9.41)$$

for some family of martingales $M_t(T)$, as above.

In the ∞-forward measure (the limit as $T^* \to \infty$) option prices c_t are given by

$$c_t Z_t = \mathbb{E}_t^\infty[c_T Z_T], \qquad (9.42)$$

where

$$Z_t = -\int_t^\infty M_t(s)\frac{\partial}{\partial s}B_0(s)\mathrm{d}s, \qquad (9.43)$$

so that Z_t is a price kernel in the ∞-forward measure. Equation (9.43) always holds. Bond prices are $B_t(T) = \mathbb{E}_t^\infty[Z_T/Z_t]$. To get an interest rate model the functional form of either Z_t or $M_t(T)$ must be specified. Jin and Glasserman show that every price kernel can be expressed in the form (9.43).

The Rational Log-normal Model

As an example, Flesaker and Hughston (96) [224] assume that Z_t can be expressed in the form

$$Z_t = A(t) + B(t)M_t, \qquad (9.44)$$

where M_t is a martingale in the ∞-forward measure, $M_0 = 1$, and $A(t)$ and $B(t)$ are positive decreasing deterministic functions with $B(t) \to 0$. Putting (9.44) into (9.42), bond prices are

$$B_t(T) = \frac{A(T) + B(T)M_t}{A(t) + B(t)M_t}, \qquad (9.45)$$

with the initial pure discount bond curve given by

$$B_0(T) = \frac{A(T) + B(T)}{A(0) + B(0)}. \qquad (9.46)$$

The choice of $A(t)$ and $B(t)$ is left free, as is the process for M_t (as long as it is a martingale). Calibration to market data is achieved by backing out the functions $A(t)$ and $B(t)$.

From (9.44) or (9.45) the short rate is

$$r_t = \frac{A'(t) + B'(t)M_t}{A(t) + B(t)M_t}. \qquad (9.47)$$

This is the rational log-normal model. The form of M_t is the heart of the modelling issue. If M_t has a geometric Brownian motion, $\mathrm{d}M_t = \sigma M_t \, \mathrm{d}z_t^\infty$, one obtains explicit formulae for caplets and swaptions (see Musiela and Rutkowski (97) [408]).

Problems with the model   Bond prices are bounded above and below, lying between upper and lower bounds determined by $A(t)$ and $B(t)$:

$$\frac{A(T)}{A(t)} \geq B_t(T) \geq \frac{B(T)}{B(t)}. \tag{9.48}$$

This means that the short rate is also constrained. Babbs (97) [37] shows that

$$-\frac{B'(t)}{B(t)} \geq r_t \geq -\frac{A'(t)}{A(t)}. \tag{9.49}$$

Writing the upper and lower bounds on the short rate as $u(t)$ and $l(t)$, Babbs shows that the model remains arbitrage free only up to the first time t that

$$\int_0^t (f_0(s) - l(s)) \mathrm{d}s \geq \frac{1}{\ln A(0)}, \tag{9.50}$$

where $f_0(t)$ is the initial instantaneous forward rate curve. Babbs gives illustrations to demonstrate that this condition can be binding. One concludes that care must be taken when implementing the rational log-normal model. One does not have complete freedom in determining $A(t)$ and $B(t)$ from market data, or condition (9.50) may be violated. In any case the bounds on r_t determined from $A(t)$ and $B(t)$ may be unreasonable.

Positive Rate Models and HJM

Jin and Glasserman (99) [323] show how the HJM framework is related to the positive rate framework of Flesaker and Hughston.

In an HJM model we have

$$\mathrm{d}f_t(T) = \alpha_t(T)\mathrm{d}t + \sum_{i=1}^N \sigma_{i,t}(T)\mathrm{d}z_{i,t}, \tag{9.51}$$

where

$$\alpha_t(T) = \sum_{i=1}^N \sigma_{i,t}(T) \left(\theta_i(t) + \int_t^T \sigma_{i,t}(s)\mathrm{d}s \right) \tag{9.52}$$

for prices of risk $\theta_i(t)$ under the objective measure. We define

$$\eta_{i,t}(T) = \frac{\sigma_{i,t}(T)}{f_t(T)} - \theta_i(t) - \int_t^T \sigma_{i,t}(s)\mathrm{d}s \tag{9.53}$$

and set

$$M_t(T) = \exp \left(\sum_{i=1}^N \left(\int_0^t \eta_{i,s}(T)\mathrm{d}z_{i,s} - \frac{1}{2} \int_0^t \eta_{i,s}^2(T)\mathrm{d}s \right) \right). \tag{9.54}$$

Then the HJM model (9.51) is a positive rate model if and only if $M_t(T)$ in (9.54) are exponential martingales for each T. If they are, then $M_t(T)$ is precisely the family of martingales required in the Flesaker–Hughston framework.

9.3.2 Square Gaussian Models

Square Gaussian models combine positive rates with some tractability, and may deserve more attention than is currently paid to them. They have been investigated by Beaglehole and Tenney (91) [57], Jamshidian (96) [311], El-Karoui et al. (92) [203] and Pelsser (96) [436].

In an n-factor square Gaussian model the short rate r_t is a sum of squares of Gaussian state variables $Y_t = (Y_{1,t}, \ldots, Y_{n,t})'$,

$$r_t = \tfrac{1}{2} Y_t' Y_t, \tag{9.55}$$

where under the EMM the process for the n-dimensional state variable Y_t is Gaussian:

$$dY_t = (a(t) + b(t)Y_t)dt + \Sigma(t)dz_t. \tag{9.56}$$

This is an n-dimensional extended Vasicek process with $a(t) \in \mathbb{R}^n$, $b(t)$ and $\Sigma(t)$ are $n \times n$ matrices, and z_t a Wiener process in $\mathbb{R}^n$.

The form of the process for r_t ensures that $r_t \geq 0$. Pure discount bond prices $B_t(T)$ are (Rogers (95) [457])

$$B_t(T) = e^{-\frac{1}{2} Y_t' Q_t Y_t + h_t' Y_t - \gamma_t}, \tag{9.57}$$

where $Q_t(T)$ is an $n \times n$ matrix satisfying the Riccati equation

$$\frac{\partial Q}{\partial t} + Qb + (Qb)' - Q\Sigma\Sigma'Q + I = 0 \tag{9.58}$$

with boundary condition $Q_T(T) = 0$, and $h_t(T)$ is a vector and $\gamma_t(T)$ a scalar given by

$$\frac{\partial h}{\partial t} = Qa + (Q\Sigma\Sigma' - b')h, \tag{9.59}$$

$$\frac{\partial \gamma}{\partial t} = h'a - \frac{1}{2}\mathrm{tr}(\Sigma'Q\Sigma) + \frac{1}{2}h'\Sigma\Sigma'h, \tag{9.60}$$

with $h_T(T) = 0$ and $\gamma_T(T) = 0$.

Solutions to these equations usually have to be computed numerically although the one-factor case may have analytic solutions.

The One-factor Square Gaussian Model

When there is a single state variable $Y = Y_1$ and a and Σ are constants the differential equations (9.58), (9.59) and (9.60) can be solved explicitly to obtain formulae for bond and bond option prices. Pelsser (96) [436] analyses this situation in detail; see also Jamshidian (95) [310]. Using Pelsser's notation we write

$$r_t = u_t^2 \tag{9.61}$$

with

$$du_t = (\theta(t) - au_t)dt + \sigma dz_t. \tag{9.62}$$

Set $y_t = u_t - \alpha(t)$ where

$$\alpha(t) = e^{-at}\sqrt{r_0} + e^{-at}\int_0^t e^{as}\theta(s)ds \tag{9.63}$$

so that

$$dy_t = -ay_t\,dt + \sigma dz_t \tag{9.64}$$

is Gaussian. Bond prices are of the form

$$B_t(T) = \exp\left(A(t,T) - B(t,T)y_t - C(t,T)y_t^2\right), \tag{9.65}$$

where

$$A(t,T) = \int_t^T \left(\frac{1}{2}\sigma^2 B^2(s,T) - \sigma^2 C(s,T) - \alpha^2(s)\right)ds, \tag{9.66}$$

$$B(t,T) = 2\int_t^T \frac{e^{\gamma s}(a+\gamma)e^{2\gamma(T-s)} + (\gamma-a)}{e^{\gamma t}(a+\gamma)e^{2\gamma(T-t)} + (\gamma-a)}\alpha(s)ds, \tag{9.67}$$

$$C(t,T) = \frac{e^{2\gamma(T-t)} - 1}{(a+\gamma)e^{2\gamma(T-t)} + (\gamma-a)}, \tag{9.68}$$

$$\gamma^2 = a^2 + 2\sigma^2. \tag{9.69}$$

The price of the European call option $c_t(T_1, T_2)$ is given by

$$c_t(T_1, T_2) = B_t(T_2)(N(d_1) - N(d_2)) - XB_t(T_1)(N(d_3) - N(d_4)), \tag{9.70}$$

where the parameters d_1, d_2, d_3, d_4, are

$$d_1 = \frac{h\tau - \nu}{\sigma\sqrt{\tau C(t,T_1)}}, \tag{9.71}$$

$$d_2 = \frac{l\tau - \nu}{\sigma\sqrt{\tau C(t,T_1)}}, \tag{9.72}$$

$$d_3 = \frac{h - M(t,T_1)}{\sigma\sqrt{C(t,T_1)}}, \tag{9.73}$$

$$d_4 = \frac{l - M(t,T_1)}{\sigma\sqrt{C(t,T_1)}}, \tag{9.74}$$

and

$$\nu = M(t,T_1) - B(T_1,T_2)\sigma^2 C(t,T_1), \tag{9.75}$$

$$\tau = 1 + 2\sigma^2 C(t,T_1)C(T_1,T_2), \tag{9.76}$$

$$h = \frac{\sqrt{d} - B(T_1,T_2)}{2C(T_1,T_2)}, \tag{9.77}$$

$$l = \frac{-\sqrt{d} - B(T_1, T_2)}{2C(T_1, T_2)}, \tag{9.78}$$

$$d = B^2(T_1, T_2) + 4C(T_1, T_2)(A(T_1, T_2) - \ln X), \tag{9.79}$$

$$M(t, T) = D(t, T)y - \int_t^T \sigma^2 D(s, T)B(s, T)\mathrm{d}s, \tag{9.80}$$

$$D(t, T) = \frac{2\gamma \mathrm{e}^{\gamma(T-t)}}{(a + \gamma)\mathrm{e}^{2\gamma(T-t)} + (\gamma - a)}. \tag{9.81}$$

9.3.3   Log-r Models

In a log-r model the short rate is the exponential of a state variable Y_t, $r_t = \mathrm{e}^{Y_t}$. This guarantees that r_t is strictly positive. The two most important log-r models are Black, Derman and Toy (90) [73] and Black and Karasinski (91) [74], for both of which good lattice implementations exist. (We discuss lattice methods in Chapter 14.) Very early examples of log-r models include Dothan (78) [170] and Courtadon (82) [145]. A related example is Brennan and Schwartz (80) [94].

For the Black and Karasinski model the state variable $Y_t \in \mathbb{R}$ follows an extended Vasicek process

$$\mathrm{d}Y_t = (a(t) + b(t)Y_t)\mathrm{d}t + \sigma(t)\mathrm{d}z_t. \tag{9.82}$$

The Black, Derman and Toy model predated the Black and Karasinski model, and was originally formulated in discrete time. The continuous time limit of the Black, Derman and Toy model gives the state variable the process

$$\mathrm{d}Y_t = \left(a(t) + \frac{1}{\sigma(t)}\frac{\partial \sigma}{\partial t}Y_t\right)\mathrm{d}t + \sigma(t)\mathrm{d}z_t, \tag{9.83}$$

so it is a special case of Black and Karasinski. The odd-looking coefficient of Y_t in the drift of Y_t arises because of the way that Black, Derman and Toy define the term structure of volatility on their lattice.

For either of these models, there is sufficient flexibility to allow both the initial term structure and term structure of volatility of a yield curve to be fitted although in many practical implementations a flat volatility may be assumed. Lattice calibration techniques will be described in Chapter 14.

It is well known that if the short rate has a log-normal process, for instance

$$\mathrm{d}r_t = \alpha(\mu - r_t)\mathrm{d}t + \sigma r_t \, \mathrm{d}z_t, \tag{9.84}$$

then the expected future value of the accumulator account, $V_t = \mathbb{E}_0\left[\exp\left(\int_0^t r_s \mathrm{d}s\right)\right]$, is unbounded even for arbitrarily small $t > 0$ (Hogan and Weintraub (93) [284], Morton (88) [403]).[3]

---

[3] Note that lattice implementations with a discrete time step may still work.

To avoid this problem, as we saw in Chapter 8, market models have been developed where the underlying state variables are discretely compounded market quoted rates. BGM models construct an entire yield curve of discretely compounded forward rates. Other market models just assume the existence of a finite set of rates. In this section we restrict our attention to factor market models with a finite number of log-normal market quoted rates. Early examples include Sandmann and Sondermann (94) [471], Musiela (94) [406] and Miltersen, Sandmann and Sondermann (97) [399].

Sandmann and Sondermann have a one-factor model whose state variable is the one year market rate $\hat{r}_t$. $\hat{r}_t$ is related to the continuously compounded annual spot rate r_t by $1 + \hat{r}_t = \exp(r_t)$.

If $\hat{r}_t$ is log-normal, so that

$$d\hat{r}_t = \mu_t \hat{r}_t \, dt + \sigma_t \hat{r}_t \, dz_t, \tag{9.85}$$

then from Itō's lemma the continuously compounded annual spot rate process is

$$dr_t = (1 - e^{-r_t})\left(\mu_t - \tfrac{1}{2}(1 - e^{-r_t})\sigma_t^2\right) dt + (1 - e^{-r_t})\sigma_t \, dz_t. \tag{9.86}$$

When r_t is large $1 - e^{-r_t} \to 1$ so r_t tends to a Brownian motion with drift $\mu_t - \tfrac{1}{2}\sigma_t^2$. When r_t is small $1 - e^{-r_t} \to r_t$ to first order in r_t so that r_t has a log-normal process. Importantly, Sandmann and Sondermann show that expected returns to bonds remain bounded in this model.

Miltersen, Sandmann and Sondermann take as their state variables a set of forward rates $f_t(T_i, \alpha_i)$ with maturity times T_i and tenors α_i, so that in terms of pure discount bond prices

$$\frac{1}{1 + \alpha_i f_t(T_i, \alpha_i)} = \frac{B_t(T_i + \alpha_i)}{B_t(T_i)}. \tag{9.87}$$

For a cap with exercise rate r_X, principal P, and exercise dates $T_0, \ldots, T_N$, set $\alpha_i = T_{i+1} - T_i$, $i = 0, \ldots, N - 1$. Suppose that forward rates $f_t(T_i, \alpha_i)$ are all log-normal so that

$$\frac{df_t(T_i, \alpha_i)}{f_t(T_i, \alpha_i)} = \mu_{i,t} \, dt + \gamma_{i,t} \, dz_t, \tag{9.88}$$

then Miltersen, Sandmann and Sondermann show that the value C_t of the cap at time $t < T_0$ is

$$C_t = P \sum_{i=0}^{N-1} \alpha_i B_t(T_{i+1})[f_t(T_i, \alpha_i)N(d_{i,1}) - r_X N(d_{i,2})], \tag{9.89}$$

where

$$d_{i,1} = \frac{1}{\sigma_t(T_i, \alpha_i)}\left[\ln \frac{f_t(T_i, \alpha_i)}{r_X} + \frac{1}{2}\sigma_t^2(T_i, \alpha_i)\right], \tag{9.90}$$

$$d_{i,2} = d_{i,1} - \sigma_t(T_i, \alpha_i), \tag{9.91}$$

$$\sigma_t^2(T, \alpha) = \int_t^T \gamma^2(s, T, \alpha) ds. \tag{9.92}$$

This is the standard Black's formula for the price of a cap in terms of caplet implied volatilities $\sigma_t(T_i, \alpha_i)$. Miltersen, Sandmann and Sondermann demonstrated that this formula is indeed legitimate. Further developments, such as the BGM model, extended this result to an entire yield curve of forward rates.

It is sometimes recommended that log-r models be used for markets like the yen where rates are very close to zero. Unfortunately a constant proportional volatility is not observed in the yen market, so that it is not clear that an unmodified log-r model is appropriate.

9.4 NON-LINEAR MODELS

To this short section belong several models that do not fall naturally into any other category. We outline them briefly here, although we meet some of them in other chapters. Their common feature is non-linearity in their drift terms. This ranges from the straightforward in the case of Marsh and Rosenfeld (83) [382] to the pathological in the case of Tice and Webber (97) [523]. We only mention each model briefly. Other non-linear models will be found elsewhere in this book.

We also include here models with non-affine volatility terms, such as Chan *et al.* (92) [124] and Andersen and Lund (96) [19], (97) [22].

Marsh and Rosenfeld (83) [382]

The short rate process is

$$dr_t = \left(ar_t^{-(1-\beta)} + br_t\right) dt + \sigma r_t^{\beta/2} dz_t, \qquad (9.93)$$

for $\beta \geq 0$. Setting $y_t = r_t^{2-\beta}$ we have $dy_t = (a + by_t)dt + c\sqrt{y_t}\,dz_t$, for constants a, b and c, so that (9.93) is reducible to affine form (see Chapter 16). Marsh and Rosenfeld estimate the model on a time series of T-bill data using maximum likelihood. They are unable to reach strong conclusions, but notice that the likelihood is higher when $\beta = 2$ than when β takes lower values.

Demmel (98) [165]

In an interesting paper Demmel (98) [165] incorporates fiscal policy into a general equilibrium framework. His short rate process emerges as

$$dr_t = \left(\sum_{i=0}^{3} a_i(r_t - b)^i\right) dt + \left(\sum_{j=1}^{2} c_j(r_t - b)^j\right) dz_t, \qquad (9.94)$$

for certain parameters a_i, b and c_j arising out of the economic model. The short rate is confined to an interval $(-\infty, r_{max})$, with $r_{max} < \infty$, and only one root of the cubic drift term occurs in the interval. Hence the process (9.94) does not support multiple equilibria.

Longstaff (89) [359], (92) [361]/Beaglehole and Tenney (92) [58]

Longstaff (89) [359], (92) [361] and Beaglehole and Tenney (92) [58] investigate a one-factor model with short rate process

$$dr_t = \kappa \left(\frac{\sigma^2}{4\kappa} - \sqrt{r_t} \right) dt + \sigma \sqrt{r_t} \, dz_t, \qquad (9.95)$$

arising originally from a general equilibrium framework, and sometimes called a double square root model. The model has an implicit boundary condition at $r_t = 0$, since $\sqrt{r_t}$ is not defined for $r_t < 0$. This is explored in detail by Goldstein and Keirstead (97) [253] and is also touched upon in Chapter 6.

Note that if y_t is a variable with process $dy_t = \mu dt + \sigma dz_t$, then $r_t = y_t^2$ has a process of the form (9.95), so that this model is an example of a square Gaussian model.

Platten (94) [440]

Platten (94) [440] investigated a two-factor double square root model in a general equilibrium framework where the state variables y_1 and y_2 have double square root processes

$$dy_{i,t} = \kappa_i \left(\frac{1}{4\kappa_i} - \sqrt{r_t} \right) dt + \sqrt{y_{i,t}} \, dz_{i,t}, \quad i = 1, 2. \qquad (9.96)$$

The short rate is a linear combination of the state variables $r_t = \theta y_1 + \phi y_2$. The short rate variance is v_t, $v_t \, dt = \mathbb{E}[dr_t \, dr_t]$, and equals $v_t = \theta^2 y_1 + \phi^2 y_2$.

As in the Longstaff and Schwartz model one may re-parameterise the model, taking as fundamental the short rate r_t and the variance v_t. Platten finds closed form solutions for bond prices.

Tice and Webber (97) [523]

This is a pathological three-factor model with two linear factors and one quadratic. Tice and Webber (97) [523] show that their model is a stochastic version of the Lorenz system of differential equations, producing chaotic solutions. The three factors in the model are the short rate r_t, the short rate reversion level x_t, and a feedback parameter p_t, with processes

$$dr_t = \alpha(x_t - r_t)dt + \sigma_r \, dz_{r,t},$$

$$dx_t = \beta(p_t r_t + (1 - p_t)\mu - x_t)dt + \sigma_x \, dz_{x,t}, \qquad (9.97)$$

$$dp_t = \gamma(\delta - \phi(x_t - \mu)(r_t - \mu) - p_t)dt + \sigma_p \, dz_{p,t}.$$

If $\phi = 0$, so that p_t had no cross-product term in its drift, then the model reduces to a three-factor affine model. The additional cross-product term is sufficient to cause the system to become chaotic.

The economic foundations of this model and its behaviour are discussed in more detail in Chapter 11.

Generalisations of CKLS

Variations of a certain three-factor model have been used by several authors as a test bed for time series estimation techniques and to explore the time series properties of the short rate. The model, arrived at by adding a stochastic mean and stochastic log-variance to the CKLS model, is

$$dr_t = \alpha(\mu_t - r_t)dt + \sigma_t r_t^{\psi} \, dz_{r,t}, \qquad (9.98)$$

$$d\left(\ln \sigma_t^2\right) = \beta\left(\phi - \ln \sigma_t^2\right) dt + \lambda dz_{\sigma,t}, \qquad (9.99)$$

$$d\mu_t = \gamma(\chi - \mu_t)dt + \sigma_\mu \sqrt{\mu_t} \, dz_{\mu,t}. \qquad (9.100)$$

The short rate, r_t, has a CKLS process. Log-variance has a Vasicek process, and the short rate mean has a CIR process. Andersen and Lund (97) [22] and Vetzal (97) [533] investigated the system (9.98) and (9.99). The full three-factor system was studied by Andersen and Lund (96a) [19], (96c) [21] as a vehicle for the EMM calibration method. This method is discussed in more detail in Chapter 17.

A second generalisation of the CKLS process has also been used for estimation purposes. This time, a more general functional form for the drift of r_t is imposed:

$$dr_t = \sum_{i=-p}^{q} \alpha_i r_t^i \, dt + \sigma r_t^{\psi} \, dz_{r,t}, \qquad (9.101)$$

where, for instance, $p = -1$, $q = 2$. This system was used by Ait-Sahalia (96) [9] and Conley *et al.* (97) [138].

The second generalisation can perhaps best be thought of as a non-parametric term structure model. It may perhaps be useful for matching to yield curves, and the form of the drift function is capable of describing multiple equilibria in the short rate process.

The three-factor generalisation has more potential as a true term structure model, but its comparative lack of tractability makes other, simpler, models much more attractive.

10

General Formulations of Interest Rate Models

This chapter goes beyond the relatively straightforward models of previous chapters. It is in three main parts. The first part generalises away from the one-parameter random variables we have been using up until now to introduce random field models (sometimes also called string models). Random fields are random variables with two or more indexes and are random in each dimension. The first random field interest rate model was Kennedy (94) [331], (97) [332], and since then other contributions have been made by Pang (96) [425], Chu (96) [131] and Goldstein (97) [252]. More recent applications include Kurbanmuradov, Sabelfeld and Schoenmakers (99) [346] and Longstaff, Santa-Clara and Schwartz (99) [364]. Pang uses a random field framework to help to calibrate Heath, Jarrow and Morton models to implied prices.

The second part generalises still further, describing the general bond pricing framework of Bjork, Kabanov and Runggaldier (97) [70], Bjork, Masi, Kabanov and Runggaldier (96) [71].

Having described a very general formulation we then specialise back down, looking at implementable models that allow interest rates to jump. We consider four categories of model: jump-augmented HJM, factor jump models, jump-augmented price kernel models, and official rate models.

An introductory section describes some of the mathematical concepts underlying models that include jumps.

10.1 JUMP PROCESSES

Figure 10.1 is a time series of UK three-month Libor. It has what appear to be clear jumps in it, at A and B, and also at other times. The jump at A accompanied the surprise announcement of sterling's entry to the ERM. The spike at B occurred during the events attendant on sterling's exit from the ERM. Figure 10.2 shows UK 'base rate' superimposed on another time series of UK three-month Libor. The base rate was a semi-official rate giving a reference level for floating rate lending that reflected the monetary stance of the UK monetary authorities. Money market rates remain close to the level of the base rate. The base rate is a pure jump process whose value is clearly related to the process of the money market rate. We investigate this in Section 10.7.

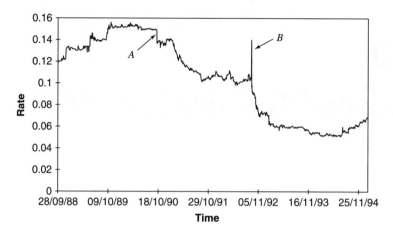

Figure 10.1   UK three-month Libor

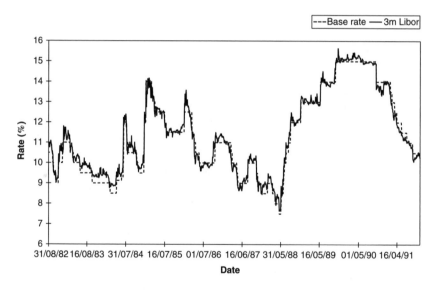

Figure 10.2   UK three-month Libor and base rate

The presence of jumps in the value process of some asset makes it difficult to hedge derivatives on that asset. A continuously rebalanced portfolio in the underlying asset cannot simultaneously hedge against both the diffusion component and the jump component of changes in the value of the derivative. Figure 10.3 is the Fed funds target rate. This is a pure jump process. Since the Fed funds rate is strongly influenced by the target rate several investigations of the Fed funds rate have also investigated the target

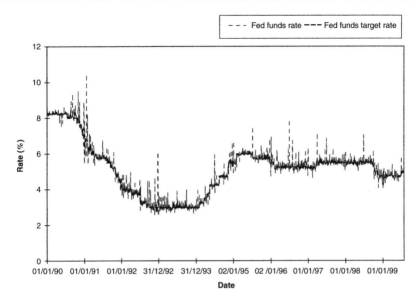

Figure 10.3 The Fed funds rate and the Fed funds target rate

rate.[1] In several markets interest rates jump when monetary authorities unexpectedly change key indicator rates. It may be possible to partially hedge against jumps if sufficient liquid futures contracts are available, but in general ordinary delta based hedging will not be effective. This poses serious theoretical and practical problems.

A pure diffusion model does not model jumps. In this section we examine processes that jump, and introduce essential concepts that we shall employ when describing models later in this chapter.

In the remainder of this section we define jumps and stopping times, and go on to define fundamental examples of jump processes: counting processes, Poisson processes and Lévy processes.

Càdlàg Processes

Suppose that X_t is a random variable. Define

$$X_{t-} = \lim_{s < t, s \to t} X_s \quad \text{and} \quad X_- = \{X_{t-}\}_{t > 0}, \tag{10.1}$$

$$X_{t+} = \lim_{s > t, s \to t} X_s \quad \text{and} \quad X_+ = \{X_{t+}\}_{t \geq 0}. \tag{10.2}$$

If X_- is well defined, then X has left limits. X is left continuous if $X = X_-$, a.s. If X_+ is well defined, then X has right limits. X is right continuous if $X = X_+$, a.s. An

---

[1] For instance Balduzzi, Bertola and Foresi (96) [47] who found that spreads between the target rate and the Fed funds rate seemed mainly driven by anticipated changes in the target rate.

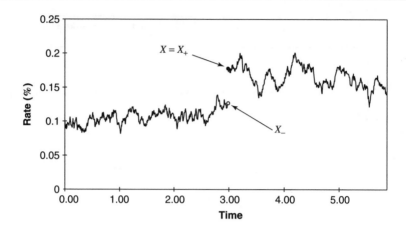

Figure 10.4 A càdlàg sample path

extremely important type of jump process is 'càdlàg' — 'continu à droite, limites à gauche' — continuous on the right, limits on the left. These processes are also called RCLL processes, 'right continuous, left limits', although càdlàg is more euphonious.

Figure 10.4 illustrates a càdlàg sample path. A jump occurs at t_0 if $X_t(\omega) \neq X_{t-}(\omega)$. In the figure there is a jump at time 3. The sample point at time 3 occurs on the upper path, so that the process is right continuous. If $X = \{X_t, \mathcal{F}_t\}_{t \geq 0}$ is adapted and càdlàg, then it has a countable number of jumps, almost surely.

The time that a jump occurs it is not predictable in the sense that it cannot be seen by looking ahead a fractional amount of time. Càdlàg processes are important because it is possible to integrate with respect to adapted càdlàg processes.

Stopping Times

A random variable $T : \Omega \to [0, \infty]$ is a stopping time if

$$\{\omega \in \Omega \mid T(\omega) \leq t\} \in \mathcal{F}_t, \quad 0 \leq t \leq \infty. \tag{10.3}$$

T should be thought of as the random time at which 'something' happens. T is a stopping time if for each time t you know whether or not the 'something' has happened. For instance, suppose that Ω is the sample space for some interest rate process, so that $r_t(\omega)$ is the value at time t of the interest rate on the path $\omega \in \Omega$. For a barrier level K let

$$T(\omega) = \inf\{t \mid r_t(\omega) \geq K\}. \tag{10.4}$$

$T(\omega)$ is the first time (since some initial time) that $r_t(\omega)$ hits the barrier at K. This will be a stopping time since you know at any time t whether you have hit K for the first time yet. On the other hand, define

$$T(\omega) = \sup\{t \leq T_{\max} \mid r_t(\omega) \leq K\}. \tag{10.5}$$

This is the last time (before time $T_{\max}$) that $r_t(\omega)$ hits the level K. This is not a stopping time because at times $t < T_{\max}$ you do not know if you have hit level K for the last time yet.

Counting Processes

Let $\{T_n\}_{n \geq 0}$ be a strictly increasing countable sequence of stopping times, with $T_0 = 0$ a.s. For instance, if $K_0 < \cdots < K_n < \cdots$, $n \geq 0$, and $r_0(\omega) = K_0$, we could define $T_n(\omega) = \inf\{t \mid r_t(\omega) \geq K_n\}$. This is the time it takes to breach the nth barrier, and is strictly increasing if, for instance, r_t is a diffusion process.

The counting process associated with $\{T_n\}_{n \geq 0}$ is $N = \{N_t\}_{t \geq 0}$, where $N_t = \Sigma_{n \geq 1} I_{\{t \geq T_n\}}$ and I is the indicator function. Then $N_t(\omega) \in \mathbb{N}$, and $N_t(\omega) = n$ if $T_n(\omega) \leq t < T_{n+1}(\omega)$. N_t counts the number of times that ω has been 'hit' by (the events referred to by the) stopping times up to time t. In the example N_t counts how may barriers have been hit by time t.

$N_0 = 0$ a.s. and N_t is adapted to $\{\mathcal{F}_t\}_{t \geq 0}$ because $\{T_n\}_{n \geq 0}$ are stopping times.

Poisson Processes

For a sequence $\{T_n\}_{n \geq 0}$ of strictly increasing stopping times, set $T = \sup_n T_n$, so that $T(\omega) = \sup_n T_n(\omega)$ along each sample path. T is the explosion time of $\{T_n\}_{n \geq 0}$.

If $T = \infty$ then the counting process N_t associated with $\{T_n\}_{n \geq 0}$ is a counting process without explosions. A counting process without explosions is càdlàg. An adapted counting process without explosions is a Poisson process if

1. For all $0 \leq s < t < \infty$, $N_t - N_s$ is independent of $\mathcal{F}_s$.
2. For all $0 \leq s < t < \infty$, $0 \leq u < v < \infty$, such that $t - s = v - u$, the distribution of $N_t - N_s$ is the same as the distribution of $N_v - N_u$, and the distribution of $N_t - N_s$ is the same as the distribution of N_{t-s}.

The first condition means that increments are independent of the past, and the second means that increments are stationary.

If N_t is a Poisson process then there exists $\lambda > 0$ such that

$$\Pr(N_t = n) = \frac{e^{-\lambda t}(\lambda t)^n}{n!}. \tag{10.6}$$

λ is the intensity of N_t; we have that $\mathbb{E}[N_t] = \lambda t$, so that λ measures the increase in expected value of N_t. Intuitively λ is the arrival rate of jumps in N_t. We also have $\mathrm{var}(N_t) = \lambda t$. If N_t is a Poisson process with intensity λ, then both $N_t - \lambda t$ and $(N_t - \lambda t)^2 - \lambda t$ are martingales.

Lévy Processes

An adapted process $\{X_t\}_{t \geq 0}$, $X_0 = 0$, is a Lévy process if

1. 'Increments are independent of the past': for all $0 \leq s < t < \infty$, $X_t - X_s$ is independent of $\mathcal{F}_s$.

2. 'Increments are stationary': for all $0 \le s < t < \infty$, the distribution of $X_t - X_s$ is the same as the distribution of X_{t-s}.

3. X_t is continuous in probability: that is, $X_t = \lim_{s \to t} X_s$ in probability (so that for all $\varepsilon > 0$, $\Pr(|X_t - X_s| > \varepsilon) \to 0$ as $\to t$).

If X_t is a Lévy process then there is a unique modification of X_t which is càdlàg and is a Lévy process. Poisson processes and Brownian motion are Lévy processes. The most general Lévy process is a combination of a Poisson process and a Brownian motion.

Compensators

If N_t is a counting process it is not a martingale since its value can only increase. However, suppose there exists a process λ_t such that $dN_t - \lambda_t \, dt$ is a martingale. If there does, then λ_t is called the intensity of N_t. In general, for a finite variation process P_t, a predictable finite variation process v_t such that $P_t - v_t$ is a martingale is called the compensator of P_t. P_t has an intensity if $dv_t = \lambda_t \, dt$.

10.2   RANDOM FIELD MODELS

A random field is a random variable parameterised by two (or more) continuous indexes. Up to now we have only considered random variables with a single index, time. In interest rate modelling it is convenient to generalise this. For a given time t, two instantaneous forward rates, $f_t(T_1)$ and $f_t(T_2)$, are random variables indexed by time to maturity, T. It is natural to represent forward rates as a random field indexed by time t and time to maturity, T. Kennedy (94) [331], (97) [332] describes a Gaussian random field model for forward rates. This section is partially based on those papers.

The correlation function $\text{corr}(dr_t(T_1), dr_t(T_2))$ between spot rates of different maturities has a structure resembling Figure 10.5. The figure shows $g(T) = \text{corr}(dr_t(T_1), dr_t(T))$, $T \in [0, T_{\max}]$ for a fixed T_1.

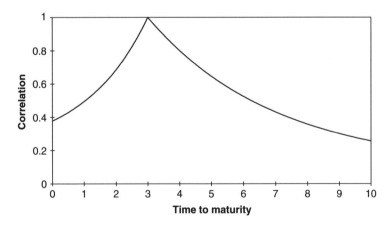

Figure 10.5   Typical correlation between spot rates

Random fields are defined by their correlation structure. A simple example is given by the Brownian sheet. $B(t, T)$ is a Brownian sheet if

$$\mathbb{E}_0[B(t_1, T_1) - B(t_2, T_2)] = 0, \tag{10.7}$$

$$\mathbb{E}_0[B(t_1, T_1)B(t_2, T_2)] = (t_1 \wedge t_2)(T_1 \wedge T_2), \tag{10.8}$$

for all t_1, T_1, t_2, T_2. For example, if B_t^1 and B_t^2 are independent Brownian motions, then $B(t, T) = B_t^1 B_T^2$ is a Brownian sheet.

A Brownian sheet would not be a suitable state variable for interest rate modelling, however. If T represented a maturity time one might require, for instance, that term structures be differentiable almost everywhere. A Brownian sample path is not differentiable almost everywhere. To achieve a more realistic yield curve we need to impose a correlation structure to relate the movements in different spot rates to one another, to more closely resemble Figure 10.5.

Suppose we have a yield curve specified as a set of instantaneous forward rates, $f_t(T)$. Suppose that forward rates are modelled as

$$f_t(T) = \mu_{t,T} + X_{t,T}, \tag{10.9}$$

where $X_{t,T}$ is a mean zero random field and $\mu_{t,T}$ is a drift term to be determined by no-arbitrage.[2] We assume that

$$\text{cov}(X_{t_1, T_1}, X_{t_2, T_2}) = c(t_1 \wedge t_2, T_1, T_2) \tag{10.10}$$

for some function c with $c(s, T_1, T_2) = c(s, T_2, T_1)$. When $X_{t,T}$ is Gaussian, so that all conditional distributions are normal, c is a function of $t_1 \wedge t_2$ if $X_{t,T}$ has independent increments in the t-direction.

In general, random field models are infinite factor, implying that

• It is not possible to hedge with finite number of instruments,
• Nor is it possible to hedge with a countable infinity of instruments.

Define $dX_{t,T}$ to be the differential in the t-direction, so that

$$\int_0^t dX_{t,T} = X_{t,T} - X_{0,T}, \tag{10.11}$$

and for $f_t(T) = \mu_{t,T} + X_{t,T}$ we have

$$df_t(T) = d\mu_{t,T} + dX_{t,T}. \tag{10.12}$$

We require that

$$\lim_{\Delta T \to 0} \text{corr}(dX_{t,T}, dX_{t,T+\Delta T}) = 1 \tag{10.13}$$

---

[2] We adopt this notation to emphasise the symmetry between t and T.

to get sufficient smoothness along the yield curve. The short rate is $r_t = f_t(t)$ and pure discount bond prices are

$$P_t(T) = \exp\left(-\int_t^T f_t(s)ds\right), \tag{10.14}$$

as usual.

10.2.1. Extended Vasicek as a Random Field Model

Suppose we have a short rate process $dr_t = (\theta(t) - a(t)r_t)dt + \sigma(t)dz_t$ under the EMM. We know that pure discount bond prices $P_t(T)$ at time t are affine:

$$P_t(T) = A(t, T)\exp(-B(t, T)r_t). \tag{10.15}$$

In terms of the initial curves $A(0, t)$ and $B(0, t)$, and denoting derivatives of B by subscripts, we have

$$B(t, T) = \frac{B(0, T) - B(0, t)}{B_t(0, t)}, \tag{10.16}$$

$$\ln A(t, T) = \ln\frac{A(0, T)}{A(0, t)} - B(t, T)\frac{\partial}{\partial t}\ln A(0, t)$$

$$- \frac{1}{2}[B(t, T)B_t(0, t)]^2 \int_0^t \left(\frac{\sigma(s)}{B_s(0, s)}\right)^2 ds. \tag{10.17}$$

$a(t)$ and $\theta(t)$ can be expressed in terms of $A(0, t)$ and $B(0, t)$:

$$a(t) = \frac{B_{t,t}(0, t)}{B_t(0, t)}, \tag{10.18}$$

$$\theta(t) = -a(t)\frac{\partial}{\partial t}\ln A(0, t) - \frac{\partial^2}{\partial t^2}\ln A(0, t)$$

$$+ [B_t(0, t)]^2 \int_0^t \left(\frac{\sigma(s)}{B_s(0, s)}\right)^2 ds. \tag{10.19}$$

Given an initial spot rate curve, $r_0(T)$, and an initial spot rate volatility curve, $\sigma_0(T)$, the initial values of A and B are

$$B(0, T) = r_0(T)\frac{\sigma_0(T)}{\sigma(0)}T \tag{10.20}$$

and

$$A(0, T) = P_0(T)\exp(B(0, T)r_0). \tag{10.21}$$

Forward rates are derived from bond prices. Pang (96) [425] shows that

$$\text{cov}\left(f_{t_1}(T_1), f_{t_2}(T_2)\right) = \frac{\partial B(0, T_1)}{\partial T_1}\frac{\partial B(0, T_2)}{\partial T_2}\int_0^{t_1 \wedge t_2} \left(\frac{\sigma(s)}{B_s(0, s)}\right)^2 ds$$

$$\equiv g(T_1, T_2)f(t_1 \wedge t_2). \tag{10.22}$$

The extended Vasicek model determines a Gaussian covariance structure. Conversely the covariance structure (10.22), where $B(0, T)$ determines $B(t, T)$ and $A(t, T)$ via equations (10.16), (10.17) and (10.21), specifies an extended Vasicek model.

10.2.2. The Risk-Adjusted Process

Under the EMM Q we have $P_t(T) = \mathbb{E}^Q \left[\exp \left(- \int_t^T r_s \, \mathrm{d}s \right) \right]$. Suppose that under Q

$$\mathrm{d}f_t(T) = \mu_{t,T}^Q \, \mathrm{d}t + \sigma_{t,T} \, \mathrm{d}z_{t,T}^Q, \tag{10.23}$$

for a Brownian sheet z^Q. Then for no-arbitrage Goldstein (97) [252] generalises Kennedy (94) [331] and shows that we must have

$$\mu_{t,T}^Q = \sigma_{t,T} \int_t^T \sigma_{t,u} c(t, T, u) \mathrm{d}u, \tag{10.24}$$

where $c(t, T, u)$ is the correlation function. Goldstein shows that (10.24) holds in the non-Gaussian case.

Equation (10.24) closely resembles the forward rate drift condition (under the EMM) of Chapter 8. In fact if $z_{t,T}^Q \equiv z_t^Q$, for all T, then $c(t, T_1, T_2) = 1$, for all T_1, T_2. The state variable is perfectly correlated in the T-direction and the equation reduces to the Heath, Jarrow and Morton forward rate drift condition. The state variable remains a function of current time but ceases to depend upon a maturity time.

The T-forward Measure

We can use the T-maturity pure discount bond, $P_t(T)$, as numeraire with the associated T-forward martingale measure F^T. Set

$$\mathrm{d}z_{t,S}^{F^T} = \mathrm{d}z_{t,S}^Q + \left[\int_t^T \sigma_{t,u} c(t, S, u) \mathrm{d}u \right] \mathrm{d}t, \tag{10.25}$$

then under F^T, $z_{t,S}^{F^T}$ is a martingale (in t) and

$$\mathrm{d}f_t(T) = \mu_{t,T}^Q \, \mathrm{d}t + \sigma_{t,T} \, \mathrm{d}z_{t,T}^Q, = \sigma_{t,T} \, \mathrm{d}z_{t,T}^{F^T} \tag{10.26}$$

is a martingale (in t) under F^T.

European Option Pricing

How might we price a European option using this model? Under the EMM Q we need to compute

$$c_t = \mathbb{E}^Q \left[H(T) \exp \left(- \int_t^T r_s \, \mathrm{d}s \right) \right], \tag{10.27}$$

where $H(T)$ is the payoff at time T, and c_t is the option value at time t. For an option on a pure discount bond, $H(T) = \max(0, B_T(U) - X)$, where X is the strike price.

If we have a finite factor model, we can use Feynman–Kac or Monte Carlo methods. For an infinite factor model these possibilities are not available. We have to solve the expectation directly, or use an approximate solution. Goldstein uses the characteristic function to help derive explicit solutions.

10.2.3 A Three-Parameter Family

To find explicit formulae it is necessary to make some much stronger assumptions. Kennedy (97) [332] imposed Markov conditions in a Gaussian setting and was able to reduce a random field model to a three-parameter family.

Gaussian Random Fields

Suppose that the random field is Gaussian. This assumption permits considerable simplifications to be made. Kennedy shows that when $X_{t,T}$ is Gaussian, relative bond prices are martingales under Q if

$$\mu_{t,T}^Q = \mu_{0,T}^Q + \int_0^t [c(t \wedge u, u, T) - c(0, u, T)] \mathrm{d}u, \tag{10.28}$$

for all $t < T$. If $X_{t,T}$ is Gaussian and relative bond prices are martingales under Q, then the covariances must be of the form

$$\mathrm{cov}\left(X_{t_1,T_1}, X_{t_2,T_2}\right) = c\left(t_1 \wedge t_2, T_1, T_2\right). \tag{10.29}$$

Markov Conditions

In a random field there are several different ways to express Markov properties. All are generalisations of the usual Markov property. Markov properties place very strong constraints on the underlying processes. $X_{t,T}$ is Markov if

1. For $0 \le t_1 \le t_2 \le t_3$, $t_1 \le T_1$, $t_3 \le T_2$, given X_{t_2,T_2} then X_{t_1,T_1} and X_{t_3,T_2} are independent.
2. For $0 \le t_1 \le t_2 \le T_1 \wedge T_2$, given X_{t_2,T_1} then X_{t_1,T_1} and X_{t_2,T_2} are independent.

Property 1 implies that $X_{t,T}$ is Markov in the t-direction for $t \le T$, with T fixed. If $X_{t,T}$ has independent increments in the t-direction, then $X_{t,T}$ has the first property.

Theorem (Kennedy) *If* $f_t(T) = f_{t,T}$ *is Markov and has independent increments, then the covariance function satisfies*

$$c(t, T_1, T_2) = v(t)g(T_1, T_2) \tag{10.30}$$

for some function v and g where v is non-decreasing and g is symmetric and non-negative definite.

Stationarity

A process is stationary if the distributional parameters of the random variable do not change through time. Formally, $X_{t,T}$ is stationary if for all $T > 0$ the joint distributions of $X_{t,T}$ are the same as those of $X_{t+u,T+u}$, for every $u > 0$. This is a strong assumption. It allows us to further pin down the covariance function.

Theorem (Kennedy) *If $f_t(T) = f_{t,T}$ is Markov, stationary, and has independent increments, then*

$$c(t, T_1, T_2) = e^{\lambda(t - T_1 \wedge T_2)} h(|T_1 - T_2|) \tag{10.31}$$

where $\lambda > 0$ and $|h(x)| \leq h(0)e^{-(1/2)\lambda x}$.

With this covariance we must have

$$\mu^Q_{t,T} = k - \int_0^{T-t} (1 - e^{\lambda(T-t-u)}) h(u) \mathrm{d}u, \tag{10.32}$$

for some constant k.

Further Markov Conditions

$X_{t,T}$ is Markov in the T-direction if for $t \leq T_1 \leq T_2 \leq T_3$, X_{t,T_1} and X_{t,T_3} are independent, given X_{t,T_2}. This is an assumption about the term structure. At any particular current time t, variations in the a spot rate of maturity time T are independent of variations in the spot rates of other maturity times.

If $X_{t,T}$ is Markov and Markov in the T-direction then it is strictly Markov. The importance of this is that the short rate process is Markov in the ordinary sense if and only if $f_{t,T}$ is strictly Markov.

Theorem (Kennedy) *If $f_t(T) = f_{t,T}$ is Markov, Markov in the T-direction, stationary, and has independent increments, then*

$$c(t, T_1, T_2) = \sigma^2 e^{\lambda t + (2\mu - \lambda)(T_1 \wedge T_2) - \mu(T_1 + T_2)} \tag{10.33}$$

for constants σ, $\lambda \geq 0$, $\mu \geq \frac{1}{2}\lambda$.

This last theorem defines a three-parameter family of models, with a highly restricted functional form for their covariance structure. The theorem is analogous to the result that the only continuous, stationary, one-parameter, Markov, Gaussian process is the Ornstein–Uhlenbeck process.

Time-changed Brownian Sheet

If $X_{t,T}$ is Gaussian and $c(t, T_1, T_2) = \sigma(t)\tau(T_1 \vee T_2)$ for two functions σ and τ that are continuous, and with $\sigma(0) = 0$, then $X_{t,T} = Z_{\sigma(t),\tau(T)}$, for a standard Brownian sheet $Z_{t,T}$. If $\tau(T)$ is decreasing then the volatility of $X_{t,T}$ decreases as T increases.

If $f_t(T) = f_{t,T}$ is Markov, Markov in the T-direction, stationary, and has independent increments, then it follows from the previous theorem that $f_{t,T}$ can be represented as

$$f_{t,T} = \mu_{t,T} + \sigma e^{-\mu T} Z_{e^{\lambda t}, e^{(2\mu - \lambda)T}}, \tag{10.34}$$

so that $f_t(T)$ is a three-parameter function of a time-changed Brownian sheet.

The Drift Function

Suppose that under Q we have $f_t(T) = \mu_{t,T} + X_{t,T}$, where $X_{t,T}$ is Gaussian with $c(t, T_1, T_2) = \sigma(t)\tau(T_1 \vee T_2)$. If $\sigma(t) = \sigma^2 t$ then $\mu_{t,T} = \mu_{0,T} + \sigma^2\tau(T)t(T - (t/2))$, is a generalised Ho–Lee Model. This process may mean revert if τ has suitable properties (see Kennedy (94) [331]), providing an important augmentation to Ho and Lee.

Suppose that $r_t = f_t(t)$ has constant volatility $a > 0$. When σ and τ are differentiable, given τ it is possible to invert the system to find σ. For example, suppose that $\tau(T) = e^{-\lambda T}$, then $\sigma(t) = (a^2/\lambda)\sinh(\lambda t)$, and

$$\text{cov}(r_t, r_s) = \frac{a^2}{\lambda}(e^{-\lambda|t-s|} - e^{-\lambda(t+s)}). \tag{10.35}$$

This is the covariance structure of an Ornstein–Uhlenbeck process; setting $Y_t = X_{t,t}$, we have $dY_t = -Y_t\,dt + a\,dz_t$ for a Wiener process z_t.

The Process for the Short Rate

With the previous assumptions, for the short rate r_t we have $r_t = \mu_{t,t} + Y_t$, and also

$$\mu_{t,t} = \mu_{0,t} + \frac{a^2}{\lambda^2}e^{-\lambda t}(\cosh(\lambda t) - 1). \tag{10.36}$$

Eliminating $\mu_{t,t}$ one obtains

$$dr_t = \lambda\left[\frac{e^{-\lambda t}}{\lambda}\frac{\partial}{\partial T}(e^{\lambda T}\mu_{0,T}) + \frac{a^2 e^{-\lambda t}}{\lambda^2}\sinh(\lambda t) - r_t\right]dt + a\,dz_t. \tag{10.37}$$

r_t reverts to a time-varying mean, contingent upon the initial yield curve $\mu_{0,T}$. The model calibrates to the initial yield curve.

Caplet Pricing

Kennedy obtains a Black's formula for the price of a caplet. If $f_t(T) = \mu_{t,T} + X_{t,T}$ is a Gaussian random field with $\text{cov}(X_{t_1,T_1}, X_{t_2,T_2}) = c(t_1 \wedge t_2, T_1, T_2)$, then the value c_0 at time 0 of a caplet with strike rate r_X, tenor τ, maturing at time T is

$$c_0 = \exp\left(-\int_0^T \mu_{0,u}\,du\right)N(d_1) - \exp\left(\tau r_X - \int_0^{T+\tau} \mu_{0,u}\,du\right)N(d_2), \tag{10.38}$$

where

$$d_1 = \frac{\tau}{\sigma}(F_0(T, T + \tau) - r_X) + \frac{1}{2}\sigma, \tag{10.39}$$

$$d_2 = d_1 - \sigma, \tag{10.40}$$

$$F_0(T, T + \tau) = \frac{1}{\tau}\int_T^{T+\tau} \mu_{0,u} \, du, \tag{10.41}$$

$$\sigma^2 = 2\int_T^{T+\tau} \int_T^u c(T, u, v) du \, dv. \tag{10.42}$$

The caplet price depends on the current term structure $\mu_{0,T}$, and the covariance structure, only.

Special Case (Goldstein)

A caplet is equivalent to a bond option. Goldstein converts the formula above into a bond option formula. Suppose that

$$c(t, T_1, T_2) = e^{\lambda(t - T_1 \wedge T_2) - \mu(T_1 + T_2)}, \tag{10.43}$$

then the value c_0 at time 0 of a pure discount bond option maturing at time T with strike X, on an underlying bond $P_t(S)$ maturing at time $S > T$, is

$$c_0 = P_0(S)N(d_1) - XP_0(T)N(d_2), \tag{10.44}$$

where

$$d_1 = \frac{1}{\sigma_P}\ln\frac{P_0(S)}{XP_0(T)} + \frac{1}{2}\sigma_P, \tag{10.45}$$

$$d_2 = d_1 - \sigma_P, \tag{10.46}$$

$$\sigma_P^2 = \frac{1}{\lambda}\frac{\sigma^2}{\mu - \lambda}(1 - e^{-2\lambda T})\left(\frac{1 - e^{-2\lambda T}}{2\lambda} - \frac{1 - e^{-(\lambda + \mu)T}}{\lambda + \mu}\right). \tag{10.47}$$

This has a very familiar looking form, and can be thought of as a generalisation of the Jamshidian formula (Chapter 7).

Pricing Swaptions

Although there is no exact formula for swaptions, there is a good approximate formula. The existence of a good approximate formula is essential for calibration to market prices. We follow Pang (96) [425].

Consider a swaption maturing at time T into a swap of tenor τ with n resets, $T < T_1, \ldots, T_n$, $T_i = T + i\tau$, and exercise rate s_X. The payoff to the swaption is

$$H(T) = \max(s_T - s_X, 0)\sum_{i=1}^n \frac{1}{(1 + \tau s_T)^{(T_i - T)/\tau}}, \tag{10.48}$$

where $s_T = (1 - P_T(T_n))/\Sigma_{i=1}^n \tau P_T(T_i)$ is the market swap rate at time T. Both s_X and s_T are supposed to be market quoted rates. Under the T-forward measure, F^T, the swaption value, is

$$c_t = P_t(T)\mathbb{E}_t^T \left[\tau \max(s_T - s_X, 0) \sum_{i=1}^n \frac{1}{(1 + \tau s_T)^{(T_i - T)/\tau}} \right]. \tag{10.49}$$

Set

$$\sigma_{i,j} = \int_T^{T_i} \int_T^{T_j} [c(T, u, v) - c(t, u, v)]\mathrm{d}v\,\mathrm{d}u. \tag{10.50}$$

Under F^T, at time t, $P_T(T_i)$ is log-normally distributed. $P_T(T_i) = \exp(X_i)$, where X_i has

$$\text{mean: } \mu = \ln \frac{P_t(T_i)}{P_t(T)} - \frac{1}{2}\sigma_i^2, \tag{10.51}$$

$$\text{variance: } \sigma_i^2 = \sigma_{i,i}, \tag{10.52}$$

and

$$\text{cov}(P_t(T_1), P_t(T_2)) = \frac{\sigma_{i,j}}{\sqrt{\sigma_{i,i}\sigma_{j,j}}}. \tag{10.53}$$

Hence, we can easily value swaptions by Monte Carlo methods; we simulate to find $P_t(T_i)$, $i = 1, \ldots, n$, and hence s_T, and find c_t from (10.49).

Approximate Formula for Swaptions

In practice, Monte Carlo methods, while effective for pricing individual instruments, are too slow to apply repeatedly as part of an optimisation procedure. For this we really need an explicit formula. While it is not possible to find an exact formula for swaptions in the random field framework, a good approximation may be found. Pang makes the following approximations:

1. The swaption payoff is

$$H(T) = \tau \max(s_T - s_X, 0) \sum_{i=1}^n \frac{1}{(1 + \tau s_T)^{(T_i - T)/\tau}}. \tag{10.54}$$

We approximate this as

$$H(T) = \tau \max(s_T - s_X, 0) \sum_{i=1}^n P_T(T_i), \tag{10.55}$$

effectively assuming that the swap rate is a good approximation to the average term structure at time T. Then

$$H(T) = \max \left(1 - \sum_{i=1}^n \tau s_X P_T(T_i) - P_T(T_n), 0 \right), \tag{10.56}$$

since $\tau s_T \Sigma_{i=1}^n P_T(T_i) = 1 - P_T(T_n)$. But this is the payoff to a put on a coupon bond, coupon rate s_X, with strike 1.

2. Assume that the value of the coupon bond at time T is log-normal.

Pang then gets a Black's formula for the value v of the swaption,

$$v = P_t(T) \left(N \left(-\frac{a}{b} \right) - \exp \left(a + \frac{1}{2}b^2 \right) N \left(-\frac{a}{b} - b \right) \right). \tag{10.57}$$

where

$$a = \ln \left(\frac{P}{\sqrt{1 + (k/P^2)}} \right), \tag{10.58}$$

$$b = \ln \left(1 + \frac{k}{P^2} \right), \tag{10.59}$$

$$P = \frac{1}{P_t(T)} \left(\sum_{i=1}^n \tau s_X P_T(T_i) + P_T(T_n) \right), \tag{10.60}$$

$$k = \tau^2 s_X^2 \sum_{i,j=1}^n c_{i,j} + c_{n,n} + 2\tau s_X \sum_{i=1}^n c_{i,n}, \tag{10.61}$$

$$c_{i,j} = \frac{P_t(T_i)P_t(T_j)}{P_t(T)^2} (\exp(\sigma_{i,j}) - 1), \tag{10.62}$$

and where $\sigma_{i,j}$ is defined in equation (10.50). He finds that his formula provides a good approximation to true swaption prices in the model.

10.3 A GENERAL MODEL

An infinite factor model that generalises random field models in much the same way that random field models generalise HJM models was developed by Bjork, Masi, Kabanov and Runggaldier (96) [71] and Bjork, Kabanov and Runggaldier (97) [70]. It provides a general framework for bond pricing which we describe in this section.

The key feature of this framework is that a hedge is going to be specified not as a vector of quantities of a finite set of hedging instruments but as a measure over a continuum of possible hedging instruments.

We take for our hedging instruments

- a continuum of bonds,
- the accumulator account.

A hedging portfolio is represented by a pair (η_t, ϕ_t). η_t is a predictable process specifying the number of units of accumulator account held in the hedge. ϕ_t is a predictable measure-valued process. $\phi_t(A)$ is the number of units held at time t of bonds with maturities in the measurable set $A \subseteq \mathbb{R}$. As in Bjork *et al.* it is necessary to assume that η_t and ϕ_t are sufficiently regular.

The value of the hedge portfolio is

$$V_t = \eta_t B_t + \int_t^\infty P_t(T)\phi_t(\mathrm{d}T), \tag{10.63}$$

where $B_t = \exp\left(\int_0^t r_s\,\mathrm{d}s\right)$ is the value of the accumulator account and $P_t(T)$ is the PDB price. The notation $\phi_t(\mathrm{d}T)$ is used as an alternative to $\mathrm{d}\phi_t$. Later we shall consider two-dimensional measure-valued functions where the present notation is clearer.

V_t is the value process for (η_t, ϕ_t). Note that ϕ_t may not have a density. If it does, we can write

$$\phi_t(\mathrm{d}T) = f_t^\phi(T)\mathrm{d}T \tag{10.64}$$

for the density f_t^ϕ.

V_t is self-financing if

$$\mathrm{d}V_t = \eta_t\,\mathrm{d}B_t + \int_t^\infty \phi_t(\mathrm{d}T)\mathrm{d}P_t(T), \tag{10.65}$$

where in general the stochastic integral has to be defined with care. For this and all technical points see Bjork $et\ al.$ (96) [71].

10.3.1   The General Case

We can consider a term structure as an element of a Banach space of continuous functions, for instance the space C of continuous functions on $[0, \infty]$, say, so that $p \in C$ is a curve of pure discount bond prices. A term structure model specifies a process in C. A hedge portfolio is an element of the dual space C^* of C, $C^* = \{f : C \to \mathbb{R} \mid f\ \text{linear}\}$. But by the Rietz representation theorem C^* is the space of measures on the positive reals $\mathbb{R}^+$, specifying for each maturity time how much of that bond is in the hedge.

In this context Bjork $et\ al.$ (96) [71] show that the short rate is the return to a portfolio of rolling over just maturing bonds. A separate hypothesis to support the existence of the short rate is not needed; the short rate exists automatically.

10.3.2   The Bond Price Process: A Special Case

Suppose the bond price process under the measure P is

$$\frac{\mathrm{d}P_t(T)}{P_{t-}(T)} = m_t(T)\mathrm{d}t + v_t(T)\mathrm{d}z_t + \int_E n_t(T, x)\mu(\mathrm{d}t, \mathrm{d}x), \tag{10.66}$$

where z_t is a Wiener process under P, $m_t(T)$ and $v_t(T)$ are the ordinary drift and volatility functions, and μ is a marked point process on a mark space E.

We may regard the mark space E as $\mathbb{R}^n$, $\mathbb{N}$ or a finite set. μ can be thought of as a jump process taking values in E. $n_t(T, x)$ is a volatility function for points $x \in E$.

Suppose that μ has a compensator $\nu(\mathrm{d}t, \mathrm{d}x)$ of the form $\nu(\mathrm{d}t, \mathrm{d}x) = \lambda(t, \mathrm{d}x)\mathrm{d}t$ so that λ is the intensity of μ and $\mu(\mathrm{d}t, \mathrm{d}x) - \nu(\mathrm{d}t, \mathrm{d}x) = \mu(\mathrm{d}t, \mathrm{d}x) - \lambda(t, \mathrm{d}x)\mathrm{d}t$ is a martingale under P.

A process of this sort is a Gaussian–Poisson process

$$\frac{dP_t(T)}{P_{t-}(T)} = m_t(T)dt + v_t(T)dz_t + \sum_{i=1}^{m} n_t^i(T)(dN_t^i - \lambda_t^i dt), \qquad (10.67)$$

where N_t^i are independent Poisson processes, with intensities λ_t^i.

Writing $P(dt, T)$ for $dP_t(T)$, in the general case we want to integrate the process

$$dV_t = \eta_t dB_t + \int_t^\infty \phi_t(dT)dP_t(T). \qquad (10.68)$$

We assume that all functions are sufficiently regular for things to work so that, for example, functions are always sufficiently differentiable, that Fubini's lemma applies (so that the order of integration can always be changed), et cetera. The integral can be interpreted as

$$V_t = \int_0^t \eta_s \, dB_s + \int_0^t \int_s^\infty m_s(T)P_{s-}(T)\phi_s(dT)ds + \int_0^t \int_s^\infty v_s(T)P_{s-}(T)\phi_s(dT)dz_s$$

$$+ \int_0^t \int_E \int_s^\infty n_s(T, x)P_{s-}(T)\phi_s(dT)\mu(ds, dx). \qquad (10.69)$$

In the general case it is necessary to integrate measure-valued processes with respect to processes in spaces of continuous functions. We do not consider the general case here. The reader interested in the mathematics this entails is referred to Bjork et al. (96) [71].

10.3.3   Relationship Between Processes

From the specification of the bond price process (10.66) Bjork et al. derive the processes for the short rate and the forward rate curve.

The Forward Rate Process

Suppose the forward rate process is

$$df_t(T) = \alpha_t(T)dt + \sigma_t(T)dz_t + \int_E \delta_t(T, x)\mu(dt, dx), \qquad (10.70)$$

then in terms of $m_t(T)$, $v_t(T)$ and $n_t(T, x)$ we have

$$\alpha_t(T) = v_t(T)\frac{\partial v_t(T)}{\partial T} - \frac{\partial m_t(T)}{\partial T}, \qquad (10.71)$$

$$\sigma_t(T) = -\frac{\partial v_t(T)}{\partial T}, \qquad (10.72)$$

$$\delta_t(T, x) = -\frac{\partial n_t(T, x)}{\partial T}\frac{1}{1 + n_t(T, x)}. \qquad (10.73)$$

The Short Rate Process

Suppose the short rate process is

$$dr_t = a_t\,dt + b_t\,dz_t + \int_E q_t(x)\mu(dt, dx),\qquad(10.74)$$

then in terms of $\alpha_t(T)$, $\sigma_t(T)$ and $\delta_t(T, x)$ we have

$$a_t = \frac{\partial f_t(t)}{\partial T} + \alpha_t(t),\qquad(10.75)$$

$$b_t = \sigma_t(t),\qquad(10.76)$$

$$q_t(x) = \delta_t(t, x).\qquad(10.77)$$

To go from the forward rate process to the bond process the relationships are

$$m_t(T) = r_t + A_t(T) + \tfrac{1}{2}|S_t(T)|^2,\qquad(10.78)$$

$$v_t(T) = S_t(T),\qquad(10.79)$$

$$n_t(T, x) = e^{D_t(T,x)} - 1,\qquad(10.80)$$

where

$$A_t(T) = -\int_t^T \alpha_t(s)ds,\qquad(10.81)$$

$$S_t(T) = -\int_t^T \sigma_t(s)ds,\qquad(10.82)$$

$$D_t(T, x) = -\int_t^T \delta_t(s, x)ds.\qquad(10.83)$$

The analogies between these expressions are clear from those for the HJM model given in Chapter 8.

10.3.4 Trading Strategies

Two trading strategies $\left(\eta_t^1, \phi_t^1\right)$ and $\left(\eta_t^2, \phi_t^2\right)$ are equivalent if they have the same value processes (defined by equation (10.63)). A strategy (η_t, ϕ_t) is n-dimensional if ϕ_t is concentrated at n distinct points almost everywhere, for all t. In other words, it is almost always possible to construct a hedge using just n bonds in the hedge. A strategy is n-reducible if it has an n-dimensional equivalent strategy but no $(n - 1)$-dimensional equivalent strategy. If all admissible trading strategies are k-reducible for $k \le n$, and at least one strategy is n-reducible, then the model is an n-factor model. A model may be countable-reducible if it is reducible to a countably infinite number of factors.

These definitions coincide with the intuitive idea of an n-factor or countable-factor model. An n-factor model is one that requires n instruments in any hedge portfolio—so that underlying the model there are only n sources of risk.

10.3.5 Existence of Martingale Measures

In the mark space setting, if Q is (locally) equivalent to P with

$$dQ_t = L_t \, dP_t, \tag{10.84}$$

for the Radon-Nikodým derivative L_t, then Bjork *et al.* show that L_t has the process

$$dL_t = L_t \Gamma_t \, dz_t + L_{t-} \int_E (\Phi_t(x) - 1)\{\mu(dt, dx) - \nu(dt, dx)\}, \tag{10.85}$$

with $L_0 = 1$ and $\mathbb{E}^P[L_t] = 1$ for all t, where Γ_t is a predictable process and $\Phi_t(x)$ is a strictly positive process. Also,

$$dz_t^Q = dz_t - \Gamma_t \, dt \tag{10.86}$$

is a Q-Wiener process and

$$\lambda^Q(t, dx) = \Phi_t(x)\lambda(t, dx) \tag{10.87}$$

is the Q-intensity of μ (the intensity of μ under the measure Q).

A martingale measure exists if

$$m_t(T) + \Gamma_t v_t(T) + \int_E \Phi_t(x) n_t(T, x)\lambda(t, dx) = r_t. \tag{10.88}$$

This is an extension of the HJM forward rate drift condition in Chapter 8. Γ_t is the market price of risk for the Wiener processes z_t, and $\Phi_t(x)$ corresponds to a market price of risk for the marked point process μ.

10.3.6 The Forward Rate Process under Q

If under the martingale measure Q we have

$$df_t(T) = \alpha_t(T)dt + \sigma_t(T)dz_t + \int_E \delta_t(T, x)\mu(dt, dx), \tag{10.89}$$

then

$$\alpha_t(T) = \sigma_t(T) \int_t^T \sigma_t(s)ds - \int_E \delta_t(T, x)e^{D_t(T,x)}\lambda^Q(t, dx) \tag{10.90}$$

and the bond price process under Q is

$$\frac{dP_t(T)}{P_{t-}(T)} = r_t \, dt + S_t(T)dz_t^Q + \int_E (e^{D_t(T,x)} - 1)\tilde{\mu}(dt, dx), \tag{10.91}$$

where $\tilde{\mu}$ is the Q-compensated process

$$\tilde{\mu}(dt, dx) = \mu(dt, dx) - \lambda^Q(t, dx)dt, \tag{10.92}$$

and $S_t(T)$ and $D_t(T, x)$ are defined by (10.82) and (10.83).

Equation (10.90) is the forward rate drift condition under the martingale measure. Note that, unlike the standard HJM framework, the drift α is not independent of the measure Q. It depends on the Q-intensity λ^Q. This makes calibration much harder in this framework.

If the mark space E is finite then the martingale measure is unique if and only if the market is complete, as usual. If E is infinite then the martingale measure is unique if and only if the market is 'approximately' complete in the following sense: For every bounded payoff function H there is a sequence of hedgeable payoffs H_i converging to H in probability.

This means that although not every payoff can be hedged, it is possible to hedge a sequence of instruments whose payoffs get arbitrarily close to the unhedgeable payoff.

Given practical trading circumstances in the market, the practical implications of being able only to 'approximately' hedge are minimal to any implementation of the model.

10.3.7   The Partial Differential Difference Equation

Suppose that r_t is Markov and that under Q

$$\mathrm{d}r_t = a_t(r_t)\mathrm{d}t + b_t(r_t)\mathrm{d}z_t + \int_E q_t(r_t, x)\mu(\mathrm{d}t, \mathrm{d}x), \qquad (10.93)$$

where a, b and q are deterministic functions, z_t is a Q-Wiener process and μ has a deterministic Q-intensity $\lambda(t, r_{t-}, \mathrm{d}x)$. Then a claim F contingent on r_t satisfies the partial differential difference equation (PDDE)

$$\frac{\partial F}{\partial t} + AF - rF = 0, \qquad (10.94)$$

$$F(T, r) = H(r), \qquad (10.95)$$

where

$$AF = a_t(r)\frac{\partial F}{\partial r} + \frac{1}{2}b_t(r)^2\frac{\partial^2 F}{\partial r^2} + \int_E [F(t, r + q_t(r, x)) - F(t, r)]\lambda(t, r, \mathrm{d}x) \qquad (10.96)$$

is the infinitesimal generator of r_t applied to F and H is determined by the payoff at maturity time T. In general this PDDE is hard to solve, but it can be solved in a few special cases such as the affine case discussed next.

10.3.8   Affine Models

Suppose that under Q

$$\mathrm{d}r_t = a_t(r_t)\mathrm{d}t + b_t(r_t)\mathrm{d}z_t + \int_E q_t(r_t, x)\mu(\mathrm{d}t, \mathrm{d}x), \qquad (10.97)$$

where $\mu(dt, dx)$ has intensity $\lambda(t, r, dx)$, and the functions $a_t(r_t)$, $b_t(r_t)$ and $q_t(r_t, x)$ are affine

$$a_t(r) = a_1(t) + a_2(t)r, \tag{10.98}$$

$$b_t(r) = (b_1(t) + b_2(t)r)^{1/2}, \tag{10.99}$$

$$q_t(r_t, x) = q_t(x), \tag{10.100}$$

$$\lambda(t, r, dx) = l_1(t, dx) + l_2(t, dx)r. \tag{10.101}$$

Bjork *et al.* show that bond prices are of the form

$$P_t(T) = e^{A(t,T) - B(t,T)r_t}, \tag{10.102}$$

where $A(t, T)$ and $B(t, T)$ satisfy the ordinary differential equations

$$\frac{\partial B}{\partial t} + a_2(t)B(t, T) - \frac{1}{2}b_2(t)B^2(t, T) + \Psi_2(t, B(t, T)) = -1, \tag{10.103}$$

$$\frac{\partial A}{\partial t} + a_1(t)B(t, T) - \frac{1}{2}b_1(t)B^2(t, T) + \Psi_1(t, B(t, T)) = -1, \tag{10.104}$$

with boundary conditions $A(T, T) = B(T, T) = 0$, where

$$\Psi_i(t, b) = \int_E \{1 - e^{-bq_t(x)}\}l_i(t, dx), \quad i = 1, 2. \tag{10.105}$$

These equations are relatively tractable and may permit explicit solutions in some circumstances. They generalise the jump–diffusion extension of the Duffie and Kan affine model.

10.3.9 Fitting an Initial Term Structure

Suppose that under Q the short rate r_t is jump-augmented Vasicek,

$$dr_t = (\theta(t) - ar_t)dt + \sigma dz_t + \int_E q_t(x)\mu(dt, dx), \tag{10.106}$$

where $\mu(dt, dx)$ has a deterministic intensity $\lambda(t, dx)$ and the reversion rate a is constant. Bjork *et al.* (95) [69] show how the model may be calibrated to any initial term structure, as long as it is twice differentiable. Suppose the initial forward rate curve is $f(0, T)$, $T \geq 0$. Set $B(t, T) = (1 - e^{-a(T-t)})/a$ and

$$g(T) = \int_0^t e^{-a(T-s)} \int_E q_s(x)e^{-B(s,T)q_s(x)}\lambda(s, dx)ds - \int_0^t e^{-a(T-s)}\sigma^2 B(s, T)ds. \tag{10.107}$$

If

$$\theta(t) = \frac{\partial f(0, t)}{\partial t} - \frac{\partial g}{\partial t} + a(f(0, t) - g(t)), \tag{10.108}$$

then the model exactly recovers the initial term structure. Compare this result with the analogous extended Vasicek form given in Chapter 7.

10.4 JUMP MODELS

A large sub-category of models attempts to capture the observed jump behaviour of interest rates in the market. That jumps exist is evident; jumps are caused by central bank action as well as by unanticipated news. Monetary authorities often use rate-setting as part of their toolkit for implementing monetary policy. As soon as an official rate is altered, the whole yield curve will shift in line with it.

The general framework described in the previous section includes jumps, but has to be specialised down to make a workable, implementable model.

We start this section by describing some properties of stochastic processes incorporating jump behaviour. We then look at the four main types of model that presently include jumps.

1. *Jump-augmented HJM models.*
    These include the models of Jarrow and Madan (91) [316], Bjork (n.d.) [64][3] Das (97) [155] and Shirakawa (91) [492].
2. *Factor jump models.*
    A number of models take ordinary factor models, such as Vasicek or Cox, Ingersoll and Ross, and augment them with jump processes. Models in this category include Das (97) [156], Baz and Das (96) [56] and Ahn and Thompson (88) [7]. Duffie, Pan and Singleton (98) [186] jump-augment the general class of affine models.
3. *Jump-augmented price kernel models.*
    Continuous time interest rate models of this type include Attari (96) [28] and Das and Foresi (96) [157].
4. *Official models.*
    These models try to explicitly model the rate-setting behaviour of the monetary authorities. Examples include Honore (98) [286] and Babbs and Webber (94) [40], (95) [41].

10.4.1 Jump-Augmented HJM

The theory of HJM models with diffusion processes is well understood. It is easy to incorporate jumps into this framework, although usually at the cost of much greater computational complexity.

Following Bjork (n.d.) [64] we specialise down the general framework of Section 10.3. Suppose N_t is a counting process with predictable intensity λ_t under P. We take the bond price process under P to be of the form (10.67),

$$\frac{\mathrm{d}P_t(T)}{P_{t-}(T)} = m_t(T)\mathrm{d}t + v_t(T)\mathrm{d}z_t + n_t(T)\mathrm{d}N_t. \tag{10.109}$$

The results of Section 10.3 relating the forward rate process and the short rate process to the bond process hold exactly as then.

---

[3] Superceded by Bjork *et al.* (96) [71].

Existence of Martingale Measures

The results of Section 10.3 simplify in this case. If Q is (locally) equivalent to P with

$$dQ_t = L_t\, dP_t, \tag{10.110}$$

for the Radon–Nikodým derivative L_t, then L_t has the process

$$dL_t = L_t g_t dz_t + L_{t-} h_t \{dN_t - \lambda(t)dt\}, \tag{10.111}$$

with $L_0 = 1$ and $\mathbb{E}^P[L_t] = 1$ for all t, where g_t and h_t are predictable processes with $h \geq -1$. Then

$$dz_t^Q = dz_t - g_t\, dt \tag{10.112}$$

is a Q-Wiener process and

$$\lambda^Q(t) = (1 + h(t))\lambda(t) \tag{10.113}$$

is the Q-intensity of N_t. A martingale measure exists if

$$m_t(T) + g_t v_t(T) + n_t(T)(1 + h(t))\lambda(t) = r_t. \tag{10.114}$$

Here, g_t is the market price of diffusion risk and h_t is the market price of (Poisson) jump risk. Equation (10.114) determines how the drift of the forward rate process must relate to the forward rate volatility and jump intensity under the EMM. Without the jump term this is just the usual HJM forward rate drift condition.

The Forward Rate Process under Q

If under the martingale measure Q we have

$$df_t(T) = \alpha_t(T)dt + \sigma_t(T)dz_t + \delta_t(T)dN_t, \tag{10.115}$$

then

$$\alpha_t(T) = \sigma_t(T)\int_t^T \sigma_t(s)ds - \delta_t(T)e^{D_t(T)}\lambda^Q(t), \tag{10.116}$$

where $D_t(T) = -\int_t^T \delta_t(s)ds$ and for $S_t(T) = -\int_t^T \sigma_t(s)ds$ the bond price process under Q is

$$\frac{dP_t(T)}{P_{t-}(T)} = r_t\, dt + S_t(T)dz_t^Q + \left(e^{D_t(T)} - 1\right)d\widetilde{N}_t, \tag{10.117}$$

where $\widetilde{N}_t$ is the compensated process $d\widetilde{N}_t = dN_t - \lambda^Q(t)dt$.

Suppose that under Q the short rate process is

$$dr_t = a_t(r_t)dt + b_t(r_t)dz_t + q_t\, dN_t, \tag{10.118}$$

where a, b and q are deterministic functions, z_t is a Q-Wiener process and N_t has deterministic Q-intensity $\lambda(t, r_{t-})$. Then a derivative F with payoff $\Phi(r)$ at time T obeys the PDDE

$$\frac{\partial F}{\partial t} + AF - rF = 0, \tag{10.119}$$

$$F(T, r) = \Phi(r), \tag{10.120}$$

where

$$A = a_t(r)\frac{\partial F}{\partial r} + \frac{1}{2}(b_t(r))^2\frac{\partial^2 F}{\partial r^2} + [F(t, r + q_t(r)) - F(t, r)]\lambda(t, r) \qquad (10.121)$$

is the infinitesimal generator of r_t. Methods exist to compute numerical solutions to this PDDE (see Chapter 12).

Shirakawa

Shirakawa (91) [492] considers an explicitly jump-augmented HJM model with

$$df_t(T) = \alpha(T - t)dt + \delta(T - t)[\beta dz_t + \gamma(dN_t - \lambda dt)], \qquad (10.122)$$

where z_t is a vector Wiener process, $\alpha(\tau)$ is the drift, β is a constant volatility, N_t is a k-dimensional Poisson process with constant intensity vector $\lambda = (\lambda_1, \ldots, \lambda_k)$, γ is a k-dimensional vector of jump sizes, $\gamma = (\gamma_1, \ldots, \gamma_k)$, and $\delta(\tau)$ is a time to maturity 'risk scaling factor'.

When z_t is one-dimensional we can solve the PDDE to get a Black's formula for the prices of pure discount bond options. However, the jump intensities in this model are constant. This is not very realistic. Jarrow and Madan (91) [316] extend Shirakawa to allow the intensities to be path-dependent.

An option pricing formula (Shirakawa) We wish to find the value c_t at time t of a European pure discount bond call option maturing at time T with strike X on a pure discount bond $P_t(S)$ maturing at time $S > T$. Suppose that z_t is one-dimensional. Then

$$c_t = P_t(S)N(d_1) - P_t(T)N(d_2), \qquad (10.123)$$

where

$$d_1 = \frac{1}{\sigma\sqrt{T - t}} \ln\frac{P_t(S)}{XP_t(T)} + \frac{1}{2}\sigma\sqrt{T - t}, \qquad (10.124)$$

$$d_2 = d_1 - \sigma\sqrt{T - t}, \qquad (10.125)$$

with

$$\sigma^2 = \sigma_t^2(T, S) = \frac{\beta^2}{T - t}\int_t^T [\xi(S - u) - \xi(T - u)]^2 \, du, \qquad (10.126)$$

where $\xi(t) = \int_0^t \delta(u)du$. When $\delta(t) = e^{-\lambda t}$ then

$$\sigma_t(T, S) = \frac{\beta}{\sqrt{T - t}}\frac{1 - e^{-\lambda(S-T)}}{\lambda}\left(\frac{1 - e^{-2\lambda(T-t)}}{2\lambda}\right)^{\frac{1}{2}}, \quad \lambda \neq 0,$$

$$\sigma_t(T, S) = \beta(S - T), \qquad\qquad\qquad\qquad \lambda = 0. \qquad (10.127)$$

This result extends the corresponding HJM formula.

10.4.2   Factor Jump Models

Various authors have tried to patch jumps into interest rate models with diffusion factors. For instance, Ahn and Thompson (88) [7] generalise the Cox, Ingersoll and Ross (CIR) model by incorporating jumps into a general equilibrium framework. They augment the processes followed by the underlying state variables by Poisson processes. Their result is a direct extension of CIR. For instance, the short rate process becomes

$$dr_t = \alpha(\mu - r_t)dt + \sigma\sqrt{r_t}\,dz_t + \delta dN_t, \qquad (10.128)$$

with α, μ, σ and δ constants, where N_t is a Poisson process with intensity πr_t, with constant π. With this simple extension Ahn and Thompson can compute the conditional mean and variance of r_t, and find an affine formula for pure discount bond prices.

Jump-Augmented Vasicek Models

Das (97) [156], Das and Foresi (96) [157] and Baz and Das (96) [56] extend the Vasicek model by adding in jumps. The short rate is modelled as

$$dr_t = \alpha(\mu - r_t)dt + \sigma dz_t + J\,dN_t, \qquad (10.129)$$

where N_t is a Poisson process with constant intensity λ and J is a random jump size. When J is exponential Bernoulli or normal it is possible to find pricing formulae.

Suppose that z_t, J and N_t are mutually independent. Then it is possible to derive the characteristic function of r_t as a function of $\mathbb{E}[J^n]$, $n \geq 1$. It is possible to compute the values of conditional moments

$$\mu_1 = \mathbb{E}[r_t \mid r_0 = r], \quad \mu_2 = \mathbb{E}[r_t^2 \mid r_0 = r], \ldots \qquad (10.130)$$

of r_t. For instance,

$$\mu_1 = \left(\mu + \frac{\lambda}{\alpha}\mathbb{E}[J]\right)(1 - e^{-\alpha t}) + re^{-\alpha t}, \qquad (10.131)$$

$$\mu_2 = (\sigma^2 + \lambda\mathbb{E}\left[J^2\right])\frac{1 - e^{-2\alpha t}}{2\alpha} + \mu_1^2, \qquad (10.132)$$

$$\cdots$$

(see Das). The conditional variance is then

$$\mu_2 - \mu_1^2 = (\sigma^2 + \lambda\mathbb{E}\left[J^2\right])\frac{1 - e^{-2\alpha t}}{2\alpha}. \qquad (10.133)$$

The Characteristic Function

The characteristic function of a random variable $r_t \mid r_0$ is the Fourier transform of $r_t \mid r_0$:

$$\phi(s \mid r_0, t) = \mathbb{E}_0\left[e^{isr_t}\right] \in \mathbb{C}, \qquad (10.134)$$

where $\mathbb{C}$ denotes the complex numbers, and $i = \sqrt{-1}$.

Moments μ_i are related to the characteristic function. In fact

$$\mu_i = \frac{\partial^i \phi}{\partial s^i}\bigg|_{s=0}. \tag{10.135}$$

The characteristic function satisfies the Kolmogorov backward equation. If r_t has the process (10.129) then

$$\frac{1}{2}\sigma^2 \frac{\partial^2 \phi}{\partial r^2} + \alpha(\mu - r)\frac{\partial \phi}{\partial r} + \lambda \mathbb{E}[\phi(r+J) - \Phi(r)] = \frac{\partial \phi}{\partial t} \tag{10.136}$$

with boundary condition $\phi(s \mid r_0, 0) = e^{isr_0}$. The general solution to (10.136) is

$$\phi(s \mid r, T) = e^{A(s|T)+B(s|T)r}, \tag{10.137}$$

where

$$A(s \mid T) = \int \left(\alpha\mu B(s \mid T) + \tfrac{1}{2}\sigma^2 B^2(s \mid T) + \lambda\mathbb{E}\left[e^{JB(s|T)} - 1\right]\right) dT, \tag{10.138}$$

$$B(s \mid T) = ise^{-\alpha T}. \tag{10.139}$$

Das solves these in special cases when the random variable J has 'easy' densities; when J is exponential Bernoulli or normal.

J is exponential Bernoulli   Suppose that J is exponential Bernoulli, with Bernoulli parameter ψ, and exponential distribution parameter β. J is positive with probability ψ, negative with probability $1 - \psi$, and $|J|$ is exponentially distributed, with parameter β. Then

$$A(s \mid T) = is\alpha\mu\frac{1 - e^{-\alpha T}}{\alpha} - \frac{1}{2}s^2\sigma^2\frac{1 - e^{-2\alpha T}}{2\alpha}$$

$$+ i\frac{\lambda}{\alpha}(1 - 2\psi)\left[\tan^{-1}\left(\frac{s}{\beta}e^{-\alpha T}\right) - \tan^{-1}\left(\frac{s}{\beta}\right)\right]$$

$$+ \frac{1}{2}\frac{\lambda}{\alpha}\ln\frac{\beta^2 + s^2 e^{-2\alpha T}}{\beta^2 + s^2}, \tag{10.140}$$

$$B(s \mid T) = ise^{-\alpha T}. \tag{10.141}$$

J is normal   Suppose that J is normally distributed. Set

$$E_n = \mathbb{E}[r_T \mid r_0, n \text{ jumps before time } T]$$

$$= \left(\mu + \frac{n}{\alpha}\mathbb{E}[J]\right)\left(1 - e^{-\alpha T}\right) + r_0 e^{-\alpha T}, \tag{10.142}$$

$$V_n = \text{var}[r_T \mid r_0, n \text{ jumps before time } T]$$

$$= \left(\sigma^2 + n\mathbb{E}\left[J^2\right]\right)\frac{1 - e^{-2\alpha T}}{2\alpha}. \tag{10.143}$$

Then, conditional on n jumps, the density function is

$$f_n \equiv f(r_T \mid r_0, n \text{ jumps before time } T)$$

$$= \frac{1}{\sqrt{2\pi V_n}} \exp\left(-\frac{(r_t - E_n)^2}{2V_n}\right). \tag{10.144}$$

So, since jumps are Poisson,

$$f(r_T \mid r_0) = \sum_{n=0}^{\infty} \frac{e^{-\lambda T}(\lambda T)^n}{n!} f_n. \tag{10.145}$$

The Transition Density Function

We have found the transition density function when J is normal. It is extremely useful to find the transition density function in the general case. Das uses an expression for the transition density function as the Fourier inverse of the characteristic function

$$f(r_{t+\tau} \mid r_t) = \frac{1}{\pi} \int_0^{\infty} \mathrm{Re}\left[e^{-isr_{t+\tau}}\phi(s \mid r_t, \tau)\right] ds, \tag{10.146}$$

where $\phi(s \mid r_t, \tau) = \mathbb{E}_t\left[e^{isr_{t+\tau}} \mid r_t\right]$ is the characteristic function. If f is known the process can be estimated using maximum likelihood methods (see Chapter 17).

Bond Prices

Suppose the process for r_t under the objective measure is

$$dr_t = \alpha(\mu - r_t)dt + \sigma dz_t + J \, dN_t, \tag{10.147}$$

with intensity λ. Under the EMM Q suppose the process becomes

$$dr_t = (\alpha(\mu - r_t) - \theta\sigma)dt + \sigma dz_t + J \, dN_t, \tag{10.148}$$

with intensity $\lambda^* = (1 - \theta^*)$. With $\tau = T - t$, bond prices $P_t(T)$ satisfy the PDDE

$$\frac{1}{2}\sigma^2 \frac{\partial^2 P}{\partial r^2} + (\alpha(\mu - r) - \theta\sigma)\frac{\partial P}{\partial r} - \frac{\partial P}{\partial \tau} + \lambda^*\mathbb{E}[P(r+J) - P(r)] = rP \tag{10.149}$$

with $P_\tau(r) = 1$. The general solution to this PDDE is

$$P_t(T) = e^{A(\tau)+B(\tau)r}, \tag{10.150}$$

where

$$B(\tau) = -\frac{1 - e^{-\alpha\tau}}{\alpha}, \tag{10.151}$$

$$A(\tau) = \int \left[(\alpha\mu - \theta\sigma)B(\tau) + \frac{1}{2}\sigma^2 B^2(\tau) + \lambda^*\mathbb{E}\left[e^{JB(\tau)} - 1\right]\right] d\tau, \tag{10.152}$$

with $A(0) = 0$.

When J is exponential Bernoulli, for instance, explicit solutions can be found (Das and Foresi (96) [157]).

Approximate Solutions

The PDDE (10.149) is equivalent to

$$\frac{1}{2}\sigma^2\frac{\partial^2 P}{\partial r^2} + (\alpha(\mu - r) - \theta\sigma)\frac{\partial P}{\partial r} - \frac{\partial P}{\partial \tau} + \lambda^* P(r)\mathbb{E}\left[e^{-JB(\tau)} - 1\right] = rP. \tag{10.153}$$

By making a second-order approximation to the exponential term Baz and Das (96) [56] are able to find approximate solutions to the PDDE. Expand out the exponential term as

$$e^{-JB(\tau)} - 1 = -JB + \tfrac{1}{2}J^2B^2 + \cdots \tag{10.154}$$

and truncate to second order. If $J \sim N(\eta, \gamma)$ then $\mathbb{E}\left[e^{-JB(\tau)} - 1\right] \sim -\eta B +\tfrac{1}{2}\left(\eta^2 + \gamma^2\right)B^2$. If this approximation is substituted into (10.149) the new PDDE can be solved explicitly as

$$P(r, \tau) = e^{-D+C(\tau)-B(\tau)r}, \tag{10.155}$$

where

$$B(\tau) = \frac{1 - e^{-\alpha\tau}}{\alpha}, \tag{10.156}$$

$$C(\tau) = -\frac{Ne^{-2\alpha\tau}}{4\alpha^3} + \frac{(\alpha M + N)e^{-\alpha\tau}}{\alpha^3} + \frac{(2\alpha M + N)\tau}{2\alpha^3}, \tag{10.157}$$

$$D = \frac{M}{\alpha^2} + \frac{3N}{4\alpha^3}, \tag{10.158}$$

with $M = \theta\sigma - \alpha\mu - \lambda^*\eta$, $N = \sigma^2 + \left(\eta^2 + \sigma^2\right)\lambda^*$.

A good approximate solution means that it is easy to calibrate the model to the yield curve.

10.4.3   Kernel Jump Models

Several authors have used the price kernel framework to investigate jump models of interest rates. Attari (96) [28] uses the Lucas framework directly (see Chapter 11), where bond prices are determined by preferences. Das and Foresi (96) [157] find a price kernel formulation for a jump-augmented Vasicek model.

Attari's Pure Jump Model

Attari (96) [28] constructs an interesting model where the random part of the underlying state variable is pure jump. By taking limits appropriately the state variable tends, in the limit, to a variety of jump-diffusion processes.

In the Lucas framework pure discount bond prices are given by

$$P_t(T) = \mathbb{E}_t \left[e^{-\rho(T-t)} \frac{u_c(T)}{u_c(t)} \right], \tag{10.159}$$

where $u_c = \partial u/\partial c$ is the derivative of the utility $u(c)$ of consumption c and ρ is a discount factor for preferences. Economic frameworks of this sort are explored in more detail in Chapter 11.

Attari assumes a particular functional form for his utility function. He uses a power utility $u_c = c^{\gamma-1}$, and assumes that consumption is a function of underlying state variables Y_t with

$$c_t = y_0 e^{gt + Y_t}, \tag{10.160}$$

$$dY_t = -\alpha Y_t \, dt + \sum_{j=1}^{J} s_j \, dN_t^j, \tag{10.161}$$

where N_t^j are Poisson processes with intensities λ_j and g is a constant. Substituting into (10.159) he obtains

$$P_t(T) = \mathbb{E}_t \left[e^{-\rho(T-t)} e^{(\gamma-1)(g(T-t)+Y(T)-Y(t))} \right]. \tag{10.162}$$

This expectation can be solved so that

$$P_t(T) = \exp(-(T-t)(\rho + g(1-\gamma)))$$

$$\times \exp\left(-(T-t) \sum_{j=1}^{J} \lambda_j (1 - I(t, T, s_j)) \right) \tag{10.163}$$

$$\times \exp\left(-(1-\gamma) \left(1 - e^{-\alpha(T-t)} \right) Y(t) \right),$$

where

$$I(t, T, s_j) = \frac{1}{T-t} \int_t^T \exp\left(-(1-\gamma)s_j e^{-(T-u)} \right) du. \tag{10.164}$$

The short rate process is found to be

$$dr_t = \alpha(\theta - r_t)dt - (1-\gamma)\alpha \sum_{j=1}^{J} s_j \, dN_t^j, \tag{10.165}$$

where $\theta = \rho + (1-\gamma)g + \Sigma_{j=1}^{J} \lambda_j (1 - e^{-(1-\gamma)s_j})$. Attari rewrites the formula for pure discount bond prices in terms of r_t. The resulting model is affine and it is possible to obtain an explicit formula for bond option prices.

Modifying the Process for y_t

Attari extends the model by

1. Allowing jump sizes have a continuous range; and
2. Allowing intensities to tend to infinity.

By take appropriate limits it is possible to obtain a variety of limiting behaviour, and it is possible to obtain bond and bond option formulae for a variety of processes. For instance, Attari finds formulae for the following processes:

1. $dr_t = \alpha(\theta - r_t)dt + (1 - \gamma)\alpha\sigma dz_t - (1 - \gamma)\alpha\Sigma_{j=1}^{J}s_j \, dN_t^j$.
2. $dr_t = \alpha(\theta(t) - r_t)dt + (1 - \gamma)\alpha\sigma x(t)dz_t - (1 - \gamma)\alpha S \, dN_t$,
   where $S \sim N(\mu_s, \sigma_s^2)$, for functions $\theta(t)$ and $x(t)$.
3. $dr_t = \alpha(\theta - r_t)dt + (1 - \gamma)\alpha c_1 \, dG_t^1 + (1 - \gamma)\alpha c_2 \, dG_t^2$,
   where G^1 and G^2 are gamma variates.

He also shows how hedging strategies can be found for derivatives in this formulation.

Price Kernels for Jump-Augmented Vasicek

Das and Foresi (96) [157] investigate a jump-augmented Vasicek model with short rate process

$$dr_t = \alpha(\mu - r_t)dt + \sigma dz_t + J \, dN_t, \qquad (10.166)$$

where $J \sim B(\psi, \beta)$ is exponential Bernoulli with Bernoulli parameter ψ and exponential parameter β, and N_t is Poisson, with constant intensity λ. They show that bond prices are determined by a price kernel:

$$P_t(t + \tau) = \mathbb{E}\left[\frac{m(t + \tau)}{m(t)}\right], \qquad (10.167)$$

where

$$-\frac{dm_t}{m_t} = r_t \, dt + \lambda dz_t + \lambda_J(dN_t - \lambda dt). \qquad (10.168)$$

They are able to obtain an explicit formula for bond prices.

Das and Foresi extend the framework by directly specifying the price kernel. They set

$$m(t) = \exp(-y_t - X_t), \qquad (10.169)$$

where

$$dX_t = \left(x_t + \tfrac{1}{2}\lambda^2\right) dt + \lambda dz_t, \qquad (10.170)$$

$$dx_t = a(b - x_t)dt + \sigma dz_t, \qquad (10.171)$$

$$y_t = y_0 \left(1 - \lambda\mu t + \sum_{j=1}^{N_t} J_j\right), \qquad (10.172)$$

with N_t a Poisson counter with intensity λ and J_j iid random jump sizes with $\mathbb{E}[J_j] = \mu$. In this framework they are able to find formulae for bond and bond options, expressed in terms of the characteristic function ϕ of J.

10.4.4 Official Rate Models

As part of their monetary regime monetary authorities control the levels of interest rates in their economies. Official rate models attempt to describe their rate-setting behaviour. Usually the rates controlled by the monetary authorities behave as if they are jump processes. Term structures are contingent upon levels of these official rates. Examples are 'Lombard' rates and 'Discount' rates. In some regimes 'Repo' rates may follow jump–diffusion processes influenced by the monetary authorities.

The controlled official rates may be

- hard ceilings or floors on market rates, or
- actual market rates themselves.

It is quite possible to incorporate official rates into models. Papers that have developed and investigated models of this type include Babbs and Webber (94) [40], (95) [41], Honore (98) [286], El-Jahel, Lindberg and Perraudin (97) [200] and Tsoi, Yang and Yeung (98) [525].

Example: An Official Corridor

Suppose that the monetary authorities publish an official floor rate D_t, the Discount rate, and a ceiling rate, L_t, the Lombard rate. These rates may be actual interest rates at which banks might theoretically deal with the monetary authorities. We assume that the monetary authorities control the levels of D_t and L_t so that $D_t \leq r_t \leq L_t$, where r_t is the short rate, and that the monetary authorities are able, if they choose, to directly influence the level of the short rate r_t.

By their behaviour in adjusting the levels of D_t and L_t the monetary authorities

1. Signal their potential willingness to defend the interval $[D_t, L_t]$;
2. By shifting D_t or L_t, the monetary authorities signal their willingness to accommodate, or restrict, movements in r_t.

We outline the model of Babbs and Webber (95) [41]. The state variables are a set of pure jump processes, Y_i, and diffusion process, X_k. The jump processes Y_i are

$$Y_i(t) = Y_i(0) + \sum_{j=1}^{J} c_{i,j} N_{i,j}, \qquad (10.173)$$

where $N_{i,j}$ are counting processes with intensities $\lambda_{i,j} = \lambda_{i,j}(Y_1, \ldots, Y_n, X_1, \ldots, X_m)$ and $c_{i,j}$ are fixed jump sizes for each $N_{i,j}$.

One way to model an official corridor is to set the Discount rate and the Lombard rate to be pure jump processes, $D_t = Y_1$, $L_t = Y_2$, and to set the short rate to be an explicit function of the official rates D_t and L_t and an additional diffusion state variable $X_t = X_1$, so that $r_t = r(D_t, L_t, X_t)$. The processes for D_t and L_t and the function r_t are set up so that $D_t \leq r_t \leq L_t$.

The market's view of authorities' actions are encoded into the intensities $\lambda_{i,j}$. A wide variety of behaviour can be accommodated.

The usual PDDE is obtained. It is usually necessary to solve it numerically, but explicit solutions may be found in special cases. For an example see El-Jahel *et al.* (97) [200].

A UK Example

Babbs and Webber (94) [40] use their framework to model the UK monetary regime as it existed in the early 1990s. The Bank of England controlled very short maturity interest rates. Effectively the short rate was moved by discrete amounts, jumping from time to time under the control of the Bank of England. The short rate itself was the official rate. In their model Babbs and Webber took their state variables to be the short rate r_t, following a pure jump process, and a 'prospective' interest rate x_t following a diffusion process,

$$\mathrm{d}r_t = \sum_{j=1}^{J} c_j \, \mathrm{d}N_{j,t}, \tag{10.174}$$

$$\mathrm{d}x_t = a(r_t, x_t)\mathrm{d}t + \sigma \, \mathrm{d}z_t, \tag{10.175}$$

where $a(r, x) = \beta(pr + (1 - p)\mu - x)$, and only a fixed number of possible jump sizes c_j, $j = i, \ldots, J$, in r_t were permitted. Jump intensities λ_j depend on $x_t - r_t$ so that when $x_t - r_t$ becomes large, the λ_j get large in such a way that a jump in r_t towards x_t becomes more likely.

In this case the PDDE takes the simple form

$$\frac{1}{2}\sigma^2 \frac{\partial^2 P}{\partial x^2} + a^*(r, x)\frac{\partial P}{\partial x} + \frac{\partial P}{\partial t} + \sum_{j=1}^{J} \lambda_j^*[P(r + c_j, x) - P(r, x)] = rP(r, x), \tag{10.176}$$

where $a^*(r, x) = a(r, x) - \theta_0\sigma$ and $\lambda_j^* = (1 - \theta_j)\lambda_j$ are risk-adjusted coefficients. This PDDE may be solved efficiently by numerical methods (see Chapter 12).

In the sterling market certain empirical regularities could be observed.

1. Libor jumps from time to time. Libor jumps when the official short rate changes and in the same direction as the change in the short rate.
2. Interbank rates lie close to the level of the official short rate. Usually three-month rates are within 0.5% and rarely greater than 1% of the short rate.
3. Long rates jump by less than short rates.
4. Libor rates appear to 'anticipate' jumps; they often move in the direction of a jump, prior to the jump occurring.

These empirical observations are mirrored by the numerical solutions of the model. Term structures depend upon the values of initial r_t and x_t, relative to μ, and have at most one hump.

In between jumps in r_t, the term structure evolves as x_t evolves. Writing l_t for a short maturity rate, such as the three-month rate, the model generates the desired behaviour:

1. l_t jumps when r_t jumps;
2. l_t stays close to r_t;
3. Longer rates jump by less than shorter rates;
4. l_t appears to 'anticipate' jumps in the sense that as x_t increases (decreases)
   (a) l_t increases (decreases),
   (b) the probability of a jump up (down) increases.
   Jumps upwards (downwards) tend to be associated with elevated (depressed) levels of l_t.

The Babbs and Webber formulation explicitly modelled the sterling regime, recognising that model parameters are controlled by authorities. Their illustrative model displayed similar empirical features to sterling.

Monetary authorities want to control levels of interest rates as part of their broader economic policies, but they can only really control only fairly short rates. Models of this sort allow policy issues to be addressed; it is possible to explore some consequences of monetary activity on the term structure in a no-arbitrage context.

11
Economic Models

Understanding the links between output, prices, interest rates, and money supply has been a major objective of economists for decades, if not centuries (see Hume *Of Money* and *Of Interest* quoted in Lucas (90) [368].) Modern macroeconomic models are most frequently set in a representative agent framework where identical agents (or a small number of distinct types of agent) make optimal decisions by maximising their utility. Optimality conditions are then used as a basis for equilibrium in the economy. Other frameworks are also used. The overlapping generations framework is potentially very powerful, although the standard two-period models are inadequate for term structure purposes. Various authors, for instance Bullard (92) [108], have explored n-period overlapping generations models.[1]

On the other hand, financial models of interest rates emphasise no-arbitrage at the expense of an economic context. This chapter is concerned with describing some concepts from economics and seeing how they can be applied to financial models of interest rates.

The first section of this chapter reviews two economic shibboleths: the expectations hypothesis and the Fisher hypothesis. Although both are useful and valuable tools in their appropriate contexts, neither—as usually formulated—can play a central role in a no-arbitrage interest rate model. They are disposed of here. The $IS-LM$-Phillips framework is discussed, and the role of the long rate is reviewed.

Section 11.2 describes a hybrid interest rate model based on a model due to Sommer (96) [500]. Sommer's no-arbitrage model is integrated with an economic sector determined by an $IS-LM$-Phillips framework.

Section 11.3 uses the $IS-LM$ framework as a direct foundation for a no-arbitrage model. A two-factor affine model based upon these relationships is described. Introducing a third factor results in a chaotic interest model. (This section is based on Tice and Webber (97) [523].)

Section 11.4 investigates hyperinflation and interest rate modelling. The Cagan hyperinflation model, derived in the $IS-LM$ framework, is shown to be related to an extended Vasicek model.

---

[1] n-period overlapping generation models appear a particularly interesting research area, as one may perhaps move on to the limiting case with n arbitrarily large. This may lead to subtle but important problems of demographics.

A major historical contribution to interest rate modelling has been the general equilibrium framework (Cox, Ingersoll and Ross (85) [147]). We describe this framework in Section 11.5. The consumption based Lucas framework is also described. The Lucas framework is far more tractable than the production based framework.

Section 11.6 discusses the price kernel and its interpretation.

11.1 ECONOMICS AND INTEREST RATES

One still finds economics textbooks where the term structure of interest rates is explained solely in terms of expectations hypotheses, preferred habitat models, and other classical mechanisms. We discuss the expectations hypothesis in the first part of this section, but the financial approach to interest rate modelling owes little to these ideas. Our objective in this section is to review some important ideas from economics; we discard what does not seem useful and exploit in future sections the ideas that are relevant.

We restrict our attention to models in continuous time. For economic models set in continuous time the period over which expectations are made, and whether rates are long or short, must be explicitly considered. In discrete time, rates, actual or expected, are frequently taken over a single period. In continuous time, as the length of a period decreases to zero, some expectations and rates need to remain 'long' rather than becoming 'instantaneous'.

We start by exploring the expectations hypothesis and the Fisher hypothesis. We then focus on macroeconomic basics, reviewing a textbook macroeconomic model. Neither representative investor models nor overlapping period models are discussed. We conclude by reviewing the part played by the long rate in economic and financial models.

11.1.1 The Expectations Hypothesis

In this book economic models of interest rates founded solely upon the expectations hypothesis or the liquidity premium hypothesis are not discussed. These models may not in general be arbitrage free, yet tests of some variant or other of the expectations hypothesis, or models based upon the assumption of the expectations hypothesis, continue to generate a large literature.

In its simplest form the expectations hypothesis claims that the current value $f(t, \tau)$ of the instantaneous forward rate for time to maturity τ is the current expected value, under the objective measure, of the future short rate, $r_{t+\tau}$ (with the possible addition of a term premium b_τ):

$$f(t, \tau) = \mathbb{E}_t[r_{t+\tau}] + b_\tau. \tag{11.1}$$

More sophisticated formulations are possible, but to the extent that arbitrage is allowed they are flawed. We have seen that (11.1) holds, with $b_\tau \equiv 0$, under the $t + \tau$-forward measure, but not in general under the objective measure. In papers investigating equation (11.1) the nature of the expectation is often not discussed. It is implicitly assumed to be the objective measure.

The literature on the expectations hypothesis is reviewed by Cook and Hahn (90) [141] who find a lack of support for it. Since then a number of articles claim to have found evidence in support of the hypothesis. These include Sola and Driffill (94) [499] who do not reject it on US data. Gerlach and Smets (97) [245] are also unable to reject it. Some articles find links between the shape of the yield curve and the expectations hypothesis. Frankel and Lown (94) [229] found a relationship to the slope of the term structure. Engle and Ng (93) [208] found that ARCH effects might help to explain the shape of the term structure. Rudebusch (95) [464] finds that interest rate targeting might explain apparent deviations from the expectations hypothesis. This view receives some support from Fuhrer (96) [232].

Other authors continue to reject the hypothesis. These include Campbell and Shiller (91) [114], Taylor (92) [519] on UK data, MacDonald and Macmillan (94) [372] using US survey data and Kugler (96) [345] in the context of regime shifts. Cuthbertson (96) [151] found inconclusive results.

It seems safe to conclude that there is no compelling theoretical or empirical reason to believe that the expectations hypothesis is a working reality in the market.

11.1.2 The Fisher Hypothesis

It is a textbook commonplace that nominal rates are equal to real rates plus expected inflation. Examined in detail by Fisher (07) [218], and known as the Fisher effect or the Fisher hypothesis, this relationship is still, after almost a century, econometrically controversial.[2] Despite much work it remains unproven except perhaps at long horizons. Recent articles finding support for the hypothesis at long horizons include Ireland (96) [305] who concludes that the 10-year rate is a good guide to expected inflation, and Boudoukh and Richardson (93) [82] who examined the Fisher effect on stock returns. The results of Engsted (93) [210] comparing a long-term rate and future realised inflation are inconclusive. Mishkin (92) [400] found only weak support for long-run effects, and no support for short-term effects. Using UK data Andrade and Clare (94) [24] found no support for short-or long-run Fisher effects.

Other studies have looked at historical data. Thies (85) [521] looks at inflation in the nineteenth century. He finds evidence for the Fisher hypothesis. Barsky and de Long (91) [54] explore the Fisher effect using pre-1914 gold production data. This should predict inflation, but their results suggest it does not.

Many difficulties surround the definition and estimation of expected inflation. Fisher himself used adaptive expectations, where expected inflation is modelled as an AR process. More recent studies assume rational expectations, where psychological expected values are assumed to be equal to mathematical expected values, and where for a continuous-time model the latter is often assumed to be equal to the drift of the

---

[2] Fisher set the proposition onto a rigorous footing. In fact the concept seems to have emerged in the 1740s in the work of Douglass. He compared interest rates on silver with those on paper money (Humphrey (83) [299]).

price process. Alternatively the Fisher relationship may be presumed to be correct, and is used to back out expectations of inflation.[3]

We shall see in Section 11.5 an arbitrage-free model in which the Fisher hypothesis does not hold.

11.1.3 A Textbook Macroeconomic Model

The standard macroeconomic model we present is an $IS-LM$–Phillips model supplemented by an expectations formation equation and a reaction equation. This model and versions of it have been studied in many places. A review is given by Kerr and King (96) [333]. Textbook treatments of the basic model may be found in, amongst others, Turnovsky (95) [526], Obstfeld and Rogoff (96) [423] and Blanchard and Fischer (89) [75].

The notation is

P_t	price level,	p_t	log price level,	
M_t	money supply,	m_t	log money supply,	
Y_t	output,	y_t	log output,	
		$\bar{y}$	'natural level' of output, a constant,	(11.2)
		r_t	nominal short rate,	
		l_t	nominal long rate,	
		π_t	expected long run future inflation.	

A standard price index is often used as a surrogate for P_t, and Y_t is often represented by GNP. M_t represents the stock of money in circulation, including short-term bank deposits. It may be measured by various aggregates. (The effects of using different aggregates has been tested by various authors.[4])

The basic $IS-LM$–Phillips equations are:

$$y_t = a - b(l_t - \pi_t), \qquad IS,$$

$$m_t - p_t = \phi y_t - \beta r_t, \qquad LM, \qquad (11.3)$$

$$\mathrm{d}p_t = f(y_t - \bar{y})\mathrm{d}t + \sigma\,\mathrm{d}z_{p,t}, \qquad \text{Phillips}$$

where a, b, ϕ, β, f and σ are constants, output y_t is presumed to be in equilibrium with income, the money supply m_t is presumed to be in equilibrium with money demand, and $z_{p,t}$ is a Wiener process (under the objective measure).

---

[3] This was assumed by Robertson (92) [456]. Unfortunately he also assumes that the short rate follows an MA process.

[4] M1 has been used by Baba *et al.* (92) [34] in an investigation of the LM relationship. After the Fed de-emphasised US M1 in 1982 Belongia and Chalfant (90) [61] investigate the implications of this for measurements of the money supply. M2 was used by Hallman, Porter and Small (91) [265] in an investigation of inflation. Dotsey and Otrok (94) [172] used M2 in an investigation using the $IS-LM$ framework to discover possible determinants of output and prices. Ireland (94) [304] compares M1 and M2 in a growth model. Feldstein and Stock (96) [213] compare a number of measures. Bullard (94) [109] looked at various measures as possible determinants of inflation. Drake (96) [175] looked at components of money demand in the UK. Taylor (93) [520] uses a broad definition of money.

The LM ('Liquidity and Money') Line

The *LM* relationship comes from an assumption of equilibrium in the money market. It is assumed that the demand for real (rather than nominal) money is increasing in y_t and decreasing in the nominal short rate r_t. Up to first order

$$\frac{M_{d,t}}{P_t} = \phi y_t - \beta r_t, \tag{11.4}$$

for money demand $M_{d,t}$ and price level P_t, where ϕ and β are positive constants. In equilibrium money demand and supply, $M_{s,t}$, are equal $M_{d,t} = M_{s,t} \equiv M_t$. Using log values on the left-hand side we arrive at (11.3, *LM*).

The IS ('Investments and Savings') Line

To first order expenditure e_t is increasing in output, y_t, and decreasing in the long real interest rate, $l_t - \pi_t$,

$$e_t = e(y_t, l_t - \pi_t) = a - b(l_t - \pi_t) + c y_t, \tag{11.5}$$

for $a, b, c > 0$, $0 < c < 1$. In equilibrium, income, y_t, and expenditure, e_t, are equal so that $e(y_t, l_t - \pi_t) = y_t$. Substituting for e_t and rearranging we get (11.3, *IS*).

The Phillips Equation

The Phillips equation comes in any number of forms. Our simple version assumes that prices vary if output y_t gets out of line with a long-term 'natural' level, $\overline{y}$. If output is too great, there is inflation and prices tend to increase; if it is too low, prices decrease.

11.1.4 Using the System

The system (11.3) is standard, but some comments are necessary. Firstly, this is a basic system somewhat crudely representing fundamental economic processes. It has to be expanded in various ways to incorporate further economic effects.

Secondly, these equations are written in continuous time. It is perhaps more usual to write them in discrete time.[5] A continuous-time formulation forces one to be careful about the timing and extent of one's information set.

Thirdly, the empirical evidence to support this framework is scant. Although the *IS–LM* framework is a basic economic workhorse, empirical support is elusive.[6] The

---

[5] In an early paper Sargent and Wallace (75) [475] use a discrete time version of the model to investigate economic control in a rational expectations framework. Howitt (92) [287] is a more recent example.

[6] Gali (92) [237] discovers it to be relevant to post-war US data, but Cutler *et al.* (97) [152] conclude that it is difficult to support the barest *IS–LM* framework, and that other variables need to be added to it.

dynamics of p_t given by the Phillips curve are very tentative.[7] At best the three equations must be seen as a linearisation of a system very close to equilibrium.

Fourthly, we distinguish between the short and long rates. While it is not unreasonable for r_t to be the short rate, the maturity of the long rate l_t and the long-run expected inflation rate π_t is arbitrary.[8] A number of authors use a single 'one-period' term for both rates.

Fifthly, in writing down the *IS* equation we have implicitly assumed the Fisher hypothesis: that the nominal interest rate is equal to the real rate plus expected inflation.[9,10]

To complete the model we need to specify the dynamics of l_t, π_t and one of r_t and m_t. Current instantaneous expected inflation v_t is often written as $v_t = \mathbb{E}[dp]/dt$. This is simply the drift term in the process for p_t,

$$v_t = \frac{\mathbb{E}[dp]}{dt} = f(y_t - \overline{y}). \tag{11.6}$$

We use an adaptive expectations model of expectations formation,

$$d\pi_t = g(v_t - \pi_t)dt, \tag{11.7}$$

where π_t is expected long-run inflation. Equation (11.7) forces expected long-run inflation to revert to the level of current expected inflation.

There are many ways that expectations can form. Rational expectations is mentioned below. A discussion of expectation formation is given in Evans and Ramey (92) [211]. Adaptive expectations are used by Stulz (86) [507]. Fukao and Benabou (93) [236] compare adaptive with forward looking expectations, after Krugman (91) [342].

The next element is a reaction equation that specifies the action taken by the monetary authorities in the exercise of economic policy. That the monetary authorities respond to economic circumstances and attempt to exercise control is beyond question. The form

---

[7] Alogoskoufis and Smith (91) [13] investigate the Phillips curve in a two-country model. Tallman (95) [513] tests the Phillips curve and extensions to it as a forecast tool for inflation levels. He finds it ineffective.

[8] Economic models, should a long rate be explicitly required, frequently use the yield on a Consol bond. This has many advantages, including a degree of tractability in certain treatments. For instance, Turnovsky and Miller (84) [527] use the yield on a Consol as a proxy for a long rate in a simple macroeconomic model (but see Clark (85) [132]. Grinols and Turnovsky (93) [261] also include a bond, but its maturity is unspecified.

[9] As we have seen, this hypothesis is in general hard to support, and arbitrage-free systems can easily be constructed where it does not hold (for instance, Bakshi and Chen (96) [45]).

[10] Other relevant references include Friedman and Kuttner (92) [230] who perform empirical work on the *LM* equation. In a classic paper Sargent and Wallace (73) [474] discuss the Gibson paradox—the tendency for prices and interest rate levels to be negatively, rather than positively, correlated. Groenewald et al. (97) [262] confirm this effect and develop a model to account for it. In another empirical paper Hafer and Kutan (97) [264] decide that money is not an explanatory factor for real output in the 1980s. In an historical study McKiernan (94) [389] decides that money shocks are more important than interest rate shocks in the period 1875–1912. Norrbin and Reffett (95) [418] conclude, in contrast to previous work, that changes in money supply are caused by both financial and technological shocks. Canova and Marrinan (96) [115] show how a form of *IS* can emerge from a ICAPM model. Smith (92) [497] is an international comparison of time series of correlations between output and prices.

of their reaction is more contentious, although attempts have been made to study it.[11] In the basic $IS-LM$–Phillips framework the reaction function will specify either r_t or m_t. Once one of these is specified the other is taken to be endogenous. We use a reaction function for r_t,

$$dr_t = h(\bar{\pi} - \pi_t)dt, \tag{11.8}$$

where $\bar{\pi}$ is a long-run inflation target and h is a reversion rate. m_t is left endogenous.

Different reaction functions are compared by Fuhrer and Moore (95a) [234], (95b) [235]. For instance, an alternative is to set

$$dm_t = h(\pi_t - \nu_t)dt + \sigma_m \, dz_{m,t}, \tag{11.9}$$

for a Wiener process $z_{m,t}$, so that m_t responds to the difference between current and long-run inflation.

The final element is an equation to determine the level of the dynamics of the long rate, l_t. This can be done in various ways. For instance, Turnovsky and Miller (84) [527] use the yield on a Consol as the long rate and relate this to the short rate. In other versions, for example Tice and Webber (97) [523], π_t is identically zero, and l_t is set equal to r_t.

The complete system can sometimes be solved. We do not present a solution method here but refer to standard textbooks such as Turnovsky (95) [526]. The system is quite flexible. For instance, it has been adapted to model hyperinflations, with no little success (see Section 11.4).

11.1.5 The Long Rate and Incomplete Markets

It is well known that the theoretical long rate, defined as the limit of spot rates as the time to maturity goes to infinity, is deterministic and can never fall (Dybvig, Ingersoll and Ross (96) [194]). This has been investigated by others including El-Karoui, Frachot and Geman (96) [201]. Several assumptions are made in reaching this conclusion. One is that the limit exists. If, for instance, long rates were cyclic in time to maturity, then they would fail to satisfy the required restrictions. Another is that traded instruments exist with arbitrarily large maturities. This assumption does not hold in real markets.[12]

Modern financial models of interest rates include a long rate. In no standard model is this rate other than a constant. Brennan and Schwartz (79) [93] used the Consol yield as a state variable. Although a specific example given in their paper was later shown to be unstable (Hogan (93) [283]), their framework remains valid. More recently Duffie, Ma and Yong (95) [184], under rather restrictive assumptions, showed that the Consol rate could sometimes be specified in terms of the other state variables in a model, and in these circumstances could not be an independent state variable. The Brennan and Schwartz model does not automatically satisfy the restrictions of Duffie *et al.*, so that their Consol rate may indeed be an independent state variable.

---

[11] For instance, Goodfriend (93) [256] investigates the Fed's reaction function for the period 1979–1992. Toma (92) [524] investigates interest rate controls using the $IS-LM$ framework. Fuhrer and Moore (95a) [234], (95b) [235] use a reaction function for the short rate.

[12] Hundred-year bonds exist in the market. These are not long enough.

An attempt to include a long rate of finite maturity was made by Sommer (96) [500]. In his model bonds exist only out to a maximum time to maturity. New bonds of this maturity are being continuously issued so that at each instant new information about the forward rate curve arrives. Sommer derives expressions for bond prices within this framework and gives an explicit example of how the arrival of information can be modelled by specifying a discovery process. His framework is limited in that he restricts his analysis to differentiable forward rate curves, and his example is based upon consistency criteria rather than expectations or some other economically motivated rationale. Nevertheless this paper is an important contribution to theory. It is reviewed and extended in the next section.

Sommer's model is unique in interest rate modelling in that it has incomplete bond markets. His just issued bond, the bond of maximum maturity, cannot be completely hedged.[13] Models such as Chen (95) [125], (96) [126] have stochastic volatility, an untraded variable, but since Chen explicitly models this factor, and since his market has a continuum of bonds, his is not an incomplete market.

Incorporating a fixed finite maximum maturity, τ, is justifiable on empirical grounds; bonds of finite but arbitrary maturity do not exist in the markets. Once τ has been set it becomes a canonical period that can be used to set the time span for long-term expectations. In the comparison below the term 'the long rate' will refer to a rate of long but finite maturity. Intuitively, this may be taken to be 20 years or so, or a period up to and beyond the maturity of the longest instrument in the market, whichever is greater, although the exact maturity is not significant.

Our discussion has indicated a need to explicitly include inflation expectations into interest rate models in a no-arbitrage way. Affine models may have the potential to build in such information by carefully specifying the process followed by long yields. However, these models completely specify the term structure of interest rates out to arbitrary maturities. This defeats our second objective, to incorporate the fact that the long rate does not exist in the markets. In the next section we review a model that does not have a long rate and which we can adapt to introduce the effects of inflation expectations.

11.2   AN ECONOMICALLY MOTIVATED FINANCIAL MODEL OF INTEREST RATES

In this section we briefly review the framework developed by Sommer (96) [500]. He shows how it is possible to model interest rates in an HJM/BGM framework when bonds of time to maturity greater than some maximum τ are not available in the market. A 'discovery' process must be specified that reveals information about newly issued bond prices. Sommer gives an example of a discovery process and prices a number of financial instruments. His choice of discovery process is determined by a desire for tractability and consistency with existing forward rate evolution. In view of the discussion in Section 11.1, we shall prefer to interpret the discovery process as reflecting beliefs about future expected inflation. Such an interpretation is consistent

---

[13] Some market models include only bonds of a certain set of maturities, but all the bonds in existence in the market are hedgeable.

with the philosophy of this chapter, in that it has an economic justification as well as being a purely statistical assumption.

Sommer requires that the forward rate curve be differentiable. This seems an unnecessary restriction but we do not seek to remedy this here. As we shall see, his model ends up with expressions similar to those in Brace, Gatarek and Musiela (although interpreted rather differently). This suggests that extensions to include càdlàg processes for the risk factors and for the discovered forward rate might resemble the extensions to Heath, Jarrow and Morton suggested by Ahn and Thompson (88) [7] and Shirakawa (91) [492].

11.2.1 Sommer's Model

Since the restriction on bonds is in terms of time to maturity it is natural to express the model in the Musiela parameterisation. Starting from an initial time 0, at time t bonds are only observed for times to maturity $x \in [0, \tau]$, where τ is the maximum time to maturity. The notation is:

$B(t, T)$, the value at time t of a PDB maturing with value 1 at time T, $t \leq T \leq t + \tau$,
$D(t, x)$, the value at time t of a PDB maturing with value 1 at time $t + x$, $0 \leq x \leq \tau$,
    so that $D(t, x) = B(t, t + x)$,
$r(t, x)$, the spot rate at time t for maturity period x, $0 \leq x \leq \tau$,
$f(t, x)$, the instantaneous forward rate at time t for time $t + x$, $0 \leq x \leq \tau$,
r_t, the instantaneous short rate at time t, as usual.

We have, as usual,

$$r(t, x) = -\frac{1}{\tau} \ln D(t, x), \tag{11.10}$$

$$f(t, x) = -\frac{1}{D} \frac{\partial}{\partial x} D(t, x) = -\frac{\partial}{\partial x} \ln D(t, x), \tag{11.11}$$

$$r_t = f(t, 0). \tag{11.12}$$

We write $\partial_x = \partial/\partial x$ for differentiation with respect to the second place variable.

At each time t only bonds of maturities in the range $[t, t + \tau]$ can be observed in the market. Only these bonds are available to trade. For convenience we define $a(T) = \max(0, T - \tau)$. For a bond maturing at time T, $a(T)$ represents the time that this bond was first observed in the market. The main result is:

Theorem (Sommer) *Suppose that*
1. *Bond prices evolve according to*

$$B(t, T) = B(a(T), T) \exp \left\{ \int_{a(T)}^{T} r_s \, dt - \int_{a(T)}^{T} \frac{1}{2} \mid \sigma(s, T - s) \mid^2 \, ds \right.$$

$$\left. - \int_{a(T)}^{T} \sigma(s, T - s)\lambda(s) ds + \int_{a(T)}^{T} \sigma(s, T - s) d\tilde{z}_s \right\}, \tag{11.13}$$

where

(a) $\tilde{z}_t$ *is a d-dimensional Brownian motion,*

(b) $\sigma(t, x)$ *is defined for* $t > 0$, $0 \le x \le \tau$, *with* $\sigma(t, 0) = 0$; *for* $t \in [a(T), T]$,
    $\sigma(t, T - t)$ *is a continuous d-dimensional process adapted to the augmented
    natural filtration of* $\tilde{z}_t$,

(c) $\partial_x \sigma$ *and* $\partial_x^2 \sigma$ *both exist and satisfy the same regularity conditions as* σ .

2. *For a given set of maturity times* T_i , $i = 1, \dots, d$, *such that* $\bigcap_{i=1}^{d} [a(T_i), T_i) \ne \emptyset$
    (that is, for all times when all d bonds are simultaneously in existence), for all
    $t \in \bigcap_{i=1}^{d} [a(T_i), T_i)$ *the* $d \times d$ *matrix* $\{\sigma(t, T_i - t)\}$ *has full rank.*

Then

1. *For* $x \in [0, \tau]$ *the forward rate process is given by*

$$\mathrm{d}f(t, x) = \left(\partial_x f(t, x) + \tfrac{1}{2} \partial_2 \mid \sigma(t, x) \mid^2 + \partial_x \sigma(t, x) \lambda(t) \right) \mathrm{d}t - \partial_x \sigma(t, x) \mathrm{d}\tilde{z}_t, \quad (11.14)$$

where $\phi(t) = \partial_x f(t, \tau)$ *is an exogenous process independent of* $\tilde{z}_t$.

2. *There exists an equivalent martingale measure* z_t *such that for* $T \le t + \tau$

$$\mathrm{d}B(t, T) = B(t, T) r_t \, \mathrm{d}t - B(t, T) \sigma(t, T - t) \mathrm{d}z_t. \quad (11.15)$$

Proof See Sommer.

Sommer derives explicit formulae for $\partial_x f(t, x)$ and $D(t, x)$ when $x < \tau$, and also derives the process for $D(t, \tau)$. Note that $D(t, \tau)$ is not in general measurable with respect to the σ -algebra $\sigma[\tilde{z}_s \mid 0 \le s \le t]$, so that a portfolio made up of existing bonds will not be able to hedge a bond newly issued for maturity τ . Sommer assumes that the process driving $\partial_x f(t, x)$ is one-dimensional, but this restriction may easily be relaxed.

Equation (11.14) is identical to the form of the process for $f(t, x)$ given by Brace, Gatarek and Musiela (97) [88]; however, the interpretation here is very different. In BGM $f(0, x)$ is given at time 0 for all $x \ge 0$ and $f(t, x)$ is defined endogenously for all $t > 0$, $x \ge 0$. Here,

1. $f(0, x)$ is known only for $0 \le x \le \tau$,
2. $f(t, x)$ is defined only for $0 \le x \le \tau$,
3. The process $\phi(t) = \partial_x f(t, \tau)$ is exogenous, and is independent of $\tilde{z}_t$.

The process $\phi(t)$ is the discovery process. At each time t the process for $f(t, \tau)$ is not completely determined by knowledge of $\tilde{z}_t$. $\phi(t)$ represents new information obtained as the value of $f(t, \tau)$ evolves.

There is another interpretation of the information discovery represented by $\phi(t)$. In the standard HJM/BGM model we have

$$\partial_x f(t, x) = \partial_x f(0, t + x) + \int_0^t \frac{1}{2} \partial_x^2 \mid \sigma(s, t + x - s) \mid^2 \, \mathrm{d}s$$

$$+ \int_0^t \partial_x^2 \sigma(s, t + x - s) \lambda(s) \mathrm{d}s - \int_0^t \partial_x^2 \sigma(s, t + x - s) \mathrm{d}\tilde{z}_s. \quad (11.16)$$

In Sommer's model we may define

$$v(t) = \phi(t) - \int_0^t \frac{1}{2} \partial_x^2 \mid \sigma(s, t + \tau - s) \mid^2 ds$$

$$- \int_0^t \partial_x^2 \sigma(s, t + \tau - s)\lambda(s)ds + \int_0^t \partial_x^2 \sigma(s, t + \tau - s)d\tilde{z}_s, \qquad (11.17)$$

so that $v(t)$ has a natural interpretation as the discovery process for $\partial_x f(0, t + \tau)$, a quantity that is not known until time $t + \tau$. Hence $v(t)$ can itself be regarded as uncovering the (initially not known) forward rate curve beyond the horizon τ.

11.2.2 A Hybrid Model

Sommer illustrates his model by specifying a process for $\phi(t)$ which he then uses to price several financial instruments. He chooses $\phi(t)$ by a consistency criterion. We choose $\phi(t)$ to be a function of economic variables to enable us to incorporate inflation expectations into the yield curve. This section follows Webber (97) [538].

We observe that Sommer's model and the $IS-LM$-Phillips framework are to some extent complimentary. Sommer's model can be regarded as a no-arbitrage engine: given an exogenous input, $\phi(t)$, it converts this into term structures, $\{r(t, x) \mid 0 \leq x \leq \tau\}$; the nature of the conversion is determined by the volatility processes $\{\sigma(t, x)\}$.

Conversely, an $IS-LM$-Phillips model may be chosen so that given interest rates as inputs it generates information about the long term. For instance, long-run expectations can be used to determine a discovery process. Figure 11.1 summarises the conceptual structure.

Term structures generated by the Sommer's no-arbitrage engine can be input into a standard $IS-LM$-Phillips framework where we may take the nominal long and short rates as inputs. Conversely long-run inflation expectations emerging from the macroeconomic model can be used to specify a discovery process in such a way that expectations of increasing inflation lead to increasing levels of the long nominal rate.

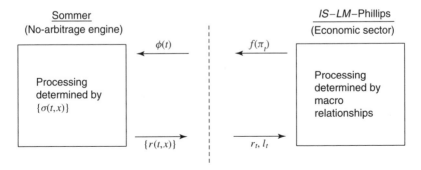

Figure 11.1   Components of the hybrid model

We have a hybrid model. It possesses a no-arbitrage financial sector and an economic sector. The financial sector contains the mathematical machinery that ensures the bond market is operating efficiently. The economic sector contains the macroeconomic dynamics underlying the market.

For illustrative purposes consider the economic sector in Figure 11.2.

The $IS-LM$ –Phillips equations are standard. The expectations formation equation (equation 'Exp' in Figure 11.2) allows three components to influence changes in expected inflation from moment to moment: long-run inflation expectations revert to the level of current inflation, increases in money supply increase expected long-run inflation, and there is a noise term. The link between the economic and the financial sectors is shown in Figure 11.3.

The financial sector generates long and short rates to feed into the economic sector. The economic model produces inflation expectations that compound into the discovery function.

The discovery function $\phi(t)$ has been chosen so that increasing inflation expectations cause the slope of the forward rate curve to rise. If expected inflation is constant the slope of the forward rate curve at time to maturity τ is discovered to be flat.

Figure 11.4 shows the result of a simulation of the model just described when the variable k has been set to zero so that there is no feedback from the economic to the financial sector. Figure 11.5 shows the situation when there is a modest amount of feedback, $k = 0.1$, with identical random shocks. The long rate is clearly influenced by the presence of an economic sector.

$$\xleftarrow{\quad f(\pi_t) \quad}$$

IS:	$y_t = a - b\,(l_t - \pi_t)$,
LM:	$m_t - p_t = cy_t - er_t$,
Phillips	$dp_t = f(y_t - \bar{y}).dt + \sigma_p.dz_p$,
Exp:	$d\pi_t = g(v_t - \pi_t)dt + j.dm_t + \sigma_\pi.dz_\pi$,
	$v_t = f(y_t - \bar{y})$,

$$\xrightarrow{\quad r_t,\ l_t \quad}$$

Figure 11.2   The economic sector

Inputs to economic sector :

$l_t = r(t,\tau)$,   specification of the long rate

$r_t = r(t,0)$,   specification of the short rate

Input to the financial sector :

$\phi(t) = k.(v_t - \pi_t) = f(\pi_t)$,   specification of the discovery function.

Figure 11.3   The financial sector

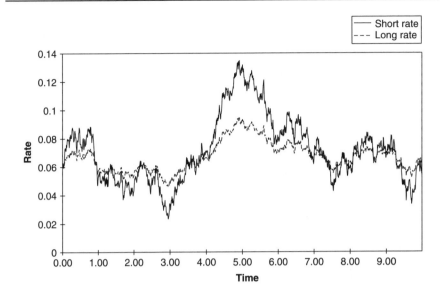

Figure 11.4   Simulated rates: no feedback

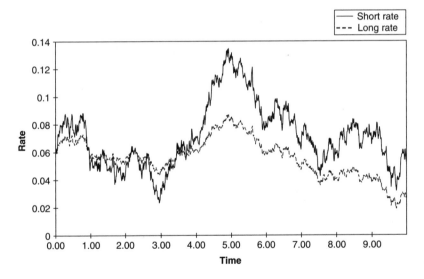

Figure 11.5   Simulated rates: modest feedback

Properties of the Hybrid Model

The hybrid model allows long-run inflation expectations to be incorporated into a no-arbitrage term-structure model. The formulation is extremely general; many choices may be made for the economic sector.

The model has a number of desirable properties. The trend of the long rate is determined by the discovery function. This means that, with suitable discovery functions, the long rate may be induced to behave in historically believable ways. The short rate process is determined by the volatility functions and by information coming in from the long end. It too may be constructed realistically. In particular it is not constrained to strongly revert within some particular range. Hyperinflation is possible in the hybrid model, with a suitable discovery function.

As formulated, the model does not allow the short rate to be determined within the economic sector. The short rate is determined within the financial sector, and there are insufficient degrees of freedom to allow a reaction function to determine m_t, the log-money supply. This is somewhat limiting as it would be valuable to explore the effect of different reaction functions within the framework of the hybrid model. An obvious extension to the hybrid framework would be to allow the short rate to be determined not in the financial sector but in the economic sector. This would require a theoretical extension of the hybrid framework, but the advantages would be very worthwhile. For valuation and hedging purposes the model could be set up to reflect economically sound prescriptions, as well as guaranteeing no-arbitrage. For economic modelling purposes, the effect of different economic assumptions could be tested in a model that guaranteed that the financial markets reacted efficiently.

11.3   AN *IS–LM* BASED MODEL

In Section 11.2 we used the IS–LM–Phillips framework to determine an economics sector in a no-arbitrage model. In this section we use the IS–LM framework directly to obtain interest rate models. Here we describe a model of Tice and Webber (97) [523]. Section 11.4 uses the Cagan model, derived from the IS–LM framework, to model situations of high inflation.

11.3.1   The General Framework

In the IS–LM framework (11.3) we have underlying state variables y_t and r_t, and equilibrium relationships between economic variables that are functions of y_t and r_t. If we assume that the equilibrium is dynamic, so that we specify the processes followed by our economic variables, then we may be able to back out the processes followed by the state variables y_t and r_t.

In general, suppose in our economy we have state variables $X_{1,t}, \ldots, X_{N,t}$, and economic variables $m_{i,t}$ and $\overline{m}_{i,t}$,

$$m_{i,t} = m_i\left(X_{1,t}, \ldots, X_{N,t}\right), \quad 1 = 1, \ldots, N, \qquad (11.18)$$

$$\overline{m}_{i,t} = \overline{m}_i\left(X_{1,t}, \ldots, X_{N,t}\right), \quad 1 = 1, \ldots, N, \qquad (11.19)$$

whose values depend on the underlying state variables. We suppose that the variable $m_{i,t}$ reverts to the level $\overline{m}_{i,t}$, so that $\overline{m}_{i,t}$ is interpreted as the equilibrium level of $m_{i,t}$.

In particular suppose that the dynamics of the equilibrium relationship are given by

$$\mathrm{d}m_{i,t} = \alpha_i(\overline{m}_{i,t} - m_{i,t})\mathrm{d}t + \sum_{j=1}^{N} \sigma_{i,j}\,\mathrm{d}z_{j,t}, \quad i = 1, \ldots, N, \tag{11.20}$$

so that m_i, $i = 1, \ldots, N$, adjusts to $\overline{m}_i$ at the rate $\alpha_i > 0$, when disturbed by the Wiener processes z_j. We assume that $\alpha = (\alpha_1, \ldots, \alpha_N)'$ and $\Sigma = \{\sigma_{i,j}\}$ are constants. If the functions $M_t = (m_{1,t}, \ldots, m_{N,t})'$ and $\overline{M}_t = (\overline{m}_{1,t}, \ldots, \overline{m}_{N,t})'$ are sufficiently regular we can invert (11.20) to find the processes followed by the vector $X_t = (X_{1,t}, \ldots, X_{N,t})'$,

$$\mathrm{d}X_t = \left(M_X^{-1}A\left(\overline{M}_t - M_t\right) - M_X^{-1}h\right)\mathrm{d}t + M_X^{-1}\Sigma\,\mathrm{d}z_t, \tag{11.21}$$

where $z_t = (z_{1,t}, \ldots, z_{N,t})'$ is a vector of Wiener processes, $A = \mathrm{diag}(\alpha)$, $M_X = \{\partial m_i/\partial X_j\}_{i,j=1,\ldots,N}$, and $h = \{h_i\}_{i=1,\ldots,N}$ is defined as

$$h_i = \frac{1}{2}\sum_{k,l,p=1}^{N}\frac{\partial^2 m_i}{\partial X_k \partial X_l}\sigma_{k,p}^X\sigma_{l,p}^X, \tag{11.22}$$

where $\sigma^X = M_X^{-1}\Sigma$.

We can now put the IS–LM relationships into this form.

11.3.2 The IS–LM Framework

We write m_d for the demand for real money and m_s for the supply of real money. Money demand, to first order, is an affine function of income y_t and nominal interest rates r_t, and so is expenditure, e_t,

$$m_{d,t} = ky_t - ur_t, \tag{11.23}$$

$$e_t = a - br_t + cy_t, \tag{11.24}$$

where k, u, a, b and c are constants. In this section we suppose that the short rate is the interest rate determining the IS relationship. We suppose that equilibrium dynamics are given by

$$\mathrm{d}m_{d,t} = \alpha(m_s - m_{d,t})\mathrm{d}t + \sigma_m\,\mathrm{d}z_{m,t}, \tag{11.25}$$

$$\mathrm{d}y_t = \beta(e_t - y_t)\mathrm{d}t + \sigma_y\,\mathrm{d}z_{y,t}, \tag{11.26}$$

so that money demand reverts to the level of money supply, m_s, a constant, and income reverts to the level of expenditure. In the money market the rate of adjustment, α, is large, whereas in the goods market the rate of adjustment, $\beta > 0$, is small.

This system fits into the general structure of the previous section. We can invert to obtain

$$\mathrm{d}r_t = \alpha_r(\beta_r + \gamma_r y_t - r_t)\mathrm{d}t + \sigma_r\,\mathrm{d}z_{r,t}, \tag{11.27}$$

$$\mathrm{d}y_t = \alpha_y(\beta_y - \gamma_y r_t - y_t)\mathrm{d}t + \sigma_y\,\mathrm{d}z_{y,t}, \tag{11.28}$$

where α_r, β_r, γ_r, α_y, β_y and γ_y are constants and we have redefined the Wiener processes.

This is a two-factor affine interest rate model, and is easy to solve. To put it into a slightly more intuitive form set $x_t = \beta_r + \gamma_r y_t$, and re-parameterise the system in terms of r and x instead of r and y. The system becomes

$$dr_t = \alpha(x_t - r_t)dt + \sigma_r \, dz_{r,t}, \tag{11.29}$$

$$dx_t = \beta(pr_t + (1 - p)\mu - x_t)dt + \sigma_x \, dz_{x,t}, \tag{11.30}$$

for constants α, β, p, μ, σ_r and σ_x.

This is a generalised Vasicek model where r_t reverts to x_t, and x_t reverts to the weighted sum of r_t and μ. It generalises the drift functions of Hull and White (93) [295], Chen (96) [126], and Sørensen (94) [501], whose models have $p = 0$. It also generalises a drift function used by Babbs and Webber (94) [40].

Models of this sort have been studied extensively by Beaglehole and Tenney (91) [57]. This section has given an economic justification for them.

The $IS-LM$ framework is used to investigate the effects of fiscal and monetary control. The monetary authorities control monetary supply and government expenditure and tax regimes. Working this through in the $IS-LM$ framework the monetary authorities control the levels of m_s and a. When expressed as (11.29) and (11.30), the monetary authorities control the value of μ. Hence μ can reasonably be time-dependent. But μ is time-varying in the Hull and White extended Vasicek model. This provides some additional economic justification for allowing time-dependent variables in these extended models.

The behaviour of the system (11.29) and (11.30) can be investigated by simulation. Putting in plausible parameter values and simulating we obtain sample paths like Figure 11.6. There appear to be cycles. These arise implicitly from the dynamics of the system and are not caused by the volatility term. The underlying dynamics can be seen by setting the volatilities to zero, $\sigma_r = \sigma_x = 0$. Figure 11.7 shows decaying cycles. In

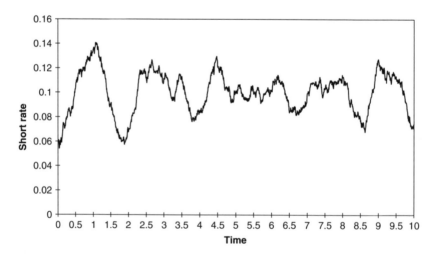

Figure 11.6   A sample path in the two-factor model

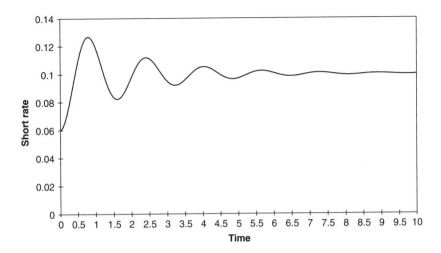

Figure 11.7 Underlying deterministic system

the noisy system if the short rate is perturbed away from the mean there is a tendency for it to overshoot the mean on its way back. This tends to preserve cycles.

11.3.3 Extending the Model: The Third Factor

In the derivation above, p was a constant. Tice and Webber extend the model to allow p to be stochastic. The variable p is related to the transactions demand for money — the average time money spends in balances. This will certainly vary through time, and Tice and Webber argue that it may even be plausible for it to be negative.

Suppose that p reverts to a mean value, $\bar{p} = \bar{p}(r, x)$,

$$dp_t = \gamma \left(\bar{p}_t - p_t \right) dt + \sigma_p \, dz_{p,t}, \tag{11.31}$$

for constant γ. Rather than assume that $\bar{p}$ is linear in r and x we expand $\bar{p}(r, x)$ about (μ, μ) and truncate, keeping only a second-order term. We have

$$\bar{p}(r, x) = \bar{p}(\mu, \mu) + \bar{p}_r(r - \mu) + \bar{p}_x(x - \mu) + \tfrac{1}{2}\bar{p}_{r,r}(r - \mu)^2$$

$$+ \tfrac{1}{2}\bar{p}_{x,x}(x - \mu)^2 + \bar{p}_{x,r}(x - \mu)(r - \mu) + \cdots, \tag{11.32}$$

where subscripts denote derivatives. Keeping only the second-order cross-term we set

$$\bar{p}(r, x) = \delta - \phi(x - \mu)(r - \mu), \tag{11.33}$$

for constants δ and ϕ, $\phi > 0$. Tice and Webber argue that this form is reasonable on behavioural grounds. We have the following three-factor system:

$$dr_t = \alpha(x_t - r_t)dt + \sigma_r \, dz_{r,t},$$

$$dx_t = \beta(p_t r_t + (1 - p_t)\mu - x_t)dt + \sigma_x \, dz_{x,t}, \tag{11.34}$$

$$dp_t = \gamma(\delta - \phi(x_t - \mu)(r_t - \mu) - p_t)dt + \sigma_p \, dz_{p,t}.$$

The processes for r and x were found by economic arguments. The process for p was not.

11.3.4 Properties of the Three-Factor Model

The system (11.34) is non-linear and its behaviour is unclear. We simulate it to investigate its behaviour. Reasonable parameter values turn out to be $(\alpha, \beta, \gamma, \mu, \delta, \phi) = (5, 0.5, \frac{5}{12}, 0.1, 23, 22\,000)$. Figure 11.8 shows a typical sample path. To get at the underlying dynamics we can once again set the volatility terms to zero, $\sigma_r = \sigma_x = \sigma_p = 0$. The behaviour of the deterministic system is shown in Figure 11.9. Note that the system with noise is not simply the curve of Figure 11.9 with noise added. The path in Figure 11.8 differs systematically from Figure 11.9, having a different sequence of high and low peaks.

r fluctuates around either high levels and low levels, alternating between these regimes. These might be interpreted as business cycles. The flips between regimes occur apparently randomly, but the system has stable statistical behaviour over time. The presence of noise can cause the system to flip differently. The average cycle time can be adjusted by scaling the reversion parameters so that it is possible to calibrate to the length of the business cycles. The path of future short rates is sensitive to initial values.

Its behaviour can be elucidated by a transformation of variables. Set

$$X_t = \frac{r_t - \mu}{s}, \tag{11.35}$$

$$Y_t = \frac{x_t - \mu}{s}, \tag{11.36}$$

$$Z_t = \delta - p_t, \tag{11.37}$$

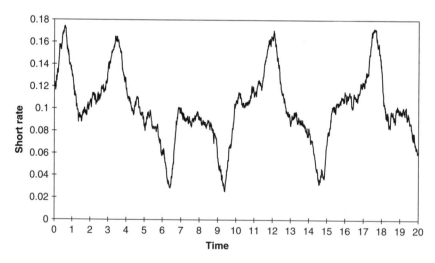

Figure 11.8 A sample path from the three-factor system

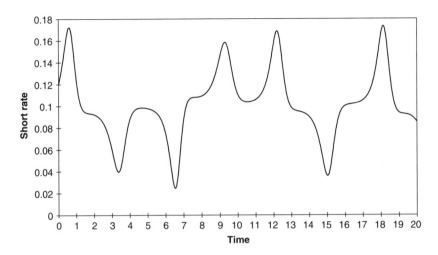

Figure 11.9 Underlying deterministic behaviour

where $s = \sqrt{1/\gamma\phi}$, and set the volatility terms to zero. The system (11.34) is transformed into

$$dX_t = \alpha(Y_t - X_t)dt, \qquad (11.38)$$

$$dY_t = \beta(\delta X_t - Z_t X_t - Y_t)dt, \qquad (11.39)$$

$$dZ_t = (X_t Y_t - \gamma Z_t)dt. \qquad (11.40)$$

With $\beta = 1$ this is the Lorenz system, which is chaotic with suitable parameter values. The Lorenz system has been very widely studied and some of its properties are quite well understood. The behaviour of r can now be interpreted as progress around an attractor.

11.3.5 The Behaviour of the Lorenz System

The behaviour of the Lorenz system depends critically on the value of δ. Set

$$\delta_H = \delta_H(\beta) = \frac{\alpha}{\beta} \frac{\alpha + \gamma + 3\beta}{\alpha - \gamma - \beta}.$$

When $\delta \leq 1$ the system has a single fixed point at $X = Y = Z = 0$, or $r = x = \mu$, $p = \delta$. In the deterministic system all points converge to this fixed point.

When $1 < \delta$, two additional fixed points emerge at

$$X = Y = \pm\sqrt{\gamma(\delta - 1)}, \quad Z = \gamma - 1. \qquad (11.41)$$

At these fixed points $r = x = \mu \pm \sqrt{(\delta - 1)/\phi}$, $p = 1$.

When $\delta_H \leq \delta$ the additional fixed points are unstable. But there is a region containing all three fixed points such that all orbits eventually enter this region and do not leave it. Since the fixed points are repelling, this implies that there is an attracting region, an attractor, which paths tend to end up close to. For our parameter values, $\delta_H = 16.94$, so $\delta = 23$ is greater than the critical value of δ_H. It is possible to argue that with $\mu = 0.1$ it is not unreasonable for $(\delta - 1) \times 10^3 \leq \phi \leq (\delta - 1) \times 10^4$. We have taken $\phi = 22\,000$.

11.3.6   Control by the Monetary Authorities

The model suggests that other forms of monetary control may be possible, besides classical fiscal and monetary measures. Three possibilities are:

1. *Direct control of p.* If the value of p can be controlled directly, perhaps by controls on credit, then attempting to keep $p = 0$ would cause r and x to remain close to mid-levels.
2. *Indirect control of p.* Suppose that the process for p could be modified by controlling the values of the parameters γ, δ or ϕ. It might then be possible to nudge the system closer to its fixed points. This would likely prove to be unstable and difficult.
3. *Control of β.* Altering the value of β alters the value of δ_H. Reducing the value of β causes the value of δ_H to increase. If β were increased until δ_H was greater than δ, the system would be taken out of the chaotic region, and could approach a fixed point (with noise). β is the speed of convergence to equilibrium in the goods market. Paradoxically, by making the market less efficient, so that it moves more slowly towards equilibrium, the market becomes non-chaotic. Too high a value for β removes a dampening effect and allows chaotic behaviour to emerge.

11.3.7   Conclusion

From the $IS-LM$ framework it is possible to obtain functional forms of the drift functions in a two-factor model. By introducing a third factor a model exhibiting chaotic behaviour was found. The model has business cycle type behaviour.

The chaotic model certainly shows that interest rate behaviour is potentially very complicated. The best that interest rate models can do is to be tractable and moderately realistic.

11.4   *IS–LM*, HYPERINFLATION AND EXTENDED VASICEK

This section explores the Cagan model of hyperinflation and its relationship to extended Vasicek term structure models. We follow Kuan and Webber (97) [343] who apply the model to the Mexican Peso crisis of 1994. In this high inflation, but non-hyperinflating economy, they fit an extended Vasicek model of the term structure and back out market expectations concerning the future levels of the money supply.

We start by describing the assumptions of the Cagan model, and show how it results in an extended Vasicek term structure model.

11.4.1   The Cagan Model

Since the seminal paper of Cagan (56) [110] hyperinflations have been regarded as test beds of monetary theory. In a hyperinflation the real economy can be ignored and only monetary effects remain. A literature review is given by Siklos (90) [494]. Capie (91) [116] reviews hyperinflations in history.

Sargent and Wallace (73) [474] re-expressed Cagan's original model using rational expectations. Attempts to estimate a key parameter of the model by Sargent (77) [473] and Salemi and Sargent (79) [469] could find only poor estimates. Empirical studies of applications of Cagan and extensions to Cagan include Engsted (93) [209] and Phylaktis and Taylor (93) [439]. Taylor (91) [518] extends Cagan to include FX effects. Miller and Zhang (97) [395] extend Cagan by suggesting an alternative demand function which may better reflect the situation pertaining in recent Eastern European hyperinflations. Nicolini (96) [415] found that hyperinflations could be ruled out if governments are rational, in a particular sense. Velasco (93) [531] uses a representative agent model to investigate stabilisation following hyperinflation.[14]

Cagan's model is an adaptation of the $IS-LM-$Phillips framework to a situation where the real economy and interest rates play no part. This is a justifiable assumption in most hyperinflations. The money supply is assumed to be controlled by the monetary authorities and is an exogenous variable.

11.4.2   Cagan and Extended Vasicek

If there is no real sector, only expected inflation is important. Time horizons become very short so that long rates cease to exist. Both income and the real interest rate can be supposed to be constant, so that the LM equation in (11.3) becomes

$$m_t - p_t = \phi y - \beta(\pi_t + k),$$
(11.42)

where k is the constant real (short) rate and π_t is current (psychological) expected inflation. There is no IS relationship or Phillips equation.

Expectation formation is crucially important. We assume adaptive expectations,

$$d\pi_t = \gamma(v_t - \pi_t)dt,$$
(11.43)

where v_t is actual current expected inflation. Write

$$dm_t = \mu_{m,t}\, dt + \sigma_{m,t}\, dz_{m,t},$$
(11.44)

$$dp_t = v_t\, dt + \sigma_p\, dz_{p,t},$$
(11.45)

---

[14] Other articles include Ferguson (96) [214] who investigates the German hyperinflation of the 1920s. Beladi, Choudhary and Parai (93) [60] test for the existence of bubbles in hyperinflations. Easterly, Mauro and Schmidt-Hebbel (95) [195] give estimates of maximum seigniorage rates in a non-linear extension of Cagan.

for the processes followed by the money supply and price level, for some μ_m, σ_m, σ_p, where

$$v_t = \frac{\mathbb{E}[dp_t]}{dt} \tag{11.46}$$

is unspecified for the moment.

We can solve this system for the nominal short rate, r_t. From (11.42) we have

$$dm_t - dp_t = -\beta \, d\pi_t. \tag{11.47}$$

Substituting in for dm_t and dp_t from (11.44) and (11.45) we find an expression for v_t:

$$v_t = \frac{\mu_{m,t}}{1 - \gamma\beta} - \frac{\gamma\beta}{1 - \gamma\beta} \pi_t, \tag{11.48}$$

so that

$$d\pi_t = \frac{\gamma}{1 - \gamma\beta}(\mu_{m,t} - \pi_t)dt + \sigma_\pi dz_{\pi,t}, \tag{11.49}$$

where σ_π is related to σ_m and σ_p,

$$\beta^2 \sigma_\pi^2 = \sigma_m^2 - 2\sigma_{mp} + \sigma_p^2. \tag{11.50}$$

Since $r_t = \pi_t + k$ we obtain

$$dr_t = \frac{\gamma}{1 - \gamma\beta}(\mu_{m,t} + k - r_t)dt + \sigma_\pi \, dz_{\pi,t}. \tag{11.51}$$

r_t is a mean-reverting process where the reversion level of r_t is the drift in money supply, $\mu_{m,t}$ (plus the real rate, k).

Two main assumptions were made in deriving (11.51). First, that in the *LM* framework the effects of the real economy can be ignored, with income and the real interest rate constant; and secondly, that anticipated inflation follows an adaptive process. The first assumption could plausibly be valid in the special circumstances of a hyperinflation. The second is more tentative. However, it is possible to argue that agents in a hyperinflating economy may be able to form no other expectations than that the monetary authorities will continue to act as they are currently acting. If corrective action by the monetary authorities to alter the extent of the hyperinflation is deemed to be implausible, and that the *de facto* inflation rate is likely to continue, then an adaptive expectations hypothesis could be supported. In the case where price increases are formally indexed to previously observed inflation then adaptive expectations may be fully justified.

Rational expectations means that $\pi_t = v_t$. From (11.48) this implies $\pi_t = \mu_{m,t}$. We do not pursue this possibility.

Equation (11.51) is an expression for the objective short rate process. The reversion level of r_t, $\mu_{m,t} + k$, is an offset from the drift of log money demand, a (possibly stochastic) function of time. This resembles a generalised Vasicek model. For the purposes of what follows we shall assume that $\mu_{m,t}$ is a deterministic function of time and not stochastic. Essentially we assume that the monetary authorities' pronouncements concerning the money supply are perfectly credible over a horizon as short as those plausible during a hyperinflation. An alternative assumption, such as a mean-reverting process for $\mu_{m,t}$, would be possible, but would entail a loss in tractability without a corresponding gain in verisimilitude. A process such as (11.51) where $\mu_{m,t}$ is deterministic is an extended Vasicek process.

The short rate process in the extended Vasicek model is of the form

$$\mathrm{d}r_t = \alpha \left(\overline{\theta}_t - r_t \right) \mathrm{d}t + \sigma \, \mathrm{d}z_t, \qquad (11.52)$$

where here $\alpha = \gamma/(1 - \gamma\beta)$ and $\overline{\theta}_t = \mu_{m,t} + k - \lambda\sigma$ (λ is a market price of risk). This is now the risk-adjusted process under the EMM.

Under our assumptions, the short rate process must be compatible with the money supply process. For instance, the expected nominal money balance is

$$\mathbb{E}_t[m_{t+s}] = m_t + \int_t^{t+s} \mu_{m,u} \, \mathrm{d}u = m_t + \int_t^{t+s} \left(\overline{\theta}_u + \lambda\sigma - k \right) \mathrm{d}u, \qquad (11.53)$$

where $\mathbb{E}_t[m_{t+s}]$ is the expected log nominal money for the time $t + s$ conditional on information known at time t.

A key feature of the extended Vasicek model is that an appropriate choice of $\overline{\theta}_t$ calibrates the model to the current yield curve. In a high inflation setting $\overline{\theta}_t$ is determined by the future drift in the (log) money supply and so the drift also determines the term structure of interest rates. Conversely, from the term structure of interest rates one may back out the drift $\mu_{m,t}$. Kuan and Webber (97) [343] undertake an empirical investigation of the Mexican crisis of 1994. They find that the term structure seemed to take account of information on the likely growth in the money supply.

11.5 THE GENERAL EQUILIBRIUM FRAMEWORK

The general equilibrium framework is extremely important in the history of interest rate modelling. Prior to martingale methods being developed and disseminated it was the only way in which no-arbitrage could be guaranteed within a model.

The idea is to construct a model of the economy in which investors maximise their utility. Prices and interest rates are determined endogenously by investors' behaviour. There is an equilibrium in which prices, output and consumption are set so that utility is maximised. In equilibrium no-arbitrage is possible since then utility would not have been maximised.

The components of the economy are

- a physical commodity,
- a production processes for the commodity,
- financial claims (including bonds),
- investors who consume the commodity and who own production processes and claims.

Investors have a utility function and attempt to maximise their expected utility of consumption. We presume that investors are identical.

There are two approaches to the problem.

In a production-based approach used by Merton (71) [393] and Cox, Ingersoll and Ross (85a) [147], (85b) [148] prices are exogenous. Consumption adjusts so that prices are consistent with equilibrium. In equilibrium consumption exactly equals output.

In the consumption-based approach due to Lucas (78) [367], and used for instance by Bakshi and Chen (96) [45], (97) [46], consumption is exogenous. Prices adjust so that consumption is consistent with equilibrium.

In the production-based approach it is difficult to find the equilibrium. It is necessary to solve Hamilton, Jacobi and Bellman (HJB) equations to find an optimum. It involves solving a non-linear PDE, which may only be feasible in special cases.

The consumption-based approach also involves a PDE, but it is more tractable.

11.5.1 Specification of the Framework

Suppose that the risk in the economy is supplied by $n + k$ Wiener processes,

$$z_t = (z_{1,t}, \ldots, z_{n+k,t})' \in \mathbb{R}^{n+k}, \tag{11.54}$$

and that there are k state variables, $Y = (Y_1, \ldots, Y_k)' \in \mathbb{R}^k$, with process

$$dY_{i,t} = \mu_i\left(t, Y_{1,t}, \ldots, Y_{k,t}\right) dt + \sum_{j=1}^{n+k} S_{i,j}\left(t, Y_{1,t}, \ldots, Y_{k,t}\right) dz_{j,t}, \tag{11.55}$$

which we write as

$$dY_t = \mu(t, Y)dt + S(t, Y)dz_t, \tag{11.56}$$

where $\mu \in \mathbb{R}^k$, $S \in \mathbb{R}^{k \times (n+k)}$, and we assume that SS' is a non-negative definite matrix and that Y_t has no accessible boundaries.

There is a single physical good and n production processes for it. The value $P_{i,t}$ of the ith production process has the process

$$dP_{i,t} = P_{i,t}\alpha_i(t, Y_{1,t}, \ldots, Y_{k,t})dt + P_{i,t}\sum_{j=1}^{n+k} G_{i,j}(t, Y_{1,t}, \ldots, Y_{k,t})dz_{j,t}, \tag{11.57}$$

where $\alpha \in \mathbb{R}^n$, $G \in \mathbb{R}^{n \times (n+k)}$, and we assume that GG' is positive definite.

The production processes should be thought of as companies with share prices $P_t = (P_{1,t}, \ldots, P_{n,t})'$.

Example: Longstaff and Schwartz

Longstaff and Schwartz (92) [365] have a production-based model. Their model has three independent Wiener processes, $z_{1,t}$, $z_{2,t}$, $z_{3,t}$, two state variables, $(X_t, Y_t) = (Y_{1,t}, Y_{2,t})$, and one production process, $P_t = P_{1,t}$. The processes for the state variables are

$$dX_t = (a - bX_t)dt + c\sqrt{X_t}\,dz_{2,t}, \tag{11.58}$$

$$dY_t = (d - eY_t)dt + f\sqrt{Y_t}\,dz_{3,t}, \tag{11.59}$$

where a, b, c, d, e and f are constants, and the process for P_t is

$$\frac{dP_t}{P_t} = (\mu X_t + \theta Y_t)dt + \sigma\sqrt{Y_t}\,dz_{1,t}, \tag{11.60}$$

where μ, θ and σ are constants. This means that

$$\alpha(t, Y_{1,t}, Y_{2,t}) = \mu X_t + \theta Y_t, \tag{11.61}$$

$$G_{1,j}(t, Y_{1,t}, Y_{2,t}) = \left(\sigma\sqrt{Y_t}, 0, 0\right).$$

in equation (11.57).

The single company in the economy can be regarded as the market index. The state variables Y_t and X_t can be thought of as the components of stock market returns related to market volatility and unrelated to market volatility, respectively.

Example: Bakshi and Chen

Bakshi and Chen (97) [46] adopt a consumption-based approach. They assume there are two independent Wiener processes, $z_{X,t}$ and $z_{Y,t}$, two state variables, $(X_t, Y_t) = (Y_{1,t}, Y_{2,t})$, and a single production process, q, representing aggregate output. The state variables follow the processes

$$dX_t = \kappa_X(\theta_X - X_t)dt + \sigma_X\sqrt{X_t}\,dz_{X,t}, \tag{11.62}$$

$$dY_t = \kappa_Y(\theta_Y - Y_t)dt + \sigma_Y\sqrt{Y_t}\,dz_{Y,t}, \tag{11.63}$$

for constants κ_X, θ_X, σ_X, κ_Y, θ_Y and σ_Y, and the process for q_t is

$$\frac{dq_t}{q_t} = (\mu_q + \beta_X X_t + \beta_Y Y_t)dt + \sigma_{qX}\sqrt{X_t}\,dz_{X,t} + \sigma_{qY}\sqrt{Y_t}\,dz_{Y,t}, \tag{11.64}$$

$$\equiv \frac{\mu_q}{q}\,dt + \frac{\sigma_q}{q}\,dz_{q,t}, \tag{11.65}$$

where μ_q, β_X, β_Y, σ_{qX} and σ_{qY} are constants.

X_t and Y_t represent market returns related to two separate sources of volatility in the market.

Note that neither Longstaff and Schwartz nor Bakshi and Chen include money in their economies. All values are real values. We see later how money can be incorporated.

11.5.2 The Investors' Problem

The economy contains identical investors maximising

$$K_t = \mathbb{E}_t \left[\int_t^{T\max} u(c_s, Y_s, s) \mathrm{d}s \right],$$ (11.66)

where u is the utility function, c_t is consumption at time t and $T_{\max}$ is a maximum time horizon. K_t is the expected utility of consumption.

Write w_t for the total wealth in the economy, and let a_i be the proportion of wealth invested in the ith production process. For both Longstaff and Schwartz and Bakshi and Chen there is a single production process so $a_1 \equiv 1$. Suppose the consumption rate is c_t at time t. Write

$$J(w_t, Y_t, t) = \max_{\omega \in \Omega} \mathbb{E}_t \left[\int_t^{T\max} u(c_s, Y_s, s) \mathrm{d}s \right],$$ (11.67)

where Ω represents the set of all investment and consumption policies, that is, the maximum is over all possible paths for $a_i(t)$ and c_t. In equilibrium no financial claims are owned so these do not appear in the policy set Ω.

J is the indirect utility function.

11.5.3 r and the Direct Utility Function

Suppose that optimal consumption follows the process

$$\mathrm{d}c_t^* = \mu_{c^*} \, \mathrm{d}t + \sigma_{c^*} \, \mathrm{d}z_t.$$ (11.68)

We show in Section 11.6 that

$$r_t = \left(-\frac{u_{c^*,t}}{u_{c^*}} \right) + \left(-\frac{c^* u_{c^*,c^*}}{u_{c^*}} \right) \left(\frac{\mu_{c^*}}{c^*} \right) - \frac{1}{2} \left(\frac{c^{*2} u_{c^*,c^*,c^*}}{u_{c^*}} \right) \left(\frac{\sigma_{c^*}}{c^*} \frac{\sigma_{c^*}'}{c^*} \right).$$ (11.69)

In equilibrium all output $q(t)$ is consumed, so that $c^*(t) = q(t)$, $u_{c^*} = u_q$, et cetera. If $u(c, Y, s) = \mathrm{e}^{-\rho s} u(c, Y)$ is time separable, then

$$r_t = \rho + \left(-\frac{q u_{q,q}}{u_q} \right) \left(\frac{\mu_q}{q} \right) - \frac{1}{2} \left(\frac{q^2 u_{q,q,q}}{u_q} \right) \left(\frac{\sigma_q}{q} \frac{\sigma_q'}{q} \right),$$ (11.70)

where μ_q and σ_q are the drift and volatility of output.

11.5.4 The Prices of Financial Claims

Suppose that F is a financial claim, such as a bond, with process

$$\frac{\mathrm{d}F_t}{F_t} = \mu_F \, \mathrm{d}t + \sigma_F \, \mathrm{d}z_t,$$ (11.71)

where σ_F is a matrix of volatilities. It is possible to show that in equilibrium

$$\mu_F - r_t = -q \frac{u_{q,q}}{u_q} \text{cov} \left(\frac{\text{d}F_t}{F_t}, \frac{\text{d}q_t}{q_t} \right), \tag{11.72}$$

and there is a vector λ such that

$$\mu_F - r_t = \sigma_F \lambda = \frac{F_Y}{F} S \lambda. \tag{11.73}$$

λ is the price of market risk vector for financial claims.

11.5.5 The Process for r

Wealth w_t follows the process

$$\text{d}w_t = (w_t a_t'(\alpha_t - r_t 1) + r w_t - c_t)\text{d}t + w_t a_t' G_t \, \text{d}z_t,$$

where 1 is the n-dimensional unit vector and α and G_t are the drift and volatility of the production processes (11.57). Suppose the optimal investment policy is $a_t^* = (a_{1,t}^*, \ldots, a_{n,t}^*)'$ and the optimal consumption rate is c_t^*. Write J_W for $\partial J / \partial W$, *et cetera*. We show in Section 11.5.9 that

$$r_t^* = a_t^{*\prime} \alpha + a_t^{*\prime} G_t G_t' a_t^* \frac{J_{w,w}}{J_w} w_t + a_t^{*\prime} G_t S_t' \frac{J_{w,Y}}{J_w}$$

$$= a_t^{*\prime} \alpha - \left(-\frac{J_{w,w}}{J_w} \right) \frac{\text{var}(w_t)}{w_t} + \frac{J_{w,Y}}{J_w} \frac{\text{cov}(w_t, Y_t)}{w_t},$$

$$= a_t^{*\prime} \alpha - \frac{\text{cov}(w_t, J_w)}{w_t J_w}, \tag{11.74}$$

since $\text{var}(w_t) = a_t^{*\prime} G_t G_t' a_t^* w_t^2$, and $\text{cov}(w_t, Y_t) = a_t^{*\prime} G_t S_t' w_t$. Note that a_t^* is the expected return on wealth optimally invested in production.

11.5.6 Specify a Utility Function

To make further progress it is necessary to be more specific about the utility function. This is chosen for tractability. Suppose that $u(c, s) = \text{e}^{-\rho s}(c^\gamma - 1)/\gamma$ is a power utility with constant discount rate ρ. u does not depend on wealth w_t, and as a consequence $-J_{wY}/J_w$ is independent of w_t and both a_t and r_t can depend on the state variables Y_t, but not on w_t.

In the limit as $\gamma \to 0$ the utility function becomes $u(c_s, s) = \text{e}^{-\rho s} \ln c_s$. It is now possible to solve explicitly for a_t^* and r_t. We have

$$a_t^* = (G_t G_t')^{-1} \alpha + \frac{1 - 1'(G_t G_t')^{-1} \alpha}{1'(G_t G_t')^{-1} 1} (G_t G_t')^{-1} 1, \tag{11.75}$$

$$r_t = \frac{1'(G_t G_t')^{-1} \alpha - 1}{1'(G_t G_t')^{-1} 1}. \tag{11.76}$$

Example: Longstaff and Schwartz

If there is a single production process, then $a^* = a = 1$. In the Longstaff and Schwartz model we have

$$G = \left(\sigma\sqrt{Y_t}, 0, 0\right) \tag{11.77}$$

so that $GG' = \sigma^2 Y_t$. This is just a scalar, so

$$r = \alpha - GG'$$
$$= \mu X_t + \theta Y_t - \sigma^2 Y_t$$
$$= \mu X_t + \left(\theta - \sigma^2\right) Y_t. \tag{11.78}$$

r_t is a linear combination of state variables. The variance of r_t is v_t. This is simply

$$v_t = \frac{\mathbb{E}[\mathrm{d}r_t \, \mathrm{d}r_t]}{\mathrm{d}t} \tag{11.79}$$

$$= \frac{\mathbb{E}\left[\left(\mu \, \mathrm{d}X_t + \left(\theta - \sigma^2\right) \mathrm{d}Y_t\right)\left(\mu \, \mathrm{d}X_t + \left(\theta - \sigma^2\right) \mathrm{d}Y_t\right)\right]}{\mathrm{d}t}$$

$$= \mu^2 c^2 X_t + \left(\theta - \sigma^2\right)^2 f^2 Y_t, \tag{11.80}$$

another linear combination of X_t and Y_t, where c and f are the volatilities of X_t and Y_t in (11.58) and (11.59). Since r_t and v_t are both linear functions of X_t and Y_t one can invert the system:

$$X_t = \frac{c^2}{\alpha} \frac{\beta r_t - v_t}{\beta - \alpha},$$

$$Y_t = \frac{f^2}{\beta} \frac{v_t - \beta r_t}{\beta - \alpha}, \tag{11.81}$$

where $\alpha = \mu c^2$ and $\beta = (\theta - \sigma^2)f^2$.

As we saw in Chapter 7, we could equally well have r_t and v_t as fundamental, instead of X_t and Y_t, and this is an alternative way to express the Longstaff and Schwartz term structure model.

It is possible to show that the price of risk for Y_t is $\lambda_Y = \left(\kappa/f^3\right)\sqrt{Y_t}$, for some constant κ. X_t has no price of risk.

Special Case: Cox, Ingersoll and Ross

The Cox, Ingersoll and Ross (85) [148] model is a special case of Longstaff and Schwartz. There is one state variable $Y_t = Y_{1,t}$ with process

$$\mathrm{d}Y_t = (\zeta + \xi Y_t)\mathrm{d}t + v\sqrt{Y_t}\,\mathrm{d}z_t, \tag{11.82}$$

where v is a $1 \times (n+k)$ vector. Cox, Ingersoll and Ross choose

$$\alpha = \hat{\alpha} Y_t,$$
$$GG' = \Omega Y_t, \tag{11.83}$$
$$GS' = \Sigma Y_t,$$

where $\hat{\alpha}$, Ω and Σ are constants. One obtains

$$\mathrm{d}r_t = \kappa(\mu - r_t)\mathrm{d}t + \sigma\sqrt{r_t}\,\mathrm{d}z_t. \tag{11.84}$$

The price of risk is $\lambda = -(\kappa/\sigma)\sqrt{r_t}$, for some constant κ. The same result can be obtained from Longstaff and Schwartz by setting $\mu = 0$ in the process for P_t.

Because they emerge from the general equilibrium framework both the Longstaff and Schwartz and the Cox, Ingersoll and Ross models are arbitrage-free.

11.5.7 Bakshi and Chen (97) [46]

Bakshi and Chen (97) [46] also obtain term structures in their framework. Once again it is necessary to specialise down before concrete results can be achieved. They suppose that

$$u(c, s) = \mathrm{e}^{-\rho s}\frac{c^{1-\gamma}}{1-\gamma}, \quad \text{for } \gamma > 0. \tag{11.85}$$

With this assumption they obtain affine term structures

$$r_t(T) = \rho + \gamma\mu_q + \frac{\alpha_x(T-t) + \alpha_y(T-t)}{T-t} + \frac{\rho_x(T-t)}{T-t}X_t + \frac{\rho_y(T-t)}{T-t}Y_t, \tag{11.86}$$

where α_x, α_y, ρ_x and ρ_y are certain deterministic functions of time to maturity. The short rate is

$$r_t = \rho + \gamma\mu_q + \gamma\left(\beta_x - \tfrac{1}{2}(1+\gamma)\sigma_{q,x}^2\right)X_t + \gamma\left(\beta_y - \tfrac{1}{2}(1+\gamma)\sigma_{q,y}^2\right)Y_t \tag{11.87}$$

for certain constants β_x and β_y.

11.5.8 Introducing Money

In a similar framework, Bakshi and Chen (96) [45] incorporate money into the utility function. They obtain both real and nominal term structures.

Their economy has one production process, with value $P_{z,t}$, and a money stock with nominal value M_t. There is a real bond, with instantaneous rate r_t, and a nominal bond, with instantaneous rate R_t. R_t is the nominal short rate and r_t is the real short rate. Investors can choose how to divide their wealth between the production process and the money stock. They gain utility from consumption and from their holding of money.

Aggregate output, y_t, has the process

$$\frac{\mathrm{d}y_t}{y_t} = \mu_y\,\mathrm{d}t + \sigma_y\,\mathrm{d}z_{y,t}, \tag{11.88}$$

and the money stock has the process

$$\frac{\mathrm{d}M_t}{M_t} = \mu_M\,\mathrm{d}t + \sigma_M\,\mathrm{d}z_{M,t}. \tag{11.89}$$

Bakshi and Chen suppose there are N financial claims in the economy, with value $P_{i,t}$, $i = 1, \ldots, N$. The price of a unit of consumption at time t is P_t^c.

Real values, denoted by lower case letters, are found by re-basing according to the value of consumption, so that real asset values are $p_{i,t} = P_{i,t}/P_t^c$, $i = 1, \ldots, N$, the real cash stock is $m_t = M_t/P_t^c$, and the real equity value is $p_{z,t} = P_{z,t}/P_t^c$ (this notation differs from that of previous sections).

Investors choose consumption and real cash balances to maximise utility. The indirect utility function is

$$J_t = \max_{c_t, m_t} \mathbb{E}_t \left[\int_t^\infty e^{-\rho(s-t)} u(c_s, m_s) ds \right]. \tag{11.90}$$

J_t is the optimal utility over all possible choices of consumption c_t and real cash stock m_t. Suppose that real asset and money stock processes are

$$\frac{dp_{i,t}}{p_{i,t}} = \mu_i \, dt + \sigma_i \, dz_{i,t}, \tag{11.91}$$

$$\frac{dm_t}{m_t} = \mu_m \, dt + \sigma_m \, dz_{m,t}, \tag{11.92}$$

with correlations $\rho_{i,y}$ between $z_{i,t}$ and $z_{y,t}$, $\rho_{i,m}$ between $z_{i,t}$ and $z_{m,t}$, and $\rho_{y,m}$ between $z_{y,t}$ and $z_{m,t}$.

Write u_c for the derivative of u with respect to c, *et cetera*. In equilibrium, when J_t is maximised, we have:

- Returns to the assets $p_{i,t}$ are

$$\mu_i - r_t = -y_t \frac{u_{c,c}}{u_c} \text{cov}_t \left(\frac{dp_{i,t}}{p_{i,t}}, \frac{dy_t}{y_t} \right) - m_t \frac{u_{c,m}}{u_c} \text{cov}_t \left(\frac{dp_{i,t}}{p_{i,t}}, \frac{dm_t}{m_t} \right) \tag{11.93}$$

$$\equiv -y_t \frac{u_{c,c}}{u_c} \sigma_i \sigma_y \rho_{i,y} - m_t \frac{u_{c,m}}{u_c} \sigma_i \sigma_m \rho_{i,m}. \tag{11.94}$$

- The real equity value is

$$p_{z,t} = \mathbb{E}_t \left[\int_t^\infty e^{-\rho(s-t)} \frac{u_c(y_s, m_s)}{u_c(y_t, m_t)} y_s \, ds \right]. \tag{11.95}$$

- The real short rate is

$$r_t = \rho - y_t \frac{u_{c,c}}{u_c} \mu_y - \frac{1}{2} y_t^2 \frac{u_{c,c,c}}{u_c} \sigma_y^2 - m_t \frac{u_{c,m}}{u_c} \mu_m$$

$$- \frac{1}{2} m_t^2 \frac{u_{c,m,m}}{u_c} \sigma_m^2 - m_t y_t \frac{u_{c,c,m}}{u_c} \sigma_y \sigma_m \rho_{y,m}. \tag{11.96}$$

- The nominal short rate is

$$R_t = \frac{u_m(y_t, m_t)}{u_c(y_t, m_t)}. \tag{11.97}$$

- Expected inflation is $i_t = r_t - r_t + \pi_t$, where π_t is a risk premium. Hence the Fisher hypothesis does not hold.

The price kernel in this economy is $p_t = e^{-\rho t} u_c(y_t, m_t)$. Suppose that

$$u(c_t, m_t) = \phi \ln c_t + (1 - \phi) \ln m_t, \tag{11.98}$$

for some weighting factor ϕ, then the nominal short rate is

$$R_t = \frac{1 - \phi}{\phi} \frac{y_t}{m_t},$$ (11.99)

where $v_t = y_t/m_t$ is the velocity of money, representing the number of times money changes hands over a period of time.

Bakshi and Chen consider two cases. If y_t and m_t have constant drifts and volatilities, then the real and nominal short rates are

$$r_t = \rho + \mu_y - \sigma_y^2,$$ (11.100)

$$R_t = \rho + \mu_m - \sigma_m^2.$$ (11.101)

In this uninteresting case both rates are constant.

Their second case is more interesting. Suppose that the output process is

$$\frac{dy_t}{y_t} = \left(\mu_y + \eta_y x_t\right) dt + \sigma_y \sqrt{x_t}\, dz_{y,t},$$ (11.102)

where

$$dx_t = \kappa_x(\theta_x - x_t)dt + \sigma_x\sqrt{x_t}\, dz_{x,t}$$ (11.103)

represents technology, and that the process for money stocks is

$$d(\ln M_t) = \mu_M\, dt + d(\ln g_t),$$ (11.104)

where

$$\frac{dg_t}{g_t} = \kappa_g\left(\theta_g - g_t\right) dt + \sigma_g\sqrt{g_t}\, dz_{g,t},$$ (11.105)

all with constant parameters. Returns to M_t revert around a level of about $\mu_M + \kappa_g\theta_g$. Bakshi and Chen show that in this case the real and nominal short rates are

$$r_t = \rho + \mu_y + \left(\eta_y - \sigma_y^2\right) x_t,$$ (11.106)

$$R_t = \frac{\left(\rho + \mu_M\right)\left(\rho + \mu_M + \kappa_g\theta_g\right)}{\rho + \mu_M + \left(\kappa_g + \sigma_g^2\right) g_t}.$$ (11.107)

The real rate depends on the state variable x_t, and the nominal rate on g_t. Their processes will be unrelated, and it will not in general hold that $r_t \leq R_t$.

The process for the nominal interest rate is quite complex. For certain a_0, a_1, b_0, b_1, $b_2 > 0$, it is

$$dR_t = \left[a_0(b_0 - b_1 R_t)(b_0 - b_2 R_t) - a_1^2(b_0 - b_1 R_t)^3\right] dt - a_1\sqrt{R_t}(b_0 - b_1 R_t)^{\frac{3}{2}}\, dz_{M,t}.$$ (11.108)

It can be shown that

$$R_t < \frac{b_0}{b_1} = \frac{\left(\rho + \mu_M\right)\left(\rho + \mu_M + \kappa_g\theta_g\right)}{\rho + \mu_M}$$

so that the variance in (11.107) is well defined.

11.5.9 The Cox, Ingersoll and Ross Framework

We now outline the derivation of equation (11.74). In the Cox, Ingersoll and Ross model there are identical agents maximising

$$K_t = \mathbb{E}_t \left[\int_t^{T\max} u(c_s, Y_s, s) \mathrm{d}s \right], \tag{11.109}$$

for a maximum time horizon $T_{\max}$, and wealth follows the process

$$\mathrm{d}w_t = (w_t a_t'(\alpha - r_t 1) + r_t w_t - c_t)\mathrm{d}t + w_t a_t' G_t \, \mathrm{d}z_t$$

$$\equiv w_t(\mu_w \, \mathrm{d}t + \sigma_w \, \mathrm{d}z_t). \tag{11.110}$$

Let Ω represent the set of all investment and consumption policies. This is the set of controls; investors choose the control in order to maximise their utility. We restrict the set of admissible controls $\omega = (a_i(t), c(t)) \in \Omega$ to be feedback controls, so that $(a_i(t), c(t))$ are $\mathcal{F}_t$-adapted; investors choose controls based upon what they have observed at each moment in time.
Set

$$K(\omega_t, w_t, Y_t, t) = \mathbb{E}_t^{w_t, Y_t} \left[\int_t^{T\max} u(c_s, Y_s, s) \mathrm{d}s \right], \tag{11.111}$$

where ω_t is the control.

Let A_t^ω be the generator of $(Y_t, w_t) \in \mathbb{R}^{k+1}$, conditional on the control ω, so that

$$A_t^\omega K = w_t \mu_w K_w + \mu' K_Y + \tfrac{1}{2} w_t^2 (\sigma_w' \sigma_w) K_{w,w} + w_t K_{w,Y} S_t \sigma_w + \tfrac{1}{2} S_t' K_{Y,Y} S_t. \tag{11.112}$$

We now apply the Hamilton, Jacobi and Bellman (HJB) theorem.

The optimal solution (HJB)   *Let $J(w, Y, t)$ solve*

$$\sup_{\omega \in \Omega} \{A_t^\omega J + u(\omega, Y, t)\} + J_t, \tag{11.113}$$

with boundary conditions

$$J(0, Y, t) = \mathbb{E}_t^Y \left[\int_t^{T\max} u(0, Y_s, s) \mathrm{d}s \right], \tag{11.114}$$

$$J(w, Y, T_{\max}) = 0,$$

then

$$J(w, Y, t) \geq K(\omega, w, Y, t), \quad \textit{for all } \omega \in \Omega, w, Y, \tag{11.115}$$

and if $\omega \in \Omega$ maximises

$$A_t^\omega J + u(\omega, Y, t), \tag{11.116}$$

for all t, w and Y, we have

$$J(w, Y, t) = K(\omega, w, Y, t), \quad \textit{for all } t, w_t, Y_t. \tag{11.117}$$

(For technical conditions and restrictions see Cox, Ingersoll and Ross (85) [147].) We assume that J and the optimal control ω^* exist and are unique. Set $\Psi = \Psi(c, a) = A_t^\omega J + u(\omega, Y, t)$. At a maximum the derivatives Ψ_c and Ψ_a of Ψ satisify

$$\Psi_c = u_c - J_w \leq 0, \tag{11.118}$$

$$\Psi_a = w_t J_w(\alpha - r_t 1) + G_t G_t' a_t w_t^2 J_{w,w} + w_t G_t S_t' J_{w,Y} \leq 0, \tag{11.119}$$

$$a_t' \Psi_a = 0, c_t \Psi_c = 0, \tag{11.120}$$

$$a_t, c_t \geq 0. \tag{11.121}$$

These conditions are necessary but not sufficient for an optimal control to exist.

It is possible to solve for a_t and c_t, in principle. In equilibrium we require a solution (r_t, a_t, c_t) such that $a_t' 1 = 1$. The problem is now

$$a^* = \arg \max_a \{a'\gamma + a'Da \mid a'1 = 1, a \geq 0\}, \tag{11.122}$$

where

$$\gamma = \alpha w J_w + GS' J_{w,Y} w, \tag{11.123}$$

$$D = \tfrac{1}{2} GG' w^2 J_{w,w}. \tag{11.124}$$

This can be solved using a Lagrange multiplier method. When a^* is optimal we have

$$r^* = \frac{\lambda^*}{w J_w} = a^{*\prime} \alpha + a^{*\prime} GG' a^* \frac{J_{w,w}}{J_w} w + a^{*\prime} GS' \frac{J_{w,Y}}{J_w} \tag{11.125}$$

$$= a^{*\prime} \alpha - \left(-\frac{J_{w,w}}{J_w}\right) \frac{\text{var}(w)}{w} - \frac{J_{w,Y}}{J_w} \frac{\text{cov}(w, Y)}{w}, \tag{11.126}$$

as required.

11.6 INTERPRETING THE PRICE KERNEL

We show how a price kernel emerges from a utility maximising framework. For further details see Duffie (92) [181]. Write K for the expected utility of consumption

$$K(c, t) = \mathbb{E}_t \left[\int_t^{T\max} u(c_s, s) ds \right], \tag{11.127}$$

where u is infinitely differentiable, and is increasing and strictly concave in consumption. Write $\Pi_t(c)$ for the price at time t of the consumption stream c_s, $s \geq t$. The investor's problem is to maximise utility, subject to the expected cost $\Pi_t(c)$ of the consumption stream being less than current wealth w,

$$J = \sup \left\{ \mathbb{E}_t \left[\int_t^{T\max} u(c_s, s) ds \right] \mid \mathbb{E}_t[\Pi_t(c)] \leq w \right\}. \tag{11.128}$$

This can be solved using a Lagrange multiplier method. The corresponding uncon-strained problem is

$$J = \sup \left\{ \mathbb{E}_t \left[\int_t^{T_{\max}} (u(c_s, s) - \lambda(p_s c_s - w)) ds \right] \right\}, \tag{11.129}$$

where p is the Rietz representation of Π and λ is the Lagrange multiplier. p is the price kernel. For optimal consumption, c_t^*, the constraint is binding, $\mathbb{E}_t \left[\int_t^{T_{\max}} p_s c_s^* ds \right] = w$. The first-order condition, since $c^* > 0$, is

$$u_c(c_t^*, t) = \lambda p_t, \quad t \in [0, T_{\max}]. \tag{11.130}$$

If p_t is a price kernel, so is λp_t, so we can identify the price kernel with the marginal utility of optimal consumption, u_c.

The Price Kernel

We show how the drift and volatility of a price kernel can be identified with the short rate process and the market price of risk. Suppose p_t is a price kernel with process

$$dp_t = \mu_p(t)dt + \sigma_p(t)dz_t, \tag{11.131}$$

and S_t is an asset with process

$$dS_t = \mu_S(t)dt + \sigma_S(t)dz_t, \tag{11.132}$$

where there is a single Wiener process z_t. Under the objective measure $S_t p_t$ is a martin-gale, $S_t p_t = \mathbb{E}_t[S_T p_T]$. It has zero drift so

$$0 = \mu_p(t)S_t + \mu_S(t)p_t + \sigma_p(t)\sigma_S(t), \tag{11.133}$$

so that

$$\frac{\mu_S(t)}{S_t} + \frac{\mu_p(t)}{p_t} = -\frac{\sigma_p(t)}{p_t} \frac{\sigma_S(t)}{S_t}. \tag{11.134}$$

If S_t is the accumulator account, then $\mu_S(t)/S_t = r_t$ and $\sigma_S(t) = 0$, so that

$$\frac{\mu_p(t)}{p_t} = -r_t, \tag{11.135}$$

the riskless short rate. Set $\theta_t = -\sigma_p(t)/p_t$. For any asset S_t we have

$$\frac{\mu_S(t)}{S_t} - r_t = \theta_t \frac{\sigma_S(t)}{S_t}, \tag{11.136}$$

so that θ_t can be interpreted as the market price of risk.

This result is straightforward to extend to the case where risk in the economy is given by a vector of Wiener processes.

The Short Rate and the Market Price of Risk

The price kernel $p_t = u_c(c_t^*, t)$ is a function of optimal consumption c_t^*. In equilibrium optimal consumption will equal output y_t. Suppose that $y_t = c_t^*$ has the process

$$dy_t = \mu_y(t)dt + \sigma_y(t)dz_t, \tag{11.137}$$

so that the process for p_t is

$$dp_t = \mu_p(t)dt + \sigma_p(t)dz_t, \tag{11.138}$$

where

$$\sigma_p(t) = u_{c,c}(y_t, t)\sigma_y(t),$$

$$\mu_p(t) = u_{c,t}(y_t, t) + u_{c,c}(y_t, t)\mu_y(t) + \tfrac{1}{2}u_{c,c,c}(y_t, t)\sigma_y^2(t). \tag{11.139}$$

This representation allows the short rate to be expressed as a function of derivatives of the utility function and of the output process

$$r_t = -\frac{\mu_p(t)}{p_t} = -\frac{u_{c,t} + u_{c,c}\mu_y + \tfrac{1}{2}u_{c,c,c}\sigma_y^2}{u_c}. \tag{11.140}$$

Similarly for the market price of risk, $\theta_t = -\sigma_p(t)/p_t$, we have

$$\frac{\mu_S(t)}{S_t} - r_t = \gamma_t \sigma_y(t)\frac{\sigma_S(t)}{S_t}, \tag{11.141}$$

where

$$\gamma_t = -\frac{u_{c,c}(y_t, t)}{u_c(y_t, t)} \tag{11.142}$$

is the Pratt–Arrow risk absolute aversion measure.

Examples

For a given utility function $u(y)$, if we make specific assumptions about the process for y_t then we have specified the evolution of the price kernel, and hence we have a term structure model. Suppose that

- the output process is

$$\frac{dy_t}{y_t} = \mu_y dt + \sigma_y dz_{y,t}, \tag{11.143}$$

  for constants μ_y and σ_y;
- the utility function is $u(y, t) = e^{-\rho t} \ln y$.

Then the price kernel is $p_t = u_c = e^{-\rho t}(1/y_t)$. Since $dp_t/p_t = -r_t dt - \theta_t dz_t$, the drift of $u_c(y_t, t)$ is the short rate. We deduce that

$$r_t = \rho + \mu_y - \sigma_y^2 \tag{11.144}$$

and the short rate is constant. This result is rather uninteresting. Suppose instead that

$$\frac{dy_t}{y_t} = m_t \, dt + \sigma_y \, dz_{y,t}, \tag{11.145}$$

$$dm_t = \alpha(\mu - m_t)dt + \sigma_m \, dz_{m,t}, \tag{11.146}$$

for constants α, μ, σ_y and σ_m. Then

$$r_t = \rho - \sigma_y^2 + m_t. \tag{11.147}$$

In this case also the short rate is identified with returns to the output process, offset by a constant. Here the short rate is mean reverting, since returns to y_t are mean reverting.

11.6.1 A Generalised Price Kernel

We have just seen that by supplying a utility function and a process for production we can construct an interest rate model. It is easy to generalise this procedure so that a large family of interest rate models can be produced.

A utility function $u(y)$ has two basic properties. First, its first derivative should be positive, so that when y is bigger so is the utility of y. Second, it is reasonable for the second derivative of u to be negative, so that diminishing returns sets in with increasing y. The production function y_t will be a submartingale.

Let $f(y, t)$ be any function such that $f > 0$ and $f_y < 0$, and let y_t be any submartingale with process $dy_t = \mu_y(y_t)dt + \sigma_y(y_t)dz_t$. We have seen that

$$r_t = -\frac{f_t + f_y \mu_y(y_t) + \frac{1}{2} f_{y,y} \sigma_y^2(y_t)}{f_y} \tag{11.148}$$

is a valid interest rate process. Choosing a log-utility function for f, $f(y, t) = e^{-\rho t} \ln y$, and a log-normal process for y_t, we have $r_t = \rho + \mu_y - \sigma_y^2$, where μ_y and σ_y are the drift and volatility of y_t. To generate any affine interest rate model set $\sigma_y \equiv \sigma$, a constant, and $\mu_y = \sum_{i=1}^{N} a_i X_{i,t}$ for state variables $X_{i,t}$ with suitable affine-type processes and a_i constant.

PART III
VALUATION METHODS

The object of interest rate modelling is often to find prices and hedge ratios for derivative instruments. This part explores the three main valuation methods, namely methods of extracting actual prices from an interest rate model.

The three techniques discussed here—finite difference methods, Monte Carlo methods and lattice methods—are extremely widely used. Monte Carlo methods are relatively straightforward methods of valuing path-dependent options of European type although fast practical implementations can be very sophisticated. These are described in Chapter 13. Finite difference methods are discussed in Chapter 12. These methods can value American style options and can sometimes be used to value path-dependent options. The third category of valuation method—lattice methods—are simpler to implement than finite difference methods but tend to be model-dependent. We meet these in Chapter 14.

The method to use depends on the model and on the application. Monte Carlo methods are easy to set up but hard to run fast. Good lattice methods exist for standard interest rate models, but may not transfer easily to other models. Finite difference methods can be difficult to implement and are probably under-used. For the brave they are a legitimate alternative to Monte Carlo methods for low-dimensional problems.

12

Finite Difference Methods

Finite difference methods have a long history in derivative modelling, and interest rate modelling in particular. The original Vasicek (77) [529] model displayed a PDE and obtained explicit solutions for it. Early papers using finite difference methods include Brennan and Schwartz (78) [92] and Courtadon (82) [144]. More recently several papers have specifically investigated the application of finite difference methods to interest rate modelling, and the particular modifications that may be made in this case. These papers include Vetzal (98) [534] aspects of which are discussed below. Some lattice methods stem from finite difference schemes (for instance Hull and White (90) [293]; see Chapter 14).

General introductions to finite difference methods include Mitchell and Griffiths (80) [401], Morton and Mayers (94) [404] and Smith (85) [496], and many others. A book specifically addressing PDE methods in derivative pricing is Wilmott, Howison and Dewynne (95) [542] and includes a discussion on finite difference methods. Books on financial derivatives frequently include some mention of finite difference methods. Examples are Wilmott (99) [541] and Hull (99) [290].

We do not discuss finite element methods. These methods and some of their applications are discussed in Zvan *et al.* (97) [547] and Forsyth *et al.* (97) [227].

In this chapter we first briefly discuss how finite difference methods can be used to value interest rate derivatives. We describe the three main finite difference methods: the explicit, implicit and Crank–Nicolson methods. The types of boundary conditions appropriate to interest rate models are reviewed. The penultimate section of this chapter covers techniques needed for N-dimensional problems. We illustrate the methods by solving numerically the Longstaff and Schwartz two-factor PDE. Finally we briefly discuss how a PDDE (partial differential difference equation) can be solved.

12.1 THE FEYNMAN–KAC EQUATION

We saw in earlier chapters that the Feynman–Kac equation provides, for 'reasonable' interest rate models, a PDE which is obeyed by the values of derivatives in that model. A derivative will satisfy the PDE with appropriate boundary conditions. It is usually the case that the PDE cannot be solved explicitly, and if this is the situation then it must be solved numerically.

Suppose that the value of an interest rate derivative, c_t, depends upon a single state variable r_t, which we may take to be the short rate. We outline some methods for the numerical solution of the PDE. The methods extend, with some considerable elaboration, to multifactor models. We discuss these in Sections 12.10–12.12.

If c_t is the value of an interest rate option at time t, then its value at time 0 satisfies the expectation

$$c_0 = \tilde{\mathbb{E}}_0 \left[c_T \frac{p_0}{p_T} \right], \tag{12.1}$$

where $\tilde{\mathbb{E}}$ is the expectation with respect to the martingale measure associated with p_t. Suppose the state variable r_t follows the process

$$dr_t = \tilde{\mu}(r_t, t)dt + \sigma(r_t, t)dz_t \tag{12.2}$$

under the EMM. Since the EMM uses the accumulator numeraire the value c of the expectation (12.1) satisfies the PDE

$$\frac{\partial c}{\partial t} + \tilde{\mu} \frac{\partial c}{\partial r} + \frac{1}{2}\sigma^2 \frac{\partial^2 c}{\partial r^2} = rc, \tag{12.3}$$

with some boundary condition at maturity time T,

$$c(T, r_T) = H(T, r_T). \tag{12.4}$$

12.1.1   Solutions to PDEs

Occasionally it is possible to obtain explicit solutions to pricing PDEs. For instance, in the extended Vasicek model bond prices $P_t(T)$ satisfy the PDE

$$\frac{\partial P}{\partial t} + (\theta(t) - ar_t) \frac{\partial P}{\partial r} + \frac{1}{2}\sigma^2 \frac{\partial^2 P}{\partial r^2} = r_t P, \quad P_T(T) = 1. \tag{12.5}$$

Substitute in a test solution $P_t(T) = e^{A(t,T)-B(t,T)r_t}$. The PDE separates out into equations for B and A:

$$\frac{\partial B}{\partial t} = aB - 1, \quad \text{with } B(T, T) = 0, \tag{12.6}$$

$$\frac{\partial A}{\partial t} = \theta(t)B - \frac{1}{2}\sigma^2 B^2, \quad \text{with } A(T, T) = 0. \tag{12.7}$$

Equation (12.6) gives $B(t, T) = \left(1 - e^{-a(T-t)}\right)/a$. Usually $\theta(t)$ is chosen so that the model values of $P_t(T)$ fit the term structure observed in the market, but if $\theta(t)$ is given a functional form it may well be possible to solve (12.7) for A, and hence for P, explicitly.

Explicit solutions can sometimes be found in other models (see Wilmott et al. (95) [542]). Unfortunately explicit solutions are rarely available and other methods need to be used.

12.2   DISCRETISING THE PDE

We solve (12.3) using numerical methods. r_t and t are discretised as

$$r_0, \ldots, r_{M+1}, \tag{12.8}$$

$$t_0, \ldots, t_{N+1} = T. \tag{12.9}$$

This creates a grid of points (r_i, t_j), $i = 0, \ldots, M + 1$, $j = 0, \ldots, N + 1$. It is sometimes convenient to use a constant grid spacing

$$\Delta_t = t_{j+1} - t_j, \quad j = 0, \ldots, N,$$

$$\Delta_r = r_{i+1} - r_i, \quad i = 0, \ldots, M,$$

although this is often not necessary.[1] Write $c_{i,j} = c(r_i, t_j)$ for the option value at the grid point (r_i, t_j). We have a grid of option prices, as in Figure 12.1. Option values at

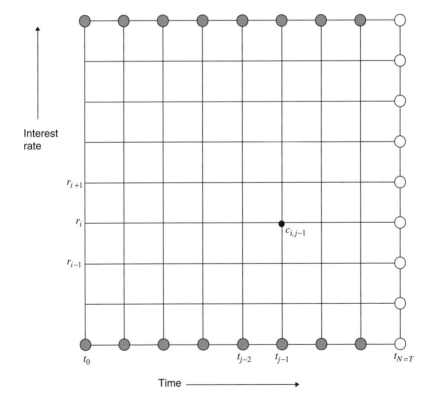

Figure 12.1   The grid of option prices

---

[1] There may often be occasions when a variable time or space mesh is desirable. For instance, a Bermudan option may be exercised at several times up to a final maturity date. It may be convenient

maturity are known, and boundary conditions will relate together option values at r_0 and r_1, and at r_M and r_{M+1}, so that, in effect, the values of c at the top and bottom of the grid are known.

For example, if the option is a call on r_t, the value of c_T at the expiry time $T = t_{N+1}$ is

$$c_{i,N+1} = \max(0, r_i - r_X), \qquad (12.10)$$

where r_X is the strike. For large values of r_t, $r_t \gg r_X$, we have $\partial c/\partial r \approx 1$ at each time t_j, so

$$\frac{c_{M+1,j} - c_{M,j}}{r_{M+1} - r_M} \approx 1. \qquad (12.11)$$

Expression (12.11) relates $c_{M+1,j}$ to $c_{M,j}$. For small values of r, $r_t \ll r_X$, $\partial c/\partial r \approx 0$, so we can approximate

$$\frac{c_{1,j} - c_{0,j}}{r_1 - r_0} \approx 0, \qquad (12.12)$$

obtaining a relationship between $c_{1,j}$ and $c_{0,j}$. These are Neumann boundary conditions determined by derivatives. We shall see in Section 12.8 how one may use boundary conditions implicitly determined by the PDE.

The object is now to fill in the rest of the grid. We can do this because option values at adjacent grid points are related. The method is to find discrete approximations for the various differentials of c which appear in the PDE (12.3). We can substitute these into the PDE and find relationships between nearby values of $c_{i,j}$. One obtains a different numerical method depending upon the particular approximations to the differentials which are used. Three types of approximation are commonly made to a derivative. At a grid point (r_i, t_j) one may approximate the derivative as:

$$\text{forward difference}: \left(\frac{\partial c}{\partial r}\right)_{i,j} \approx \frac{c_{i,j+1} - c_{i,j}}{r_{j+1} - r_j}, \qquad (12.13)$$

$$\text{backwards difference}: \left(\frac{\partial c}{\partial r}\right)_{i,j} \approx \frac{c_{i,j} - c_{i,j-1}}{r_j - r_{j-1}}, \qquad (12.14)$$

$$\text{central difference}: \left(\frac{\partial c}{\partial r}\right)_{i,j} \approx \frac{c_{i,j+1} - c_{i,j-1}}{r_{j+1} - r_{j-1}}. \qquad (12.15)$$

The different approximations are illustrated in Figure 12.2. From the figure it is clear that the central difference approximation is a better approximation to the derivative of c at r_i than either of the other two. Indeed it is usually (but not always) the preferred approximation. The time derivative is usually approximated as a backwards difference, however.[2]

---

to adjust the time discretisation to ensure that exercise times coincide with time steps. If the grid is non-uniform the numerical approximations we shall make to the derivatives in (12.3) have to be adjusted appropriately. This is straightforward.

[2] A central difference approximation for $\partial c/\partial t$ turns out to be unworkable.

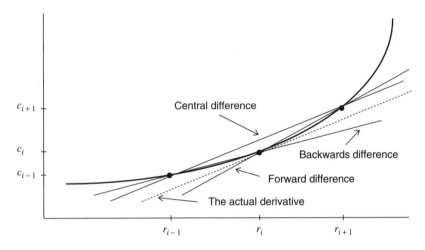

Figure 12.2   Three discrete approximations to the first derivative

There are two possible numerical errors associated with approximating derivatives in this way. The first is discretisation error, the error due to using a discrete approximation to the derivative. The second type of error is round-off error, introduced because numbers are truncated during calculation. A numerical method is convergent if the discretisation error may be made arbitrarily small by taking a finer and finer grid. The finer the grid, the more accurately a discrete approximation to a derivative may be expected to become, but the number of computations will increase, resulting in a likelihood of greater truncation error. A method is stable if the round-off error remains bounded as the grid gets finer. A method is likely to be stable if round-off errors can cancel each other out, rather than compound one another.

12.3   SIMPLIFYING THE PDE

Before attempting to discretise the PDE (12.3) it should be simplified as much as possible. This will increase the stability and robustness of a numerical solution method. For instance, consider the Black–Scholes PDE satisfied by an option, c_t, on a traded stock, S_t, following a geometric Brownian motion with constant volatility σ,

$$\frac{\partial c}{\partial t} + rS\frac{\partial c}{\partial S} + \frac{1}{2}\sigma^2 S^2 \frac{\partial^2 c}{\partial S^2} = rc. \qquad (12.16)$$

This PDE can be simplified in two ways:

1. *Remove the rc term on the right-hand side.*
   Make the substitution

$$c = e^{rt}v \qquad (12.17)$$

so that v is the value of c discounted back to time 0. v satisfies the PDE

$$\frac{\partial v}{\partial t} + rS\frac{\partial v}{\partial S} + \frac{1}{2}\sigma^2 S^2 \frac{\partial^2 v}{\partial S^2} = 0 \tag{12.18}$$

with the appropriately modified boundary condition.

2. *Remove the dependence on S from the coefficients of the PDE.*
Change the independent variable from S to $R = \ln S$, and set $u(R, t) = v\left(e^R, t\right)$. Then

$$\frac{\partial u}{\partial t} + \left(r - \frac{1}{2}\sigma^2\right)\frac{\partial u}{\partial R} + \frac{1}{2}\sigma^2 \frac{\partial^2 u}{\partial R^2} = 0. \tag{12.19}$$

u is the (discounted) option value expressed as a function of the total return to the stock. This equation in u has constant coefficients and is much more stable than (12.18)

In general each PDE must be considered on its own merits. For the interest rate PDE (12.3) method 1 is difficult to apply, but a transformation analogous to 2 can occasionally be useful. If an interest rate process is $dr_t = \tilde{\mu}(r_t, t)dt + \sigma(r_t, t)dz_t$ under the EMM, define $R(r, t) = \int^r (1/\sigma(s, t))ds$ and set $u(R(r), t) = v(r, t)$. Then $dR_t = m(r_t, t)dt + dz_t$ for some drift $m(r_t, t)$ and

$$\frac{\partial u}{\partial t} + m(r_t, t)\frac{\partial u}{\partial R} + \frac{1}{2}\frac{\partial^2 u}{\partial R^2} = 0, \tag{12.20}$$

with a constant diffusion coefficient.

We discuss transformations further in Section 12.10 when we investigate N-dimensional PDEs.

12.3.1 Transformation to a Compact Set

State variables may often take values on the entire real line. An interest rate process may be unbounded above, so that although rates are usually confined to moderate levels their density is non-zero at arbitrarily high levels. Also, it may only be at large values of r that good approximations to boundary conditions are made. For instance, as $r \to \infty$ a PDB price $B_t(T \mid r) \to 0$. Unfortunately the boundary condition $B_t(T \mid r_{M+1}) = 0$ may only be a valid approximation when r_{M+1} is very large.

To overcome this problem the state space can be transformed to map the real line onto a bounded subset, I. Let $x \in \mathbb{R}$. Possibilities are to set

1. $z = \arctan x$. Then $z \in I = (-\pi/2, \pi/2) \subseteq [-\pi/2, \pi/2]$.
2. $z = N^{-1}(x)$, where N is the normal distribution function. Then $z \in I = (0, 1) \subseteq [0, 1]$.
3. $z = (1 + x)^{-1}$. Then $z \in (0, 1] \subseteq [0, 1]$.

After a transformation of this sort, the PDE is defined on the interval I, not the whole of $\mathbb{R}$. A uniform discretisation of I is effectively discretising the whole of $\mathbb{R}$, so that the problems noted above are overcome. The cost is that the transformed PDE may have awkward coefficients. Unfortunately this may be a necessary evil.

Table 12.1   Types of boundary
conditions

Type	Specifies
Dirichlet	c
Neumann	$\frac{\partial c}{\partial r}$
Robin	$\frac{\partial c}{\partial r} = ac + b,$

12.3.2   Boundary Conditions

At the upper and lower boundaries we can specify boundary conditions in a number
of ways. Table 12.1 lists the commoner types. The simplest is the Dirichlet boundary
condition which specifies the value of c at the boundary.

On the grid, boundary conditions are used to specify $c_{0,j}$ and $c_{M+1,j}$ as affine functions
of $c_{1,j}$ and $c_{2,j}$, and $c_{M-1,j}$ and $c_{M,j}$. The system must remain tridiagonal, or nearly
tridiagonal, so that it is easy to solve, as we see below.

At the boundary we have, for example with Robin conditions,

$$\frac{1}{\Delta_r}\left(c_{1,j} - c_{0,j}\right) = a\left(c_{1,j} + c_{0,j}\right)/2 + b, \tag{12.21}$$

which specifies how $c_{0,j}$ is obtained from $c_{1,j}$.

Note that the approximation to c in Equation (12.21) is centred. It is much more
accurate to use the centred value $\frac{1}{2}\left(c_{1,j} + c_{0,j}\right)$ than, for instance, using the value of
$c_{1,j}$ (see Morton and Mayers (94) [404]).

12.4   EXPLICIT METHODS

We need to find approximations for derivatives at the grid point (i, j). In explicit finite
difference methods, a central difference approximation is used for both the first and
second derivatives with respect to r, and a backward difference approximation for the
time derivative. The space derivatives are approximated using option values at time j.
Assuming a constant grid spacing we obtain:

$$\left(\frac{\partial c}{\partial r}\right)_{i,j} \approx \frac{c_{i+1,j} - c_{i-1,j}}{2\Delta_r}, \tag{12.22}$$

$$\left(\frac{\partial^2 c}{\partial r^2}\right)_{i,j} = \frac{\partial\left(\frac{\partial c}{\partial r}\right)}{\partial r} \approx \frac{1}{\Delta_r}\left(\frac{c_{i+1,j} - c_{i,j}}{\Delta_r} - \frac{c_{i,j} - c_{i-1,j}}{\Delta_r}\right) \tag{12.23}$$

$$= \frac{c_{i+1,j} - 2c_{i,j} + c_{i-1,j}}{(\Delta_r)^2}, \tag{12.24}$$

$$\left(\frac{\partial c}{\partial t}\right)_{i,j} \approx \frac{c_{i,j} - c_{i,j-1}}{\Delta_t}. \tag{12.25}$$

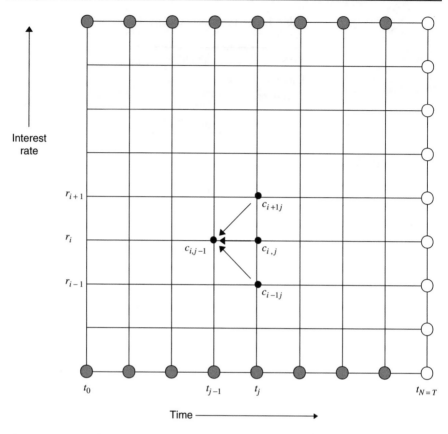

Figure 12.3 Working backwards through the grid in the explicit method

(The backwards difference approximation for $\partial c/\partial t$ is a forwards difference in reverse time.) We substitute these approximations into the PDE (12.3)

$$\frac{\partial c}{\partial t} + \tilde{\mu}\frac{\partial c}{\partial r} + \frac{1}{2}\sigma^2\frac{\partial^2 c}{\partial r^2} = rc, \qquad (12.26)$$

which becomes

$$\frac{c_{i,j} - c_{i,j-1}}{\Delta_t} + \tilde{\mu}_{i,j}\frac{c_{i+1,j} - c_{i-1,j}}{2\Delta_r} + \frac{1}{2}\sigma_{i,j}^2\frac{c_{i+1,j} - 2c_{i,j} + c_{i-1,j}}{(\Delta_r)^2} = r_i c_{i,j}, \qquad (12.27)$$

where $\tilde{\mu}_{i,j}$ and $\sigma_{i,j}^2$ are computed using r_i and t_j.[3] We can rearrange (12.27) to get

$$A_{i,j}c_{i+1,j} + B_{i,j}c_{i,j} + C_{i,j}c_{i-1,j} = c_{i,j-1}, \qquad (12.28)$$

---

[3] We have discretised c as $c_{i,j}$ on the right-hand side of (12.26).

where

$$A_{i,j} = \frac{1}{2}\tilde{\mu}_{i,j}\frac{\Delta_t}{\Delta_r} + \frac{1}{2}\sigma_{i,j}^2\frac{\Delta_t}{(\Delta_r)^2}, \tag{12.29}$$

$$B_{i,j} = 1 - \sigma_{i,j}^2\frac{\Delta_t}{(\Delta_r)^2} - r_i\Delta_t, \tag{12.30}$$

$$C_{i,j} = -\frac{1}{2}\tilde{\mu}_{i,j}\frac{\Delta_t}{\Delta_r} + \frac{1}{2}\sigma_{i,j}^2\frac{\Delta_t}{(\Delta_r)^2}, \tag{12.31}$$

The value $c_{i,j-1}$ at time t_{j-1} is a function of the values of the three points $c_{i+1,j}$, $c_{i,j}$ and $c_{i-1,j}$ at time t_j. Using (12.28) one works backwards through the grid from time t_{N+1} to time t_0, one layer at a time, as in Figure 12.3. The solution at maturity time $T = t_{N+1}$ is known. Given a set of values of $c_{i,j}$ at time t_j one uses (12.28) to find values of $c_{i,j-1}$ at time t_{j-1}.

At the very top and bottom of the grid the appropriate boundary conditions, which depend on the particular instrument one is valuing, must be incorporated. For instance, if we specify that $\partial c/\partial r = 0$ at the lower boundary, say, then we set $c_{0,j-1} = c_{1,j-1}$. Once $c_{1,j-1}$ has been found, $c_{0,j-1}$ is determined.

12.5 IMPLICIT METHODS

In the explicit finite difference method approximations for space derivatives at grid point (i, j) are computed using option values at time t_j. This results in a method where option values at time t_{j-1} are obtained as explicit functions of option values at time t_j. The implicit finite difference method uses option values at time t_{j-1} to compute space derivatives in the PDE. This gives a method where option values at time t_{j-1} are implicitly determined from those at time t_j. An option value at time t_{j-1} will depend upon every option value at time t_j. The advantage in doing this is that rounding errors will tend to cancel one another out. The approximations used are:

$$\left(\frac{\partial c}{\partial r}\right)_{i,j} \approx \frac{c_{i+1,j-1} - c_{i-1,j-1}}{2\Delta_r}, \tag{12.32}$$

$$\left(\frac{\partial^2 c}{\partial r^2}\right)_{i,j} \approx \frac{c_{i+1,j-1} - 2c_{i,j-1} + c_{i-1,j-1}}{(\Delta_r)^2}, \tag{12.33}$$

$$\left(\frac{\partial c}{\partial t}\right)_{i,j} \approx \frac{c_{i,j} - c_{i,j-1}}{\Delta_t}. \tag{12.34}$$

If these are substituted into the PDE, we obtain

$$\frac{c_{i,j} - c_{i,j-1}}{\Delta_t} + \tilde{\mu}_{i,j}\frac{c_{i+1,j-1} - c_{i-1,j-1}}{2\Delta_r} + \frac{1}{2}\sigma_{i,j}^2\frac{c_{i+1,j-1} - 2c_{i,j-1} + c_{i-1,j-1}}{(\Delta_r)^2} = r_i c_{i,j}. \tag{12.35}$$

This is rearranged to obtain

$$A_{i,j}c_{i+1,j-1} + B_{i,j}c_{i,j-1} + C_{i,j}c_{i-1,j-1} = c_{i,j}, \quad i = 1, \ldots, M, \tag{12.36}$$

where

$$A_{i,j} = \frac{1}{1 - r_i \Delta_t} \left(-\frac{1}{2}\tilde{\mu}_{i,j}\frac{\Delta_t}{\Delta_r} - \frac{1}{2}\sigma_{i,j}^2 \frac{\Delta_t}{(\Delta_r)^2} \right), \qquad (12.37)$$

$$B_{i,j} = \frac{1}{1 - r_i \Delta_t} \left(1 + \sigma_{i,j}^2 \frac{\Delta_t}{(\Delta_r)^2} \right), \qquad (12.38)$$

$$C_{i,j} = \frac{1}{1 - r_i \Delta_t} \left(\frac{1}{2}\tilde{\mu}_{i,j}\frac{\Delta_t}{\Delta_r} - \frac{1}{2}\sigma_{i,j}^2 \frac{\Delta_t}{(\Delta_r)^2} \right). \qquad (12.39)$$

Equation (12.36) expresses the value of a time t_j object $c_{i,j}$ in terms of three time t_{j-1} objects, $c_{i+1,j-1}$, $c_{i,j-1}$ and $c_{i-1,j-1}$ (see Figure 12.4). As for the explicit method, we can work backwards through the grid from known option values at maturity time $T = t_{N+1}$, although here the method is more complex. (12.36) is a system of M linear equations expressing unknown values $c_{i,j-1}$ in terms of known values of $c_{i,j}$.

There are modified equations at $i = 0$ and $i = M + 1$, depending on the upper and lower boundary conditions. For instance, with a Robin boundary condition,

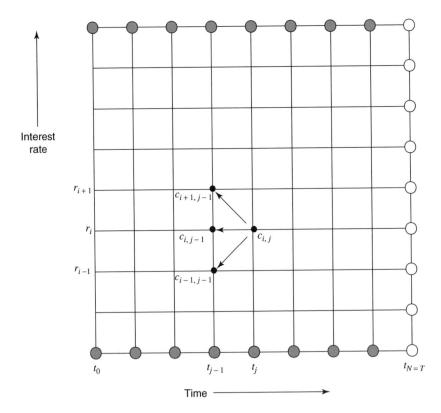

Figure 12.4 Working backwards through the grid in the implicit method

the relationship

$$c_{0,j-1} \left(\frac{1}{\Delta_r} + \frac{1}{2}a \right) = c_{1,j-1} \left(\frac{1}{\Delta_r} - \frac{1}{2}a \right) - b, \tag{12.40}$$

derived from (12.21) replaces equation (12.36) for $i = 0$.

The complete system is tri-diagonal and easy numerical solution methods exist. This is discussed further below.

12.6 THE CRANK–NICOLSON METHOD

The Crank–Nicolson method can be thought of as an average of an explicit and an implicit scheme. It has advantages over both, but there are some limitations to its use. Let $\Theta \in [0, 1]$ be a constant. The Crank–Nicolson scheme uses the following approximations for the derivatives at grid point (i, j):

$$\left(\frac{\partial c}{\partial r} \right)_{i,j} \approx (1 - \Theta) \frac{c_{i+1,j} - c_{i-1,j}}{2\Delta_r} + \Theta \frac{c_{i+1,j-1} - c_{i-1,j-1}}{2\Delta_r},$$

$$\left(\frac{\partial^2 c}{\partial r^2} \right)_{i,j} \approx (1 - \Theta) \frac{c_{i+1,j} - 2c_{i,j} + c_{i-1,j}}{(\Delta_r)^2}$$

$$+ \Theta \frac{c_{i+1,j-1} - 2c_{i,j-1} + c_{i-1,j-1}}{(\Delta_r)^2}, \tag{12.41}$$

$$\left(\frac{\partial c}{\partial t} \right)_{i,j} \approx \frac{c_{i,j} - c_{i,j-1}}{\Delta_t}.$$

When $\Theta = 0$ this gives the explicit scheme. $\Theta = 1$ gives the implicit scheme. The Crank–Nicolson scheme is given by $\Theta = \frac{1}{2}$. Set $\alpha = \Delta_t/(\Delta_r)^2$ and $v(r, t) = \frac{1}{2}\sigma^2(r, t)$ and define

$$m_{i,j} = -2\alpha v_{i,j}, \tag{12.42}$$

$$u_{i,j} = \alpha v_{i,j} \left(v_{i,j} + \frac{1}{2}\tilde{\mu}_{i,j}\Delta_r \right), \tag{12.43}$$

$$l_{i,j} = \alpha v_{i,j} \left(v_{i,j} - \frac{1}{2}\tilde{\mu}_{i,j}\Delta_r \right). \tag{12.44}$$

When the approximations (12.41) are substituted into (12.3) we obtain:[4]

$$- (1 - \Theta)u_{i,j}c_{i+1,j} - (1 - r_i\Delta_t + (1 - \Theta)m_{i,j})c_{i,j} - (1 - \Theta)l_{i,j}c_{i-1,j}$$

$$= \Theta u_{i,j}c_{i+1,j-1} - (1 - \Theta m_{i,j})c_{i,j-1} + \Theta l_{i,j}c_{i-1,j-1}, \tag{12.45}$$

for $i = 1, \ldots, M$. This is a tri-diagonal system of equations. This can be clearly seen by expressing (12.45) in matrix form. For simplicity we impose constant values of the

---

[4] The zeroth-order term, c, has been discretised as $c \approx c_{i,j}$. We have seen that we could also consider using a discretisation such as $c \approx \frac{1}{2} \left(c_{i,j} + c_{i,j-1} \right)$.

option at the boundary; that is, we specify values for $c_{0,j}$ and $c_{M+1,j}$, $j = 0, \ldots, N$. Define

$$c_j = \begin{pmatrix} c_{1,j} \\ c_{2,j} \\ \vdots \\ c_{M,j} \end{pmatrix} \quad \text{and} \quad B_j = \begin{pmatrix} l_{1,j}\left((1 - \Theta)c_{0,j} + \Theta c_{0,j-1}\right) \\ 0 \\ \vdots \\ 0 \\ u_{M,j}\left((1 - \Theta)c_{M+1,j} + \Theta c_{M+1,j-1}\right) \end{pmatrix} \quad (12.46)$$

c_j is the vector of option values at time t_j and B_j is a vector carrying the boundary conditions for time t_j. Set

$$M_j = \begin{pmatrix} m_{1,j} & u_{1,j} & 0 & 0 & \cdots & 0 \\ l_{2,j} & m_{2,j} & u_{2,j} & 0 & \cdots & 0 \\ 0 & \ddots & \ddots & \ddots & \ddots & \vdots \\ \vdots & \ddots & \ddots & \ddots & \ddots & 0 \\ 0 & \cdots & 0 & l_{M-1,j} & m_{M-1,j} & u_{M-1,j} \\ 0 & \cdots & 0 & 0 & l_{M,j} & m_{M,j} \end{pmatrix} \quad (12.47)$$

and $P = \text{diag}\{1 - r_i\Delta_t\}$. Then the vector of option values satisfies the matrix equation

$$\left(-P - (1 - \Theta)M_j\right)c_j = \left(-I + \Theta M_j\right)c_{j-1} + B_j. \quad (12.48)$$

If c_j is known, then the left-hand side of (12.48) is known. Because M_j is tri-diagonal the system (12.48) can be solved easily using standard row-reduction techniques to find the unknown vector c_{j-1}. For solution methods see Morton and Mayers (94) [404], Press *et al.* (92) [441], *et cetera*.

12.7 COMPARISON OF METHODS

The choice of methods depends upon the degree of difficulty of implementation which one is prepared to accept and the appropriateness of the method for the application in hand. The explicit method is

- Stable and convergent if $\alpha = \Delta_t/(\Delta_r)^2 \leq \frac{1}{2}$ (when volatilities have been normalised to 1). If $\alpha > \frac{1}{2}$ errors may grow uncontrollably.
- Easy to implement.
- May not require explicit boundary conditions (see below).
- Only first-order accurate in time.

In contrast, the implicit method is

- Always stable and convergent: small-scale fluctuations caused by rounding errors tend to cancel each other out because of the averaging introduced when the tri-diagonal system of equations is solved.
- Slightly harder to implement than the explicit method.

- Almost as fast as the explicit method.
- Usually requires explicit boundary conditions (see below).
- First-order accurate in time.

The Crank–Nicolson method is

- As stable as the fully implicit method.
- Slightly harder to implement than the other two methods.
- Cannot handle discontinuous boundary conditions.
- Second-order accurate in time.

In practice the Crank–Nicolson method is often preferred. Even though it is the most complicated method to implement its inherent stability means that a much larger time step may be made resulting in large overall computational savings. Although it cannot cope with certain types of boundary conditions—those with discontinuous payoffs such as those arising from range options—one overcomes this problem by inserting a few implicit steps leading away from the final maturity time before switching over to Crank–Nicolson steps just away from the boundary. Just before time zero one should also insert a few fully implicit steps to average out any short-range noise frozen in by the Crank–Nicolson method.

12.8 IMPLICIT BOUNDARY CONDITIONS

For a parabolic PDE, different numerical methods have different requirements for boundary conditions. Since in an implicit method all option values at time t_j contribute to each option value at time t_{j-1}, these methods normally require boundary conditions to be supplied explicitly. An explicit method does not. The explicit method allows boundary conditions to be determined by the PDE, rather than requiring the provision of separate additional conditions.

In Vetzal (98) [534] it is argued that for interest rate dependent claims it is unnecessary to provide explicit boundary conditions. In many interest rate models $|\mu(r, t)| \longrightarrow \infty$ as $r \longrightarrow \pm\infty$, and $\sigma^2(r, t)$ does not increase as fast as $|\mu(r, t)|$. This implies that the differential equation (12.3) is convection dominated—dominated by the first derivative—which in turn implies that for neither explicit nor for implicit methods should boundary conditions be imposed; rather, they should be determined implicitly from the differential equation itself.

To obtain an implicit relationship at the bottom boundary do two Taylor series expansions about r_0:

$$c(r_1) \approx c(r_0) + \frac{\partial c}{\partial r}\Delta_r + \frac{1}{2}\frac{\partial^2 c}{\partial r^2}(\Delta_r)^2 , \tag{12.49}$$

$$c(r_2) \approx c(r_0) + 2\frac{\partial c}{\partial r}\Delta_r + \frac{1}{2}\frac{\partial^2 c}{\partial r^2}(2\Delta_r)^2 . \tag{12.50}$$

These two equations may be solved to find approximations for $(\partial c/\partial r)_{0,j}$ and $\left(\partial^2 c/\partial r^2\right)_{0,j}$ at r_0:

$$\left(\frac{\partial c}{\partial r}\right)_{0,j} \approx \frac{-c_{2,j} + 4c_{1,j} - 3c_{0,j}}{2\Delta_r}, \tag{12.51}$$

$$\left(\frac{\partial^2 c}{\partial r^2}\right)_{0,j} \approx \frac{c_{2,j} - 2c_{1,j} + c_{0,j}}{(\Delta_r)^2}. \tag{12.52}$$

Similarly at the top boundary one obtains:

$$\left(\frac{\partial c}{\partial r}\right)_{M+1,j} \approx \frac{c_{M-1,j} - 4c_{M,j} + 3c_{M+1,j}}{2\Delta_r}, \tag{12.53}$$

$$\left(\frac{\partial^2 c}{\partial r^2}\right)_{M+1,j} \approx \frac{c_{M-1,j} - 2c_{M,j} + c_{M+1,j}}{(\Delta_r)^2}. \tag{12.54}$$

These two pairs of approximations form the basis of the approximation used at top and bottom boundaries, instead of the usual central approximations. They are derived solely from the differential equation and do not depend upon the characteristics of any particular derivative security. Note that this method only applies to interest rate products where the drift and volatility functions have the appropriate behaviour. For equities, volatilities are likely to scale to roughly the same order as the drift term, and so an implicitly determined boundary condition is likely to be inappropriate. Equations (12.52) and (12.54) are essentially imposing the condition that $\partial^3 c/\partial r^3 = 0$ at the boundary.

For a fully implicit scheme one adjusts the recurrence relationship between time t_{j-1} and time t_j as follows:

For $i = 1, \ldots, M$ use the normal relationship:

$$A_{i,j}c_{i+1,j-1} + B_{i,j}c_{i,j-1} + C_{i,j}c_{i-1,j-1} = c_{i,j}, \quad i = 1, \ldots, M,$$

$$A_{i,j} = \frac{1}{1 - r_i\Delta_t}\left(-\frac{1}{2}\tilde{\mu}_{i,j}\frac{\Delta_t}{\Delta_r} - \frac{1}{2}\sigma_{i,j}^2\frac{\Delta_t}{(\Delta_r)^2}\right),$$

$$B_{i,j} = \frac{1}{1 - r_i\Delta_t}\left(1 + \sigma_{i,j}^2\frac{\Delta_t}{(\Delta_r)^2}\right),$$

$$C_{i,j} = \frac{1}{1 - r_i\Delta_t}\left(\frac{1}{2}\tilde{\mu}_{i,j}\frac{\Delta_t}{\Delta_r} - \frac{1}{2}\sigma_{i,j}^2\frac{\Delta_t}{(\Delta_r)^2}\right).$$

For $i = 0$ the relationship is

$$A_{0,j}c_{2,j-1} + B_{0,j}c_{1,j-1} + C_{0,j}c_{0,j-1} = c_{0,j},$$

$$A_{0,j} = \frac{1}{1 - r_0\Delta_t}\left(\frac{1}{2}\tilde{\mu}_{0,j}\frac{\Delta_t}{\Delta_r} - \frac{1}{2}\sigma_{0,j}^2\frac{\Delta_t}{(\Delta_r)^2}\right),$$

$$B_{0,j} = \frac{1}{1 - r_0\Delta_t}\left(-2\tilde{\mu}_{0,j}\frac{\Delta_t}{\Delta_r} + \sigma_{0,j}^2\frac{\Delta_t}{(\Delta_r)^2}\right),$$

$$C_{0,j} = \frac{1}{1 - r_0\Delta_t}\left(1 + \frac{3}{2}\tilde{\mu}_{0,j}\frac{\Delta_t}{\Delta_r} - \frac{1}{2}\sigma_{0,j}^2\frac{\Delta_t}{(\Delta_r)^2}\right).$$

For $i = M + 1$ the relationship is:

$$A_{M+1,j}c_{M-1,j-1} + B_{M+1,j}c_{M,j-1} + C_{M+1,j}c_{M+1,j-1} = c_{M+1,j},$$

$$A_{M+1,j} = \frac{1}{1 - r_{M+1}\Delta_t}\left(-\frac{1}{2}\tilde{\mu}_{M+1,j}\frac{\Delta_t}{\Delta_r} - \frac{1}{2}\sigma_{M+1,j}^2\frac{\Delta_t}{(\Delta_r)^2}\right),$$

$$B_{M+1,j} = \frac{1}{1 - r_{M+1}\Delta_t}\left(2\tilde{\mu}_{M+1,j}\frac{\Delta_t}{\Delta_r} + \sigma_{M+1,j}^2\frac{\Delta_t}{(\Delta_r)^2}\right),$$

$$C_{M+1,j} = \frac{1}{1 - r_{M+1}\Delta_t}\left(1 - \frac{3}{2}\tilde{\mu}_{M+1,j}\frac{\Delta_t}{\Delta_r} - \frac{1}{2}\sigma_{M+1,j}^2\frac{\Delta_t}{(\Delta_r)^2}\right).$$

This can be put into matrix form. Set $c_j = (c_{0,j}, \ldots, c_{M+1,j})$ and

$$M_j = \begin{pmatrix} C_{0,j} & B_{0,j} & A_{0,j} & 0 & \cdots & 0 \\ C_{1,j} & B_{1,j} & A_{1,j} & 0 & \cdots & 0 \\ 0 & \ddots & \ddots & \ddots & \ddots & \vdots \\ \vdots & \ddots & \ddots & \ddots & \ddots & 0 \\ 0 & \cdots & 0 & C_{M,j} & B_{M,j} & A_{M,j} \\ 0 & \cdots & 0 & C_{M+1,j} & B_{M+1,j} & A_{M+1,j} \end{pmatrix}, \qquad (12.55)$$

then

$$M_{j-1}c_{j-1} = c_j. \qquad (12.56)$$

M_{j-1} is not tri-diagonal, but it is simple to tri-diagonalise by eliminating $A_{0,j}$ and $C_{M+1,j}$. Standard tri-diagonal algorithms then apply to derive c_{j-1} iteratively from c_j, starting from the known values of c_{N+1}.

12.9 FITTING TO AN INITIAL TERM STRUCTURE

An interest rate model will generate its own particular set of term structures. These will not, in general, coincide with term structures observed in the market. However, there is a very strong desire amongst practitioners to use only models that can reproduce, either exactly or very closely, the term structures actually observed. If derivatives are valued with a model that has been calibrated to the current term structure then their values are in some sense consistent with the observed term structure. One's intuitive feeling is that prices that are consistent in this way are in some sense 'more accurate' then prices that are not consistent. Of course, this does not mean these consistent prices are 'correct'.

Given an (arbitrary) interest rate model there are various methods available to adapt it to enable it to generate any given term structure (within reason). These include allowing some coefficients in the risk-adjusted processes for the state variables to be time dependent, allowing the market price of risk to be time-dependent, and adjusting options prices directly. The lattice method of Hull and White adjusts the reversion level of a mean reverting process so that observed term structures are recovered. We discuss this method in a later chapter. Here we briefly discuss alternative procedures.

12.9.1   Making the Market Price of Risk Time-Dependent

Suppose that the sole state variable is the short rate r_t whose objective process is

$$\mathrm{d}r_t = \mu(r_t, t)\mathrm{d}t + \sigma(r_t, t)\mathrm{d}z_t. \tag{12.57}$$

Pure discount bond prices $B_t(T)$ satisfy the PDE

$$\frac{\partial B}{\partial t} + \tilde{\mu}\frac{\partial B}{\partial r} + \frac{1}{2}\sigma^2\frac{\partial^2 B}{\partial r^2} = rB, \tag{12.58}$$

where $\tilde{\mu}(r, t) = \mu(r, t) - \lambda(r, t).\sigma(r, t)$ for the price of risk function $\lambda(r, t)$, and with boundary condition $B_t(T) = 1$. Suppose that $\lambda(r, t)$ decomposes as

$$\lambda(r, t) = \theta(t)\psi(r), \tag{12.59}$$

for some function $\theta(t)$ and a given function $\psi(r)$. Uhrig and Walter (95) [528] propose that $\theta(t)$ should be chosen so that solutions to (12.58) recover the observed term structure. They suggest the following method.

Under an implicit scheme (12.58) is solved on a grid where for each time t_j one finds a vector $B_j = \left(B_{0,j}, \ldots, B_{M+1,j}\right)'$ of pure discount bond prices. We have seen that there is a matrix M_{j-1} such that $M_{j-1}B_{j-1} = B_j$, where the coefficients of M_{j-1} depend on $\tilde{\mu}$ and σ^2. Since $\tilde{\mu}(r, t)$ depends on $\theta(t)$, M_{j-1} is also a function of $\theta_{j-1} = \theta(t_{j-1})$. If the current short rate is r_{i_0}, for some $i_0 \in \{0, \ldots, M + 1\}$, then the current term structure is determined by $B_{i_0,j}$, $j = 0, \ldots, N + 1$. Working backwards from $j = N + 1$ one successively chooses θ_{j-1} for each $j - 1$ so that $B_{i_0,j-1}$ has the correct observed value.

The drawbacks of this method are that

1. It involves a numerical search for each θ_{j-1}; and
2. It supposes that the time-dependent component of the market price of risk is an appropriate object to adjust in order to fit the current term structure.

Although the second point is not a fundamental objection *per se* it is nevertheless a restriction when one considers that there may be arguments as least as strong in favour of fitting to the current term structure by adjusting μ or σ.

The scheme can be considered as an alternative, of a particular form, to the Hull and White lattice method, in that the time dependence of the risk-adjusted drift is modified so that market bond prices are recovered.

12.9.2   Direct Adjustment of Option Prices

This method allows the values of European style instruments to be adjusted to be consistent with the initial term structure. It was first suggested by Dybvig (89) [193] and has been investigated more recently by Vetzal (98) [534].

Suppose that pure discount bond prices $B_t(T, r_t)$ are contingent upon the value of the short rate r_t. Let $\underline{r}_t$ be a deterministic function of time and set $R_t = r_t + \underline{r}_t$. Write

$B_t(T, R_t)$ and $B_t(T, \underline{r}_t)$ for the values of pure discount bonds contingent upon the values of R_t and $\underline{r}_t$. Then

$$B_t(T, r_t + \underline{r}_t) = B_t(T, r_t)B_t(T, \underline{r}_t), \qquad (12.60)$$

where

$$B_t(T, \underline{r}_t) = \exp\left(-\int_t^T \underline{r}_s \, ds\right). \qquad (12.61)$$

Suppose that market pure discount bond prices are $P_t(T)$. Given a process for r_t, under some pricing measure, one may compute the model term structure given by $B_t(T, r_t)$. Set

$$\underline{r}_s = -\frac{\partial}{\partial s}\left(\ln \frac{P_t(s)}{B_t(s, r_t)}\right), \quad s > t. \qquad (12.62)$$

$\underline{r}_t$ is a deterministic function and $P_t(T) = B_t(T, r_t)\exp\left(-\int_t^T \underline{r}_s \, ds\right)$. The main result is due to Dybvig.

The value of a European claim with payoff at time T

$$H_T(R_T, P_T(T_1), \ldots, P_T(T_N)) \qquad (12.63)$$

under R_T has the same value as a claim with payoff

$$B_t(T, \underline{r}_t)H_T(r_T + \underline{r}_T, B_T(T_1, r_T)B_T(T_1, \underline{r}_t), \ldots, B_T(T_N, r_T)B_T(T_N, \underline{r}_t)) \qquad (12.64)$$

under r_t.

The consequence is that for any interest rate model where the short rate, r_t, is the sole state variable, option prices found under r_t can be modified to be consistent with the initial term structure. Simply value them (under r_t) with adjusted boundary conditions and discount by $B_t(T, \underline{r}_t)$.

This method has significant advantages over that of Uhrig and Walter. It is much easier to find $\underline{r}_t$ than it is to find $\theta(t)$. For instance, suppose that under the EMM r_t has the process $dr_t = \tilde{\mu}(r_t, t)dt + \sigma(r_t, t)dz_t$, then it can be verified (by direct substitution) that the market prices of pure discount bonds, $P_t(T)$, satisfy the PDE

$$\frac{\partial P}{\partial t} + \tilde{\mu}\frac{\partial P}{\partial r} + \frac{1}{2}\sigma^2\frac{\partial^2 P}{\partial r^2} = \left(r_t + \underline{r}_t\right)P, \qquad (12.65)$$

where $\underline{r}_t$ is defined by (12.62). It is easier to recursively back out $\underline{r}_t$ from (12.65) than it is to back out $\theta(t)$ from the method of Uhrig and Walter.

The adjustment (12.60) may be best regarded as a perturbation to the model bond price $B_t(T, r_t)$. If model prices are very dissimilar to market prices the adjustment $B_t(T, \underline{r}_t)$ will be large. It may be preferable in this case to use an alternative interest rate model with term structures closer to those observed in the market.

12.10 FINITE DIFFERENCE METHODS IN N DIMENSIONS

Finite difference methods in N dimensions pose special problems both in theory and in practical implementation. N-factor interest rate models naturally generate N-dimensional PDEs and hence finite difference methods in N dimensions. We shall meet several examples below. Such is the difficulty of solving them that Monte Carlo methods are often preferred in practice to solving N-dimensional problems when N is greater than 3 or 4 (unless there are special features that make finite difference methods possible).

In this section we discuss so-called operator splitting finite difference schemes. There are other methods that could be used, and we mention these briefly, but we do not discuss them in detail.

We shall see that many schemes are only first-order accurate in time which, because of the computational demands of a higher dimensional problem, is unattractive. We may sometimes be able to implement a second-order scheme for the sort of PDEs we meet in interest rate modelling, but special care must be taken to ensure that boundary conditions are also second-order accurate in time. A second-order scheme with first-order boundary conditions is really only a first-order scheme.

In higher dimensions, even more so than in one dimension, it is crucially important to transform away as much of the structure in the PDE as possible. Unfortunately in interest rate models it is often the case that simplifying the second-order terms in the PDE has the effect of ruining the first-order terms.

We conclude with an example of a scheme for a particular two-dimensional problem: numerically solving the PDE for the Longstaff and Schwartz model.

There are a number of good sources for finite difference methods in N dimensions. A good general book is Morton and Mayers (94) [404]. Marchuk (90) [379] is a detailed theoretical treatise of the Russian school. Mitchell and Griffiths (80) [401] cover stability aspects in some detail. Gourlay and McKee (77) [260] discuss the hopscotch method. Clewlow (90) [133] reviews several methods.

There are a number of general applications orientated books that cover some aspects of these methods. Hoffman (93) [282] is one example. Press *et al.* (92) [441] also have a section on this problem.

12.10.1 Introduction to N-dimensional Problems

In finance there are frequent examples of N-factor models. Options on the values of two stocks, where, for example, each stock has a standard log-normal process, satisfy a two-factor PDE. Diff swaps and other cross market instruments, where the underlying factors might be interest rates and an FX rate, will obey a multifactor PDE. The value of corporate debt is implicitly contingent upon the firm's asset value and also on the term structure, even in the most simplistic models. Models with stochastic volatility, and any multifactor interest rate model, generate multifactor PDEs.

We have seen that if $v_0 = \widetilde{E}_0[c_T p_0/p_T]$ then v_0 satisfies a particular partial differential equation. Option prices satisfy this PDE, with boundary conditions determined by the option. Suppose the state variables of our model are $X_t = \left(X_{1,t}, \ldots, X_{N,t}\right)'$ (so that we have an N-factor model). Suppose that under the EMM X_t has the process

$$dX_t = b(X_t)dt + \sigma(X_t)dz_t, \qquad (12.66)$$

with $z_t \in \mathbb{R}^N$. Set $a_{i,j} = \frac{1}{2}\left(\sigma\rho\sigma'\right)_{i,j}$, where ρ is the correlation matrix for z_t. If c is an option, then c satisfies the PDE

$$\frac{\partial c}{\partial t} + \sum_{i=1}^{N} b_i(X)\frac{\partial c}{\partial X_i} + \sum_{i,j=1}^{N} a_{i,j}(X)\frac{\partial^2 c}{\partial X_i \partial X_j} = rc, \qquad (12.67)$$

on some domain D, assumed rectilinear, with some boundary condition at time T determined by the option payoff, assumed to be computable at time T,

$$c(T, X_T) = H(T, X_T), \qquad (12.68)$$

and other boundary conditions elsewhere on ∂D.

Numerically solving the PDE becomes exponentially more difficult as N increases. When $N = 1$ one may use the relatively easy methods of Sections 12.4, 12.5 and 12.6. When $N = 2$ one must immediately begin to use more elaborate methods. These are feasible for $N = 2$. For $N = 3$ applying these methods become problematical. For $N \geq 4$, unless the problem has a special structure that enables the methods to work, one is recommended to use Monte Carlo methods.

The Longstaff and Schwartz (92) [365] model has two factors (r_t, v_t). Under the EMM these state variables obey the processes

$$dr_t = \left((\alpha\gamma + \beta\eta) - \frac{\beta\delta - \alpha\xi}{\beta - \alpha}r_t - \frac{\delta - \xi}{\beta - \alpha}v_t\right)dt \qquad (12.69)$$

$$+ \left(\frac{\alpha\beta r_t - \alpha v_t}{\beta - \alpha}\right)^{\frac{1}{2}} dz_{1,t} + \left(\frac{\beta v_t - \alpha\beta r_t}{\beta - \alpha}\right)^{\frac{1}{2}} dz_{2,t}, \qquad (12.70)$$

$$dv_t = \left((\alpha^2\gamma + \beta^2\eta) - \frac{\alpha\beta(\delta - \xi)}{\beta - \alpha}r_t - \frac{\beta\xi - \alpha\delta}{\beta - \alpha}v_t\right)dt \qquad (12.71)$$

$$+ \left(\frac{\alpha^3\beta r_t - \alpha^3 v_t}{\beta - \alpha}\right)^{\frac{1}{2}} dz_{1,t} + \left(\frac{\beta^3 v_t - \alpha\beta^3 r_t}{\beta - \alpha}\right)^{\frac{1}{2}} dz_{2,t}, \qquad (12.72)$$

where $z_{1,t}$ and $z_{2,t}$ are uncorrelated; see Chapter 7.

The Fong and Vasicek (91) [226] model has state variables (r_t, v_t) with processes

$$dr_t = \alpha(\mu - r_t)dt + \sqrt{v_t}\,dz_{r,t}, \qquad (12.73)$$

$$dv_t = \delta(\kappa - v_t)dt + \lambda\sqrt{v_t}\,dz_{v,t}, \qquad (12.74)$$

and $dz_{r,t}\,dz_{v,t} = \rho dt$ are correlated. We write down the PDEs satisfied by option values c in these two models.

For Longstaff and Schwartz the PDE in (r_t, v_t) is

$$\frac{\partial c}{\partial t} + a(r,v)\frac{\partial c}{\partial r} + b(r,v)\frac{\partial c}{\partial v} + d(r,v)\frac{\partial^2 c}{\partial r^2} + e(r,v)\frac{\partial^2 c}{\partial r\partial v} + f(r,v)\frac{\partial^2 c}{\partial v^2} = rc, \qquad (12.75)$$

where a and b are affine in r and v and d, e and f are linear in r and v. This is complicated but it is possible to simplify things considerably. We know that r_t and v_t are linear combinations of two other state variables X_t and Y_t,

$$r_t = gX_t + hY_t, \tag{12.76}$$

$$v_t = g^2 c^2 X_t + h^2 f^2 Y_t \tag{12.77}$$

(see Chapters 7 and 11), where g and h are constants and

$$dX_t = (a - bX_t)\,dt + c\sqrt{X_t}\,dz_{1,t}, \tag{12.78}$$

$$dY_t = (d - eY_t)\,dt + f\sqrt{Y_t}\,dz_{2,t}, \tag{12.79}$$

with $z_{2,t}$ and $z_{3,t}$ independent. In terms of X_t and Y_t,

$$\frac{\partial c}{\partial t} + (a - bX)\,\frac{\partial c}{\partial X} + (d - eY)\,\frac{\partial c}{\partial Y} + c^2 X \frac{\partial^2 c}{\partial X^2} + f^2 Y \frac{\partial^2 c}{\partial Y^2} = rc, \tag{12.80}$$

a PDE that is simple enough to attempt to solve numerically (it has no cross term). For Fong and Vasicek we have immediately

$$\frac{\partial c}{\partial t} + \alpha\,(\mu - r)\,\frac{\partial c}{\partial r} + \delta\,(\kappa - v)\,\frac{\partial c}{\partial v} + v\frac{\partial^2 c}{\partial r^2} + 2\lambda\rho v\frac{\partial^2 c}{\partial r \partial v} + \lambda^2 v\frac{\partial^2 c}{\partial v^2} = rc. \tag{12.81}$$

Transforming the PDE

Given a general PDE of the form

$$\frac{\partial c}{\partial t} + \sum_{i=1}^{N} b_i\,(X)\,\frac{\partial c}{\partial X_i} + \sum_{i,j=1}^{N} a_{i,j}\,(X)\,\frac{\partial^2 c}{\partial X_i \partial X_j} = rc \tag{12.82}$$

it is crucially important to transform away as much structure as possible. For instance, one might

1. Change variables to make $a_{i,i}$ constant.
2. Rotate variables to remove cross terms.
3. Attempt to remove zeroth- and first-order terms.

Ideally one would like to put the equation in the form

$$\frac{\partial c}{\partial t} + \sum_{i=1}^{N} \frac{\partial^2 c}{\partial X_i^2} = 0, \tag{12.83}$$

where the derivatives have constant unit coefficients. It is possible, in principle, to solve the Beltrami equations to transform away the cross terms and the state dependent coefficients on the second-order terms. Unfortunately this transformation will usually enormously complicate the coefficients of the first-order terms. It is only possible to reduce (12.82) to the form (12.83) in special cases, for example when the state variables are log-normal with constant drifts and volatilities. The transformation is likely to fail even for the simplest stochastic volatility model.

If it is necessary to compactify the PDE, as in Section 12.3.1, it may not be feasible to simplify the PDE.

Using a standard transformation the process

$$dX_{i,t} = b_i(X_t) dt + \sigma_i(X_i) dz_{i,t} \tag{12.84}$$

can have its diffusion coefficient transformed away. Set

$$Y_i(X) = \int^X \frac{1}{\sigma_i(x)} dx. \tag{12.85}$$

Y_i has volatility identically 1, if it is well defined. For example, the log-normal process

$$dX_t = \mu X_t dt + \sigma X_t dz_t \tag{12.86}$$

has the transformation

$$Y = \int^X \frac{1}{\sigma x} dx = \frac{1}{\sigma} \ln X, \tag{12.87}$$

so that

$$dY_t = \left(\frac{\mu}{\sigma} - \frac{1}{2} \sigma \right) dt + dz_t. \tag{12.88}$$

In this case the drift term is also now constant.

For the Longstaff and Schwartz processes for X and Y one can set

$$x = \frac{2}{c} \sqrt{X}, \tag{12.89}$$

$$y = \frac{2}{f} \sqrt{Y}. \tag{12.90}$$

x and y have constant volatilities but their drift terms are no longer linear.

If the PDE (12.82) has been derived from a financial model with prices contingent upon the values of underlying state variables it is always possible to transform away the cross terms. Barring degeneracy, one finds linear combinations of the state variables that are uncorrelated with one another. These combinations become the new state variables. In the new state variables equation (12.82) has no cross term.

In the Fong and Vasicek model one can remove the cross term. If one also sets one diffusion coefficient to zero the linear structure of the drift terms is destroyed.

If r were constant the zeroth term can be removed by setting $c = e^{rt}u$. This is not so useful for an interest rate model, although a more general transformation of the form $c = e^{f(r,t)}u$ can sometimes help.

Notation

In this section we use the following notation. Note that it varies slightly from the notation used previously in this chapter. If there are two or three state variables we call them x, y and z. We allow t and x, y, z to take on discrete values on a rectilinear grid:

$$t \in \{t_0, \ldots, t_{M_t} = T\}, \qquad t_{i+1} - t_i = \Delta_t,$$

$$x \in \{x_0, \ldots, x_{M_x+1}\}, \qquad x_{i+1} - x_i = \Delta_x,$$

$$y \in \{y_0, \ldots, y_{M_y+1}\}, \qquad y_{i+1} - y_i = \Delta_y, \qquad (12.91)$$

$$z \in \{z_0, \ldots, z_{M_z+1}\}, \qquad z_{i+1} - z_i = \Delta_z.$$

The time step size Δ_t does not need to be constant, but we require the space step sizes Δ_x, Δ_y, Δ_z to be constant. This defines a regular N-dimensional grid in the space dimensions, with $(M_t + 1)(M_x + 2)(M_y + 2)(M_z + 2)$ points. In practice M_t, M_x, M_y and M_z may be of order 10^2 or 10^3, so that there are 10^8 to 10^{12} points on the grid. This is enormous, and it is crucially important to

- Make the grid as small as possible, for instance by using larger step sizes;
- Be computationally efficient when evaluating the grid.

Write $c_{i,j,k}^n$ for the option value $c\left(x_i, y_j, z_k, t_n\right)$ on the grid, and write $c^n = \{c_{i,j,k}^n\}$, a three-dimensional tensor for each n. Write ∂_t for $\partial/\partial t$, ∂_x for $\partial/\partial x$, et cetera, $\partial_{x,x}$ (or ∂_x^2) for $\partial^2/\partial x^2$, $\partial_{x,y}$ for $\partial^2/\partial x \partial y$, et cetera. We make discrete approximations to these operators on the grid. Define the discrete operators δ_t, δ_x, δ_x^2, $\delta_{x,y}$, et cetera,

$$\delta_t c_{i,j,k}^n = \frac{1}{\Delta_t}\left(c_{i,j,k}^n - c_{i,j,k}^{n-1}\right), \qquad (12.92)$$

$$\delta_x c_{i,j,k}^n = c_{i+1,j,k}^n - c_{i-1,j,k}^n. \qquad (12.93)$$

$$\delta_x^2 c_{i,j,k}^n = \delta_{x,x} c_{i,j,k}^n \qquad (12.94)$$

$$= c_{i+1,j,k}^n - 2c_{i,j,k}^n + c_{i-1,j,k}^n, \qquad (12.95)$$

$$\delta_{x,y} c_{i,j,k}^n = c_{i+1,j+1,k}^n - c_{i+1,j-1,k}^n - c_{i-1,j+1,k}^n + c_{i-1,j-1,k}^n, \qquad (12.96)$$

in the interior of the grid.

$$\delta_t c^n = \frac{1}{\Delta_t}\left\{c_{i,j,k}^n - c_{i,j,k}^{n-1}\right\}_{i,j,k}, \qquad (12.97)$$

$$\delta_x^2 c^n = \left\{c_{i+1,j,k}^n - 2c_{i,j,k}^n + c_{i-1,j,k}^n\right\}_{i,j,k}, \qquad (12.98)$$

et cetera, are the operators applied to c^n (suitably modified at the boundary of the grid).

Cross terms $\delta_{x,y} c_{i,j,k}^n$ are very awkward to deal with. Not only does each cross term add four (un)knowns to the system we have to solve, but it turns out to be hard to solve for these terms using an implicit method. We will assume in most of what follows that the cross terms have been transformed out of the PDE (12.82) by an appropriate change of variables.

In general we want to discretise the PDE

$$\frac{\partial c}{\partial t} + \sum_{i=1}^N b_i(X) \frac{\partial c}{\partial X_i} + \sum_{i,j=1}^N a_{i,j}(X) \frac{\partial^2 c}{\partial X_i \partial X_j} = rc \qquad (12.99)$$

$$\equiv \partial_t c + \sum_{i=1}^{N} b_i\,(X)\,\partial_i c + \sum_{i,j=1}^{N} a_{i,j}\,(X)\,\partial_{i,j} c = rc. \tag{12.100}$$

For simplicity we first consider the simpler PDE (12.83)

$$\partial_t c + \sum_{i=1}^{N} \partial_{i,i} c = 0. \tag{12.101}$$

We consider the general case in Section 12.11. On the grid we replace the continuous differential operators by their discrete analogues. As usual there are three main types of discretisation:

1. An explicit scheme: spacial operators act at time t_n,

$$\delta_t c^n + \left(\sum_{i=1}^{N} \frac{1}{\Delta_i^2}\delta_{i,i}\right) c^n = 0. \tag{12.102}$$

2. An implicit scheme: spacial operators act at time t_{n-1},

$$\delta_t c^n + \left(\sum_{i=1}^{N} \frac{1}{\Delta_i^2}\delta_{i,i}\right) c^{n-1} = 0. \tag{12.103}$$

3. The Crank–Nicolson scheme: spacial operators act at time $t_{n-1/2}$,

$$\delta_t c^n + \left(\sum_{i=1}^{N} \frac{1}{\Delta_i^2}\delta_{i,i}\right) \frac{c^n + c^{n-1}}{2} = 0. \tag{12.104}$$

It is useful to express these relationships in a slightly different form. Expand out the time derivative and re-arrange, setting $v_{i,i} = \Delta_t/\Delta_i^2$. The schemes become:

1. The explicit scheme:

$$c^{n-1} = \left(1 + \sum_{i=1}^{N} v_{i,i}\delta_{i,i}\right) c^n. \tag{12.105}$$

2. The implicit scheme:

$$\left(1 - \sum_{i=1}^{N} v_{i,i}\delta_{i,i}\right) c^{n-1} = c^n. \tag{12.106}$$

3. The Crank–Nicolson scheme:

$$\left(1 - \frac{1}{2}\sum_{i=1}^{N} v_{i,i}\delta_{i,i}\right) c^{n-1} = \left(1 + \frac{1}{2}\sum_{i=1}^{N} v_{i,i}\delta_{i,i}\right) c^n. \tag{12.107}$$

The explicit scheme is, as usual, a set of explicit linear equations. With suitable modifications at the boundary, (12.105) is a set of $\Pi_{i=1}^{N}M_i$ linear equations, each one relating

$2N + 1$ known values at time t_n to one unknown value at time t_{n-1}. Of course this is easy to do. The scheme is first-order accurate in time and is stable if $\sum_{i=1}^{N} v_{i,i} \leq \frac{1}{2}$. Unfortunately the explicit method is poorly behaved. For stability a small value of Δ_t is required, leading to a large grid.

The implicit scheme produces a set of linear equations each with $2N + 1$ unknown values at time t_{n-1} on the left-hand side and one known value at time t_n on the right-hand side. In principle this is a solvable matrix equation. Unfortunately it is a difficult matrix inversion, computationally hard in N dimensions.

When $N = 1$, the matrices on the left-hand sides of (12.106) and (12.107) are tri-diagonal and are very easy to invert to express the time t_{n-1} unknown values in terms of the known values at time t_n. When $N \geq 2$, the matrix is not tri-diagonal and is hard to invert. There is no simple algorithm as there is in the tri-diagonal case. With three state variables, at each time step the implicit scheme has $(M_x + 2)\,(M_y + 2)\,(M_z + 2)$ linear equations in seven unknowns. To solve we need to invert a $(M_x + 2)\,(M_y + 2)\,(M_z + 2) \times (M_x + 2)\,(M_y + 2)\,(M_z + 2)$ matrix. This is not possible unless the matrix has a special structure.

In fact the matrix is sparse, and is highly structured ('banded pentadiagonal'). One can attempt to use matrix methods, such as SOR (successive over-relaxation), but we do not consider these ideas here.

Method of Attack

One can easily solve tri-diagonal systems. The methods we describe are based upon breaking up the calculations at each time step into pieces, each one of which involves at most a tri-diagonal inversion. These methods are generically called operator splitting methods.

Other methods can be tried. We have already mentioned matrix methods where one attempts to invert the sparse matrix directly. Other methods include Galerkin approximations, where one tries to find approximate solutions to c^{n-1} using simple functions such as piecewise polynomials, and Hopscotch methods, which use different discretisations at different points on the grid.[5] We do not discuss these methods here.

12.11   OPERATOR SPLITTING

Operator splitting is a general name given to a category of finite difference schemes in N dimensions in which a differential operator is decomposed into a linear sum of simpler operators.

Schemes of the type include the ADI scheme, the AFI scheme and LOD schemes (see below). So-called corrector schemes also fall into this category.

In this section we discuss operator splitting schemes. We discuss boundary conditions and non-commuting operators, showing how the former can be obtained and the latter accommodated.

---

[5] An early paper on the hopscotch method is Gourlay (70) [259].

12.11.1 Operator Splitting

Suppose we have a parabolic PDE

$$\partial_t c + Ac = 0, \qquad (12.108)$$

where A is a differential operator defined on a rectilinear domain D, with boundary condition $c(0) = H$, for some function H at time 0, and other consistent boundary conditions elsewhere on ∂D.

In general, operator splitting has two stages. First, split A into linear components, and secondly factorise the discretisation of each component. Each component of A is evolved over the entire time step Δ_t. Each factor is evolved over a fraction of Δ_t.

Splitting A into linear components gives schemes that are only first order in time, whereas a good factorisation may be second order in time. If there is a stable tractable factorisation of the whole of A there is no need to split A into components.

Suppose $A = A_1 + \cdots + A_R$ splits into a linear sum of components. Suppose that $\delta_{A_r}^{\Delta_t}$ is a discretisation scheme for A_r, when the time step is Δ_t. For each time step, to go from time t_n to time t_{n-1}, say, set

$$c_{i,j,k}^{n,0} = c_{i,j,k}^n \qquad (12.109)$$

and iterate as

$$\frac{c_{i,j,k}^{n,r} - c_{i,j,k}^{n,r-1}}{\Delta_t} = \delta_{A_r}^{\Delta_t} c_{i,j,k}^{n,r-1}, \quad r = 1, \ldots, R, \qquad (12.110)$$

$$\text{or, } c_{i,j,k}^{n,r} = \left(1 + \Delta_t \delta_{A_r}^{\Delta_t}\right) c_{i,j,k}^{n,r-1}, \qquad (12.111)$$

where $\delta_{A_r}^{\Delta_t} c_{i,j,k}^{n,r}$ could stand for an explicit, implicit or Crank–Nicolson scheme, say. Finally, set

$$c_{i,j,k}^{n-1} = c_{i,j,k}^{n,R}. \qquad (12.112)$$

Each operator is applied to an intermediate value obtained from the previous operator. Intermediate values are not at intermediate times; they are merely intermediate steps in the calculation.

Example: $\partial_t c + \left(\partial_{x,x} + \partial_{y,y}\right) c = 0$

For $N = 2$ consider equation (12.108) with $A = \partial_{x,x} + \partial_{y,y}$, and set $A_1 = \partial_{x,x}$ and $A_2 = \partial_{y,y}$. The operator A_1 can be discretised in various ways. For an explicit scheme define

$$\delta_{A_1}^{\Delta_t} c^n = \frac{1}{\Delta_x^2} \delta_x^2 \{c_{i,j,k}^n\}. \qquad (12.113)$$

For an implicit scheme define

$$\delta_{A_1}^{\Delta_t} c^n = \frac{1}{\Delta_x^2} \delta_x^2 \{c_{i,j,k}^{n-1}\}, \qquad (12.114)$$

and for a Crank–Nicolson scheme define

$$\delta_{A_1}^{\Delta_t} c^n = \frac{1}{2} \frac{1}{\Delta_x^2} \delta_x^2 \left\{ c_{i,j,k}^n + c_{i,j,k}^{n-1} \right\}. \tag{12.115}$$

An implicit scheme can be implemented by setting

$$\delta_{A_1}^{\Delta_t} c^n = \frac{1}{\Delta_x^2} \delta_x^2 \{ c_{i,j,k}^{n,1} \}, \tag{12.116}$$

$$\delta_{A_2}^{\Delta_t} c^n = \frac{1}{\Delta_y^2} \delta_y^2 \{ c_{i,j,k}^{n,2} \}, \tag{12.117}$$

with $c_{i,j,k}^{n-1} = c_{i,j,k}^{n,2}$. The scheme with (12.116) and (12.117) can be re-expressed as

$$\left(1 - v_{x,x} \delta_{x,x} \right) c_{i,j,k}^{n,1} = c_{i,j,k}^n, \tag{12.118}$$

$$\left(1 - v_{y,y} \delta_{y,y} \right) c_{i,j,k}^{n-1} = c_{i,j,k}^{n,1}, \tag{12.119}$$

where $v_{x,x} = \Delta_t / \Delta_x^2$ and $v_{y,y} = \Delta_t / \Delta_y^2$. This is a fully implicit scheme, and is unconditionally stable and first order in time. It is called the AFI (approximate factorisation implicit) scheme. Each individual step is tri-diagonal. Each time step needs approximately $M_x + M_y$ tridiagonal inversions. Boundary conditions for level $c^{n,1}$ are obtained from (12.119).

We can eliminate $c_{i,j,k}^{n,1}$ from (12.118) and (12.119). Operate on each side of (12.119) by $1 - v_{x,x} \delta_{x,x}$, to get

$$\left(1 - v_{x,x} \delta_{x,x} \right) \left(1 - v_{y,y} \delta_{y,y} \right) c_{i,j,k}^{n-1} = c_{i,j,k}^n, \tag{12.120}$$

so that, expanding out the product,

$$\left(1 - v_{x,x} \delta_{x,x} - v_{y,y} \delta_{y,y} + v_{x,x} v_{y,y} \delta_{x,x} \delta_{y,y} \right) c_{i,j,k}^{n-1} = c_{i,j,k}^n, \tag{12.121}$$

This is the fully implicit scheme for $A = \partial_{x,x} + \partial_{y,y}$, but with an additional order Δ_t^2 term. The AFI scheme can be regarded as a second-order perturbation of the fully implicit scheme.

Accuracy of a Crank–Nicolson scheme

A Crank–Nicolson splitting scheme in two dimensions is (with time step Δ_t)

$$\left(1 - \tfrac{1}{2} v_{x,x} \delta_{x,x} \right) c_{i,j,k}^{n,1} = \left(1 + \tfrac{1}{2} v_{x,x} \delta_{x,x} \right) c^n, \tag{12.122}$$

$$\left(1 - \tfrac{1}{2} v_{y,y} \delta_{y,y} \right) c_{i,j,k}^{n-1} = \left(1 + \tfrac{1}{2} v_{y,y} \delta_{y,y} \right) c_{i,j,k}^{n,1}. \tag{12.123}$$

Each step is tri-diagonal. As before, we can eliminate $c_{i,j,k}^{n,1}$. (Note that the operators $1 - \tfrac{1}{2} v_{x,x} \delta_{x,x}$ and $1 + \tfrac{1}{2} v_{y,y} \delta_{y,y}$ commute.)

$$\left(1 - \tfrac{1}{2} v_{x,x} \delta_{x,x} \right) \left(1 - \tfrac{1}{2} v_{y,y} \delta_{y,y} \right) c_{i,j,k}^{n-1} = \left(1 + \tfrac{1}{2} v_{x,x} \delta_{x,x} \right) \left(1 + \tfrac{1}{2} v_{y,y} \delta_{y,y} \right) c^n, \tag{12.124}$$

so expanding out,

$$\left(1 - \tfrac{1}{2}v_{x,x}\delta_{x,x} - \tfrac{1}{2}v_{y,y}\delta_{y,y} + \tfrac{1}{4}v_{x,x}v_{y,y}\delta_{x,x}\delta_{y,y}\right)c^{n-1}$$
$$= \left(1 + \tfrac{1}{2}v_{x,x}\delta_{x,x} + \tfrac{1}{2}v_{y,y}\delta_{y,y} + \tfrac{1}{4}v_{x,x}v_{y,y}\delta_{x,x}\delta_{y,y}\right)c^n. \tag{12.125}$$

Compare this with the full Crank–Nicolson scheme,

$$\left(1 - \tfrac{1}{2}v_{x,x}\delta_{x,x} - \tfrac{1}{2}v_{y,y}\delta_{y,y}\right)c^{n-1} = \left(1 + \tfrac{1}{2}v_{x,x}\delta_{x,x} + \tfrac{1}{2}v_{y,y}\delta_{y,y}\right)c^n. \tag{12.126}$$

The difference between the split scheme and the full Crank–Nicolson scheme is

$$\tfrac{1}{4}v_{x,x}v_{y,y}\delta_{x,x}\delta_{y,y}\left(c^{n-1} - c^n\right) \sim \tfrac{1}{4}\Delta_t v_{x,x}v_{y,y}\delta_{x,x}\delta_{y,y}\delta_t. \tag{12.127}$$

This is of order Δ_t^3, the same magnitude of error as the Crank–Nicolson scheme itself.

For stability conditions see Marchuk (90) [379]. For the scheme as a whole to be stable, it is unnecessary for each part to be stable. An explicit scheme is stable, and first order in t, if $\|c^n\| \le \|H\|$ in the L^2 norm.

If each operator A_r is one dimensional, these schemes are called LOD (locally one dimensional) schemes. The fully implicit LOD scheme for $A = \partial_{x,x} + \partial_{y,y}$ is sometimes called 'the' LOD scheme. In general, there are severe problems in obtaining correct boundary conditions for LOD schemes.

Cross Terms

Consider the PDE

$$\partial_t c + \left(a_{x,x}\partial_{x,x} + 2a_{x,y}\partial_{x,y} + a_{y,y}\partial_{y,y}\right)c = 0, \tag{12.128}$$

with $a_{xx}a_{yy} - a_{xy}^2 > 0$. Marchuk (90) [379] describes a scheme to incorporate the cross term in a computationally feasible way. Set

$$A_1 = a_{x,x}\partial_{x,x} + a_{x,y}\partial_{x,y}, \tag{12.129}$$

$$A_2 = a_{x,y}\partial_{x,y} + a_{y,y}\partial_{y,y}, \tag{12.130}$$

and $v_{x,y} = \Delta_t/4\Delta_x\Delta_y$. Discretise the PDE as

$$\left(1 - v_{x,x}\delta_{x,x}\right)c_{i,j,k}^{n,1} = \left(1 + v_{x,y}a_{x,y}\delta_{x,y}\right)c^n, \tag{12.131}$$

$$\left(1 - v_{y,y}\delta_{y,y}\right)c_{i,j,k}^{n,2} = \left(1 + v_{x,y}a_{x,y}\delta_{x,y}\right)c_{i,j,k}^{n,1}, \tag{12.132}$$

and set

$$c_{i,j,k}^{n-1} = c_{i,j,k}^{n,2}. \tag{12.133}$$

This is implicit in δ_x^2 and δ_y^2 but explicit in $\delta_{x,y}$ so that it is computationally acceptable. It is first order in time.

Boundary Conditions

Considerable care is needed with boundaries. It is not correct to use boundaries at time t_{n-1} when computing intermediate values $c_{i,j,k}^{n,r}$. To do so introduces extra inaccuracies of order Δ_t. LOD schemes are therefore usually only order Δ_t.

One advantage of LOD schemes is that it is only necessary to supply boundary conditions in one dimension at a time.

12.11.2 Factorising the Discretisation

Factorisation is the key to obtaining second-order approximations. We discretise each component of A. Suppose the rth component of A, A_r, decomposes into a linear sum, $A_r = A_{r,1} + \cdots + A_{r,Q}$. Suppose $\delta_{A_{r,q}}^{\Delta_t}$ is a discretisation for the whole of A_r that is stable for $A_{r,q}$. Then set

$$\delta_{A_r}^{\Delta_t} = \delta_{A_{r,1}}^{\Delta_t/Q} + \cdots + \delta_{A_{r,Q}}^{\Delta_t/Q}. \tag{12.134}$$

For each r the time step is divided into Q parts. The scheme iterates one factor $\delta_{A_{r,q}}^{\Delta_t}$ at a time over a time step of size Δ_t/Q,

$$\frac{c_{i,j,k}^{n-q/Q,r-1} - c_{i,j,k}^{n-(q-1)/Q,r-1}}{\Delta_t/Q} = \delta_{A_{r,q}}^{\Delta_t/Q} c_{i,j,k}^{n-(q-1)/Q,r-1}, \tag{12.135}$$

for $q = 1, \ldots, Q$. At the end of the Qth iteration for the rth component set $c^{n,r} = c^{n-1,r-1}$ and move on to the next component.

Each $c_{i,j,k}^{n-q/Q,r-1}$ is now correctly interpreted as being for time $t_{n-q/Q}$. We now know how to do the boundaries correctly.

This is also called a fractional step scheme. In practice a factorisation will be applied to the whole of A so that $R = 1$ in (12.110).

Example: The ADI Scheme for $N = 2$

The ADI (Alternating directions implicit) scheme was created by Peaceman and Rachford (55) [431]. We apply it to the PDE $\partial_t c + (\partial_{x,x} + \partial_{y,y}) c = 0$. We use one component, $A = A_1 = \partial_{x,x} + \partial_{y,y}$, and factorise it as follows. Let

$$A_{1,1} = \partial_{x,x}, \tag{12.136}$$

$$A_{1,2} = \partial_{y,y}. \tag{12.137}$$

with factorisation

$$\delta_{A_{1,1}}^{\Delta_t/2} c^n = \frac{1}{\Delta_y^2} \delta_{y,y} c^n + \frac{1}{\Delta_x^2} \delta_{x,x} c^{n-1/2}, \tag{12.138}$$

$$\delta_{A_{1,2}}^{\Delta_t/2} c^{n-1/2} = \frac{1}{\Delta_y^2} \delta_{y,y} c^{n-1} + \frac{1}{\Delta_x^2} \delta_{x,x} c^{n-1/2}. \tag{12.139}$$

The first half step is implicit in x and explicit in y. The second half step is implicit in y and explicit in x. We can write the scheme (12.138) and (12.139) with (12.134) as

$$\left(1 - \tfrac{1}{2} v_{x,x} \delta_{x,x}\right) c^{n-1/2} = \left(1 + \tfrac{1}{2} v_{y,y} \delta_{y,y}\right) c^n, \tag{12.140}$$

$$\left(1 - \tfrac{1}{2} v_{y,y} \delta_{y,y}\right) c^{n-1} = \left(1 + \tfrac{1}{2} v_{x,x} \delta_{x,x}\right) c^{n-1/2}. \tag{12.141}$$

Each step is tri-diagonal and stable. (12.140) and (12.141) together represent the ADI scheme, alternating implicit and explicit steps in each direction.

ADI and Crank–Nicolson

Because the operator $1 - \frac{1}{2}v_{x,x}\delta_{x,x}$ commutes with $1 + \frac{1}{2}v_{x,x}\delta_{x,x}$, we can eliminate $c^{n-1/2}$ from (12.138) and (12.139). Multiply both sides of (12.141) by $1 - \frac{1}{2}v_{xx}\delta_{xx}$ to obtain

$$\left(1 - \tfrac{1}{2}v_{y,y}\delta_{y,y}\right)\left(1 - \tfrac{1}{2}v_{x,x}\delta_{x,x}\right)c^{n-1} = \left(1 + \tfrac{1}{2}v_{y,y}\delta_{y,y}\right)\left(1 + \tfrac{1}{2}v_{x,x}\delta_{x,x}\right)c^n. \quad (12.142)$$

Expanding out

$$\left(1 - \tfrac{1}{2}v_{x,x}\delta_{x,x} - \tfrac{1}{2}v_{y,y}\delta_{y,y} + \tfrac{1}{4}v_{x,x}v_{y,y}\delta_{x,x}\delta_{y,y}\right)c^{n-1}$$

$$= \left(1 + \tfrac{1}{2}v_{x,x}\delta_{x,x} + \tfrac{1}{2}v_{y,y}\delta_{y,y} + \tfrac{1}{4}v_{x,x}v_{y,y}\delta_{x,x}\delta_{y,y}\right)c^n. \quad (12.143)$$

The full Crank–Nicolson scheme is

$$\left(1 - \tfrac{1}{2}v_{x,x}\delta_{x,x} - \tfrac{1}{2}v_{y,y}\delta_{y,y}\right)c^{n-1} = \left(1 + \tfrac{1}{2}v_{x,x}\delta_{x,x} + \tfrac{1}{2}v_{y,y}\delta_{y,y}\right)c^n. \quad (12.144)$$

The difference between the ADI scheme and the full Crank–Nicolson scheme is

$$\tfrac{1}{4}v_{x,x}v_{y,y}\delta_{x,x}\delta_{y,y}\left(c^{n-1} - c^n\right) \sim \tfrac{1}{4}\Delta_t v_{x,x}v_{y,y}\delta_{x,x}\delta_{y,y}\delta_t. \quad (12.145)$$

This is a term of order Δ_t^3. Just as before, we can consider the ADI scheme to be a perturbed Crank–Nicolson method. It is second-order accurate in time.

The ADI Scheme in N Dimensions

It is easy to generalise the ADI scheme. For the PDE

$$\partial_t c + \sum_{i=1}^{N} \partial_{i,i} c = 0, \quad (12.146)$$

one can use the factorisation

$$\left(1 - \frac{1}{N}v_{1,1}\delta_{1,1}\right)c^{n-1/N} = \sum_{i=2}^{N}\left(1 + \frac{1}{N}v_{i,i}\delta_{i,i}\right)c^n,$$

$$\vdots \qquad \vdots$$

$$\left(1 - \frac{1}{N}v_{j,j}\delta_{j,j}\right)c^{n-j/N} = \sum_{\substack{i=1 \\ i\neq j}}^{N}\left(1 + \frac{1}{N}v_{i,i}\delta_{i,i}\right)c^{n-(j-1)/N}, \quad (12.147)$$

$$\vdots \qquad \vdots$$

$$\left(1 - \frac{1}{N}v_{N,N}\delta_{N,N}\right)c^{n-1} = \sum_{i=1}^{N-1}\left(1 + \frac{1}{N}v_{i,i}\delta_{i,i}\right)c^{n-1+1/N}.$$

Unfortunately this scheme is not unconditionally stable for $N > 2$.

The General ADI Method

For the PDE

$$\partial_t c + Ac = 0, \tag{12.148}$$

suppose that $A = A_1 + \cdots + A_Q$. The ADI scheme generalises as

$$\frac{c_{i,j,k}^{n-q/Q} - c_{i,j,k}^{n-(q-1)/Q}}{\Delta_t/Q} = \delta_{A_q}^{\Delta_t/Q} c_{i,j,k}^{n-(q-1)/Q} + \sum_{\substack{i=1 \\ i \neq q}}^{Q} \delta_{A_i}^{\Delta_t/Q} c_{i,j,k}^{n-q/Q}, \tag{12.149}$$

for $q = 1, \ldots, Q$, where on each step the qth operator is implicit, and the rest are explicit. If $Q = 2$, this is a perturbed Crank–Nicolson scheme for A.

The Douglas–Rachford Correction Scheme

Douglas and Rachford (56) [174] described an important predictor–corrector scheme. In three dimensions the scheme is

$$\left(1 - v_{x,x}\delta_{x,x}\right) c^{n,1} = \left(1 + v_{y,y}\delta_{y,y} + v_{z,z}\delta_{z,z}\right) c^n, \tag{12.150}$$

$$\left(1 - v_{y,y}\delta_{y,y}\right) c^{n,2} = c^{n,1} - v_{y,y}\delta_{y,y}c^n, \tag{12.151}$$

$$\left(1 - v_{z,z}\delta_{z,z}\right) c^{n-1} = c^{n,2} - v_{z,z}\delta_{z,z}c^n. \tag{12.152}$$

The first equation obtains a predictor $c^{n,1}$ of c^{n-1}, the subsequent equations correct the predictor. This scheme is order 1 in time.

In two dimensions the scheme is

$$\left(1 - v_{x,x}\delta_{x,x}\right) c^{n,1} = \left(1 + v_{y,y}\delta_{y,y}\right) c^n, \tag{12.153}$$

$$\left(1 - v_{y,y}\delta_{y,y}\right) c^{n-1} = c^{n,1} - v_{y,y}\delta_{y,y}c^n. \tag{12.154}$$

Eliminating $c^{n,1}$ one gets

$$\left(1 - v_{x,x}\delta_{x,x}\right)\left(1 - v_{y,y}\delta_{y,y}\right) c^{n-1} = \left(1 + v_{x,x}v_{y,y}\delta_{x,x}\delta_{y,y}\right) c^n. \tag{12.155}$$

This differs from a full implicit method by

$$v_{x,x}v_{y,y}\delta_{x,x}\delta_{y,y}\left(c^{n-1} - c^n\right) \sim \Delta_t v_{x,x}v_{y,y}\delta_{x,x}\delta_{y,y}\delta_t, \tag{12.156}$$

which is an order 3 perturbation of full implicit method.

General Correction Scheme

Douglas and Gunn (64) [173] generalised the Douglas and Rachford scheme. Suppose that we have a scheme in which

$$(1 - A)c^{n-1} = Bc^n, \tag{12.157}$$

where $A = A_1 + \cdots + A_Q$, and $1 - A$ and B are not invertible, but $1 - A_q$ is for each q. Douglas and Gunn showed that the predictor–corrector scheme

$$(1 - A_1)\, c^{n,1} = Bc^n + \sum_{q=2}^{Q} A_q c^n, \tag{12.158}$$

$$\left(1 - A_q\right) c^{n,q} = c^{n,q-1} - A_q c^n, \quad q = 2, \ldots, Q, \tag{12.159}$$

$$c^{n-1} = c^{n,Q}, \tag{12.160}$$

is equivalent to

$$(1 - A)\, c^{n,1} = Bc^n - \sum_{\pi \in I} A_\pi \left(c^{n-1} - c^n \right), \tag{12.161}$$

where

$$I = \{(i_1, \ldots, i_m) \mid i_1 < \cdots < i_m\}, \tag{12.162}$$

$$A_\pi = A_{i_1} \ldots A_{i_m}. \tag{12.163}$$

The predictor–corrector scheme is a perturbation of the original specification (12.157), and is a computable approximation to it.

Boundary Conditions

The big difference between the ADI scheme and the Crank–Nicolson LOD method is that the ADI scheme can do the boundary conditions properly. This advantage only holds for rectilinear grids, but these are normal for financial applications.

For a two-dimensional ADI scheme it is easy to see that

$$c^{n-1/2} = \tfrac{1}{2} \left(c^n + c^{n-1} \right) + \tfrac{1}{4} v_{y,y} \delta_{y,y} \left(c^{n-1} - c^n \right). \tag{12.164}$$

(12.164) can be used to get boundary conditions for $c^{n-1/2}$ from those for c^n and c^{n-1}.

In the two-dimensional Douglas–Rachford scheme it is easy to see that

$$c^{n,1} = c^{n-1} - v_{y,y} \delta_{y,y} \left(c^{n-1} - c^n \right). \tag{12.165}$$

This is used to get boundary conditions for $c^{n,1}$ from those for c^n and c^{n-1}.

With the correct boundary conditions ADI is second-order accurate in time. For LOD schemes in general there is no way of expressing intermediate values in terms of c^n and c^{n-1}, so that it is impossible to find proper boundary conditions.

Non-commuting Operators

Consider the PDE

$$\partial_t c + Ac = 0, \tag{12.166}$$

where $A = A_1 + \cdots + A_R$ and A_q may depend on the state variables x_i. In general the operators will not commute, $A_q A_p \neq A_p A_q$, and the previously described schemes do not work. Instead we can use a two-cycle operator splitting scheme applied over two time steps.

1. Set $c_{i,j,k}^{n,0} = c_{i,j,k}^{n}$ and

$$\frac{c_{i,j,k}^{n,r} - c_{i,j,k}^{n,r-1}}{\Delta_t} = \delta_{A_r}^{\Delta_t} c_{i,j,k}^{n,r-1}, \quad r = 1, \ldots, R, \tag{12.167}$$

set $c_{i,j,k}^{n-1} = c_{i,j,k}^{n,R}$.

2. Set $c_{i,j,k}^{n-1,0} = c_{i,j,k}^{n-1}$ and for $r = 1, \ldots, R$,

$$\frac{c_{i,j,k}^{n-1,r} - c_{i,j,k}^{n-1,r-1}}{\Delta_t} = \delta_{A_{R+1-r}}^{\Delta_t} c_{i,j,k}^{n-1,r-1}, \tag{12.168}$$

set $c_{i,j,k}^{n-2} = c_{i,j,k}^{n-1,R}$.

The second step, to go from time t_{n-1} to time t_{n-2}, is the same as the first step, from time t_n to time t_{n-1}, but the order of operators is reversed at the second stage. Marchuk (90) [379] discusses these methods in detail.

12.12 A TWO-DIMENSIONAL PDE

This section illustrates the methods discussed in Sections 12.10 and 12.11. We solve numerically the two-dimensional Longstaff and Schwartz PDE

$$\frac{\partial c}{\partial t} + (a - bx)\frac{\partial c}{\partial x} + (d - ey)\frac{\partial c}{\partial y} + ux\frac{\partial^2 c}{\partial x^2} + vy\frac{\partial^2 c}{\partial y^2} = (gx + hy)c, \tag{12.169}$$

for the option price c where a, b, d, e, u, v, g and h are constants. Points to notice are:

- The PDE (12.169) has no cross term.
- We can only make diffusion coefficients constants by ruining the convection coefficients.
- We do not get rid of the zeroth term.

Since the cross term is already absent, and no further transformation seems sensible, we solve (12.169) directly. For illustration, we do not compactify the PDE.

A Crank–Nicolson Scheme for the PDE

We use a Crank–Nicolson scheme. Write the PDE as

$$\partial_t c + \left((a - bx)\partial_x + (d - ey)\partial_y + ux\partial_{x,x} + vy\partial_{y,y}\right)c = (gx + hy)c. \tag{12.170}$$

Since we cannot get rid of the zeroth-order term we discretise it in Crank–Nicolson fashion as $c = \frac{1}{2}\left(c^{n-1} + c^n\right)$. We set

$$\delta_t c^n + L\frac{c^n + c^{n-1}}{2} = 0, \tag{12.171}$$

where

$$L = v_{x,x}\, ux\delta_{x,x} + w_x\, (a - bx)\, \delta_x - gx1 \tag{12.172}$$

$$+ v_{y,y}\, vy\delta_{y,y} + w_y\, (d - ey)\, \delta_y - hy1. \tag{12.173}$$

where $w_x = \Delta_t/2\Delta_x$ and $w_y = \Delta_t/2\Delta_y$.
To implement a split of L we set

$$L_x = v_{x,x}\, u\delta_{x,x} + w_x\, (a - bx)\, \delta_x - \Delta_t gx1, \tag{12.174}$$

$$L_y = v_{y,y}\, v\delta_{y,y} + w_y\, (d - ey)\, \delta_y - \Delta_t hy1, \tag{12.175}$$

then the full Crank–Nicolson scheme is

$$\left(1 - \tfrac{1}{2}L_x - \tfrac{1}{2}L_y\right) c^{n-1} = \left(1 + \tfrac{1}{2}L_x + \tfrac{1}{2}L_y\right) c^n. \tag{12.176}$$

We use an ADI two-step method:

$$\left(1 - \tfrac{1}{2}L_x\right) c^{n-1/2} = \left(1 + \tfrac{1}{2}L_y\right) c^n, \tag{12.177}$$

$$\left(1 - \tfrac{1}{2}L_y\right) c^{n-1} = \left(1 + \tfrac{1}{2}L_x\right) c^{n-1/2}. \tag{12.178}$$

Note that

- $1 - \tfrac{1}{2}L_x$ and $1 - \tfrac{1}{2}L_y$ are tri-diagonal.
- $1 - \tfrac{1}{2}L_x$ commutes with $1 + \tfrac{1}{2}L_x$ (and with $1 \pm \tfrac{1}{2}L_y$).

Order of Convergence

Eliminating $c^{n-1/2}$ we have

$$\left(1 - \tfrac{1}{2}L_x\right)\left(1 - \tfrac{1}{2}L_y\right) c^{n-1} = \left(1 + \tfrac{1}{2}L_x\right)\left(1 + \tfrac{1}{2}L_y\right) c^n \tag{12.179}$$

or

$$\left(1 - \tfrac{1}{2}L_x - \tfrac{1}{2}L_y + \tfrac{1}{4}L_xL_y\right) c^{n-1} = \left(1 + \tfrac{1}{2}L_x + \tfrac{1}{2}L_y + \tfrac{1}{4}L_xL_y\right) c^n. \tag{12.180}$$

This differs from the full Crank–Nicolson scheme by

$$\tfrac{1}{4}L_xL_y\left(c^{n-1} - c^n\right) \sim \Delta_t \tfrac{1}{4}L_xL_y\partial_t, \tag{12.181}$$

which is third order in t. As usual, we can regard this method as a perturbation of a full Crank–Nicolson method. The method is second order in time.

General Two-dimensional Case

We can use the same analysis for the general PDE

$$\partial_t c + \left(a\partial_x + b\partial_y + u\partial_{x,x} + v\partial_{y,y}\right) c = ec, \tag{12.182}$$

where a, b, u, v, e are now functions of x and y. Set

$$L_x = v_{x,x} u \delta_{x,x} + w_x a \delta_x - \tfrac{1}{2} \Delta_t e 1, \tag{12.183}$$

$$L_y = v_{y,y} v \delta_{y,y} + w_y b \delta_y - \tfrac{1}{2} \Delta_t e 1. \tag{12.184}$$

It is still possible to use the scheme

$$\left(1 - \tfrac{1}{2} L_x\right) c^{n-1/2} = \left(1 + \tfrac{1}{2} L_y\right) c^n, \tag{12.185}$$

$$\left(1 - \tfrac{1}{2} L_y\right) c^{n-1} = \left(1 + \tfrac{1}{2} L_x\right) c^{n-1/2}. \tag{12.186}$$

It does not matter that L_x and L_y do not now commute. We still get

$$\left(1 - \tfrac{1}{2} L_x\right) \left(1 - \tfrac{1}{2} L_y\right) c^{n-1} = \left(1 + \tfrac{1}{2} L_x\right) \left(1 + \tfrac{1}{2} L_y\right) c^n, \tag{12.187}$$

and this differs from the full Crank–Nicolson method by a term of order 3. The non-commuting operators are all in the perturbation term $\tfrac{1}{4} L_x L_y \left(c^{n-1} - c^n\right)$. The intermediate boundary condition is still

$$c^{n-1/2} = \tfrac{1}{2} \left(c^n + c^{n-1}\right) - \tfrac{1}{4} L_y \left(c^{n-1} - c^n\right). \tag{12.188}$$

We use (12.188) to get boundary conditions for $c^{n-1/2}$ from those at c^n and c^{n-1}.

Boundary Conditions

We value a bond and a bond option in the Longstaff and Schwartz model. We need to investigate the boundary conditions for the finite difference method.

We know that $B_t(\tau) = \exp(a(\tau) - b(\tau)r - c(\tau)v)$, and $r = px + qy$, $v = fx + gy$, for constants p, q, f and g. We can re-parameterise to express the bond price in terms of x and y instead of r and v, obtaining

$$B_t(\tau) = \exp\left(A(\tau) - B(\tau)x_t - C(\tau)y_t\right), \tag{12.189}$$

$$\frac{\partial B}{\partial x} = -B(\tau) B_t(\tau), \tag{12.190}$$

$$\frac{\partial B}{\partial y} = -C(\tau) B_t(\tau). \tag{12.191}$$

Taking limits as x and y go to zero and to $+\infty$ we obtain Table 12.2.

Boundary values for the bond option can be found from those for the bond. Table 12.2 enables us to specify Neumann boundaries for large values of x and y, but does not help us to obtain boundary conditions as $x, y \to 0$. Neither Dirichlet nor Neumann boundaries work since values on the boundary for one state variable still depend upon the other.

We are led to consider implicit boundaries as in Section 12.8. At the $i = 0$ boundary we approximate $\partial c / \partial x$ and $\partial^2 c / \partial x^2$ as

$$\frac{\partial c}{\partial x} = \frac{-c_2 + 4c_1 - 3c_0}{\Delta_x^2}, \tag{12.192}$$

Table 12.2   Limits for x and y

Limits: x	$x \to \infty$	$x \to 0$
B	0	$\exp\left(A\left(\tau\right) - C\left(\tau\right)y_t\right)$
$\dfrac{\partial B}{\partial x}$	0	$-B\left(\tau\right)\exp\left(A\left(\tau\right) - C\left(\tau\right)y_t\right)$
Limits: y	$y \to \infty$	$y \to 0$
B	0	$\exp\left(A\left(\tau\right) - B\left(\tau\right)x_t\right)$
$\dfrac{\partial B}{\partial y}$	0	$-C\left(\tau\right)\exp\left(A\left(\tau\right) - B\left(\tau\right)x_t\right)$

$$\frac{\partial^2 c}{\partial x^2} = \frac{c_2 - 2c_1 + c_0}{\Delta_x^2}. \tag{12.193}$$

Similarly at the $i = M_x + 1$ boundary we approximate the derivatives as

$$\frac{\partial c}{\partial x} = \frac{c_{M-1} - 4c_M + 3c_{M+1}}{2\Delta_x}, \tag{12.194}$$

$$\frac{\partial^2 c}{\partial x^2} = \frac{c_{M-1} - 2c_M + c_{M+1}}{\Delta_x^2}. \tag{12.195}$$

We use these approximations at the top and bottom boundaries, not the usual ones. This gives a nearly tri-diagonal system which is easy to invert.

Even though we appear to have a Neumann boundary condition for large values of x and y we nevertheless use implicit boundaries at large values also. This is because $\partial B / \partial x \to 0$ only when x is very large, relative to normal values. We want to extend the grid only out as far as is necessary, and preferably no further out than those values of x and y that are reasonably likely to affect prices. $\partial B / \partial x$ only gets close to zero when x is ~ 10, say. This corresponds to interest rates of 1000%, far outside the range we are interested in. By using an implicit condition when x is large we do not need to go out that far.[6]

We could, of course, transform the state space, as discussed in Section 12.3.1, but we do not do so for this illustration.

Figure 12.5 shows a term structure produced by the finite difference method compared with the explicit solution. The finite difference method used $M_x = M_y = 50$ and $M_t = 100$, with $T = 100$.[7] The method has obviously not converged at this refinement of the mesh. Figure 12.6 shows the effect of increasing the number of space steps from 50 to 500 (over the same range), keeping the time step the same. Convergence is better at the short end but with this grid and time step there is still considerable bias away from short maturities.

---

[6] Although the implicit boundary must not be imposed at too small values of x and y.

[7] Model parameter values were $a = 0.05$, $b = 0.2$, $d = 0.01$, $e = 0.15$, $g = 0.5$, $h = 0.6$, and term structures were computed for $x = 0.061$ and $y = 0.081$.

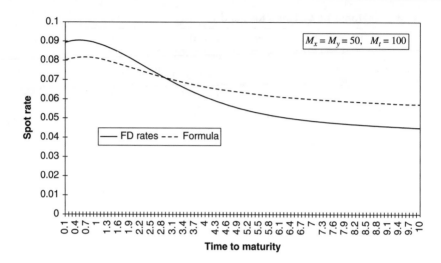

Figure 12.5   Comparison of term structures: $M_x = M_y = 50$

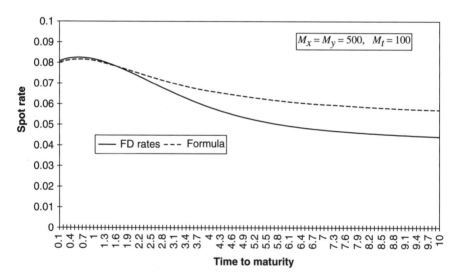

Figure 12.6   Comparison of term structures: $M_x = M_y = 500$

12.13   SOLVING A PDDE

Models with jumps give PDDEs (partial differential difference equations) to solve. It is quite feasible to solve these numerically. In this section we show how a particular PDDE arises in a jump–diffusion model and show how it can be presented in a form suitable for numerical solution. We briefly show how it might be solved numerically.

12.13.1 An Example PDDE

In the jump–diffusion model of Babbs and Webber (94) [40] the short rate, r_t, satisfies a pure jump process

$$dr_t = c_j \, dN_j, \qquad (12.196)$$

where each N_j is a point process with jump intensities $\lambda_j \equiv \lambda_j (r_t, x_t, t)$. c_j is the size of the jump in r_t if event N_j occurs, for example $c_j = \pm 0.0025, \pm 0.005$, etc. There is a single diffusion state variable x_t with process

$$dx_t = a (r_t, x_t, t) \, dt + \sigma dz_t, \qquad (12.197)$$

for some drift function $a (r_t, x_t, t)$.

Write $P (t, T, r_t, x_t)$ for the value at time t of a pure discount bond maturing at time T. P satisfies the differential equation

$$\frac{\partial P}{\partial t} + a^* (r, x) \frac{\partial P}{\partial x} + \frac{1}{2} \sigma^2 \frac{\partial^2 P}{\partial x^2} + \sum_{j=1}^{J} \lambda_j^* \left[P \left(r + c_j, x \right) - P (r, x) \right] = rP (r, x),$$

$$(12.198)$$

with boundary condition $P (T, T, r_t, x_t) = 1$, where

$$a^* = a - \theta_0 \sigma, \qquad (12.199)$$

$$\lambda_j^* = (1 - \theta_j) \lambda_j, \qquad (12.200)$$

are the risk-adjusted coefficients.

The PDDE (12.198) can be re-formulated as an equation on a vector valued underlying state variable. We assume there is a countable set of possible values for r_t, $\{r_i\}_{i \in I}$. Write $P_i (t, T, x_t) = P (t, T, r_i, x_t)$, then (12.198) can be re-written as

$$\frac{\partial P_i}{\partial t} + a_i^* \frac{\partial P_i}{\partial x} + \frac{1}{2} \sigma_i^2 \frac{\partial^2 P_i}{\partial x^2} + \sum_{k \neq i} \lambda_{k,i}^* [P_k - P_i] = r_i P_i, \qquad (12.201)$$

where $\lambda_{k,i}^*$ is the risk-adjusted price of risk for a jump from r_i to r_k, and a_i^* and σ_i have an i subscript to emphasise their r dependency.

Write $P = \{P_i\}_{i \in I}$ for the vector of bond prices contingent upon the level r_i. Write

$$D_i = \frac{\partial}{\partial t} + a_i^* \frac{\partial}{\partial x} + \frac{1}{2} \sigma_i^2 \frac{\partial^2}{\partial x^2},$$

and set $D = \text{diag} (D_i)$. Suppose that I is a finite set, $N = |I|$. Let Ω be the coefficient matrix

$$\Omega = \begin{pmatrix} r_1 + \sum_{k \neq 1} \lambda_{k,1}^* & \cdots & -\lambda_{i,1}^* & \cdots & -\lambda_{N,1}^* \\ \vdots & \ddots & \vdots & & \vdots \\ -\lambda_{1,i}^* & \cdots & r_i + \sum_{k \neq i} \lambda_{k,i}^* & \cdots & -\lambda_{N,i}^* \\ \vdots & & \vdots & \ddots & \vdots \\ -\lambda_{1,N}^* & \cdots & -\lambda_{i,1}^* & \cdots & r_N + \sum_{k \neq N} \lambda_{k,N}^* \end{pmatrix}. \qquad (12.202)$$

Ω is a known matrix which may depend on x_t. The PDDE (12.198) is equivalent to the system of equations

$$DP = \Omega P. \qquad (12.203)$$

This system can be solved. Re-arrange (12.201) as

$$\frac{\partial P_i}{\partial t} + a_i^* \frac{\partial P_i}{\partial x} + \frac{1}{2}\sigma_i^2 \frac{\partial^2 P_i}{\partial x^2} = \left(r_i + \sum_{k \neq i} \lambda_{k,i}^* \right) P_i - \sum_{k \neq i} \lambda_{k,i}^* P_k. \qquad (12.204)$$

The left-hand side involves the single component P_i of the vector P. The right-hand side has terms in P_i but also in the other components of P. The left-hand side can be discretised using a Crank–Nicolson scheme. On the right-hand side the P_i term can also be discretised this way. It is sufficient to discretise the $\sum_{k \neq i} \lambda_{k,i}^* P_k$ terms explicitly to yield a workable finite difference method.

13

Valuation: The Monte Carlo Method

The value of a derivative is the expected discounted payoff under the EMM. The value of this expectation can be found by direct evaluation, or, if this is not possible, by finding the PDE which it obeys and solving it. While finite difference methods are useful, the direct numerical evaluation of the expectation by numerical integration techniques such as Monte Carlo is an equally valid approach.

The basic Monte Carlo method is very straightforward, but an effective implementation requires improvements of various degrees of sophistication. The two main requirements are for effective methods of making the basic method run faster and methods for generating 'good' sample paths. There are a number of reviews of the Monte Carlo method and its elaborations. These include Broadie and Glasserman (97) [100] and Boyle *et al.* (97) [85], amongst others. Wilmott (99) [541] and Rebonato (98) [448] have sections on the Monte Carlo method, as does Hull (99) [290]. Dupire and Savine (98) [192] is an excellent review of a number of sophisticated techniques.

In this section we discuss the basic Monte Carlo method, speed-up methods, and techniques of sample path generation and regularisation. Finally, we discuss how Monte Carlo methods may be calibrated to market data.

13.1 THE BASIC MONTE CARLO METHOD

The basic Monte Carlo method is extremely easy to implement. In this introductory section we describe the basic method and discuss some of its properties. We show how it can be applied to multifactor models and to path-dependent options, and how it can be used to compute hedge ratios. We also discuss the limitations of the method.

Suppose an interest rate model has a single state variable, r_t, which we may take to be the short rate. We wish to value a derivative with payoff $H(T)$, possibly path-dependent, at time T. Under the EMM P the value V_0 of the derivative at time $t = 0$ is the expected discounted payoff

$$V_0 = \mathbb{E}_0^P \left[e^{-\int_0^T r_s \, ds} H(T) \right], \tag{13.1}$$

where $\mathbb{E}_0^P$ is the expectation under P at time $t = 0$. In general the value of the derivative is given by an expression of the form

$$V_0 = \mathbb{E}_0^P \left[\widetilde{H}(T, \omega) \right],$$ (13.2)

where P is some pricing measure, $\widetilde{H}(T, \omega)$ is the payoff normalised by the numeraire associated with P, and $\omega \in \Omega$ is a sample point in the path space $\Omega \equiv \Omega(x_1, \ldots, x_k)$ of the state variables $x = (x_1, \ldots, x_k)$. The expectation is an integral over Ω:

$$V_0 = \int_\Omega \widetilde{H}(T, \omega) dP.$$ (13.3)

If x was a discrete time process, taking values only at times $0 = t_0 < t_1 < \cdots < t_N = T$, the integral would become

$$V_0 = \int_{-\infty}^{+\infty} \cdots \int_{-\infty}^{+\infty} \widetilde{H}(T, x_{1,0}, \ldots, x_{k,N}) p(x_{1,0}, \ldots, x_{k,N}) dx_{1,0} \ldots dx_{k,N},$$ (13.4)

where $x_{l,j}$ is the value of the state variable x_l at time t_j, for a density function p over the complete set $\{x_{l,j}\}_{l=1,\ldots,k, j=0,\ldots,N}$. This is a $k \times (N + 1)$-dimensional integral. If (13.4) is to be a good approximation to (13.3), then N must be large and it is not possible to use an 'ordinary' numerical integration method to compute the integral.

In this case a Monte Carlo integration method may be appropriate. The idea is to sample the joint density of $\{x_{l,j}\}_{l=1,\ldots,k, j=0,\ldots,N}$ to obtain M sample points, $x^{(i)} = \left(x_1^{(i)}, \ldots, x_k^{(i)} \right)$, $i = 1, \ldots, M$, $x_l^{(i)} = \left(x_{l,0}^{(i)}, \ldots, x_{l,N}^{(i)} \right)$, from the sample space Ω. A single sample point is a path of values of x. The value of the derivative is estimated to be

$$\widetilde{V}_0 = \frac{1}{M} \sum_{i=1}^{M} \widetilde{H} \left(x_1^{(i)}, \ldots, x_k^{(i)} \right).$$ (13.5)

This is the Monte Carlo estimate of the value of the derivative. Sampling the density is done by evolving the state variables from their initial values under the risk-adjusted processes. Suppose the short rate r_t is the only state variable, whose process under the EMM is

$$dr_t = \mu(r, t) dt + \sigma(r, t) dz_t.$$ (13.6)

Starting from an initial value of r_0 at time 0, we use a discrete approximation for the process (13.6) to evolve r_t up to time T. The path we have found is a sample from the space of paths, Ω. The payoff $H(T, r_T)$ along this sample path is computed. The value of $H(T, r_T)$ will depend upon the random numbers generated in order to evolve r_t, so the simulation must be repeated many times to expect to accurately reflect the distribution of $H(T, r_T)$. The sampled values of $H(T, r_T)$ are discounted back to time $t = 0$, using the generated values of r_t as discount rates, and the arithmetic average of these discounted values is the Monte Carlo estimate of the value of the derivative.

This process can be broken up into stages:

1. Divide the period $[0, T]$ into N time steps. Set $\Delta t = T/N$.
2. Compute M sample paths $r_t^{(i)}, i = 1, \ldots, M$, for $t = 0, \Delta t, \ldots, T$. For $i = 1, \ldots, M$ set $r_0^{(i)} = r_0$, the value of r at time 0. At each time step the next value

of $r_t^{(i)}$ is found from its discretised process. For instance, the Euler discretisation of (13.6) is

$$r_{t+\Delta t}^{(i)} = r_t^{(i)} + \mu\left(r_t^{(i)}, t\right) \Delta t + \sigma\left(r_t^{(i)}, t\right) \sqrt{\Delta t}\, \varepsilon_{t+\Delta t}, \tag{13.7}$$

where $\varepsilon_{t+\Delta t} \sim N(0, 1)$, $t = 0, \ldots, T - \Delta t$, is a sequence of independent standard normal variables.

3. Obtain values $r_T^{(i)}$, $i = 1, \ldots, M$, at time T
4. Compute $H\left(T, r_T^{(i)}\right)$, $i = 1, \ldots, M$, and discount back to time 0 using the generated values of the short rate r_t; that is, compute

$$V_0^{(i)} = e^{-\sum_{t=0}^{T-\Delta t} r_t^{(i)} \Delta t} H\left(T, r_T^{(i)}\right), \quad i = 1, \ldots, M. \tag{13.8}$$

$V_0^{(i)}$ is the value at time 0 of the derivative along the i'th sample path.

5. The Monte Carlo estimate $\tilde{V}_0$ of the value V_0 of the derivative at time 0 is the average of the $V_0^{(i)}$ that is,

$$\tilde{V}_0 = \frac{1}{M} \sum_{i=1}^{M} V_0^{(i)}. \tag{13.9}$$

Because it is necessary to have the distribution of the sample paths as close to the actual distribution as possible, we need to use a sensible discretisation method. A Euler method with a sufficiently small step size Δt would suffice.

Note that the time step Δt need not be constant. It may be desirable to vary the time step if, for example, a derivative has cash flows or reset dates at irregular intervals. In this case it may be necessary to ensure that one generates samples of r_t at these irregular times. If sample paths are required with values of r_t at times t_j, $j = 1, \ldots, N$, the method described above can be adapted by evolving $r_{t_j}^{(i)}$ according to

$$r_{t_{j+1}}^{(i)} = r_{t_j}^{(i)} + \mu\left(r_{t_j}^{(i)}, t\right) \Delta t_{j+1} + \sigma\left(r_{t_j}^{(i)}, t\right) \sqrt{\Delta t_{j+1}}\, \varepsilon_{t_{j+1}}, \tag{13.10}$$

where now $\Delta t_{j+1} = t_{j+1} - t_j$ and $\varepsilon_{t_{j+1}} \sim N(0, 1)$, $j = 0, \ldots, N - 1$. Although in what follows we may often assume a constant time step, a variable time step can usually be incorporated in the manner just described.

It is possible to simulate several state variables at once, and therefore multifactor models do not in principle present a practical difficulty for the Monte Carlo method.

Another advantage of Monte Carlo methods is that they handle path-dependent products as easily as path-independent ones. However, their big disadvantage is that they are profligate users of computing time and power; typically, M might be of the order of 10 000 (without speed-ups), and N might be of the order of 1 000 time steps per year so that 10 000 000 iterations of (13.10) are required for each year of simulation. For this reason various speed-up methods have been devised to make Monte Carlo simulations significantly easier and faster, thereby considerably reducing the number of sample paths required and allowing larger time steps to be used.

13.1.1 Simulating for the Value of the Underlying

If the payoff to the derivative depends on the value of some underlying instrument, rather than depending directly on the value of the state variable r_T, in order to compute the value of the payoff at time T it is necessary first to find a value of the underlying instrument. For instance, suppose that we are attempting to value a bond option. The payoff at time T depends on the value of the underlying bond at time T. If no other means are possible, for instance if no explicit formulae for the bond price exist, then it may be necessary to find the bond value by continuing the simulation. The simulation is continued up to the maturity date of the underlying bond. The bond payoff is then discounted back to time T to give a value of the bond at time T along this particular sample path. The bond value can then be used to compute the payoff to the option at time T.

We consider this example in more detail. Write $c_t(T_1, T_2)$ for the value at time t of a European call option maturing at time T_1 on a pure discount bond maturing at time $T_2 > T_1$. The exercise price of the option is X. We wish to obtain an estimate $\tilde{c}_0(T_1, T_2)$ of the value of a call option at time $t = 0$.

We suppose the sole state variable is the short rate r_t. r_t is evolved up to time T_2, obtaining a series $r_0, \ldots, r_{T_2 - \Delta t}$ (with time step Δt). The sample path value at time T_1 of the pure discount bond $B_{T_1}(T_2)$ is its discounted payoff

$$\tilde{B}_{T_1}(T_2) = e^{-\sum_{t=T_1}^{T_2 - \Delta t} r_t \Delta t} \cdot 1. \tag{13.11}$$

The payoff to the option along this path is equal to $\max\left(0, \tilde{B}_{T_1}(T_2) - X\right)$. The payoff is discounted back from time T_1 to time 0 to obtain the value of the call option along this sample path:

$$V_0 = e^{-\sum_{t=0}^{T_1 - \Delta t} r_t \Delta t} \max\left(0, \tilde{B}_{t_1}(T_2) - X\right). \tag{13.12}$$

We repeat this process M times and take the average of $V_0^{(i)}, i = 1, \ldots, M$, to get a Monte Carlo estimate $\tilde{V}_0$ of the value of the call option at time $t = 0$. Note that if the payoff $\max\left(0, \tilde{B}_{T_1}(T_2) - X\right)$ has value zero, then V_0 along this path can immediately be set to zero, thus reducing the amount of computation required.

In practice when a sample path has been evolved up to time r_{T_1}, to find a value for $\tilde{B}_{T_1}(T_2)$ it is preferable to evolve several paths $r_t^{(i)}$ for $t = T_1, \ldots, T_2 - \Delta t$, obtaining several values for

$$\tilde{B}_{T_1}^{(i)}(T_2) = e^{-\sum_{t=T_1}^{T_2 - \Delta t} r_t^{(i)} \Delta t} \cdot 1 \tag{13.13}$$

and setting $\tilde{B}_{T_1}(T_2)$ to be the arithmetic average of the $\tilde{B}_{T_1}^{(i)}(T_2)$. This produces much more stable values for the payoffs of the derivative at time T_1, which in turn reduces the variance of the final estimate of the value of the derivative. It is well worth the extra computational effort.

13.1.2   Multifactor Models

An interest rate model may have several state variables, like the Fong and Vasicek model, for example. In this case there are two state variables, the short rate r_t and the variance of the short rate, v_t, with processes

$$dr_t = \alpha(\mu_r - r_t)dt + \sqrt{v_t}\,dz_t, \qquad (13.14)$$

$$dv_t = \beta(\mu_v - v_t)dt + \sigma\sqrt{v_t}\,dw_t, \qquad (13.15)$$

where α, μ_r, β, μ_v and σ are constants and z_t and w_t are Wiener processes. We use a Euler discretisation to give

$$r_{t+\Delta t} = r_t + \alpha(\mu_r - r_t)\Delta t + \sqrt{v_t}\,\sqrt{\Delta t}\,\varepsilon_{t+\Delta t}, \qquad (13.16)$$

$$v_{t+\Delta t} = v_t + \beta(\mu_v - v_t)\Delta t + \sigma\sqrt{v_t}\,\sqrt{\Delta t}\,\eta_{t+\Delta t}, \qquad (13.17)$$

where now ε_t, $\eta_t \sim N(0, 1)$ are standard normal variates which may be correlated. At each time step we evolve both v_t and r_t to obtain $v_{t+\Delta t}$ and $r_{t+\Delta t}$. At time T we will have values for both v_T and r_T.

To value a call option $c_0(T_1, T_2)$ under Fong and Vasicek both r_t and v_t are simulated up to time T_2. The sample path of values of r_t are used to find values $\widetilde{B}_{T_1}(T_2)$, and hence the payoff to the option at time T_1, and finally the value of the option at time 0, as before.[1] Although the sample path of values of v_t are not used directly in the valuation equations, they influence the sample path of r_t.

Although using Monte Carlo for multiple state variables is very easy, the number of sample paths required to achieve a given level of accuracy goes up with the power of the number of state variables. If N paths are needed for one state variable, N^2 are needed with two state variables. Inevitably, the accuracy of Monte Carlo methods in multifactor models is reduced.

13.1.3   Path-Dependent Instruments

These are easily valued with Monte Carlo methods; indeed, they are hardly more difficult than other instrument types. A sample path of interest rates or state variables $r_0, \ldots, r_T$ is generated as usual, and the payoff $H(T, r_T)$ at time T is computed and discounted back to time $t = 0$. However, $H(T, r_T)$ may now depend on the entire sample path $r_0, \ldots, r_T$ instead of just the terminal value r_T.

As an example consider a lookback call option with payoff

$$H(T, r_T) = r_T - \min_{t=0,\ldots,T} r_t. \qquad (13.18)$$

The payoff is the difference between the final value r_T and the minimum value of r_t achieved between times $t = 0$ and $t = T$. The value V_0 of the lookback along a

---

[1] In the Fong and Vasicek model explicit solutions exist for pure discount bond prices.

particular sample path $r_0, \ldots, r_T$ is

$$
V_0 = e^{-\sum_{t=0}^{T-\Delta t} r_t \Delta t} \left(r_T - \min_{t=0,\ldots,T} r_t \right). \tag{13.19}
$$

As usual, we compute V_0 for M paths and then take the average.

If the option contract specifies when resets take place, care should be taken to ensure that time steps occur at these times.

13.1.4 Computing Hedge Ratios

Monte Carlo methods can be used to compute hedge ratios (the 'Greeks') at relatively little additional computing cost. For instance, the delta hedge ratio can easily be obtained. For a derivative with value $c(r)$ contingent upon a state variable r, then the delta with respect to r is $\partial c / \partial r$. Using a central difference approximation,

$$
\frac{\partial c}{\partial r} \approx \frac{c(r + \Delta r) - c(r - \Delta r)}{2\Delta r}. \tag{13.20}
$$

To find the delta hedge ratio we need both $c(r + \Delta r)$ and $c(r - \Delta r)$. Suppose we want to compute the delta at an initial value r_0. Two sample paths, r_t^+ and r_t^-, are generated simultaneously, the first from a starting value of $r_0 + \Delta r$, the second from a starting value of $r_0 - \Delta r$. The two sample paths are computed using a single set of random numbers ε_t, $t = 0, \Delta t, \ldots, T - \Delta t$,

$$
r_{t+\Delta t}^+ = r_t^+ + \mu \left(r_t^+, t \right) + \sigma \left(r_t^+ \right) \sqrt{\Delta t}\, \varepsilon_{t+\Delta t} \text{ for } r_0^+ = r_0 + \Delta r, \tag{13.21}
$$

$$
r_{t+\Delta t}^- = r_t^- + \mu \left(r_t^-, t \right) + \sigma \left(r_t^- \right) \sqrt{\Delta t}\, \varepsilon_{t+\Delta t} \text{ for } r_0^- = r_0 - \Delta r, \tag{13.22}
$$

where μ and σ are the drift and volatility of the state variable r under the pricing measure. Using the sample paths r_t^+ a Monte Carlo estimate c^+ of the value of $c(r + \Delta r)$ is found, and similarly an estimate c^- of the value of $c(r - \Delta r)$ is found using sample paths for r_t^-. The Monte Carlo estimate of the delta hedge ratio is

$$
\left. \frac{\partial c}{\partial r} \right|_{r_0} = \frac{c^+ - c^-}{2\Delta r}. \tag{13.23}
$$

Other hedge ratios may be calculated in a similar manner.[2]

Note that generating the two paths using the same set of ε_t means that the difference $c(r + \Delta r) - c(r - \Delta r)$ is properly simulated. If $c(r + \Delta r)$ and $c(r - \Delta r)$ are each found separately, using their own separate sets of ε_t, the error in the difference $c(r + \Delta r) - c(r - \Delta r)$ would have been compounded.

---

[2] If $\partial c / \partial r$ and $\partial c / \partial t$ have both been calculated, a value of $\partial^2 c / \partial r^2$ can be found by substitution into (12.3)

An alternative to the procedure just described is to simulate directly for the value of $\partial c/\partial r$. Since $c = \mathbb{E}[\tilde{H}]$, under mild conditions we have

$$\frac{\partial c}{\partial r} = \mathbb{E}\left[\frac{\partial \tilde{H}}{\partial r}\right]. \tag{13.24}$$

Here $\partial \tilde{H}/\partial r$ is the terminal value of the delta which is known, presumably, if $\tilde{H}$ is. A Monte Carlo method can be used on (13.24) directly to estimate $\partial c/\partial r$.

13.1.5 Limitations of Monte Carlo Methods

The two main disadvantages of the Monte Carlo method are first that it cannot easily be used to value some types of derivatives, and secondly that it never gives the same answer twice. The second disadvantage can be overcome, in practical terms, by specifying a tolerance level—the standard error—at which the Monte Carlo solution will be accepted. The first disadvantage cannot so easily be remedied.

Options with Free Boundaries

Although Monte Carlo methods are extremely useful, there are some types of instruments which they cannot value. These have so-called 'free boundaries'.

A simple example is the American put, written on some underlying, S_t. An American type option may be exercised at any time between the time of agreement and the expiry date of the option. At every time t up to the final maturity time T there will be some critical value S_t^* of the underlying such that it is optimal to exercise the option if S_t falls below the critical value S_t^*. The set of critical values $\{S_t^*\}_{0 \leq t \leq T}$ forms the early exercise boundary. The option should be exercised if the early exercise boundary is hit by the path of the underlying. (The location of the early exercise boundary depends upon the assumptions made about the process followed by the underlying.) The early exercise boundary is the free boundary—its location is not given explicitly but is determined implicitly by performing an optimisation.

Because a Monte Carlo method works by evolving the underlying state variables forward through time it cannot know when it is optimal to exercise—it cannot locate the free boundary.[3] Several authors (Broadie and Detemple (96) [98], Carr and Yang (97) [118], (98) [119], Longstaff and Schwartz (98) [366], Andersen (99) [17], Miltersen (99) [398] and Pedersen (99) [435] for instance) have proposed techniques to adapt the Monte Carlo method to value American style instruments, but on the whole these methods are computationally highly intensive, and although promising their value is yet to be proved.

Other authors, for instance Ho, Stapleton and Subrahmanyam (91) [281] with a related discussion in Broadie and Detemple (96) [98], have proposed methods based upon extrapolating from the prices of Bermudan options to the price of an American

---

[3] By contrast, a finite difference method works backwards from final maturity. At each step it is possible to determine whether exercise should take place.

option. A Bermudan option may be exercised at a discrete set of times, possibly only two or three, up to a final maturity date. It is possible to value Bermudan options with a small number of exercise times by Monte Carlo methods. Ho *et al.* show how it is possible to extrapolate from the values of Bermudans with an increasing but small number of exercise times to find an approximate value for the American option over the same period.

The Monte Carlo Estimate as a Random Variable

A serious problem with the Monte Carlo method is the fact that only probabilistic estimates of the values of instruments are found—not an exact value. Repeating a Monte Carlo estimate will give a different value for the derivative. The accuracy of the final estimate depends upon the number of sample paths used, which means that it may take some considerable time to obtain a sufficiently accurate result.

A Monte Carlo estimate is a random variable, with a mean and a variance. It is possible to find the standard error of the estimate. Suppose we have computed M simulated values of a financial instrument, $V_0^{(i)}$, $i = 1, \ldots, M$. The Monte Carlo estimate of the value of the instrument is

$$\widetilde{V}_0 = \frac{1}{M} \sum_{i=1}^{M} V_0^{(i)}. \tag{13.25}$$

The standard error of this estimate is s, where

$$s^2 = \frac{1}{(M-1)^2} \sum_{i=1}^{M} \left(V_0^{(i)} - \widetilde{V}_0 \right)^2. \tag{13.26}$$

The standard error decreases with the square root of the number of sample paths; to reduce the standard error by half it is necessary to generate four times as many sample paths. This means that it may take many sample paths to reduce the standard error to an acceptable level. The Monte Carlo method is really only practicable if speed-up methods are used to reduce the number of sample paths that need to be generated to achieve a standard error of a given size.

13.2   SPEED-UP METHODS

In this section we discuss the various speed-up methods which have been developed to enable Monte Carlo methods to reach specified levels of standard error in relatively short times. The two main techniques used are the antithetic variate method and the control variate method. The control variate method has been described by Hull and White (88) [291], Clewlow and Carverhill (94) [134], and Clewlow and Strickland (98) [137].

13.2.1   The Antithetic Variate Method

This method generates two sample paths at a time, r_t^+ and r_t^-, for the state variable r_t. The two sample paths start at the same point, $r_0^+ = r_0^-$. At each time step t, a standard normal innovation $\varepsilon_{t+\Delta t}$ is generated. The sample path r_t^+ is evolved using $\varepsilon_{t+\Delta t}$; the sample path r_t^- is evolved using $-\varepsilon_{t+\Delta t}$, so that the two sample paths come from a single set of ε_t. Under the EMM, say,

$$r_{t+\Delta t}^+ = r_t^+ + \mu\left(r_t^+, t\right)\Delta_t + \sigma\left(r_t^+, t\right)\sqrt{\Delta t}\,\varepsilon_{t+\Delta t}, \tag{13.27}$$

$$r_{t+\Delta t}^- = r_t^- + \mu\left(r_t^-, t\right)\Delta_t + \sigma\left(r_t^-, t\right)\sqrt{\Delta t}(-\varepsilon_{t+\Delta t}). \tag{13.28}$$

Discounted payoffs are calculated separately along the two sample paths r_t^+ and r_t^- to find two values, V^+ and V^-. The average $V_0 = \frac{1}{2}\left(V_0^+ + V_0^-\right)$ is the derivative value found from this pair of paths. The process is repeated M times, obtaining M values $V_0^{(i)}$, $i = 1, \ldots, M$. The antithetic estimate of the value of the derivative is $\tilde{V}_0 = (1/M)\sum_{i=1}^M V_0^{(i)}$.

The point of the method is that the variance of V_0 may well be significantly less than the variance achieved with a non-antithetic method. Because of the way that the sample paths are generated, V_0^+ may be negatively correlated to V_0^-. If it is, V_0 will have a lower variance than V_0^+ or V_0^-. We have

$$\text{var}\left(\frac{V_0^+ + V_0^-}{2}\right) = \frac{1}{4}\text{var}\left(V_0^+\right) + \frac{1}{2}\text{cov}\left(V_0^+, V_0^-\right) + \frac{1}{4}\text{var}\left(V_0^-\right) \tag{13.29}$$

$$= \frac{1}{2}\text{var}\left(V_0^+\right)\left(1 + \text{corr}\left(V_0^+, V_0^-\right)\right) \tag{13.30}$$

$\left(\text{since } \text{var}\left(V_0^+\right) = \text{var}\left(V_0^-\right)\right)$. If corr $\left(V_0^+, V_0^-\right)$ is close to -1, var (V_0) may be much smaller than var $\left(V_0^+\right)$, and as long as corr $\left(V_0^+, V_0^-\right) < 1$, one gets at least some variance reduction.

Whether the correlation between V_0^+ and V_0^- is negative or not depends upon the process followed by r_t and the payoff structure of the derivative being valued. For an 'ordinary' process, when $\Delta r_t^+ = r_{t+\Delta t}^+ - r_t^+$ is positive, Δr_t^- will be negative and vice versa, so that r_T^+ and r_T^- are negatively correlated for some terminal time T. If the payoff to the derivative is monotonic in r_T then V_0^+ and V_0^- will be negatively correlated. For instance, a call on r_t has this property, and so the antithetic method is likely to give computational savings in this case. However, the payoff

$$H_T = |r_T - r_X|, \tag{13.31}$$

for a straddle with a strike rate r_X, may not be positively correlated to r_T (conditional on the initial value, r_0). The antithetic variate method may not produce savings in this case.

This technique can reduce the variance of V_0 by as much as a factor of 10 or 20, and it is fast, since generating r_t^- in addition to r_t^+ is cheap in terms of computing time. The antithetic variate method can always be incorporated as part of a Monte Carlo method since its implementation (as opposed to its efficiency) does not depend upon the characteristics of the individual derivative being valued. It is recommended that this technique is included as an option in any half-way serious Monte Carlo implementation.

13.2.2   Control Variates

The control variate method is a highly effective speed-up method, when it can be used. Its disadvantage is that its implementation depends on the characteristics of the instrument being valued, so that in the worse case, in effect, a fresh implementation is required for each new instrument that comes along.

The method relies upon being able to generate a value d on each sample path with the properties that

1. d is positively correlated to V, the value of the derivative on the same sample path, and
2. The expected value of d is zero, $\mathbb{E}[d] = 0$.

If a d can be found with these properties, then for some number β define

$$V' = V - \beta d. \tag{13.32}$$

The variance of V' is

$$\mathrm{var}(V') = \mathrm{var}(V) - 2\beta \, \mathrm{cov}(V, d) + \beta^2 \, \mathrm{var}(d). \tag{13.33}$$

This variance is minimised if $\beta = \mathrm{cov}(V, d) / \mathrm{var}(d)$. Then $\mathbb{E}[V'] = \mathbb{E}[V - \beta d] = \mathbb{E}[V]$, but $\mathrm{var}(V') \leq \mathrm{var}(V)$. For the variance minimising value of β we find

$$\mathrm{var}(V') = \mathrm{var}(V)(1 - \mathrm{corr}^2(V, d)). \tag{13.34}$$

If the absolute value of the correlation between d and V is close to 1, then $\mathrm{var}(V')$ will be very small.

It is clear that if a d can be found that is highly correlated to V, then very large computational savings may be made.

d is called the control variate. The method is flexible enough to be able to include more than one control variate at a time, if suitable control variates can be found. Fortunately there are standard methods of finding control variates related to the construction of hedge portfolios for the instrument being valued. A very commonly used control variate is the delta control variate, which is found from the value of a delta hedged hedging portfolio for the underlying instrument. (This technique was used by Clewlow and Carverhill (94) [134].) The control variate 'works' because the value of a delta hedge is highly correlated to the value of the instrument it is hedging.

Suppose the value c_t of a derivative is contingent upon the value of some underlying instrument B_t. For instance, c_t might be a call option on some pure discount bond B_t. When B_t is traded a delta hedge for c_t is long $\partial c_t / \partial B$ units of B_t and short $c_t - (\partial c_t / \partial B) B_t$ of cash. Hence the cost of putting on the hedge at time t_0 is

$$\frac{\partial c_{t_0}}{\partial B} B_{t_0} - c_{t_0}. \tag{13.35}$$

At each subsequent time t_i, the hedge must be adjusted. The cost of the adjustment will be

$$\left(\frac{\partial c_{t_i}}{\partial B} - \frac{\partial c_{t_{i-1}}}{\partial B} \right) B_{t_i}, \tag{13.36}$$

representing the additional cash that must be put into (or taken out of) the portfolio at time t_i. At time $T = t_N$, cash of value $(\partial c_{t_{N-1}}/\partial B)B_{t_N}$ is recovered. The total cost discounted back to time t_0 is

$$D = \left(\frac{\partial c_{t_0}}{\partial B} B_{t_0} - c_{t_0} \right) + \sum_{i=1}^{N-1} \left(\frac{\partial c_{t_i}}{\partial B} - \frac{\partial c_{t_{i-1}}}{\partial B} \right) B_{t_i} \exp \left(-\sum_{j=0}^{i-1} r_{t_j} \Delta t \right)$$

$$- \frac{\partial c_{t_{N-1}}}{\partial B} B_{t_N} \exp \left(-\sum_{i=0}^{N-1} r_{t_i} \Delta t \right)$$

$$= -\sum_{i=0}^{N-1} \frac{\partial c_{t_i}}{\partial B} \left(B_{t_{i+1}} - B_{t_i} e^{r_{t_i} \Delta t} \right) \exp \left(-\sum_{j=0}^{i} r_{t_j} \Delta t \right) - c_{t_0}. \qquad (13.37)$$

We set

$$d = \sum_{i=0}^{N-1} \frac{\partial c_{t_i}}{\partial B} \left(B_{t_{i+1}} - B_{t_i} e^{r_{t_i} \Delta t} \right) \exp \left(-\sum_{j=0}^{i} r_{t_j} \Delta t \right). \qquad (13.38)$$

d is the present value of the additional cash that needs to put into the delta hedge after the option premium has been received. The expected value of d is zero, since on average the additional cash injection is zero.

If the underlying is not traded, for instance if it is an interest rate, the control variate (13.38) can still be used. Under the EMM (13.38) can be written as

$$d = \sum_{i=0}^{N-1} \frac{\partial c_{t_i}}{\partial B} \left(\Delta B_{t_{i+1}} - \mathbb{E}_{t_i} \left[\Delta B_{t_i} \right] \right) \exp \left(-\sum_{j=0}^{i} r_{t_j} \Delta t \right). \qquad (13.39)$$

It can be verified that $\mathbb{E}[d] = 0$ and that $|\text{corr}(d, c)| > 0$ so that d is a potential control variate. d can be computed step by step along a Monte Carlo sample path as long as the value $\partial c_{t_i}/\partial B$ of the delta hedge ratio can be computed. In fact, getting an exact value for $\partial c_{t_i}/\partial B$ is very likely to be extremely difficult. Fortunately, as long as a reasonable approximation to the value of $\partial c_{t_i}/\partial B$ is used, d will still be highly correlated to c. In fact a quite crude approximation often turns out to do quite well.

Example of Using Control Variates

Clewlow and Strickland (97) [136] apply a control variate technique to the Fong and Vasicek model. They show how a pure discount bond option may be valued using delta and vega control variates.

The Fong and Vasicek model has two state variables, the short rate r_t and the short rate variance v_t. Their processes are

$$dr_t = \alpha(\mu_r - r_t)dt + \sqrt{v_t}\, dz_t, \qquad (13.40)$$

$$dv_t = \beta(\mu_v - v_t)dt + \sigma\sqrt{v_t}\, dw_t, \qquad (13.41)$$

where μ_r, μ_v, α, β and σ are constants and $dz_t dw_t = \rho \, dt$. r_t and v_t can be simulated using a Euler scheme

$$\Delta r_t = \alpha(\mu_r - r_t)\Delta t + \sqrt{v_t}\sqrt{\Delta t}\,\varepsilon_t^1, \qquad (13.42)$$

$$\Delta v_t = \beta(\mu_v - v_t)\Delta t + \sigma\sqrt{v_t}\sqrt{\Delta t}\,\varepsilon_t^2, \qquad (13.43)$$

where $\left(\varepsilon_t^1, \varepsilon_t^2\right)$ are bivariate standard normal with correlation ρ. In the Fong and Vasicek model there are closed form solutions for pure discount bond prices. This means that it is only necessary to simulate to the maturity of the option, at which point the value of the underlying can be computed with no further simulation.

The delta control variate for the state variable r_t will be denoted by x. For the jth path, $j = 1, \dots, M$, Clewlow and Strickland calculate $x^{(j)}$ as

$$x^{(j)} = \sum_{i=0}^{N-1} \frac{\partial c_{t_i}}{\partial r}\left(\Delta r_{t_i} - \mathbb{E}\left[\Delta r_{t_i}\right]\right). \qquad (13.44)$$

(Dropping the discount term does not effect the control variate properties.) The value $\partial c_{t_i}/\partial r$ of the delta is not known in the Fong and Vasicek model but an approximation can easily be found. The value of the option delta is known in the extended Vasicek model (from the Jamshidian formula (Chapter 7)). This delta can be used instead of the true Fong and Vasicek delta. Although it is an approximate value—in effect it is the Fong and Vasicek delta with the stochastic volatility component removed—it is quite a good approximation.

Let $\delta(r_t, t)$ be the Vasicek/Jamshidian delta. In the Euler discretisation we have $\Delta r_{t_i} = \mathbb{E}\left[\Delta r_{t_i}\right] + \sqrt{v_{t_i}}\sqrt{\Delta t_i}\,\varepsilon_{t_i}^1$, so for the jth sample path set

$$x^{(j)} = \sum_{i=0}^{N-1} \delta\left(r_{t_i}, t_i\right)\sqrt{v_{t_i}}\sqrt{\Delta t_i}\,\varepsilon_{t_i}^1. \qquad (13.45)$$

Calculate the set $\left(c^{(j)}, x^{(j)}\right)$, $j = 1, \dots, M$, where $c^{(j)}$ is the option value computed on the jth sample path. The control variate method requires the calculation of the parameter $\beta = \mathrm{cov}(c, x)/\mathrm{var}(x)$. Upon inspection this is just the coefficient of $x^{(j)}$ in the regression of $x^{(j)}$ against $c^{(j)}$. Performing the regression we have

$$c^{(j)} = a + bx^{(j)} + \eta_j, \qquad (13.46)$$

where a and b are the regression parameters and η_j is the error term. The control variate estimate is just the regression parameter a, that is, the value of $c = a + bx$ when $x = 0$. The easiest way to visualise the procedure is to plot the points $\left(c^{(j)}, x^{(j)}\right)$ in a scatter diagram, and superimpose the regression line on the graph.

The intercept of the regression line with the c-axis is the control variate estimate of the option value. Clewlow and Strickland report a variance reduction of a factor of 200. The extra computation the method requires increases the computer time by a factor of 4, so that overall a saving of a factor of 50 is achieved. This is a considerable saving over a basic Monte Carlo method.

Clewlow and Strickland go on to investigate the effect of incorporating a vega control variate, corresponding to a portfolio hedged against changes in the state variable v_t. The vega control variate for the jth path is

$$y^{(j)} = \sum_{i=0}^{N-1} \frac{\partial c_{t_i}}{\partial v} \left(\Delta v_{t_i} - \mathbb{E} \left[\Delta v_{t_i} \right] \right). \tag{13.47}$$

Once again, there is no exact formula available but a good approximation for $\partial c_t / \partial v$ can be found from the Jamshidian formula for the extended Vasicek model.

Let $\gamma(r_t, t)$ be the Vasicek/Jamshidian vega. Set

$$y^{(j)} = \sum_{i=0}^{N-1} \gamma \left(r_{t_i}, t_i \right) \sigma \sqrt{v_{t_i}} \sqrt{\Delta t_i} \, \varepsilon_{t_i}^2. \tag{13.48}$$

Calculate the set $\left(c^{(j)}, x^{(j)}, y^{(j)} \right)$, $j = 1, \ldots, M$. Regress $c^{(j)}$ against $x^{(j)}$ and $y^{(j)}$ to obtain

$$c^{(j)} = a + bx^{(j)} + cy^{(j)} + \eta_j, \tag{13.49}$$

where a, b and c are the regression parameters and η_j is the error term. The control variate estimate is the parameter a, as before. Although Clewlow and Strickland report that additional savings are not so great in this case, nevertheless it can be seen that adding in one or more extra control variates is a relatively straightforward procedure. Further discussion of the method, including pseudo code, can be found in Clewlow and Strickland (98) [137].

The control variate method can be used in conjunction with the antithetic variate method, allowing considerable computational savings to be made.

13.3 SAMPLING ISSUES

In this section we discuss a number of very important modifications that allow much better sampling of relevant distributions. The better the sampling, the more accurate the estimates found, and the fewer the number of samples that need to be generated.

The methods discussed include how to generate normal random variates; better matching to a given density using stratified sampling and moment matching methods; discretisation and methods of simulation; using distributional information; Brownian bridge techniques; sampling from the unit hypercube using partial stratified sampling and Latin hypercube sampling; and the use of quasi-random numbers.

13.3.1 Generating Random Numbers

A practical problem with Monte Carlo methods is the requirement of a good random number generator. It is important that a good robust generator is used; possible problems with the output from poor generators include

- serial correlations
- cycling of numbers
- poor distributions.

Many if not all random number generators are pseudo-random number generators that produce a seemingly random stream of numbers by a deterministic algorithm. One pseudo-random number method recommended by Park and Miller (88) [428] is

$$I_{i+1} = aI_i \pmod{m}. \tag{13.50}$$

where $a = 7^5$ and $m = 2^{31} - 1$. The set $\{I_i\}$ is a reasonable good sequence of uniform random variates.[4]

An example of a poor random number generator would be a function returning a uniform pseudo-random integer in some range $[0, RAND\_MAX]$, where $RAND\_MAX$ is set to too small a value, 32 767, say. This generator would cycle after at most 32 767 numbers had been generated. Since even a small Monte Carlo programme might require over a million random numbers, this generator would be wholly inadequate.

13.3.2 Obtaining a Normal Distribution

A standard random number generator might generate uniform variates, $u \sim U[0, 1]$. There are various techniques available to transform uniform variates into, for example, the normal variates that are required by most Monte Carlo implementations. We describe four methods of performing the transformation.

1. *A basic method.* Generate $u_i \sim U[0, 1]$, $i = 1, \ldots, 12$, and set

$$\varepsilon = \sum_{i=1}^{12} u_i - 6. \tag{13.51}$$

ε has mean zero and variance one, but its kurtosis is approximately 0.15 (a normal distribution has a kurtosis of three). Also, $|\varepsilon| \leq 6$ so rare events (those more than six away from zero) are precluded by this method.

This is a simple method that is very easy to implement and is satisfactory for rough and ready work. However, it is inadequate for any serious application.

2. *The Box–Muller method.* Generate two independent uniform variates, $u_1, u_2 \sim U[0, 1]$, and set

$$\varepsilon_1 = \sqrt{-2 \ln u_1} \cos 2\pi u_2, \tag{13.52}$$

$$\varepsilon_2 = \sqrt{-2 \ln u_1} \sin 2\pi u_2, \tag{13.53}$$

then $\varepsilon_1, \varepsilon_2 \sim N(0, 1)$ are independent standard normal variates.

---

[4] At the time of writing it is possible to obtain series of random numbers derived from the decay of atomic nuclei, which are an ideal source of pure random numbers. It is however uncertain as to whether these stored series are long enough to use for very large scale Monte Carlo simulations.

This method generates variates that are correctly distributed, but it is relatively expensive to compute. Furthermore, if (u_1, u_2) are not independent, or if there is any autocorrelation in the sequence of uniform variates, then this structure will carry over to the normal variates $(\varepsilon_1, \varepsilon_2)$.[5]

3. *The polar rejection method.* Generate two independent uniform variates, $u_1, u_2 \sim$ U$[-1, +1]$. Compute $w = u_1^2 + u_2^2$. If $w < 1$, then set

$$\varepsilon_1 = \sqrt{-2\frac{\ln w}{w}}\, u_1, \tag{13.54}$$

$$\varepsilon_2 = \sqrt{-2\frac{\ln w}{w}}\, u_2. \tag{13.55}$$

If $w \geq 1$ reject the current pair of uniform variates and generate another pair (u_1, u_2).

This method has similar problems to the Box–Muller method but is quicker and is recommended as long as all the normal variates it generates are used.

4. *The inverse transform method.* This is a method that can be used to obtain variates from very general distributions. Suppose that we would like to generate variates with a distribution F which could be, for example, the normal distribution function

$$F(x) = \frac{1}{\sqrt{2\pi}} \int_{-\infty}^{x} e^{-\frac{1}{2}t^2}\, dt. \tag{13.56}$$

If $u \sim$ U$[0, 1]$ then $F^{-1}(u)$ is N$(0, 1)$.

For this method to work well fast approximations for F^{-1} are required. For a normal distribution such approximations exist. See, for instance, Moro (95) [402], and Marsaglia *et al.* (94) [381], amongst others.

The inverse transform method is recommended if a suitable approximation for F^{-1} can be found. Otherwise the polar rejection method can be used.

13.3.3   Stratified Sampling

A Monte Carlo method requires the generation of random numbers that reflect some desired underlying density. Unfortunately, random numbers have a habit of being unpredictable. A histogram plot of 1000 numbers sampled from a normal distribution will yield a sample density that looks roughly normal but which has obvious irregularities and possibly quite large deviations from the underlying normal density. Stratified sampling tries to improve upon nature by enforcing a close approximation by the sample to the underlying density. It tries to build in a guaranteed good match. In outline, the method is as follows:

---

[5] Whenever vectors $u_t = (u_{1,t}, \ldots, u_{n,t}) \in [0, 1]^n$ are being generated it is sensible to visually inspect scatter plots of $(u_{i,t}, u_{j,t})_{t=1,\ldots,N}$ for various pairs (i, j). Any obvious structure is a clear indication of dependence.

1. Sample $u_1, \ldots, u_N \sim U[0, 1]$.
2. Set

$$v_i = \frac{i-1}{N} + \frac{u_i}{N}, \quad i = 1, \ldots, N.$$

3. Set $w_i = F^{-1}(v_i)$.

w_i lies between the $100 \times ((i-1)/N)$th and $100 \times (i/N)$th percentiles of F. The construction guarantees that F is sampled uniformly in the sense that there is one variate in each percentile band. Of course $\{w_i\}_{i=1,\ldots,N}$ is a highly autocorrelated set. If this is a problem, as it sometimes is, then after the set $\{w_i\}_{i=1,\ldots,N}$ has been constructed it can be randomly permuted to yield a series without serial correlation. However, if the stratified sample is used to provide a set of terminal values, say, then autocorrelation is irrelevant.

Stratified sampling is a popular technique to improve the accuracy with which the underlying distribution is sampled. This results in fewer sample paths being required to give the desired density of coverage of the underlying distribution, and hence a given standard error can be achieved with fewer sample paths.

Stratified sampling can be combined with moment matching, described below, and is often used with Brownian bridge techniques described in Section 13.3.8.

13.3.4 Moment Matching

Suppose we have generated samples $r_T^{(i)}$, $i = 1, \ldots, M$, from a distribution F. $r_T^{(i)}$ can be adjusted to ensure that, for example, the sample mean and standard deviation exactly match those of F.

Suppose that F has mean μ and standard deviation σ, and that the sample mean and standard deviation of the $r_T^{(i)}$ are $\tilde{\mu}$ and $\tilde{\sigma}$. Then set

$$\underline{r}_T^{(i)} = \mu + \sigma \frac{r_T^{(i)} - \tilde{\mu}}{\tilde{\sigma}}, \quad i = 1, \ldots, M. \tag{13.57}$$

The set of $\underline{r}_T^{(i)}$ now has mean μ and standard deviation σ, so that the first and second moments of F are matched.

The method can be extended so that various moments of F are matched. It is clear this is a useful technique for financial applications. A related technique can be used to calibrate Monte Carlo estimates to market data; see below.

13.3.5 Discretisation

To simulate a one-dimensional process such as $dr_t = \mu(r_t, t)dt + \sigma(r_t, t)dz_t$ one must first discretise it. We have previously seen the Euler discretisation, where the process is discretised as

$$r_{t+\Delta t} = r_t + \mu(r_t, t)\Delta t + \sigma(r_t, t)\sqrt{\Delta t}\,\varepsilon_{t+\Delta t}, \tag{13.58}$$

with $\varepsilon_{t+\Delta t} \sim N(0, 1), t = 0, \ldots, T - \Delta t$, a sequence of independent standard normal variables. This is not the only way that the process can be discretised, however. The Euler discretisation is an 'order 0.5 strong Taylor scheme' (see Kloeden and Platen (95) [336]) and only generates good sample paths when Δt is very small. If Δt is too large the terminal distribution is very likely to be biased. Using a very small time step is not usually a problem, and in implementing a Monte Carlo method one should normally use a Euler scheme with Δt sufficiently small. However, one needs to be aware of other possible schemes.

For instance, the Milshtein discretisation is an 'order 1.0 strong Taylor scheme' (Kloeden and Platen). Its more rapid convergence means that one may use bigger time steps to achieve the same accuracy as the Euler scheme. The Milshtein scheme discretises the process as

$$r_{t+\Delta t} = r_t + \mu(r_t, t)\Delta t + \sigma(r_t, t)\sqrt{\Delta t}\,\varepsilon_{t+\Delta t} + \tfrac{1}{2}\sigma(r_t, t)\sigma'(r_t, t)\Delta t\left(\varepsilon_{t+\Delta t}^2 - 1\right). \quad (13.59)$$

This is the Euler scheme with an additional second-order term. Note that the expected value of the additional term is zero. With several state variables, including stochastic volatility, the Milshtein scheme becomes very complex; see for instance Miltersen (99) [398] who describes a version of the Milshtein scheme which he uses to simulate an HJM model.

A number of people have used higher order schemes in simulation; see for instance Andersen (96) [16].

Despite the increased accuracy of the Milshtein scheme, our experience has shown that in typical interest rate applications the extra computation required is too great relative to the gains extracted. Other, even more complex schemes are possible but for simulation it is generally better to stick with a Euler scheme with a small enough time step Δt.

13.3.6   Predictor–Corrector Simulation

There are other techniques available that attempt to compensate for the bias in the Euler scheme. A predictor–corrector method uses an Euler step to predict the value of the next simulated value, and then adds a correction to adjust the predictor for bias. Different versions are possible. We describe a method used by Goldman *et al.* (95) [251].

For a state variable r_t with process $dr_t = \mu(r_t, t)dt + \sigma(r_t, t)dz_t$ set

$$\underline{r}_{t+\Delta t} = r_t + \mu(r_t, t)\Delta t + \sigma(r_t, t)\sqrt{\Delta t}\,\varepsilon_{t+\Delta t} \qquad (13.60)$$

and

$$r_{t+\Delta t} = r_t + \left[\alpha\underline{\mu}(r_t, t) + (1 - \alpha)\underline{\mu}\left(\underline{r}_{t+\Delta t}, t\right)\right]\Delta t$$
$$+ \left[\beta\sigma(r_t, t) + (1 - \beta)\sigma\left(\underline{r}_{t+\Delta t}, t\right)\right]\sqrt{\Delta t}\,\varepsilon_{t+\Delta t}, \qquad (13.61)$$

where

$$\underline{\mu}(r_t, t) = \mu(r_t, t) - \beta\sigma(r_t, t)\frac{\partial \sigma}{\partial r}\bigg|_{(r_t, t)}. \qquad (13.62)$$

(There is freedom to choose the values of the weighting parameters α and β.) Equation (13.60) constructs the predictor $\underline{r}_{t+\Delta t}$ as a normal Euler step. The corrected value, $r_{t+\Delta t}$, is obtained by evolving on from r_t using a modified drift function (13.62). Both the drift and the volatility in (13.61) are computed as a weighted average of values at r_t and at $\underline{r}_{t+\Delta t}$. Kloeden and Platen (95) [336] describe this as an order 1.0 predictor–corrector scheme. They also describe higher order schemes.

13.3.7 Using Distributional Information

Sometimes the conditional density of the state variable is known. For instance, for the Vasicek process $dr_t = \alpha(\mu - r_t)dt + \sigma dz_t$, where μ and σ are constants, the conditional density $r_{t+\Delta t} \mid r_t$ is normal,

$$r_{t+\Delta t} \mid r_t \sim N(\mu_t, \sigma_t), \tag{13.63}$$

where

$$\mu_t = \mu + e^{-\alpha \Delta t}(r_t - \mu), \tag{13.64}$$

$$\sigma_t^2 = \frac{\sigma^2}{2\alpha}(1 - e^{-2\alpha \Delta t}). \tag{13.65}$$

The exact distribution is simulated by setting

$$r_{t+\Delta t} = \mu_t + \sigma_t \varepsilon_{t+\Delta t}, \tag{13.66}$$

for $\varepsilon_{t+\Delta t} \sim N(0, 1)$.

A second example is given by Scott (96) [484]. When r_t has a Cox, Ingersoll and Ross square root process, $dr_t = \alpha(\mu - r_t)dt + \sigma\sqrt{r_t}\,dz_t$, the conditional density of $r_{t+\Delta t} \mid r_t$ is non-central chi-squared. In fact

$$r_{t+\Delta t} = r_t + \frac{c_i}{2}Y_i, \tag{13.67}$$

where $c_i = (\sigma^2/2\alpha)(1 - e^{-\alpha\Delta t})$, and $Y_i \sim \chi^2(\upsilon, \lambda_i)$ is non-central chi-squared with $\upsilon = 4\alpha\mu/\sigma^2$ degrees of freedom, and non-centrality parameter $\lambda = 2c_i e^{-\alpha\Delta t}r_t$. This may form the basis of a Monte Carlo method, as Scott demonstrates.

13.3.8 Stratified Sampling and a Brownian Bridge

In many applications it may be important to ensure the terminal distribution of the underlying asset is as accurately reflected as possible. For instance, a European style option only has cash flows at a single final maturity date, so the density on this date is of special importance.[6] Stratified sampling is a method that finds a more uniform

---

[6] Of course, since the terminal payoffs have to be discounted (under the EMM) back to time 0, the primary object of interest is still the pricing measure over the space of paths, Ω. However, the terminal density nevertheless plays a distinguished role. Using a T-forward measure the terminal density (under F^T) is crucial.

sampling from any given density. In the context of a Monte Carlo method, stratified sampling can be combined with a Brownian bridge technique to ensure that the density that is stratified is the density at some final date. The technique is applied to find sample paths of an underlying Wiener process z_t. Sample paths for z_t must then be transformed into sample paths for the state variable using one of the techniques discussed above.

Suppose that we want to generate sample paths $r_{t_0}^{(i)}, \ldots, r_{t_N}^{(i)}, i = 1, \ldots, M$, of the process $dr_t = \mu(r_t, t)dt + \sigma(r_t, t)dz_t$. (Here we explicitly allow for a non-constant time step.)

We generate sample paths $z_{t_0}^{(i)}, \ldots, z_{t_N}^{(i)}, i = 1, \ldots, M$, of Wiener processes z_t, which may then be appropriately transformed. Increments in z_t must have the property that $\sqrt{\Delta t_j} \cdot \varepsilon_{j+1} = z_{t_{i+1}}^{(i)} - z_{t_i}^{(i)}$, where $\varepsilon_{j+1} \sim N(0, 1)$ are independent standard normal variates.

The method proceeds as follows:

1. Obtain a set of $z_{t_N}^{(i)}, i = 1, \ldots, M$, by stratified sampling from $N(0, t_N - t_0)$.
2. Fill in from $0 = z_{t_0}^{(i)}$ up to $z_{t_N}^{(i)}$ by constructing a Brownian bridge, for each i.

A Brownian bridge is a sample path from a Brownian motion that has pre-specified start and end values. The difficulty in the construction is to ensure that all conditional distributions are correct and consistent with the underlying Brownian motion. That is, given z_{t_0} and z_{t_N} one must construct $z_{t_j}, j = 1, \ldots, N - 1$, so that z_{t_j} have the correct conditional distributions.

The construction is recursive. The following is a forward construction. Suppose we have already constructed $z_{t_0}, \ldots, z_{t_j}$. Set

$$z_{t_{j+1}} = \frac{t_N - t_{j+1}}{t_N - t_j} z_{t_j} + \frac{t_{j+1} - t_j}{t_N - t_j} z_{t_N} + \sqrt{\frac{(t_N - t_{j+1})(t_{j+1} - t_j)}{t_N - t_j}} \varepsilon_{j+1}, \tag{13.68}$$

where $\varepsilon_{j+1} \sim N(0, 1)$ is standard normal.

Rather than a forward construction, a bisection construction gives better control over the generated sample paths. Starting with $j^- = 0$, $j^+ = N$ and $j^m = \lfloor N/2 \rfloor$ or $\lceil N/2 \rceil$, one sets

$$z_{t_{j^m}} = \frac{t_{j^+} - t_{j^m}}{t_{j^+} - t_{j^-}} z_{t_{j^-}} + \frac{t_{j^m} - t_{j^-}}{t_{j^+} - t_{j^-}} z_{t_{j^+}} + \sqrt{\frac{(t_{j^+} - t_{j^m})(t_{j^m} - t_{j^-})}{t_{j^+} - t_{j^-}}} \varepsilon_{j^m}. \tag{13.69}$$

One then performs the construction twice more, first with $j^- = 0$, $j^+ = j^m$ and then with $j^- = j^m$, $j^+ = N$, with j^m chosen to about mid-way between j^- and j^+ in each case. The procedure then continues to 'fill in the gaps'. It is easy to implement as a recursive computer routine.

The set of $z_{t_j}, j = 1, \ldots, N$, constructed either way, is a discretely sampled Wiener process conditional on z_{t_0} and z_{t_N}. The normalised increments $\varepsilon_{j+1} = (z_{t_{j+1}} - z_{t_j})/\sqrt{\Delta t_j}$ can now be inserted into (13.10), or some variant thereof, to obtain a sample path for r_t.

If we have a set of $z_{t_N}^{(i)}, i = 1, \ldots, M$, $z_{t_N}^{(i)} \sim N(0, t_N - t_0)$, obtained by stratified sampling, then the procedures just described generate M sample paths with a stratified terminal density. The terminal density normally has the greatest influence on the ultimate value of an option, so it is often the most important to stratify. The bisection construction allows the density at time $t_{N/2}$, the next most important density (conditional on the terminal density), to be stratified too in a straightforward way.

This method is heavily used in serious Monte Carlo applications. It deserves to be used more widely in interest rate applications.

As an aside, the Brownian bridge construction can be used to demonstrate the existence of a Wiener process[7] (see for instance Karatzas and Shreve (91) [329]).

13.3.9 Sampling the Unit Hypercube

To value a derivative security we require a numerical method of evaluating the integral

$$V_0 = \int_{-\infty}^{+\infty} \dots \int_{-\infty}^{+\infty} \widetilde{H}(x_1, \dots, x_k) f(x_1, \dots, x_k) dx_1 \dots dx_k, \qquad (13.70)$$

where $x_1, \dots, x_k$ represent the state variables sampled $N + 1$ times, and where $\widetilde{H}$ is the discounted payoff function. Although the number of state variables may be comparatively small, the number of time steps N will be large. With daily resets over two years a one-factor model would require the computation of a 500-dimensional integral. This is certainly beyond the abilities of a finite difference technique, and also poses considerable problems for a Monte Carlo method.

To see the nature of the problem, use an inverse transformation to write

$$V_0 = \int_0^1 \dots \int_0^1 \widetilde{H}(x_1, \dots, x_k) F^{-1}(u_1, \dots, u_k) du_1 \dots du_k, \qquad (13.71)$$

where F is the distribution corresponding to f, and $(u_1, \dots, u_k)$ are U[0, 1]^k, a uniform sample from the unit hypercube. If k is large, obtaining a uniform sample from the unit hypercube [0, 1]^k is decidedly non-trivial. For instance, it is not possible to perform a full stratified sample in k dimensions when k becomes large: to find a stratified sample with N bins in each dimension requires the generation of N^k sample points. This number rapidly explodes—we are hit by the 'curse of dimensionality'.

A non-stratified sample, where each $u_i, i = 1, \dots, k$, is an independent uniform variate drawn from [0, 1], is likely to be very patchy. It will give poor coverage of the entire hypercube, unless the size of the sample is of the same order—or greater—as that of a stratified sample.

Partial Stratified Sampling

As an alternative it is quite feasible to perform a partial stratified sampling, a hybrid method that uses stratified sampling in a small number of 'key' dimensions, and ordinary Monte Carlo sampling in the other dimensions.

---

[7] This is not trivial.

For instance, for $k' < k$, obtain random variates $v_1, \ldots, v_{k'}$ by stratified sampling of the unit hypercube $[0, 1]^{k'}$, and obtain $u_{k'+1}, \ldots, u_k$ by ordinary Monte Carlo sampling. $(v_1, \ldots, v_{k'}, u_{k'+1}, \ldots, u_k)$ is then a partially stratified sample of $[0, 1]^k$. Some care must be taken in using this approach, however. For instance, one must be aware of how the uniform distribution on $[0, 1]^k$ transforms into the desired distribution F. The stratified dimensions have to be chosen appropriately or they may map onto unimportant directions in F.

Latin Hypercube Sampling

One very effective technique of sampling the unit hypercube $[0, 1]^k$ is the Latin hypercube method. The simplest version finds a sample of N points from $[0, 1]^k$ so that marginal distributions in each dimension are correctly stratified. The unit hypercube $[0, 1]^k$ is divided into N^k bins by stratifying each dimension into N bins. The Latin hypercube method selects N of the N^k bins and picks one point in each by ordinary Monte Carlo sampling. The key idea is to choose the sample of N bins so that every one-dimensional co-space has a sample point of each of its N co-bins; that is, orthogonal projections down onto each dimension project a single sample point into each of the bins along that dimension.

The technique is better illustrated by a diagram than by words or equations. Figure 13.1 illustrates a full stratified sample for $k = 2$ and $N = 5$. A total of 5^2 bins are created and a single Monte Carlo sample is drawn from each. A Latin hypercube sample resembles Figure 13.2. A two-dimensional array has two co-spaces; one is the set of rows of the array, and the other is the set of columns. In the figure each row and each column of the array has exactly one bin in it from which a sample has been taken.

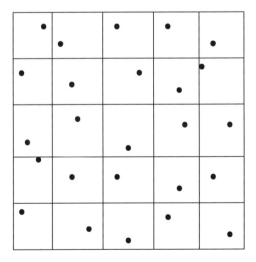

Figure 13.1 A full stratified sample: $k = 2$, $N = 5$

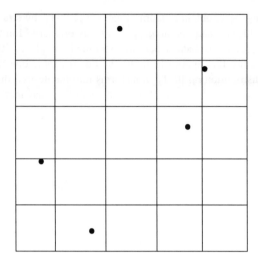

Figure 13.2   A Latin hypercube Sample: $k = 2$, $N = 5$

Projecting down each column, or across each row, gives exactly one sample point in each of the N possible slots. This means that the marginal distributions are stratified correctly.

A Latin hypercube sample is constructed as follows. Sample k permutations, $\pi_1, \ldots, \pi_k$, of $\{1, \ldots, N\}$, so that each π_j, $j = 1, \ldots, k$, is a re-ordering of the set $\{1, \ldots, N\}$ and $\pi_j(i)$ is the index of the i after being permuted by π_j. Let $u_j(i)$, $j = 1, \ldots, k$, $i = 1, \ldots, N$, be U[0, 1]. Set

$$v_j(i) = \frac{\pi_j(i) - 1}{N} + \frac{u_j(i)}{N}. \tag{13.72}$$

Let $v(i) = (v_1(i), \ldots, v_k(i))'$, then $v(i)$, $i = 1, \ldots, N$, is a Latin hypercube sample of size N in dimension k.

For a k-dimensional hypercube there are k orders of Latin hypercube. A scheme of order l, $1 \leq l \leq k$, projects down onto each l-dimensional co-space of $[0, 1]^k$ with the correct marginal distributions. We have just described the first-order scheme. We can construct lth order schemes for a k-dimensional hypercube as follows. An lth order scheme selects points from N^l cells out of the total of N^k in the hypercube. Select the first cell at random from the full set of N^k. Eliminate all cells belonging to any $k - l$-dimensional hyperplane that contains it. Each successive point is randomly chosen from the currently uneliminated cells. When the cell is selected all cells belonging to any $k - l$-dimensional hyperplane that contains it are eliminated.

The Latin hypercube method is a highly effective method of sampling high dimensional spaces, and is widely used in the Monte Carlo evaluation of certain path-dependent options. The drawback of the method is that it is not possible to directly estimate standard errors. The size of standard errors has to be estimated by work-around methods.

13.3.10   In-Cell Symmetric Sampling

Any stratified sampling method can be improved by augmenting it with an in-cell symmetric sample. Suppose we have selected a point

$$v(i) = (v_1(i), \ldots, v_k(i))' = (w_1(i) + u_1(i), \ldots, w_k(i) + u_k(i))', \qquad (13.73)$$

where $w_j(i) = w_{j,i}/N$ for some $w_{j,i} \in \{0, \ldots, N-1\}$, and $u_j(i) = u_{j,i}/N$ for $u_{j,i} \sim U[0,1]$. The in-cell symmetric point to $v(i)$ is

$$\hat{v}(i) = (v_1(i), \ldots, v_k(i))' = \left(w_1(i) + \frac{1}{N} - u_1(i), \ldots, w_k(i) + \frac{1}{N} - u_k(i)\right)', \quad (13.74)$$

the point diametrically opposite $v(i)$ across the cubelet. One uses $v(i)$ to find one option value, $c(i)$, and $\hat{v}(i)$ to find another, $\hat{c}(i)$. The new estimate of c is $\frac{1}{2}(c(i) + \hat{c}(i))$. The average of the in-cell symmetric estimates is the Monte Carlo estimate of the option value.

Figure 13.3 shows an in-cell symmetric Latin hypercube sample of the unit square with $N = 50$. Points evidently come in pairs, one pair per squarelet, symmetrically

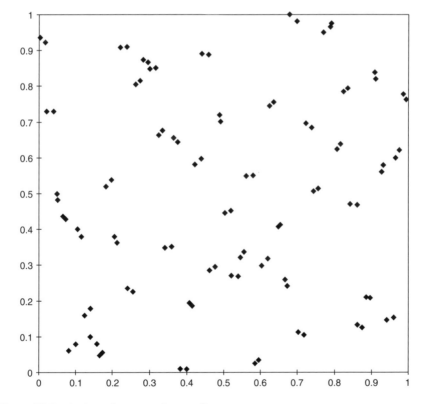

Figure 13.3   An in-cell symmetric sampling

placed about the centre of the square. Using the inverse transformation to convert to a bivariate normal distribution gives the scatter plot shown in Figure 13.4.

The in-cell symmetric sampling method works because it is a much better way of estimating an average value of the option in each cubelet. Figure 13.5 represents the integration of a function over an interval. The point v_0 is at the centre of the interval. v and $\hat{v}$ represent a pair of in-cell symmetric samples from the interval. The area under the line (E,F) is the volume estimate if the function is evaluated at the mid-point v. The area underneath the line (C,D) is the in-cell symmetric sample estimate. If only v was chosen the area under the line (A,B) would have been the estimate. If the function has curvature, the estimate provided by (C,D) is better than that provided using the endpoints (G,H).

The Monte Carlo approximation given by (A,B) is better than the regular approximation given by (E,F), in the sense that it converges faster to the true value as the mesh size decreases, as soon as the dimension of the cubelet is five or greater. The in-cell symmetric estimate converges faster still, and is always faster than the regular approximation.

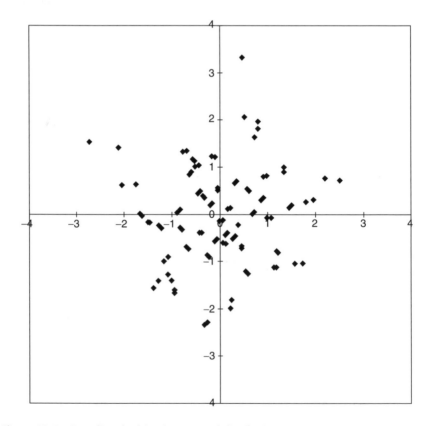

Figure 13.4   Sampling the bivariate normal distribution

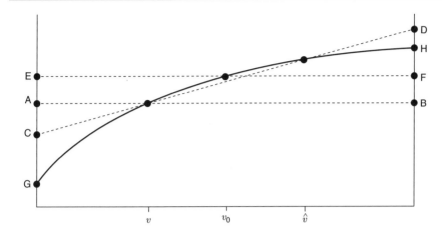

Figure 13.5   In-cell symmetric sampling and integration

The in-cell symmetric approximation works best because it more accurately approximates the underlying integral if the function to be integrated has curvature, on average. In gives a better approximation within each cell, and if the curvature of the function varies from cell to cell—sometimes positive and sometimes negative—errors across different cells will tend to cancel out.

13.3.11   Quasi-Random Numbers

Quasi-random numbers, also called sub-random numbers or low discrepancy sequences, are an alternative to randomly generating sampling points in the unit hypercube.[8] Instead of selecting numbers randomly, a sequence of quasi-random numbers systematically samples $[0, 1]^k$, ensuring that it is sampled 'uniformly', so that, for example, gaps tend to be filled in.[9] A sequence of quasi-random numbers in k dimensions is a set of points $\phi(j) = (\phi_1(j), \ldots, \phi_k(j))$, $j = 1, \ldots, N$, so that $[0, 1]^k$ is evenly covered with points. For example, the first few two-dimensional points of a sequence of quasi-random numbers, called the Halton numbers, are

$$\left(\tfrac{1}{2}, \tfrac{1}{3}\right), \left(\tfrac{1}{4}, \tfrac{2}{3}\right), \left(\tfrac{3}{4}, \tfrac{1}{9}\right), \left(\tfrac{1}{8}, \tfrac{4}{9}\right), \left(\tfrac{5}{8}, \tfrac{7}{9}\right), \left(\tfrac{3}{8}, \tfrac{2}{9}\right), \left(\tfrac{7}{8}, \tfrac{5}{9}\right). \qquad (13.75)$$

This sequence is illustrated in Figure 13.6. It is evident from the plot that the sequence has repeating patterns, but is filling up the square fairly evenly.

Once the sequence $\phi(j) \in [0, 1]^k$ has been found it can be used to evaluate the integral (13.71), as described above.

The use of quasi-random numbers in derivative pricing is described by Brotherton-Ratcliffe (94) [101], Papageorgiou and Traub (96) [427], Joy, Boyle and Tan (94) [327],

---

[8] The name 'quasi-random' is misleading since the numbers are deterministically generated and do not pretend to be random.

[9] There is a rather more precise definition related to the 'discrepency' of the sequence. See Niederreiter (92) [416] for more details.

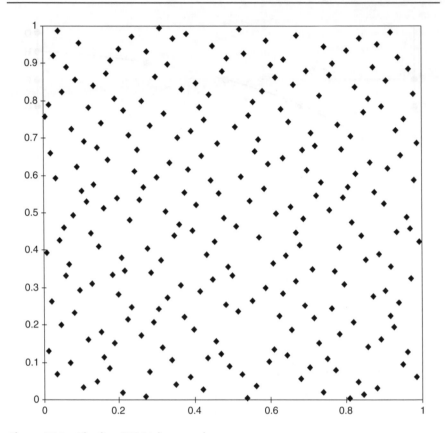

Figure 13.6   The first 250 Halton numbers

Boyle and Tan (97) [87], and Paskov (96) [429]. Paskov and Traub (95) [430] and
Acworth, Broadie and Glasserman (97) [4] compare quasi-random number based
methods with standard Monte Carlo methods.

  We describe the construction of the Halton sequence and the Faure sequence. In
practice both the Faure sequence and the Sobol' sequence are superior to the Halton
sequence. The Sobol' sequence is too complex to allow a description here, but fast
implementations are described in, for instance, Bratley and Bennett (88) [90] and Press
et al. (92) [441].

Constructing the Halton Sequence

Let $p_1, \ldots, p_k$ be the first k prime numbers. For each k, each integer n has a unique
representation

$$n = \sum_{i=0}^{\infty} a_k(i)(p_k)^i, \quad 0 \le a_k(i) < p_k, \quad a_k(i) \in \mathbb{Z}. \quad (13.76)$$

Set

$$\phi_k(n) = \sum_{i=0}^{\infty} a_k(i) \cdot (p_k)^{-i-1}, \tag{13.77}$$

so that $0 < \phi_k(n) < 1$. The k-dimensional Halton sequence is $(\phi_1(n), \ldots, \phi_k(n))$, $n = 1, \ldots, \infty$. (Note that only finite $a_j^1(n)$ are non-zero.)

The Halton sequence has some undesirable properties. For instance, points in successive dimensions are highly correlated, which makes this sequence unsuited for use in numerical integration.

Constructing the Faure Sequence

This is described by Joy *et al.* (94) [327] amongst others. Let p be the smallest prime greater than $\max(k, 2)$. For each n, k Faure numbers are generated recursively. Suppose that $n = \Sigma_{j=0}^{\infty} a_j^1(n) p^j$, $0 \leq a_j^1(n) < p$. Set

$$\phi_p^1(n) = \sum_{j=0}^{\infty} a_j^1(n) p^{-j-1}. \tag{13.78}$$

For $1 \leq s \leq k$, $\phi_p^s(n)$ is defined as

$$\phi_p^s(n) = \sum_{j=0}^{\infty} a_j^s(n) p^{-j-1}, \tag{13.79}$$

where $a_j^s(n)$ are defined recursively. Suppose all $a_j^{s-1}(n)$ are known, then set

$$a_j^s(n) = \sum_{i \geq j}^{\infty} \frac{i!}{j!(i-j)!} a_j^{s-1}(n) \bmod p. \tag{13.80}$$

The sequence of k-dimensional vectors $\{\phi_p^\bullet(n)\}_{n=1,2,\ldots}$ is the k-dimensional Faure sequence we require.

We have noted that Faure and Sobol' sequences perform better than Halton sequences. Sobol' sequences are cheaper to compute than Faure sequences, and may even be as fast as pseudo-random numbers.

There is conflicting evidence of the effectiveness of quasi-random numbers in numerical integration. A number of studies have compared quasi-random with Monte Carlo simulation. Although some of these studies report that quasi-random numbers perform better than Monte Carlo, it is not always clear when effective speed-up methods are used in conjunction with the Monte Carlo method; it is hard to come up with a clear comparison. As a rule of thumb, a Monte Carlo method, used with effective speed-ups, is likely to be of comparable speed to a method based on quasi-random numbers.

13.3.12 Calibrating a Monte Carlo Method

By allowing certain parameters to be time-dependent, we have seen that it is possible to calibrate a one-factor model to the term structure of interest rates. Such a calibration is achieved during the course of a finite difference or lattice implementation by adjusting the parameter value at each time step so that the market value of some variable, such as a spot rate, is matched by the model. A similar idea may be applied to a Monte Carlo implementation. It is possible to calibrate a Monte Carlo method to reproduce the market values of certain chosen instruments. These methods are the Monte Carlo analogy to the extended Vasicek model, and are related to moment matching methods.[10] The idea was developed by Duan and Simonato (95) [179] and described in Broadie and Glasserman (97) [100]. Duan and Simonato applied the method to Asian equity option valuation, but the method applies equally well to interest rate products.

For instance, we may wish to implement a Monte Carlo method to value bond options while simultaneously recovering a given set of bond prices. Under the EMM P we have

$$B_0(T) = \mathbb{E}_0^P \left[e^{-\int_0^T r_s \, ds} \right].$$
(13.81)

Simulate M paths $r_{t_0}^{(i)}, \ldots, r_{t_N}^{(i)}$, $i = 1, \ldots, M$, for the short rate r_t and set

$$\underline{P}_j = \frac{1}{M} \sum_{i=1}^{M} \exp \left(-\Delta t_j \sum_{k=0}^{j-1} r_{t_k}^{(i)} \right), \quad j = 1, \ldots, N.$$
(13.82)

$\underline{P}_j$ is the simulated value of the t_j maturity pure discount bond. The simulated forward rate is

$$\underline{F}_j = \frac{1}{\Delta t_j} \ln \frac{\underline{P}_j}{\underline{P}_{j+1}}.$$
(13.83)

The generated values of the short rate are now offset so that the simulated prices exactly recover observed pure discount bond prices. Suppose that the market value of the pure discount bond of maturity t_j is P_j, $j = 1, \ldots, N$. The market forward rate for the period $[t_j, t_{j+1}]$ is

$$F_j = \frac{1}{\Delta t_j} \ln \frac{P_j}{P_{j+1}}.$$
(13.84)

The simulated short rate values are offset by the difference between the simulated and market forward rates. Set

$$\underline{r}_{t_j}^{(i)} = r_{t_j}^{(i)} + F_j - \underline{F}_j.$$
(13.85)

Putting $\underline{r}_{t_j}^{(i)}$ into (13.82) instead of $r_{t_j}^{(i)}$ recovers the market prices of pure discount bonds, P_j, $j = 1, \ldots, N$. The offset simulated short rates $\underline{r}_{t_i}^{(j)}$ can now be used to price bond option values, or any other derivative. The values obtained are now consistent with the term structure of interest rates.

In this example we have illustrated how the method may be used to calibrate to the term structure. It is not difficult to extend the method so that other types of instrument are correctly priced. For instance, one could ensure that a set of at-the-money (ATM) caps was priced to reproduce market values. Other instruments, such as swaptions,

---

[10] Of course, the methods apply more generally than just to affine models or others in which explicit solutions are known.

could then be valued consistent with the selected cap prices. However, only a restricted set of instruments may be calibrated to at a time. So, for instance, one could not simultaneously calibrate both to a term structure and to a set of cap prices.

The method is most appropriately used if the model comes close to fitting market data so that the offsetting (13.85) can be regarded as a perturbation of the original values $r_{t_j}^{(i)}$. If the required adjustments are large, then one may question whether one should not be using a different underlying model.

Broadie and Glasserman (97) [100] point out a number of problems associated with the method.

1. The choice of which market prices should be calibrated to is problematic.
2. Price estimates are biased unless M is large.
3. Paths are no longer independent. This means that it is not possible to directly estimate standard errors.

Also, the generated values $r_{t_j}^{(i)}$ need to be stored and then transformed. This may place a considerable burden on computer memory.

Despite these problems, these calibration methods are a powerful weapon in the Monte Carlo armoury and could be more widely used.

13.4 SIMULATION METHODS FOR HJM MODELS

HJM models have some special features that can be exploited in a Monte Carlo method. We describe the sledgehammer simulation approach that works when all else fails, but is cumbersome and troublesome. One-factor HJM models have an easier simulation, whatever the form of the volatility function. We describe this and then give another simulation method for Markovian one-factor volatilities.

An excellent source of information on methods for HJM models is Clewlow and Strickland (98) [137], who present pseudo-code algorithms for several of the methods sketched here.

13.4.1 The Sledgehammer Simulation Approach

Suppose that the forward rate process is

$$\mathrm{d}f_t(T) = \alpha(t, T)\mathrm{d}t + \sum_{i=1}^{n} \sigma_i(t, T)\mathrm{d}z_{i,t}, \tag{13.86}$$

where z_t is an $\mathbb{R}^n$ valued Wiener process under the objective measure Q and

$$\alpha(t, T) = -\sum_{i=1}^{n} \sigma_i(t, T)\left(\lambda_i(t) - \int_t^T \sigma_i(t, s)\mathrm{d}s\right). \tag{13.87}$$

Under the EMM P, one obtains the drift of $f_t(T)$ by setting $\lambda_i(t) = 0$, $i = 1, \ldots, n$, in (13.87), so that

$$\alpha(t, T) = \sum_{i=1}^{n} \sigma_i(t, T) \int_t^T \sigma_i(t, s) \mathrm{d}s. \tag{13.88}$$

We use as our example the European bond option, $c_t(T, S)$, where $t < T < S$, with strike X. The sledgehammer Monte Carlo approach evolves the entire forward rate curve. Starting from time t, the forward rate curve is simulated up to time T where the value of the pure discount bond, $B_T(S)$, and hence the option payoff, $\max(0, B_T(S) - X)$, is found. The payoff is then discounted back to time t, and an average value over many sample paths is found, in the usual way.

Discretising the Forward Rate Curve

We need to evolve forward rates for all maturities between time t and a maximum maturity time S. The time to maturity interval $[t, S]$ is discretised into M intervals. Set $\Delta T = (S - t)/M$ and $t = T_0, \ldots, T_M = S$, where $T_{j+1} = T_j + \Delta T$. Similarly current time $[t, T]$ is split into K intervals with $\Delta t = (T - t)/K$ and $t = t_0, \ldots, t_K = T$, with $t_{k+1} = t_k + \Delta t$. It is a practical requirement that Δt should be an integer multiple of ΔT, so that $\{t_0, \ldots, t_K\} \subset \{T_0, \ldots, T_M\}$. For simplicity we assume that $\Delta t = \Delta T$. A path of forward rate curves can now be simulated. We describe the procedure in a moment.

Along a particular simulation path, at the option maturity time $T = t_K$, the value of the underlying bond is

$$B_T(S) = B_{t_K}(T_M) = \exp\left[-\sum_{j=K}^{M-1} f_{t_K}(T_j)\Delta T\right]. \tag{13.89}$$

The payoff $\max(0, B_{t_K}(T_M) - X)$ is discounted back to time t using the simulated values of the short rate, $f_{t_i}(t_i)$, $i = 0, \ldots, K - 1$, along this path of forward rate curves:

$$V = \exp\left[-\sum_{i=0}^{K-1} f_{t_i}(t_i)\Delta t\right] \max(0, B_{t_K}(T_M) - X). \tag{13.90}$$

As usual, many values of V are calculated and their average is the Monte Carlo estimate for $c_t(T, S)$.

The Simulation

For $k = 0, \ldots, K - 1$, $i = 1, \ldots, n$, generate normal random variates $\varepsilon_{i,k} \sim N(0, 1)$, iid.

For each $j = 1, \ldots, M - 1$, and for $0 < k < j$, evolve $f_{t_k}(T_j)$ as

$$f_{t_{k+1}}(T_j) = f_{t_k}(T_j) + \alpha(t_k, T_j)\Delta t + \sum_{i=1}^{n} \sigma_i(t_k, T_j)\sqrt{\Delta t}\, \varepsilon_{i,k}. \tag{13.91}$$

For a fixed maturity T_j, current time can only evolve up to time T_j before the forward rate of that maturity ceases to exist. The forward rate drift $\alpha(t_k, T_j)$ is calculated using a discretised version of (13.88), for example,

$$\alpha(t_k, T_j) = \sum_{i=1}^{n} \sigma_i(t_k, T_j) \sum_{l=k}^{K-1} \sigma_i(t_k, T_l) \Delta T. \tag{13.92}$$

The evolution (13.91) is in general very messy. $\sigma_i(t_k, T_j)$ may be path-dependent, and in any case $\alpha(t_k, T_j)$ depends on values of $\sigma_i(t_k, T_j)$ for a range of maturities. The method must be implemented with care. Computational demands are also high. To simulate the path of forward rate curves, accuracy requires a small time step. However, if this entails a small maturity step a considerable amount of computation will be necessary.

13.4.2   One-factor HJM with a General Volatility Function

Although with n-dimensional general volatility functions it may be necessary to use the sledgehammer Monte Carlo approach, when $n = 1$ it is possible to find an improved, robust Monte Carlo procedure for bond options. Carverhill and Pang (95) [121] show that for the bond option $c_t(T, S)$,

$$c_t(T, S) = \widetilde{\mathbb{E}}_t \left[e^{-\int_t^T r_u \, du} \max(0, B_T(S) - X) \right] \tag{13.93}$$

$$= \widetilde{\mathbb{E}}_t[\max(0, B_T(S)Y_t(T, S) - XY_t(T, T)], \tag{13.94}$$

under the EMM where

$$Y_t(T, S) = \exp \left[\int_t^T v(u, S) dz_u - \frac{1}{2} \int_t^T v^2(u, S) du \right], \tag{13.95}$$

and $v(t, T) = -\int_t^T \sigma(t, s) ds$, as in Section 8.2.1. One now simulates for $Y_t(T, S)$ and $Y_t(T, T)$, rather than for $f_t(T)$. The call option value is found from (13.94) by normal Monte Carlo methods. (Note that there is no discounting in (13.94).) The simulation itself is quite straightforward. For $k = 0, \ldots, N$, set $t = t_0, \ldots, t_N = T$, where $t_{k+1} = t_k + \Delta t$, $\Delta t = (T - t)/N$. Generate standard normal variates $\varepsilon_k \sim N(0, 1)$ iid and set

$$Y_t(T, S) = \exp \left[\sum_{k=1}^{N} v(t_k, S)\sqrt{\Delta t}\, \varepsilon_k - \frac{1}{2} \sum_{k=1}^{N} v^2(t_k, S) \Delta t \right], \tag{13.96}$$

$$Y_t(T, T) = \exp \left[\sum_{k=1}^{N} v(t_k, T)\sqrt{\Delta t}\, \varepsilon_k - \frac{1}{2} \sum_{k=1}^{N} v^2(t_k, T) \Delta t \right]. \tag{13.97}$$

$Y_t(T, S)$ and $Y_t(T, T)$ do not require a complicated simulation, and the method is easy to implement.

13.4.3   Pricing for Markovian One-Factor Volatilities

When volatilities are Markovian, lattice approaches become available. We describe a simulation method due to Ritchken and Sankarasubramanian (95) [454]. A lattice method due to Li, Ritchken and Sankarasubramanian (95) [351] is presented in Chapter 14.

Suppose we have a Ritchken and Sankarasubramanian volatility function

$$\sigma(r, t, T,) = \sigma(r, t)e^{-\int_t^T k(s)ds} = \sigma(r, t)k(t, T). \tag{13.98}$$

It is possible to show that pure discount bond prices are given by

$$B_t(T) = \frac{B_0(T)}{B_0(t)} \exp\left(-\frac{1}{2}\beta^2(t, T)\phi(t) + \beta(t, T)\psi(t) \right), \tag{13.99}$$

where

$$\phi_t = \int_0^t \sigma^2(r_t, s, t,)ds, \tag{13.100}$$

$$\psi_t = f_0(t) - r_t, \tag{13.101}$$

and

$$\beta(t, T) = \int_t^T k(t, u)du. \tag{13.102}$$

$\beta(t, T)$ is a deterministic function, so bond prices $B_t(T)$ can be regarded as functions of two state variables, ϕ_t and r_t (since ψ_t is just a transform of r_t). These state variables may either be simulated directly, or evolved in a lattice.

The simulation approach   If $\sigma(r, t, T) = \sigma(r, t)k(t, T)$ is a Ritchken and Sankarasubramanian volatility function, then the processes for r_t and ϕ_t are

$$dr_t = \mu(t)dt + \sigma(r_t, t)dz_t, \tag{13.103}$$

$$d\phi_t = (\sigma^2(r_t, t) - 2k(t)\phi_t)dt, \tag{13.104}$$

where

$$\mu(t) = k(t)\psi_t + \phi_t + \sigma(r_t, t)\lambda(t) + \frac{\partial}{\partial t}f_0(t)$$

under the objective measure Q and $\lambda(t)$ is the price of risk. The process for ϕ_t is deterministic. For a Monte Carlo simulation, discretise the processes for r_t and ϕ_t and simulate (under P, so that $\lambda(t)$ is set to zero).

Ritchken and Sankarasubramanian point out that sometimes suitable control variates might be available. For instance, suppose $\sigma(r_t, t) = \sigma r_t^\gamma$ and $k(t) \equiv k$ are constant. Then if $\gamma = 0$, the model is just a standard extended Vasicek. This has explicit solutions for instruments such as bond options. These solutions can be used as control variates for the corresponding simulation problem.

Calibrating with Ritchken and Sankarasubramanian Volatilities

Bliss and Ritchken (95) [78] give a procedure whereby the current values of the functions ϕ_t and ψ_t can be backed out of observations of the current term structure. For these volatilities we have

$$B_t(T) = \frac{B_0(T)}{B_0(t)} \exp\left(-\frac{1}{2}\beta^2(t, T)\phi_t + \beta(t, T)\psi_t\right) \qquad (13.105)$$

as before. For times $s < t < t + \tau$, continuous forward rates of tenor τ are $f_s(t, t + \tau) = (1/\tau)\int_t^{t+\tau} f_s(u)\mathrm{d}u$. From equation (13.105) we get an expression for the forward rate $f_s(t, t + \tau)$ in terms of $\beta(t, T)$, ϕ_t and ψ_t:

$$f_t(t, t + \tau) = f_0(t, t + \tau) + \frac{1}{\tau}\left(\beta(t, t + \tau)\psi_t - \frac{1}{2}\beta^2(t, t + \tau)\phi_t\right). \qquad (13.106)$$

$f_t(t, t + \tau)$ is just the spot rate $r_t(t + \tau)$. The change in the value of $f_t(t, t + \tau)$ over a short time interval Δt is $\Delta f_t(t, t + \tau) = f_t(t, t + \tau) - f_{t-\Delta t}(t, t + \tau)$ so that

$$\Delta f_t(t, t + \tau) = \frac{1}{\tau}\left(\beta(t, t + \tau)\psi_t - \frac{1}{2}\beta^2(t, t + \tau)\phi_t\right). \qquad (13.107)$$

From the term structure observed at two successive times one may compute $\Delta f_t(t, t + \tau)$ in equation (13.107). Selecting two reference maturities, τ_1 and τ_2, and obtaining two values, $\Delta f_t(t, t + \tau_1)$ and $\Delta f_t(t, t + \tau_2)$, it is possible to eliminate ϕ_t and ψ_t, so that

$$\Delta f_t(t, t + \tau) = \Delta f_t(t, t + \tau_1)H_1(\tau) + \Delta f_t(t, t + \tau_2)H_2(\tau), \qquad (13.108)$$

where

$$H_1(\tau) = \frac{\tau_1\beta(t, t + \tau)[\beta(t, t + \tau_2) - \beta(t, t + \tau)]}{\tau\beta(t, t + \tau_1)[\beta(t, t + \tau_2) - \beta(t, t + \tau_1)]}, \qquad (13.109)$$

$$H_2(\tau) = \frac{\tau_2\beta(t, t + \tau)[\beta(t, t + \tau) - \beta(t, t + \tau_1)]}{\tau\beta(t, t + \tau_2)[\beta(t, t + \tau_2) - \beta(t, t + \tau_1)]}. \qquad (13.110)$$

From a set of observations of Δf_t at varying maturities, and given a functional form for $\beta(t, T)$, it is possible from (13.108), (13.109) and (13.110) to calibrate $\beta(t, T)$ to changes in market prices from day to day. By selecting further reference maturities one can calibrate ϕ_t and ψ_t. Bliss and Ritchken develop statistics for this procedure.

14

Lattice Methods

In Chapter 12 we saw how finite difference methods could be used to solve the pricing PDE for derivative securities. For some types of process an apparently simpler alternative is available. Lattice methods are a half-way house between Monte Carlo methods and finite difference methods. A continuous state variable is approximated as a discrete variable on a lattice. We shall see that there are connections with both Monte Carlo and finite difference methods.

Lattice methods were introduced for log-normal processes in the late 1970s by Cox, Ross and Rubinstein (79) [149], and the binomial method (for FX and equity derivatives) has been a reliable workhorse ever since. Because interest rate processes are mean reverting, trying to use a naive binomial method does not work; it does not have sufficient flexibility. Effective lattice methods for interest rates were introduced by Ho and Lee (86) [280], Hull and White (93) [295], (94) [297], and Black, Derman and Toy (BDT) (90) [73].[1] The Heath, Jarrow and Morton (HJM) model can also be implemented on a lattice, for some types of volatility functions (Li, Ritchken and Sankarasubramanian (95) [351]).

Jamshidian (91) [309] introduced the method of forward induction and placed lattice methods on a securer theoretical footing, also enabling them to be readily calibrated to market prices.

Lattice methods have come to be vital to the derivatives industry. They are the method of choice for pricing American and Bermudan instruments, since Monte Carlo methods are unsuitable here despite recent developments.

In this chapter we first discuss lattice methods, setting up a general framework. We show how to price on lattices, illustrating with the lattice methods of Hull and White, Black, Derman and Toy, and Schmidt (97) [479]. The Li, Ritchken and Sankarasubramanian lattice for HJM models is presented. We show how lattices can be calibrated to market prices. Hybrid lattice and Monte Carlo methods are briefly described and we conclude by discussing the implementation of non-recombining lattices.

---

[1] The original Ho and Lee lattice was binomial. The Black, Derman and Toy lattice is also binomial, but it evolves the entire term structure giving it much more flexibility.

14.1   INTRODUCTION TO LATTICE METHODS

We set up a theoretical framework for interest rate lattice methods that is sufficiently general to include all the main lattice methods currently in use. We show how prices can be obtained in this general framework, and then illustrate using some well-known methods.

14.1.1   The Interest Rate Lattice

A lattice $\mathcal{L} = (\mathcal{N}, \mathcal{A}, \mathcal{S}, \underline{X}, p, t, r)$ has seven elements to it.

- A finite set $\mathcal{N}$ of nodes and a set $\mathcal{A} \subseteq \mathcal{N} \times \mathcal{N}$ of arcs together define the branching on the lattice.
- A state space $\mathcal{S}$, a state variable $\underline{X} : \mathcal{N} \to \mathcal{S}$, a set of probabilities $p : \mathcal{A} \to \mathbb{R}^+$, and a time $t : \mathcal{N} \to \mathbb{R}$ define a discrete process on the lattice.
- A function $r : \mathcal{S} \to \mathbb{R}$ giving the spot rate $r(\underline{X}(N))$ at each node $N \in \mathcal{N}$ determines prices on the lattice.

The lattice is directed in that each arc runs from a node at an earlier time to a node at a later time. We may refer to the lattice $(\mathcal{N}, \mathcal{A}, \mathcal{S}, \underline{X}, p, t, r)$ as the process $\underline{X}$ under the EMM.

To set things up consistently as an interest rate model we need a little more notation. Write t_j, $j = 1, \ldots, M$, for the set of discrete times in the lattice and write $\mathcal{N}_j$ for the set of nodes at time t_j. Set $N_j = |\mathcal{N}_j|$ so that $\mathcal{N}_j$ can be indexed as $\mathcal{N}_j = \{(i, j)\}_{i=1,\ldots,N_j}$, with $t(i, j) = t_j$. If $((i, j), (k, l))$ is in $\mathcal{A}$, then $j < l$. Write $\underline{X}_{i,j}$ for the value $\underline{X}(i, j)$ of the state variable at node (i, j). We write $\underline{X}_j$ for the random variable taking possible values in the set $\{\underline{X}_{i,j}\}_{i=1,\ldots,N_j}$ at time t_j.

For a node $(i, j) \in \mathcal{N}_j$ the set of successor nodes to (i, j) is the set $\mathcal{B}_{i,j} = \{(k, l) \mid ((i, j), (k, l)) \in \mathcal{A}\}$. It is the set of nodes that node (i, j) branches to. Similarly set $\mathcal{C}_{i,j} = \{(k, l) \mid ((k, l), (i, j)) \in \mathcal{A}\}$. $\mathcal{C}_{i,j}$ is the set of predecessor nodes to node (i, j).

Write $p_{k,l;i,j}$ for the probability $p((i, j), (k, l)) \in \mathbb{R}^+$. It is the probability of branching to (k, l), conditional on being at (i, j). The probability function must have the property that for all nodes $(i, j) \in \mathcal{N}$,

$$\sum_{(k,l) \in \mathcal{B}_{i,j}} p_{k,l;i,j} = 1. \tag{14.1}$$

Figure 14.1 illustrates a general lattice process. Arrows represent a sample of allowed transitions, each of which has a probability associated with it.

The illustrated process has irregular branching. This is fine in principle, but would be hard to implement or to calibrate. Instead it is natural to make the assumption that the process $\underline{X}$ decomposes into increments from one time to the next time, so that $\mathcal{B}_{i,j} \subseteq \mathcal{N}_{j+1}$, for all $j = 1, \ldots, M - 1$. Figure 14.2 illustrates this. Allowable transitions are from time t_j to t_{j+1} only. It is also natural to demand that all nodes (except at time t_1) have a non-empty predecessor set, $\mathcal{C}_{i,j}$, and that all nodes (except those at time t_M) have a non-empty successor set, $\mathcal{B}_{i,j}$.

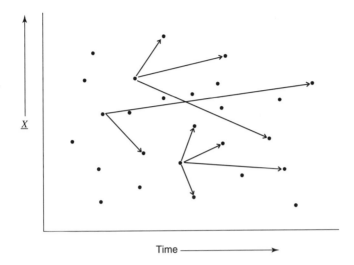

Figure 14.1 Branching with conditional observation times

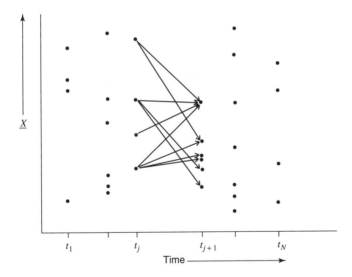

Figure 14.2 Branching with unconditional observation times

A lattice fulfilling these conditions will be called a simple lattice. The branching may still be irregular.

We write $\Delta_j = t_{j+1} - t_j$ for the time step at time t_j. On a simple lattice all spot rates at time t_j will be for maturity Δ_j, so that they define discount factors to get back from time t_{j+1} to time t_j. In a consistent arbitrage-free term structure model an entire term structure can be found for each state of the lattice. This means that the function $r(\underline{X}_{i,j})$

extends to a function (also denoted by r)

$$r : \mathcal{S} \times \mathbb{R}^+ \to \mathbb{R}, \qquad r\left(\underline{X}_{i,j}, \tau\right) \mapsto r_{i,j}(\tau), \tag{14.2}$$

where $r_{i,j}(\tau)$ is the time τ to maturity spot rate, such that $r_{i,j}\left(\Delta_j\right) = r\left(\underline{X}_{i,j}\right)$. We shall see later that the space of such extensions may be highly constrained. We suppose that the set $\{(i, j)\}_{i=1,\ldots,N_j}$ is ordered so that $r_{k,j}(\Delta_j) \geq r_{i,j}(\Delta_j)$ if $k \geq i$.

Note that there is no reason why the set $\{r_{i,j}(\tau)\}_{i=1,\ldots,N_j}$ should contain N_j distinct values. In a two-factor lattice, where one factor is the spot rate, there will be several nodes for each value of r at each time.

Given a lattice with the properties as described we see how it is possible to price derivative securities (on the lattice).

A Lattice Method

To have a lattice method we have to specify a set of lattices,

$$\mathcal{L}^{(n)} = \left(\mathcal{N}^{(n)}, \mathcal{A}^{(n)}, \mathcal{S}, \underline{X}^{(n)}, p^{(n)}, t^{(n)}, r^{(n)}\right), \quad n > 0, \tag{14.3}$$

for a common state space $\mathcal{S}$, such that as $n \to \infty$ the discrete random variable $\underline{X}_j^{(n)}$ converges to a continuous-time random variable X_t and $r^{(n)}$ converges to the short rate process r_t. Typically $\underline{X}_j^{(n)}$ is defined on a finer and finer mesh as n increases. In an implementation of a lattice method n may be a parameter whose value is chosen so that prices on the lattice are found to a required degree of accuracy, relative to 'true' prices in the underlying continuous-time model.[2]

A lattice method will guarantee that $\underline{X}_j^{(n)}$ converges, although usually at the expense of increased computation and storage requirements. As n increases, the time mesh $\Delta_t = \max\{\Delta_j\}$ will decrease. As an important practical consideration, we need the set $\mathcal{N}_j^{(n)}$ to grow slowly, if at all, as both n and j increase. In many methods $N_j^{(n)}$ is a function of j only and $N_j = N_j^{(n)}$ might be linear or a small order polynomial in j. For instance, one could have $\Delta_j = 1/n$. In a non-recombining trinomial tree (see below) we have $N_j = 3^{j-1}$. Since in a typical (recombining) lattice j might be of the order of 1000, it is evident that a non-recombining method has to be designed and implemented with care.

$\{r_{i,j}(\Delta_j)\}$ and p implicitly vary with Δ_t. Define $\Delta_{i,j} = |r_{i+1,j}(\Delta_j) - r_{i,j}(\Delta_j)|$ (we have assumed the nodes (i, j) are ordered) and set $\Delta_r = \max_{i,j} \Delta_{i,j}$. Convergence requires that

$$\Delta_r \to 0 \text{ as } \Delta_t \to 0, \tag{14.4}$$

in an appropriate limit. Usually $\Delta_{i,j}$ is a function of Δ_{j-1} as a consequence of ensuring that $\underline{X}$ does converge to the correct limit.

Schmidt (97) [479] establishes when convergence takes place. Some lattices can be thought of as finite difference methods. In this case standard techniques can be used to

---

[2] In fact a lattice is a perfectly good arbitrage-free discrete-time model in its own right and does not need to be thought of only as an approximation to a continuous-time model.

establish convergence and stability. We do not discuss these here, but see, for instance, Morton and Mayers (94) [404].

14.1.2 Types of Lattice

The branching in a lattice is determined by the pair $(\mathcal{N}, \mathcal{A})$. Set $N_{i,j} = |\mathcal{B}_{i,j}|$. This is the order of branching at node (i, j). If $N_{i,j} \equiv k$, a constant, then the lattice is order k. If $k = 2$ the lattice is binomial, if $k = 3$ the lattice is trinomial. A typical lattice method evolves from a single root node at time t_1, so that $N_1 = 1$. A grid method has the same number of nodes at each time step (see below).

Recombining Lattices

A recombining lattice has the property that 'N_j grows only slowly in j'. For instance, if $N_{j+1} \le N_j + k$, for some fixed k, then the lattice is recombining. For our purposes we define a lattice to be recombining if N_j is bounded by a polynomial in j, but other definitions could also be acceptable.[3] The importance of having a recombining lattice is that in practical implementations the storage and computational requirements remain firmly under control. A non-recombining lattice, with N_j growing exponentially, say, poses severe implementation problems.

A much stricter definition of a recombining lattice is possible. Restricting ourselves to the case of a trinomial lattice, suppose $\mathcal{B}_{i,j} = \{u_{i,j}, v_{i,j}, w_{i,j}\} \subseteq \mathcal{N}_{j+1}$, with $r(u_{i,j}) \ge r(v_{i,j}) \ge r(w_{i,j})$. Set $(i, j)^u = u_{i,j}$, $(i, j)^m = v_{i,j}$, $(i, j)^d = w_{i,j}$. For a strictly recombining lattice we require that

$$(i, j)^{u,d} = (i, j)^{m,m} = (i, j)^{d,u}, \tag{14.5}$$

$$(i, j)^{m,u} = (i, j)^{u,m}, (i, j)^{m,d} = (i, j)^{d,m}. \tag{14.6}$$

This is illustrated in Figure 14.3. This is a very strong set of conditions that puts severe restrictions upon the process. For instance, the lattice may not converge to a continuous

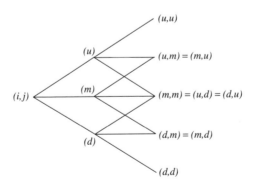

Figure 14.3 A strictly recombining lattice

---

[3] For instance, that N_j grows linearly in j.

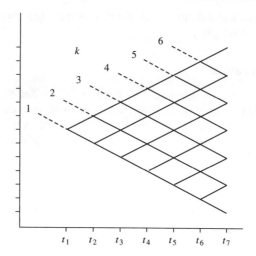

Figure 14.4   A regular standard binomial lattice

process whose volatility depends on the value of the state variable. For recombining lattices in the weaker sense it may be possible to allow level dependent volatilities.

Standard binomial branching   In a standard binomial lattice each node branches to two adjacent nodes at the next time, $\mathcal{B}_{i,j} = \{(k+1, j+1),(k, j+1)\}$, for all (i, j), for some k. A regular standard binomial lattice has $N_j = j$ and $\mathcal{B}_{i,j} = \{(i+1, j+1),(i, j+1)\}$, leading to the branching shown in Figure 14.4. This lattice is strictly recombining. The BDT lattice is of this type.

Standard trinomial branching   In a standard trinomial lattice the branching is

$$\mathcal{B}_{i,j} = \{(n_{i,j}+1, j+1), (n_{i,j}, j+1), (n_{i,j}-1, j+1)\}, \qquad (14.7)$$

for some $n_{i,j}$ so that

$$p_{n_{i,j}+1,j+1;i,j} = p^u \geq 0, \qquad (14.8)$$

$$p_{n_{i,j},j+1;i,j} = p^m \geq 0, \qquad (14.9)$$

$$p_{n_{i,j}-1,j+1;i,j} = p^d \geq 0, \qquad (14.10)$$

$$p_{k,j+1;i,j} = 0, \text{ otherwise.} \qquad (14.11)$$

A regular standard trinomial lattice has $n_{i,j} = i + 1$. This branching is illustrated in Figure 14.5.

It is strictly recombining. An example is the Schmidt lattice. The Hull and White lattice has a regular standard trinomial lattice with modified branching at the top and bottom. It is shown in Figure 14.6.

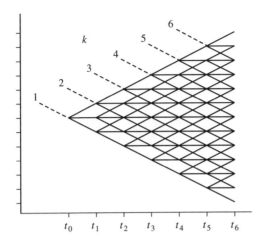

Figure 14.5   A regular standard trinomial lattice

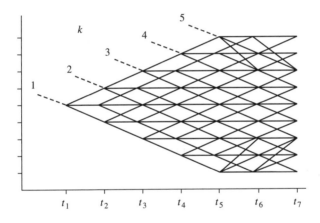

Figure 14.6   A modified regular standard trinomial lattice

Non-recombining Lattices

A completely non-recombining lattice has the property that $\mathcal{B}_{i,j} \cap \mathcal{B}_{l,j} = \emptyset$, $i \neq l$. For a lattice of order k, $N_j = k^{j-1}$ is increasing exponentially. An example of a completely non-recombining lattice is shown in Figure 14.7.

Lattices for non-Markovian processes are non-recombining (see Sections 14.7).

Regular Lattices

Lattices are often regular, in that for each j

$$\{\underline{X}_{i,j}\} \subseteq \{\underline{X}_{i,j+1}\} \subseteq \{\underline{X}_{i,N}\} \equiv \{\underline{X}_i\}, \tag{14.12}$$

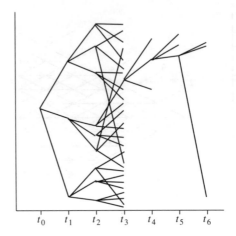

Figure 14.7 A completely non-recombining lattice with sample branching

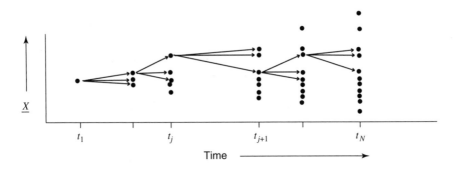

Figure 14.8 Regular trinomial branching

so that the set of possible values taken by $\underline{X}$ is augmented at each time step. In a regular grid $\underline{X}$ takes the same set of possible values at each time j:

$$\{\underline{X}_{i,j}\} = \{\underline{X}_{i,j+1}\} = \{\underline{X}_{i,N}\} \equiv \{\underline{X}_i\}. \tag{14.13}$$

Figure 14.8 illustrates a regular trinomial lattice, showing a sample branching. Figure 14.9 shows part of a regular trinomial grid. An explicit finite difference method can be regarded as having a grid of this sort. An implicit grid has branching of order $N_j \equiv N$. Each node effectively branches to all nodes on the next layer.

14.1.3 Pricing on a Lattice

Pricing on a lattice is straightforward. At its heart, pricing is just a discrete form of expected discounted payoff. The discrete process is assumed to be under the EMM. We describe first the ordinary pricing method. It turns out to be a considerable simplification,

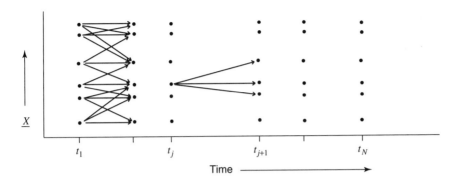

Figure 14.9   A regular trinomial grid

and the key for calibration on a lattice, if one first constructs prices of Arrow–Debreu securities. A useful method is forward induction, due to Jamshidian (91) [309].

We describe pricing on a simple lattice, but analogous results hold on more general lattices.

Derivative Securities

A derivative is defined by a payoff function $H : \mathcal{S} \times \mathbb{R} \to \mathbb{R}$, where the payoff at node (i, j) is $H\left(\underline{X}_{i,j}, t_j\right)$. We shall write this as $H_{i,j}$. We treat derivatives as if their payoffs were of American type. For a European option $H_{i,j}$ is undefined unless $j = M$.

The payoff to a pure discount bond maturing at time t_M is 1 at each node (i, M). The payoff to a caplet at a terminal node is

$$H_{i,M} = \exp(-r_{i,M}(\tau)\tau) \max(l_{i,M}(\tau) - l_X, 0), \tag{14.14}$$

where $l_{i,M}(\tau)$ is the Libor rate of tenor τ at node (i, M), $r_{i,M}(\tau)$ is the τ to maturity spot rate, and l_X is the exercise rate. Both $l_{i,M}(\tau)$ and $r_{i,M}(\tau)$ must be computable from a knowledge of the value of the state variable, $\underline{X}_{i,M}$, and the spot rate function, r.

Expected Discounted Payoffs

At a terminal node the value $V_{i,M}$ of the instrument equals its payoff, $V_{i,M} = H_{i,M}$. The backwards induction method proceeds, just like a finite difference method, by sweeping backwards through the tree calculating expected discounted payoffs as it goes. Suppose that the value of an instrument is known for all nodes at times $t_k > t_j$. For a node at time t_j the value $V_{k,l}$ of the instrument is known for all successor nodes $(k, l) \in \mathcal{B}_{i,j}$. Then set

$$V_{i,j} = \exp(-r_{i,j}(\Delta_j)\Delta_j) \sum_{(k,l) \in \mathcal{B}_{i,j}} p_{k,l;i,j} V_{k,l}. \tag{14.15}$$

This is just the expected discounted payoff for a discrete process.

American Options

As long as the payoff when exercised, $H_{i,j}$, can be computed at each node (i, j) the value of an American style option can be computed. Suppose we have values $V_{l,k}$ for the option at all nodes in $\mathcal{N}_k$, $k \geq j + 1$. At a node $(i, j) \in \mathcal{N}_j$ set

$$V_{i,j}^u = \exp(-r_{i,j}(\Delta_j)\Delta_j) \sum_{(k,l) \in \mathcal{B}_{i,j}} p_{k,l;i,j} V_{k,l}. \tag{14.16}$$

This is the value at node (i, j) of the option if unexercised there. Set

$$V_{i,j} = \max\{V_{i,j}^u, H_{i,j}\}, \tag{14.17}$$

the maximum of the exercised and unexercised values. This is the value of the option at (i, j) if the option is exercised optimally.

Note that if there is an exact solution for the European version of an American option, at the very last time step in a lattice iteration the exact price can be used instead of the lattice price. Broadie and Detemple (96) [98] report much smoother convergence as the number of time steps increases (in an equity example). This means that it may be possible to apply the Richardson extrapolation.

In the Richardson extrapolation a lattice is constructed with $2m$ time steps up to time T. Option values are simultaneously found for the full $2m$ steps, V_{2m}, and also for the lattice with only m steps (each twice as large), V_m. The Richardson extrapolated option value is $V = 2V_{2m} - V_m$. When applicable, when V_{2m} converges smoothly enough to its asymptotic value, Richardson extrapolation can give more accurate solutions at relatively little cost. Richardson extrapolation is examined in depth in Marchuk and Shaidurov (83) [380].

Another key technique can be used if option payoffs are piecewise polynomial. Ordinary call and put payoffs are of this type. One arranges, if possible, for nodes of the lattice to occur at values of the state variables where the second derivative of the payoff is not defined. For instance, if pricing a caplet on a one-dimensional tree for the short rate r_t, one constructs the lattice so that the exercise rate r_X is at a node on the lattice, $r_X = r_{i,m}$ for some terminal node (i, m). When this is possible much smoother, faster convergence can be achieved.

Recently Figlewski and Gao (99) [216] have described a modified lattice which reduces the pricing error when payoffs are non-linear. Their adaptive mesh scheme has a much finer mesh for a few time steps just prior to maturity. Figlewski and Gao report much faster convergence for both European and American options.

Exploiting Exact Solutions

Some particularly tractable models have exact solutions for certain instruments, such as pure discount bonds or bond options. Where available these exact solutions can be exploited. For instance, to compute the value of a bond option on a lattice it is usually necessary to take the lattice out to the maturity of the underlying bond. The value of the bond at the maturity date of the option can then be found. If bond prices can be calculated explicitly, then the value of the underlying can be found at the maturity date of the option without the need to take the lattice out any farther.

Pruning the Lattice

Many lattice methods produce a grid that over-samples the tails of the distribution of its state variables. For instance, with a reasonable time step, the Hull and White lattice extends out many standard deviations from the mean of the short rate. Instead of computing the entire lattice, the lattice can be truncated at some upper and lower bounds on the values of its state variables. The contribution to the payoff represented by the tails is (for reasonable options) negligible. This technique is discussed in Gandhi and Hunt (97) [241].

Brownian Bridge Discount Factors

Gandhi and Hunt (97) [241] also describe a Brownian bridge technique that can sometimes be used to obtain very fast accurate prices. It can be implemented for the Hull and White lattice and McCarthy and Webber (99) [386] use it in their non-recombining scheme.

A conventional lattice scheme, as defined in Section 14.1.1, discounts back at each node using an approximation to the spot interest rate at that node. Gandhi and Hunt point out that since the level of the spot rate is known not only at the start of a branch, but also at the end of a branch, it is possible to use a Brownian bridge technique to get exact discount factors. Given the known option values $V_{t+\Delta t}$ at time $t + \Delta t$, the option value V_t at time t is

$$V_t = \mathbb{E}\left[V_{t+\Delta t}\exp\left(-\int_t^{t+\Delta t} r_s ds\right) \mid r_t\right] \tag{14.18}$$

$$= \mathbb{E}\left[V_{t+\Delta t}\mathbb{E}\left[\exp\left(-\int_t^{t+\Delta t} r_s ds\right) \mid r_t, r_{t+\Delta t}\right] \mid r_t\right]. \tag{14.19}$$

In the extended Vasicek model Gandhi and Hunt solve this expression to give

$$V_t = \alpha_{t,t+\Delta t}e^{-\beta_{t,t+\Delta t}r_t}\mathbb{E}[V_{t+\Delta t}e^{-\gamma_{t,t+\Delta t}r_{t+\Delta t}} \mid r_t] \tag{14.20}$$

for computable values $\alpha_{t,t+\Delta t}$, $\beta_{t,t+\Delta t}$ and $\gamma_{t,t+\Delta t}$. On a lattice this becomes

$$V_{i,j} = \alpha_{t,t+\Delta t}e^{-\beta_{t,t+\Delta t}r_{i,j}} \sum_{(k,l)\in\mathcal{B}_{i,j}} p_{k,l;i,j}e^{-\gamma_{t,t+\Delta t}r_{k,l}} V_{k,l}. \tag{14.21}$$

Each branch from a node now has its own discount factor, conditional on the level of rate at the successor node.

If the conditional discount factors can be computed, as in the extended Vasicek model, this technique is immensely powerful. Considerable improvements can be made if only an approximation to the true conditional discount factors can be found.

Arrow–Debreu Securities

Arrow–Debreu securities are extremely important both conceptually and in practical implementations of lattice methods. $AD_{i,j}$ is the security with payoff 1 in state (i, j), and 0 elsewhere. We use the notation

$$Q_{i,j} = \text{value of } AD_{i,j} \text{ in state } (1, 1), \tag{14.22}$$

$$Q_{i,j;k,l} = \text{value of } AD_{i,j} \text{ in state } (k, l), \quad \text{for } l \le j. \tag{14.23}$$

Obviously $Q_{i,j} = Q_{i,j;1,1}$ and

$$Q_{i,j;k,l} = \begin{cases} 1 & \text{when } (k, l) = (i, j), \\ 0 & \text{when } l = j, k \ne i. \end{cases} \tag{14.24}$$

If one can generate $Q_{i,j;k,l}$, then it is possible to use the lattice to price anything. Write $\delta_{i,j}(k)$ for the value in state (i, j) of a pure discount bond maturing at time t_{j+k}. The value in state $(1, 1)$ of the pure discount bond maturing at time t_j is $\delta_{1,1}(j - 1) = \Sigma_{i \in \mathcal{N}_j} Q_{i,j}$. Conditional on being in state (k, l), $l < j$, the value of the bond is $\delta_{k,l}(j - l) = \Sigma_{i \in \mathcal{N}_j} Q_{i,j;k,l}$. The value in state $(1, 1)$ of a bond option maturing at time t_j on a pure discount bond maturing at time t_n, $n > j$, with exercise price X is

$$c_{1,1}(t_j, t_n) = \sum_{i \in \mathcal{N}_j} Q_{i,j} \max \left(\sum_{m \in \mathcal{N}_n} Q_{m,n;i,j} - X, 0 \right). \tag{14.25}$$

Arrow–Debreu securities can be valued as expected discounted payoffs in the usual way. $H_{i,M} = 1_{i,M}$ has value 1 in state (i, M) and 0 elsewhere. We apply (14.15) to find $Q_{i,j} = Q_{i,j;1,1}$ iteratively using

$$Q_{i,j;k,l} = \exp(-r_{k,l}(\Delta_l)\Delta_l) \sum_{(m,n) \in \mathcal{B}_{k,l}} p_{m,n;k,l} Q_{i,j;m,n}. \tag{14.26}$$

This is the backwards induction method for pricing Arrow–Debreu securities.

Forward Induction

An alternative to backwards induction is the forward induction method. It is an application of the law of iterated expectation; for all times $t_1 < t_2 < t_3$ and processes X_t we have

$$\mathbb{E}\left[X_{t_3} \mid \mathcal{F}_{t_1}\right] = \mathbb{E}\left[\mathbb{E}\left[X_{t_3} \mid \mathcal{F}_{t_2}\right] \mid \mathcal{F}_{t_1}\right]. \tag{14.27}$$

For a payoff function H_T and price kernel $Z(t, T)$, $Z(t, T) = \exp\left(-\int_t^T r_s ds\right)$ say, we take $X_T = H_T Z(t, T)$ so that the value V_{t_1} at time t_1 of a derivative with payoff H_{t_3} at time t_3 is

$$V_{t_1} = \mathbb{E}\left[H_{t_3} Z(t_1, t_3) \mid \mathcal{F}_{t_1}\right] = \mathbb{E}\left[\mathbb{E}\left[H_{t_3} Z(t_2, t_3) \mid \mathcal{F}_{t_2}\right] \mid \mathcal{F}_{t_1}\right]. \tag{14.28}$$

On a lattice, for times $t_1 < t_j < t_{j+1}$ and payoff $H_{i,j+1} = 1_{i,j+1}$ at time t_{j+1}, we have

$$Q_{i,j+1} = \mathbb{E}\left[1_{i,j+1} Z(t_1, t_{j+1}) \mid \mathcal{F}_{t_1}\right] = \mathbb{E}\left[\mathbb{E}\left[1_{i,j+1} Z(t_j, t_{j+1}) \mid \mathcal{F}_{t_j}\right] \mid \mathcal{F}_{t_1}\right]. \tag{14.29}$$

But on a lattice the information set at time t_j is just the state (k, j) at time t_j so

$$\mathbb{E}\left[1_{i,j+1}Z\left(t_j, t_{j+1}\right) \mid \mathcal{F}_{t_j}\right] = \exp\left(-r_{k,j}\left(\Delta_j\right)\Delta_j\right) p_{i,j+1;k,j}, \qquad (14.30)$$

conditional on being in state $(k, j) \in \mathcal{C}_{i,j+1}$ at time t_j, and

$$Q_{i,j+1} = \sum_{(k,j)\in\mathcal{C}_{i,j+1}\subseteq\mathcal{N}_j} \exp\left(-r_{k,j}(\Delta_j)\Delta_j\right) p_{i,j+1;k,j}Q_{k,j}. \qquad (14.31)$$

This expression is the forward induction relationship. A knowledge of Arrow–Debreu security prices for time t_j enables us to determine them for time t_{j+1}. It is possible to sweep forward through the lattice calculating Arrow–Debreu security one layer at a time, starting from $Q_{1,1} = 1$.

Finding a set of Arrow–Debreu security prices moving once through the lattice using (14.31) is far more efficient than repeatedly using (14.26). However, (14.26) does compute conditional values $Q_{i,j;k,l}$ for each payoff $H_{i,j} = 1_{i,j}$. We can also get the same conditional values from forward induction:

$$Q_{i,j+1;k,l} = \mathbb{E}\left[1_{i,j+1}Z\left(t_l, t_{j+1}\right) \mid \mathcal{F}_{t_l}\right] = \mathbb{E}\left[\mathbb{E}\left[1_{i,j+1}Z\left(t_j, t_{j+1}\right) \mid \mathcal{F}_{t_j}\right] \mid \mathcal{F}_{t_l}\right], \qquad (14.32)$$

leading to

$$Q_{i,j+1;k,l} = \sum_{(m,n)\in\mathcal{C}_{i,j+1}\subseteq\mathcal{N}_j} \exp\left(-r_{m,n}\left(\Delta_j\right)\Delta_j\right) p_{i,j+1;m,n}Q_{m,n;k,l}, \qquad (14.33)$$

with $Q_{i,j+1;i,j+1} = 1$.

Convergence in a Lattice Method

A lattice method constructs a family of lattices that converges to some continuous time limit. Often one is given a continuous-time process and wants to construct a set of lattices that converges to it. For example, suppose we are given a continuous process $dr_t = \mu(r_t, t)dt + \sigma(r_t, t)dz_t$ for the short rate, and we have constructed a standard trinomial lattice with the short rate as the state variable. For a given value $r_{i,j}$ of the short rate we may be able to compute

$$E_{i,j} = \mathbb{E}\left[r_{t_{j+1}} - r_{t_j} \mid r_{t_j} = r_{i,j}\right], \qquad (14.34)$$

$$V_{i,j} = \text{var}\left[r_{t_{j+1}} - r_{t_j} \mid r_{t_j} = r_{i,j}\right]. \qquad (14.35)$$

If explicit formulae are unavailable one may approximate for $E_{i,j}$ and $V_{i,j}$. For instance, when Δ_t is small $E_{i,j}$ and $V_{i,j}$ can be found to order Δ_t directly from the process for r_t:

$$E_{i,j} = \mu\left(r_{i,j}, t_j\right)\Delta_t, \qquad (14.36)$$

$$V_{i,j} = \sigma^2\left(r_{i,j}, t_j\right)\Delta_t. \qquad (14.37)$$

On the trinomial lattice we have

$$\mathbb{E}\left[\underline{r}_{j+1} - \underline{r}_j \mid \underline{r}_j = r_{i,j}\right] = \sum_{(k,l)\in\mathcal{B}_{i,j}} p_{k,l;i,j}\left(r_{k,l} - r_{i,j}\right) \qquad (14.38)$$

$$\equiv p^u\Delta_r^u + p^m\Delta_r^m + p^d\Delta_r^d \qquad (14.39)$$

(where p^u, p^m and p^d, and Δ^u_r, Δ^m_r and Δ^d_r, the up, middle and down probabilities and jump sizes, are defined in the obvious way) and

$$\text{var}\left[\underline{r}_{j+1} - \underline{r}_j \mid \underline{r}_j = r_{i,j}\right] = \mathbb{E}\left[\left(\underline{r}_{j+1} - \underline{r}_j\right)^2 \mid \underline{r}_j = r_{i,j}\right]$$

$$- \mathbb{E}^2\left[\underline{r}_{j+1} - \underline{r}_j \mid \underline{r}_j = r_{i,j}\right] \qquad (14.40)$$

$$= p^u\left(\Delta^u_r\right)^2 + p^m\left(\Delta^m_r\right)^2 + p^d\left(\Delta^d_r\right)^2$$

$$- \left(p^u\Delta^u_r + p^m\Delta^m_r + p^d\Delta^d_r\right)^2. \qquad (14.41)$$

The lattice is constructed so that

$$\mathbb{E}\left[\underline{r}_{j+1} - \underline{r}_j \mid \underline{r}_j = r_{i,j}\right] = E_{i,j}, \qquad (14.42)$$

$$\text{var}\left[\underline{r}_{j+1} - \underline{r}_j \mid \underline{r}_j = r_{i,j}\right] = V_{i,j}. \qquad (14.43)$$

If the lattice has been sensibly constructed one expects p^u, p^m, $p^d > 0$ and $\underline{r}_j \to r_t$ as $\Delta_t \to 0$.

Using Actual Moments

In the previous section $E_{i,j}$ and $V_{i,j}$ were approximated by moments derived from a Euler discretisation of the underlying state variables. This is quick, easy, universally applicable, and crude. If the true conditional moments of the continuous-time process for the underlying state variables is known, then these should be used instead of the Euler approximations. They are known for tractable processes such as extended Vasicek and Cox, Ingersoll and Ross (CIR).

Scott (96) [484], in the context of a Monte Carlo simulation, uses exact moments for a multifactor CIR process, and a sophisticated Brownian bridge method to simulate discount factors.

14.2 ISSUES IN CONSTRUCTING A LATTICE

We discuss some general issues in constructing lattices, including evolving a vector of spot rates, multiple factors, a change of variable technique, and computing hedge ratios.

14.2.1 Evolving a Vector

We may want to evolve a vector on a lattice, for example a term structure. The BDT lattice evolves $r_t(T_i)$, $i = 1, \ldots, N$, calibrating to an initial term structure of volatility. Lattice implementations of HJM models may evolve $f_t(T_i)$ (or $r_t(T_i)$), $i = 1, \ldots, N$.

It is just as easy to evolve a vector or a continuous function as it is to evolve a single state variable. The difficulty is to ensure convergence to an underlying continuous-time model.

In a continuous term structure model it is always possible to compute, if only numerically, the entire yield curve at each state of the model. The same is true on a lattice. We may as well suppose that we evolve an entire term structure through the lattice, not just the state variable. In practice the term structure is likely to be represented as a vector $\{r_{i,j}(\tau_k)\}_{k=0,\ldots,K_j}$, $\tau_k = k\Delta_j$, where $K_j\Delta_j$ is the maximum time to maturity for spot rates at time t_j.[4] Given spot rates $r_{i,j}(\tau_k)$ one has conditional discount factors

$$\delta_{i,j}(k) = \exp(-r_{i,j}(\tau_k)\tau_k), \quad k = 1, \ldots, K_j, \tag{14.44}$$

as before. For completeness we can define $\delta_{i,j}(0) = 1$.

In addition to the forward and backward induction equations there is now an additional term structure consistency condition

$$\delta_{i,j}(k) = \delta_{i,j}(1) \sum_{(l,j+1)\in\mathcal{B}_{i,j}} p_{l,j+1;i,j}\delta_{l,j+1}(k-1), \quad k = 2, \ldots, K_j. \tag{14.45}$$

This expresses the conditional value of the pure discount bond maturing at time $t_j + \tau_k$ as its expected discounted value from time t_{j+1}. For a given K_j, only $K_j - 1$ values at time t_{j+1} are affected. Spot rates of maturity K_j at time t_{j+1} can in principle be chosen arbitrarily.[5]

Suppose that we have constructed a lattice out to a maximum time t_M and that we need no discount factors for times beyond t_M. At node $(1, 1)$ we require $K_1 = M$, and at subsequent times we have $K_j = M + 1 - j$.

Suppose that we have evolved a term structure forward through the lattice up to time t_j. At time t_{j+1} there are $N_{j+1}(K_j - 1)$ unknown spot rates to find. At each node (i, j), equation (14.45) is a set of $K_j - 1$ conditions, giving a total of $N_j(K_j - 1)$ relationships. There are $(N_{j+1} - N_j)(K_j - 1)$ degrees of freedom remaining.

In a binomial lattice $N_{j+1} - N_j = 1$, so there is only one degree of freedom for each maturity time k. In the BDT model this degree of freedom is used to specify a common spot rate volatility (see below).

In a trinomial lattice $N_{j+1} - N_j = 2$, so there are two degrees of freedom for each maturity time k. The trinomial Hull and White lattice uses a certain parameter set to specify the initial term structure. These parameters are re-used to generate term structures at subsequent nodes (see Section 14.3.1).

A quartomial lattice, of order four, has $N_{j+1} - N_j = 3$. At each time step it is theoretically possible to incorporate three separate innovations to the term structure.

Lattice methods place very strong constraints on the evolution allowed for term structures in the model, but seem to have the potential to implement three-factor Markov HJM models.

14.2.2 Multiple Factors

Models with multiple factors can be implemented on lattices. Suppose the state space in an n-factor model is $\mathbb{R}^n$, so that $\underline{X} : \mathcal{N} \to \mathbb{R}^n$. It may be possible to decompose a

---

[4] Whether the short rate $r_{i,j}(0)$ is computed or not is a matter of convenience. It is not strictly required, although some lattice methods use it as an approximation to the spot rate $r_{i,j}(\Delta_j)$.

[5] The continuous-time analogy is Sommer's model described in Chapter 11.

lattice for $\underline{X} = (\underline{X}^1, \ldots, \underline{X}^n)' \in \mathbb{R}^n$ as a product of separate lattices for each $\underline{X}^i$. An n-factor model would require an n-dimensional lattice.

In principle these implementations are no different to the one-dimensional case. In practice they can be difficult to implement successfully: it can be awkward to correctly handle correlations between factors.

Multifactor lattice methods for general asset pricing have been proposed by Boyle (88) [84], Boyle, Evnine and Gibbs (89) [86], Madan, Milne and Shefrin (89) [374], Kamrad and Ritchken (91) [328], Chen (96) [126], Das (97) [155], Tang and Lange (99) [514], and McCarthy and Webber (99) [386].

Heath, Jarrow and Morton (90) [274] and Heath *et al.* (92) [276] propose a more parsimonious trinomial scheme for the two-factor version of the HJM whole yield curve model. It is described by Jarrow and Turnbull (96) [318], Clewlow and Strickland (98) [137] and McCarthy and Webber.

In the HJM lattice the branching from a point $(z_{1,t}, z_{2,t})$ is $(z_{1,t+\Delta t}, z_{2,t+\Delta t}) = (z_{1,t}, z_{2,t}) + s \cdot (a_i, b_i)$, $i = 1, 2, 3$, where the branching probabilities are given in Table 14.1 and $s = \sqrt{\Delta t}$. The tableau for this scheme is shown in Figure 14.10. It is an isosceles triangle. The scheme recombines for z_t.

A branching step in a simple two-dimensional product lattice is illustrated in Figure 14.11. The lattice is trinomial in each dimension. On each step the number of nodes is $N_j = (2j - 1)^2$. Each node $(i', j', j + 1)$ at time $j + 1$ has the product

Table 14.1 Branching probabilities: HJM scheme

i	(a_i, b_i)	Probability
1	$(1, 0)$,	0.5
2	$(-1, \sqrt{2})$,	0.25
3	$(-1, -\sqrt{2})$,	0.25

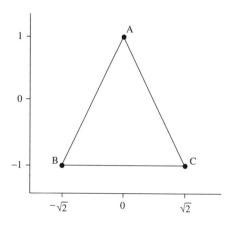

Figure 14.10 Branching for the HJM trinomial scheme

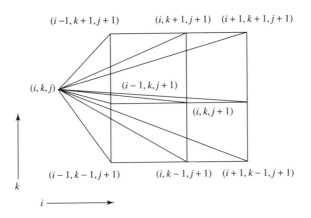

Figure 14.11   Two-dimensional branching

probability $p_{i',j';i,j} = p_{i';i}\,p_{j';j}$. This is an inefficient way of sampling a two-factor distribution.

A Recombining Tree for Poisson–Gaussian HJM Models

Das (97) [155] suggests a two-dimensional lattice method for Poisson–Gaussian HJM models with Markov volatilities and binomial jumps. The forward rate process for each maturity time is discretised as

$$f_{t+\Delta t}(T) = f_t(T) + \alpha_t(T)\Delta t + \sigma(T)\sqrt{\Delta t}\,\varepsilon_t + JN_t, \tag{14.46}$$

where $\varepsilon_t \sim N(0, 1)$, and

$$J = \begin{cases} \mu + \gamma, & \text{probability } \frac{1}{2}, \\ \mu - \gamma, & \text{probability } \frac{1}{2}, \end{cases} \tag{14.47}$$

$$N_t = \begin{cases} 1, & \text{probability } \underline{\lambda}\Delta t, \\ 0, & \text{probability } 1 - \underline{\lambda}\Delta t. \end{cases} \tag{14.48}$$

ε_t, J and N_t are assumed to be independent. We have a two-dimensional lattice, the product of two one-dimensional lattices.

The entire forward rate curve is evolved in the lattice. μ and γ determine the skewness and kurtosis of f. We write $\lambda = \underline{\lambda}\Delta t$. Branching in the ε_t plane is shown in Figure 14.12 and in the JN_t plane in Figure 14.13. With a Gaussian volatility $\sigma(T)$ the lattices recombine in each plane separately. In the JN_t plane it is not strictly recombining. There are $\frac{1}{2}(k + 1)(k + 2)$ nodes at time step k. At each node in the tree there are six branches, as in Figure 14.14.

Under the EMM the function $\alpha_t(T)$ is determined by $\sigma(T)$, and the processes for J and N_t, as in Chapter 10. Das states that on the lattice there are fast recursive procedures to calculate $\alpha_t(T)$.

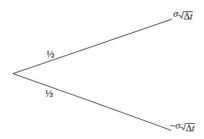

Figure 14.12   Branching in the ε_t plane

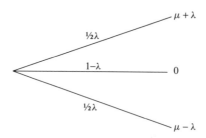

Figure 14.13   Branching in the JN_t plane

$$f_{t+\Delta t}(T) = f_t(T) + \alpha_t(T)\,\Delta t + \text{sum of column and row labels}$$

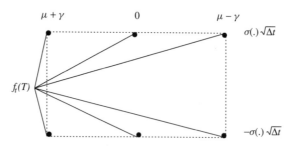

Figure 14.14   Combined branching

An Alternative Two-factor Branching

An alternative to the product branching of Figure 14.11 is the hexagonal branching of Figure 14.15, described by McCarthy and Webber (99) [386]. The probability of branching to each node is given alongside it. The figure illustrates branching for two uncorrelated processes, $dx = \sigma_x dz_{x,t}$ and $dy = \sigma_y dz_{y,t}$, but is easily adapted to incorporate correlations. There are $3j(j-1)+1$ nodes at time t_j.

This form of recombining branching has the advantage that it more closely samples the joint distribution of x and y. The low probability corners of the ordinary product branching are not sampled.

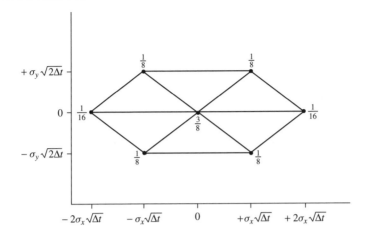

Figure 14.15   Hexagonal branching

One hexagonal step can be constructed as a composition of two trinomial steps (with different trinomial branching at each alternate step) but in a recombining model it is better to construct the hex-step in one go.

A Three-factor Icosahedral Branching

McCarthy and Webber (99) [386] describe a recombining three-dimensional lattice based on an oblate icosahedron. They define a measure of the effectiveness of a lattice scheme. By their measure the general icosahedral scheme is significantly more efficient than, for instance, a crude three-factor product scheme.

14.2.3   A Change of Variable

Suppose that

$$\mathrm{d}r_t = \mu(r_t, t)\mathrm{d}t + \sigma(r_t, t)\mathrm{d}z_t. \tag{14.49}$$

r_t will not have a strictly recombining lattice method if $\sigma(r_t, t)$ depends on r_t. If $\sigma(r_t, t)$ does depend on r_t it is possible to change variables so that the lattice evolves a variable with constant volatility. This is explored in detail by Nelson and Ramaswamy (90) [410]. Set

$$y(r, t) = \int^r \frac{1}{\sigma(s, t)}\mathrm{d}s, \tag{14.50}$$

then y_t has the process

$$\mathrm{d}y_t = \left(\frac{\mu(r_t, t)}{\sigma(r_t, t)} - \frac{1}{2}\frac{\partial\sigma(r, t)}{\partial r}\bigg|_{r_t} - \int_0^{r_t} \frac{\partial\sigma(s, t)}{\partial t}\frac{1}{\sigma^2(s, t)}\mathrm{d}s \right)\mathrm{d}t + \mathrm{d}z_t. \tag{14.51}$$

This has constant unit variance and a standard recombining lattice can be constructed for y_t. For example, suppose that r_t is a positive valued CIR process, $dr_t = \alpha(\mu - r_t)dt + \sigma\sqrt{r_t}\,dz_t$. Then $y_t = (2/\sigma)\sqrt{r_t}$ and

$$dy_t = \frac{\alpha}{2y_t}\left(\frac{4\alpha\mu - 2}{\alpha\sigma^2} - y_t^2\right)dt + dz_t. \tag{14.52}$$

y_t is mean reverting and positive, since r_t is, and $\sigma(r_t)$ is monotonic in r_t, although this may not be obvious from (14.52) alone.

The transformation (14.50) can be very effective, and 'works' for the standard volatility functions normally used in interest rate processes. Care must be taken, however, if r_t is bounded or if $\sigma(r_t, t)$ has zeros or becomes arbitrarily close to zero. For example, for a CKLS volatility function, $\sigma(r_t, t) = \sigma r_t^\gamma$ with $\gamma > 1$, then $y_t = (1/\sigma(1 - \gamma))r_t^{1-\gamma}$ becomes unbounded as $r_t \to 0$. See Nelson and Ramaswarmy for further details. If y_t is not mean reverting then some lattice methods, such as the Hull and White lattice, will fail.

14.2.4 Computing Hedge Ratios

Hedge ratios may be found very easily. Suppose that $S = \mathbb{R}$. One method is to approximate deltas and gammas at time t_1 by those at time t_2 or time t_3. As $\Delta_t \to 0$ these approximations tend to the true continuous-time values at time t_1. Let $V_{i,j}$ be the value of the derivative at node (i, j). The approximations for the trinomial and binomial lattices are shown in Tables 14.2 and 14.3. These equations come from a quadratic approximation. When the spacing in $\underline{X}$ is constant they reduce to the usual central difference approximations to the first and second derivatives.

Alternatively, a faster convergence is obtained by taking the lattice back one step and starting it off from time $t_0 = t_1 - \Delta_t$ for a trinomial lattice, or from time $t_{-1} = t_1 - 2\Delta_t$

Table 14.2 Hedge ratio approximations in a trinomial lattice

Trinomial

$$\frac{\partial V}{\partial \underline{X}} = \frac{V_{1,2}(\underline{X}_{2,2} - \underline{X}_{3,2})}{(\underline{X}_{1,2} - \underline{X}_{3,2})\,(\underline{X}_{1,2} - \underline{X}_{2,2})} + \frac{V_{2,2}(2\underline{X}_{2,2} - \underline{X}_{1,2} - \underline{X}_{3,2})}{(\underline{X}_{2,2} - \underline{X}_{3,2})(\underline{X}_{2,2} - \underline{X}_{1,2})} + \frac{V_{3,2}(\underline{X}_{2,2} - \underline{X}_{1,2})}{(\underline{X}_{3,2} - \underline{X}_{1,2})(\underline{X}_{3,2} - \underline{X}_{2,2})}$$

$$\frac{\partial^2 V}{\partial \underline{X}^2} = \frac{2V_{1,2}}{(\underline{X}_{1,2} - \underline{X}_{3,2})(\underline{X}_{1,2} - \underline{X}_{2,2})} + \frac{2V_{2,2}}{(\underline{X}_{2,2} - \underline{X}_{3,2})(\underline{X}_{2,2} - \underline{X}_{1,2})} + \frac{2V_{3,2}}{(\underline{X}_{3,2} - \underline{X}_{1,2})(\underline{X}_{3,2} - \underline{X}_{2,2})}$$

Table 14.3 Hedge ratio approximations in a binomial lattice

Binomial

$$\frac{\partial V}{\partial \underline{X}} = \frac{V_{2,2} - V_{1,2}}{\underline{X}_{2,2} - \underline{X}_{1,2}}$$

$$\frac{\partial^2 V}{\partial \underline{X}^2} = \frac{2V_{1,3}}{(\underline{X}_{1,3} - \underline{X}_{3,3})(\underline{X}_{1,3} - \underline{X}_{2,3})} + \frac{2V_{2,3}}{(\underline{X}_{2,3} - \underline{X}_{3,3})(\underline{X}_{2,3} - \underline{X}_{1,3})} + \frac{2V_{3,2}}{(\underline{X}_{3,3} - \underline{X}_{1,3})(\underline{X}_{3,3} - \underline{X}_{2,3})}$$

for a binomial lattice. The approximations in Tables 14.2 and 14.3 can then be applied directly to time t_1. It is usually possible to arrange that $r_{2,1}$ has a value equal to today's spot rate.

14.3 EXAMPLES OF LATTICE METHODS

We present the lattices for four methods: the Hull and White lattice, the BDT lattice, the Schmidt lattice, and the Li, Ritchken and Sankarasubramanian lattice. Hull and White and BDT are the two most important interest rate model implementations currently in use. They are tractable and quick, but lack the flexibility for more sophisticated applications. They are industry bread and butter.

14.3.1 The Hull and White Lattice

The Hull and White (94) [297] lattice method is a lattice implementation of the extended Vasicek model. The short rate process is

$$dr_t = (\theta(t) - ar_t)dt + \sigma dz_t \tag{14.53}$$

under the EMM. Although analytic solutions are available for some simple instruments, in general numerical solutions are needed. The Hull and White lattice is specified in Table 14.4. The lattice is the same as that in Figure 14.6. Branching at the top and bottom of the lattice is modified so that the probabilities remain positive there. $i_{\max}$ is determined by the need to have positive probabilities. A usual choice is the smallest integer greater than $(1 - \sqrt{2/3})/a\Delta_t \sim 0.184/a\Delta_t$ (the smallest integer for which the modified branching is possible). α_j is chosen so that the model can be calibrated to the initial term structure.

Since r is the identity we write $\underline{r}$ for $\underline{X}$. Probabilities are determined by the three relationships

$$p^u + p^m + p^d = 1, \tag{14.54}$$

$$\Delta_r^u p^u + \Delta_r^m p^m + (-\Delta_r^d)p^d = \mu_{i,j}\Delta_j = E_{i,j}, \tag{14.55}$$

$$(\Delta_r^u)^2 p^u + (\Delta_r^m)^2 p^m + (-\Delta_r^d)^2 p^d = \sigma_{i,j}^2 \Delta_j + (\mu_{i,j}\Delta_j)^2 = V_{i,j} + (E_{i,j})^2, \tag{14.56}$$

where $\mu_{i,j} = \theta_j - ar_{i,j}$, $\sigma_{i,j} = \sigma$ and the steps sizes are given in Table 14.5. The lattice is stable if all three probabilities are positive (Hull and White (90) [293]).

The lattice can be used whenever the short rate r_t is a function of a state variable x_t, $r_t = f(x_t)$, and the state variable process is extended Vasicek:

$$dx_t = (\theta(t) - ax_t)dt + \sigma dz_t. \tag{14.57}$$

This includes the Black, Derman and Toy process and the square Gaussian process.

Although we have taken care to specify the altered branching at the top and bottom of the lattice, in practice the lattice is likely to be pruned before the short rate reaches the level at which the altered branching takes place.

Table 14.4   The Hull and White lattice

$\left.\begin{array}{c} \mathcal{N} \\ \mathcal{A} \end{array}\right\}$ = modified regular standard trinomial lattice,

$S = \mathbb{R}$,

$X_{i,j} = \alpha_j + i\Delta_r$, with $i_{\max} \le i \le -i_{\max}$ and $\Delta_r = \sigma\sqrt{3\Delta_t}$,

$i = i_{\max}$
$p_{i,j}^u = \frac{7}{6} + \frac{1}{2}(a^2 i^2 \Delta_t^2 - 3ai\Delta_t)$
$p_{i,j}^m = -\frac{1}{3} - a^2 i^2 \Delta_t^2 + 2ai\Delta_t$
$p_{i,j}^d = \frac{1}{6} + \frac{1}{2}(a^2 i^2 \Delta_t^2 - ai\Delta_t)$
$i_{\max} < i < -i_{\max}$
$p_{i,j}^u = \frac{1}{6} + \frac{1}{2}(a^2 i^2 \Delta_t^2 - ai\Delta_t)$
$p_{i,j}^m = \frac{2}{3} - a^2 i^2 \Delta_t^2$
$p_{i,j}^d = \frac{1}{6} + \frac{1}{2}(a^2 i^2 \Delta_t^2 + ai\Delta_t)$
$i = -i_{\max}$
$p_{i,j}^u = \frac{1}{6} + \frac{1}{2}(a^2 i^2 \Delta_t^2 - ai\Delta_t)$
$p_{i,j}^m = -\frac{1}{3} - a^2 i^2 \Delta_t^2 + 2ai\Delta_t$
$p_{i,j}^d = \frac{7}{6} + \frac{1}{2}(a^2 i^2 \Delta_t^2 - 3ai\Delta_t)$

$t(i, j) = j\Delta_t$, for some Δ_t,

$r(\underline{X}_{i,j}) = \underline{X}_{ij}$, the identity.

Table 14.5   Step sizes in the Hull and White lattice

	$i = i_{\max}$	$i_{\max} < i < -i_{\max}$	$i = -i_{\max}$
$\Delta_r^u =$	0	$+\Delta_r$	$+2\Delta_r$
$\Delta_r^m =$	$-\Delta_r$	0	$+\Delta_r$
$\Delta_r^d =$	$-2\Delta_r$	$-\Delta_r$	0

14.3.2   The Black, Derman and Toy Lattice

We have seen that a lattice with binomial branching, in which the state variable is a vector of spot rates, is highly constrained. In evolving from time t_j to time t_{j+1}, once a term structure has been specified at just one node in $\mathcal{N}_{j+1}$, then all the other states are determined (for a given set of probabilities). The Black, Derman and Toy (90) [73] lattice chooses the set of term structures at time t_{j+1} by a volatility type condition.

We set

$$\sigma_{i,j+1}(k) = \frac{1}{2}\frac{r_{i+1,j+1}(k)}{r_{i,j+1}(k)} = \frac{1}{2}\frac{\ln \delta_{i+1,j+1}(k)}{\ln \delta_{i,j+1}(k)}. \tag{14.58}$$

Table 14.6 Specification of the BDT lattice

$\left.\begin{array}{c} \mathcal{N} \\ \mathcal{A} \end{array}\right\}$ = regular standard binomial branching,

$S = \mathbb{R}^M$,

$\underline{X}_{i,j} = (r_{i,j}(k))_{k=1,\ldots,M+1-j}$, found from $\delta_{1,1}(k)$ and $\sigma_2(k)$,

$(r_{i,j}(k), k$ greater than M, are undefined),

$p(a) = \frac{1}{2}$, for $a \in \mathcal{A}$,

$t(i, j) = j\Delta_t$,

$r(\underline{X}_{i,j}) = \pi_1(\underline{X}_{i,j}) = r_{i,j}(1)$.

The BDT condition is that

$$\sigma_{1,j+1}(k) = \cdots = \sigma_{N_j-1,j+1}(k) \equiv \sigma_{j+1}(k) \qquad (14.59)$$

are equal for every $i = 1, \ldots, N_{j+1} - 1$.

This gives $N_j(K_j - 1)$ conditions for $K_j - 1$ unknowns. It turns out, however, that this apparent over-specification is not mis-specified and that given a set $\sigma_2(k)$, $k = 1, \ldots, M - 1$, of initial volatilities, it is possible to consistently and uniquely determine $\sigma_j(k)$ for $j \geq 3$, $k = 1, \ldots, M + 1 - j$.

The BDT lattice requires as input data an initial term structure $\delta_{1,1}(k) = \exp(-r_{1,1}(k)\Delta_t)$, $k = 1, \ldots, M$, and the initial volatilities $\sigma_2(k)$. These completely determine the state variable throughout the lattice.

The specification of the BDT lattice is given in Table 14.6.

14.3.3 The Schmidt Lattice

This method was described in Schmidt (97) [479]. It is a general lattice for one-factor models. It contains as special cases the extended Vasicek model, the BDT log-r model, Black and Karasinski, and many others. The underlying state variable is a time-changed Wiener process

The method can be applied when the short rate is an explicit function of a Wiener process. If the SDE, $dr_t = \mu(t, r_t)dt + \sigma(t, r_t)dz_t$, has a solution, $r_t = G(t, z_t)$ for some known function G, then G is used as the spot rate function in the lattice specification. The solution may involve a time-changed Wiener process.

Solutions to SDEs

Given an SDE

$$dX_t = \mu(t, X_t)dt + \sigma(t, X_t)dz_t, \qquad (14.60)$$

one may be able to solve it as $X_t = G(t, z_t)$. For example, if X_t has a geometric Brownian motion,

$$dX_t = \mu X_t dt + \sigma X_t dz_t, \qquad (14.61)$$

then X_t is a function of z_t,

$$X_t = X_0 \exp \left(\left(\mu - \tfrac{1}{2}\sigma^2 \right) t + \sigma z_t \right). \tag{14.62}$$

However, if X_t has an absolute diffusion process,

$$dX_t = X_t dt + dz_t, \tag{14.63}$$

X_t can only be expressed as an integral with respect to z_t,

$$X_t = e^t X_0 + \int_0^t e^{t-s} dz_s. \tag{14.64}$$

The solution is path-dependent for this case.

In general an acceptable solution could involve a time change.

Time-changed Wiener Processes

For a Wiener process, z_t, and a strictly increasing deterministic function $h(t)$, set $w_t = z_{h(t)}$. w_t is a time-changed Brownian motion. The effect of a time change is to speed up or slow down the Wiener process. It is equivalent to having a time varying volatility. In fact one may show that

$$dw_t = \sqrt{\frac{\partial h}{\partial t}} \, d\tilde{z}_t, \tag{14.65}$$

for some Wiener process $\tilde{z}_t$. For example, suppose $h(t) = e^{at}$, with $a = 0.3$. A sample path for z_t is shown in Figure 14.16. Figure 14.17 shows the corresponding time-changed sample path for w_t. The process is clearly speeded up for $\sqrt{\partial h / \partial t} > 1$, that is, for $t > -(\ln a)/a \sim 4$, but runs more slowly for $t < 4$.

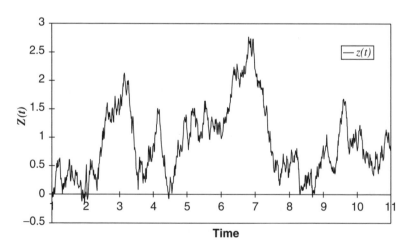

Figure 14.16   A Wiener sample path

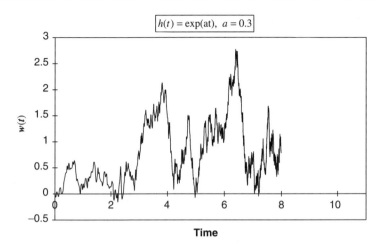

Figure 14.17 The time-changed sample path

Schmidt's Method

Suppose the short rate process can be written as

$$r_t = F(f(t) + g(t)z_{h(t)}),$$ (14.66)

where z_t is a Wiener process, h and F are strictly increasing functions, g is positive and F, f, g and h are all continuous. Schmidt's lattice is for processes of this sort. For example, in the extended Vasicek model the short rate process is

$$dr_t = (\theta_t - a_t r_t)dt + \sigma_t dz_t,$$ (14.67)

where θ_t, a_t and σ_t are all deterministic functions of time. The solution to this SDE is

$$r_t = F(f(t) + g(t)z_{h(t)}),$$ (14.68)

where

$$F(x) \equiv x,$$ (14.69)

$$g(t) = \exp\left(\int_0^t -a_s ds\right),$$ (14.70)

$$h(t) = \int_0^t \left(\frac{\sigma_s}{g(s)}\right)^2 ds,$$ (14.71)

$$f(t) = g(t)\left(r_0 + \int_0^t \frac{\theta_s}{g(s)} ds\right).$$ (14.72)

The Black and Karasinski model has $r_t = \exp(\xi_t)$, where $d\xi_t = (\theta_t - a_t\xi_t)dt + \sigma_t dz_t$. The solution is $r_t = F(f(t) + g(t)z_{h(t)})$ where

$$F(x) = \exp(x),$$ (14.73)

$$g(t) = \exp\left(-\int_0^t a_s ds\right),$$ (14.74)

$$h(t) = \int_0^t \left(\frac{\sigma_s}{g(s)}\right)^2 ds,$$ (14.75)

$$f(t) = g(t)\left(\ln r_0 + \int_0^t \frac{\theta_s}{g(s)} ds\right).$$ (14.76)

The continuous-time limit of the Black, Derman and Toy lattice is a restriction of Black and Karasinski with $a_t = -(\partial \sigma_t/\partial t)(1/\sigma_t)$, so $g(t) = \sigma_t/\sigma_0$ and $h(t) = t\sigma_0^2$. So for Black, Derman and Toy the short rate is $r_t = F(f(t) + \sigma_t z_t)$.

Other models that fit Schmidt's specification are square Gaussian models and the Sandmann and Sondermann (94) [471] model.

The Schmidt Lattice

Schmidt describes a general multinomial lattice. Here we describe the trinomial version. We suppose that the short rate process is

$$dr_t = \mu(t, r_t)dt + \sigma(t, r_t)dz_t$$ (14.77)

with solution of the form

$$r_t = F(f(t) + g(t)z_{h(t)}).$$ (14.78)

The method constructs a lattice for $w_t = z_{h(t)}$. The lattice is specified in Table 14.7.

The lattice is illustrated in Figure 14.18. We assume that both the space step Δ_w and the time step Δ_t are constant (it is not necessary to demand that Δ_t is fixed). It is necessary for the space step to satisfy the condition $h(t_j) - h(t_{j-1}) < (\Delta_w)^2$ to ensure

Table 14.7 Specification of the Schmidt lattice

$$\left.\begin{array}{c} \mathcal{N} \\ \mathcal{A} \end{array}\right\} = \text{regular standard trinomial lattice,}$$

$S = \mathbb{R},$

$\underline{X}_{i,j} = i\Delta_w$ for $-j \le i \le +j$ and $h(t_j) - h(t_{j-1}) < (\Delta_w)^2$,

$p_{i,j}^u = \dfrac{1}{2}\dfrac{h(t_{i+1}) - h(t_i)}{\Delta_w^2}$

$p_{i,j}^m = 1 - p_{i,j}^u - p_{i,j}^d$

$p_{i,j}^d = \dfrac{1}{2}\dfrac{h(t_{i+1}) - h(t_i)}{\Delta_w^2}$

$t(i, j) = j\Delta_t,$ for some $\Delta_t,$

$r(\underline{X}_{i,j}) = F(f(t) + g(t)\underline{X}_{i,j}).$

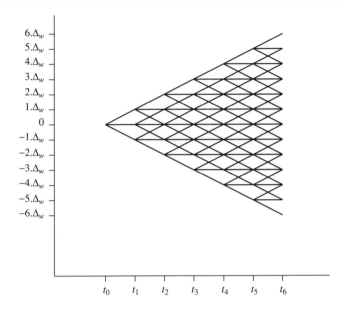

Figure 14.18   The lattice for w_t

that probabilities are positive. We assume that Δ_w and Δ_t have been chosen so that this condition is satisfied. For the lattice to converge to w_t at each branch we require

$$\mathbb{E}\left[w_{t_{j+1}}\right] = w_{t_j},$$ (14.79)

$$\operatorname{var}\left[w_{t_{j+1}}\right] = h(t_{j+1}) - h(t_j).$$ (14.80)

These conditions are satisfied by the probabilities given above.

An advantage of Schmidt's method is that the terminal distribution r_M is sampled much better that the regular sampling of the Hull and White lattice or the BDT lattice. However, it still over-samples the tail of the distribution of w_t.

14.3.4   The Li, Ritchken and Sankarasubramanian Lattice

Li, Ritchken and Sankarasubramanian (95a) [351], (95b) [352] describe a lattice approach for HJM models with one-factor Markovian volatilities. It is an approximate lattice method in that the lattice does not keep track of every state that the system could potentially reach.

The method is in fact very general. It assumes that there are two state variables y_t and ϕ_t with processes

$$\mathrm{d}y_t = m(y_t, \phi_t, t)\mathrm{d}t + \sigma \mathrm{d}z_t,$$ (14.81)

$$\mathrm{d}\phi_t = n(y_t, \phi_t, t)\mathrm{d}t,$$ (14.82)

for some functions m and n. Strictly, y_t is the sole state variable. In fact ϕ_t will be path-dependent and in practice it is not possible to store all its possible values at every node. Instead, ϕ_t is treated as if it were a second auxiliary state variable.

The method could be used when y_t is a transformed log-normal FX process and ϕ_t was an average (on the lattice) along the path of y_t. In the interest rate case Li, Ritchken and Sankarasubramanian apply the method when forward rates have a Ritchken and Sankarasubramanian volatility function.

Suppose we have a one-factor Markovian HJM model $df_t(T) = \alpha(t, T)dt + \sigma(r_t, t, T)dz_t$, where $\sigma(r, t, T,) = \sigma(r, t)e^{-\int_t^T k(s)ds}$. We saw in Chapter 8 that under the EMM the short rate process is

$$dr_t = \mu(t)dt + \sigma(r_t, t)dz_t, \tag{14.83}$$

$$d\phi_t = (\sigma^2(r_t, t) - 2k(t)\phi_t)dt, \tag{14.84}$$

where $\mu(t) = k(t)\psi_t + \phi_t + \partial f_0(t)/\partial t$ with $\psi_t = f_0(t) - r_t$ for an initial forward rate curve $f_0(t)$.

We change variables from r_t to y_t, $y_t(r) = \int_0^r (1/\sigma(s, t))ds$, where we assume that this is well defined and invertible so that we can transform back to obtain r_t from y_t. In terms of y_t and ϕ_t we have

$$dy_t = m(y_t, \phi_t, t)dt + dz_t, \tag{14.85}$$

$$d\phi_t = n(y_t, \phi_t, t)dt, \tag{14.86}$$

where

$$m(y_t, \phi_t, t) = \frac{\partial y}{\partial t}y_t + \mu(t)\frac{\partial y}{\partial r} + \frac{1}{2}\sigma^2(y_t, t)\frac{\partial^2 y}{\partial r^2}, \tag{14.87}$$

$$n(y_t, \phi_t, t) = \sigma^2(y_t, t) - 2k(t)\phi_t. \tag{14.88}$$

The two state variables are evolved in a binomial lattice for y_t. Because y_t has constant variance, the lattice is recombining. The method evolves y_t while keeping track of a set of possible values for ϕ_t at each node in the lattice.

Discretise time as $t_j = j\Delta t$, $j = 0, \ldots, M$, and space as $y_i = y_0 + i\sqrt{\Delta t}$, $i = -N, \ldots, N$. N must be chosen to be sufficiently large so that the process for y_t does not branch outside the range $[y_{-N}, y_N]$ up to time t_M. At each node (i, j) of the tree we find and store m values of ϕ_t. At node (i, j) these are labelled $\phi_{i,j;k}$, $k = 1, \ldots, m$. A completely specified state on the tree is a triplet $(y_i, t_j; \phi_{i,j;k})$, which is abbreviated to $(i, j; k)$. For each state $(i, j; k)$ we shall find a value of the derivative, $c(y_i, t_j; \phi_{i,j;k}) \equiv c_{i,j;k}$.

The procedure is the usual roll-forward–roll-backwards induction method, modified to keep track of the values of ϕ_t.

1. Roll forward through the tree to get the states $(i, j; k) = (y_i, t_j, \phi_{i,j;k})$, and the probabilities for each branch.
2. Calculate the payoff at maturity at each node $(i, M; k)$, $i = -N, \ldots, N$, $k = 1, \ldots, m$.
3. Roll backwards through the tree to find the option price at each node $(i, j; k)$.

As we roll forward through the tree, it is not possible to keep track of all the values of ϕ_t that could be generated. At any node (i, j), we would ideally calculate one value of $\phi_{i,j}$ for each path getting to (i, j). The number of possible paths explodes as j increases, so instead of storing all possible values that ϕ_t could take at node (i, j), only m representative values in between the maximum and minimum values at each node are stored. The m values, $\phi_{i,j;k}$, $k = 1, \ldots, m$, will be equally spaced between the maximum and minimum achievable values of ϕ_t at that node.

Evolving Forwards

The branching for y_t is standard binomial. For every state $(i, j; k)$ at node (i, j), there is a value of J such that y_i evolves to either y_J at node $(J, j + 1)$ or to y_{J-1} at node $(J - 1, j + 1)$ where, for $m_{i,j;k} = m\left(y_i, \phi_{i,j}(k), t_j\right)$, J is determined by

$$y_0 + J\sqrt{\Delta t} \geq y_i + m_{i,j;k}\Delta t \geq y_0 + (J - 1)\sqrt{\Delta t}. \qquad (14.89)$$

At each time t_j some nodes will not be reached from any nodes at time t_{j-1}. These nodes can be ignored.

The up and down branching probabilities $p^u_{i,j;k}$ and $p^d_{i,j;k}$ are given by

$$p^u_{i,j;k} = \frac{\left(m_{i,j;k}\Delta t + y_i\right) - y_{J-1}}{y_J - y_{J-1}} = 1 - p^d_{i,j;k}. \qquad (14.90)$$

These probabilities give the correct expected value, and as the mesh size tends to zero also give the correct variance. Figure 14.19 illustrates the binomial branching from node (i, j).

For the two successor nodes $(J, j + 1)$ and $(J - 1, j + 1)$, and for each value $\phi_{i,j;k}$ at node (i, j) compute

$$\phi_{J,j+1|i,j;k} = \phi_{J-1,j+1|i,j;k} = \phi_{i,j;k} + \left(\sigma^2\left(y_i, t_j\right) - 2k\left(t_j\right)\phi_{i,j;k}\right)\Delta t. \qquad (14.91)$$

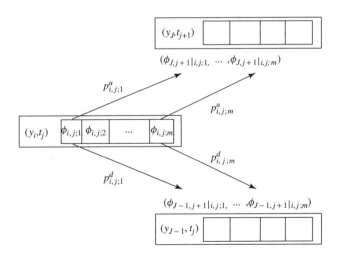

Figure 14.19 Branching from node (i, j)

The set $\phi_{J,j+1|i,j;k}$, $k = 1, \ldots, m$, are the values of ϕ_t that could be reached at node $(J, j + 1)$ from the set of states $(i, j; k)$ at node (i, j), and similarly for $\phi_{J-1,j+1|i,j;k}$. Temporarily store these values for each node and repeat the procedure for $\phi_{J,j+1|i,j;k}$ and $\phi_{J-1,j+1|i,j;k}$ for every state $(i, j; k)$ at time j. Then for every node $(i, j + 1)$ at time t_{j+1} set

$$\phi_{J,j+1;1} = \min_{i,k} \phi_{J,j+1|i,j;k}, \tag{14.92}$$

$$\phi_{J,j+1;m} = \max_{i,k} \phi_{J,j+1|i,j;k}, \tag{14.93}$$

and

$$\phi_{J,j+1;k+1} = \phi_{J,j+1;1} + \frac{k}{m-1}[\phi_{J,j+1;m} - \phi_{J,j+1;1}], \quad k = 1, \ldots, m - 2. \tag{14.94}$$

These values $\phi_{J,j+1;k}$, $k = 1, \ldots, m$, are stored at node $(J, j + 1)$, $J = -N, \ldots, N$. For each node $(i, j + 1)$ at time t_{j+1} this construction finds the set of all possible values of ϕ_t that could have been reached at this node, given the values of ϕ_t that have been stored at nodes (i, j) at time t_j. From this full range of values the maximum and the minimum values are retained, and $m - 2$ equally spaced intermediate values are computed and stored.

Evolving Backwards

We suppose that at the maturity time t_M we can compute option values $c(y_i, t_M; \phi_{i,M;k}) \equiv c_{i,M;k}$. Suppose we have already found option values $c_{i,j+1;k}$ for all nodes $(i, j + 1; k)$. We want to compute values $c_{i,j;k}$ at the previous time t_j. The method is a modification of the standard binomial expected discounted value calculation. For each state $(i, j; k)$ at time t_j we shall compute a value $c_{i,j;k}$,

$$c_{i,j;k} = e^{-r_{i,j}\Delta t}(p_{i,j;k}^u c_{J,j+1|i,j;k} + p_{i,j;k}^d c_{J-1,j+1|i,j;k}), \tag{14.95}$$

where $c_{J,j+1|i,j;k}$ and $c_{J-1,j+1|i,j;k}$ are option values found by interpolation and $r_{i,j}$ is the value of the short rate corresponding to y_i at time t_j. See Figure 14.20. For instance, to find $c_{J,j+1|i,j;k}$:

1. Compute $\phi_{J,j+1|i,j;k}$ from (14.91).
2. Find l such that $\phi_{J,j+1;l+1} \geq \phi_{J,j+1|i,j;k} \geq \phi_{J,j+1;l}$.
3. From the known values of $c_{J,j+1;l+1}$ and $c_{J,j+1;l}$ linearly interpolate to find $c_{J,j+1|i,j;k}$.

The value $c_{J-1,j+1|i,j;k}$ is found similarly. These two values can be inserted into (14.95) so that the value of $c_{i,j;k}$ can be found. This procedure is repeated for every state $(i, j; k)$ at time t_j to fill up option values for time t_j. Evolving backwards through the grid a value $c_{1,1}$ is found for the initial state $(1,1)$.

Although the procedure looks complicated, it is simply keeping track of how m different values of ϕ_t evolve forward from each node (i, j), and keeping just a representative set of m values at each successor node.

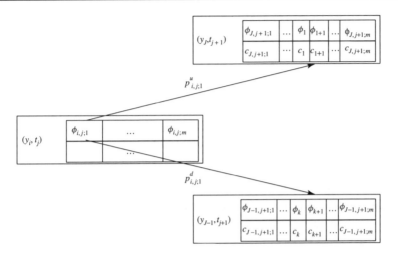

Figure 14.20   Evolving backwards

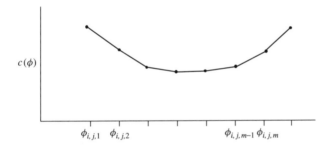

Figure 14.21   Piecewise linear approximation to $c(\phi)$

Ideally a lattice for a path-dependent state variable ϕ_t would calculate at each node (i, j) a function $c(\phi) = c(y_i, t_j, \phi)$ for all possible values of ϕ. This is usually infeasible. The Li, Ritchken and Sankarasubramanian lattice approximates $c(\phi)$ as a piecewise linear function defined on a bounded interval, as in Figure 14.21. In effect $c(\phi)$ is approximated as a first-order spline with equally spaced knot points (see Chapter 15). This is simple, but suggests improvements.

1.   Knot points could be spaced at unequal intervals, being more concentrated at points where $c(\phi)$ has greater curvature.
2.   A more sophisticated interpolation method could be used, for instance quadratic or cubic splines.

Alternatively the unknown curve $c(\phi)$ could modelled parametrically by some function f with a small parameter set θ, $c(\phi) \sim f(\phi \mid \theta)$. At each node (i, j) a parameter set $\theta_{i,j}$ is chosen so that $f(\phi \mid \theta_{i,j})$ best fits $c_{i,j;k}$. One then sets $c_{J,j+1|i,j;k} = f(\phi_{J,j+1|i,j;k} \mid \theta_{i,j})$.

14.4 CALIBRATION TO MARKET PRICES

An implied tree is a lattice that is calibrated, at least partially, to market prices; $\{\underline{X}_{i,j}\}$ and $p_{k,j+1;i,j}$ are chosen so that the lattice recovers certain market prices. A lattice can in principle fit to:

1. Pure discount bond prices, so that the lattice recovers the initial term structure;
2. At-the-money cap prices, so that a volatility term structure is recovered;
3. Cap and bond options prices, to recover the full volatility smile;
4. Swaption prices, recovering the correlation structure.

Many lattice methods can be calibrated to the initial term structure. The Hull and White lattice has an easy calibration, while for methods that evolve the entire term structure, such as Black, Derman and Toy, or Heath, Jarrow and Morton, an initial term structure is input as an initial condition. The two most popular lattice methods, Hull and White, and Black, Derman and Toy, can each also calibrate to a term structure of volatility. A full implied tree calibrates to the entire volatility smile. This is not usually done in interest rate models, but see Chapter 19.

At the time of writing the authors know of no lattice method that successfully calibrates to the correlation structure.

The process of calibration, given the theory we have developed so far, is straightforward. Calibration usually proceeds by

1. Determining a lattice $\mathcal{L} = (\mathcal{N}, \mathcal{A}, \mathcal{S}, \underline{X}, p, t, r)$ for some underlying state variable $\underline{X}$, with spot rate function r;
2. Replacing the function r with $\hat{r}$ and probabilities p with $\hat{p}$, so that $\hat{\mathcal{L}} = (\mathcal{N}, \mathcal{A}, \mathcal{S}, \underline{X}, \hat{p}, t, \hat{r})$ recovers the desired market prices.

Here we discuss only calibration to term structures of interest rates and volatilities. We mention three calibration methods: the Hull and White method, the BDT method, and Schmidt's method.

On the lattice $\mathcal{L}$ we are able to compute Arrow–Debreu security prices, and conditional pure discount bond prices

$$\delta_{k,l}(j-l) = \sum_{(i,j) \in \mathcal{N}_j} Q_{i,j;k,l} \tag{14.96}$$

for (k, l), $l < j$. There is a second expression for the value $\delta_{k,l}(j - l)$. To generate a certain payoff of 1 at time t_j buy a quantity $\exp(-r(\underline{X}_{i,j-1})\Delta_{j-1})$ of the pure security for each node $(i, j - 1) \in \mathcal{N}_{j-1}$. Whatever the state of the world at time t_{j-1}, the portfolio generates 1 at time t_j. The cost of the portfolio, conditional on having been in state (k, l), is

$$\delta_{k,l}(j-l) = \sum_{(i,j-1) \in \mathcal{N}_{j-1}} Q_{i,j-1;k,l} \exp(-r(\underline{X}_{i,j-1})\Delta_{j-1}). \tag{14.97}$$

This expresses pure discount bond prices as a function of the spot rates and the Arrow–Debreu security prices for the previous time. This will serve as the kernel of an iterative calibration method.

We suppose that the function $r : S \to \mathbb{R}$ is governed by a set of parameters θ, $r(\underline{X}_{i,j-1}) \equiv r(\underline{X}_{i,j-1} \mid \theta)$. The function $\hat{r}$ will be identical to r except that θ becomes time-dependent.

14.4.1 Fitting to Term Structures

Suppose that we observe in the market a discount curve $\hat{\delta}(k) = \hat{\delta}_{1,1}(k)$, the pure discount bond maturing at time t_{k+1}, $k = 1, \ldots, M$, and a volatility term structure $\hat{v}(k)$. (We discuss the meaning of $\hat{v}(k)$ in a moment.) We want to find $\hat{r}$ such that $\widehat{\mathcal{L}}$ recovers $\hat{\delta}(k)$ and $\hat{v}(k)$.

Fit to $\hat{\delta}(k)$ Only

Choose a parameter $\alpha \in \theta$. Iterate forward through the lattice one layer at a time, choosing values α_j of α at each time t_j to fit to $\hat{\delta}(j)$. Suppose that we have constructed

1. Values $\widehat{Q}_{i,j}$ of Arrow–Debreu securities for the lattice $\widehat{\mathcal{L}}$ up to and including time t_j;
2. Values α_l of α, $l = 1, \ldots, j - 1$.

The procedure is to

1. Choose α_j so that $\hat{\delta}(j) = \sum_{(i,j) \in \mathcal{N}_j} \widehat{Q}_{i,j} \exp\left(-r(\underline{X}_{i,j} \mid \alpha_j) \Delta_j\right)$.
2. Given α_j, set $\widehat{Q}_{i,j+1} = \sum_{(k,j) \in \mathcal{N}_j} \exp\left(-r\left(\underline{X}_{i,j} \mid \alpha_j\right) \Delta_j\right) p_{i,j+1;k,j} \widehat{Q}_{k,j}$.

Since $\widehat{Q}_{1,1} = 1$ and α_1 is chosen so that $\hat{\delta}(1) = \exp\left(-r\left(\underline{X}_{1,1} \mid \alpha_1\right) \Delta_1\right)$, the procedure can be initialised and the calibration undertaken.

Not all parameters $\alpha \in \theta$ might be suitable for use in the procedure. Usually a parameter associated to the drift of the short rate, for instance the mean reversion level, is more appropriate than a parameter affecting only the volatility term.

Fitting to $\hat{\delta}(k)$ and to $\hat{v}(k)$

We need to define the volatility term structure. In the market this may be an ATM cap volatility, or a term structure of caplet volatilities backed out from a Black's formula. BDT use a definition based upon the volatility of the discrete spot rate in their binomial lattice. We adopt a definition similar to Schmidt's.

First, we define conditional probabilities in the lattice. Let $q_{k,l;i,j}$ be the probability of hitting node (k, l) conditioned on being at node (i, j) at time $t_j < t_l$. Then $q_{k,l;k,l} = 1$ and

$$q_{k,l;i,j} = \sum_{(m,n) \in \mathcal{C}_{k,l}} q_{m,n;i,j} p_{k,l;m,n}. \tag{14.98}$$

These quantities can be computed, as usual, by iterating forward through the lattice. $q_{k,l} = q_{k,l;1,1}$ is the probability of reaching (k, l) from the initial node $(1,1)$.

We define $v(j)$ to be the variance of the one-period discount factor $\delta_j(j + 1) = \exp\left(-r\left(\underline{X}_{i,j}\right)\Delta_j\right)$ conditional on being in state $(1,1)$:

$$v(j) = \text{var}\left[\ln \delta_j(j + 1)\right].$$ (14.99)

Since $\text{var}[x] = \mathbb{E}\left[x^2\right] - \mathbb{E}^2[x]$ we have

$$v(j) = \mathbb{E}\left[\left(\ln \delta_j(j + 1)\right)^2\right] - \mathbb{E}^2\left[\ln \delta_j(j + 1)\right]$$ (14.100)

$$= \sum_{(i,j)\in\mathcal{N}_j}\left(-r\left(\underline{X}_{i,j}\right)\Delta_j\right)^2 q_{i,j} - \left(\sum_{(i,j)\in\mathcal{N}_j}-r(\underline{X}_{i,j})\Delta_j q_{i,j}\right)^2.$$ (14.101)

Identify two parameters $\alpha, \beta \in \theta$. We choose values α_j and β_j for α and β at each time t_j so that

$$\hat{\delta}(j) = \sum_{(i,j)\in\mathcal{N}_j}\hat{Q}_{i,j}\exp\left(-r\left(\underline{X}_{i,j} \mid \alpha_j, \beta_j\right)\Delta_j\right),$$ (14.102)

$$\hat{v}(j) = \sum_{(i,j)\in\mathcal{N}_j}\left(-r\left(\underline{X}_{i,j} \mid \alpha_j, \beta_j\right)\Delta_j\right)^2 q_{i,j} - \left(\sum_{(i,j)\in\mathcal{N}_j}-r\left(\underline{X}_{i,j} \mid \alpha_j, \beta_j\right)\Delta_j q_{i,j}\right)^2.$$
(14.103)

As before, the procedure iterates forward through the lattice, at each layer first finding values of α_j and β_j to fit (14.102) and (14.103) and then finding Arrow–Debreu security prices for the next layer. A numerical method will be needed to find values of α_j and β_j that fit to $\hat{\delta}(j)$ and $\hat{v}(j)$.

We mention how these ideas are applied in three lattice models.

1. *Hull and White.* In the Hull and White lattice we have $r\left(\underline{X}_{i,j} \mid \alpha\right) = \alpha + i\Delta_r$. α can be used to calibrate to the yield curve.
2. *Black, Derman and Toy.* An initial term structure and an initial volatility are supplied as data to set up the lattice.
3. *Schmidt.* The model can be calibrated by the usual methods. Given a set of pure discount bond prices the function f can be chosen to recover them. An appropriate choice of g and h calibrates the lattice to the volatilities of pure discount bonds.

Hull and White (93) [295] describe a procedure that adapts the standard Hull and White extended Vasicek lattice to calibrate to a term structure of volatility, based on the short rate process

$$dr_t = (\theta(t) - a(t)r_t)dt + \sigma dz_t.$$ (14.104)

Clewlow and Strickland (98) [137] give a pseudo-code implementation of this and other lattice methods.

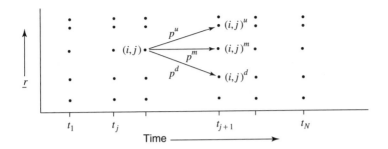

Figure 14.22   Branching on a trinomial grid

14.5   THE EXPLICIT FINITE DIFFERENCE METHOD

Suppose we approximate the short rate r_t on a grid, as in Figure 14.22. Let the short rate process be $dr_t = \mu(r_t, t)dt + \sigma(r_t, t)dz_t$ and set $\mu_{i,j} = \mu(r_{i,j}, t_j)$ and $\sigma_{i,j} = \sigma(r_{i,j}, t_j)$. For a small time step Δ_j,

$$E_{i,j} = \mathbb{E}\left[r_{t_{j+1}} - r_{t_j} \mid r_{t_j} = r_{i,j}\right] \sim \mu_{i,j}\Delta_j, \tag{14.105}$$

$$V_{i,j} = \text{var}\left[r_{t_{j+1}} - r_{t_j} \mid r_{t_j} = r_{i,j}\right] \sim \sigma_{i,j}^2 \Delta_j. \tag{14.106}$$

For branching probabilities p^u, p^m and p^d we can fit to these approximations for $E_{i,j}$ and $V_{i,j}$, obtaining

$$p^u + p^m + p^d = 1,$$
$$\Delta_u p^u + \Delta_m p^m + (-\Delta_d)p^d = \mu_{i,j}\Delta_j, \tag{14.107}$$
$$(\Delta_u)^2 p^u + (\Delta_m)^2 p^m + (-\Delta_u)^2 p^d = \sigma_{i,j}^2 \Delta_j,$$

where Δ_u, Δ_m, Δ_d are the up, middle and down $\underline{r}$-steps. If the grid spacing is regular, so that $\{r_{i,j}\} = \{r_{i,j+1}\}$, $\Delta_j \equiv \Delta_t$ and $\Delta_u = \Delta_d$, $\Delta_m = 0$, then (14.107) can be solved to obtain

$$p^u = \frac{1}{2}\mu_{i,j}\frac{\Delta t}{\Delta r} + \frac{1}{2}\sigma_{i,j}^2\frac{\Delta t}{(\Delta r)^2}, \tag{14.108}$$

$$p^d = 1 - \sigma_{i,j}^2\frac{\Delta t}{(\Delta r)^2}, \tag{14.109}$$

$$p^m = -\frac{1}{2}\mu_{i,j}\frac{\Delta t}{\Delta r} + \frac{1}{2}\sigma_{i,j}^2\frac{\Delta t}{(\Delta r)^2}. \tag{14.110}$$

We saw in Chapter 12 that the explicit finite difference method obtains these probabilities. (In that chapter there is an additional $r\Delta t$ term in the expression corresponding to (14.109). This is because there discounting is already included.)

A grid implementation does not require that $\sigma(r_t) \equiv \sigma$ is a constant. However, we require that $\Delta_m = 0$ and that the probabilities p^u, p^m and p^d are positive. This, combined with an r_t-dependent volatility function, puts constraints on the grid spacing.

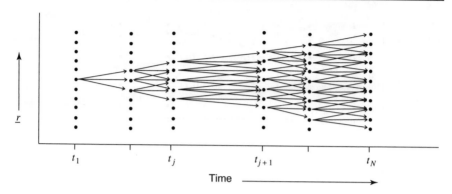

Figure 14.23 A trinomial lattice imbedded in a grid

At the boundary of a grid it is necessary to modify the branching, either by incorporating an explicit boundary condition or by altering the approximation used for the derivatives.

Relationship to the Hull and White Lattice

The explicit finite difference method effectively approximates the conditional variance $V_{i,j}$ as

$$V_{i,j} = \text{var}\left[r_{t_{j+1}} - r_{t_j} \mid r_{t_j} = r_{i,j}\right] \sim \sigma_{i,j}^2 \Delta_j. \tag{14.111}$$

Alternatively, the variance could be approximated to second order as

$$V'_{i,j} = \text{var}\left[r_{t_{j+1}} - r_{t_j} \mid r_{t_j} = r_{i,j}\right] \sim \sigma_{i,j}^2 \Delta_j + \left(\mu_{i,j}\Delta_j\right)^2. \tag{14.112}$$

The difference between (14.111) and (14.112) is just a term of order $(\Delta_j)^2$. As $\Delta_j \to 0$, both approximations converge correctly to the continuous underlying process. If the second approximation (14.112) to the conditional variance is used we recover the probabilities for the Hull and White lattice. Hence the Hull and White lattice can be considered as a segment of a modified explicit grid (Figure 14.23). Alternatively, an explicit finite difference method can be thought of as the simultaneous evolution of several overlapping lattices, each with a first-order approximation to the variance. Vetzal (98) [534] explores this in greater detail.

14.6 LATTICES AND THE MONTE CARLO METHOD

A path in a lattice is a sequence of nodes starting from a node at time t_1, ending at time t_M, such that each node can be reached directly from the preceding node. It is a set of nodes $P = (p_i, q_i)_{i=1,\ldots,i_P}$ such that $q_1 = 1$, $q_{i_P} = M$ and $(p_{i+1}, q_{i+1}) \in \mathcal{B}_{p_i,q_i}$ for $i = 1, \ldots, i_P - 1$. Write $\mathcal{P}$ for the set of all distinct paths in a lattice. The probability

$p(P)$ of a path $P = (p_i, q_i)_{i=1,\ldots,i_P} \in \mathcal{P}$, and the discount factor $\delta(P)$ along P, are

$$p(P) = \prod_{i=1}^{i_P-1} p_{p_{i+1},q_{i+1};p_i,q_i}, \tag{14.113}$$

$$\delta(P) = \prod_{i=1}^{i_P-1} \exp\left(-r_{p_i,q_i}\left(\Delta_{q_i}\right)\Delta_{q_i}\right) \tag{14.114}$$

$$= \exp\left(-\sum_{i=1}^{i_P-1} r_{p_i,q_i}\left(\Delta_{q_i}\right)\Delta_{q_i}\right). \tag{14.115}$$

For a European option with payoff function $H_{i,M}$ write $H(P) = H_{i,i_P}$ for the payoff on the terminal node of a path P.

For simplicity we suppose that $N_1 = 1$ and that the lattice is simple, so that $i_P = M$. By construction, from (14.115) we have that $\Sigma_{P\in\mathcal{P}} p(P) = 1$ and for any European option with payoff function $H_{i,M}$ the value V_{t_1} of the option at time t_1 is

$$V_{t_1} = \sum_{P\in\mathcal{P}} p(P)\delta(P)H(P). \tag{14.116}$$

But this is just the payoff to a highly regularised Monte Carlo method, where only a finite sample of ordered paths is allowed, and each is weighted by its relative frequency in the population, $p(P)$. We saw in Chapter 13 that numerical integration schemes which select sample paths in an ordered regular fashion are out-performed by schemes incorporating a random element. Lattice schemes are used, however, because they allow easy calibration to market prices, and are easier to implement compared with fast Monte Carlo schemes.

A lattice method does not sample extreme sample paths in the sense that at each time step there is explicitly a minimum and a maximum allowed value of $r(N)$, $N \in \mathcal{N}_j$. Only as Δ_t goes to zero do these extreme values become unbounded, for a fixed time $t = j\Delta_t$.

The Monte Carlo method generates a lattice in which $N_{1,1} = K$, for K very large and $p_{k,2;1,1} = 1/K$, and for all other nodes $N_{i,j} = 1$ and $p_{k,l;i,j} = 1$. Figure 14.24 illustrates this.

14.6.1 Hybrid Lattices and Monte Carlo Schemes

It is possible to relax a strict lattice scheme to incorporate some of the potential advantages of a Monte Carlo scheme. For instance, replace the very last step in a simple lattice with a single antithetic Monte Carlo step, as in Figure 14.25.

Using antithetic branching at the final step makes little difference if the payoff function is piecewise linear.

On a hybrid lattice one constructs Arrow–Debreu security prices as usual up to time t_{M-1}. The derivative value will be

$$V = \sum_{(i,M-1)\in\mathcal{N}_{M-1}} \exp(-r_{i,M-1}(\Delta_{M-1})\Delta_{M-1})H_i Q_{i,M-1}, \tag{14.117}$$

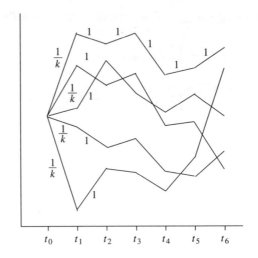

Figure 14.24 A Monte Carlo lattice

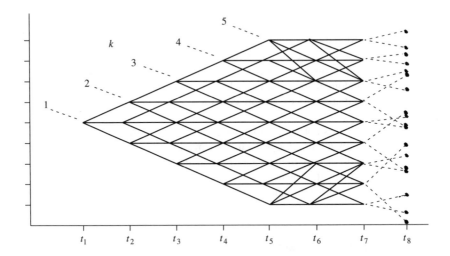

Figure 14.25 A hybrid lattice scheme

where H_i is the payoff computed from the evolved values of the state variables at node $(i, M - 1)$.

14.7 NON-RECOMBINING LATTICES

Heath, Jarrow and Morton models specify a vector of volatility functions $\sigma = (\sigma_1(t, T, \omega), \ldots, \sigma_d(t, T, \omega))$ for $f_t(T)$ which determine how the yield curve varies from one time to the next. Lattice implementations of these models are inherently path-dependent, leading to non-recombining lattices. In a recombining lattice the slow growth of N_j severely constrains the evolution of the term structure, the opposite of that required for path-dependent models.

We shall see that there is a great deal in common between Monte Carlo methods and non-recombining lattice methods. They use similar sampling and regularisation methods, for example Brownian bridge techniques. The key objectives are to get a correct distribution at maturity and to sample the path-dependency as well as possible by using regularisation methods.

For non-recombining lattices it is helpful to use a slightly different parameterisation of the nodes in the lattice. Suppose we have a completely non-recombining lattice of order k. At each node (i, j) we label the arcs in $\mathcal{B}_{i,j}$, the successor set to (i, j), by the numbers $0, \dots, k - 1$. Since there is a unique path leading to each node we can label the node by the sequence of arcs leading to it from the initial node $(1, 1)$, $P = ((1, 1), (i_2, 2), \dots, (i_j, j)) \equiv (b_1, \dots, b_{j-1})$, where each $b_i \in \{0, \dots, k - 1\}$. There is a one-to-one correspondence between paths $P = (b_1, \dots, b_{M-1}) \in \mathcal{P}$ and base-k representations of the numbers $0, \dots, 3^{M-1}$, given by $P = \sum_{i=1}^{M-1} b_i k^{M-1-i}$.

The Underlying Lattice for z_t

In many lattice methods one is evolving a state variable $\underline{X}_j \in \mathbb{R}^n$ as an approximation to a continuous n-dimensional process $dX_t = \mu(X_t, t)dt + \sigma(X_t, t)dz_t$. If one demands a regular space step for $\underline{X}_j$, one may sample unimportant regions of the state space. It is preferable, where possible, to construct a lattice which samples $\underline{X}_j$ better. One way of doing this is to construct a lattice for the n-dimensional Wiener process z_t, and from this find a lattice for $\underline{X}_j$. The lattice for $\underline{X}_j$ is likely to be non-recombining.

A standard binomial lattice for $z_t \in \mathbb{R}$ is $\mathcal{L} = (\mathcal{N}, \mathcal{A}, \mathcal{S}, \underline{X}, p, t, r)$, specified in Table 14.8.

A standard trinomial lattice for $z_t \in \mathbb{R}$ is $\mathcal{L} = (\mathcal{N}, \mathcal{A}, \mathcal{S}, \underline{X}, p, t, r)$, as shown in Table 14.9. k is a free parameter. Hull and White choose $k = 3$.[6]

Table 14.8   The standard binomial lattice

$$\left.\begin{matrix} \mathcal{N} \\ \mathcal{A} \end{matrix}\right\} = \left\{ \begin{matrix} \{(i, j) \mid j = 1, \dots, M, i = 1, \dots, N_j, N_j = j\} \\ \{(i, j; i, j + 1), (i, j; i + 1, j + 1)\} \end{matrix} \right.$$

$\mathcal{S} = \mathbb{R}$,

$\underline{X}_{i,j} = (2i - 1 - j)\Delta_z$, with $\Delta_z^2 = \Delta_t$,

$p, \quad p^u = p^d = \frac{1}{2}$,

$t(i, j) = j\Delta_t$, for some Δ_t,

$r(\underline{X}_{i,j})$,   (undefined).

---

[6] k is often chosen to match the kurtosis of the underlying continuous-time process.

Table 14.9   The standard trinomial lattice

$$\left.\begin{array}{c} \mathcal{N} \\ \mathcal{A} \end{array}\right\} = \begin{cases} \{(i,j)|j=1,\ldots,M, i=1,\ldots,N_j, N_j = 2j-1\} \\ \{(i,j;i,j+1),(i,j;i+1,j+1),(i,j;i+2,j+1)\} \end{cases}$$

$$\mathcal{S} = \mathbb{R},$$

$$\underline{X}_{i,j} = (i-j-1)\Delta_z, \text{ with } \Delta_z^2 = k\Delta_t, k > 1$$

$$p, \quad p^u = p^d = \frac{1}{2k}, p^m = \frac{k-1}{k},$$

$$t(i,j) = j\Delta_t, \text{ for some } \Delta_t,$$

$$r(\underline{X}_{i,j}), \quad \text{(undefined).}$$

Given a lattice for z_t one obtains a (non-recombining) lattice for X_t. For instance, one could implement a lattice for the Vasicek process this way. Suppose the initial value of the short rate is $r_{1,1}$. Given a path $p = ((i_1, 1), (i_2, 2), \ldots, (i_M, M))$, $i_1 = 1$, through the lattice for z_t, we have

$$r_{i_{k+1}, k+1} = r_{i_k, k} + \alpha(\mu - r_{i_k, k})\Delta_t + (i_{k+1} - i_k - 1)\Delta_z. \tag{14.118}$$

Evidently, different paths arriving at the same node (i_M, M) will produce different values of $r_{i,M}$.[7] (McCarthy and Webber point out (14.118) is a bad discretisation.)

Although these non-recombining lattices converge as $M \to \infty$, the number of nodes increases too fast, so that computational limits may be reached well before a suitable degree of convergence is achieved. Even in one dimension a completely non-recombining trinomial tree has over a million nodes in 14 time steps. It is clear from Table 14.10 that non-recombining trees have to have far fewer time steps than recombining lattices.

There are several techniques available to circumvent the problem. Some of these are discussed in McCarthy and Webber (99) [386] (see Section 14.7.2) who find that when certain conditions are met it is possible to find accurate prices with very few time steps.

Table 14.10   Comparison of number of time steps

Type of lattice	Number of nodes as a function of M	Value of M giving $\sim 10^6$ nodes
Recombining		
Binomial	$\frac{1}{2}M(M+1)$	1414
Trinomial	M^2	1000
Grid	M^2	1000
Non-recombining		
Binomial	$2^M - 1$	20
Trinomial	$3^M - 1$	14

---

[7] If the SDE for r_t can be solved, as in Schmidt (97) [479], a recombining lattice for z_t gives a recombining lattice for r_t.

14.7.1 Pricing on a Non-Recombining Lattice

It is feasible to use for non-recombining lattices the same methods that we developed for recombining lattices. Non-recombining lattices can be implemented by iterating around the lattice, requiring only a very small amount of information to be stored at any time.

Suppose that we have already generated a completely non-recombining lattice for $\underline{X}_{i,j}$, so that we have known values $\underline{X}_{i,j}$ and known branching. (In fact in a practical implementation, the lattice for $\underline{X}_{i,j}$ will itself also be generated iteratively as a minor extension of the procedure we are about to describe.)

We iterate though the lattice considering each path $P_i = (b_{i,1}, \ldots, b_{i,M-1})$, $i = 1, \ldots, 3^{M-1}$, in turn starting with path $P_1 = (0, \ldots, 0)$. Write $\underline{X}_{i,j}$ for the value of the state variable at time t_j along path P_i. We maintain a vector $V = (V_1, \ldots, V_{M-1})$ of partially accumulated prices.

Step 0. Set $i = 0$ and $V = (0, \ldots, 0)$.

Step 1. Increment $i \leftarrow i + 1$.
Compute the payoff $H_{i,M}$ at the terminal node $\underline{X}_{i,M}$ along path $P_i = (b_{i,1}, \ldots, b_{i,M-1})$ where $b_{i,j} = \lfloor i/k^{M-1-j} \rfloor \bmod k$.
Compute the discounted probability weighted value

$$V'_{M-1} = \exp\left(-r\left(\underline{X}_{i,M-1}\right) \Delta_{M-1}\right) p_{i,M;i,M-1} H_{i,M}. \tag{14.119}$$

Accumulate $V_{M-1} \leftarrow V_{M-1} + V'_{M-1}$.

Step 2. If $b_{i,M-1} = k - 1$ set $l = M$.
Loop: Decrement $l \leftarrow l - 1$. If $l = 1$ then goto *Finish*.
For an American option compute the payoff $H_{i,l}$ and set $V_l \leftarrow \max(H_{i,l}, V_l)$.
Compute the discounted probability weighted value

$$V'_{l-1} = \exp(-r(\underline{X}_{i,l-1})\Delta_{l-1}) p_{i,l;i,l-1} V_l. \tag{14.120}$$

Accumulate $V_{l-1} \to V_{l-1} + V'_{l-1}$. Set $V_l = 0$.
If $b_{i,l-1} = k - 1$ goto *Loop*, or else go back to Step 1.
Finish: The value V_1 is the expected discounted derivative value for time t_1.

With this procedure storage requirements are minimal.

14.7.2 Requirements for an Effective Non-Recombining Lattice

McCarthy and Webber (99) [386] apply the algorithm of Section 14.7.1 to a three-factor icosahedral branching scheme. At each node the branching is to the vertices of a regular icosahedron in z-space. They find that it is possible to obtain relatively fast and accurate prices as long as three requirements are met.

First, in evolving forward through the lattice it is essential to use distributional information about the underlying process, so that the moments of the process on the lattice match the moments of the continuous-time process over a discrete time step.

McCarthy and Webber show how it is possible to avoid clustering nodes at the terminal and intermediate times.

Second, it must be possible to determine, to a good approximation, the payoff to the derivative at the exercise time of the option, so that it is not necessary to evolve the lattice beyond the maturity time of the option.

Third, it is necessary to be able to discount back accurately through the lattice. McCarthy and Webber found that the Brownian bridge technique of Gandhi and Hunt (97) [241] was very effective on their lattice.

In these circumstances they find that the time step can be of the order of magnitude of a year, in some cases, while still obtaining acceptable accuracy.

14.8 CONCLUSIONS

We have seen in this chapter how general lattices can be constructed; how several factors can be evolved simultaneously; and how non-recombining lattices can be implemented. Lattice methods are extremely flexible and very tractable. Standard lattice methods are widely used, though not perhaps to their full potential.

PART IV
CALIBRATION AND ESTIMATION

The process of fitting an interest rate model to historical and current market data is known as estimation; the process is often called calibrating a model if the parameters of the models are being estimated from current market data. All useful yield curve models have a number of parameters which are 'floating'—they may be adjusted until the model fits the available data, within reasonable limits. Part IV deals with all the estimation and calibration techniques used in the market.

Chapter 15 discusses how the yield curve may be extracted from market data using non-parametric techniques, including spline methods.

In Chapter 16 we discuss how a series of fitted yield curves can be used to estimate volatility functions for whole yield curve models. The technique, principal components analysis (PCA), can also be applied to current market prices to calibrate directly to implied volatility and covariance structures. PCA can also be used to investigate the topology of state space underlying the market. We introduce interest rate models defined on non-linear state spaces.

Chapters 17 and 18 are about estimating model parameters from historical data. Since interest rate distributions are not normal, a number of sophisticated techniques are necessary to find the values of the floating parameters; familiar techniques based on least squares are ineffective. We describe the general method of moments and maximum likelihood techniques, including simulation based approaches. Chapter 18 looks at filtering methods and at GARCH based methods.

Chapter 19 investigates implied pricing. The drift and volatility functions of an interest rate process may be extracted from market prices of caps, floors and swaptions. These functions depend on the level of the rate as well as current time, so they determine a surface of drifts and volatilities. If a complete set of caplets existed, then their implied volatilities, parameterised by the strike and time to maturity, can be directly related to the drift and volatility surfaces. In practice it is an enormous challenge to fit a model to this whole surface. For pricing purposes, workarounds are usually available but are unsatisfactory. This chapter discusses how a model may be calibrated to the entire volatility surface, and explains how a number of the difficulties involved may be overcome.

15

Modelling the Yield Curve

In previous chapters we have seen how interest rate models can be used to price a variety of derivative securities, both in theory and in practice. Before a model can be used it must be calibrated, and the fundamental object to calibrate against is the yield curve. This can mean one of two things: either the model is calibrated against the instruments from which the yield curve is constructed, so that one matches Libor rates and swap rates, for instance; or else the yield curve is modelled non-parametrically from the market rates and then the model is calibrated to the whole estimated curve.

The latter idea is particularly relevant to HJM models. From a sequence of yield curves, estimated on successive days, sets of volatility components can be derived. We see how this may be done in Chapter 16.

In this chapter we investigate how the yield curve may be fitted non-parametrically. We start by discussing some general issues, showing how the money market curve and the government bond market curve can both be approached by an equivalent methodology. We show how a naive approach to yield curve modelling fails dismally, but then describe several reasonable methods that can be used successfully to model the yield curve.

We first discuss spline techniques. These are now widely used, both as regression splines and as smoothing splines. Then we review the Nelson and Siegel family of curves. The limitations of these curves for interest rate modelling is demonstrated.

In a short section we describe a relatively new and little pursued approach based on kernel approximations to the yield curve.

Finally we review the classical LP and regression methods in the light of our previous discussion.

Comparisons of various types of fitting techniques have been made by a number of authors. The articles of Gourieroux and Scaillet (94) [258] and Bliss (96) [77] are particularly useful, although Dahlquist and Svensson (96) [153] is also good, but more restricted in scope. Other reviews include Ferguson and Raymar (98) [215] and Bekdache and Baum (94) [59].

A book that reviews many methods in the area is Anderson *et al.* (96) [23].

15.1 STRIPPING THE YIELD CURVE

In this section we show that in both the bond market and the money market similar methods may be applied to obtain a set of discount factors, and hence spot rates, from market data.

In each market there will be set of basic instruments with

- Known or imputed future cashflows, and
- Known or imputed current market value.

This is particularly clear in the bond market where the basic instruments are coupon bonds, but in the money market also we may interpret market quoted rates as a relationship between cashflows and market values.

15.1.1 The Bond Market

Suppose there is a set of n liquid bonds, with market values P_i, $i = 1, \ldots, n$, and cashflows $c_{i,j}$ to bond i at time t_j, $j = 1, \ldots, m$. For example, cashflows might be biannual coupon payments, with a final payment of principal and coupon at the bond maturity date. $C = \{c_{i,j}\}_{i=1,\ldots,n, j=1,\ldots,m}$ is the cashflow matrix and $P = \{P_i\}_{i=1,\ldots,n}$ is the price vector.

C and P, and a knowledge of discount factors for times t_j, $j = 1, \ldots, m$, are the information universe for simple coupon bonds. Bonds with call features require additional information, for instance in the form of volatilities. They are more complicated derivatives that in general will require numerical methods to enable them to be valued and hedged correctly.

We illustrate with an example from the UK government bond (gilt) market. Figure 15.1 gives summary information for nine gilts for the 4 September 1996. UK gilt prices are quoted as 'clean' prices. To obtain the price actually paid—the 'dirty' price—one calculates an amount of accrued interest deemed to have been earned since the last coupon date and adds it to the clean price. This calculation is performed in the table.

The pattern of cashflows in known, and one can generate the cashflow matrix C. For these bonds the first part of C is shown in Figure 15.2. C is a sparse matrix with most entries zero. It has one column for each time that a cashflow can arise. Since in

Bond Data		(04/09/96)					Calculating the dirty price			
	Name	Clean price	coupon (%)	Prior coupon	Next coupon	maturity date	time to maturity	ex div ?	Accrued interest	Dirty price
bond 1:	con 10 96	100.7813	10	15/05/96	15/11/96	15/11/96	0.20	0	3.0410959	103.82235
bond 2:	ex 93/4 98	104.8125	9.75	19/07/96	19/01/97	19/01/98	1.38	0	1.2287671	106.04127
bond 3:	ex 121/4 99	113.0313	12.25	26/03/96	26/09/96	26/03/99	2.56	0	5.4034247	118.43467
bond 4:	con 9 00	106.2813	9	03/03/96	03/09/96	03/03/00	3.50	1	0	106.28125
bond 5:	tr 7 01	98.84375	7	06/05/96	06/11/96	06/11/01	5.18	0	2.3013699	101.14512
bond 6:	tr 93/4 02	110.875	9.75	27/08/96	27/02/97	27/08/02	5.98	0	0.1869863	111.06199
bond 7:	tr 81/2 05	104.1875	8.5	07/06/96	07/12/96	07/12/05	9.27	0	2.0493151	106.23682
bond 8:	tr 73/4 06	98.59375	7.75	08/03/96	08/09/96	08/09/06	10.02	1	-0.106164	98.487586
bond 9:	tr 9 08	107.3438	9	13/04/96	13/10/96	13/10/08	12.12	0	3.5260274	110.86978

Figure 15.1 Market prices of UK gilts

The matrix of cash flows (Just the first few columns)									
date:	26/09/96	13/10/96	06/11/96	15/11/96	07/12/96	19/01/97	27/02/97	03/03/97	08/03/97	26/03/97
time:	0.06	0.11	0.18	0.20	0.26	0.38	0.48	0.50	0.51	0.56
bond 1:	0	0	0	105	0	0	0	0	0	0
bond 2:	0	0	0	0	0	4.875	0	0	0	0
bond 3:	6.125	0	0	0	0	0	0	0	0	6.125
bond 4:	0	0	0	0	0	0	0	4.5	0	0
bond 5:	0	0	3.5	0	0	0	0	0	0	0
bond 6:	0	0	0	0	0	0	4.875	0	0	0
bond 7:	0	0	0	0	4.25	0	0	0	0	0
bond 8:	0	0	0	0	0	0	0	0	3.875	0
bond 9:	0	4.5	0	0	0	0	0	0	0	0

Figure 15.2 The gilt cashflow matrix (partial)

this sample no two bonds have cashflows on the same date, each column has a single non-zero entry.

15.1.2 The Money Market

Money market data can be put into the same price—cashflow form as we found for the bond market. One analyses each instrument type to determine the size of the cashflows associated to them and their timing. For this purpose we may only consider instruments with no option features. We describe the cashflow and price structure associated with several money market instruments. In practice one needs to get the day count fraction right. We have, for instance:

1. *Libor.* Libor rate L, tenor τ: pay 1 at time 0, receive $1 + \tau L$ at time τ.
2. *FRAs.* FRA rate f, tenor τ, for time t_1: pay 0 at time 0. Pay 1 at time t_1, receive $1 + \tau f$ at time $t_1 + \tau$.
3. *Swaps.* Swap rate s, tenor τ: treat these like par coupon bonds. Pay 1 at time 0, receive τs at the coupon dates, and receive $1 + \tau s$ at the final payment date.
4. *Forward Start Swaps.* Forward start swap rate s, tenor τ, start date t_0: treat like forward start bonds. Pay 1 at time t_0, receive τs at the coupon dates, and receive $1 + \tau s$ at the final payment date.

Figure 15.3 summarises money market data for the US dollar on the 6 October 1997.
For the sake of this example we shall pretend that futures rates may be taken as FRAs. Figure 15.4 presents the price vector and cashflow matrix. The first column of the table is the vector P giving the notional price, at time zero, of each instrument. Libor and swaps have notional value 1 at time zero. FRAs and forward start swaps have value zero at time zero. An attempt has been made to incorporate the correct day bases for each instrument type.
The cashflow matrix has properties just as bad as that found for the gilt example.

15.1.3 Either Market

We have shown that in both the bond and the money markets we can find a vector P of current prices, and a matrix C of cashflows. We expect to be able to find a vector $\hat{\delta}$

USD Money Market Data, 6 October 1997		
Days	Period	rate, %
	spot	
1	o/n	5.59375
33	1m	5.625
91	3m	5.71875
91	Oct-97	94.27
91	Nov-97	94.26
91	Dec-97	94.24
91	Mar-98	94.23
91	Jun-98	94.18
91	Sep-98	94.12
91	Dec-98	94
	2	6.01253
	3	6.10823
	4	6.16
	5	6.22
	7	6.32
	10	6.42
	15	6.56
	20	6.56
	30	6.56

Figure 15.3   USD money market data

	Price'	Cashflow matrix (Partial)													
date:		08/10/97	09/10/97	15/10/97	10/11/97	19/11/97	17/12/97	08/01/98	14/01/98	18/02/98	18/03/98	17/06/98	16/09/98	08/10/98	16/12/98
time:		0	0.00274	0.019178	0.090411	0.115068	0.191781	0.252055	0.268493	0.364384	0.441096	0.690411	0.939726	1	1.189041
libor: act/360	1	1.000155	0	0	0	0	0	0	0	0	0	0	0	0	0
	1	0	0	1.005156	0	0	0	0	0	0	0	0	0	0	0
	1	0	0	0	0	0	1.014615	0	0	0	0	0	0	0	0
futures: act/360	0	0	-1	0	0	0	0	1.014484	0	0	0	0	0	0	0
	0	0	0	0	-1	0	0	0	1.014509	0	0	0	0	0	0
	0	0	0	0	0	-1	0	0	0	1.01456	0	0	0	0	0
	0	0	0	0	0	0	0	0	0	-1	1.014585	0	0	0	0
	0	0	0	0	0	0	0	0	0	0	-1	1.014712	0	0	0
	0	0	0	0	0	0	0	0	0	0	0	-1	0	1.014863	
	0	0	0	0	0	0	0	0	0	0	0	0	0	-1	
swaps: act/360	1	0	0	0	0	0	0	0	0	0	0	0	0	0.060125	0
	1	0	0	0	0	0	0	0	0	0	0	0	0	0.061082	0
	1	0	0	0	0	0	0	0	0	0	0	0	0	0.0616	0
	1	0	0	0	0	0	0	0	0	0	0	0	0	0.0622	0
	1	0	0	0	0	0	0	0	0	0	0	0	0	0.0632	0
	1	0	0	0	0	0	0	0	0	0	0	0	0	0.0642	0
	1	0	0	0	0	0	0	0	0	0	0	0	0	0.0656	0
	1	0	0	0	0	0	0	0	0	0	0	0	0	0.0656	0
	1	0	0	0	0	0	0	0	0	0	0	0	0	0.0656	0

Figure 15.4   USD data: cashflows and notional prices

of discount factors so that

$$P = C\hat{\delta} + \varepsilon, \tag{15.1}$$

where the errors ε are small.

We do not expect ε to be identically zero. In practice prices are never exactly simultaneous, and bid–offer spreads introduce noise into quoted prices. Theoretically when ε is non-zero there may be arbitrage opportunities in the market. Normally, if not always, either the arbitrage is a figment caused by, for instance, non-synchronous data, or else prices are insufficiently out of line to make a profit once transaction costs are taken into account.

One might attempt to find $\hat{\delta}$ in equation (15.1) directly using OLS regression. The unconstrained solution to the linear programming problem,

$$\delta^* = \arg\min_{\hat{\delta}} \left\{ \varepsilon' \varepsilon \mid \varepsilon = P - C\hat{\delta} \right\}, \tag{15.2}$$

is

$$\delta^* = (C'C)^{-1} C'P. \tag{15.3}$$

Unfortunately finding $\hat{\delta}$ this way does not work very well. The matrix C has too many columns compared with the length of the vector P, and too many zeros. For example, Carleton and Cooper (76) [117] tried to find a term structure from coupon bond data. They were able to find a data set in which a large number of bonds had cashflows on the same four dates each year, so that C was not entirely full of zeros. The regression method still has big problems. There are as many parameters as there are cashflow dates, and there is nothing to regularise the discount factors found from the regression; each discount factor is only coincidentally related to those of similar maturity. This results is an extremely ragged set of implied spot rates and an even worse set of implied forward rates.

Figure 15.5 shows the results of using this approach in a simple example. Coupon bond prices were generated using a set of 'actual' spot rates. To represent trading noise, et cetera, the prices were randomly perturbed by Gaussian noise with a standard deviation of 10 basis points. The figure shows actual forward rates, and the forward rates recovered from the perturbed prices. Although the actual forward rates lie on a smooth curve, the recovered forward rates do not; they reflect the noise introduced

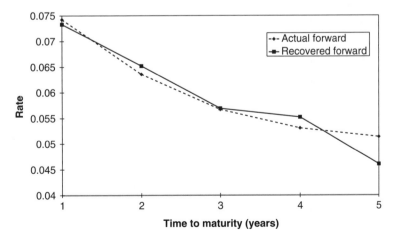

Figure 15.5   Actual and perturbed forward rates

into the bond prices. We conclude that the direct regression approach is inadequate for modelling the yield curve.

In the money market optimising equation (15.1) may not be the most appropriate way to obtain the vector $\hat{\delta}$. Instead, one may attempt to recover market quoted rates, a procedure likely to be more acceptable to traders. Suppose that M is a vector of market quoted rates. Given C and $\hat{\delta}$ one may reconstruct model quoted rates $\hat{M} = \hat{M}\left(C, \hat{\delta}\right)$. The optimisation is now

$$\delta^* = \arg\min_{\hat{\delta}} \left\{ \left(M - \hat{M}\right)' \left(M - \hat{M}\right) \right\}. \tag{15.4}$$

This will in general produce a different set of discount factors to the original optimisation, but will suffer the same problems as before.

In the bond market, instead of fitting to the market prices of coupon bonds one may instead minimise the error in the imputed values of pure discount bond prices. For a discount curve $\delta(\tau) = \delta(\tau \mid \theta)$ depending on some parameter set θ, Gourieroux and Scaillet (94) [258] explore a kernel method (see Section 15.6) using the optimisation

$$\theta^* = \arg\min_{\theta} \left\{ \varepsilon'\varepsilon \mid P = C(\delta_\theta + \varepsilon) \right\}, \tag{15.5}$$

where $\delta_\theta = (\delta(\tau_1 \mid \theta), \ldots, \delta(\tau_m \mid \theta))'$ is the vector of discount factors conditional on θ. If one may assume that $\text{var}(\varepsilon) = \omega^2 \Lambda$, where Λ is diagonal, then this criterion is equivalent to

$$\theta^* = \arg\min_{\theta} (P - C\delta_\theta)'(C\Lambda C')^{-1}(P - C\delta_\theta); \tag{15.6}$$

that is, the method imposes a particular weighting matrix on errors at different maturities. If $\delta_\theta = X\theta$, for a loading matrix X whose columns represent basis vectors, then

$$\theta^* = \left[X'C'(C\Lambda C')^{-1}CX\right]^{-1} X'C'(C\Lambda C')^{-1}P.$$

This is a readily computable explicit formula for the parameter values θ.

Comparing (15.5) with (15.2) it is not obvious in general whether one should fit to market prices or to discount factors. A clear trading preference is to optimise (15.2).

15.1.4   Polynomial Approximation

It is well known that a polynomial of sufficiently high degree can approximate arbitrarily closely any continuous function (on a closed interval) so it is tempting to use a polynomial approximation to the yield curve.

Given a set of m points $\{\tau_k, \delta_k\}_{k=1,\ldots,m}$ on the plane (with distinct values of τ_k) a Lagrange polynomial of degree m will pass through every point. For $k = 1, \ldots, m$ set

$$\phi_k(\tau) = \prod_{i=1, i\neq k}^{m} \frac{\tau - \tau_i}{\tau_j - \tau_i}. \tag{15.7}$$

These are a set of basis functions. Define

$$\delta(\tau) = \sum_{k=1}^{m} \delta_k \phi_k(\tau), \tag{15.8}$$

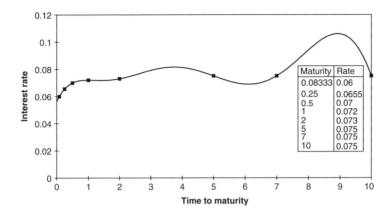

Figure 15.6   Lagrange polynomial curve fitting

then $\delta(\tau_k) = \delta_k$, $k = 1, \ldots, m$. $\delta(\tau)$ is a polynomial that passes through each of the points (τ_k, δ_k) at maturities τ_k. Figure 15.6 shows a typical Lagrange polynomial fit to a specified set of data points. The inadequacies of the fit are obvious. The polynomial is out of control in between the data points, and its behaviour at the extremes of the data set $[0, t_{\max}]$ can be very bad. Forward curves near 0 and $t_{\max}$ are very badly behaved. Since $\mid \delta(t) \mid \to \infty$ as $t \to \pm\infty$, it cannot be used to extrapolate outside the interval $[0, t_{\max}]$.

More subtle is the non-locality of the approximation; small changes in the data can have large non-local effects. The effect of a small change in a single data point is shown in Figure 15.7. The three-month point has been perturbed by 5 basis points from 6.55% to 6.6%. The fit is now ridiculous.

If an exact fit to the data set does not work, an approximate fit may do better. Chambers, Carleton and Waldman (84) [123] used a third-degree polynomial approximation

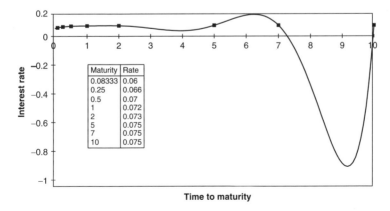

Figure 15.7   Lagrange polynomial fit to perturbed data

to the spot rate curve, for instance, and reported good results. Unfortunately the yield curve is not usually close to being a third-, or fourth- or higher degree polynomial. Fitting a low-order polynomial to a curve that is not of this type leads to the same types of problems as encountered by Lagrange polynomials, albeit on a smaller scale.

15.2 FITTING USING PARAMETERISED CURVES

For a vector P of current prices and a matrix C of cashflows we want to find a vector $\hat{\delta}$ of discount factors so that $P = C\hat{\delta} + \varepsilon$, where the errors ε are small. We have seen that finding $\hat{\delta}$ directly using OLS regression does not work.

A better approach is to let $\delta(\tau)$ be a function of time to maturity, defined for all maturity times $t \in [0, \infty)$, and then to set $\hat{\delta} = (\delta(\tau_1), \ldots, \delta(\tau_m))'$, where $\{\tau_k\}_{k=1,\ldots,m}$ is the set of cashflow times. If the function $\delta(\tau)$ depends on a small number of parameters, $\delta(\tau) = \delta(\tau \mid a, b, \ldots)$, then fitting the curve involves choosing an optimal set of parameters. For example, the Nelson and Siegel functions are

$$\delta(\tau) = \delta(\tau \mid a, b, c, d) = a + (b + c\tau)e^{-d\tau}, \tag{15.9}$$

a four-parameter family of curves. One chooses $\{a, b, c, d\}$ to make $\varepsilon = P - C\hat{\delta}$ small, for instance by minimising $\varepsilon'\varepsilon$.

This procedure is much more stable than OLS regression. There are only a few parameters to estimate, four in the case of Nelson and Siegel, instead of one parameter for every cashflow time. The resulting curve really is a curve, not a set of independent discount factors.

15.2.1 Types of Curves

The curves commonly used in fitting the term structure can be separated into two main types. Firstly there are parametric curves derived from interest rate models, for example Longstaff and Schwartz term structures, or Fong and Vasicek term structures. Secondly there are non-parametric curves. These are general curve-fitting families including, for example, B-splines and Nelson and Siegel curves, that do not derive from an interest rate model. (Non-parametric curves also depend upon a set of parameters.)

Non-parametric curves are used to calibrate interest rate models such as extended Vasicek or HJM where an initial yield curve is an input to the model. A time series of stripped curves can be used to obtain volatility functions for HJM models by principal component analysis.

Families of curves may be 'linear' or 'non-linear'. A linear family forms a vector space with a set of basis elements, so that every curve in the family can be represented as a linear combination of basis functions. Because of this property, 'linear' curves are easy to optimise to get a 'best' fit.

A non-linear family of curves does not have a set of basis functions and a curve in the family cannot be represented as a sum of other simpler curves. It may be difficult to optimise to find the curve in the family that provides a best fit.

Table 15.1 Families of curves

Examples of curves	Linear	Non-linear
Parametric	Affine term structures	Tice and Webber
Non-parametric	Splines	Nelson and Siegel

Table 15.1 gives examples of families of curves of each type.

Affine term structures are a linear family of curves for the spot rate curve, not the discount curve. For a fixed set of parameter values a term structure is determined as an element of a vector space whose coordinates are the set of values of the state variables of the model.

Tice and Webber (97) [523] term structures arise from a chaotic model of interest rates, and so are pathologically non-linear.

We discuss splines and Nelson and Siegel curves in later sections.

15.2.2 Using a Basis

The existence of a basis makes it very easy to work with linear families of curves. In a linear family the function $\delta(\tau)$ can be represented as

$$\delta(\tau) = \sum_{k=1}^{K} \lambda_k \phi_k(\tau), \tag{15.10}$$

for some fixed set of functions $\phi_k(\tau)$, $k = 1, \ldots, K$. The set $\{\phi_k(\tau)\}_{k=1,\ldots,K}$ is the set of basis functions. The function $\delta(\tau)$ is determined by the vector $\lambda = (\lambda_1, \ldots, \lambda_K)'$. It is simple to find Λ to obtain an optimal fit, by the least squares criterion.

We require $P = C\hat{\delta} + \varepsilon$. Set $\Phi = \{\phi_k(\tau_j)\}_{k=1,\ldots,K, j=1,\ldots,m}$, so that $\hat{\delta} = \Phi'\lambda$, and set $D = C\Phi'$. Now we only have to find λ so that

$$P = D\lambda + \varepsilon. \tag{15.11}$$

This is easily done using a regression technique. There are now only K parameters to find. Typically, in a term structure problem, K may be as small as six or seven, for a suitable set of basis functions.

Example: Affine Yield Models

In an affine model spot rates are affine in the state variables X_i,

$$r_t(\tau) = A_0(\tau) + \sum_{i=1}^{n} A_i(\tau)X_{i,t}, \tag{15.12}$$

where $\{A_i(\tau)\}_{i=1,\ldots,n}$ is a set of basis functions determined by the model and depending on the parameters of the model. We suppose that we have a set of working estimates of the values of the parameters of the model but need to infer values of the state variables $X_{i,t}$, which may not be directly observable.

Suppose spot rates $R_t(\tau_j)$ are observed at maturities $\tau_1, \ldots, \tau_m$. We adopt the viewpoint that the model fits the market accurately and that discrepancies are due to random noise, so that $R_t(\tau_j) = r_t(\tau_j) + \varepsilon_{t,j}$, where $\varepsilon_{t,j}$ are Gaussian errors.

Write

$$R_t = (R_t(\tau_1), \ldots, R_t(\tau_m))', \quad a = (A_0(\tau_1), \ldots, A_0(\tau_m))',$$

$A = \{A_i(\tau_j)\}_{i=1,\ldots,n, \, j=1,\ldots,m}$ and $\varepsilon_t = (\varepsilon_{t,1}, \ldots, \varepsilon_{t,m})'$.

Then

$$R_t = a + AX_t + \varepsilon_t, \tag{15.13}$$

where X_t is the vector of state variables. This is linear, and it is easy to back out from it values of X_t that provide a best fit.

Alternatively and preferably one can look at changes R_t over one time period. Set $\Delta R_t = R_{t+1} - R_t$, then

$$\Delta R_t = A \Delta X_t + \eta_t, \tag{15.14}$$

where η_t are errors in the fit to changes in R_t. One is far happier supposing that η_t are Gaussian errors than that ε_t in (15.13) are. A disadvantage of (15.14) is that only changes ΔX_t in X_t are found, so that an initial value X_0 of the vector of state variables needs to be supplied.

15.3   FITTING THE YIELD CURVE USING SPLINES

Splines are a linear non-parametric interpolation method. There are several ways of using them. The most straightforward method is regression splines. This method has some problems, however. A regression spline curve may oscillate too much and it is sensitive to modelling parameters. As a result it may not produce a good curve at too long or too short maturities.

An improved technique is the smoothing spline method. It requires a parameter controlling the degree of curvature that is tolerated in a fitted curve. For yield curve estimation this parameter should be maturity dependent.

Spline methods are described by de Boor (78) [161] and Dierckx (95) [168], *et cetera*.

15.3.1   Splines and B-Splines

A kth-order spline is a piecewise polynomial approximation, with polynomials of degree k, differentiable $k - 1$ times everywhere.

The points $\{\xi_0, \ldots, \xi_n\}$, $\xi_p < \xi_{p+1}$, $p = 0, \ldots, n - 1$, where adjacent polynomials meet, are called knot points. A kth-order spline has to be differentiable $k - 1$ times at every knot point ξ_p, $p = 1, \ldots, n - 1$. A piecewise cubic polynomial is a curve $s(\tau)$ that is a polynomial of degree three on each interval $[\xi_p, \xi_{p+1}]$, $p = 0, \ldots, n - 1$. It is a spline if it is twice differentiable at each ξ_p, $p = 1, \ldots, n - 1$.

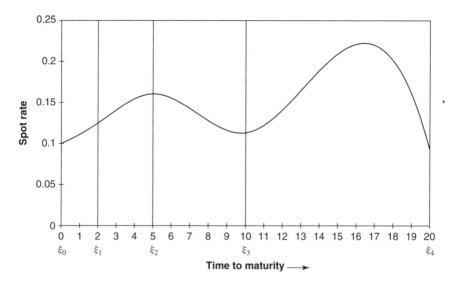

Figure 15.8 A cubic spline; knots are at {0, 2, 5, 10, 20}

Cubic Splines

A cubic spline is a spline of order three; it is a piecewise cubic polynomial that is everywhere twice differentiable. At each knot point:

1. Slopes on each side must match,
2. Curvatures from each side must match.

Figure 15.8 is a cubic spline. Vertical lines mark the locations of the knot points. On each interval the curve is a cubic polynomial. It is clear that a large variety of shapes is possible, with the possibility of up to one hump and one trough in each interval.

A general cubic spline is given by the formula

$$s(\tau) = \sum_{i=0}^{3} a_i \tau^i + \frac{1}{3!} \sum_{p=1}^{n-1} b_p (\tau - \xi_p)_+^3, \qquad (15.15)$$

where $(\tau - \xi_p)_+ = \max(\tau - \xi_p, 0)$. The first part of the formula is a cubic polynomial. The second part is differentiable only twice at the knot points. For a spline with $n + 1$ knots $\{\xi_0, \ldots, \xi_n\}$, a cubic spline has $n + 3$ parameters, $\{a_0, \ldots, a_3, b_1, \ldots, b_{n-1}\}$, and in general a kth degree spline has $n + k$ parameters.

$s(\tau)$ is a linear combination of the functions

$$\left\{\tau^i\right\}_{i=0,\ldots,3}, \qquad \left\{(\tau - \xi_p)_+^3\right\}_{p=1,\ldots,n-1}, \qquad (15.16)$$

and so these functions provide a basis for the space of cubic splines (conditional on the knot points). This is a poor choice of basis functions since the functions in (15.16) are unbounded. For modelling the yield curve a set of basis functions should be bounded, and preferably zero outside some compact set. This makes computation easy and stable, and local in the sense that only a few basis functions would be non-zero at any particular maturity time.

Equation (15.15) is not a very useful way of writing down a spline. It is much more convenient to find a set of basis functions and to represent general splines as linear combinations of these. A good set of basis functions are the B-splines.

For fixed set of knots $\{\xi_0, \dots, \xi_n\}$ and for $p = 0, \dots, n - 4$, set

$$B_p(\tau) = \sum_{j=p}^{p+4} \left(\prod_{i=p, i \neq j}^{p+4} \frac{1}{\xi_i - \xi_j} \right) (\tau - \xi_p)_+^3. \tag{15.17}$$

$B_p(\tau)$ are cubic B-splines. $B_p(\tau)$ is only non-zero on the interval $[\xi_p, \xi_{p+4}]$. Figure 15.9 shows a B-spline defined by knot points at $\{0, 1, 6, 8, 11\}$. The curve has a characteristic hump, but the exact shape depends on the location of the knot points. The B-spline is zero outside the range $[\xi_p, \xi_{p+4}] = [0, 11]$.

Out of Interval Knot Points

$n + 3$ parameters are required to define a spline so $n + 3$ functions are needed to form a basis. Equation (15.17) enables us to define $n - 3$ B-splines using knots $\xi_0, \dots, \xi_n$. A further six basis functions are required. These are found by the trick of defining additional 'out of interval' knot points.

Introduce extra knots $\xi_{-3}, \xi_{-2}, \xi_{-1}, \xi_{n+1}, \xi_{n+2}, \xi_{n+3}$ with

$$\xi_{-3} < \xi_{-2} < \xi_{-1} < \xi_0 < \cdots < \xi_n < \xi_{n+1} < \xi_{n+2} < \xi_{n+3}. \tag{15.18}$$

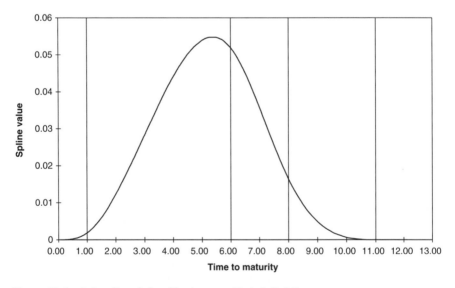

Figure 15.9   A B-spline defined by knots at $\{0, 1, 6, 8, 11\}$

It is now possible to define $B_p(\tau)$ for $p = -3, \ldots, n-1$, giving $n+3$ B-splines. The basis is the set of functions $\{B_p(\tau)\}_{p=-3,\ldots,n-1}$ restricted to the interval $[\xi_0, \xi_n]$. It is straightforward to show that these functions do indeed give a basis for the set of cubic splines on $[\xi_0, \xi_n]$.

15.3.2 Using B-Splines

The B-spline approximating function on $[\xi_0, \xi_n]$ is

$$\delta(\tau) = \delta(\tau \mid \lambda_{-3}, \ldots, \lambda_{n-1}) = \sum_{p=-3}^{n-1} \lambda_p B_p(\tau), \tag{15.19}$$

where $\lambda = (\lambda_{-3}, \ldots, \lambda_{n-1})'$ are coefficients to be determined by the fit. For cashflow times $\tau_1, \ldots, \tau_m$ define $B = \{B_p(\tau_j)\}_{p=-3,\ldots,n-1, j=1,\ldots,m}$ and $\hat{\delta} = (\delta(\tau_1), \ldots, \delta(\tau_m))'$, so that $\hat{\delta} = B'\lambda$. Now

$$\delta^* = \arg\min_{\hat{\delta}} \left\{ \varepsilon'\varepsilon \mid \varepsilon = P - C\hat{\delta} \right\} \tag{15.20}$$

has the same minimum errors, $\varepsilon'\varepsilon$, as the equivalent regression

$$\lambda^* = \arg\min_{\lambda} \left\{ \varepsilon'\varepsilon \mid \varepsilon = P - D\lambda \right\}, \tag{15.21}$$

where $D = CB'$ is known. Equation (15.21) can be solved easily using OLS regression. There are only $n+3$ parameters to be found, where the number of 'in interval' intervals, n, may be as small as three.

Example of Using B-splines: Steeley (91) [506]

Steeley (91) [506] was amongst the first authors to use B-splines to estimate term structures. He estimated the UK gilt term structure using closing mid-market prices of high coupon gilts, for each week in the period March 1986 to October 1987.[1] Importantly, Steeley obtained error intervals for his estimates.

He used cubic B-splines with $n = 3$. Knots were at the points

Knot:	ξ_{-3}	ξ_{-2}	ξ_{-1}	ξ_0	ξ_1	ξ_2	ξ_3	ξ_4	ξ_5	ξ_6
Location:	-3	-2	-1	0	5	10	40	45	50	60

(15.22)

giving an estimation interval $[0, 40]$. In-interval knot points chosen so that approximately equal number of bonds mature in each of the three 'in interval' intervals. Steeley reports good results for his method.

Steeley (n.d.) [503] went on to use the stripped yield curves to analyse the components of yield curve movements.

---

[1] In the UK low coupon bond prices are distorted by tax effects. The distortion is reduced by restricting the data sample to high coupon bonds.

The unconstrained problem   The solution to the unconstrained regression

$$\lambda^* = \arg\min_{\lambda} \left\{ \varepsilon' \varepsilon \mid \varepsilon = P - D\lambda \right\} \tag{15.23}$$

is

$$\lambda^* = \left(D'D\right)^{-1} D'P. \tag{15.24}$$

This is extremely easy to solve; since D is a small matrix it can even be done on a spreadsheet.

The constrained problem   It is reasonable to demand that $\delta(0) = 1$. This ties down the left-hand side of the discount curve and should give a better fit at the short end. We write $W = (B_{-3}(0), \ldots, B_{n-1}(0))'$ for the vector of values of the B-splines at 0, and set $w = 1$. The constraint is the requirement that $W\lambda = w$, so we solve the constrained problem

$$\lambda^{\#} = \arg\min_{\lambda} \left\{ \varepsilon' \varepsilon \mid \varepsilon = P - D\lambda, W\lambda = w \right\}. \tag{15.25}$$

The solution to the constrained problem is

$$\lambda^{\#} = \lambda^* + \frac{\left(W'W\right)^{-1} B'}{B \left(W'W\right)^{-1} B'} \left(w - W\lambda^*\right). \tag{15.26}$$

Solutions found from (15.26) do indeed provide a better fit at the short end than solutions found from (15.24).

An Example of a B-spline Fit

We return to the gilt data presented in Section 15.1. The maximum bond maturity is 12.12 years. We use knots at $\{-20, -5, -2, 0, 1, 6, 8, 11, 15, 20, 25, 30\}$ so that the estimation interval is $[0, 15]$. We leave a discussion of the appropriateness of this choice of knots for the moment, merely noting for now that we are fitting a set of nine bonds with eight B-splines. Figure 15.10 shows the B-spline basis for these knot points. Solving for the unconstrained problem (15.24) we find values $\lambda = (13.2, 11.5, 8.5, 7.7, 6.9, 6.4, -6.0, 917.6)$ (to one decimal place), producing the yield curve estimate in Figure 15.11. The figure shows both the spline estimate and also a plot of the bond redemption yields.

Although useless for most purposes the redemption yields give an indication of the approximate location and shape of the actual yield curve. The redemption yield curve shows no sign of any anomalous behaviour in the term structure. If an approximating curve fits some bond price exactly, then it would automatically recover the redemption yield for that bond on the redemption yield curve. With eight splines fitting to only nine bonds one expects that prices, and hence redemption yields, would be closely fitted.

The spline curve is evidently a bad fit. Its behaviour at both short and long maturities is abysmal, and at middle maturities it also appears to have excess curvature. Like a Lagrange polynomial approximation it passes through (or very closely to) a certain

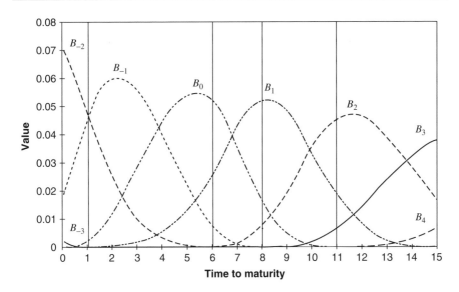

Figure 15.10   B-spline basis: knots at $\{-20, -5, -2, 0, 1, 6, 8, 11, 15, 20, 25, 30\}$

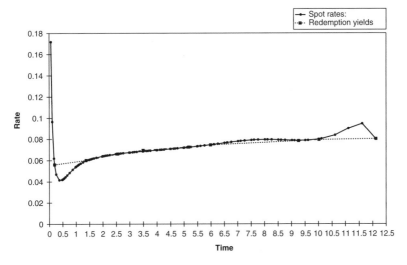

Figure 15.11   A poor B-spline estimate of the yield curve

set of points, but its behaviour in between those points can be very poor. It is badly overfitting because

1. too many splines have been used in the approximation, and
2. in any case the knots are badly positioned.

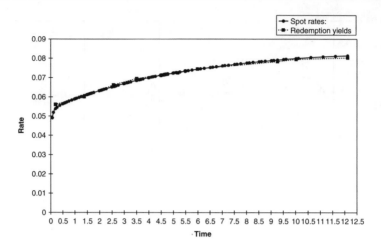

Figure 15.12   An improved B-spline estimate of the yield curve

If a fit were 'reasonable' and stable one might expect each B-spline to contribute roughly equally to the approximating curve, so that each element of λ was roughly the same order of magnitude. An examination of the λ giving the approximating curve in Figure 15.11 reveals that although most elements of λ have absolute value in the range 5 to 15, λ_3 is -6 and λ_4 is 917. The reason for this is that the choice of knots has left B_4 almost zero at the final bond's maturity date. A better choice of knots, such as those determining Figure 15.12, would overcome this problem.

Compare Figure 15.11 with Figure 15.12. Five splines were used to construct this curve, with knots $\xi = \{-10, -5, -2, 0, 4, 15, 20, 25, 30\}$. The curve looks much superior to before, but by the criterion of equation (15.24) the fit is worse. The curve no longer reconstructs bond prices as well as before. For instance, Bond 1 maturing in 0.2 of a year is a pure discount bond. Its price is more or less exactly recovered by the curve in Figure 15.11. The curve in the second figure overprices it by five basis points compared with a one basis point error in the first curve. The second curve has a root mean square error of 0.13 compared with an error of 0.07 for the first curve.

An improved fit can be found by imposing the constraint at zero, but the arbitrariness of the method is evident. The results are extremely sensitive to the number and location of the knot points, and there is no optimal way of selecting them. Also, if we believe that Figure 15.12 shows a better curve than that in Figure 15.11 then the criterion we have used in (15.23) is incorrect.

15.3.3   Smoothing Splines

The normal least squares criterion is to choose $\lambda = (\lambda_{-3}, \ldots, \lambda_{n-1})'$ to minimise

$$c_1 = (P - CB'\lambda))^2. \tag{15.27}$$

We saw in the previous section that there is cause to be dissatisfied with this criterion. An alternative is to use a smoothing criterion. There are several different forms of smoothing criteria. They all have in common the willingness to relax criterion (15.23) in order to achieve a fit with less curvature, measured in some way.

Natural Smoothing Splines

For $\delta(\tau) = \sum_{p=-3}^{n-1} \lambda_p B_p(\tau)$, we set

$$c_2 = \int_{\xi_0}^{\xi_n} \left(\frac{\partial^j \delta}{\partial \tau^j} \right)^2 d\tau, \qquad (15.28)$$

with $j = k - 1$ for a kth-degree spline. For cubic splines $k = 2$. c_2 is a measure of the total curvature of the spline approximation $\delta(\tau)$. The natural smoothing criterion is

$$\lambda^* = \arg \min_{\lambda} \{ c_2 \mid c_1 \leq S \} \qquad (15.29)$$

for some constant S. S is the smoothing factor which determines the relative importance of c_1 and c_2.

A spline of degree k is natural if

$$\left. \frac{\partial^{k-1} \delta}{\partial \tau^{k-1}} \right|_{\xi_0} = \left. \frac{\partial^{k-1} \delta}{\partial \tau^{k-1}} \right|_{\xi_n} = 0. \qquad (15.30)$$

Criterion (15.29) is an appealing criterion to use in the light of the result that, for an arbitrary j, c_2 is minimised, subject to $c_1 \leq S$, by a natural spline of degree $2j - 1$, with knots at the data points.

Smoothing splines are splines that optimise a criterion that incorporates a smoothing condition. They reduce the amount of curvature in $\delta(\tau)$ at the expense of a worse fit by the criterion c_1. Other smoothing criteria are

$$c_2 = \int_{\xi_0}^{\xi_n} \left| \frac{\partial^j \delta}{\partial \tau^j} \right| d\tau, \qquad (15.31)$$

$$c_2 = \int_{\xi_0}^{\xi_n} \left(\frac{\partial \delta}{\partial \tau} \right)^2 d\tau, \qquad (15.32)$$

amongst others. We highlight a jump-smoothness criterion.

A Jump-smoothing Criterion

This is a criterion described by Dierckx (95) [168]. For a cubic spline the third derivative is discontinuous at the knot points and the size of the discontinuity is a measure of the curvature of the spline. Set

$$c_3 = \sum_{p=0}^{n} \left\{ \frac{\partial^j \delta}{\partial \tau^j}(\xi_p^+) - \frac{\partial^j \delta}{\partial \tau^j}(\xi_p^-) \right\}, \qquad (15.33)$$

where $j = k$ for a kth-degree spline. We choose λ and $\xi = (\xi_{-3}, \ldots, \xi_{n+3})$ by the criterion

$$(\lambda^*, \xi^*) = \arg\min_{\lambda, \xi}\{c_3 \mid c_1 \leq S\}, \tag{15.34}$$

for some constant smoothing factor S.

c_3 measures the curvature in $\delta(\tau)$ as the sum of the jumps in the kth derivative at the knot points. For algorithms and properties of this criterion see Dierckx (95) [168].

Applications of Smoothing Splines

Various authors have compared different types of smoothing splines and their relative success at fitting the term structure. Maximal smoothness splines were introduced by Adams and Van Deventer (94) [6]. Smoothing splines were also used by Fisher, Nychka and Zervos (95) [220] and Tanggaard (95) [516]. Waggoner (97) [536] recommends the use of weighted penalty roughness splines. A comparison of some of these methods may be found in Bliss (96) [77]. We review several of these techniques.

Maximal smoothness splines Adams and Van Deventer (94) [6] used a criterion based on the smoothness of the forward rate curve $f(\tau \mid \lambda, \xi)$ defined from a spline approximation $\delta(\tau \mid \lambda, \xi)$ of the discount curve. For a vector of bond prices P with cashflow times τ_i, $i = 1, \ldots, m$, set

$$c_4 = \int_0^T \left(\frac{\partial^2 f(\tau \mid \lambda, \xi)}{\partial \tau^2}\right)^2 d\tau + \theta'(P - C\delta), \tag{15.35}$$

where θ is a vector of Lagrange multipliers. A maximal smoothness spline selects λ, ξ and θ to minimise the criterion c_4. It can be shown that, conditional on $\{\tau_i\}_{i=1,\ldots,m}$, a function f optimising c_4 is a quartic spline, with knots at $0 = \tau_0 < \tau_1 < \cdots < \tau_m < \tau_{m+1} = T = T_{\max}$, of the form

$$f(t) = f_i(t) = a_i + b_i t + c_i t^4 \tag{15.36}$$

on each interval $[\tau_i, \tau_{i+1}]$. (a_i, b_i, c_i, $i = 1, \ldots, m$ must satisfy certain compatibility conditions.) There are two free end conditions, so we may impose $f'(T_{\max}) = 0$ and $a_0 = r_0$, the short rate.

Adams and Van Deventer compared six methods, including regression splines on δ, regression splines on the spot rate curve $r(\tau)$, exponential splines (see below), and linear interpolation on yields. In brief they found that fitting to prices produced a smoother yield curve than fitting to yields.

Criteria c_4 is not the only smoothing criteria that could be used. Adams and Van Deventer mention

$$c_4' = \int_0^T \frac{\left|\dfrac{\partial^2 f(\tau)}{\partial \tau^2}\right|}{\left(\dfrac{\partial f(\tau)}{\partial \tau}\right)^2 + 1} d\tau + \theta'(P - C\delta), \tag{15.37}$$

and several other plausible criteria can be devised. They are not interchangeable; each emphasises a particular property of the data and will result in different fits to the yield curve.

Smoothing spline criterion   The smoothing spline criterion is c_5 where

$$c_5 = \theta \int_0^T \left(\frac{\partial^2 h(\tau \mid \lambda, \xi)}{\partial \tau^2} \right)^2 d\tau + (P - C\delta(\tau \mid \lambda, \xi))^2. \tag{15.38}$$

h is some invertible function of the yield curve. θ is the smoothing or roughness parameter.

Fisher, Nychka and Zervos (95) [220] used this criterion in a study of US bond data. They used a number of knots equal to about a third of the number of bonds. As usual the knot spacing was fixed so that an equal number of bonds was in each interval. They compare the results of splining h when h is either the discount curve $\delta(\tau)$, or the curve $k(\tau) = \tau r(\tau)$, the forward rate curve.

For both simulated and real data they found that the best results were achieved by splining the forward rate curve.

The choice of θ?   In the Fisher, Nychka and Zervos method the choice of the parameter θ is crucial. Is there an optimal choice for θ? One way is to choose θ to minimise the 'general cross validation criterion', GCV(λ). For a given value of θ set $\delta_\theta = \delta(\tau \mid \lambda^*, \xi^*, \theta)$, where $(\lambda^*, \xi^*) = \arg\min_{(\lambda, \xi)} c_5$. δ_θ is the optimal discount curve for the given value of θ. One way of measuring the error in the approximation is as $E(\theta) = \mathrm{tr}(S_\theta)$ where S_θ is a diagonal matrix such that $S_\theta P = C\delta_\theta$. If δ_θ reproduces bond prices perfectly then S_θ is the identity matrix, and $E(\theta) = M$ is the number of bonds in the sample. $E(\theta)$ can be thought of as representing the 'number of bond prices' explained by the fit found using the parameter θ.

Set

$$\mathrm{GCV}(\theta) = \frac{\mathrm{MSE}(\theta)}{(M - \eta E(\theta))^2} \tag{15.39}$$

where $\mathrm{MSE}(\lambda) = (P - C\delta_\theta)^2$ is the residual sum of squares. GCV(θ) tries to get the best fit by minimising MSE(θ) while simultaneously minimising the mispricing measured by $E(\theta)$.

η is a 'tuning' parameter. Fisher, Nychka and Zervos take $\eta = 2$, as does Waggoner who reproduces their methodology (see below). Tanggaard uses $\eta = 1$. The choice of η is itself prone to the same criticism as the choice of θ. Instead of arbitrarily choosing θ, one has to arbitrarily choose η.

Weighted penalty roughness splines   The criteria described above apply the same value of θ at every maturity in the term structure. In effect, curvature at any maturity is penalised equally. However, the yield curve is prone to have much more curvature at the short end than at the long end. Waggoner (97) [536] allowed θ to depend on time to maturity τ, $\theta \equiv \theta(\tau)$. Specifically he set

$$\theta(\tau) = 0.1, \qquad 0 \le \tau < 1,$$

$$\theta(\tau) = 100, \qquad 1 \le \tau < 10, \qquad\qquad (15.40)$$

$$\theta(\tau) = 100\,000, \qquad 10 \le \tau,$$

and optimised the criteria c_6 applied to the forward rate curve f:

$$c_6 = \int_0^T \theta(\tau) \left(\frac{\partial^2 f(\tau \mid \lambda)}{\partial \tau^2} \right)^2 d\tau + (P - C\delta(\tau \mid \lambda))^2. \qquad (15.41)$$

A time-varying θ allows the approximating curve to have greater curvature where θ is small. Waggoner compared this method with simple regression splines and with ordinary smoothing splines. He strongly recommends the use of a time-varying roughness penalty. The GCV criterion is not recommended.

15.4 NELSON AND SIEGEL CURVES

These are a family curves with relatively few parameters, sometimes advocated by economists. They succeed fairly well in capturing the overall shape of the yield curve, as long as it is not too complex, and as long as good accuracy is not required. There are several different versions of this family of curves.

Nelson and Siegel: This is the original family described by Nelson and Siegel (85) [412]. There are four parameters $(\beta_0, \beta_1, \beta_2, k)$. The curve is $f_0(\tau)$,

$$f_0(\tau) = \beta_0 + (\beta + \beta_2 \tau) e^{-k\tau}. \qquad (15.42)$$

Svensson: This is a six-parameter family due to Svensson (94) [511], extending the Nelson and Siegel family by the addition of a second exponential decay term. With parameters $(\beta_0, \beta_1, \beta_2, \beta_3, k_1, k_2)$ the curves $f_1(\tau)$ are

$$f_1(\tau) = \beta_0 + (\beta_1 + \beta_2 \tau) e^{-k_1 \tau} + \beta_3 \tau e^{-k_2 \tau}. \qquad (15.43)$$

Wiseman: Wiseman (94) [544] described a family with $n + 1$ exponential decay basis elements. There are $2 \times (n + 1)$ parameters, $\{\beta_j, k_j\}_{j=0,\dots,n}$, with curves $f_2(\tau)$,

$$f_2(\tau) = \sum_{j=0}^n \beta_j e^{-k_j \tau}. \qquad (15.44)$$

Bjork and Christensen: These curves are Wiseman with polynomial coefficients. Bjork and Christensen (97) [67] devised these with a particular purpose in mind, which we discuss below. The curves are $f_3(\tau)$,

$$f_3(\tau) = \sum_{j=0}^n p_j(\tau) e^{-k_j \tau}, \qquad (15.45)$$

where $p_j(\tau)$ is a polynomial of fixed degree n_j. There are $(n + 1)(n_j + 2)$ parameters.

15.4.1 Examples of Curves

We describe only the original Nelson and Siegel curves, although our comments apply to a greater or lesser extent to the other families as well. With only four parameters the original Nelson and Siegel curves have limited flexibility. Although they can generate term structures with one hump, they cannot model 'spoon-shaped' curves with a hump and a trough. It is not possible to match arbitrary term structures with sufficient precision. For finance purposes they are rough and ready, and are not suitable for accurate 'no-arbitrage' modelling. They have the advantage that they are very easy to compute, and the variety of shapes they generate is sufficient to describe the outline of the yield curve perhaps nine-tenths of the time.

15.4.2 The Forward Rate Curve

One may choose to use Nelson and Siegel curves to model either the forward rate curve or the spot rate curve. They are not suited to model the discount curve. If the forward rate curve is

$$f_0(\tau) = \beta_0 + (\beta_1 + \beta_2\tau)e^{-k\tau}, \tag{15.46}$$

then the spot rate curve is

$$r(\tau) = \beta_0 + \left(\beta_1 + \frac{\beta_2}{k}\right)\frac{1 - e^{-k\tau}}{k\tau} - \frac{\beta_2}{k}e^{-k\tau}. \tag{15.47}$$

The short rate is $r(0) = \beta_0 + \beta_1$ and the long rate is $\lim_{\tau\to\infty} r(\tau) = \beta_0$, so that β_0 and β_1 have a very direct intuition. k and β_2 control the location and height of the hump.

Figures 15.13 and 15.14 show examples of Nelson and Siegel curves which illustrate their characteristic shape.

There are superficial similarities between equation (15.47) and Vasicek term structures given by

$$r(\tau) = r_\infty + (r_0 - r_\infty)\frac{1 - e^{-\alpha\tau}}{\alpha\tau} + \frac{\sigma^2\tau^2}{4\alpha}\left(\frac{1 - e^{-\alpha\tau}}{\alpha\tau}\right)^2. \tag{15.48}$$

The forward rate curves of each incorporate an exponential decay, but that is as far as the similarity goes.

Using Nelson and Siegel Curves

We use Nelson and Siegel curves to fit to the UK gilt prices presented in Section 15.1. We solve the non-linear problem

$$(\beta_0^*, \beta_2^*, \beta_2^*, k^*) = \arg\min_{(\beta_0, \beta_1, \beta_2, k)}\left\{\varepsilon'\varepsilon \mid \varepsilon = P - C\hat{\delta}(\tau \mid \beta_0, \beta_1, \beta_2, k)\right\}, \tag{15.49}$$

where $\hat{\delta}(\tau)$ is a vector of discount factors obtained from a Nelson and Siegel forward rate curve. The curve is illustrated in Figure 15.15. The fitted curve is remarkably

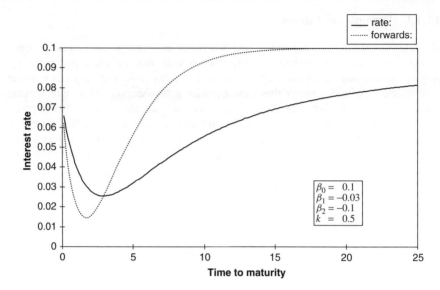

Figure 15.13   Nelson and Siegel forward and spot curves (A)

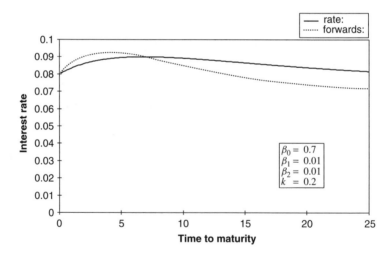

Figure 15.14   Nelson and Siegel forward and spot curves (B)

smooth, although this may not be unexpected. If anything, the curve is too smooth. It does not fit the curve well at the short end, over-pricing the short maturity bond by five basis points. The root mean square error is 13 basis points, comparable with a spline fit with five B-splines.

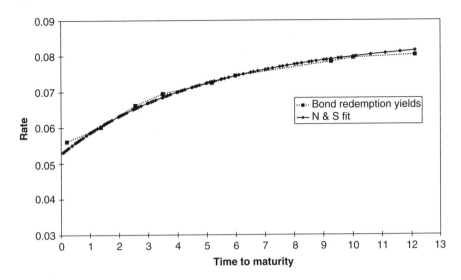

Figure 15.15   Nelson and Siegel fitted to UK gilt prices

15.5   COMPARISON OF FAMILIES OF CURVES

We compare four of the families of curves that we have met so far. The comparison is based upon three criteria:

- Flexibility: do the curves fit a wide range of term structures?
- Tractability: are the curves easy to compute?
- Consistency: are the curves compatible with a yield curve model?

The first two criteria are self-explanatory. To be useful a family of curves must be usable and also appropriate for the purpose of modelling yield curves. The final criterion is more theoretical.

Given a family of curves, $\mathcal{R}$, suppose that the initial term structure $r_0(\tau)$ belongs to $\mathcal{R}$. Is there an interest rate model such that if $r_0(\tau)$ evolves according to the model, all subsequent term structures are also in $\mathcal{R}$? If the family $\mathcal{R}$ has this property then it is consistent with that interest rate model. Bjork and Christensen (97) [67] show that their curves are consistent with the Hull and White (90) [292] extended Vasicek term structure model. On the other hand, they also show that Nelson and Siegel curves are not consistent with any interest rate model.

Table 15.2 compares Nelson and Siegel curves with cubic B-splines, affine curves, and Bjork and Christensen curves. The main advantage of Nelson and Siegel curves is their simplicity. This is also their Achilles' heel.

B-splines are very flexible and are suitable for non-parametric yield curve stripping. Affine curves, even from a two- or three-factor model, are perhaps surprisingly flexible. They are consistent as term structures and can be used as if they were non-parametric families, although this may have to be done with care.

Table 15.2 Comparison of curves

Comparison of curves	Nelson and Siegel	B-spline	Affine	Bjork and Christensen
Flexibility	$\sim$	Yes	Yes	Yes
Simplicity	Yes	$\sim$	$\sim$	$\sim$
Consistency	No	$\sim$	Yes	Yes

Bjork and Christensen's curves are flexible and consistent. Of course, the unrestricted form of their curves has too many parameters to be part of a sensible non-parametric estimation method.

15.6 KERNEL METHODS OF YIELD CURVE ESTIMATION

This section describes the work of Gourieroux and Scaillet (94) [258] and Tanggaard (92) [515] who use kernel methods to estimate a yield curve. Kernels centred at cashflow times are used to allow information at different parts of the yield curve to influence other parts of the curve.

As usual, one has a vector of coupon bond prices P and a corresponding cashflow matrix C. The discount curve $\delta(\tau) = \delta(\tau \mid \theta)$ depends on some parameter set θ. Optimising on the discount curve

$$\theta^* = \arg\min_{\theta} \left\{ \varepsilon'\varepsilon \mid P = C(\delta_{\theta} + \varepsilon) \right\} \tag{15.50}$$

when $\text{var}(\varepsilon) = \omega^2 \Lambda$, for a diagonal matrix Λ and volatility ω, one has

$$\theta^* = \arg\min_{\theta}(P - C\delta_{\theta})'(C\Lambda C')^{-1}(P - C\delta_{\theta}). \tag{15.51}$$

When an entry in Λ is small the corresponding element of ε is tightly determined. When an element in Λ is large the corresponding element in ε is only loosely specified.

15.6.1 Local Regression

A kernel method uses kernel functions to find a set of matrices $\left\{ \Lambda_{\tau_i} \right\}_{i=1,...,m}$, one for each cashflow time. The optimal parameters are $\left\{ \theta_{\tau_i} \right\}_{i=1,...,m}$, one set for each cashflow time. The matrix Λ_{τ_i} is constructed so that ε_{τ_i} is found with greatest precision. This means that the parameters θ_{τ_i} give a best fit locally, near τ_i, to the yield curve.

Given a kernel function K and a bandwidth h (see Chapter 6) we construct the weighting matrix

$$\Lambda_{\tau_i} = \text{diag}\left(\left\{ K_h(\tau_i - \tau_j)^{-1} \right\}_{j=1,...,m} \right). \tag{15.52}$$

Λ_{τ_i} measures how far away τ_i is from each τ_j, $j = 1, \ldots, m$, as measured by the kernel function K_h. For cashflow times τ_i, select θ_{τ_i} to solve

$$\theta_{\tau_i} = \arg\min_{\theta}(P - C\delta_{\theta})'\left(C\Lambda_{\tau_i}C' \right)^{-1}(P - C\delta_{\theta}). \tag{15.53}$$

The cashflow at maturity τ_j makes a contribution to the yield curve at τ_i determined by its distance from τ_i, as measured by K_h. We find parameters θ_{τ_i} indexed by τ_i.

Example: Gourieroux and Scaillet

Gourieroux and Scaillet (94) [258] fitted the Vasicek model by local regression. For the short rate process $dr_t = (\alpha + \beta r_t)dt + \sigma dz_t$, under the EMM, the parameter set is $\theta = (\beta, \alpha, \sigma^2, r_0)$, where r_0 is the short rate, a free parameter in the estimation. The spot rate curve was modelled as a Vasicek curve.

Gourieroux and Scaillet used Epanechnikov kernels and tried various bandwidths. They found that

1. When τ is large, h has little effect.
2. When τ is small, the results are quite sensitive to h.

Example: Tanggaard (92) [515]

Tanggaard (92) [515] estimated the term structure directly. Suppose that the discount curve is a one-parameter exponential decay

$$\delta_\theta(\tau) = e^{-\tau\theta}. \tag{15.54}$$

A local estimate of θ_τ is just an estimate of the spot rate of maturity τ, so that the set $\{\theta_\tau\}_{\tau \geq 0}$ is just the spot rate curve.

Tanggaard used a Gaussian kernel, with a heuristically determined bandwidth. He used both simulated and actual data and concluded, like Gourieroux and Scaillet, that the short end was harder to fit than the long end. Linton et al. (98) [353] develop the method further. Testing the method against US Treasury bonds their yield curve usually recovers bond prices to within 1% of their market values.

Despite the appealing intuition of this application of the kernel method, it is not clear how effective it is at modelling the yield curve.

15.7 LP AND REGRESSION METHODS

This section briefly reviews classical LP and the regression methods. The literature is venerable. The older methods fail if they do not incorporate a basis. We use the framework proposed by Prisman (90) [442].

LP methods were described in early papers by Schaefer (81) [476], (82) [477] and Nelson and Schaefer (83) [411]. Regression methods were used by Chambers et al. (84) [123], McCulloch (71) [387], McCulloch (75) [388], Shea (84) [487], Shea (85) [488] and Vasicek and Fong (82) [530], and Steeley (89) [504], (90) [505]. We have described Steeley's work in Section 15.3.2. McCulloch seems to have been the first person to use splines in term structure estimation, although McCulloch (71) [387] has methodological problems. Vasicek and Fong (82) [530] proposed a method called 'exponential splines', but this method was criticised by Shea (85) [488].

This section can be regarded as providing examples of methods discussed in previous sections of this chapter.

15.7.1   Background to the Methods

As usual we have a vector of prices, P, and a matrix of cashflows C. In a perfect world there would exist a vector of discount factors δ such that $P = C\delta$. An exact fit is not expected in the bond market. In the money market methods such as those described in Chapter 5 give an exact fit but have many other drawbacks. One way of investigating the consistency of prices and cashflows is to solve the dual LP to the original LP used to find δ.

If prices really were inconsistent and costs did not prevent an arbitrage opportunity, the arbitrage profit could be found as follows. Buy quantities x_i of bond i, $i = 1, \ldots, M$. Set $x = (x_1, , x_M)'$. The possible arbitrage profit is

$$\text{L1:} \qquad V = \min_x \left\{ x'P \mid x'C \geq 0 \right\}. \qquad (15.55)$$

This is the value of the cheapest portfolio with non-negative cashflows. Arbitrage is possible if $V < 0$. Write x^* for an optimal x.

- Either $x^{*\prime}P$ is unbounded, in which case there is no δ such that $C\delta = P$. This implies unlimited arbitrage profit.
- Or $x^{*\prime}P = 0$, then there is a δ such that $C\delta = P$. No arbitrage is possible in this case.

In practice, of course, the problem as posed is unrealistic. More realistic constraints need to be imposed. These include

- *Restrictions on short sales*: going short may not possible, and in any case may be too expensive.
- *Restrictions on long positions*: the extent to which one may go long is constrained by position limits imposed on a book, and ultimately by the fact that there is only a finite supply of bonds.
- *Potential profit is limited by costs*: costs include the cost of forming the arbitrage portfolio and the cost of holding, monitoring and liquidating it.

It is necessary to incorporate idealised versions of these realistic constraints into L1. Usually 'arbitrage' only exists within the bid–offer spread and so is unattainable.

No Short Sales

If one cannot hold negative quantities of bonds, so that $x_i \geq 0$ for all i, L1 is modified to become L2:

$$\text{L2:} \qquad V = \min_x \left\{ x'P \mid x'C \geq 0, x \geq 0 \right\}. \qquad (15.56)$$

This is solvable, with $V = 0$, only if there is a term structure δ such that $C\delta \leq P$. For positive C and P this is possible with $\delta \equiv 0$, when $x \equiv 0$ solves L2.

If for bond i we had $\Sigma_{j=1}^{n} c_{i,j} \delta_j = P_i$, so that bond i is correctly priced, then we may have $x_i > 0$. If $\Sigma_{j=1}^{n} c_{i,j} \delta_j < P_i$, the market price P_i of bond i is too expensive compared with its 'theoretical price' $\Sigma_{j=1}^{n} c_{i,j} \delta_j$, and we will have $x_i = 0$.

Efficient bonds   A bond is efficient if its theoretical price equals its market price, so that $\Sigma_{j=1}^{n} c_{i,j} \delta_j = P_i$. An efficient bond may be held by an investor. Unfortunately there is no reason why any bonds should be efficient. One way of ensuring that efficient bonds exist is to assume that investors require some positive cashflow stream, $s = \{s_j\} \neq 0$, where s_j is the cashflow required at time t_j (Schaefer (81) [476], (82) [477]; Nelson and Schaefer (83) [411]).

The cheapest portfolio that generates s is

$$\text{L2}' : \qquad V = \min_{x} \left\{ x'P \mid x'C \geq s, x \geq 0 \right\}. \tag{15.57}$$

The dual of L2$'$ is

$$\text{L3:} \qquad V = \max_{\delta} \left\{ s'\delta \mid C\delta \leq P, \delta \geq 0 \right\}. \tag{15.58}$$

Although this guarantees that efficient bonds now exist one is left with the problem of choosing s.

Incorporating Costs

Prisman (90) [442] showed how including costs in the LP approach provided a link to the regression approach. Suppose that the costs of setting up, holding, and eventually liquidating a portfolio with quantities x is $f(x)$. The available arbitrage profit is

$$\text{L4:} \qquad V = \min_{x} \left\{ x'P + f(x) \mid xC \geq 0 \right\}. \tag{15.59}$$

A no short sales constraint is equivalent to a cost structure of the form

$$f(x) = 0, \qquad \text{if all } x_i \geq 0, \tag{15.60}$$

$$f(x) = \infty, \qquad \text{if } x_i < 0, \text{ for some bond } i. \tag{15.61}$$

Set $\varepsilon = P - C\delta$. The dual to L4 is L5

$$\text{L5:} \qquad V = \min_{\delta} \left\{ f^*(P - C\delta) \mid \delta \geq 0 \right\}, \tag{15.62}$$

where

$$f^*(\varepsilon) = \sup_{x} \left\{ \varepsilon'x - f(x) \right\} \tag{15.63}$$

is the maximum arbitrage profit. The optimal term structure minimises the maximum potential arbitrage profit.

Special case   Suppose $f(x) = \frac{1}{2} x'x$, so that costs are proportional to the square of the transaction size. Then $f^*(\varepsilon) = \frac{1}{2} \varepsilon'\varepsilon$. L5 becomes

$$\text{L6:} \qquad V = \min_{\delta} \left\{ \frac{1}{2} \varepsilon'\varepsilon \mid P = C\delta + \varepsilon, \delta \geq 0 \right\}. \tag{15.64}$$

But this is simply standard OLS regression.

This shows that if there is no δ such that $P = C\delta$, estimating δ by regressing P against $C\delta$ is equivalent to setting up an arbitrage when costs are quadratic in transaction volume.

Two Ways of Finding δ

We have seen that there are two distinct ways of finding a vector of discount factors:

1. Choose a stream of cashflows s. Then solve L3 (or L2$'$).
2. Choose a cost function $f(x)$. Then solve L4 (or L5). It is possible to choose $f(x)$ so that L4 is a least squares regression.

Method 1 is called the LP approach.
Method 2, with $f(x) = \frac{1}{2}\varepsilon'\varepsilon$, is called the regression approach.

15.7.2   Examples of Applications

In practice, C is almost singular. We have seen that attempting to directly apply an OLS method does not work. It is necessary to supply a parameterised curve, and estimate its parameter values.

Polynomial Approximation to the Spot Curve

Chambers, Carleton and Waldman (84) [123] used a polynomial approximation to spot rates. They assumed that $r(\tau) = \Sigma_{j=1}^{J} x_j t^{j-1}$ so that $\delta(\tau) = e^{-\tau r(\tau)} = \exp\left(\Sigma_{j=1}^{J} x_j t^{j-1}\right)$. They made no explicit assumptions about short sales or costs, but solved L6 so that ε could be assumed to be the measurement error. They used non-linear regression to regress P_i against $\Sigma_{k=1}^{m} c_{i,k} \exp\left(\Sigma_{j=1}^{J} x_j t^{j-1}\right)$. Using polynomials of degree three they claimed to get good fits to the spot rate curve. However, the spot rate curve is usually not very close to being a cubic polynomial.

Cubic Splines

Shea (84) [487] solved L6 on a sample of long-term Japanese discount bonds. In the Japanese secondary market these are untaxed so that tax effects can be ignored.

Shea imposed the condition that $\delta(0) = 1$. The remaining degrees of freedom—location of knot points, the boundary condition at the right boundary—were estimated in the regression. He later imposed the further constraint that

$$\left.\frac{\partial s}{\partial t}\right|_{t_{max}} = \frac{1}{2}\left.\frac{\partial s}{\partial t}\right|_{t_{max}-1}. \tag{15.65}$$

This curvature condition greatly increased the precision of his fit.

Exponential Splines

Exponential splines were proposed by Vasicek and Fong (82) [530]. The idea is to ensure that the exponential decay character of $\delta(\tau)$ is imposed on the data by a transformation of the time axis.

Define $x = 1 - e^{-\alpha\tau}$ and set $G(x) = \delta(\tau)$. The transformation maps $\tau \in [0, \infty)$ onto $x \in [0, 1)$. Now fit $G(x)$ by polynomial splines, $s(x)$. The fit $s(x)$ is then transformed back to obtain $\delta(\tau) = s(1 - e^{-\alpha\tau})$. Vasicek and Fong claimed good results for this method. Various problems were noted by Shea (85) [488] and Adams and Van Deventer (94) [6].

One may have very little data for x near 1, and there are problems in estimating α. In evaluating the method Shea uses B-splines to estimate $G(x)$.

The key idea of the exponential splines method is to mimic the exponential decay of the discount curve $\delta(\tau)$. Vasicek and Fong point out that a simple polynomial curve cannot mimic this decay. However, a piecewise polynomial curve, such as splines, can fit an exponential decay arbitrarily closely.

Other Suggested Re-parameterisations

Siegel and Nelson (88) [493] noticed that if one supposes that $r(\tau) = r(\infty) + c/\tau + g(\tau)$, where $g(\tau) \to 0$, as $\tau \to \infty$, then the spot rate curve can be re-parameterised. Set $x = 1/\tau$ and define $Y(x) = r(1/x) = r(\tau)$.

Siegel and Nelson suggest that it may be better to fit $Y(x)$ rather than $r(\tau)$. However, no rigorous justification is given.

Not that the condition holds if $g(\tau)$ levels off fast enough, for example if $g(\tau) \sim g(\infty) + ke^{-\lambda\tau}$ as $\tau \to \infty$. This is not unreasonable so that it makes some sense to investigate this re-parameterisation. However, it is not clear what the positive advantages of it might be.

Tanggaard (95) [516] suggests that one should fit to $Y(\tau) = (1 + \tau)r(\tau)$. This ensures that $\partial r/\partial \tau \to 0$ as $\tau \to \infty$ and has other reasonable properties.

Miltersen (92) [397] fits the forward rate curve as $f(t) = \gamma + Q(t)e^{-\gamma t}$, where $Q(t)$ is a low-order polynomial in t. He reports good results on his data set.

15.7.3 Conclusions

We make three conclusions from this section.

First, one must appropriately account for tax. The early papers of McCulloch (71) [387] and Carleton and Cooper (76) [117] simply ignored tax issues. Shea (84) [487], (85) [488] deliberately chooses a market when taxes are can be ignored. McCulloch (75) [388] and Steeley (89) [504] assume a single effective tax rate, appropriately in the case of Steeley. To give tax a proper treatment it is necessary to include different tax clientele. Schaefer (82) [477] and Nelson and Schaefer (83) [411] both do this.

Second, one should distinguish between quantifiable frictions and measurement noise, so far as this is possible.

Third, for simplicity of computation, if for no other reason, some form of spline approximation for $\delta(\tau)$ should be used.

16

Principal Components Analysis

This chapter revisits volatility structures in a very general setting. So far we have only considered models whose underlying state space is essentially just a vector space. However there is no reason to suppose that 'real' state space is as simple as this. Motivated by a discussion of principal components analysis (PCA) we move on to consider interest rate models defined on more topologically complicated objects: manifolds.

We start by discussing PCA of both historical term structure data and also of covariances implied from market prices. We introduces the notion of a non-linear underlying state space. We discuss interest rate models on manifolds, and give an example of a model defined on a circle. We conclude with an empirical analysis of UK data.

Principal components analysis has been a key technique in yield curve analysis for only 10 years. Early papers applying PCA (or factor analysis) include Litterman and Scheinkman (88) [354], (91) [355], Steeley (90) [505] and Carverhill and Strickland (92) [122]. Knez, Litterman and Scheinkman (94) [338] attempt to interpret the factors they find in the dollar market. Frachot, Janci and Lacoste (92) [228] is an early paper applying PCA specifically in the context of an HJM term structure model (see also the original Heath, Jarrow and Morton papers). Rebonato (98) [448] discusses PCA applied to interest rates in some detail. Wilmott (99) [541] discusses PCA in the context of estimating volatilities for HJM models.

We do not discuss factor analysis in this chapter. The difference between the two methods is that PCA finds explanatory factors that maximise successive contributions to the variance, effectively explaining variation as a diagonal matrix, whereas factor analysis tries to explain as much of the off-diagonal behaviour of the variation as possible. Principal components are essentially unique. Factors are unique only up to multiplication by an orthonormal matrix; orthogonal rotations of components—effectively changes of basis—cannot be distinguished.

General references to PCA methods include Flury (88) [225] and Jolliffe (86) [324]. A paper discussing some pitfalls in the use of principal components is Hadi and Ling (98) [263]. We do not discuss statistical tests here; see Flury, for instance.

Parts on this chapter are based on Nunes and Webber (97) [422].

16.1 VOLATILITY STRUCTURES

In previous chapters we have given a number of examples of the term structure of volatility determined by interest rate models. We have seen a variety of volatility structures used by Heath, Jarrow and Morton models.

In any interest rate model we can, in principle, write down the process followed by spot rates in the model. For the purposes of this chapter the volatility of spot rates of different maturities will be taken as the term structure of volatility, rather than the forward rate volatility curve of the HJM framework.

Example: Vasicek

In the Vasicek model spot rates $r_t(\tau, r_t)$ are

$$r_t(\tau, r_t) = r_\infty + (r_t - r_\infty)\frac{1 - e^{-\alpha\tau}}{\alpha\tau} + \frac{\sigma^2\tau}{4\alpha}\left(\frac{1 - e^{-\alpha\tau}}{\alpha\tau}\right)^2, \tag{16.1}$$

for the long rate r_∞ and parameters α and σ. The process for $r_t(\tau, r_t)$ is

$$dr_t(\tau, r) = \frac{1 - e^{-\alpha\tau}}{\alpha\tau}dr_t \tag{16.2}$$

$$= \mu(\tau, r_t)dt + \sigma(\tau)dz_t, \tag{16.3}$$

where

$$\mu(\tau, r_t) = \frac{1 - e^{-\alpha\tau}}{\tau}(\mu - r_t), \tag{16.4}$$

$$\sigma(\tau) = \frac{1 - e^{-\alpha\tau}}{\alpha\tau}\sigma. \tag{16.5}$$

$\sigma(\tau)$ is the Vasicek volatility structure. The forward rate process is $df_t(\tau) = \mu_f(\tau)dt + \sigma_f(\tau)dz_t$, where

$$\sigma_f(\tau) = \frac{\partial}{\partial\tau}\tau\sigma(\tau, r_t) = \sigma e^{-\alpha\tau}, \tag{16.6}$$

for some drift function $\mu_f(\tau)$. $\sigma_f(\tau)$ is the HJM volatility function.

Example: Cox, Ingersoll and Ross

In the Cox, Ingersoll and Ross (CIR) model spot rates are

$$r_t(\tau) = \frac{A(\tau)}{\tau} + \frac{B(\tau)}{\tau}r_t, \tag{16.7}$$

where

$$B(t, \tau) = \frac{\sinh\gamma\tau}{\gamma\cosh\gamma\tau + \frac{1}{2}a\sinh\gamma\tau} \tag{16.8}$$

with $2\gamma = \sqrt{a^2 + 2\sigma^2}$. The process followed by spot rates is

$$dr_t(\tau) = \frac{B(\tau)}{\tau} dr_t,$$ (16.9)

so that the CIR volatility structure is

$$\sigma(\tau, r_t) = \frac{\sinh \gamma\tau}{\left(\gamma \cosh \gamma\tau + \frac{1}{2}a \sinh \gamma\tau\right)\tau}\sigma r_t^{\frac{1}{2}}.$$ (16.10)

Example: Ho and Lee

If r_t has the process

$$dr_t = \theta(t)dt + \sigma dz_t$$ (16.11)

under the EMM, then spot rates are

$$r_t(T, r_t) = r_t - \frac{1}{6}\sigma^2(T - t)^2 + \frac{1}{\tau}\int_t^T \theta(s)(T - s)ds.$$ (16.12)

Hence the spot rate process is

$$dr_t(T, r_t) = dr_t - \theta(t)(T - t)dt.$$ (16.13)

The volatility function is σ, a constant,

$$\sigma(\tau, r_t) \equiv \sigma.$$ (16.14)

This volatility structure is particularly unrealistic. It is an empirical fact that volatility declines for increasing maturities. With this volatility structure the yield curve explodes.

Example: Heath, Jarrow and Morton

If the forward rate structure in Heath, Jarrow and Morton (HJM) is

$$df_t(T) = \alpha(t, T, \omega)dt + \sigma(t, T, \omega)dz_t,$$ (16.15)

where z_t is an $\mathbb{R}^d$-valued Brownian motion, then we have seen that the spot rate process is

$$dr_t(T) = \frac{1}{T - t}\left(r_t(T) - r_t + b(t, T) - \frac{1}{2}a^2(t, T)\right)dt + a(t, T)dz_t,$$ (16.16)

where

$$a = (a_1, \ldots, a_d)',$$ (16.17)

$$a_i(t, T, \omega) = -\int_t^T \sigma_i(t, s, \omega)ds, \quad i = 1, \ldots, d,$$ (16.18)

$$b(t, T, \omega) = -\int_t^T \alpha(t, s, \omega)ds + \frac{1}{2}\sum_{i=1}^d a_i^2(t, T, \omega).$$ (16.19)

The spot rate volatility functions are

$$a_i(t, T, \omega) = -\int_t^T \sigma_i(t, s, \omega)\mathrm{d}s, \quad i = 1, \ldots, d. \tag{16.20}$$

A change $\Delta z_{i,t}$ in the ith Wiener component causes a change

$$r_t(T) \to r_t(T) + a_i(t, T, \omega)\Delta z_{i,t} \tag{16.21}$$

in the whole term structure.

Example: Affine Models

In these models, by construction, the spot rate curve is an affine function of the state variables,

$$r(\tau, X_t) = -\frac{A(\tau)}{\tau} - \frac{B(\tau)}{\tau}X_t, \tag{16.22}$$

for certain functions A and B, where $X_t \in \mathbb{R}^m$, $\mathrm{d}X_t = (aX_t + b)\mathrm{d}t + \Sigma V\mathrm{d}z_t$, with

$$V = \mathrm{diag}\left(\sqrt{\alpha_1 + \beta_1 X_t}, \ldots, \sqrt{\alpha_m + \beta_m X_t}\right), \tag{16.23}$$

Σ a constant matrix, and $z_t \in \mathbb{R}^m$ an m-dimensional Wiener process. The spot rate process is

$$\mathrm{d}r(\tau, X_t) = -\frac{B(\tau)}{\tau}\mathrm{d}X_t, \tag{16.24}$$

$$= \mu(\tau, X_t)\mathrm{d}t + \sigma(\tau, X_t)\mathrm{d}z_t, \tag{16.25}$$

where

$$\mu(\tau, X_t) = -\frac{B(\tau)}{\tau}(aX_t + b), \tag{16.26}$$

$$\sigma(\tau, X_t) = -\frac{B(\tau)}{\tau}\Sigma V. \tag{16.27}$$

The coefficient of the ith Wiener process in (16.25) is the function

$$\sigma_i(\tau, X_t) = -\sum_{j=1}^m \frac{B_j(\tau)}{\tau}\Sigma_{j,i}\sqrt{\alpha_i + \beta_i X_t}. \tag{16.28}$$

This model has a set of m spot rate volatility functions, $\sigma_i(\tau, X_t)$, $i = 1, \ldots, m$, which are multiplied by changes in the uncorrelated Wiener processes, $z_{i,t}$. It may be more intuitive to regard $B_j(\tau)$, $j = 1, \ldots, m$, as the volatility functions even though these are multiplied by changes in X_t, which are not independent processes and may be quite complicated. We see in Section 16.5 that it may be more realistic to think in terms of (16.24) rather than (16.25).

16.2 IDENTIFYING EMPIRICAL VOLATILITY FACTORS

It is possible to identify surrogate volatility factors from market data by applying PCA to a time series of historical term structures.

Suppose the state variables in a model are $X_t \in \mathbb{R}^m$. In order to be able to apply PCA we must be able to express the process for $r_t(\tau) \equiv r(\tau, X_t)$ in the form

$$dr(\tau, X_t) = \mu(\tau, X_t)dt + \sigma(\tau)dz_t, \qquad (16.29)$$

where $\sigma(\tau)$ does not depend on X_t and the z_t are uncorrelated.

It may be more natural to express term structures as

$$dr(\tau, X_t) = \mu(\tau, X_t)dt + \sigma(\tau)dX_t, \qquad (16.30)$$

where $\sigma(\tau)$ does not depend on X_t, but where the $\sigma(\tau)$ have a complicated dependency. Unfortunately it would be significantly harder to extract components in this case.

16.2.1 Principal Components Analysis

Suppose we observe spatial data, so that at time t_i, $i = 1, \ldots, n + 1$, we observe $r_{t_i}(\tau_j)$, $j = 1, \ldots, k$. The procedure is:

1. Calculate the differences $d_{i,j} = r_{t_{i+1}}(\tau_j) - r_{t_i}(\tau_j)$. The $d_{i,j}$ are regarded as observations of a random variable, d_j.
2. Form the covariance matrix $\Sigma = \text{cov}(d_1, \ldots, d_k)$. Write $\Sigma = \{\Sigma_{i,j}\}$ where $\Sigma_{i,j} = \text{cov}(d_i, d_j)$.
3. Find a matrix P such that $P' = P^{-1}$ and $P\Sigma P'$ is diagonal. (We assume that Σ is not degenerate.) We may suppose that P has been chosen so that

$$P\Sigma P' = \text{diag}(\lambda_1, \ldots, \lambda_k), \qquad (16.31)$$

   with $\lambda_1 \geq \cdots \geq \lambda_k$. Write $P = \{p_{i,j}\}$.
4. Set

$$e_i = \sum_j p_{i,j}d_j, \quad i = 1, \ldots, k. \qquad (16.32)$$

e_i is a random variable and

$$\text{cov}(e_i, e_j) = \text{cov}\left(\sum_p p_{i,p}d_p, \sum_q p_{j,q}d_q\right) \qquad (16.33)$$

$$= \sum_{p,q} p_{i,p} \, \text{cov}(d_p, d_q)p_{j,q} \qquad (16.34)$$

$$= \delta_{i,j}\lambda_j, \qquad (16.35)$$

where $\delta_{i,j}$ is the Kronecker delta. e_i and e_j are uncorrelated unless $i = j$, when $\text{var}(e_j) = \lambda_j$.

The principal components are the k vectors $\{p_{i,j}\}_{j=1,\ldots,k}$, $i = 1, \ldots, k$. A blip in the ith variable, e_i, causes the term structure to alter by a multiple of $\{p_{i,j}\}_{j=1,\ldots,k}$. Suppose that all e_j are zero apart from e_i. Since $d_j = p_{i,j}e_i$ a blip in e_i causes the change $r_t(\tau_j) \to$ $r_t(\tau_j) + p_{i,j}e_i$ in $r_t(\tau_j)$.

$p_i(\tau_j) = p_{i,j}$ is the volatility component corresponding to e_i. Since $P\Sigma P' = \text{diag}(\lambda_1, \ldots, \lambda_k)$,

$$\Sigma p'_i = \lambda_i p'_i, \tag{16.36}$$

where p_i is the ith row of P. λ_i is the eigenvalue associated with the eigenvector p_i.

Using the Components

Write $e_{i,p}$ for the value of e_i at time t_p. Set $f_{i,p} = \sum_{j=1}^{p} e_{i,j}$, so that $\Delta f_{i,p} = e_{i,p}$. We can now write

$$\Delta r_{t_p}(\tau_j) = \sum_{i=1}^{k} p_i(\tau_j) \Delta f_{i,p}, \tag{16.37}$$

where by construction $f_{i,p}$ and $f_{j,p}$ are uncorrelated, $i \neq j$.

We would like to extend the procedure in discrete time to the continuous-time case, and define

$$dr_t(\tau) = \mu_t(\tau)dt + \sum_{i=1}^{k} p_i(\tau)df_i \tag{16.38}$$

$$= \mu_t(\tau)dt + \sum_{i=1}^{k} p_i(\tau)\sqrt{\lambda_i}\,dz_i. \tag{16.39}$$

This is an HJM structure in spot rate form; f_1 has greatest variance λ_1, f_2 has next highest, *et cetera*. We know that in the HJM model the drift function $\mu_t(\tau)$ is determined by the volatility functions $p_i(\tau)$, whereas the empirical derivation of the components effectively assumed that the drift was identically zero. In practice it is usually assumed that the empirical components $p_i(\tau)$ fit the continuous-time model with the correct drift.

16.2.2   Examples of Principal Components Analysis

There have been many published articles on PCA applied to interest rate term structures. We restrict ourselves to three examples: two early studies by Steeley (90) [505] and by Carverhill and Strickland (92) [122], and an analysis by Nunes and Webber. The seminal paper in this area is Litterman and Scheinkman (91) [355] who investigated factors in bond yields (this paper is strictly a factor analysis paper rather than a PCA paper).

Components are usually found to have particular shapes. The first component is roughly flat and corresponds to a parallel shift in the term structure. The second component is downward sloping and causes the term structure to tilt. The third component is hump-shaped and causes the term structure to flex. Higher order components have progressively more wiggles.

The importance of a component p_i is determined by the size of the corresponding eigenvalue, λ_i, which indicates the amount of variance explained by p_i. The key statistic is the proportion of the total variance explained by p_i, $\nu_i = \lambda_i / \sum_{i=1}^{k} \lambda_i$. The first component will often explain 80%–90% or more of the variance, depending on the data set, confirming that parallel shifts are the most usual term structure movement. The first three components between them may explain 90%–95% of the variance. Higher order components are often regarded as noise and eliminated from further analysis.

Example: Analysis of UK Money Market Data (Nunes and Webber)

Nunes and Webber (97) [422] investigated the structure of UK money market rates using seven years' data, from September 1988 to February 1995. The data are observations of three-month, six-month and 12-month Libor, and two-, three-, four-, five-, seven- and ten-year swap rates. This gives 1609 observations of a vector with nine components. PCA will find components $p_i = (p_{i,1}, \ldots, p_{i,9})$, $i = 1, \ldots, 9$, such that

$$\Delta r_t(\tau_j) = \sum_{i=1}^{9} p_{i,j} \Delta w_{i,t} + \varepsilon_{t,j}, \tag{16.40}$$

with $w_t = (w_{1t}, \ldots, w_{9t})$ uncorrelated and $\varepsilon_{t,j}$ is residual noise.

The results of the analysis are presented in the following table:

	Global PCA								
	p_1	p_2	p_3	p_4	p_5	p_6	p_7	p_8	p_9
Eigenvalue:	0.0400	0.0128	0.0037	0.002	0.0018	0.0006	0.0003	0.0003	0.0002
Percentage:	64.6%	20.7%	5.9%	3.6%	2.9%	0.9%	0.5%	0.4%	0.3%
Cumulative:	64.6%	85.3%	91.3%	94.9%	97.8%	98.7%	99.3%	99.7%	100.0%
	Eigenvectors								
3 months	−0.3158	0.4693	−0.7280	0.3652	0.1272	0.0068	−0.0106	0.0166	−0.0052
6 months	−0.3439	0.4747	0.0636	−0.8043	0.0714	−0.0074	0.0086	−0.0151	−0.0006
1 year	−0.3748	0.4251	0.6772	0.4678	0.0348	−0.0035	0.0064	−0.0004	0.0024
2 years	−0.3531	−0.1542	−0.0512	−0.0116	−0.6412	0.5280	−0.3859	0.0910	−0.0410
3 years	−0.3423	−0.1962	−0.0596	0.0056	−0.3755	−0.1344	0.7666	−0.2053	0.2280
4 years	−0.3354	−0.2463	−0.0218	−0.0079	−0.0591	−0.5075	−0.0657	0.1918	−0.7240
5 years	−0.3309	−0.2634	−0.0157	−0.0108	0.0886	−0.4640	−0.4018	0.1606	0.6406
7 years	−0.3057	−0.2957	−0.0021	0.0015	0.3883	0.1851	−0.1641	−0.7716	−0.1086
10 years	−0.2903	−0.3065	0.0201	−0.0210	0.5132	0.4426	0.2656	0.5396	0.0050

$$\tag{16.41}$$

Since the data are nine dimensional, a total of nine components are computed. However, in common with other studies in various currencies, such as Wilson (94) [543], *et cetera*. Nunes and Webber find that a very high proportion of the variation in interest rate term structures is explained by just three components. The first component alone counts for 65%, the second and third components between them accounting for an additional 26%. As a result of this analysis they conclude that three components are significant, so that $m = 3$.

The first three components explain about 90% of the total variance. This is significantly less than the first three components explain in other studies, cited below, but here seven years' data are being used. Intuitively one expects to find more variation than might be found in one year, so one does not expect to explain as much. Offsetting this Nunes and Webber use quoted rates which might be expected to explain more variation than if stripped rates were used. Also, using fewer than nine rates, the first three factors might be expected to explain proportionately move.

PCA analysis assumes the underlying process is a diffusion; jumps are not allowed. It is an empirical reality that the data do jump, for instance due to interest rate setting by the monetary authorities. Before doing the PCA it is necessary to remove jumps from the data. Nunes and Webber found that leaving jumps in does affect the results. Only 12 points were removed from the data set.

Nunes and Webber worked with rates themselves, and did not strip them to get spot rates. Since they were performing a data reduction exercise this is legitimate; the components only need to explain variation in quoted rates, not in stripped rates. We elaborate on this in Section 16.5.2.

The first three components are plotted in Figure 16.1. The market quoted rates appear to behave as if they were partitioned by maturity into rates of one year or less (that is, Libor rates) and rates of two years or more (that is, swap rates).

The first component moves Libor and swaps up and down together. The second component causes Libor and swap rates to move in opposite directions. The third component causes Libor rates to pivot, while swap rates are largely unaffected.

On the basis of this evidence it would seem that when setting rates traders behave as if they regard Libor rates and swap rates as independent blocks, either moving up and down relatively independently, or else Libor rates are rotated, with the 12-month rate going in one direction and the three-month going in the other.

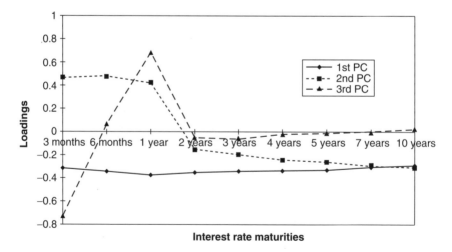

Figure 16.1   The three most significant components

This conclusion is rather different to that generally reported in the literature. In other studies the data are usually stripped to obtain a spot rate curve before a PCA is performed.

Example: Analysis for UK Gilts (Steeley)

Steeley (90) [505] computed principal components and variances for term structures found from closing mid-market prices of high coupon fixed interest gilts in the period March 1986–March 1987. He stripped the yield curve using B-splines. He found that on this data set the first component accounts for about 90% of variance and the first three account for approximately 98%.

It is quite normal in relatively short time series of data to find that the first three components explain a very high proportion of the variance. We have seen that over longer time periods a much lower proportion may be explained.

Sterling Money Market (Carverhill and Strickland)

Carverhill and Strickland (92) [122] used UK money market rates: six-month and 12-month Libor, and two-, three-, four-, five-, seven-, ten-year swap rates, from April 1989 to August 1990. Carverhill and Strickland found the first three factors accounted for 99.7% of variance. This is an extremely high proportion even for PCA. Part of the reason for this may lie in the data set chosen by Carverhill and Strickland. It was a period when term structures in the UK were highly inverted, and in some sense at an extreme in their range of movement. One may hypothesise that at an extreme fewer modes of variation are available to the underlying processes, and hence an analysis of this sort has a higher explanatory power.

Comparison

A reassuringly similar pattern of components were found in both the gilt market and the money market. A problem with the analysis in both cases is that components are estimated only over a relatively short period of historical data. If the estimation is performed over successive (short) time periods, then although the broad picture remains the same the detail varies considerably—apparently by far more than simple statistical variation would account for. We speculate that over a relatively short time period the state variables underlying an interest rate model do not sample a very large region in their state space. Over successive periods they tend to move more extensively and may sample regions remote enough that the character of the term structures changes in a manner detectable by PCA. We explore these ideas in Section 16.4. The model involves the concept of processes on general manifolds.

16.3   CALIBRATING WHOLE YIELD CURVE MODELS

Random field models provide a natural framework within which to calibrate Gaussian HJM models. Pang (96) [425] showed how random field models can be used to obtain an empirically derived covariance matrix. Taking principal components enables us to find volatility factors for a whole yield curve model.

We start by showing how the HJM model can be expressed as a random field model and is determined by a covariance matrix. We then outline Pang's procedure for deriving the empirical covariance matrix from the prices of caps and swaptions.

16.3.1 HJM as a Random Field Model (Pang)

A Gaussian version of the HJM model is

$$\mathrm{d}f_t(T) = \alpha_t(T)\mathrm{d}t + \sigma_t(T)\mathrm{d}z_t, \tag{16.42}$$

where z_t is an n-dimensional Wiener process and $\alpha_t(T) = \sigma_t(T)\int_t^T \sigma_t(s)\mathrm{d}s$ under the EMM Q. Forward rates are

$$f_t(T) = f_0(T) + \int_0^t \alpha_s(T)\mathrm{d}s + \int_0^t \sigma_s(T)\mathrm{d}z_s, \tag{16.43}$$

so immediately the covariance structure is

$$\mathrm{cov}(f_{t_1}(T_1), f_{t_2}(T_2)) = \int_0^{t_1 \wedge t_2} \sigma_s(T_1)\sigma_s(T_2)\mathrm{d}s$$

$$\equiv c(t_1 \wedge t_2, T_1, T_2). \tag{16.44}$$

If the rates $f_t(T)$ are stationary then

$$c(t, T_1, T_2) = \int_0^t g(T_1 - s, T_2 - s)\mathrm{d}s + h(T_1, T_2). \tag{16.45}$$

Pang assumes that $h(T_1, T_2) = 0$ so that $c(0, T_1, T_2) = 0$ and initially forward rates are uncorrelated to one another. Pang formulates the model in terms of g, the covariance density. He shows that

1. $f_t(T)$ is continuous in T if $g(u, v)$ is continuous and bounded.
2. Forward rates are differentiable in T, so that $\partial f_t(T)/\partial T$ exists and is continuous, if $\partial_g^2(u, v)/\partial_u\partial_v$ is continuous and bounded.
3. Spot rate covariance is given by

$$\mathrm{cov}(\mathrm{d}r_t(T_1), \mathrm{d}r_t(T_2)) = \frac{1}{\tau_1}\frac{1}{\tau_2}\int_0^{\tau_1}\int_0^{\tau_2} g(u, v)\mathrm{d}v\mathrm{d}u, \tag{16.46}$$

where $\tau_1 = T_1 - t$, $\tau_2 = T_2 - t$, and stationarity is assumed.

Of these, the last property is crucial. It gives the relationship between the covariance matrix for spot rates and the function g.

16.3.2 Kennedy and HJM

Kennedy (94) [331] derives closed form formulae for caps and swaptions in the Gaussian random field framework. However, no formulae are available for other instruments. It is much easier to price other instruments within a finite factor HJM model rather than an infinite factor random field model.

To do this we approximate the (possibly) infinite factor random field model by an HJM model whose volatility components are found as the leading principal components of the implied spot rate covariance matrix.

The HJM Approximation Procedure (Pang)

Assuming that there are sufficient liquid caps and swaptions in the market for the method to work, we proceed in five stages:

1. Given $c(t, T_1, T_2)$, there is an exact formula for caps and a good approximate formula for swaptions. We can express $c(t, T_1, T_2)$ as a function of $g(u, v)$.
2. Fit $g(u, v)$ to the market prices of caps and swaptions. We can find values of $g(u, v)$ for (u, v) taking values on a grid[1] and linearly interpolate in between grid points. This is quick to do because there are explicit formulae for cap and swaption prices.
3. For a given set of maturities τ_i, $i = 1, \ldots, n$, we form the spot rate covariance matrix,

$$C = \{c_{i,j}\}, c_{i,j} = \frac{1}{\tau_i} \frac{1}{\tau_j} \int_0^{\tau_i} \int_0^{\tau_j} g(u, v) \mathrm{d}v \mathrm{d}u, \qquad (16.47)$$

   where the integral is computed numerically.
4. Find the principal components of C, that is, the matrix P such that $P'\mathrm{diag}(\lambda_1, \ldots, \lambda_k)P = C$, where $p_{j,i}$ is the eigenvector and λ_i is the corresponding eigenvalue of C.
5. For some $k < n$, use p_i, $i = 1, \ldots, k$, as the volatility functions for a Gaussian HJM model.

This procedure obtains a set of k volatility functions, derived from current market prices. In practice one might seek to regularise the solutions by imposing some functional form, or curvature property, upon them.

The approximations enable rapid calculations of swaption prices to be made in the optimisation part of the calibration procedure. Pang finds that

- The approximate formula for swaptions works well, and allows fast calibration;
- A Gaussian random field model calibrates well to caps and swaptions;
- A three-factor Gaussian HJM model fits reasonably well to caps and swaptions. A one-factor HJM model fits surprisingly well.

Calibrating an HJM model to implieds is far more effective than calibrating from a covariance matrix derived from historical term structure data.

16.4   PROCESSES ON MANIFOLDS

Interest rate models explicitly or implicitly define a state space S. For the Vasicek model $S = \mathbb{R}$. In the CIR model $S = \mathbb{R}^+$ and in the Longstaff and Schwartz model the state

---

[1] Pang takes $(u, v) \in \{0, 2, 4, 6, 8, 10\}^2$.

space is

$$S = \left\{ (r, v) \mid \frac{v}{\alpha} > r > \beta v \right\}, \qquad (16.48)$$

for certain constants α and β. This model is specified by the dynamics (under risk neutrality) of the state variables $X_t = (r_t, v_t) \in S$ and by a function defining the short rate

$$r_t = \pi_1(X_t) = X_{1,t}. \qquad (16.49)$$

The Longstaff and Schwartz model is a Duffie and Kan affine model; the state variables follow semi-affine processes, as in equation (7.6), defined on an open set in $\mathbb{R}^n$, for $n = 2$.

When we investigate the results of PCA in more detail, regarding it as a technique for data reduction, we find it useful to consider more general state spaces. In particular we suppose that the state space S may be endowed with the structure of an s-dimensional manifold.

A manifold is a topological space where every point is surrounded by an open set diffeomorphic to an open set in $\mathbb{R}^s$, for some fixed dimension s. s is the dimension of the manifold. For instance, the circle S^1 is a manifold because every point on the circle is contained in a segment diffeomorphic to an open set in $\mathbb{R}$. S may be considered as a subset of $\mathbb{R}^n$, $S \subseteq \mathbb{R}^n$, where we choose n to be the smallest integer for which a diffeomorphic imbedding exists. Every manifold can be regarded as a subset of $\mathbb{R}^n$, for some n, in this way.

The evolution of the system is described by a stochastic processes X_t taking values in S. We discuss stochastic processes on manifolds in Section 16.4.4.

We suppose that we are given a function $r_0 : S \to \mathbb{R}$, where $r_0(x)$ is interpreted as the value of the short rate as a function of the state $x \in S$.

A term structure model is thus specified by the triple (S, X_t, r_0) where

- S is the state space, an s-dimensional manifold imbeddible into $\mathbb{R}^n$, say;
- X_t is a process defined on S, the state at time t;
- $r_0 : S \to \mathbb{R}$ is the short rate map.

In the Vasicek model $S = \mathbb{R}$, X_t has the process $dX_t = \alpha(\theta - X_t)dt + \sigma dz_t$ on $S = \mathbb{R}$ and $r_0 = 1$ is the identity map. In a general affine model $S = \mathbb{R}^n$, $X_t \in S = \mathbb{R}^n$ has an affine process as described in Chapter 7 and $r_0 = a + b'X_t$ is an affine function.

Hughston (94) [288] develops a framework for arbitrage-free pricing on a general Riemannian state space. As well as r_0 he defines the asset price process $S_t^i : S \to \mathbb{R}$, $i = 1, \ldots, n$, and a vector field λ identifiable as a market price of risk. We only require the existence of r_0 since, along with Duffie and Kan, we shall be working in a risk-neutral world.

Bjork and Christensen (99) [68] investigate processes confined to manifolds and seek to discover the local invariance properties of manifolds that are consistent with interest rate evolution.

The process X_t has a natural co-ordinate decomposition induced by the imbedding of S into $\mathbb{R}^n$, $X_t = (X_{1,t}, \ldots, X_{n,t})$, in the canonical basis. It may happen that the model is formulated so that the short rate is itself a component of the state variable, $X_{1,t}$ say. Then the function r_0 is simply the projection of X_t onto $X_{1,t}$.

$\mathcal{S}$ itself may be a manifold of dimension strictly less than n. An example of a manifold with dimension strictly less than its imbedding dimension is the $(n-1)$-sphere

$$\mathcal{S} = S^{n-1} = \{(x_1, \dots, x_n) \in \mathbb{R}^n \mid x_1^2 + \cdots + x_n^2 = 1\}, \qquad (16.50)$$

and an example of a process X_t taking values in S^{n-1} is $X_t = Y_t/R_t$, where Y_t is any process defined on $\mathbb{R}^n \setminus 0$ and $R_t = \sqrt{Y_{1t}^2 + Y_{2t}^2 + \cdots + Y_{nt}^2}$.

In this example X_t takes values in S^{n-1}, a space of dimension $n-1$. Of course, it is not possible to endow S^{n-1} with global co-ordinates, and so we are led to consider local co-ordinates at each $x \in S^{n-1}$. At a point $x \in S^{n-1}$ co-ordinates on the tangent space $T_x S^{n-1}$ to x on S^{n-1} may be augmented by the normal n_x to S^{n-1} in $\mathbb{R}^n$ to give co-ordinates around x in $\mathbb{R}^n$. A basis for these co-ordinates is a linear transformation of the canonical basis of $\mathbb{R}^n$. The process X_t has a representation in these co-ordinates in which the component of X_t along n_x is zero. (If it did not, then the process X_t would not be confined to the manifold; see Rogers and Williams (87) [459].) This implies that the volatility matrix ρ of X_t has rank strictly less than n, since otherwise X_t could randomly move in n dimensions and would not be constrained to lie in an $n-1$-dimensional subspace.

Suppose the process for X_t is

$$dX_t = \alpha dt + \rho dz_t, \qquad (16.51)$$

for some functions α and ρ, under the risk-adjusted measure.

In general at a point $x \in \mathcal{S} \subseteq \mathbb{R}^n$ it is possible to find a co-ordinate patch (L_x, U_x) with $x \in U_x$, U_x open in $\mathbb{R}^n$, with basis vectors $L_x = (L_{1,x}, \dots, L_{n,x})$ so that $(L_{s+1,x}, \dots, L_{n,x})$ span the normal subspace to $\mathcal{S}$ at x, $(L_{1,x}, \dots, L_{p,x})$ span the random subspace of X at x,[2] and either $p = s$ or $p = s - 1$. In the former case the system is of full random rank: ρ is of rank s so at a point $x = X_t \in \mathcal{S}$ the columns of ρ span $T_x\mathcal{S}$, the tangent space to $\mathcal{S}$ at x. In the latter case $L_{s,x}$ may be taken to be the deterministic direction of the system at x_t, that is the drift vector $\mu(X_t)$, and rank ρ is $s - 1$. Figure 16.2 illustrates a system $L = (L_1, L_2, L_3)$.

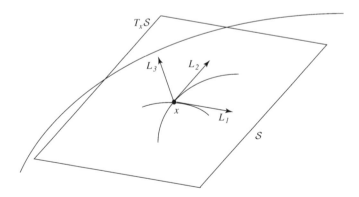

Figure 16.2 A basis defined at the point x

---

[2] That is, the subspace of the tangent space $T_x\mathcal{S}$ spanned by the columns of ρ.

The figure shows the tangent space $T_x S$ at a point $x \in S$. L_1 and L_2 span the tangent space, L_3 spans the normal subspace at x.

Why should one consider generalising the state space to be an arbitrary manifold to S? Empirically, it might turn out to be necessary to do so. Furthermore, as we shall see, a model defined on a manifold S need not necessarily be inconsistent with a Duffie and Kan affine model, at least locally.

We exclude jump behaviour from the process X_t. If jumps are possible then one may be led to consider disconnected state spaces. For instance, the jump–diffusion model considered by Babbs and Webber (94) [40], (95) [41] has a disconnected state space where components are labelled by the (discrete) values of the short rate. The state space in a jump–diffusion model such as Ahn and Thompson (88) [7] may not be disconnected if the state process can diffuse between any two points in the state space. Even in this instance one may question whether or not the state space is homotopically trivial.

Prices $B_t(X_t, T)$ of pure discount bonds at time t may be found as solutions to the partial differential equation

$$r_0 B = \frac{1}{2} \, \text{tr}\left(\rho' \frac{\partial^2 B}{\partial X^2} \rho \kappa \right) + \alpha \frac{\partial B}{\partial X} + \frac{\partial B}{\partial t}, \tag{16.52}$$

with boundary condition $B_T(X, T) = 1$, defined in $\mathbb{R}^n$. Term structures $r_t(\tau) = r_t(\tau, X_t)$ are then found from the bond prices $B_t(X_t, T) = \exp(-r_t(\tau, X_t)\tau)$ as usual.

PCA can be applied to historical data if the underlying state variables are stationary. Since we intend to use PCA in an empirical investigation of this framework, we require that the system defined by equation 16.51 has no explicit time dependence in α or ρ.

The short rate map $r_0 : S \to \mathbb{R}$ can be extended to a map $r : S \to C^+ = \{f : \mathbb{R}^+ \to \mathbb{R} \mid f \text{ continuous}\}$ defined by

$$r(X_t)(\tau) = r_t(\tau, X_t). \tag{16.53}$$

$r(x)$ is the entire term structure at the point x. We presume that the system is non-degenerate in the sense that r is a diffeomorphism of S onto its image $\mathcal{R} = r(S)$.

We wish to describe the image space $\mathcal{R}$ and relate this to the domain S. A space of interest is the smallest vector subspace T of C^+ that contains $\mathcal{R}$. Although r is a diffeomorphism, by assumption, it need not in general be the case that $\dim \mathcal{R} = n$. We are particularly interested in the case when T is finite dimensional, $T \subseteq \mathbb{R}^m$. This is a key assumption. We are interested in compatible theories (S, X_t, r_0) such that T is finite dimensional. Define $\pi_0(f) = f(0)$ and $r_0 = \pi_0 r$, then we have the commutative diagram shown in Figure 16.3.

If $T \subseteq \mathbb{R}^m$ spans a finite dimensional subspace of C^+ then we can find a set of m functions, $B_1, \ldots, B_m \in C^+$, such that for all $x \in S$ there exists $y = (y_1, \ldots, y_m) \in \mathbb{R}^m$ such that

$$-\tau r(\tau, x) = B_1(\tau) y_1 + \cdots + B_m(\tau) y_m, \tag{16.54}$$

where we have written the basis elements in this form for convenience and consistency with Duffie and Kan.

The choice of the basis functions $B_1, \ldots, B_m$ is of course not unique. Duffie and Kan demonstrate that, with their assumptions, a basis can be found in which $y_1 \equiv 1$.

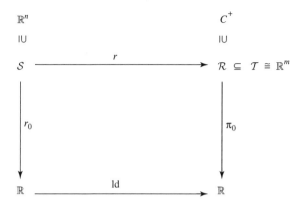

Figure 16.3 The structure of a term structure model

Given a choice of basis functions in $\mathcal{T} \subseteq \mathbb{R}^m$, r can be regarded as a map associating to each $x \in \mathcal{S}$ an element $y \in \mathbb{R}^m$ where y is defined as above. By assumption r is a monomorphism. If $X_t \in \mathcal{S}$ follows the process $dX_t = \alpha(X_t)dt + \rho(X_t)dz_t$, where $z_t \in \mathbb{R}^n$ and $dz_t dz_t' = \kappa dt$, then the process for $Y_t = r(X_t)$ is $dY_t = \mu(Y_t)dt + \sigma(Y_t)dz_t$ where

$$\mu(Y_t) = \frac{\partial r(\tau, x)}{\partial x}\alpha(X_t) + \frac{1}{2}\,\mathrm{tr}\left(\rho \frac{\partial^2 r(\tau, x)}{\partial x^2}\rho\kappa\right), \tag{16.55}$$

$$\sigma(Y_t) = \frac{\partial r(\tau, x)}{\partial x}\rho(X_t), \tag{16.56}$$

for $X_t = r^{-1}(Y_t)$.

16.4.1 Properties of Affine Models

Suppose that X_t is a process in $\mathbb{R}^m$, $dX_t = \mu(X_t)dt + \sigma(X_t)dz_t$. Write $P(\tau, X_t)$ for the value of the τ-maturity pure discount bond in state X_t, and $r(\tau, X_t)$ for the corresponding τ-maturity spot rate. If the model is affine, then

$$\ln P(\tau, X_t) = -\tau r(\tau, X_t) = A(\tau) + B(\tau)'X_t, \tag{16.57}$$

where

$$A(\tau), B_1(\tau), \ldots, B_m(\tau) \in C^+. \tag{16.58}$$

Under the EMM the drift of dP/P is equal to the short rate so denoting partial differentiation with respect to τ by τ subscripts we have

$$r_t(X_t) = -A_\tau(\tau) - B_\tau(\tau)X_t + B(\tau)'\mu(X_t) \tag{16.59}$$

$$+ \tfrac{1}{2}B'(\tau)\sigma(X_t)\kappa\sigma'(X_t)B(\tau), \tag{16.60}$$

where $r_t(X_t) = -A_\tau(0) - B_\tau(0)'X_t$ is the short rate and κ is the correlation matrix (Duffie and Kan (96) [183]).

The property of being affine, given in Equation 16.57, means that $r(\tau, X_t)$ belongs to T, an m-dimensional linear subspace of C^+. $\{A(\tau), B_1(\tau), \ldots, B_m(\tau)\}$ is a basis for T. The state space S can be identified with $\mathcal{R} = \{A(\tau) + B(\tau)'X_t\} \subseteq T$.

Under these conditions Duffie and Kan show that

$$\mu(X_t) = a + bX_t, \tag{16.61}$$

$$\sigma(X_t)\kappa\sigma'(X_t) = c + dX_t, \tag{16.62}$$

are both affine functions of X_t. A process X_t whose drift and volatility satisfy (16.61) and (16.62) will be called a semi-affine process.

Duffie and Kan assume that $\sigma(X_t)$ has full rank, and every $x \in \mathcal{R}$ has a neighbourhood $U \subseteq \mathcal{R}$ such that U is open in $\mathbb{R}^m$. These assumptions can be relaxed. In particular we investigate processes that can be reduced to semi-affine form, and the implications of this for term structure models.

16.4.2   Reducibility to Semi-Affine Form

Suppose that Y_t is a process is $\mathbb{R}^n$,

$$dY_t = a(Y_t)dt + b(Y_t)dz_t, \tag{16.63}$$

for $a(Y_t), z_t \in \mathbb{R}^n$, $b(Y_t) \in \mathbb{R}^{n \times n}$. We say that Y_t is reducible to semi-affine form if there exists a twice differentiable map $U : \mathbb{R}^n \to \mathbb{R}^m$, such that $U_t = U(Y_t)$ has semi-affine form. For example, for $n = m = 1$ the drift and volatility of $U(Y_t)$ are

$$\mu(U) = a(Y)U_Y + \tfrac{1}{2}b^2(Y)U_{YY}, \tag{16.64}$$

$$\sigma(U) = b(Y)U_Y, \tag{16.65}$$

where we require

$$\mu(U) = a_1 U + a_2, \tag{16.66}$$

$$\sigma(U) = \sqrt{b_1 U + b_2}, \tag{16.67}$$

for some $a_1, a_2, b_1, b_2 \in \mathbb{R}$. In this case if U exists it has the form

$$U(Y) = \begin{cases} \dfrac{1}{b_1}V(Y)^2 - \dfrac{b_2}{b_1}, & b_1 \neq 0, \\[2ex] b_2 \displaystyle\int \dfrac{1}{b(Y)}dY, & b_1 = 0, \end{cases} \tag{16.68}$$

where $V(Y)$ is

$$V(Y) = k + \frac{b_1}{2}\int \frac{1}{b(Y)}dY, \tag{16.69}$$

for some constant k. Given $b(Y)$, $a(Y)$ must be of the form

$$a = \frac{1}{2}bb_Y + f\frac{b}{V} + \frac{a_1}{b_1} + bV, \tag{16.70}$$

where $f = a_2 - b_2 - \tfrac{1}{4}b_1$.

Examples

We consider a number of important special cases when $n = m = 1$.

- $b(Y) = 1$, then $a(Y) = \frac{1}{2}a_1 Y + k$, so that

$$U(Y) = \begin{cases} \dfrac{1}{b_1}\left(k + \dfrac{b_1}{2}Y\right)^2 - \dfrac{b_2}{b_1}, & b_1 \neq 0, \\ b_2 Y, & b_1 = 0. \end{cases} \tag{16.71}$$

The second possibility is trivial. Choosing $k = b_2 = 0$ in the first case we obtain $U(Y) = (b_1/4)Y^2$, which is essentially the transformation used in the quadratic Gaussian model.

- $b(Y) = Y^{1/2}$, then we can choose $a(Y) = a_1 Y + a_2$, so that

$$U(Y) = Y \tag{16.72}$$

is the identity.

- $b(Y) = Y$, then $a(Y) = Y \ln kY^{\frac{1}{2}a_1}$, so

$$U(Y) = \left(k + \frac{b_1}{2}\ln Y\right)^2 - \frac{b_2}{b_1}. \tag{16.73}$$

- $b(Y) = -\sqrt{1 - Y^2}$, then we can choose $a(Y) = -\frac{1}{2}Y$, and

$$U(Y) = \sin^{-1} Y, \ Y \in [-1, 1]. \tag{16.74}$$

Suppose we are investigating an interest rate model $(\mathcal{S}, Y_t, r_0)$ and $U : \mathbb{R}^n \to \mathbb{R}^m$ exists such that the process $X_t = U(Y_t)$ is semi-affine. When X_t is semi-affine the short rate in a model for which X_t is the state variable is just $B_\tau(0)'X_t$ where $B(\tau) = (B_1(\tau), \ldots, B_m(\tau))$ is defined in equation 16.54. Hence for a well-defined model we require that

$$r_0(Y) = \pi_0 U(Y) = B_\tau(0)'U(Y). \tag{16.75}$$

That is, r_0 is a linear multiple of $U(Y)$. When $n = m = 1$ we must have that

$$r_0(Y) = (k_1 + k_2 c_t)(l_1 + l_2 c_t), \tag{16.76}$$

where $c_t = \int (1/b(Y))\mathrm{d}Y$.

For instance, if $b(Y) \equiv b$, a constant, then $r_0(Y)$ must be at most quadratic in Y. When $b(Y) = Y$, $r_0(Y)$ must be quadratic in $\ln Y$. For $b(Y) = -\sqrt{1 - Y^2}$ a compatible choice of r_0 is

$$r_0(Y) = k_1 + k_2 \sin^{-1} Y. \tag{16.77}$$

In this case, since Y can be interpreted as $\sin \theta$, where θ is the angular coordinate of the circle, the short rate is just an affine function of θ, where it is defined.

16.4.3 Reduction to Semi-Affine Form

Suppose we have a term structure model defined on a manifold $S \subseteq \mathbb{R}^n$. Given a process X_t on S, we may be able to reduce it to semi-affine form in $\mathbb{R}^m$. We would then have a Duffie and Kan affine term structure model.

Given (S, X_t, r_t) we need to find a map $r : S \to \mathcal{R} \subseteq C^+$, such that

1. $\mathcal{R} = r(S) \subseteq T$, is a finite dimensional subspace of C^+,
2. $Y_t = r(X_t)$ is semi-affine,
3. Figure 16.3 commutes.

r maps (S, X_t, r_0) onto $(\mathcal{R}, r(X_t), \pi_0(r))$. Normally it is not possible to find a map r. However, we show below that locally, in a neighbourhood of each point $x \in S$, it is possible to find such a map. The implications are that if one only has a limited amount of empirical data, one may be able to fit it accurately by an affine term structure model. Only if one has a large amount of data, so that it cannot all lie within a single coordinate patch, will one be unable to fit an affine model.

16.4.4 Examples of Processes on Manifolds

Having set up a term structure modelling framework couched in terms of processes on manifolds, it behoves us to demonstrate that such processes can be defined and can be computed with. We give two constructions. For further details see Rogers and Williams (87) [459].

Suppose that $f : \mathbb{R}^n \to \mathbb{R}^m$ is C^∞ and that $m = \dim \mathrm{Im} f$. Let M be the zero set of f, $M = \{x \in \mathbb{R}^n \mid f(x) = 0\}$. If $\det(\partial f_i / \partial x_j)_{i=1,\dots,m, j=1,\dots,n} \neq 0$ on M, then M can be given the structure of a $\dim f^{-1}(0) = n - m$ dimensional manifold.

It is easy to construct processes on M. As an example of the general construction suppose $f : \mathbb{R}^n \to \mathbb{R}$ is C^∞ and suppose its zero set M is a manifold, as above. The unit normal to M at $x \in M$ is

$$n(x) = \left| \frac{\partial f}{\partial x} \right|^{-1} \frac{\partial f}{\partial x}. \qquad (16.78)$$

The projection operator onto $T_x M$ at x is

$$P(x) = I - n(x) \circ n(x)'. \qquad (16.79)$$

If z_t is a Brownian motion in $\mathbb{R}^n$, then the process X_t satisfying

$$dX_t = -\tfrac{1}{2} \mathrm{div}\,(n) n(X_t) dt + P(X_t) dz_t, \qquad (16.80)$$

where

$$\mathrm{div}(n) = \frac{\partial n_1}{\partial x_1} + \cdots + \frac{\partial n_n}{\partial x_n}, \qquad (16.81)$$

is a process confined to $M \subseteq \mathbb{R}^n$.

For example, the circle is a one-dimensional manifold definable as the zero set of the function $f : \mathbb{R}^2 \to \mathbb{R}$, $f(x, y) = x^2 + y^2 - 1$,

$$M = S^1 = \{(x, y) \in \mathbb{R}^2 \mid x^2 + y^2 = 1\}. \tag{16.82}$$

Then

$$n(x, y) = \begin{pmatrix} x \\ y \end{pmatrix}, \tag{16.83}$$

$$P(x, y) = \begin{pmatrix} 1 - x^2 & -xy \\ -xy & 1 - y^2 \end{pmatrix}, \tag{16.84}$$

$$\operatorname{div}(n) = 2, \tag{16.85}$$

and the process

$$dX_t = -\begin{pmatrix} x \\ y \end{pmatrix} dt + \begin{pmatrix} 1 - x^2 \\ -xy \end{pmatrix} dz_{1,t} + \begin{pmatrix} -xy \\ 1 - y^2 \end{pmatrix} dz_{2,t} \tag{16.86}$$

is a process confined to S^1.

Alternatively, suppose M is defined as the zero points of f, as before. If $X_t \in M$, for all t, then $f(X_t) \equiv 0$. Suppose the process for X_t is $dX_t = \mu dt + \sigma dz_t$. If $f(X_t) \equiv 0$ then $df = 0$, so that

$$0 = \mu(f) = f_X \mu + \tfrac{1}{2}\sigma' f_{XX}\sigma, \tag{16.87}$$

$$0 = \sigma(f) = f_X \sigma. \tag{16.88}$$

Choose $\sigma(x)$ so that $f_X \sigma = 0$; that is, the columns of $\sigma(x)$ are orthogonal to

$$f_X = n(x)|f_X|, \tag{16.89}$$

and choose μ so that $f_X \mu + \tfrac{1}{2}\sigma' f_{XX}\sigma = 0$; for example, choose $\mu = -N f_X/|f_X|^2$, where $N = \tfrac{1}{2}\sigma' f_{XX}\sigma$. If μ satisfies this relationship, so does $\mu + k\sigma$, for some scalar k.

A process confined to the circle For example, for $f : \mathbb{R}^2 \to \mathbb{R}$, $f(x, y) = x^2 + y^2 - 1$, the zero set is the circle as before. Then $(f_x, f_y) = 2(x, y)$ and $f_{XX} = 2I$. Set $\sigma(x, y) = \begin{pmatrix} -y \\ x \end{pmatrix}$, so that $f_x \sigma = 0$. Then $\sigma' f_{XX}\sigma = 2$. Define μ so that $f_X \mu = -1$; for example,

$$\mu(x, y) = -\frac{1}{2}\begin{pmatrix} x \\ y \end{pmatrix} + k\begin{pmatrix} -y \\ x \end{pmatrix}. \tag{16.90}$$

Then the process

$$dX_t = \left(-\frac{1}{2}\begin{pmatrix} X_{1,t} \\ X_{2,t} \end{pmatrix} + k\begin{pmatrix} -X_{2,t} \\ X_{1,t} \end{pmatrix}\right) dt + \begin{pmatrix} -X_{2,t} \\ X_{1,t} \end{pmatrix} dz_t, \tag{16.91}$$

for $z_t \in \mathbb{R}$, is confined to $M = S^1$.

Another process defined on S^1 Let X_t be an arbitrary continuous process taking values in $\mathbb{R}$. Define

$$Y_t = (Y_{1,t}, Y_{2,t}) = \pi(X_t) = (\cos X_t, \sin X_t). \tag{16.92}$$

$\pi : \mathbb{R} \to S^1$ is the projection from $\mathbb{R}$ onto the unit circle in the plane. The components of $Y_t \in S^1 \subseteq \mathbb{R}^2$ obey the process

$$d\begin{pmatrix} Y_{1,t} \\ Y_{2,t} \end{pmatrix} = -\frac{1}{2}\begin{pmatrix} Y_{1,t} \\ Y_{2,t} \end{pmatrix} dX_t \cdot dX_t + \begin{pmatrix} -Y_{2,t} \\ Y_{1,t} \end{pmatrix} dX_t. \tag{16.93}$$

If $X_t = z_t$ is a Brownian motion in $\mathbb{R}$ then

$$d\begin{pmatrix} Y_{1,t} \\ Y_{2,t} \end{pmatrix} = -\frac{1}{2}\begin{pmatrix} Y_{1,t} \\ Y_{2,t} \end{pmatrix} dt + \begin{pmatrix} -Y_{2,t} \\ Y_{1,t} \end{pmatrix} dz_t. \tag{16.94}$$

For $dX_t = \mu dt + \sigma dz_t$,

$$d\begin{pmatrix} Y_{1,t} \\ Y_{2,t} \end{pmatrix} = \left[\mu \begin{pmatrix} -Y_{2,t} \\ Y_{1,t} \end{pmatrix} - \frac{1}{2}\sigma^2 \begin{pmatrix} Y_{1,t} \\ Y_{2,t} \end{pmatrix}\right] dt + \sigma \begin{pmatrix} -Y_{2,t} \\ Y_{1,t} \end{pmatrix} dz_t. \tag{16.95}$$

Motion on the circle is generated via the covering of S^1 by $\mathbb{R}$. The inverse mapping, on $[-1, 1]$, is given by

$$X_t = \cos^{-1} Y_{1,t} = \sin^{-1} Y_{2,t}. \tag{16.96}$$

In general suppose there is a process X_t taking values in a domain $D \subseteq \mathbb{R}^m$, such that (D, X_t) satisfies the Duffie and Kan conditions. Then if $\pi : \mathbb{R}^m \to S$ covers a manifold S such that the image of D also covers S, and if the fibre is a discrete set, then the process X_t in $\mathbb{R}^m$ defines a process Y_t in S, such that there is a lifting of Y_t into $\mathbb{R}^m$, once a base point $\pi^{-1}(Y_0)$ is specified. For instance, suppose that

$$dX_t = (a + bX_t)dt + \sqrt{X_t}\, dz_t \tag{16.97}$$

in $\mathbb{R}$. Then its projection onto S^1 is given by $Y_t = (Y_{1,t}, Y_{2,t}) = \pi(X_t) = (\cos X_t, \sin X_t)$, and

$$d\begin{pmatrix} Y_{1,t} \\ Y_{2,t} \end{pmatrix} = \begin{pmatrix} -aY_{2,t} - \frac{1}{2}Y_{1,t}\sigma^2 \cos^{-1} Y_{1,t} - bY_{2,t} \sin^{-1} Y_{2,t} \\ -aY_{1,t} - \frac{1}{2}Y_{2,t}\sigma^2 \sin^{-1} Y_{2,t} - bY_{1,t} \cos^{-1} Y_{1,t} \end{pmatrix} dt$$
$$- \sigma^2 \begin{pmatrix} Y_{2,t}\sqrt{\sin^{-1} Y_{2,t}} \\ Y_{1,t}\sqrt{\cos^{-1} Y_{1,t}} \end{pmatrix} dz_t. \tag{16.98}$$

Given an X_0 such that $\pi(X_0) = Y_0$, any process on S^1 satisfying the SDE above can be uniquely lifted to a process X_t in $\mathbb{R}$. Furthermore, since X_t is a Duffie and Kan process it possesses affine term structures. These are inherited by Y_t on S^1.

A process on a sphere Let X_t be an arbitrary process taking values in $\mathbb{R}^n \setminus 0$. Set $r_t^2 = X_{1,t}^2 + \cdots + X_{n,t}^2$, and define $Y_t = X_t/r_t$. Y_t takes values on $S^{n-1} \subseteq \mathbb{R}^n$. The definition is symmetric, so that the process looks the same under orthogonal transformations. This is an example where the dimension of the embedded manifold is strictly less than the dimension of the embedding space.

A process confined to the sphere   For $f : \mathbb{R}^3 \to \mathbb{R}$, $f(x, y) = x^2 + y^2 + z^3 - 1$, the zero set is the sphere

$$M = S^2 = \left\{ (x, y, z) \in \mathbb{R}^3 \mid x^2 + y^2 + z^2 - 1 = 0 \right\}. \tag{16.99}$$

Then $(f_x, f_y, f_z) = 2(x, y, z)$ and $f_{XX} = 2I$. We can choose $\sigma_1(X), \sigma_2(X) \in \mathbb{R}^3$ so that

$$f_X \cdot (\sigma_1, \sigma_2) = 0, \tag{16.100}$$

and

$$\sigma_i \cdot \sigma_j = \delta_{i,j}. \tag{16.101}$$

Hence we can choose

$$\mu(X) = -\frac{f_X}{|f_X|^2} + \sigma \cdot \begin{pmatrix} k_1 \\ k_2 \end{pmatrix} \tag{16.102}$$

as before.

Another processes on the sphere   For $Y_t = (Y_{1,t}, Y_{2,t}, Y_{3,t})' \in \mathbb{R}^3$, define

$$dY_t = \mu(Y_t)dt + \sigma(Y_t)dz_t \tag{16.103}$$

by

$$\mu(Y_t) = -1 \begin{pmatrix} Y_{1,t} \\ Y_{2,t} \\ Y_{3,t} \end{pmatrix} + \alpha \begin{pmatrix} -Y_{2,t} \\ Y_{1,t} \\ 0 \end{pmatrix} + \frac{\beta}{2} \begin{pmatrix} 0 \\ 0 \\ -Y_{3,t} \end{pmatrix}, \tag{16.104}$$

$$\sigma(Y_t) = \begin{pmatrix} Y_{1,t}\dfrac{Y_{3,t}}{\sqrt{1 - Y_{3,t}^2}} & -\sqrt{\dfrac{\beta}{2}}\, Y_{3,t}\dfrac{Y_{2,t}}{\sqrt{1 - Y_{3,t}^2}} \\[4mm] Y_{2,t}\dfrac{Y_{3,t}}{\sqrt{1 - Y_{3,t}^2}} & \sqrt{\dfrac{\beta}{2}}\, Y_{3,t}\dfrac{Y_{1,t}}{\sqrt{1 - Y_{3,t}^2}} \\[4mm] \sqrt{1 - Y_{3,t}^2} & 0 \end{pmatrix}, \quad Y_{3,t} \neq \pm 1. \tag{16.105}$$

This process is confined to a set

$$S^2 = \left\{ Y \mid Y_1^2 + Y_2^2 + Y_3^2 = 1 \right\}. \tag{16.106}$$

The parameterisation is well defined and finite, except at the poles, $Y_{3,t} \neq \pm 1$, a set of measure zero. (We may only use this parameterisation in circumstances where it is legitimate.) The random increments in Y_t are confined to the tangent plane at Y_t; the drift term compensates the process so that it is confined to the unit sphere. It rotates about the Y_3 axis at a rate α, while reverting to the $Y_3 = 0$ plane at a rate β. Figure 16.4 shows a sample path from this process. The rate has been chosen so that the process

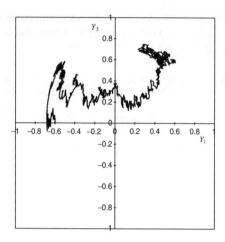

Figure 16.4   Sample path of a process confined to a sphere

orbits relatively rapidly about the Y_3 axis. The figure shows the projection onto the $Y_2 = 0$ plane.

In general to construct a process confined to S^{n-1}, for $Y_t \in \mathbb{R}^n$, define $\mu(Y_t) = ((1-n)/2)Y_t$, and let $\sigma(Y_t)$ be an $n \times n - 1$ matrix whose columns are of unit modulus and span the $n - 1$-dimensional subspace tangent to S^{n-1} at Y_t.

Construction by projection   Suppose a process X_t is defined on a manifold M. If $\phi : M \to N$ then $\phi(X_t)$ is a process defined on N. The examples above are mappings from $\mathbb{R}^2$ and $\mathbb{R}$, respectively, onto S^1.

The Moebius strip, $\mathbb{M}$, can be constructed as a quotient of $S^1 \times \mathbb{R}$. For $(\theta, x) \in S^1 \times \mathbb{R}$, define an equivalence relationship $\sim$ by

$$(\theta, x) \sim (\theta + \pi, -x). \tag{16.107}$$

Set $\mathbb{M} = (S^1 \times \mathbb{R})/\sim$.

Processes on $\mathbb{M}$ can be generated from processes taking values in the trivial covering bundle. For instance, a process taking values in $S^1 \times \mathbb{R}$ can be projected down onto $\mathbb{M}$ via the covering map. This process thus defined on $\mathbb{M}$ is well defined and topologically distinct from the process on $S^1 \times \mathbb{R}$. Since $S^1 \times \mathbb{R}$ can itself be covered by $\mathbb{R} \times \mathbb{R}$, a semi-affine process in $\mathbb{R}^2$ generates a process in $\mathbb{M}$ that has affine term structures.

Figure 16.5 shows the sample path for a process on $\mathbb{M}$. It was generated from a two-dimensional semi-affine process, (θ_t, r_t),

$$\mathrm{d}\begin{pmatrix} \theta_t \\ r_t \end{pmatrix} = \left[\begin{pmatrix} 0 \\ \alpha\mu_r \end{pmatrix} + \begin{pmatrix} \mu_\theta & 0 \\ 0 & -\alpha \end{pmatrix} \begin{pmatrix} \theta_t \\ r_t \end{pmatrix} \right] \mathrm{d}t + (\theta_t \; r_t) \begin{pmatrix} \sigma_\theta & 0 \\ 0 & \sigma_r \end{pmatrix} \begin{pmatrix} \mathrm{d}z_\theta \\ \mathrm{d}z_r \end{pmatrix}. \tag{16.108}$$

$(\theta_t, r_t) \in \mathbb{R}^2$ was projected down onto $\mathbb{M} \subseteq \mathbb{R}^3$ by the mapping

$$(\theta_t, r_t) \longmapsto (a\cos 2\theta_t + r_t \cos \theta_t, a\sin 2\theta_t + r_t \sin \theta_t, r_t \sin \theta_t), \tag{16.109}$$

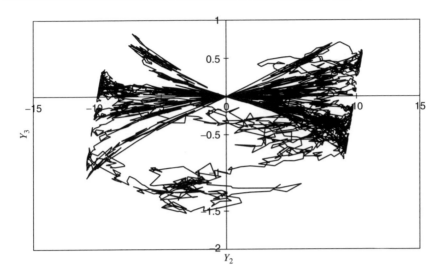

Figure 16.5 Sample path on a Moebius strip

where $a > 0$ is a scale constant defining a radius. The figure shows the sample path looking 'side on' at the Moebius strip. It is rotating about the Y_3 axis.

16.4.5 An S^1 Interest Rate Model

A process on the circle S^1 may not be expressed in finite dimensional semi-affine form. However, it is perfectly feasible to define term structure models upon it. Suppose the underlying state variable is W_t where

$$dW_t = \alpha(W_t, \omega)dt + \rho(W_t, \omega)dz_t, \qquad (16.110)$$

under the risk-neutral measure, for some parameter set ω, and α and ρ are periodic in W_t:

$$\alpha(W_t, \omega) = \alpha(W_t + 2\pi, \omega), \qquad (16.111)$$

$$\rho(W_t, \omega) = \rho(W_t + 2\pi, \omega), \qquad (16.112)$$

Bond prices satisfy the PDE

$$\alpha(W_t)P_W + \tfrac{1}{2}\rho^2(W_t)P_{W,W} + P = r(W_t)P, \qquad (16.113)$$

where subscripts denote partial differentiation, and where we impose the boundary conditions

$$P(W_T, T) = 1, P(W_t, t) = P(W_t + 2\pi, t). \qquad (16.114)$$

Since everything is periodic in W_t, solutions are defined on $\theta_t = W_t \bmod 2\pi$, which is just the circle S^1.

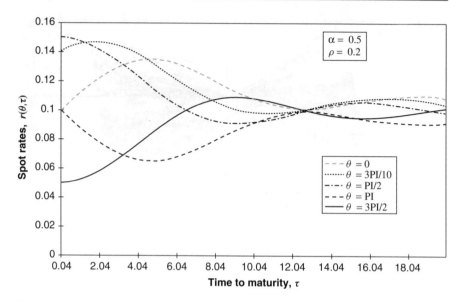

Figure 16.6   Term structures; various initial values of θ

The PDE is easy to solve numerically. For example, take α and ρ to be constants, and set $r(X_t) = a + b \sin X_t$. The model has a surprising broad spectrum of behaviour. Term structures can be damped waves or they can be monotonic. Figure 16.6 shows term structures computed when α and ρ are constants, $\alpha = 0.5$, $\rho = 0.2$, with $r(X, Y) = 0.1 + 0.05X$. These distinctive term structures are unlike those produced by models defined on $\mathbb{R}^n$.[3]

Figure 16.7 shows a sample path of the short rate. The short rate is driven up and down in the interval $I = [a - b, a + b]$ as (X, Y) travels around the circle. r cannot take values outside of I so that interest rates are positive in this model if $a > b$.

16.4.6   Local Reduction to Semi-Affine Form

When does the map $r : S \to T \cong \mathbb{R}^m$ exist? We have seen that in general it might be hard to find.

An alternative is to use local co-ordinates. Instead of defining r on the whole of S, define it only on open sets in S making up co-ordinate patches on the manifold. Since S is an s-dimensional manifold there exists a co-ordinate system $\{(U_i, \phi_i)\}$ with $U_i \subseteq S$, such that $\bigcup U_i = S$, where $\phi_i : U_i \to \mathbb{R}^s$ are diffeomorphisms. If $\mathbb{R}^s$ possesses a semi-affine process X_t, then $\phi_i^{-1}(X_t)$ is a process on U_i that ϕ_i reduces to semi-affine form. Hence affine term structures can be defined on U_i.

---

[3] The location of the humps can be controlled if, for instance, α is allowed to be a function of time.

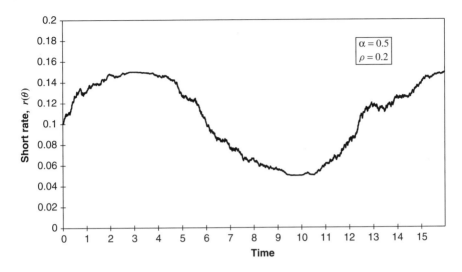

Figure 16.7 Simulation of the short rate process

There are serious problems with this construction:

1. Different patches (ϕ_i, U_i) give different term structure decompositions.
2. A reducible process on (ϕ_i, U_i) will not in general extend to a reducible process on S.
3. Co-ordinate patches are not 'canonical'. One prefers a definition that does not depend on a particular choice of co-ordinate patch.

One solution is to use covering spaces. A manifold M covers a manifold N with fibre F if

1. There exists a diffeomorphism $\pi : M \to N$ which is onto.
2. For all $x \in N$, $\pi^{-1}(x) \cong F$.
3. For all $x \in N$, there exists an open set $U \subseteq N$, with $x \in U$, such that $\pi^{-1}(U) \cong U \times F$.

We are interested in coverings with a discrete fibre so that $F = \{f_i\}_{i \in I}$, for some discrete index set I, and the set $U \times F$ can be decomposed into a sum of components each diffeomorphic to U, $U \times F = \bigcup_{i \in I} U \times \{f_i\}$.

For example, $\mathbb{R}$ covers the circle S^1. Define

$$\pi : \mathbb{R} \to S^1, \tag{16.115}$$

$$\pi(\theta) = (\cos\theta, \sin\theta). \tag{16.116}$$

This is a covering of S^1 by $\mathbb{R}$, with fibre $\mathbb{Z}$. The inverse map is only defined on open sets $U \subseteq [0, 2\pi]$,

$$\pi^{-1}(\cos\theta, \sin\theta) = \theta + 2n\pi, \quad \text{for some } n \in \mathbb{Z}, \theta \in U. \tag{16.117}$$

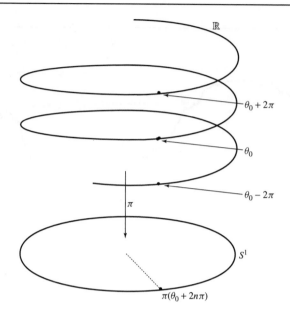

Figure 16.8   Covering S^1 by $\mathbb{R}$

Figure 16.8 illustrates the mapping. The inverse mapping is defined once a base point is supplied.

Coverings with Discrete Fibre

Suppose that F is discrete; for example, if $F \cong \mathbb{Z}$, then

1. Processes on M project down to processes on N.
2. Processes in N lift to processes in M, at least locally.

Suppose that X_t is a process on N. Since F is discrete the inverse mapping is easy to define, at least locally, once a base point is given.

For $X_0 \in N$ find a base point $X_0^\uparrow$ such that $\pi(X_0^\uparrow) = X_0$. In a neighbourhood U of X_0, we have $\pi^{-1}(U) \cong U \times F$. Suppose $X_0^\uparrow \in U \times \{f\}$, for some $f \in F$. Then $\pi \mid U \times \{f\}$ is a diffeomorphism. For $X_t \in U$ define $X_t^\uparrow$ by

$$X_t^\uparrow = (\pi_{U \times \{f\}})^{-1}(X_t). \tag{16.118}$$

This lift is unique, on U, once $X_0^\uparrow$ is fixed.

Local Reduction to Semi-affine Form

Given (S, X_t, r_0), suppose there exists a covering

$$\pi : \mathbb{R}^m \to S, \tag{16.119}$$

with discrete fibre F, where the process X_t on $\mathcal{S}$ is induced from a semi-affine process on $\mathbb{R}^m$ by the covering map π. For all $x \in \mathcal{S}$, we can find an open set U, $x \in U \subseteq \mathcal{S}$, and a map r^U,

$$r^U : U \subseteq \mathcal{S} \to r^U(U) = \mathbb{R}^U \subseteq \mathbb{R}^m, \tag{16.120}$$

such that

$$\left(\mathbb{R}^U, r^U(X_t), \pi_0 \left(r^U \right) \right) \tag{16.121}$$

reduces X_t to semi-affine form.

The properties of coverings and covering spaces have been very deeply studied. For introductions to the area see Husemoller (85) [302] or Wolf (84) [545]. Examples of coverings are afforded by coverings of S^{n-1}. Both $O(n)$ and $SO(n)$ cover S^{n-1} with fibre $O(n-1)$ and $SO(n-1)$, respectively, which correspond to the stabiliser subgroups of points on S^{n-1}. S^3 covers S^2; S^3 is diffeomorphic to the group $SU(2)$ which has a double covering of $SO(3)$ which in turn covers S^2.

Coverings with discrete fibres may be found by taking quotients of spaces with respect to discrete groups of symmetries. For instance, a quotient of S^2 by a finite rotation group gives a discrete cover of the quotient space. The only complete connected 2-manifolds covered by $\mathbb{R}^2$ are the cylinder $S^1 \times \mathbb{R}$, the torus $S^1 \times S^1$, the Moebius strip $\mathbb{M}$, the Klein bottle, or $\mathbb{R}^2$ itself (see Wolf).

16.5   ANALYSIS OF DYNAMICAL SYSTEMS

Affine models are quite tractable, but are they realistic? We shall conclude on theoretical grounds that locally affine models are good approximations to a process on an underlying finite dimensional manifold. However, a model will need re-calibrating as the underlying state variables evolve around the manifold.

We want to investigate financial data, in particular interest rates. There are two different ideas:

1. Look at a single time series, for example a time series of the short rate. We could then use GMM or maximum likelihood methods to estimate parameter values for the objective process. Unfortunately estimating from a single time series is unsatisfactory. Results are often inconclusive, and are in any case based upon a limited subset of the available data.
2. Look at several time series at once; for example, the whole term structure observed at some fixed set of times to maturity. PCA analysis is an excellent data reduction method in this case.

16.5.1   Spatial Data

In a physical system, at each moment in time it is often possible to measure data at different points in space. This is called spatial data. There is an analogous structure in interest rate data. At each time there is an entire term structure of interest rates, and indeed a surface of volatility data (implied volatilities for options for different times to maturity and exercise price).

Our method shall be:

1. Identify a set of spatial data, for example a set of bond prices or money market rates.
2. Standardise the data, for example by computing (or interpolating to find) spot rates with fixed times to maturity
3. Do a PCA to identify the underlying factors. We regard PCA as a mapping into an imbedding space. For example, perform a PCA on $r_t(\tau)$, the time τ to maturity spot rate at time t. Suppose we find n components $\sigma_i(\tau)$ such that

$$r_{t+1}(\tau) - r_t(\tau) = \sum_{i=1}^{n} \sigma_i(\tau) \left(w_{t+1}^i - w_t^i \right) + \varepsilon_t(\tau), \tag{16.122}$$

where $\varepsilon_t(\tau)$ is residual noise. Set $w_t = \left(w_t^1, \ldots, w_t^n \right)'$. We then identify the state of the system with $w_t \in \mathbb{R}^n$. n is the imbedding dimension.
4. Analyse the dynamics of w_t.

16.5.2   Empirical Results

We reported the results of Nunes and Webber (97) [422] in Section 16.2.2. PCA was used to perform a global analysis of the data to establish a basis of $\mathcal{T} \subseteq C^+$.

A further step, reported in their paper, is to perform a local analysis. A PCA was made of subperiods. The purpose of the local analysis was to relate local bases to the global basis to allow an investigation of the evolution of the system in global co-ordinates.

Since Nunes and Webber were seeking only to construct a basis for $\mathcal{T} \subseteq C^+$, for which a stripped curve is unnecessary, they worked directly with market rates, leading to the results shown in Section 16.2.2.

They found nine components $p_i = (p_{i,1}, \ldots, p_{i,9})$, $i = 1, \ldots, 9$, such that

$$\Delta r_t(\tau_j) = \sum_{i=1}^{9} p_{i,j} \Delta w_{i,t} + \varepsilon_{t,j}, \tag{16.123}$$

with $w_t = (w_{1t}, \ldots, w_{9t})$ uncorrelated and $\varepsilon_{t,j}$ is residual noise. $p = (p_1, \ldots, p_9)'$ is a basis for the set $C = \{p : \{1, 2, \ldots, 9\} \to \mathbb{R}\}$. In the HJM framework $w_{i,t} = \sum_{s=0}^{t-1} \Delta w_{i,s}$ are independent. In Duffie and Kan $w_{i,t}$ are semi-affine processes, but w_t has full rank in $\mathbb{R}^9$.

16.5.3   The State Space, $\mathcal{T}$

Suppose there are precisely three components. Decompose term structures as

$$\Delta r_t(\tau_j) = \sum_{i=1}^{3} p_{i,j} \Delta w_{i,t} + \varepsilon_{t,j}, \tag{16.124}$$

so that

$$r_t(\tau_j) = r_0(\tau_j) + \sum_{i=1}^{3} p_{i,j} w_{i,t} + \eta_{t,j}. \tag{16.125}$$

There is a one-to-one correspondence between

$$r_t(\tau) = (r_t(\tau_1), \ldots, r_t(\tau_k)) \quad \text{and} \quad w_t = (w_{1,t}, w_{2,t}, w_{3,t}). \tag{16.126}$$

The map

$$r_t(\tau) \to w_t \tag{16.127}$$

embeds the state space $\mathcal{S}$ into $\mathcal{T}$, a finite dimensional subspace of $\mathbb{R}^3$. $\mathcal{W} = \{w_t\}$ is the empirical realisation of $\mathcal{R} = \text{Im}(\mathcal{S})$. To study $\mathcal{S}$ it is only necessary to study the set $\mathcal{W}$.

16.5.4   The Set $\mathcal{W}$: Term Structures Embedded into $\mathcal{T}$

Nunes and Webber obtained a set $\mathcal{W}$ from their data by PCA. Figures 16.9–16.11 show various projections of $\mathcal{W}$.

One's first impression is that w_t is not a process with independent increments, so that its dynamics are non-trivial. This feature is only verifiable from statistical tests. Plots like Figures 16.9–16.11 can be very misleading and should not be construed as illustrating structure unless the structure can be tested for. In fact in this case the series fails tests for no serial correlation and stability on subsets.

Suppose that $\mathcal{W}$ lies on a manifold $\mathcal{R}$, the image of $\mathcal{S}$ in $\mathbb{R}^3$. There are only a limited number of possibilities for $\mathcal{R}$, if one requires a degree of symmetry. The dimension of $\mathcal{R}$ may be 3 or 2 or 1.

1. $\mathcal{R}$ is a 3-manifold? Since $\mathcal{R}$ is embedded in $\mathbb{R}^3$, it must be a subset of $\mathbb{R}^3$. It may have holes, or it might be a Duffie and Kan affine system.
2. $\mathcal{R}$ is a 2-manifold? If it is covered by $\mathbb{R}^2$ then it must be one of $S^1 \times \mathbb{R}$, $S^1 \times S^1$, $\mathbb{M}$, the Klein bottle, or $\mathbb{R}^2$.

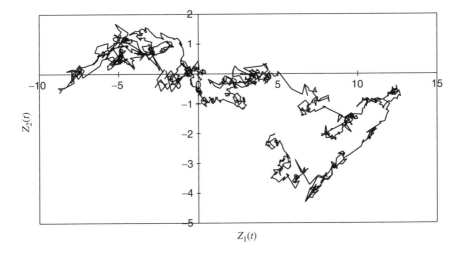

Figure 16.9   Scatter plot: second and first components (28 September 1988 to 3 February 1995)

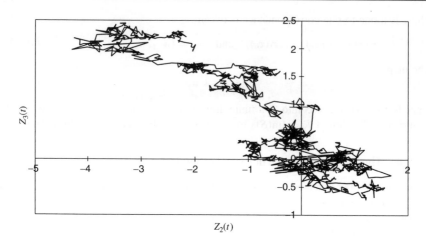

Figure 16.10 Scatter plot: third and second components (28 September 1988 to 3 February 1995)

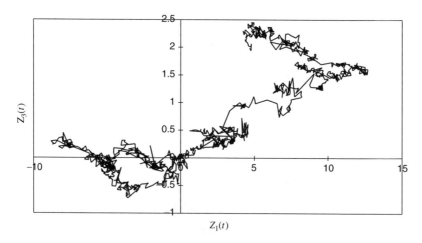

Figure 16.11 Scatter plot: third and first components (28 September 1988 to 3 February 1995)

3. $\mathcal{R}$ is a 1-manifold? It must be either S^1 or $\mathbb{R}$.

Note that the embedding may be very complex. For example, a 1-manifold in $\mathbb{R}^3$ may have accumulation points. For instance, define $\phi : \mathbb{R} \to \mathbb{R}^2$ as $\phi(t) = (\theta_t, r_t)$, in polar co-ordinates, with $\theta_t = t$, $r_t = 1/t$. As another example, a 1-manifold in $\mathbb{R}^3$ may be a chaotic orbit. For instance, the deterministic version of the Tice and Webber model has chaotic orbits

$$t \to (r_t, x_t, p_t) \in \mathbb{R}^3 \tag{16.128}$$

(in their notation; see Chapter 11). Suppose $X_t \in \mathbb{R}$ is semi-affine, then $\phi(X_t) = (r_{X_t}, x_{X_t}, p_{X_t})$ maps X_t onto a chaotic orbit in $\mathbb{R}^3$.

In their paper Nunes and Webber perform further analyses on the set $\mathcal{W}$. They attempt to model the data as a two-factor process or a cylinder. Their two factors are

$$d\theta_t = (a\theta_t + b)dt + \sqrt{c + d\theta_t}\, dz_t^\theta, \tag{16.129}$$

$$dr_t = (ar_t + b)dt + \sqrt{c + dr_t}\, dz_t^r, \tag{16.130}$$

where (via a transformation) (θ_t, r_t) represent the polar coordinates of a point in $\mathcal{W}$. They fit the model using a quasi-maximum likelihood method, but find that the diagnostics are not particularly good.

16.6 CONCLUSIONS

We have seen that PCA analysis can be used to calibrate Heath, Jarrow and Morton models, at least those with Gaussian volatility functions. We can do this using historical term structure data or using an implied covariance matrix.

Going a step beyond this, we used the volatility functions as basis functions to reduce the dimensions of the state space. We explored how interest rate models might be defined on non-linear state spaces and defined a model defined on the circle.

We conclude that affine co-ordinates can easily be imposed, at least locally, in any term structure model if a suitable covering can be found. We expect volatility components to be time-varying as the local covering varies at different points in the state space.

The key idea is to analyse dynamics in $\mathcal{T}$, to permit $\mathcal{S}$ to be a non-trivial manifold, and to reduce to semi-affine form via coverings. An affine structure is a local phenomena and may not extend globally.

17

Estimation Methods: GMM and ML

Interest rate models contain parameters that must be estimated by calibrating to market data. It is usually preferable to estimate parameter values from prices by some implied calibration method. Despite this it is still necessary to estimate parameter values from time series. This is done, for instance, to look at the behaviour of strategies over time, to compare implied to historical parameter estimates, and to investigate the time series behaviour of implieds.

We saw in Chapter 5 that naive ordinary least squares (OLS) methods are unsuitable for calibrating interest rate models. Here we discuss the two main methods suitable for financial applications. These are

1. *The General Method of Moments (GMM)* (Hansen (82) [267]). This method compares certain functions of the sample, called moments, with their theoretical values. Parameter values are chosen so that the values of the theoretical moments are close to their sample values.
2. *Maximum Likelihood (ML) methods* (Lo (86) [356], (88) [357]). These methods are most appropriate if the transition density function of observables in the model is known. ML is then an efficient method for finding parameter values. Variations of the method can be used if an explicit form of the transition density function is not known, but then it may be computationally intensive to obtain accurate estimates.

Both methods are statistically 'proper', in that they have known tests and diagnostics. Neither method should be used unless proper diagnostics are used to assess the results. An estimate without diagnostics is almost as bad as no estimate at all, since it may lead one to accept, and make decisions based upon, an ill-specified model.

In this chapter we describe both the general method of moments and the maximum likelihood method. We discuss the practical implementation of each method and give examples of variations of the basic method. In particular we describe the efficient method of moments (EMM) (also known as the simulated methods of moments (SMM)) and simulated maximum likelihood (SML).

GMM has been used by Heston (88) [279], Gibbons and Ramaswamy (93) [247], and Longstaff and Schwartz (92) [365] for estimating parameters of one-and two-factor

CIR processes. Chan *et al* (92) [124], Vetzal (97) [533] and Bliss and Smith (98) [79] have used GMM to estimate CKLS processes and extensions.

ML has been used to estimate one-and two-factor CIR type models by Brown and Dybvig (86) [103], Brown and Schaefer (94) [105], Edsparr (92) [197], Chen and Scott (93) [128], Pearson and Sun (94) [432], Ball and Torous (96) [51] and Brandt and Santa-Clara (99) [89], and many others. By transforming their non-linear model into CIR form, Marsh and Rosenfeld (83) [382] are able to use ML to estimate it. Broze *et al.* (93) [106], Nowman (97a) [419], (97b) [420] and Honore (98) [286] use ML to estimate CKLS type models.

EMM has been used by Duffie and Singleton (93) [188] in a general asset pricing context, by Dai and Singleton (98) [154] to estimate three-factor affine models, and by Andersen and Lund (97) [22], (96a) [19], (96b) [20] and (96c) [21] for two-and three-factor extensions of the CKLS model.

There are many excellent textbooks which describe these methods. Good references include Campbell, Lo and MacKinlay (97) [113], Davidson and MacKinnon (93) [158] Hamilton (94) [266], and many others. Gourieroux and Monfort (96) [257] look specifically at simulation methods.

17.1 GMM ESTIMATION

Suppose we have a set of observations, r_t, whose evolution depends upon a set of parameters θ,

$$\theta = (\theta_1, \ldots, \theta_k)'. \tag{17.1}$$

For example, in the Vasicek model θ could be

$$\theta = (\alpha, \sigma, r_\infty)' \tag{17.2}$$

(see Chapter 5). It will be possible to find functions $f_i(r_t \mid \theta)$, $i = 1, \ldots, m$, $m \geq k$, such that

$$\mathbb{E}[f_i(r_t \mid \theta)] = 0. \tag{17.3}$$

Given such a set of such functions one may compute sample estimates of $\mathbb{E}[f_i(r_t \mid \theta)]$, $i = 1, \ldots, m$. The GMM estimates $\hat{\theta}$ of θ are those values of θ that set the sample estimates as close to zero as possible. In the 'classic' method of moments the number of parameters equals the number of functions. When $m = k$ it should be possible to set the f_i exactly to zero. One finds values $\hat{\theta}$ of θ such that

$$\frac{1}{N} \sum_{t=1}^{N} f_i(r_t \mid \hat{\theta}) = 0, \quad i = 1, \ldots, k. \tag{17.4}$$

$\hat{\theta}$ are the classic method of moments estimates of θ.

We shall immediately relax the assumption that $m = k$. Set $f = (f_1, \ldots, f_m)$, and define $\hat{\theta}$ to be

$$\hat{\theta} = \arg \min_\theta f' W f \tag{17.5}$$

for some positive definite weighting matrix W. This is the GMM estimate of θ, contingent upon W and f. For a least squares method W is the identity matrix or a diagonal matrix. We discuss the appropriate choice of weighting matrix in Section 17.1.2.

A disadvantage of the method is that $\hat{\theta}$ depends on which functions $\{f_i\}_{i=1,\ldots,m}$ have been chosen. We discuss good choices below. f will be chosen to be related to the moments of r_t.

17.1.1 Example: Chan, Karolyi, Longstaff and Sanders

Chan, Karolyi, Longstaff and Sanders (CKLS) (92) [124] is a standard early example of the use of GMM in interest rate parameter estimation. Although its methodology and conclusions have been subsequently extended (Bliss and Smith (98) [79], Brenner et al. (96) [96], Andersen and Lund (97) [22]) it remains an illuminating illustration of the method. Chan, Karolyi, Longstaff and Sanders estimated a discrete-time version of the process

$$dr_t = \alpha(\mu - r_t)dt + \sigma r_t^\gamma \, dz_t.$$

They used a Euler discretisation

$$r_{t+1} = a + br_t + \sigma r_t^\gamma u_{t+1}. \tag{17.6}$$

The parameter set is $\theta = (a, b, \sigma, \gamma)'$. Set $\varepsilon_{t+1} = r_{t+1} - (a + br_t)$, so that $\varepsilon_{t+1} = \sigma r_t^\gamma u_{t+1}$. If the model is correctly specified, then $\varepsilon_{t+1} \sim N(0, \sigma^2 r_t^{2\gamma} \Delta t)$ is normal iid, ε_{t+1} is serially uncorrelated with r_t, et cetera. This immediately gives us an abundance of moment conditions:

- $\varepsilon_{t+1} \sim N(0, \sigma^2 r_t^{2\gamma} \Delta t)$:

$$\mathbb{E}[\varepsilon_{t+1}] = 0, \tag{17.7}$$

$$\mathbb{E}[\varepsilon_{t+1}^2 - \sigma^2 r_t^{2\gamma} \Delta t] = 0, \tag{17.8}$$

$$\mathbb{E}[\varepsilon_{t+1}^3] = 0, \text{ et cetera} \tag{17.9}$$

- ε_{t+1} is serially uncorrelated:

$$\mathbb{E}[\varepsilon_{t+1}\varepsilon_t] = 0, \tag{17.10}$$

$$\mathbb{E}[\varepsilon_{t+1}\varepsilon_{t-1}] = 0, \text{ et cetera} \tag{17.11}$$

- ε_{t+1} is serially uncorrelated with r_t:

$$\mathbb{E}[\varepsilon_{t+1}r_t] = 0, \tag{17.12}$$

$$\mathbb{E}[(\varepsilon_{t+1}^2 - \sigma^2 r_t^{2\gamma} \Delta t)r_t] = 0, \text{ et cetera} \tag{17.13}$$

Given a value for θ we can compute sample moments. For instance, sample moments for moments (17.7), (17.8), (17.12) and (17.13) are

$$(17.7): \qquad f_1 = \frac{1}{N}\sum_{t=1}^{N}(r_{t+1} - a - br_t),$$

$$(17.8): \qquad f_2 = \frac{1}{N}\sum_{t=1}^{N}((r_{t+1} - a - br_t)^2 - \sigma^2 r_t^{2\gamma}\Delta t),$$

$$(17.12): \qquad f_3 = \frac{1}{N}\sum_{t=1}^{N}(r_{t+1} - a - br_t)r_t,$$

$$(17.13): \qquad f_4 = \frac{1}{N}\sum_{t=1}^{N}((r_{t+1} - a - br_t)^2 - \sigma^2 r_t^{2\gamma}\Delta t)r_t.$$

We choose a, b, σ and γ to set f_1, f_2, f_3 and f_4 to zero, for instance by minimising

$$J(a, b, \sigma, \gamma) = f_1^2 + f_2^2 + f_3^2 + f_4^2. \qquad (17.14)$$

The GMM estimates of a, b, σ and γ are

$$(\hat{a}, \hat{b}, \hat{\sigma}, \hat{\gamma}) = \arg\min_{(a,b,\sigma,\gamma)} J(a, b, \sigma, \gamma). \qquad (17.15)$$

Chan, Karolyi, Longstaff and Sanders choose precisely the four moments f_1, f_2, f_3 and f_4 above to estimate the four parameters (a, b, σ, γ), an implementation of the classical method of moments. They famously concluded that $\gamma \sim 1.5$. We shall have more to say about this conclusion in Section 17.2.4.

17.1.2   Over-Estimation and the Weighting Matrix

Four unknowns require four equations, but we can find many different moments. In general we want to estimate k parameters by setting $m > k$ equations to 0. With only k parameters, it will not in general prove possible to set all m equations to 0. In practice, it is necessary to define a criteria function and attempt to minimise the criteria.

This procedure is called over-estimation. GMM improves with over-estimation, but if there is too much over-estimation the method ends up fitting the quirks of the sample.

In equation (17.15) we minimised the least squares criteria. This is actually suboptimal, in general. There is an optimal choice of weighting matrix, W. Given an $m \times m$ matrix, W, set

$$J_W(\theta) = f'Wf, \qquad (17.16)$$

so that the GMM estimates of (a, b, σ, γ) relative to W are $\hat{\theta} = (\hat{a}, \hat{b}, \hat{\sigma}, \hat{\gamma})$,

$$\hat{\theta} = \arg\min_{\theta} J_W(\theta). \qquad (17.17)$$

An optimal choice for W is the sample estimate of the asymptotic covariance minimising matrix (Hansen (82) [267], and Campbell, Lo and MacKinlay). Set

$$S = \lim_{N \to \infty} \mathbb{E} \left[\frac{1}{N} \sum_{t=1}^{N} \sum_{s=1}^{N} f_t f_s' \right]. \tag{17.18}$$

The optimal choice for W is for it to be a consistent estimator of S^{-1}. Its practical estimation has been discussed by Newey and West (87) [414] and Andrews (91) [26]; see Vetzal (97) [533]. For our purposes we simply set

$$W = \left(\frac{1}{N} \sum_{t=1}^{N} f_t f_t' \right)^{-1}, \tag{17.19}$$

so that

$$(W^{-1})_{i,j} = \frac{1}{N} \sum_{t=1}^{N} f_{t,i} f_{t,j}, \tag{17.20}$$

where $f_t = (f_{t,1}, \ldots, f_{t,m})$, $f_{t,i} = f_i(r_t \mid a, b, \sigma, \gamma)$.[1] W depends on a, b, σ and γ. Minimising (17.16) is a non-linear optimisation problem. A number of computer packages are available to perform GMM by optimising (17.16).

17.1.3 Pros and Cons of GMM

With a good optimiser GMM is reasonably fast. A big advantage of GMM is that its use does not require a knowledge of the distribution of ε_t, just its moments f.

A disadvantage is that it ignores the transition density function, should it be available. GMM only uses information about the moments f, and does not make use of other possible information. There is also the problem of the choice of which moments to use. The latter problem has an answer, as we see in Sections 17.2.1 and 17.2.2.

17.2 IMPLEMENTATION ISSUES

In this section we explore how in general moment conditions might be obtained. We show how one may hypothesis test in GMM, including how to decide if the model estimated by GMM fits the data or not. We present several examples of the use of GMM. These include Longstaff and Schwartz (92) [365], Vetzal (97) [533] and Bliss and Smith (98) [79].

---

[1] We are implicitly assuming that $f_t(\theta)$ are serially uncorrelated.

17.2.1 Obtaining Moment Conditions

Suppose a process X_t depends on a parameter vector θ. Given a function f, one may in principle compute the theoretical expected value $g(\theta)$ of f:

$$g(\theta) = \mathbb{E}[f(X) \mid \theta]. \tag{17.21}$$

For the moment we relax the restriction that $g(\theta) \equiv 0$. Given observations $\hat{X}_t$, the sample moment $\hat{f}$ is computed as

$$\hat{f} = \frac{1}{N} \sum_{t=1}^{N} f(\hat{X}_t). \tag{17.22}$$

We want to choose θ so that $\hat{f} = g(\theta)$. When f is vector valued, θ is chosen so that

$$\hat{\theta} = \arg \min_{\theta} J(\theta) = (\hat{f} - g)' W(\theta)(\hat{f} - g), \tag{17.23}$$

for a weighting matrix W, as before. The estimated value $\hat{\theta}$ of θ depends on the functions f that we have chosen. This poses two questions. First, since the choice of f may seriously influence the results of the estimation procedure, how should f be chosen? Second, how can $g(\theta)$ be calculated?

17.2.2 Selecting Moments

As we have seen, it is possible to generate moments from the standardised residuals. For example, Vetzal (97) [533] and Melino and Turnbull (91) [391] use the moments

$$
\begin{array}{ll}
\varepsilon_t^m, & m = 1, 2, 3, \ldots, \\
|\varepsilon_t^m|, & m = 1, 2, 3, \ldots, \\
\varepsilon_t \varepsilon_{t-s}, & s = 1, 2, 3, \ldots, \\
\varepsilon_t^2 \varepsilon_{t-s}^2, & s = 1, 2, 3, \ldots, \\
|\varepsilon_t \varepsilon_{t-s}|, & s = 1, 2, 3, \ldots, \\
|\varepsilon_t| |\varepsilon_{t-s}|, & s = 1, 2, 3, \ldots.
\end{array} \tag{17.24}
$$

When $\varepsilon_t \sim N(0, 1)$ iid, it is possible to find explicit formulae for the expected values of the functions above. Vetzal and Melino and Turnbull estimate the two-factor stochastic volatility model:

$$dr_t = (a + br_t)dt + \sigma_t r_t^\gamma \, dz_{1,t}, \tag{17.25}$$

$$d(\ln \sigma_t) = (c + d \ln \sigma_t)dt + \xi \, dz_{2,t},$$

with $dz_{1,t} \, dz_{2,t} = \rho dt$. Set

$$\varepsilon_t = \frac{r_t - a\Delta_t - (1 + b\Delta_t)r_{t-1}}{r_{t-1}^\gamma \sqrt{\Delta_t}} = \sigma_{t-1} e_t, \tag{17.26}$$

where $e_t \sim N(0, 1)$ iid, and σ_{t-1} is log-normal. It is possible to compute the theoretical moments in this case too (see Melino and Turnbull).

In general computing the theoretical moments $g(\theta)$ might be a serious practical problem. The solution is to generate f so that by construction, $g(\theta)$ has known values, for instance $g(\theta) \equiv 0$. Hansen and Scheinkman (95) [268] show how it is possible to generate many moments with this property. They give two constructions. Given an n-dimensional stationary stochastic process X_t with infinitesimal generator A, Hansen and Scheinkman show that:

1. For any function f for which Af is well defined,

$$\mathbb{E}[Af(x) \mid \theta] = 0. \tag{17.27}$$

2. If X_t^* is the reverse time process of X_t (see Hansen and Scheinkman) and A^* is the infinitesimal generator of X^*, then for any functions f and h, for which Af and A^*h are well defined,

$$\mathbb{E}[Af(x)h(x) - f(x)A^*h(x) \mid \theta] = 0. \tag{17.28}$$

In practice, since X_t^* might be hard to compute, moments of the first type above are easiest to find. There are more than enough of these.

17.2.3 Hypothesis Testing and Diagnostics

There are two main tests. The first is an overall test of mis-specification. It can be used to test whether restrictions of a model still fit the data. The second are t-statistics for individual parameters.

The GMM Omnibus Test

Suppose that we have found estimates $\hat{\theta}$ of θ as

$$\hat{\theta} = \arg \min_\theta J(\theta) = f'(\theta)W(\theta)f(\theta), \tag{17.29}$$

for a moment vector f and the optimal weighting matrix W. Suppose there are N observations, then

$$R = NJ(\hat{\theta}) \tag{17.30}$$

is χ^2 with $|f| - |\theta|$ degrees of freedom.

t-Statistics for Individual Parameters

For a GMM estimation with an optimal weighting matrix W, parameter estimates are asymptotically normal, $\sqrt{N}(\hat{\theta} - \theta) \sim N(0, \Sigma)$ with covariance matrix

$$\Sigma = (f'_\theta W f_\theta)^{-1} f'_\theta W \hat{S} W f_\theta (f'_\theta W f_\theta)^{-1}, \tag{17.31}$$

where f_θ is the derivative of f with respect to θ, and $\hat{S}$ is an estimator of S. For our purposes we can approximate $\hat{S} = W^{-1}$, and $\Sigma = (f'_\theta W f_\theta)^{-1}$.

To compute t-statistics for θ_i, we can use the sample estimate $\hat{\theta}_i$ with standard error $\sqrt{\Sigma_{ii}}$. For less approximate methods the reader is referred to Campbell, Lo and MacKinlay, *et cetera*.

17.2.4   Illustrating the Method

We illustrate GMM by fitting the CKLS model to a time series of UK three-month Libor. We use daily data from September 1988 to November 1994, shown in Figure 17.1. From the discussion in Chapter 5 we do not expect the model to fit the data.

The process is discretised as

$$r_{t_{i+1}} = a + br_{t_i} + \sigma r_{t_i}^\gamma \sqrt{\Delta t}\, \varepsilon_{t_{i+1}}, \qquad (17.32)$$

where $a = \alpha\mu\Delta t$ and $b = 1 - \alpha\Delta t$ and we use the moments f_1 to f_4 in Equations 17.7 to 17.13. The optimal weighting matrix was used.

Finding parameter values proves to be difficult. The function $J(\theta)$ seems to be relatively flat over a wide range of values of θ; the fit is equally bad everywhere. An optimiser finds local minima, conditional on the initial values for θ given to it. The parameters σ and γ are especially hard to find (since many combinations of σ and γ give similar sets of values for σr_t^γ that fit the data equally badly). Our implementation

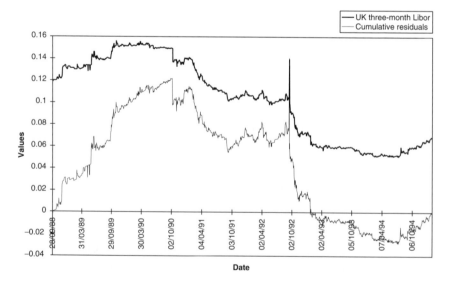

Figure 17.1   UK three-month Libor and the cumulative residuals

came up with the following sets of parameter values, amongst others:

α	μ	σ	γ	
0.240	0.069	0.14	0.73	(17.33)
0.239	0.069	0.13	0.69	
0.238	0.069	0.021	0.12	

α and μ are apparently quite stable, but σ and γ are very sensitive to initial values. Adding further moments makes no difference to the fit or to the quality of the estimates.

Of course, the problem is that the model is not the DGP for the time series. This is formally confirmed by checking the omnibus statistic, which firmly rejects the model. Informally, compare the cumulative normalised residuals, $w_{t_i} = \sum_{j=0}^{i-1} \varepsilon_{i_j}$, found from the parameter set in the last row of the table, with the original data set. Both sets are plotted in Figure 17.1.[2] The shape of the cumulative residuals is very similar to the original time series. This means that very little of the structure of the original series is being explained by the model. Furthermore, if (17.32) were the DGP, then the series w_{t_i} would be cumulative normal iid. However it fails any test for this.

The original series has various features that lead us to suspect that it is not a realisation of a CKLS process. For instance, it has a single large swing from high to low levels, and it has very obvious outliers. We can re-test the series with the major outlier eliminated, but this leads to equally poor results (in fact, depending on initial parameter values, we can find $b > 1$, implying a mean fleeing process).

The period September 1991 to September 1992 looks relatively flat, so we might expect the CKLS model to fit the data better in this region. In fact, we find results that are just as bad as before. The values obtained for the parameters, from different initial values, look more stable:

α	μ	σ	γ	
15.4	0.105	0.490	1.57	(17.34)
15.4	0.105	0.456	1.54	
15.4	0.105	0.503	1.58	

μ is at roughly the mean of the series, and the high level of α reflects the implicitly high degree of mean reversion, but the variation in σ and γ is still large enough to significantly affect pricing. The model still badly fails the omnibus test. For an informal test, plotting the cumulative residuals alongside the data series again shows striking similarities.

The conclusion is that GMM may indeed be a good method of finding parameters. However, if the model just does not fit the data the results from any estimation procedure, including GMM, will be poor. Any estimation procedure must be used with a clear awareness of the appropriateness of the model for the data set.

---

[2] The cumulative residuals have been scaled to give them a comparable magnitude to the data series.

17.2.5   Examples

We give three examples of the use of GMM: Longstaff and Schwartz (92) [365], Vetzal (97) [533], and Bliss and Smith (98) [79]. Longstaff and Schwartz use GMM simultaneously on spot rates of several different maturities. Vetzal uses a 'hard' set of moments on a single time series. Bliss and Smith use GMM to determine whether a regime shift occurred.

In a term structure model where yield curve data are available it is much better to use spot rates of several different maturities all at once, if possible, rather than relying on a single time series. The method then exploits the model term structure to obtain calibration on much shorter time series. An impediment is the need to be able to compute model term structures very rapidly, which in practice means having an explicit formula, or least a very fast approximate formula.

Longstaff and Schwartz (two-factor CIR)

In the Longstaff and Schwartz model there is an explicit formula for spot rates, $r_t(\tau \mid \theta)$, conditional upon a parameter set θ:

$$r_t(\tau \mid \theta) = A(\tau \mid \theta) + B(\tau \mid \theta)r_t + C(\tau \mid \theta)v_t, \tag{17.35}$$

where r_t is the short rate, v_t is the short rate variance, and A, B and C are functions of time to maturity τ depending on θ (see Chapter 7).

Suppose we observe empirical term structures $y_t(\tau)$. We can compare the empirical day-to-day changes in the term structure, $\Delta y_t(\tau) = y_{t+1}(\tau) - y_t(\tau)$, with changes in the model term structures $\Delta r_t(\tau) = r_{t+1}(\tau) - r_t(\tau)$. Let $\varepsilon_t(\tau)$ be the deviations between model and empirical changes,

$$\varepsilon_t(\tau) = \Delta r_t(\tau) - \Delta y_t(\tau)$$

$$= B(\tau)\Delta r_t + C(\tau)\Delta v_t - \Delta y_t(\tau). \tag{17.36}$$

If the model is correctly specified, then $\varepsilon_t(\tau)$ can be interpreted as observation error, which may reasonably be assumed to be normal iid in t, and independent for each τ. This served as the basis for Longstaff and Schwartz's estimation procedure.

Longstaff and Schwartz used observations of spot rates at eight maturities,

$$r_t(\tau_i), \quad i = 1, \ldots, 8, \tag{17.37}$$

and for each maturity they used three moments,

$$\varepsilon_t(\tau_i), \varepsilon_t(\tau_i)\Delta r_t, \varepsilon_t(\tau_i)\Delta v_t, \quad i = 1, \ldots, 8, \tag{17.38}$$

making 24 moments in all. Theoretical values of the moments are zero. $\varepsilon_t(\tau)$ does not depend on A, and B and C depend on only four parameters of the model. Estimates just for these four parameters may be obtained. Hence the omnibus test

$$J(\hat{\theta}) = f'(\hat{\theta})W(\hat{\theta})f(\hat{\theta}) \tag{17.39}$$

is $\chi^2(20)$. Longstaff and Schwartz found that their model was not rejected by the data.

Vetzal (97) [533]

Vetzal used GMM to compare a one-and a two-factor version of a model by their ability to

- fit the short rate process,
- fit to bond option prices.

His first factor is the CKLS short rate process,

$$dr_t = (a + br_t)dt + \sigma r_t^{\gamma} dz_{1,t}. \tag{17.40}$$

The second factor is a stochastic volatility factor,

$$d(\ln \sigma_t) = (c + d \ln \sigma_t) dt + \xi dz_{2,t}, \tag{17.41}$$

with $dz_{1,t} dz_{2,t} = \rho dt$. Vetzal used the same moments as Melino and Turnbull, namely 34 moments for seven unknowns; he found it necessary, like Melino and Turnbull, to fix the value of γ rather than attempting to estimate it. He restricted γ to the values $\gamma = 0, \frac{1}{2}, 1$.

$\xi = 0$ is strongly rejected by the specification tests, so that one concludes volatility may indeed be stochastic. Vetzal found that overall the two-factor model fitted the yield curve best, especially for $\gamma = 1$.

CKLS Revisited

Chan, Karolyi, Longstaff and Sanders estimated the CKLS short rate specification,

$$dr_t = \alpha(\mu - r_t)dt + \sigma r_t^{\gamma} dz_t, \tag{17.42}$$

using four moments to estimate four parameters. Figure 17.2 shows a time series similar to the data set used in their estimation. The figure shows monthly observations of the Fed funds rate; CKLS used a USD one-month T-bill rate from 1964 to 1989. Note that this time series has an apparent regime shift in the period 1979 to 1982, corresponding to the Fed experiment. Chan, Karolyi, Longstaff and Sanders performed a specification test; the period before September 1979 was compared with the period after September 1979.

Chan, Karolyi, Longstaff and Sanders found that they could not reject the hypothesis that same parameters fit both periods.

These results were questioned by Bliss and Smith. The two main problems are:

1. The data were of dubious quality. What Chan, Karolyi, Longstaff and Sanders used as a one-month T-bill time series in fact contained interest rates of very variable maturities.
2. The regime periods were mis-specified. The Fed experiment stopped in October 1982 so the specification test should compare the period [Sept 79, Oct 82] against the rest.

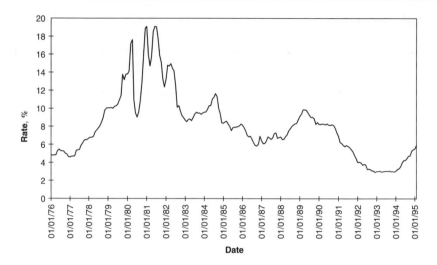

Figure 17.2 The Fed funds rate: 1976–1995

The second problem gives an example of a specification test. Bliss and Smith repeated the analysis, using both the same data as Chan, Karolyi, Longstaff and Sanders and also an improved data set, specifying the new test period. They set

$$r_{t+1} = (a + d_1 D_t) + (b + d_2 D_t) r_t + \varepsilon_t, \tag{17.43}$$

$$\varepsilon_t^2 = (\sigma^2 + d_3 D_t) r_t^{2(\gamma + d_4 D_t)} + \eta_t. \tag{17.44}$$

D_t is an indicator variable, $D_t = 1$ if t ∈ [Sept 79, Oct 82], 0 otherwise. d_i, $i = 1, 2, 3, 4$, measure changes in parameter values, inside and outside of the test period. If $d_i \neq 0$ there has been a regime shift.

The Estimation Procedure

First, fit the unrestricted model to find estimates of $\theta = (a, d_1, b, d_2, \sigma, d_3, \gamma, d_4)'$. Bliss and Smith use eight moments

$$f(\theta) = (\varepsilon_t, \varepsilon_t r_{t-1}, \eta_t, \eta_t r_{t-1}, \varepsilon_t D_t, \varepsilon_t D_t r_{t-1}, \eta_t D_t, \eta_t D_t r_{t-1})', \tag{17.45}$$

to find an estimate

$$\hat{\theta} = \arg \min_\theta J(\theta) = f' W(\theta) f,$$

where W is the optimal weighting matrix.

Second, fit the restricted model to find estimates of $\theta = (a, d_1, b, d_2, \sigma, d_3, \gamma, d_4)$, where d_i are constrained to be zero, using the same moments. They find an estimate

$$\tilde{\theta} = \arg \min_\theta J(\theta) = f' W(\theta) f,$$

where W is the same matrix as in the first step.

Finally, The test statistic is $R = N \left(J(\hat{\theta}) - J(\tilde{\theta}) \right)$. This is χ^2 with four degrees of freedom.

Bliss and Smith found that

- There is indeed a regime shift in the test period: (a) parameter estimates differ significantly, and (b) the no-change hypothesis is rejected;
- A model with moderate values of γ can fit the data, once the regime shift is accounted for.

Although this is just one example it is clear that model calibration in general may be very sensitive to the assumptions underlying the calibration. An un-compensated for regime shift can fatally throw off parameter estimates, making the 'calibrated' model useless for practical application.

17.2.6 GMM and Alternative Discretisation Schemes

The examples we have seen above all relied on a Euler discretisation of the underlying processes. There is no reason why a more sophisticated discretisation should not be employed. In fact a better discretisation should result in better parameter estimates. Baadsgaard *et al.* (96) [33] compared estimates from time series based on simulation using different discretisations of the process

$$\mathrm{d}y_t = (\theta + \alpha y_t)\mathrm{d}t + \rho y_t^\gamma \, \mathrm{d}z_t, \tag{17.46}$$

with the same four moments as Chan *et al.* They found that whatever discretisation scheme they used, large sample sizes were required, say 1500 observations, for GMM or else parameter estimates were biased. The process was simulated by

- Euler: this gave awful results.
- Milshtein: the results here were not much better.
- Itō–Taylor (see Kloeden and Platen (95) [336]: '1.5 strong'):

$$y_{t+1} = y_t + \mu \Delta_t + \sigma \Delta_z + \tfrac{1}{2}\sigma\sigma'(\Delta_z^2 - \Delta_t) + \mu'\sigma\Delta_w$$

$$+ \tfrac{1}{2}\left(\mu\mu' + \tfrac{1}{2}\sigma^2\mu''\right)\Delta_t^2 + \left(\mu\sigma' + \tfrac{1}{2}\sigma^2\sigma''\right)(\Delta_z\Delta_t - \Delta_w)$$

$$+ \tfrac{1}{2}\sigma\left(\sigma\sigma'' + (\sigma')^2\right)\left(\tfrac{1}{3}\Delta_z^2 - \Delta_t\right)\Delta_z, \tag{17.47}$$

where $\mu = \theta + \alpha y_t$, $\sigma = \rho y_t^\gamma$, $\Delta_w \sim N(0, \tfrac{1}{3}\Delta_t^3)$, $\mathbb{E}[\Delta_w \Delta_z] = \tfrac{1}{2}\Delta_t^2$, and $'$ denotes differentiation with respect to y_t.

Baadsgaard *et al.* found that there was still some bias, but the results were much better.

The paper concludes that for a GMM estimation of a financial model one should *always* use a higher order Itō–Taylor discretisation, and *never* use a Euler discretisation. However, the paper does not indicate how the estimation improves if the number of moments used in the estimation increases.

17.3   THE EFFICIENT METHOD OF MOMENTS (EMM)

Also known as a minimum χ^2 estimation, this method is used and described by Gallant and Tauchen (95) [239], (96) [240], Gallant and Long (97) [238], Andersen and Lund (97) [22] and Dai and Singleton (98) [154], amongst others. Given a structural model with parameters θ we want not only to estimate θ but also to test hypotheses and to have diagnostics to help improve the model.

GMM requires the computation of expectations

$$g(\theta) = \mathbb{E}[f(X) \mid \theta], \tag{17.48}$$

or else a selection of moments $f(X)$ whose expectations are known, for instance known to be zero. Unfortunately, one may not be able to compute g for suitable f, and the Hansen and Scheinkman moments may not be appropriate. If there are hidden variables, it may not be possible to compute the sample moments. However, it is possible to use a simulation procedure.

17.3.1   Simulated Method of Moments (SMM)

We follow Duffie and Singleton (93) [188]. Given a structural model for X_t and parameters θ, we want to compute theoretical values of $\mathbb{E}[f(X_t) \mid \theta]$. One way is to simulate a long sample path $\hat{X}_t \mid \theta$. Using this sample path we can compute an estimate

$$\hat{g}(\theta) = \frac{1}{N} \sum_{t=1}^{n} f\left(\hat{X}_t \mid \theta\right) \tag{17.49}$$

of $g(\theta)$. $\hat{g}(\theta)$ can now be used to compute the GMM objective function, $J(\theta)$,

$$J(\theta) = (\tilde{f} - \hat{g}(\theta))' W (\tilde{f} - \hat{g}(\theta)t), \tag{17.50}$$

where

$$\tilde{f} = \frac{1}{N} \sum_{t=1}^{N} \tilde{f}\left(\tilde{X}_t\right) \tag{17.51}$$

is computed from the observed data series $\tilde{X}_t$, and W is a weighting matrix. Estimated parameters are

$$\hat{\theta} = \arg\min_{\theta} J(\theta), \tag{17.52}$$

as usual.

Problems with the Method

The method as described above is computationally very expensive. It requires repeated simulation of sample paths $\hat{X}_t \mid \theta$, for successive sets of parameter values θ. The optimal W,

$$W = S^{-1}, \tag{17.53}$$

where

$$S = \frac{1}{N} \sum_{t=1}^{N} \left(\tilde{f}_t - \hat{g}(\theta) \right) \left(\tilde{f}_t - \hat{g}(\theta) \right)', \tag{17.54}$$

also depends on θ and must be re-computed on every iteration.

Also, the method gives no guidance on an optimal choice of moments f.

17.3.2 The Scores Vector

Given a transition density $p(X_{t+1} \mid X_t; \theta)$, the conditional density of $\tilde{X}_{N+1}$ given $\tilde{X}_1 \dots, \tilde{X}_N$ is

$$L\left(\tilde{X}_{N+1}, \theta \right) = p_0(\tilde{X}_1 \mid \theta) \prod_{i=1}^{N} p\left(i+1, \tilde{X}_{i+1}; i, \tilde{X}_i \mid \theta \right). \tag{17.55}$$

L is a density so

$$\int L(X, \theta) dX = 1. \tag{17.56}$$

Therefore

$$\frac{\partial}{\partial \theta} \int L(X, \theta) dX = \int \frac{\partial}{\partial \theta} L(X, \theta) dX = 0. \tag{17.57}$$

But

$$\frac{\partial L}{\partial \theta} = \frac{\partial \ln L}{\partial \theta} L \tag{17.58}$$

so

$$0 = \int \frac{\partial \ln L}{\partial \theta} L dX = \mathbb{E} \left[\frac{\partial \ln L}{\partial \theta} \right]. \tag{17.59}$$

Hence $\partial \ln L / \partial \theta$ defines a set of moment conditions. $\partial \ln L / \partial \theta$ is called the scores function or scores vector. It can be used directly in a classical method of moments.

17.3.3 Efficient Moments

We follow Gallant and Tauchen (96) [240]. Suppose that the structural model is the DGP, with transition density $p(X_{t+1} \mid X_t; \theta)$. Then optimal moments are

$$f(\theta) = \frac{\partial}{\partial \theta} \ln p(X_{t+1} \mid X_t; \theta), \tag{17.60}$$

that is, the scores function of the density.

We have $g(\theta) = \mathbb{E}[f(\theta)] = 0$. If p were known, then we could use the maximum likelihood method. Usually, of course, p is not known, but it is possible to use an approximation here for p in Equation 17.60.

We define an 'auxiliary model', i.e. a density

$$q(X_{t+1} \mid Y_t; \rho), \tag{17.61}$$

where $Y_t = (X_t, \ldots, X_{t-L})$ are lags of X_t, and ρ is a parameter vector. q should be 'close to' p, but computable.

The procedure is as follows:

1. Fit q to the data $\widetilde{X}_t$, $t = 1, \ldots, N$, by, for example, a quasi-ML method (see Section 17.5.1). Obtain parameter estimates $\hat{\rho}$ of ρ.
2. Compute the sample moments as

$$f(\theta, \hat{\rho}) = \int \frac{\partial}{\partial \theta} \ln q\left(X_{t+1} \mid Y_t; \hat{\rho}\right) dp\left(X_t \mid \theta\right), \qquad (17.62)$$

by some method, for example by Monte Carlo integration. Generate a long sample path $\hat{X}_t \mid \theta$ and set

$$\hat{f}(\theta, \hat{\rho}) = \frac{1}{n} \sum_{t=1}^{n} \frac{\partial}{\partial \theta} \ln q\left(\hat{X}_t \mid \theta; \hat{\rho}\right). \qquad (17.63)$$

The sample moment is derived from the observations $\widetilde{X}_t$ via $\hat{\rho}$ and the density q. q is chosen to facilitate the computation of (17.63).
3. Set

$$J(\theta) = \hat{f}(\theta, \hat{\rho})' W \hat{f}(\theta, \hat{\rho}), \qquad (17.64)$$

for the optimal matrix W and set

$$\hat{\theta} = \arg \min_{\theta} J(\theta). \qquad (17.65)$$

This is the EMM estimate of θ.

The Weighting Matrix W

This is the usual form, as in Section 17.1.2. Set

$$S = \frac{1}{N} \sum_{t=1}^{N} \left(\frac{\partial}{\partial \theta} \ln q\left(\widetilde{X}_t \mid \hat{\rho}\right)\right) \left(\frac{\partial}{\partial \theta} \ln q\left(\widetilde{X}_t \mid \hat{\rho}\right)\right)'. \qquad (17.66)$$

Then $W = S^{-1}$.

If q is a good approximation to p, then W is close to optimal. We only have to compute W once, which considerably reduces the computational load of EMM.

17.3.4   Test Statistics

The omnibus statistic is

$$R = NJ(\hat{\theta}). \qquad (17.67)$$

This is χ^2 with $|\theta| - |\rho|$ degrees of freedom.

We can also test for over-specification. If there are constraints of the form $h(\theta) = 0 \in \mathbb{R}^q$, then define

$$\underline{\theta} = \arg \min_{\theta} \hat{f}(\theta, \hat{\rho})' W \hat{f}(\theta, \hat{\rho}) \mid h(\theta) = 0. \qquad (17.68)$$

Set $R = N \left(J(\underline{\theta}) - J\left(\hat{\theta}\right) \right)$. This is χ^2 with q degrees of freedom.

It is easy to find an approximation for the standard errors of individual parameters. Set $s_i = \sqrt{S_{ii}}$. This is a cheap estimate of the standard error of θ_i (an under-estimate of the true value). The t-statistic is then $\left(\sqrt{N}/s_i\right) f\left(\hat{\theta}, \hat{\rho}\right)$. The estimated covariance matrix of θ is $(1/N) \left(\hat{f}'_\theta S^{-1} \hat{f}_\theta \right)$, where $\hat{f}_\theta$ is the derivative of $\hat{f}$ with respect to θ.

17.3.5 Choice of Auxiliary Model

Gallant and Tauchen (96) [240] suggest two types of model:

- Neural net scores (Eller *et al.* (95) [204])
- A semi-non-parametric framework (SNP).

Since the SNP approach appears to be generally preferred, we do not describe the neural net method here. Implementing an SNP density for a time series $\widetilde{X}_t, t = 1, \ldots, N$, is a two-stage procedure.

1. 'Normalise' $\widetilde{X}_t$. Approximate $\widetilde{X}_t$ as, for instance, a GARCH process.
2. Expand out the density. Approximate the density of the normalised process as a perturbed normal density.

To normalise $\widetilde{X}_t$ we find an amenable process that approximates it. For instance, one could use a GARCH process conditional on the lags $Y_t = \left(\widetilde{X}_t, \ldots, \widetilde{X}_{t-L}\right)$ of $\widetilde{X}_{t+1}$. Calculate the conditional mean $\mu_{Y_{t-1}}$ and covariance matrix $R_{Y_{t-1}}$ of the approximating process and set

$$z_t = R_{Y_{t-1}}^{-1} \left(\widetilde{X}_t - \mu_{Y_{t-1}}\right). \qquad (17.69)$$

If $\widetilde{X}_t$ is fitted reasonably well by the approximating process, then z_t will be 'more normal' than $\widetilde{X}_t$. The procedure 'pre-whitens' $\widetilde{X}_t$. The approximating process will have a parameter set Ψ. For examples see Andersen and Lund (97) [22], Dai and Singleton (98) [154], Gallant and Long (97) [238], and Gallant and Tauchen (96) [240].

If the approximating process is reasonable, then z_t will be approximately normal. We expand out the density of z_t by expressing it as a weighted average of standard normal densities, weighted by powers z_t^i and Y_t^j. We set

$$q(X_{t+1} \mid Y_t; \rho) = c(Y_t, \rho) \left(\varepsilon_0 + h(z_t \mid Y_t)^2\right) n(z_t), \qquad (17.70)$$

where $n(z_t)$ is the standard normal density, $h(z_t \mid Y_t)$ is a polynomial in z_t and Y_t, ε_0 is a small constant, and $c(Y_t, \rho)$ is a normalisation coefficient so that q integrates up to 1. For simplicity h may have the form $\sum_{i=0}^{K_z} \sum_{j=0}^{K_x} a_{i,j} x_{t-j}^j z_t^i$, where $a_{0,0}$ is normalised to one, and cross terms in Y_t^j are dropped. ρ is then the set $(\varepsilon_0, \{a_{i,j}\}, \Psi)$.

17.3.6 Example: Andersen and Lund

Andersen and Lund (97) [22] fit a process of the form

$$dr_t = \alpha(\mu - r_t)dt + \sigma r_t^\gamma \, dz_{1,t}, \tag{17.71}$$

$$d(\ln \sigma_t^2) = \beta(\kappa - \ln \sigma_t^2)dt + \xi dz_{2,t}, \tag{17.72}$$

to the short rate by observing the short rate only. A normalising process used by Andersen and Lund is

$$\Delta r_t = \phi_0 + \phi_1 r_{t-1} + \sum_{i=1}^{s-1} \phi_{1+i}\Delta r_{t-i} + r_{t-1}^\gamma \sqrt{h_t} \, z_t,$$

$$\ln h_t = \omega + \sum_{i=1}^{p} \beta_i \ln h_{t-i} + (1 + \alpha_1 L + \ldots + \alpha_q L^q)\left(\theta_1 z_{t-1} + \theta_2 u(z_{t-1}) - \sqrt{\frac{2}{\pi}}\right),$$

$$\tag{17.73}$$

where L is the lag operator, and $u(z) \sim |z|$ is a twice differentiable approximation to the modulus function. Equations 17.73 are an EGARCH volatility specification. In practice a low-dimensional GARCH process suffices. Set $(p, q) = (1, 1)$ or $(1, 2)$, so that for (17.69) we have

$$\mu_{Y_{t-1}} = \phi_0 + \phi_1 r_{t-1} + \sum_{i=1}^{s-1} \phi_{1+i}\Delta r_{t-i}, \tag{17.74}$$

$$R_{Y_{t-1}} = r_{t-1}^\gamma \sqrt{h_t}. \tag{17.75}$$

For the density expansion Andersen and Lund used a polynomial h of the form

$$h(z_t \mid Y_t) = \sum_{i=0}^{K_z} \sum_{j=0}^{K_x} a_{i,j} x_{t-j}^j z_t^i, \tag{17.76}$$

with one lag of $\widetilde{X}_t$ and

$$K_x = 0 \text{ or } 1,$$

$$K_z = 4 \text{ or } 6 \text{ or } 8.$$

Results Using a similar data set to CKLS, Andersen and Lund find that $\gamma \sim 0.5$. In order for specification tests to fail to reject the model a third factor was found to be required. Andersen and Lund (96a) [20], (96c) [21] introduced a stochastic mean term,

$$d\mu_t = \beta_\mu(\kappa_\mu - \mu_t)dt + \xi_\mu \, dz_{3,t}. \tag{17.77}$$

They found that

- (17.71) + (17.72) provided a reasonable fit;
- (17.71) + (17.77) gave a poor fit;
- (17.71) + (17.72) + (17.77) gave a fit marginally better than (17.71) + (17.72).

The interpretation of these results hinges on the hypothesis that the data set has a regime shift in the period [Sept 79, Oct 82]. A model will not fit this data set unless it is sufficiently 'stretchy'. Introducing equation (17.72) does it.

17.3.7 Example: Dai and Singleton

Dai and Singleton (98) [154] wanted to fit an affine $M_2(3)$ model to dollar data. The data set is daily observations of spot rates for three maturities each day, so each observation $\widetilde{X}_t$ is a 3-vector. Given a set of parameters for the $M_2(3)$, model spot rates were found by solving the Riccati partial differential equation.

The normalising process used one lag and sets

$$\mu_{Y_{t-1}} = \phi_0 + \phi_1 \widetilde{X}_{t-1}. \tag{17.78}$$

An upper triangular matrix with constant off-diagonal terms was used for $R_{Y_{t-1}}$, with terms in the leading diagonal affine in two lags of $|\widetilde{X}_t - \mu_{Y_{t-1}}|$. The polynomial $h(z_t \mid Y_t) = \sum_{i=0}^{4} \sum_{k=0}^{3} a_{i,j} z_{k,t}^i$, containing no cross terms in z_t^i, was used in the density expansion.

Dai and Singleton found that the general $M_2(3)$ model is not rejected, but that the restriction to the Chen model is rejected.

17.4 MAXIMUM LIKELIHOOD METHODS

Maximum likelihood methods find parameter values for which the actual outcome has the maximum probability; they choose parameter values so that the actual outcome lies at the mode of the density function over sample paths. This can be calculated using the transition density function.

Suppose we have a time series r_{t_i}, $i = 1, \ldots, N$, whose transition densities,

$$p(t_2, r_{t_2}; t_1, r_{t_1} \mid \theta), \tag{17.79}$$

are known. The process is assumed to be Markov. The density depends upon the parameter set θ.

Example: Vasicek

For the short rate process

$$dr_t = \alpha(\mu - r_t)dt + \sigma dz_t \tag{17.80}$$

conditional distributions are normal. Given r_{t_1} at time t_1, the density of r_{t_2} at time t_2 is

$$p(t_2, \bullet; t_1, r_{t_1} \mid \theta) \sim N\left(\mu + (r_{t_1} - \mu)e^{-\alpha\Delta t}, \frac{\sigma^2}{2\alpha}(1 - e^{-2\alpha\Delta t})\right), \tag{17.81}$$

where $\Delta t = t_2 - t_1$, and $N\left(\mu, \sigma^2\right)$ is the normal density function with mean μ and variance σ^2.

Example: CIR

The short rate process is

$$dr_t = \alpha(\mu - r_t)dt + \sigma r_t^{\frac{1}{2}} dz_t. \tag{17.82}$$

Conditional distributions are not normal. Given r_{t_1} at time t_1 the density of r_{t_2} at time t_2 is

$$p(t_2, r_{t_2}; t_1, r_{t_1} \mid \theta) = ce^{-u-v} \left(\frac{v}{u}\right)^{\frac{q}{2}} I_q(2\sqrt{uv}), \tag{17.83}$$

where

$$c = \frac{2\alpha}{\sigma^2(1 - e^{-\alpha \Delta t})},$$

$$u = cr_{t_1}e^{-\alpha \Delta t},$$

$$v = cr_{t_2}, \tag{17.84}$$

$$q = \frac{2\alpha \mu}{\sigma} - 1,$$

and I_q is the modified Bessel function of the first kind of order q (see Abramowitz and Stegun (65) [3]).

The distribution function is non-central χ^2, $\chi^2(2cr_{t_2}; 2q + 2, 2u)$, with $2q + 2$ degrees of freedom, non-centrality parameter $2u$. The first and second moments are:

$$\mathbb{E}[r_{t_2} \mid r_{t_1}] = r_{t_1}e^{-\alpha \Delta t} + \mu\left(1 - e^{-\alpha \Delta t}\right), \tag{17.85}$$

$$\text{var}[r_{t_2} \mid r_{t_1}] = r_{t_1}\frac{\sigma^2}{\alpha}\left(e^{-\alpha \Delta t} - e^{-2\alpha \Delta t}\right) + \mu\frac{\sigma^2}{2\alpha}\left(1 - e^{-\alpha \Delta t}\right)^2. \tag{17.86}$$

17.4.1   The Maximum Likelihood Method

Suppose we have observed a time series r_{t_i}, $i = 1, \dots, N$, with transition densities

$$p(t_{i+1}, r_{t_{i+1}}; t_i, r_{t_i} \mid \theta). \tag{17.87}$$

The joint density of these observations is

$$p(r_{t_1}, \dots, r_{t_N} \mid \theta) = p_0(r_{t_1} \mid \theta) \prod_{i=1}^{N-1} p(t_{i+1}, r_{t_{i+1}}; t_i, r_{t_i} \mid \theta), \tag{17.88}$$

where p_0 is some prior density for r_{t_1}. The likelihood function is

$$L(\theta) = \prod_{i=1}^{N-1} p(t_{i+1}, r_{t_{i+1}}; t_i, r_{t_i} \mid \theta). \tag{17.89}$$

An estimate for θ is found as $\hat{\theta} = \arg\max_\theta L(\theta)$. $\hat{\theta}$ is the maximum likelihood estimate of θ. Maximising L places the observed time series at the maximum of the joint density function.

It may be more convenient to maximise $\ln L$ instead of L. Since $\ln$ is monotonically increasing, maximising $\ln L$ also maximises L. One has the alternatives:

- Maximum likelihood: choose θ so that $\partial L/\partial\theta = 0$.
- Maximum log-likelihood: choose θ so that $\partial \ln L/\partial\theta = L'/L = 0$.

In general, the optimisation will involve non-linear methods

17.4.2 Vasicek: Doing it Properly

For the Vasicek process

$$\mathrm{d}r_t = \alpha(\mu - r_t)\mathrm{d}t + \sigma\mathrm{d}z_t, \tag{17.90}$$

with parameters $\theta = \{\alpha, \mu, \sigma\}$, the transition density function is

$$p(t_{i+1}, r_{t_{i+1}}; t_i, r_{t_i} \mid \theta) = (2\pi\,\mathrm{var}_{t_i})^{-\frac{1}{2}} \exp\left(-\tfrac{1}{2}v^2(r_{t_i}, r_{t_{i+1}}, \Delta t_i)\right), \tag{17.91}$$

where for $\Delta t_i = t_{i+1} - t_i$

$$\mathrm{var}_{t_i} = \frac{\sigma^2}{2\alpha}(1 - e^{-2\alpha\Delta t_i}), \tag{17.92}$$

$$v(r_{t_i}, r_{t_i+1}, \Delta t_i) = \frac{r_{t_{i+1}} - \left(\mu + \left(r_{t_i} - \mu\right)e^{-\alpha\Delta t_i}\right)}{\sqrt{\mathrm{var}_{t_i}}}. \tag{17.93}$$

The likelihood function is L:

$$L = \prod_{i=1}^{N-1} \left(2\pi\frac{\sigma^2}{2\alpha}(1 - e^{-2\alpha\Delta t_i})\right)^{-\frac{1}{2}} \exp\left(-\frac{1}{2}v^2(r_{t_i}, r_{t_i+1}, t_i)\right). \tag{17.94}$$

If observations are at equal time increments, $\Delta t_i \equiv \Delta t$, then

$$L = \left(2\pi\frac{\sigma^2}{2\alpha}(1 - e^{-2\alpha\Delta t})\right)^{-\frac{N-1}{2}} \exp\left(-\frac{1}{2}\sum_{i=1}^{N-1} v^2(r_{t_i}, r_{t_i+1}, \Delta t)\right), \tag{17.95}$$

and the log-likelihood function is

$$\ln L = -\frac{N-1}{2}\ln 2\pi - \frac{N-1}{2}\ln\left(\frac{\sigma^2}{2\alpha}(1 - e^{-2\alpha\Delta t})\right) - \frac{1}{2}\sum_{i=1}^{N-1} v^2\left(r_{t_i}, r_{t_i+1}, \Delta t\right). \tag{17.96}$$

The maximum log-likelihood estimates of $\theta = \{\alpha, \mu, \sigma\}$ are

$$\hat{\theta} = \arg\max_\theta \ln L(\theta). \tag{17.97}$$

17.4.3 Vasicek: Doing it Naively

Quite often the transition density function is unknown. We see below that a variant of the full maximum likelihood method can then be employed. We apply it here as a naive approach to estimating the Vasicek process. Using the Euler discretisation the discrete time process is

$$r_{t+\Delta t} = a + br_t + \sigma\sqrt{\Delta t}\,\varepsilon_t, \tag{17.98}$$

where $a = \alpha\mu\Delta t$, $b = 1 - \alpha\Delta t$, and $\varepsilon_t \sim N(0, 1)$. The transition density function of the process (17.98) is

$$p(t_2, \bullet; t_1, r_{t_1} \mid \theta) \sim N(a + br_t, \sigma^2\Delta t). \tag{17.99}$$

We can implement a maximum likelihood method using this approximation to the true density (17.81). Given observations $\{r_{t_i}\}_{i=1,\dots,N}$, $t_{i+1} - t_i = \Delta t_i$, set

$$\varepsilon_{t_i} = \frac{r_{t_{i+1}} - (a + br_{t_i})}{\sigma\sqrt{\Delta t_i}}.$$

The likelihood function is:

$$L(\theta) = \prod_{i=1}^{N-1}(2\pi\sigma^2\Delta t_i)^{-\frac{1}{2}}\exp\left(-\tfrac{1}{2}\varepsilon_{t_i}^2\right)$$

$$= (2\pi\sigma^2\Delta t)^{-\frac{N-1}{2}}\exp\left(-\frac{1}{2}\sum_{i=1}^{N-1}\left(\frac{r_{t_{i+1}} - (a + br_{t_i})}{\sigma\sqrt{\Delta t}}\right)^2\right), \tag{17.100}$$

for $\Delta t_i \equiv \Delta t$ constant. This has a maximum when $\partial L/\partial\theta = 0$. So at a maximum

$$0 = \frac{\partial L}{\partial b} = \frac{1}{\sigma^2\Delta t}L(\theta)\sum_{t=1}^{N-1}r_{t_i}\left(r_{t_{i+1}} - (a + br_{t_i})\right),$$

$$0 = \frac{\partial L}{\partial a} = \frac{1}{\sigma^2\Delta t}L(\theta)\sum_{t=1}^{N-1}\left(r_{t_{i+1}} - (a + br_{t_i})\right). \tag{17.101}$$

Solving for a and b gives the same result as OLS regression. This is the naive maximum likelihood estimator of a and b.

17.4.4 Properties of the Estimator

We follow Campbell, Lo and MacKinlay (97) [113]. Suppose that $\hat{\theta}$ is the ML estimate of θ. As N grows large, $\hat{\theta}$ has the asymptotic distribution $\sqrt{N}(\hat{\theta} - \theta) \sim N(0, I^{-1}(\theta))$, where $I(\theta)$ is the information matrix defined as

$$I(\theta) = -\lim_{N\to\infty}\mathbb{E}\left[\frac{1}{N}\frac{\partial^2 L(\theta)}{\partial\theta\partial\theta'}\right], \tag{17.102}$$

where $L(\theta)$ is the log-likelihood function. The information matrix is also equal to

$$I(\theta) = \lim_{N \to \infty} \mathbb{E}\left[\frac{1}{N} \frac{\partial L(\theta)}{\partial \theta} \frac{\partial L(\theta)}{\partial \theta'} \right], \tag{17.103}$$

and so $I(\theta)$ can be estimated as the sample variance of the scores vector $\partial \ln p_i(\theta)/\partial \theta$,

$$I(\theta) = -\frac{1}{N-1} \sum_{i=1}^{N-1} \frac{\partial \ln p_i(\theta)}{\partial \theta} \frac{\partial \ln p_i(\theta)}{\partial \theta'}, \tag{17.104}$$

where $p_i = p(t_{i+1}, r_{t_{i+1}}; t_i, r_{t_i} \mid \theta)$ is the transition density at the ith step.

Restrictions

For $L(\theta) = \sum_{i=1}^{N-1} \ln p_i$ the ML estimate $\hat{\theta}$ of θ is

$$\hat{\theta} = \arg\max_{\theta} L(\theta). \tag{17.105}$$

Suppose that m restrictions are imposed upon θ, by requiring $h(\theta) = 0 \in \mathbb{R}^m$. Set

$$\underline{\theta} = \arg\max_{\theta} L(\theta) \mid h(\theta) = 0. \tag{17.106}$$

Define the statistic R,

$$R = 2N(L(\hat{\theta}) - L(\underline{\theta})), \tag{17.107}$$

then R is χ^2 with m degrees of freedom.

17.5 HIERARCHY OF PROCEDURES

The basic maximum likelihood method can be adapted in various ways, leading to a hierarchy of procedures.

1. *Maximum likelihood, in full.* This requires the transition density to be known.
2. *Quasi-maximum likelihood.* If the transition densities are not known it may be possible to find reasonable approximations to them. The quasi-maximum likelihood method uses a quick and dirty approximation when the continuous-time process is given.
3. *Normal approximation.* This can be used if the first and second conditional moments of the process are known.
4. *Simulated maximum likelihood.* This is used when the transition density is not known, but when accuracy is more important than speed.

17.5.1 Quasi-Maximum Likelihood

A process

$$dr_t = \mu(t, r_t)dt + \sigma(t, r_t)dz_t \tag{17.108}$$

can be discretised using a Euler approximation

$$r_{t+\Delta t} = r_t + \mu(t, r_t)\Delta t + \sigma(t, r_t)\sqrt{\Delta t}\, \varepsilon_t, \tag{17.109}$$

where $\varepsilon_t \sim N(0, 1)$. The quasi-maximum likelihood method uses the approximation that $r_{t+\Delta t}$ is normal with mean $r_t + \mu(t, r_t)\Delta t$ and variance $\sigma^2(t, r_t)\Delta t$.

For observations $\{r_{t_i}\}_{i=1,\ldots,N}$, where $t_{i+1} - t_i = \Delta t$ is constant, say, we maximise QL where

$$QL = -\frac{N-1}{2} \ln 2\pi - \frac{1}{2} \sum_{i=1}^{N-1} \ln \left(\sigma^2\left(t_i, r_{t_i}\right)\Delta t\right) - \frac{1}{2} \sum_{i=1}^{N-1} \left(\frac{r_{t_{i+1}} - r_{t_i} - \mu\left(t_i, r_{t_i}\right)\Delta t}{\sigma\left(t_i, r_{t_i}\right)\sqrt{\Delta t_i}}\right)^2.$$

(17.110)

This method assumes that Δt is small enough so that increments $\Delta r_t = r_{t+\Delta t} - r_t$ are approximately normal. Since this is only reasonable when Δt is very small, the quasi-maximum likelihood method gives biased estimates except in the limit as $\Delta t \to 0$.

Note that the method may be extended by using a Milshtein or Itō–Taylor discretisation instead of a Euler approximation.

17.5.2   Normal Approximation

Suppose the first and second moments of the transition density are known,

$$\mathbb{E}[r(s) \mid r(t)] = f_1(r(t), r(s), s - t), \tag{17.111}$$

$$\text{var}[r(s) \mid r(t)] = f_2(r(t), r(s), s - t), \tag{17.112}$$

for known functions f_1 and f_2. The normal approximation assumes that $r_{t+\Delta t}$ is normal with mean $f_1(r(t), r(s), s - t)$ and variance $f_2(r(t), r(s), s - t)$, for $s = t + \Delta t$. One now maximises QL where

$$QL = -\frac{N-1}{2} \ln 2\pi - \frac{1}{2} \sum_{i=1}^{N-1} \ln f_2(r_{t_{i+1}}, r_{t_i}, \Delta t) - \frac{1}{2} \sum_{i=1}^{N-1} \frac{(r_{t_{i+1}} - f_1(r_{t_{i+1}}, r_{t_i}, \Delta t))^2}{f_2(r_{t_{i+1}}, r_{t_i}, \Delta t)}.$$

(17.113)

This method is a better approximation than the quasi-likelihood method, because it uses the actual moments, not surrogate ones. It assumes that Δt is small enough so that $r_{t+\Delta t} \sim N(f_1, f_2)$.

17.5.3   Simulated Maximum Likelihood

Sometimes called the approximate maximum likelihood method, this method has been developed and used by Pedersen (95) [433], Santa-Clara (95) [472], and Honore (98) [286], and others. It can be used if the first and second moments of the transition density are not known and if a quasi-likelihood estimate is not good enough. The transition density is approximated by a simulation technique.

Suppose the Euler approximation to r_t is

$$r_{t_{i+1}} = r_{t_i} + \mu(t_i, r_{t_i})\Delta t_i + \sigma(t_i, r_{t_i})\sqrt{\Delta t_i}\,\varepsilon_{t_i}, \quad \Delta t_i = r_{t_{i+1}} - r_{t_i}. \tag{17.114}$$

If Δt is very small, then over a single time step we have

$$p\left(t + \Delta t, r_{t+\Delta t}; t, r_t \mid \theta\right) \sim \hat{p}\left(t + \Delta t, r_{t+\Delta t}; t, r_t \mid \theta\right), \tag{17.115}$$

where

$$\hat{p}\left(t + \Delta t, r_{t+\Delta t}; t, r_t \mid \theta\right) = N\left(r_t + \mu(t, r_t)\Delta t_i, \sigma^2(t, r_t)\Delta t\right), \tag{17.116}$$

the normal density function.

For each observation r_{t_i} at time t_i we shall simulate M sample paths, each with a step size of $\Delta t_i / N$, up to time $t_{i+1} - \Delta t_i / N$ just before the next observation time. Let $k = 1, \ldots, N - 1$, $m = 1, \ldots, M$, and set

$$r_0^m = r_{t_i}, \tag{17.117}$$

$$r_{k+1}^m = r_k^m + \mu\left(t_i + k\frac{\Delta t_i}{N}, r_k^m\right)\frac{\Delta t_i}{N} + \frac{1}{\sqrt{n}}\sigma\left(t_i + k\frac{\Delta t_i}{N}, r_k^m\right)\sqrt{\frac{\Delta t_i}{N}}\,\varepsilon_k^m,$$

where ε_k^m are $N(0, 1)$ iid, $k = 1, \ldots, n$, $m = 1, \ldots, M$. This generates a sample of M interest rates, r_{N-1}^m, $m = 1, \ldots, M$, which, on the assumption that $\Delta t_i / N$ is small, is a 'good' sample from the actual distribution of $r_{t_{i+1} - (\Delta t_i / N)} \mid r_{t_i}$.

Now define

$$\tilde{p}\left(t_{i+1}, r_{t_{i+1}}; t_i, r_{t_i} \mid \theta\right) = \frac{1}{M}\sum_{m=1}^{M} \hat{p}\left(t_{i+1}, r_{t_{i+1}}; t_{i+1} - \frac{\Delta t_i}{N}, r_{N-1}^m \mid \theta\right). \tag{17.118}$$

Because $\Delta t_i / N$ is small, the density of $r_{t_{i+1}} \mid r_{t_{i+1} - (\Delta t_i / N)}$ is well approximated by $\hat{p}(t_{i+1}, r_{t_{i+1}}; t_{i+1} - \Delta t_i / N, r_{N-1}^m \mid \theta)$. Since we have generated a good sample of $r_{t_{i+1} - (\Delta t_i / N)} \mid r_{t_i}$, $\tilde{p}$ is a good approximation to the true transition density p:

$$p\left(t_{i+1}, r_{t_{i+1}}; t_i, r_{t_i} \mid \theta\right)$$

$$= \int p\left(t_{i+1} - \frac{\Delta t_i}{N}, r; t_i, r_{t_i} \mid \theta\right) p\left(t_{i+1}, r_{t_{i+1}}; t_{i+1} - \frac{\Delta t_i}{N}, r \mid \theta\right) dr \tag{17.119}$$

$$\approx \int p\left(t_{i+1} - \frac{\Delta t_i}{N}, r; t_i, r_{t_i} \mid \theta\right) \hat{p}\left(t_{i+1}, r_{t_{i+1}}; t_{i+1} - \frac{\Delta t_i}{N}, r \mid \theta\right) dr \tag{17.120}$$

$$\approx \frac{1}{M}\sum_{m=1}^{M} \hat{p}\left(t_{i+1}, r_{t_{i+1}}; t_{i+1} - \frac{\Delta t_i}{N}, r_{N-1}^m \mid \theta\right). \tag{17.121}$$

As N gets large, the approximated transition density converges to the true density. Figure 17.3 illustrates what is going on.

The approximated log-likelihood function is now

$$\ln L = \sum_{i=1}^{N-1} \tilde{p}\left(t_{i+1}, r_{t_{i+1}}; t_i, r_{t_i} \mid \theta\right). \tag{17.122}$$

The likelihood is approximated by generating auxiliary variables.

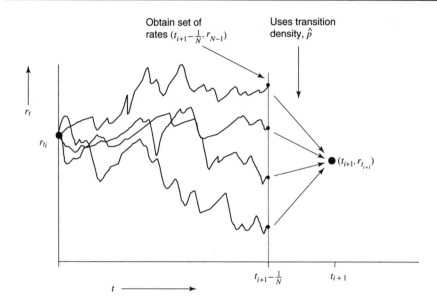

Figure 17.3   The transition between each observation

17.5.4   Illustration of the Method

We apply ML to fit the CKLS model to the UK three-month Libor series we used in Section 17.2.4. We established there that the model does not fit the data. When we run ML we find parameter values $\alpha = 0.254$, $\mu = 0.070$, $\sigma = 0.032$ and $\gamma = 1.10$. The parameters obtained by ML are much more robust with respect to initial values given to the optimiser. The surface $\ln L(\theta)$ appears to have a much better defined maximum and so has better optimisation properties than the GMM surface $J(\theta)$. This does not mean these parameter estimates are any better than the GMM estimates. Of course, they fail the specification test. The cumulative residuals are shown in Figure 17.4. The plot resembles the original data series, informally confirming the test results.

If a model fits the data, then both GMM and ML will return good estimates of the model parameters. If a model does not fit the data, then no estimation procedure is capable of finding a fit.

17.5.5   Example of Maximum Likelihood: Pearson and Sun

Many authors use ML to estimate interest rate processes, for example Chen and Scott (93) [128], Pearson and Sun (94) [432], Honore (98) [286], Nowman (97) [420], and others. Usually the ML method is used to estimate a Gaussian or CIR process; in these cases the transition density function is known so the method is easiest to apply.

Pearson and Sun estimate a two-factor CIR process, applying ML to bond prices. They work in the framework of the three-factor CIR model (CIR (85) [148]). The

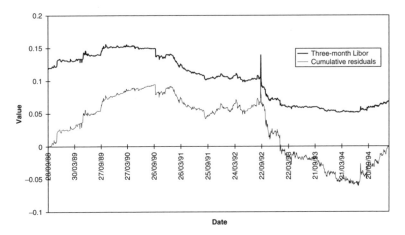

Figure 17.4 Comparison of UK three-month Libor and cumulative residuals

three state variables are the price level p_t, the real interest rate $r'_t = \underline{r} + r_t$, where $\underline{r}$ is a constant, and the inflation rate $y'_t = \underline{y} + y_t$, where $\underline{y}$ is a constant. The processes followed by the state variables are

$$dp_t = y_t p_t \, dt + \sigma_p p_t \sqrt{y_t} \, dz_{p,t}, \tag{17.123}$$

$$dy_t = \kappa_y \left(\mu_y - y_t \right) dt + \sigma_y \sqrt{y_t} \, dz_{y,t}, \tag{17.124}$$

$$dr_t = \kappa_r \left(\mu_r - r_t \right) dt + \sigma_r \sqrt{r_t} \, dz_{r,t}, \tag{17.125}$$

with $dz_{y,t} \, dz_{p,t} = \rho dt$, but $z_{r,t}$ is independent of either, under the EMM.

If nominal bond values are contingent upon y_t and r_t only, then this is a two-factor affine term structure model with

$$B_t(T) = A(\tau)C(\tau) \exp(-B(\tau)r_t - D(\tau)y_t), \tag{17.126}$$

for certain functions A, C, B, D of $\tau = T - t$, and parameter set $\theta = \{\underline{r}, \underline{y}, \kappa_y, \kappa_r, \mu_y, \mu_r, \sigma_p, \sigma_y, \sigma_r, \rho\}$. The short rate is

$$\tilde{r}_t = \underline{r} + \underline{y} + r_t + (1 - \sigma_p^2)y_t. \tag{17.127}$$

Estimation Procedure

In this model the conditional joint density for r_t and y_t is known. Pearson and Sun assume that (r_t, y_t) is not observed. Instead they assume that a pair of bond prices, $(P_t(\tau_1), P_t(\tau_2))$, is observed. From the two bond prices it is possible to back out r_t and y_t, and it is possible also to find the conditional joint density of $(P_t(\tau_1), P_t(\tau_2))$.

Pearson and Sun find

1. the joint density of (r_t, y_t);
2. (r_t, y_t) in terms of $(P_t(\tau_1), P_t(\tau_2))$;
3. the conditional joint density of $(P_t(\tau_1), P_t(\tau_2))$.

They make no allowance for observation error. An alternative procedure would be to treat r_t and y_t as hidden variables, whose values must be imputed from the term structure. If one assumes that bond prices are observed with measurement error, one can then incorporate more bonds into the estimation.

Conditional Joint Density of $(P_t(\tau_1), P_t(\tau_2))$

For the two-factor CIR model the transition density $p((r_s, y_s); (r_t, y_t) \mid \theta)$ is known explicitly. We write $(r_t, y_t) = g((P_t(\tau_1), P_t(\tau_2)))$. Since bond prices $P_t(\tau)$ are affine in (r_t, y_t) there is an easy expression for g. Write $P_{t,i}$ for $P_t(\tau_i)$. The joint conditional density for $(P_{t,1}, P_{t,2})$ is

$$q((P_{s,1}, P_{s,2}) \mid (P_{t,1}, P_{t,2})) = J\, p(g(P_{s,1}, P_{s,2}); g(P_{t,1}, P_{t,2}) \mid \theta), \qquad (17.128)$$

where

$$J = \begin{vmatrix} \dfrac{\partial r_s}{\partial P_{s,1}} & \dfrac{\partial r_s}{\partial P_{s,2}} \\[2mm] \dfrac{\partial y_s}{\partial P_{s,1}} & \dfrac{\partial y_s}{\partial P_{s,2}} \end{vmatrix} = \frac{1}{(B(\tau_1)D(\tau_2) - B(\tau_2)D(\tau_2))P_{s,1}P_{s,2}}. \qquad (17.129)$$

Suppose we have N observations $(P_{t_i,1}, P_{t_i,2})$, $i = 1, \ldots, N$, of the bond prices. The likelihood function is

$$L(\theta) = \sum_{i=1}^{N-1} \ln q((P_{t_{i+1},1}, P_{t_{i+1},2}) \mid (P_{t_i,1}, P_{t_i,2})). \qquad (17.130)$$

In fact Pearson and Sun use a slight generalisation of this procedure. Instead of using pure discount bonds, they want to use (in effect) coupon bond data (actually, the observed values of portfolios of bonds and bills). Two portfolio values, Q_1 and Q_2 are observed. Q_1 has coupons $c_{1,j}$ at time $t_{1,j}$ and Q_2 has coupons $c_{2,j}$ at time $t_{2,j}$. Their values are

$$Q_i = \sum c_{i,j} P_t(\tau_{i,j}), \quad i = 1, 2. \qquad (17.131)$$

Given Q_1 and Q_2 one can back out the values of r_t and y_t that generated them, as before, although now there is no exact formula. So, as before, one obtains a conditional joint density of (Q_1, Q_2).

Using maximum likelihood, Pearson and Sun calculate parameter values from three different pairs of portfolios,

- two bond portfolios,
- a bill and a bond portfolio,
- two bill portfolios.

If only bills are used in the estimation, the likelihood surface is too flat and it is not possible to get proper parameter estimates. In the other two cases Pearson and Sun claim to obtain reasonable results.

They also test the one-factor CIR against the two-factor model. The one-factor CIR model was rejected in favour of the two-factor model.

18
Further Estimation Methods

This chapter investigates several further important estimation methods. We shall be chiefly concerned with estimating models when there are hidden variables—state variables that cannot be directly observed. Before parameters can be estimated the values of these state variables must be inferred. Filtering techniques are used for this purpose. Sometimes filtering techniques may be inappropriate, in which case approximate techniques can be used. GARCH time series can be used in this context.

Interest rates can be modelled directly as GARCH processes. As long as a model is arbitrage-free and calibrates to the market the form of the underlying time series is not, in itself, too crucial (although some formulations may be more convenient in some situations than others). We discuss this use of GARCH in this chapter. Finally, in a brief section, we review artificial neural networks (ANNs) which are occasionally used to assist parameter estimation.

Filtering methods are used by Pennacchi (91) [437], Babbs and Nowman (97) [38], (99) [39], and Elliott, Fischer and Platen (97) [205] to estimate Gaussian affine models. General affine models are estimated by Lund (97) [370] and Duan and Simonato (95) [180]. Lund (97) [371] uses a non-linear filter by estimating an affine model directly from coupon bond data.

18.1 INTRODUCTION

In many modelling situations there is a system evolving, but only parts of it can be observed directly. For example,

- *Stochastic volatility models.* A stock price S_t can be observed directly but its underlying volatility σ_t cannot. A simple stochastic volatility model is

$$dS_t = \mu S_t dt + \sigma_t S_t dz_{s,t},$$

$$d\sigma_t = \alpha(\mu - \sigma_t)dt + \gamma\sqrt{\sigma_t}\,dz_{\sigma,t},$$

(18.1)

where z_s and z_σ are independent. α and γ can be chosen to ensure that σ remains positive. Values for σ_t might be inferred from option prices, but how might they be inferred directly from a time series of term structure data?

- *Dynamic mean term structure models.* One can observe interest rates r_t, but the underlying mean reversion level x_t is not observed. This could be modelled as a two-factor affine model:

$$\mathrm{d}r_t = \alpha(x_t - r_t)\mathrm{d}t + \sigma_r \mathrm{d}z_{r,t}, \qquad (18.2)$$

$$\mathrm{d}x_t = \beta(\mu - x_t)\mathrm{d}t + \sigma_x \mathrm{d}z_{x,t}, \qquad (18.3)$$

where z_r and z_x are independent.

Before parameters can be estimated, one must first infer the values of the hidden variables, σ_t for the stochastic volatility model and x_t for the dynamic mean model. There are several possibilities for estimating in this situation.

Case I: Hidden Variables Appear in Observables' Drift

If the system is linear, then Kalman filtering, described below, can be used. If the system is non-linear, then either

1. give up, or go on to Case II,
2. use extended Kalman filtering.

Case II: Hidden Variables do not Appear in Observables' Drift, or if the System is Non-linear

If one is prepared to compromise on generality, then an approximate method might be used. If one is not prepared to compromise on generality, then either

1. give up, or
2. work hard, by estimating using an efficient method of moments, perhaps.

The first section of this chapter looks at Kalman filtering. The second looks at GARCH approximation methods.

18.2   FILTERING APPROACHES TO ESTIMATION

These methods are very efficient, when they can be applied. Estimates are improved as new data arrive. There are a number of examples of the method being used in term structure estimation, and more are appearing all the time. The Kalman filter has been applied to both Gaussian and CIR type affine models. Affine models are particularly suited for estimating using the Kalman filter because of their linear structure. Non-linear models are harder to estimate by the standard filter. Also, in the affine case there are sometimes explicit formulae for the yield curve. This means that it is possible to use spot rates of different maturities in the estimation procedure.

In the Gaussian case examples are due to Babbs and Nowman (99) [39] and Lund (97) [370], who estimate a two-factor generalised Vasicek model. Both Lund and Babbs and Nowman observe eight spot rates with maturities between one and 10 years.

In the CIR case there are examples due to Ball and Torous (96) [51], Duan and Simonato (95) [180] and again Lund (97) [370].

- Ball and Torous use a filter to illustrate a unit root problem. They fit CIR to two sets of three yields with maturities $\left(\frac{1}{12}, 1, 5\right)$ years and $\left(\frac{1}{12}, \frac{1}{2}, 1\right)$ years.
- Duan and Siminato investigate the general affine case. As illustrations they fit one- and two-factor CIR to rates of maturities up to nine months.

Other applications of the filter are described by Pennacchi (91) [437] and Jegadeesh and Pennacchi (96) [321].

18.2.1 The Form of the Kalman Filter

The Kalman filter uses data observed in the market to infer values for unobserved state variables. Parameter values can then be estimated using, for example, maximum likelihood methods. Consider the double mean reverting model

$$dr_t = \alpha(x_t - r_t)dt + \sigma_r dz_{r,t}, \tag{18.4}$$

$$dx_t = \beta(\mu - x_t)dt + \sigma_x dz_{x,t}, \tag{18.5}$$

and suppose that up to time t one has observed a series $\{r_1, \ldots, r_{t-1}\}$. At time t one observes the value r_t. Next one infers the value $\tilde{x}_t$ of the unobserved state variable x_t at time t. Finally one estimates values of the parameters α, β, μ, σ_r and σ_x. When the next value, r_{t+1}, arrives the procedure is repeated, so that fresh estimates of α, β, μ, σ_r and σ_x are made.

In practice one would try to incorporate spot rates for several different maturities in the estimation procedure, since the shape of the term structure is sensitive to the values of the underlying state variables.

Strictly, the Kalman filter is a linear estimation method. Suppose we have a vector of observables $y_t = (y_{1,t}, \ldots, y_{n,t})'$, and a vector of state variables $a_t = (a_{1,t}, \ldots, a_{m,t})'$. To use the Kalman filter it must be possible to write the model in the form

$$y_t = Z_t(\theta)a_t + d_t(\theta) + \varepsilon_t, \qquad \text{the measurement equation,}$$

$$a_{t+1} = T_t(\theta)a_t + c_t(\theta) + R_t(\theta)\eta_t, \qquad \text{the system equation,} \tag{18.6}$$

where θ is a set of parameters, Z_t, T_t and R_t are matrices, d_t and c_t are vectors, ε_t is Gaussian noise with variance H_t, and η_t is Gaussian noise with variance Q_t. Z_t, T_t, R_t, d_t, c_t, H_t and Q_t may depend on y_{t-1}, but not on y_t, so that it is possible to compute them at time t. The system (18.6) may arise as a discretisation of an underlying continuous time system.

Equations (18.6) define a linear conditional Gaussian system.

Example: Double Mean Reverting Model

We discretise the double mean reverting model (18.4) and (18.5) as

$$r_{t+\Delta t} = \alpha \Delta t x_t + (1 - \alpha \Delta t)r_t + \sigma_r \sqrt{\Delta t}\, \varepsilon_t, \tag{18.7}$$

$$x_{t+\Delta t} = (1 - \beta \Delta t)x_t + \beta \mu \Delta t + \sigma_x \sqrt{\Delta t}\, \eta_t. \tag{18.8}$$

so that $\theta = \{\alpha, \beta, \mu, \sigma_r, \sigma_x\}$ is the set of parameters. If r_t is observed at daily intervals then $\Delta t = \frac{1}{260}$, say. Let us suppose that r_t is observable, and that x_t is a hidden state variable. To put (18.7) in the form (18.6), y_t is set to be $r_{t+\Delta t}$, and then the other terms in (18.6) are

$$Z_t = \alpha \Delta t, \tag{18.9}$$

$$T_t = (1 - \beta \Delta t), \tag{18.10}$$

$$R_t = \sigma_x \sqrt{\Delta t}, \tag{18.11}$$

$$H_t = \sigma_r^2 \Delta t, \tag{18.12}$$

$$Q_t = \text{Id}, \tag{18.13}$$

$$d_t = (1 - \alpha \Delta t)r_t, \tag{18.14}$$

$$c_t = \beta \mu \Delta t. \tag{18.15}$$

This is now in the correct form to apply the filter. Note that in the generalised Vasicek model an exact conditional process can be used instead of the Euler discretisation of (18.7) and (18.8). We explore this model further in Section 18.2.3.

Example: Longstaff and Schwartz

This continuous-time model has two state variables, the short rate r_t and its variance V_t, with processes of the form

$$\begin{aligned} dr_t &= e(a - bV_t - r_t)dt + \sqrt{V_t}\,dz_{r,t}, \\ dV_t &= f(c - dr_t - V_t)dt + \sqrt{W_t}\,dz_{V,t}, \end{aligned} \tag{18.16}$$

where

$$W_t = \frac{\alpha^3}{\beta - \alpha}(\beta r_t - V_t) - \frac{\beta^3}{\beta - \alpha}(V_t - \alpha r_t) \tag{18.17}$$

for certain parameters α and β, functions of a, b, c and d. The short rate r_t is observable; its variance V_t is not. We can discretise (18.16) as

$$\begin{aligned} r_{t+\Delta t} &= -eb\Delta t V_t + (1 - e\Delta t)r_t + ea\Delta t + \sqrt{V_t \Delta t}\,\varepsilon_t, \\ V_{t+\Delta t} &= (1 - ft)V_t + f(c - dr_t)\Delta t + \sqrt{W_t \Delta t}\,\eta_t, \end{aligned} \tag{18.18}$$

with W_t as above. $\theta = \{a, b, c, d, e, f\}$ is the set of parameters and

$$Z_t = -eb\Delta t, \tag{18.19}$$

$$T_t = (1 - f\Delta t), \tag{18.20}$$

$$R_t = \sqrt{W_t \Delta t}, \tag{18.21}$$

$$H_t = V_t \Delta t, \tag{18.22}$$

$$Q_t = \text{Id}, \tag{18.23}$$

$$d_t = (1 - e\Delta t)r_t + ea\Delta t, \tag{18.24}$$

$$c_t = f(c - dr_t)\Delta t. \tag{18.25}$$

This is now in the correct form to apply the filter.[1]

Alternatively, in the Longstaff and Schwartz model we know that $r_t(\tau) = A(\tau) + B(\tau)x_t + C(\tau)y_t$ for functions A, B and C and certain unobserved state variables x_t and y_t. The filter could be applied to infer values of x_t and y_t from observations of spot rates $r_t(\tau)$ of various maturity times.

Example: Stochastic Volatility Model

The stochastic volatility model (18.26)

$$dS_t = \mu S_t dt + \sigma_t S_t dz_{s,t},$$

$$d\sigma_t = \alpha(\beta - \sigma_t)dt + \gamma dz_{\sigma,t}. \tag{18.26}$$

can be discretised as

$$S_{t+\Delta t} = 0.\sigma_t + (1 + \mu\Delta t)S_t + \sigma_t c\sqrt{\Delta t}\,\varepsilon_t,$$

$$\sigma_{t+\Delta t} = (1 - \alpha\Delta t)\sigma_t + \alpha\beta\Delta t + \gamma\sqrt{\Delta t}\,\eta_t. \tag{18.27}$$

$\theta = \{\mu, \alpha, \beta, \gamma\}$ is the set of parameters and we can write

$$Z_t = 0, \tag{18.28}$$

$$T_t = (1 - \alpha\Delta t),$$

$$R_t = \gamma\sqrt{\Delta t},$$

$$H_t = \sigma_t^2 S_t^2 \Delta t,$$

$$Q_t = \text{Id},$$

$$d_t = (1 + \mu\Delta t)S_t,$$

$$c_t = \alpha\beta\Delta t.$$

This is now in the correct form, but Z_t is 0. We shall discover that the filter requires Z_t to be invertible, so we cannot apply the filter in this case.

18.2.2 The Kalman Filter Procedure

We now describe the filter. At time $t - 1$ we shall have current estimates of the state variables a_{t-1}, the variance P_{t-1} of a_{t-1}, and the parameters, θ_{t-1}. (Initial estimates of a_0 and P_0 need to be supplied.) There are three steps.

---

[1] Strictly, the current values of W_t and V_t should not appear in the volatility functions R_t and H_t. In implementations lagged values may be used.

1. The prediction step. We find
   - $a_{t|t-1}$, the forecast of a_t at time $t - 1$,
   - $P_{t|t-1}$, the forecast of P_t at time $t - 1$.
   At time t get a new observation, y_t.
2. The update step. Using y_t, compute estimates of a_t and P_t.
3. The parameter estimation step. Using a_t and P_t, compute an estimate θ_t of θ.

We examine each step in turn. Our emphasis is to state the results, rather than to prove them. A good account of the filter and its derivation can be found in Harvey (89) [272], for instance.

The Prediction Step

Forecasts are simply the unbiased conditional estimates,

$$a_{t|t-1} = T_t a_{t-1} + c_t, \tag{18.29}$$

$$P_{t|t-1} = T_{t-1} P_{t-1} T'_{t-1} + R_{t-1} Q_{t-1} R'_{t-1}. \tag{18.30}$$

The Update Step

When y_t has been observed, the forecast error v_t is

$$v_t = y_t - Z_t a_{t|t-1} - d_t. \tag{18.31}$$

The variance F_t of v_t is

$$F_t = Z_t P_{t|t-1} Z'_t + H_t. \tag{18.32}$$

The new estimates a_t and P_t, in terms of v_t and F_t, are

$$a_t = a_{t|t-1} + P_{t|t-1} Z'_t F_t^{-1} v_t, \tag{18.33}$$

$$P_t = P_{t|t-1} - P_{t|t-1} Z'_t F_t^{-1} Z_t P_{t|t-1}. \tag{18.34}$$

These are the variance minimising conditionally unbiased estimators of a_t and P_t. The Kalman filter is optimal in that it is the best estimator in the class of linear estimators.

The Parameter Estimation Step

It is natural, but not essential, to use maximum likelihood to estimate parameter values. Set

$$QL = -\frac{nt}{2} \ln 2\pi - \frac{1}{2} \sum_{i=1}^{t} \ln F_t - \frac{1}{2} \sum_{i=1}^{t} v'_t F_t^{-1} v_t. \tag{18.35}$$

Since the forecast error is Gaussian, (18.35) is the maximum likelihood estimator to best explain the observed values of y_t. Both F_t and v_t depend upon θ. θ_t is chosen to maximise QL.

An alternative procedure that avoids a separate estimation step is to estimate the parameters θ_t as part of the filter. One must then suppose that θ_t is evolving through time as part of the system equation. The model (18.6) is extended to give evolution equations for θ_t:

$$y_t = Z_t(\theta_t)a_t + d_t(\theta_t) + \varepsilon_t,$$

$$a_{t+1} = T_t(\theta_t)a_t + c_t(\theta_t) + R_t(\theta_t)\eta_t, \tag{18.36}$$

$$\theta_{t+1} = D_t(\kappa_t)\theta_t + e_t(\kappa_t) + V_t(\kappa_t)\xi_t,$$

where D_t and V_t are matrices, e_t is a vector, ξ_t is a vector of Gaussian noise with variance G_t, and κ_t is a small set of parameters which may be taken to be known constants. The vector of unobserved state variables is now extended to $a^* = (a \mid \theta)'$. For an example of the approach see Rogers and Zane (98) [460]. Note that the model (18.36) is now unlikely to be linear so that the ordinary filter cannot be used. Instead one must use an extended filter, described in Section 18.3 below.

18.2.3 Example: Double Mean Reverting Model

For a given model there is usually no unique way of applying the filter. It depends on what data are available, and the tractability of the model. We give two examples of using the filter to estimate a generalised Vasicek model. The first method uses data from along the term structure; the second just uses short rate data. As might be expected, the first method is far more robust.

Calibration Using Term Structure Data

Babbs and Nowman (97) [38], (99) [39] use the filter to fit, in effect, the double mean reverting process

$$dr_t = \alpha(x_t - r_t)dt + \sigma_r dz_{r,t}, \tag{18.37}$$

$$dx_t = \beta(\mu - x_t)dt + \sigma_x dz_{x,t} \tag{18.38}$$

(under the EMM) to the term structure. Observations are spot rates $R_{t,k}$, the spot rate at time t for time to maturity τ_k, for a fixed set of times to maturity, $\tau_1, \ldots, \tau_n$. The state variables are r_t and x_t, where the short rate is not assumed to be observable. The parameter set is $\theta = \{\alpha, \beta, \mu, \sigma_r, \sigma_x\}$.

Theoretical spot rates for maturities τ_k are explicit functions of the state variables

$$r_t(\tau_k \mid \theta) = r_{t,k} = A_0(\tau_k \mid \theta) + A_1(\tau_k \mid \theta)r_t + A_2(\tau_k \mid \theta)x_t, \tag{18.39}$$

where A_0, A_1 and A_2 are known functions of τ and the parameter set θ.

The estimating assumption is that observed rates are theoretical rates plus Gaussian noise:

$$R_{t,k} = r_{t,k} + \varepsilon_{t,k}. \tag{18.40}$$

This can now be put into Kalman filter form. Set $R_t = (R_{t,1}, \ldots, R_{t,n})'$. The measurement equation is

$$R_t = Z_t \begin{pmatrix} r_t \\ x_t \end{pmatrix} + c_t + \varepsilon_t, \tag{18.41}$$

where Z_t is an $n \times 2$ matrix

$$Z_t(k, 1) = A_1(\tau_k), \tag{18.42}$$

$$Z_t(k, 2) = A_2(\tau_k), \tag{18.43}$$

c_t is an n-dimensional vector

$$c_t(k) = A_0(\tau_k), \tag{18.44}$$

and ε_t is n-dimensional noise.

The system equation is

$$\begin{pmatrix} r_{t+1} \\ x_{t+1} \end{pmatrix} = \begin{pmatrix} 1 - \alpha\Delta t & \alpha\Delta t \\ 0 & 1 - \beta\Delta t \end{pmatrix} \begin{pmatrix} r_t \\ x_t \end{pmatrix} + \begin{pmatrix} 0 \\ \beta\mu\Delta t \end{pmatrix} + \varepsilon_t, \tag{18.45}$$

as before. Babbs and Nowman use a more sophisticated discretisation scheme employing the true conditional moments (18.39), instead of a Euler approximation.

Babbs and Nowman use spot rates for $n = 8$ maturities and solve the system using 'Gauss'. They find that the two-factor version of their model seems able to explain much of the variation in the US term structure in their sample, 1987–1996, but the repeated maximum likelihood estimation was extremely time consuming.

Calibration Using Only Short Rate Data

It is both necessary and desirable to fit to rates of both long and short maturities. Attempting to apply the filter when there is just a single observable does not work very well, particularly if the data set has features that the theoretical model does not describe. We attempt to use the filter to fit the double mean reverting model to a time series of UK three-month Libor, taking the three-month Libor rate to be a surrogate for the short rate and the sole observable.

Apart from the problems we introduce by using a surrogate for the short rate, in using just a single rate as an observable we make the estimation over-sensitive to the behaviour of that rate. We do not capture the behaviour of the yield curve as a whole. While there may be contexts in which this may not be altogether bad, we must expect that parameter estimates will be much less stable than they would be if more maturity dates were used.

The effects on the imputed values of the unobserved state variable x_t of the parameters of the model are shown in Figures 18.1 and 18.2. Figure 18.1 shows the filtered series x_t when $\alpha = 0.2$, $\beta = 0.25$, $\mu = 0.07$, $\sigma_r = 0.05$, and $\sigma_x = 0.05$. The initial value of x_t is set equal to the initial value of r_t. The reversion rate α of r_t to x_t is relatively small, so r_t does not closely track the imputed values of x_t. Figure 18.2 shows what happens

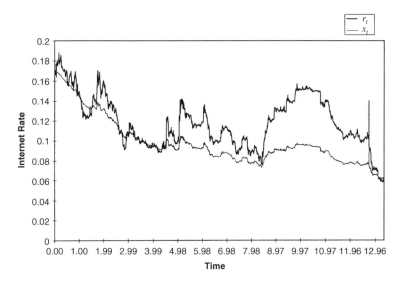

Figure 18.1   Filtered values of x_t: low α

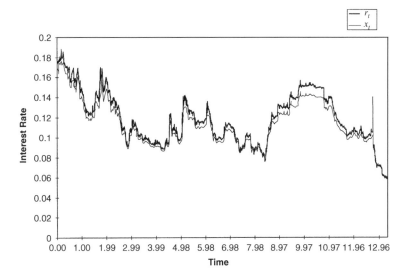

Figure 18.2   Filtered values of x_t: high α

when $\alpha = 5$ and all the other parameters are the same. r_t now tracks x_t quite closely. The likelihood value is higher in the first figure than the second.

We extend the method by introducing a second observable, the slope of the term structure at the short end. It can be shown (for instance by expanding out $r_t(\tau)$ in a Taylor series expansion in r_t and x_t at $\tau = 0$) that the slope of the term structure at

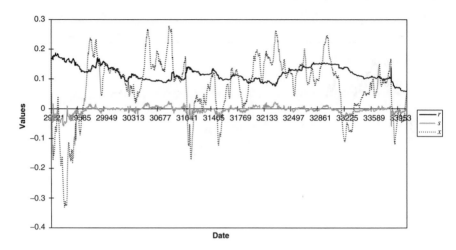

Figure 18.3 Filtered values of x_t: found from r_t and s_t

$\tau = 0$ is the drift of r_t under the EMM:

$$s_t = \tfrac{1}{2}(\alpha(x_t - r_t) - \lambda\sigma), \tag{18.46}$$

where λ is the market price of risk, which we take here to be a constant. Our premise is now that we observe r_t and s_t and have to infer x_t. For simplicity, r_t and s_t are approximated as

$$r_t = \text{3m Libor}, \tag{18.47}$$

$$s_t = \frac{\text{6m Libor} - \text{3m Libor}}{\frac{1}{4}}. \tag{18.48}$$

Figure 18.3 shows the inferred values of x_t and the observed series r_t and x_t, with the same parameter values as in Figure 18.1, and with $\lambda = 0$, $\sigma_s = 0.05$. The inferred values x_t are now far more volatile. They are evidently over-sensitive to noise in the slope between three-month and six-month Libor. The estimation is not improved if better methods are used to extract a short rate and a slope from the money market rates; essentially the model does not fit the data (the two short rate series), and tinkering with it does not help

18.2.4   Example: Generalised Vasicek

Lund (97) [370] estimates an affine Gaussian model where the short rate r_t decomposes as a linear function of the state variables $X_t = (X_{1,t}, \ldots, X_{m,t})'$ with weighting vector $w = (w_1, \ldots, w_m)'$,

$$r_t = w'X_t. \tag{18.49}$$

Under the EMM, X_t has the process

$$dX_t = (a - BX_t)dt + Gdz_t, \qquad (18.50)$$

where a is an m-dimensional vector, B is an $m \times m$ matrix, and G is an $m \times d$ matrix, where all these are constants, and z_t is a d-dimensional Wiener process.

Bond prices are of the form

$$B_t(\tau) = \exp\left(A_0(\tau) + A_1'(\tau)X_t\right), \qquad (18.51)$$

for $A_0 : \mathbb{R}^+ \to \mathbb{R}$ and $A_1 : \mathbb{R}^+ \to \mathbb{R}^m$. Since X_t is conditionally normally distributed, we also have

$$B_t(\tau) = \exp\left(-\mathbb{E}_t[I] + \tfrac{1}{2}\operatorname{var}_t[I]\right), \qquad (18.52)$$

where

$$I_t(\tau) = \int_t^{t+\tau} r_s ds = w' \int_t^{t+\tau} X_s ds, \qquad (18.53)$$

and $\mathbb{E}$ and var are computed under the EMM. It is possible to find computable expressions for $A_0(\tau)$ and $A_1(\tau)$. Theoretical spot rates are of the form $r_t(\tau \mid \theta) = Z_t(\tau \mid \theta)X_t + d_t(\tau \mid \theta)$, where

$$d_t(\tau \mid \theta) = \frac{-A_0(\tau \mid \theta)}{\tau}, \qquad (18.54)$$

$$Z_t(\tau \mid \theta) = \frac{-A_1'(\tau \mid \theta)}{\tau}, \qquad (18.55)$$

and where $\theta = \{a, B, G\}$ is the parameter set.

The estimation premise is that there is noise in the system. At time t we observe a vector of rates

$$R_t = (R_{1,t}, \ldots, R_{n,t})' \qquad (18.56)$$

for a fixed set of times to maturity $\tau_1, \ldots, \tau_n$. Lund supposes that the observed rates R_t are the theoretical model rates with added Gaussian noise $\varepsilon_{k,t} \sim N(0, H(\varphi))$, for some set of parameters φ. We have

$$R_{k,t} = r_t(\tau_k) + \varepsilon_{k,t}, \qquad (18.57)$$

$$= Z_t(\tau_k \mid \theta)X_t + d_t(\tau_k \mid \theta) + \varepsilon_{k,t}. \qquad (18.58)$$

This constitutes the measurement equation of the system.

It is easy to show that

$$\mathbb{E}_t[X_s] = e^{-B(s-t)}X_t + \int_t^s e^{-B(s-u)}adu, \quad t \le s. \qquad (18.59)$$

From this we immediately obtain the discrete time evolution of X_t,

$$X_{t+1} = c_t(\theta) + T_t(\theta)X_t + \eta_t, \qquad (18.60)$$

where

$$c_t(\theta) = \int_t^{t+1} a e^{-B(s-u)} du,$$

$$T_t(\theta) = e^{-B((t+1)-t)},$$

(18.61)

and $\eta_t \sim N(0, V_t(\theta))$, where

$$V_t(\theta) = \int_t^{t+1} e^{-B(s-u)} GG' e^{-B'(s-u)} du.$$

(18.62)

Equation (18.60) is the system equation. This is now in an appropriate form for the filter. Lund (97) [371] extends the analysis to the general affine case.

18.3   THE EXTENDED KALMAN FILTER

The Kalman filter is well-defined for linear systems specified by (18.6). In many systems a linear specification is inappropriate—or simply wrong. What happens if observables and state variables have non-linear dependencies? Suppose

$$y_t = f(a_t, \varepsilon_t),$$

(18.63)

$$a_{t+1} = g(a_t, \eta_t),$$

(18.64)

where f and g are non-linear and ε_t and η_t are Gaussian noise as before. The strict Kalman filter does not apply to this situation. The extended Kalman filter expands f and g out in a first-order Taylor series (see Harvey (89) [272]).

Suppose that

$$y_t = f(a_t, t) + \varepsilon_t,$$

(18.65)

$$a_{t+1} = g(a_t, t) + R(a_t, t)\eta_t,$$

with var $(\varepsilon_t) = H_t$ and var $(\eta_t) = Q_t$. At time $t - 1$ we will have estimates $\hat{a}_{t-1}$ and $\hat{a}_{t|t-1}$ of a_{t-1} and $a_{t|t-1}$. Expand f and g in Taylor series, up to first order:

$$f(a_t, t) \approx f(\hat{a}_{t|t-1}, t) + f'(\hat{a}_{t|t-1}, t)(a_t - \hat{a}_{t|t-1}),$$

$$g(a_t, t) \approx g(\hat{a}_t, t) + g'(\hat{a}_t, t)(a_t - \hat{a}_t).$$

(18.66)

(We shall compute $\hat{a}_t$ at the start of the update step.) The linearised system and measurement equations are

$$y_t = f'(\hat{a}_{t|t-1}, t)a_t + f(\hat{a}_{t|t-1}, t) - f'(\hat{a}_{t|t-1}, t)a_{t|t-1} + \varepsilon_t,$$

(18.67)

$$a_{t+1} = g'(\hat{a}_t, t)a_t + g(\hat{a}_t, t) - g'(\hat{a}_t, t)\hat{a}_t + R(\hat{a}_t, t)\eta_t.$$

(18.68)

Set

$$Z_t = f'(\hat{a}_{t|t-1}, t),$$

(18.69)

$$T_t = g'(\hat{a}_t, t),$$

(18.70)

$$R_t = R(\hat{a}_t, t),$$

(18.71)

for each time t. The prediction equations are

$$\hat{a}_{t|t-1} = g(\hat{a}_{t-1}, t),$$ (18.72)

$$P_{t|t-1} = T_{t-1}P_{t-1}T'_{t-1} + R_{t-1}Q_{t-1}R'_{t-1},$$ (18.73)

and the update equations are

$$\hat{a}_t = \hat{a}_{t|t-1} + P_{t|t-1}Z'_tF_t^{-1}(y_t - f(\hat{a}_{t|t-1}, t)),$$ (18.74)

$$P_t = P_{t|t-1} - P_{t|t-1}Z'_tF_t^{-1}Z_tP_{t|t-1},$$ (18.75)

where $F_t = Z_tP_{t|t-1}Z'_t + H_t$. The system has been linearised and the standard Kalman filter can now be applied.

Unfortunately this method does not work very well. It only gives reasonable results when f and g are already close to being linear so that we are justified in ignoring higher order terms in (18.66) (Tice (98) [522]).

An alternative is to use the Kitagawa algorithm or a related method (Kitagawa (87) [335], Jiang and Kitagawa (92) [322] and Tanizaki and Mariano (95) [517]). The idea is to approximate the underlying unknown density by piecewise linear functions. The method suffers from the 'curse of dimensionality' and does not usually perform very well either.

The non-linear filter was successfully implemented by Lund (97) [371] to estimate parameters from a time series of coupon bond data.

18.3.1 Example: A Chaotic Three-Factor Model

In this section we apply the Kalman filter to a non-linear model of Tice and Webber (97) [523]. Elaborations of the basic filter are discussed in Tice (98) [522]. We investigate two estimation procedures. For this model, unlike the affine Gaussian case, there is no explicit solution available to find spot rates as functions of the state variables. Although it would be possible to use simulation-based methods to find theoretical spot rates, so that one could use rates of different times to maturity in the estimation, we do not do so here. Instead we illustrate the problems encountered if too few inappropriate observables are used.

The model has three factors: the short rate r_t, the mean reversion level x_t of r_t, and a coupling parameter p_t. The dynamics are

$$dr_t = \alpha(x_t - r_t)dt + \sigma_r dz_{r,t},$$ (18.76)

$$dx_t = \beta(p_tr_t + (1 - p_t)\mu - x_t)dt + \sigma_x dz_{x,t},$$ (18.77)

$$dp_t = \gamma(\delta - \phi(x_t - \mu)(r_t - \mu) - p_t)dt + \sigma_p dz_{p,t}.$$ (18.78)

As we saw in Chapter 11 this is actually a system with deterministic chaos. We use this example to give two illustrations of the use of the filter. Neither is a viable estimation method; a good estimation procedure for this model needs term structure data and a means of rapidly computing term structures from the model.

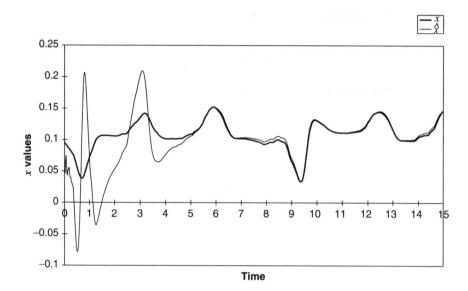

Figure 18.4   Actual and inferred values of x_t

The Short Rate is the Only Observable

In the first illustration we suppose that only r_t can be observed and that values for both x_t and p_t have to be inferred. The filter is benchmarked by running it against data simulated under the model with known parameter values. The DGP parameter values are $\alpha = 5$, $\beta = 0.5$, $\gamma = 0.4166667$, $\mu = 0.1$, $\delta = 23$, $\phi = 43456.79$, $\sigma_r = 0.05$, $\sigma_x = \sigma_p = 0$, $r_0 = 0.09$, $x_0 = 0.095$ and $p_0 = 10$.

Figure 18.4 shows the convergence of the inferred values of x_t to the actual values when α, β, γ, μ, ϕ, and σ_r are the DGP values, $\sigma_x = \sigma_p = 0.05$, $x_0 = 0.05$ and $p_0 = 1$. x_t converges to its true values after a few cycles. Similarly, Figure 18.5 shows the convergence of the inferred values of p_t to the actual values. This also settles down after a few cycles, but does not achieve the same accuracy as x_t.

Unfortunately it is not possible to obtain reliable estimates of the parameters of the model, even if one starts off with initial estimates quite close to the true values. There are too few observables, the model is too non-linear, and life is short.

The Short Rate and the Slope at the Short End are Observed

As in Section 18.2.3, suppose now that we can observe the slope s_t of the term structure at $\tau = 0$, in addition to the short rate r_t. From observations of r_t and s_t we have to infer x_t and p_t. Using the same parameter values and initial estimates as in the previous section, and $\sigma_s = 0.5$, we obtain the convergence shown in Figures 18.6 and 18.7. Convergence is now faster to the true values. Unfortunately it is still not possible to use the filter to estimate parameter values.

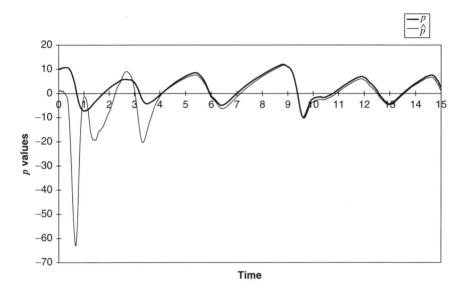

Figure 18.5 Actual and inferred values of p_t

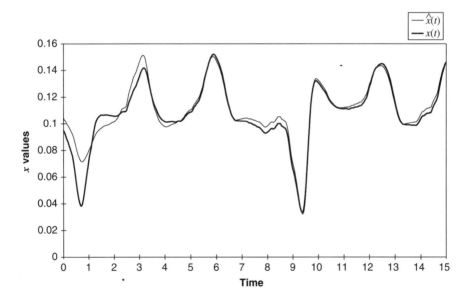

Figure 18.6 Actual and inferred values of x_t

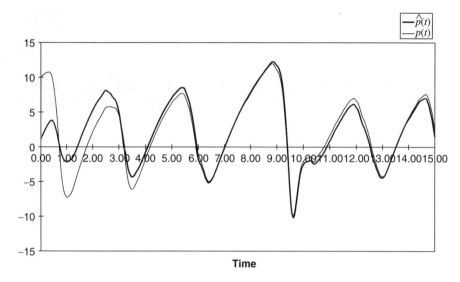

Figure 18.7 Actual and inferred values of p_t

18.3.2 Square Root Filtering Methods

The standard Kalman filter propagates the variance P_t of the estimate of a_t. This can lead to instabilities; in an ill-conditioned system there is no guarantee that $P_{t|t-1}$ remains positive definite, for instance. Instead of propagating $P_{t|t-1}$, square root methods propagate the Choleski factor $P_{t|t-1}^{1/2}$ of $P_{t|t-1}$. $P_{t|t-1}^{1/2}$ is the 'square root' of $P_{t|t-1}$ in the sense that

$$P_{t|t-1} = P_{t|t-1}^{1/2} \left(P_{t|t-1}^{1/2} \right)' . \tag{18.79}$$

(We assume that Choleski factors exist for Q_t and R_t.)

By propagating the square root we guarantee that the covariance matrices remain symmetric and positive definite. This ensures that we have much greater numerical stability. These methods can solve systems where the ordinary filter becomes unstable; for instance, systems like those in Section 18.3.1 above (with certain parameter values). For more information see Tice (98) [522] and Verhaegen and Van Dooren (86) [532].

18.4 GARCH MODELS

Many authors have demonstrated, and market practitioners have always known, that financial time series have non-constant variance; volatilities change through time. This has significant practical implications and needs to be modelled, when appropriate. In situations where filtering methods cannot be used, so that a stochastic volatility cannot be estimated directly, it may be sensible to restrict the specification of the stochastic volatility process to something that can be estimated. One such specification is GARCH.

In this section we describe the GARCH(p, q) time series specification and how it may be estimated and tested. ARCH (AutoRegressive Conditional Heteroscedasticity), models were introduced by Engle (82) [207] and GARCH (Generalised ARCH) by Bollerslev (86) [80]. We briefly discuss alternative formulations and modifications of GARCH. Finally, we describe the use of GARCH in term structure modelling.

18.4.1 Overview of Procedure

It is possible to use GARCH models if the variance of a time series has no additional specific innovations. There are three steps. Suppose that we have a time series y_t.

1. Model y_t as, for example, an ARMA process, with residuals ε_t,

$$y_t = \phi_1 y_{t-1} + \cdots + \phi_q y_{t-p} - \theta_1 \varepsilon_{t-1} - \cdots - \theta_q \varepsilon_{t-q} + \varepsilon_t. \tag{18.80}$$

ARMA combines autoregression and a moving average. The discrete-time process (18.80) can be written compactly as

$$\phi(L) y_t = \theta(L) \varepsilon_t, \tag{18.81}$$

where L is the lag operator and $\phi(L)$ and $\theta(L)$ are polynomials in L,

$$\phi(L) = 1 - \phi_1 L - \cdots - \phi_q L^q, \tag{18.82}$$

$$\theta(L) = 1 - \theta_1 L - \cdots - \theta_p L^p. \tag{18.83}$$

2. Model ε_t as a GARCH process,

$$\varepsilon_t \sim N(0, h_t), \tag{18.84}$$

where h_t satisfies a time series relationship such as, for example,

$$h_t = \alpha_0 + \alpha_1 \varepsilon_{t-1}^2, \text{ ARCH(1) specification,}$$

$$h_t = \alpha_0 + \alpha_1 \varepsilon_{t-1}^2 + \beta_1 h_{t-1}, \text{ GARCH(1, 1) specification.} \tag{18.85}$$

3. Confirm that
   (a) residuals have the correct properties,
   (b) y_t has the correct properties.

18.4.2 GARCH (p, q)

The idea is to explain the way that volatility is seen to vary through time. In a GARCH model the conditional variance h_t, $\varepsilon_t \sim N(0, h_t)$, follows the discrete-time process

$$h_t = \alpha_0 + \alpha(L) \varepsilon_t^2 + \beta(L) h_t, \tag{18.86}$$

where α and β are polynomials in L, the lag operator,

$$\alpha(L)\varepsilon_t^2 = \alpha_1\varepsilon_{t-1}^2 + \cdots + \alpha_q\varepsilon_{t-q}^2, \tag{18.87}$$

$$\beta(L)h_t = \beta_1 h_{t-1} + \cdots + \beta_p h_{t-p}.$$

h_t has an ARCH process if $\beta(L) = 0$. Note that (18.86) can be re-arranged as

$$\varepsilon_t^2 = (\alpha(L) + \beta(L))\varepsilon_t^2 + (1 - \beta(L))\left(\varepsilon_t^2 - h_t\right). \tag{18.88}$$

$\varepsilon_t^2 - h_t$ has mean zero and is serially uncorrelated, so it is an innovation (it is chi-squared). (18.88) is an ARMA (m, p) representation for ε_t^2, where $m = \max(p, q)$.

Also note that if the roots of $1 - \beta(L)$ are outside the unit circle, then rearranging (18.86) we have

$$h_t = (1 - \beta(L))^{-1}\alpha(L)\alpha_0 + (1 - \beta(L))^{-1}\alpha(L)\varepsilon_t^2. \tag{18.89}$$

This is an ARCH(∞) representation of h_t. This means that h_t is affected by very long lags. An implication is that GARCH is parsimonious compared with ARCH; the influence of very long lags can be obtained with small values of p and q.

18.4.3 Properties of GARCH

GARCH models have only a single stream of innovations, ε_t. Although there are innovations in h_t, they are functions of the innovations ε_t, and thus do not constitute a separate source of risk. This makes GARCH an inappropriate technique, in general, for discretising a multifactor term structure model with true stochastic volatility. The relationship of discrete-time ARCH and GARCH models to underlying continuous-time processes and their convergence properties is investigated by Nelson (90) [409] and Duan (97) [178].

When used in situations where it is appropriate, it is usually unnecessary to have high values of p or q. It is possible to get good results with $p, q \le 2$. Other points to notice are:

1. ε_t affects h_t only via $|\varepsilon_t|$, so the volatility of y_t cannot depend on whether y_t is increasing or decreasing.
2. A large quantity of data is required for reliable parameter estimates.
3. There is a trade-off (as ever) between an in-sample fit and an out-of-sample forecast.
4. The GARCH method was devised to obtain heteroscedastic residuals. It is bad at long-run forecasting, but good at short-term forecasts.
5. h_t must be positive. This puts constraints upon α_i and β_i.

Ensuring that h_t is Positive

We have

$$h_t = \alpha_0 + \alpha(L)\varepsilon_t^2 + \beta(L)h_t. \tag{18.90}$$

h_t will be positive if

$$\alpha_0 > 0, \quad \alpha_i, \beta_i \geq 0. \tag{18.91}$$

This condition is certainly sufficient, but it is too strong. For instance, if it is possible to re-express (18.90) in an MA(∞) representation,

$$h_t = \alpha_0^* + \sum_{i=1}^{\infty} \alpha_i^* \varepsilon_{t-i}^2, \tag{18.92}$$

then h_t is positive if $\alpha_0^* > 0$, $\alpha_i^* \geq 0$. For GARCH(1, 2) this is equivalent to requiring $\alpha_0 > 0$, $\alpha_1, \beta_1 \geq 0$, $\alpha_1 \beta_1 + \alpha_2 \geq 0$, *et cetera*. α_2 is not required to be positive and may be negative.

Moments of a GARCH Process

It is possible to compute the moments of a GARCH process. For instance, for GARCH(1, 1) we have

$$\mathbb{E}\left[\varepsilon_t^2\right] = \mathbb{E}[h_t] = \alpha_0 + (\alpha_1 + \beta_1)\mathbb{E}\left[\varepsilon_{t-1}^2\right]. \tag{18.93}$$

This can be iterated. It converges to

$$\mathbb{E}\left[\varepsilon_t^2\right] = \sigma_\varepsilon^2 = \frac{\alpha_0}{1 - (\alpha_1 + \beta_1)}, \tag{18.94}$$

if $\alpha_1 + \beta_1 < 1$. Similarly, for GARCH(p, q) the unconditional variance σ_ε^2 is finite if

$$\sum_{i=1}^{q} \alpha_i + \sum_{i=1}^{p} \beta_i < 1. \tag{18.95}$$

Hence, GARCH is unconditionally homoscedastic.

The autocovariances of GARCH(p, q) are zero, $\mathbb{E}[\varepsilon_t \varepsilon_{t-k}] = 0$, for $k \geq 1$; hence a GARCH process is weakly stationary if $\sigma_\varepsilon^2 < \infty$.

18.4.4 Estimating GARCH Processes

Either GMM or maximum likelihood methods may be used. Maximum likelihood is quite straightforward in this case. Suppose we have a GARCH series y_{t_i}, $i = 0, \ldots, n$ with transition densities

$$p\left(t_i, y_{t_i}, t_{i-1}, y_{t_{i-1}} \mid \theta\right), \quad i = 1, \ldots, n, \tag{18.96}$$

depending upon a parameter set θ. For a GARCH process, $\varepsilon_t \sim N(0, h_t)$, and successive ε_t are independent, so

$$p\left(t_i, \varepsilon_{t_i}, t_{i-1}, \varepsilon_{t_{i-1}} \mid h_t\right) = p(\varepsilon_t) = (2\pi h_t)^{-\frac{1}{2}} \exp\left(\frac{-\varepsilon_t^2}{2h_t}\right) \tag{18.97}$$

is just the normal density function with h_t depending on α_0, α_i and β_i. The likelihood function is just

$$L = \prod_{i=1}^{n} p\left(t_i, y_{t_i}, t_{i-1}, y_{t_{i-1}} \mid \theta\right) \qquad (18.98)$$

as usual.

Example: ARCH(1) = *GARCH*(1, 0)

Suppose we have modelled a time series y_t as ARMA(p, q),

$$y_t = \phi_1 y_{t-1} + \cdots + \phi_q y_{t-p} - \theta_1 \varepsilon_{t-1} - \cdots - \theta_q \varepsilon_{t-q} + \varepsilon_t. \qquad (18.99)$$

If there is an AR(∞) representation we can write

$$\varepsilon_t = y_t + \sum_{i=1}^{\infty} \phi_i^* y_{t-i}, \qquad (18.100)$$

where the ϕ_i^* are known functions of the parameter set $\{\phi, \ldots, \phi_p, \theta_1, \ldots, \theta_q\}$. We have

$$\varepsilon_t \sim N(0, h_t), \quad h_t = \alpha_0 + \alpha_1 \varepsilon_{t-1}^2. \qquad (18.101)$$

The likelihood function is $L(\theta)$,

$$L(\theta) = \prod_{t=1}^{n} (2\pi h_t)^{-\frac{1}{2}} \exp\left(\frac{-\varepsilon_t^2}{2h_t}\right). \qquad (18.102)$$

It is more convenient to use the log-likelihood function $\ln L$,

$$\ln L = -\frac{n}{2} \ln 2\pi - \frac{1}{2} \sum_{t=1}^{n} \ln h_t - \frac{1}{2} \sum_{t=1}^{n} \frac{\varepsilon_t^2}{h_t}. \qquad (18.103)$$

For GARCH(1, 0) the parameter set is $\theta = (\alpha_0, \alpha_1)'$. Set $u_t = \left(1, \varepsilon_{t-1}^2\right)'$, so that $h_t = u_t'\theta$. Then

$$\frac{\partial \ln L}{\partial \theta} = \sum_{t=1}^{n} \frac{1}{2h_t} \left(\frac{\varepsilon_t^2}{h_t} - 1\right) u_t. \qquad (18.104)$$

Finding the zeros of (18.104) requires algorithms suitable for this non-linear case. A popular method is the Berndt, Hall, Hall and Hausman (74) [62] (BHHH) algorithm. Maximum likelihood estimation of GARCH processes is now standard in various computer packages.

18.4.5   Testing

In addition to tests associated to ML there are various other specification tests available for GARCH processes. We content ourselves with describing just two, both for ARCH processes.

Does ARCH Fit the Data (i)?

The LM test can be applied to ARCH (Engle (82) [207]). For $\text{ARCH}(q) = \text{GARCH}(0, q)$:

1. Estimate $y_t = \beta x_t + \hat{\varepsilon}_t$.
2. Regress

$$\hat{\varepsilon}_t = \alpha_0 + \alpha_1 \hat{\varepsilon}_{t-1}^2 + \cdots + \alpha_q \hat{\varepsilon}_{t-q}^2 + u_t. \tag{18.105}$$

Note the R^2.

3. Under H_0: $\alpha_1 = \cdots = \alpha_q = 0$ (no ARCH) use the LM statistic:

$$nR^2 \sim \chi^2(q) \tag{18.106}$$

where n is the number of observations.

This test can easily be generalised. For example, for AARCH (see Section 18.5.1) regress

$$\hat{\varepsilon}_t = \alpha_0 + \sum_{i,j=1}^{q} \alpha_{i,j} \hat{\varepsilon}_{t-i}^2 \hat{\varepsilon}_{t-j}^2. \tag{18.107}$$

Then $nR^2 \sim \chi^2 \left(\frac{1}{2} q(q+1) \right)$.

Does ARCH Fit the Data (ii)?

It is possible to use the portmanteau statistic Q. The test is

1. Find the residuals $\hat{\varepsilon}_t$ from an estimation of y_t.
2. Compute the sample autocorrelation function (SACF) of $\hat{\varepsilon}_t^2$:

$$\hat{r}(k) = \frac{\sum_{t=k+1}^{n} \left(\hat{\varepsilon}_t^2 - \hat{\sigma}^2 \right) \left(\hat{\varepsilon}_{t-k}^2 - \hat{\sigma}^2 \right)}{\sum_{t=1}^{n} \left(\hat{\varepsilon}_t^2 - \hat{\sigma}^2 \right)^2}, \tag{18.108}$$

where $\hat{\sigma}^2 = (1/n) \sum_{t=1}^{n} \hat{\varepsilon}_t^2$.

3. The asymptotic variance of $\hat{r}(k)$ is n^{-1}. Compute the portmanteau statistic

$$Q = n(n+2) \sum_{k=1}^{m} \frac{\hat{r}(k)}{n-k}. \tag{18.109}$$

Q is asymptotically $\chi^2(m)$ if $\hat{\varepsilon}_t^2$ are independent. This allows us to reject the hypothesis of no ARCH.

18.5 EXTENSIONS OF GARCH

Many extensions of the GARCH process described above have been experimented with. The idea is to try to account for more subtle relationships in the volatility. For instance, autocorrelations, the positivity of h_t, an asymmetric effect of ε_t on h_t, and other features. In this section we very briefly define AARCH, QARCH, log-ARCH, NARCH, E-GARCH, I-GARCH, and GARCH-M. A number of these are discussed by Campbell, Lo and MacKinlay (97) [113]. Shephard (96) [489] is an excellent review of ARCH and GARCH applications to finance including a discussion of some of the alternatives listed here.

These refinements do not seem really appropriate for no-arbitrage interest rate modelling, but we include them for reference. If the initial model does not fit, tweaking it will not improve it significantly.

18.5.1 Allowing Lagged Covariances to Affect h_t

The AARCH and QARCH extensions of GARCH allow h_t to be influenced by lagged covariances.

AARCH (augmented ARCH)

h_t is specified as

$$h_t = \alpha_0 + \sum_{i,j=1}^{q} \varepsilon_{t-i} A_{i,j} \varepsilon_{t-j}, \tag{18.110}$$

$$= \alpha_0 + \underline{\varepsilon}_\tau' A \underline{\varepsilon}_\tau, \tag{18.111}$$

where $\underline{\varepsilon}_\tau' = (\varepsilon_{t-1}, \dots, \varepsilon_{t-q})$, and A is a constant matrix. When A is diagonal AARCH(q) is ARCH(q). AARCH permits off-diagonal terms to be significant.

QARCH (quadratic ARCH)

Specify h_t as

$$h_t = \alpha_0 + \sum_{i,j=1}^{q} \varepsilon_{t-i} A_{i,j} \varepsilon_{t-j} + \sum_{i=1}^{q} B_i \varepsilon_{t-i}$$

$$= \alpha_0 + \underline{\varepsilon}_\tau' A \underline{\varepsilon}_\tau + B \underline{\varepsilon}_\tau. \tag{18.112}$$

Shocks to h_t can depend on the sign of ε_t as well as the absolute magnitude of ε_t.

18.5.2 Avoiding Negative h_t

The log-ARCH and NARCH extensions address the problem of negative estimates of h_t (when parameters are unconstrained).

log-ARCH

h_t is specified as

$$\ln h_t = \alpha_0 + \alpha_1 \ln \varepsilon_{t-1}^2 + \cdots + \alpha_q \ln \varepsilon_{t-q}^2, \tag{18.113}$$

then $h_t > 0$ is guaranteed.

NARCH (non-linear ARCH)

Specify h_t as

$$h_t = \left((\alpha_0)^\delta + \alpha_1 \left(\varepsilon_{t-1}^2 \right)^\delta + \cdots + \alpha_q \left(\varepsilon_{t-q}^2 \right)^\delta \right)^{1/\delta}, \tag{18.114}$$

with

$$\sum_{i=1}^{q} \alpha_i = 1, \quad a_0 > 0, \alpha_i \geq 0, \delta > 0. \tag{18.115}$$

When $\delta = 1$ NARCH reduces to ARCH(q). When $\delta \to 0$ NARCH becomes log-ARCH.

18.5.3   Allowing sign(ε_t) to Matter

The E-GARCH method tries to build in some asymmetry, so that sign (ε_t) matters. Set

$$u_t = \frac{\varepsilon_t}{\sqrt{h_t}} \sim N(0, 1) \tag{18.116}$$

and specify

$$\ln h_t = \alpha_0 + \sum_{i=1}^{q} \alpha_i g(u_{t-i}) + \sum_{i=1}^{p} \beta_i \ln h_{t-i}, \tag{18.117}$$

where g is an asymmetric function of u_t. For instance, one could try

$$g(u_t) = \theta u_t + \gamma(|u_t| - \alpha \mathbb{E}[|u_t|]). \tag{18.118}$$

Since $\mathbb{E}[|u_t|] = \sqrt{2/\pi}$ is a constant, g in (18.118) has mean 0 and constant variance (if finite) so it is an innovation, hence E-GARCH is ARMA(p, q) in $\ln h_t$.
$g(u_t)$ is asymmetric. In fact

$$\begin{aligned} g(u_t) &= (\theta + \gamma)u_t - \alpha\gamma\sqrt{2/\pi}, \quad \text{if } u_t > 0, \\ g(u_t) &= (\theta - \gamma)u_t - \alpha\gamma\sqrt{2/\pi}, \quad \text{if } u_t < 0. \end{aligned} \tag{18.119}$$

18.5.4   Building in a Unit Root

Empirically it is often found that

$$\sum_{i=1}^{q} \alpha_i + \sum_{i=1}^{p} \beta_i \sim 1, \tag{18.120}$$

so that the process (18.86) is close to having a unit root. I-GARCH (integrated GARCH) imposes a unit root; one requires that

$$\sum_{i=1}^{q} \alpha_i + \sum_{i=1}^{p} \beta_i = 1. \tag{18.121}$$

For GARCH(1, 1)

$$h_t = \alpha_0 + \alpha_1 \varepsilon_{t-1}^2 + \beta_1 h_{t-1}. \tag{18.122}$$

If $\alpha_1 + \beta_1 = 1$, then I-GARCH(1, 1) is

$$h_t = \alpha_0 + \alpha_1 \varepsilon_{t-1}^2 + (1 - \alpha_1) h_{t-1}, \tag{18.123}$$

and

$$\mathbb{E}_t \left[\varepsilon_{t+s}^2 \right] = s\alpha_0 + h_t, \tag{18.124}$$

so that the estimated variance grows without limit. We conclude that an I-GARCH process is not weakly stationary, but it could be strongly stationary. Shocks to h_t are persistent (like a random walk). In cases where this is an appropriate assumption I-GARCH may be a good modelling hypothesis.

18.5.5 Allowing Variance to Influence Returns

In financial returns series, higher variance is often associated with higher returns. GARCH-M (GARCH in the mean) builds this in as an assumption. Specify

$$y_t = \xi x_t + \delta g(h_t) + \varepsilon_t, \tag{18.125}$$

where x_t is an underlying explanatory process. $g(h_t)$ models the influence of variance upon the series y_t. If y_t is a returns series then δ represents a price of risk.

ε_t is modelled as ARCH or GARCH. For example, set $g(h_t) = h_t$ and $\xi = 0$, then conditional upon information Ω_{t-1} known at time $t - 1$,

$$y_t = \delta h_t + \varepsilon_t, \quad \varepsilon_t \mid \Omega_{t-1} \sim N(0, h_t), \tag{18.126}$$

$$h_t = \alpha_0 + \alpha_1 \varepsilon_{t-1}^2. \tag{18.127}$$

In this case we have

$$\mathbb{E} \left[\varepsilon_t^2 \right] = \frac{\alpha_0}{1 - \alpha_1}, \tag{18.128}$$

and it is possible to show that

$$\mathbb{E}[y_t] = \delta \alpha_0 \left(1 + \frac{\alpha_1}{1 - \alpha_1} \right), \tag{18.129}$$

$$\text{var}[y_t] = \frac{\alpha_0}{1 - \alpha_1} + \frac{(\delta \alpha_1)^2 2\alpha_0^2}{(1 - \alpha_0)^2 \left(1 - 3\alpha_1^2 \right)}. \tag{18.130}$$

The second term is 0 if δ is 0 so that the process reduces to an ARCH(1) process.

18.6 INTEREST RATE MODELS AND GARCH

GARCH methods have recently begun to be used in various aspects of interest rate modelling. They have been used for some time in the analysis of financial time series, including interest rate series, but these uses have often been exercises in econometrics and not in the context of the consistent estimation of an arbitrage-free system. Uses include

1. Estimating continuous-time interest rate models;
2. Approximating empirical densities;
3. Approximating processes;
4. As a sound basis for no-arbitrage pricing;
5. As a basis for no-arbitrage pricing.

Care is required if doing 1. GARCH is not equivalent to stochastic volatility, in the continuous-time modelling sense. Since it does not introduce an extra source of risk it does not reproduce a stochastic volatility.

Uses 2 and 3 are not quite identical. Brenner, Harjes and Kroner (96) [96] are modelling an underlying process, and do not attempt to do more than 3. In particular they are not attempting to price derivatives.

On the other, hand Andersen and Lund (97) [22] and Dai and Singleton (98) [154] do 2. These authors want an approximate auxiliary density to enable them to estimate their underlying processes. It does not matter where it comes from. Using a GARCH specification they find a ballpark density for the short rate process (see Chapter 17).

Use 4 is somewhat preferable to 5.

18.6.1   Example: Longstaff and Schwartz

The Longstaff and Schwartz two-factor model is

$$dr_t = \alpha(a - bV_t - r_t)dt + \sqrt{V_t}\,dz_{r,t},$$
$$dV_t = \beta(c - dr_t - V_t)dt + \sqrt{W_t}\,dz_{r,t}, \tag{18.131}$$

where W_t is a linear function of V_t and r_t. To estimate their model Longstaff and Schwartz initially discretised it as

$$r_t - r_{t-1} = \alpha_0 + \alpha_1 r_{t-1} + \alpha_2 h_t^2 + h_t\varepsilon_t,$$
$$h_t^2 = \beta_0 r_{t-1} + \beta_1 h_{t-1}^2 + \beta_2 \varepsilon_{t-1}^2 + \beta_3, \tag{18.132}$$
$$\varepsilon_t \sim N(0, 1), \text{ iid}.$$

h_t is supposed to correspond to V_t, but innovations in h_t do not incorporate a second separate source of risk. Longstaff and Schwartz recognised the inadequacies of this method and turned to a GMM alternative.

18.6.2   Price Kernel in Discrete Time

Duan (96a) [176], (96b) [177] uses a price kernel, and standard methods, to obtain a short rate process in discrete time. His method is rigorous and arbitrage-free. He obtains, under the objective measure P,

$$r_t - r_{t-1} = \alpha_0 + \alpha_1 r_{t-1} + (\beta_0 + \beta_1 r_{t-1})W_{t-1},$$

$$W_{t-1} = \frac{(\varepsilon_{t-1} - \psi)^2 - (1 + \psi^2)}{\sqrt{2 + 4\psi^2}}, \tag{18.133}$$

$$\varepsilon_{t-1} \sim N(0, 1), \text{ iid,}$$

where

$$\mathbb{E}[W_{t-1}] = 0, \qquad \mathbb{E}\left[W_{t-1}^2\right] = 1. \tag{18.134}$$

Duan shows how to transform to the accumulator measure Q. Bond option prices are found by simulation under Q. Since the model is arbitrage-free in discrete-time, and not a discrete time approximation to a continuous-time model, there is no need to worry about the choice of discretisation scheme.

18.6.3   Modelling the Short Rate Process

Brenner, Harjes and Kroner (96) [96] model the short rate process as a GARCH process. They do not try to price anything, emphasising an investigation into the behaviour of short rate volatility, so their methodology is quite acceptable. The short rate process is modelled as

$$r_t - r_{t-1} = \alpha_0 + \alpha_1 r_{t-1} + \varepsilon_{t-1},$$

$$\varepsilon_{t-1} \sim N(0, h_{t-1}) \tag{18.135}$$

They set up four different specifications for volatility. Set $\eta_{t-1} = \min(\varepsilon_{t-1}, 0)$.

1. A GARCH(1, 1) specification for non-level-dependent volatility:

$$h_t^2 = \Psi_t^2 r_{t-1}^{2\gamma}, \tag{18.136}$$

$$\Psi_t^2 = a_0 + a_1 \varepsilon_{t-1}^2 + b_1 \Psi_{t-1}^2.$$

2. A GARCH(1, 1) specification for non-level-dependent volatility, modified to incorporate asymmetrical effects:

$$h_t^2 = \Psi_t^2 r_{t-1}^{2\gamma}, \tag{18.137}$$

$$\Psi_t^2 = a_0 + a_1 \varepsilon_{t-1}^2 + b_1 \Psi_{t-1}^2 + a_2 \eta_{t-1}^2.$$

3. A specification for h_t^2 incorporating feedback from the observable r_t:

$$h_t^2 = a_0 + a_1 \varepsilon_{t-1}^2 + b_1 h_{t-1}^2 + a_2 r_{t-1}^{2\gamma}. \tag{18.138}$$

4. A specification for h_t^2 incorporating feedback from the observable r_t, and also including possible asymmetrical effects:

$$h_t^2 = a_0 + a_1 \varepsilon_{t-1}^2 + b_1 h_{t-1}^2 + a_2 r_{t-1}^{2\gamma} + a_3 \eta_{t-1}^2. \tag{18.139}$$

Conclusions

Brenner, Harjes and Kroner fit the four specifications to three-month T-bill data over the period 1973–1990, and compare their results with CKLS. They conclude that

1. Serial correlation effects exist that the CKLS specification fails to capture. On the other hand CKLS + GARCH over-emphasises serial correlation effects.
2. CKLS argue that level-dependent effects in volatility are of primary importance. Brenner *et al.* argue that stochastic volatility effects are of equal importance.
3. More generally Brenner *et al.* conclude that stochastic volatility, serial correlation, and other effects need to be incorporated into interest rate models before they adequately explain short rate time series.

We do not find ourselves demurring from these conclusions.

18.6.4   Summary

GARCH processes and their variants have a role to play in providing insights into interest rate modelling. They stem from an econometric context, however, and (except in special situations, such as Duan's GARCH models) seem to be inappropriate for direct use in arbitrage-free pricing. However, there has been a fair amount of recent work on the application of GARCH based models, and one may expect to see further advances in the use of GARCH in option pricing.

18.7   ARTIFICIAL NEURAL NETS (ANNs)

Despite its suggestive nomenclature ANNs can be regarded as essentially just a curve-fitting and interpolation method. In this section we describe ANNs but do not attempt to apply them to interest rate modelling.

There are many textbooks on ANNs. Some examples with differing approaches are Bishop (95) [63], Haykin (94) [273] and Hertz *et al.* (91) [278].

18.7.1   Definition of an ANN

An ANN is a collection of functions whose dependencies are represented as a network. A node represents a particular function. An arc represents one function supplying an input into another.

Suppose we have a set $\mathcal{N}$ of N nodes, $\mathcal{N} = \{N_i, \quad i = 1, \ldots, N\}$, and arcs $\mathcal{A} \subseteq \mathcal{N} \times \mathcal{N}$. For example, Figure 18.8 shows a simple network with $N = 5$ and $\mathcal{A} = \{(1, 2), (4, 3), (1, 3), (5, 2), (5, 3)\}$.

Write f_i for the function represented by node N_i. At each node there is an input set and an output set. At node N_i the input set is $\mathcal{I}_i$,

$$\mathcal{I}_i = \{j \in \mathcal{N} \mid (j, i) \in \mathcal{A}\}. \tag{18.140}$$

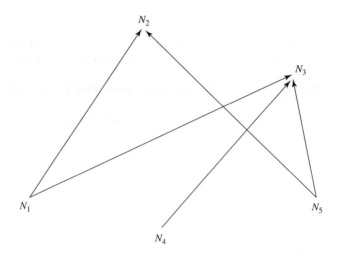

Figure 18.8   An example of a network

The output set at node N_i is $\mathcal{O}_i$,

$$\mathcal{O}_i = \{ j \in \mathcal{N} \mid (i, j) \in \mathcal{A} \}. \tag{18.141}$$

$\mathcal{I}_i$ are the nodes from which the function f_i at node N_i obtains its arguments; $\mathcal{O}_i$ represents the nodes to which f_i is an argument. f_i has $|\mathcal{I}_i|$ arguments. Writing $\hat{f}_i$ for the value of the function f_i,

$$\hat{f}_i = f_i \big(\hat{f}_k \mid k \in \mathcal{I}_i \big). \tag{18.142}$$

A node with $|\mathcal{I}_i| = 0$ is an input node. A node with $|\mathcal{O}_i| = 0$ is an output node. Write $\mathcal{I}, \mathcal{O} \subseteq \mathcal{N}$ for the sets of input and output nodes, respectively. Input nodes supply values that are input into the network. Output nodes supply values that represent the output of the network.

18.7.2   Typical Network Architecture

An ANN is specified by the underlying network. Different types of network cause an ANN to behave in qualitatively different ways. A forward feed network has no feedback loops. It can compute solutions explicitly. We do not consider networks with feedback here.

Figure 18.9 illustrates a typical forward feed architecture. It has an input layer containing only input nodes, an output layer with only output nodes, and the remaining 'hidden' nodes in between.

For $q = |\mathcal{I}|$, $p = |\mathcal{O}|$, an ANN is a function

$$A : \mathbb{R}^q \rightarrow \mathbb{R}^p, \tag{18.143}$$

Input
layer   Hidden layers   Output
                                                                      layer

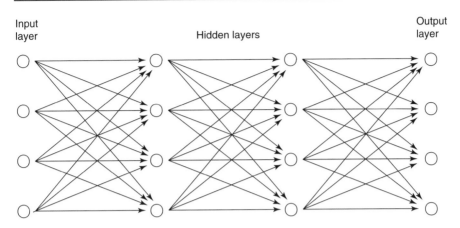

Figure 18.9   A typical forward feed network architecture

defined by $f = \{f_i\}_{i=1,...,N}$ and the network architecture. It is a fact that any continuous function can be approximated by a two-layer network.

18.7.3   Special Cases

Two families of ANN are often used in applications.

1. *Multilayer perceptron.* All functions (except at input nodes) decompose as

$$\hat{f}_i = f\left(w_i\left(\hat{f}_k \mid k \in I_i\right)\right), \tag{18.144}$$

where f is fixed function and w_i are affine functions,

$$w_i\left(\hat{f}_k \mid k \in I_i\right) = w_{i,0} + \sum_{k \in I_i} w_{i,k}\hat{f}_k. \tag{18.145}$$

f is called the activation function. w_i are called the discriminant functions.

2. *Radial basis function network.* Hidden layer nodes have non-linear functions, for example Gaussian kernels. Output layer nodes may have linear functions. The network may have only one hidden layer.

Multilayer perceptrons are supposed to be better at global approximation, for instance extracting components from a set of yield curves. Radial basis function networks are supposed to be superior for local approximation, for instance curve-fitting.

18.7.4   The Activation Function, f

There are a number of standard functional forms often used for the activation function f.

1. The threshold function

$$f(x) = 0, x \leq 0,$$
$$= 1, x > 0. \tag{18.146}$$

2. The logistic sigmoid function

$$f(x) = \frac{1}{1 + e^{-x}}. \tag{18.147}$$

3. The tanh function

$$f(x) = \frac{e^x - e^{-x}}{e^x + e^{-x}}. \tag{18.148}$$

Other functional forms are often used in radial basis function networks, for instance,

$$f(x) = e^{-\frac{1}{2}x^2}, \tag{18.149}$$

$$f(x) = x^2 \ln x, \tag{18.150}$$

$$f(x) = \left(x^2 + \sigma^2\right)^{-\alpha}, \tag{18.151}$$

and others.

18.7.5 The Discriminant Functions, w_i

At node i, the discriminant function w_i is

$$w_i\left(\hat{f}_k \mid k \in I_i\right) = w_{i,0} + \sum_{k \in I_i} w_{i,k} \hat{f}_k. \tag{18.152}$$

$w_{i,0}$ is called the threshold or bias, and $\{w_i\}$ is called the weight vector. Specification (18.152) has be relaxed to give a generalised linear discriminant where

$$w_i\left(\hat{f}_k \mid k \in I_i\right) = w_{i,0} + \sum_{j=1}^{m} w_{i,j} \phi_j\left(\{\hat{f}_k\}\right), \tag{18.153}$$

and where ϕ_j, $j = 1, \ldots, m$, is a fixed set of basis functions. We shall assume that all networks are of this form.

18.7.6 Key Idea: Training/Learning

Suppose we are supplied with a partially known map

$$g : \mathbb{R}^q \rightarrow \mathbb{R}^p. \tag{18.154}$$

The map g is partially known in the sense that we are given a finite set of pairs $\{(x_n, g(x_n))\}_{n=1,\ldots,M}$ for $x_n \in \mathbb{R}^q$. That is, we are given a set of values of g evaluated at M points in $\mathbb{R}^q$. This is a realistic modelling situation. For instance, we may suppose that changes in the yield curve from day to day are determined by certain state variables that we can observe in the market. We could suppose, for instance, that changes in the entire yield curve are determined solely by changes in spot rates of a few fixed times to maturity. We can observe changes in the state variables, and we can observe changes in the yield curve as a whole, but the functional relationship between the two may be illusive. ANNs can be used as fitting and interpolation methods to help in this situation.

We want to construct an ANN with q input nodes and p output nodes, such that g is closely approximated by the ANN function

$$A : \mathbb{R}^q \to \mathbb{R}^p, \tag{18.155}$$

defined by f and $\{w_{i,k}\}$. That is, for a chosen function f, we want to find a set $w = \{w_{i,k}\}$ so that $g \sim A$.

In turns out to be possible to do this using a simple optimisation procedure, at least for simple examples. For more complicated, more realistic situations it may be hard to apply the procedure and get convergence to a set of suitable w.

There are two phases. The first is to train the net. The second is to then use the net in place of the function g.

The Training Method

This is an iterative method. We are given a set of training data $\{(x_n, g(x_n))\}_{n=1,\ldots,M}$. We start with some initial values w^0. At step $n - 1$ we have found values w^{n-1}. For step n:

1. Evaluate the network at the next data point x_n and compute

$$A_n = A(x_n \mid w^{n-1}). \tag{18.156}$$

$A_n = (A_{n,1}, \ldots, A_{n,p})'$ is a vector in $\mathbb{R}^p$. The error is e_n is measured as

$$e_n = A_n - g(x_n). \tag{18.157}$$

2. Alter w^{n-1} to obtain w^n such that

$$A(x_n \mid w^n) - g(x_n) < |e_n|. \tag{18.158}$$

This crucial step is called back propagation, and is described below.
3. Go to step 1.

Back Propagation

The back propagation method described here is actually an implementation of a simple descent method. It sweeps through the network starting from the output nodes, finding new values of $w_{j,i}^n$ as it proceeds.

Computation at an output node   For each $i \in \mathcal{O}$ compute

$$e_{n,i} = A_{n,i} - g_i(x_n). \tag{18.159}$$

This is the error at node i (that is, the error in the ith component of A). For $j \in \mathcal{I}_i$ set

$$w_{j,i}^n = w_{j,i}^{n-1} + \Delta w_{j,i}, \qquad (18.160)$$

where

$$\Delta w_{j,i} = -\eta \hat{f}_j \delta_i^n \qquad (18.161)$$

for a constant learning rate η and

$$\delta_i^n = e_{n,i} \left. \frac{\partial f_i}{\partial x} \right|_{\hat{f}_i}. \qquad (18.162)$$

We can now work back through the network, layer by layer.

Computation at a hidden node   We want to find new values $w_{j,i}^n$ at node N_i, $j \in \mathcal{I}_i$. Suppose we have computed δ_k^n for all $k \in \mathcal{O}_i$. Simply set

$$\Delta w_{j,i}^n = -\eta \hat{f}_j \delta_i^n, \qquad (18.163)$$

where

$$\delta_i^n = \frac{\partial f_i}{\partial x} \sum_{k \in \mathcal{O}_i} \delta_k^n w_{i,k}^n. \qquad (18.164)$$

We can sweep backwards through the network adjusting $w_{j,i}^{n-1}$ at successive nodes as we go.

It is possible to show that this procedure converges in a quadratic system. In a more complicated system convergence is not guaranteed.

18.7.7   Uses in Finance

The aspect of ANNs we have described above is their use as a non-parametric interpolation method. There are many potential uses in interest rate modelling. For instance, in fitting the yield curve, and in fitting to cap and swaption prices.

ANNs are often used to assist in forecasting; in other words, the detection of an underlying structure in financial time series that might be used in trading applications. The purpose is to provide signal detection for position taking.

The difficulty with the procedure as described are many.

1. The model may be mis-specified in that the inputs and outputs to the ANN, and hence our assumptions about the function g, are wrong. The inputs we have selected may not in fact explain the outputs we observe.
2. The training data may be inadequate in that it may not sample very much of the state space.
    (a) We would not expect a model trained on a data set containing inverted yield curves to perform well when yield curves were 'normal'.
    (b) A model trained on data from the period of the Fed experiment would not be expected to perform well in other periods.

3. At a practical level the training procedure may simply not converge.
4. Even if an ANN seems to work, one may have no idea why it is working. It is purely non-parametric and provides no intuition as to what is going on. This has been described, with good reason, as 'scary'. A seemingly well trained ANN may suddenly cease to provide good forecasts, for no apparent reason.

19

Interest Rates and Implied Pricing

One would like to be able to back out from the prices of interest rate derivatives in the market, information about the implied interest rate density function. This would enable us to price other, perhaps exotic or less liquid, securities from the implied density. In the equity and FX markets there are often plenty of liquid instruments that one can calibrate to and implied pricing is significantly easier than in the interest rate markets where there are usually fewer liquid instruments. One may have at-the-money (ATM) cap and swaption prices but very little information on out-of-the-money or in-the-money prices.

Breeden and Litzenberger (78) [91] and Banz and Miller (78) [52] first showed how a complete knowledge of European call and put prices was sufficient to enable the risk-neutral density of the underlying stochastic asset to be derived. Practical applications of these concepts hit problems of numerical instability. A number of numerical methods have been developed. For example, lattice methods have been developed by Dupire (94) [191], Rubinstein (94) [462], Jackwerth and Rubinstein (96) [307], Derman and Kani (94) [166], Derman, Kani and Chriss (96) [167], Jackwerth (97) [306], Barle and Cakici (95) [53], *et cetera*. Implied grid methods are due to Andersen (96) [16] and Lagnado and Osher (97a) [347], (97b) [348]. It is normally necessary to employ a regularisation method, in effect smoothing over the input data so that outputs have greater stability (Levin (98) [350], Cont (98) [140]).

There is a sizeable implied pricing literature for the equity and FX markets, but there is relatively little for interest rate markets, although contributions include Amin and Morton (94) [14], Amin and Ng (97) [15], Andersen and Andreasen (98) [18] and Coutant, Jondeau and Rockinger (98) [146].

In this chapter we investigate problems with implied pricing and discuss some of the solutions that have been found. We start by reviewing the relationship between prices, the interest rate density function and implied and local volatilities. We show how in theory, but not in practice, the density can be extracted from a set of option prices. We then discuss possible practical implementation of the schemes, including regularisation issues. Finally we discuss how tails might be patched onto the implied density.

Parts of this chapter are based on Kuan and Webber (98) [344].

19.1 PROBLEMS WITH INTEREST RATE MODELS

To use an interest rate model one must first calibrate it. The Longstaff and Schwartz model, with state variables the short rate r_t and the short rate variance v_t, with processes

$$dr_t = (\alpha - \beta r_t - \gamma v_t)dt + \sqrt{v_t}\,dz_{1,t}^Q, \qquad (19.1)$$

$$dv_t = (\delta - \varepsilon r_t - \phi v_t)dt + \sqrt{w(r_t, v_t)}\,dz_{2,t}^Q, \qquad (19.2)$$

under the accumulator measure Q, has six parameters, $\theta = \{\alpha, \beta, \gamma, \delta, \varepsilon, \phi\}$. θ, and the current values of r_t and v_t, are chosen to match market prices, normally the yield curve, cap and swaption prices, *et cetera*. Calibration is simplified by the existence of explicit formulae for pure discount bonds and pure discount bond options. With the Longstaff and Schwartz model, and more generally for any interest rate model:

- One may be able to get reasonable fits to prices, but it is not possible to fit every price.
- Parameter values estimated on one day are different from those found on the next day. Market prices are not consistent with model prices and market dynamics are not consistent with model dynamics

There are several ways around these problems. If one requires the tractability of some particular model, it may be possible to extend the model, making some parameters deterministic functions of time. We have seen this technique used with extended Vasicek and extended CIR models, and other affine models can be given the same treatment. A model suitably extended will be able to fit exactly to the current term structure and to a term structure of volatility. It may also be able to calibrate to a volatility smile.

Rather than extending an existing model, a more fundamental way around the problem is to back out the model directly from market prices, giving an 'implied' model. The implied model should, for instance, fit the volatility smile.

Suppose that at time t we can observe, or can impute, a complete set of caplet prices. That is, we know caplet prices $c_t(r_X, T)$ for all exercise rates $r_X > 0$, and times of maturity $T > t$. We have Black's implied volatilities $\sigma_t(r_X, T)$,

$$c(r_X, T) = B(r_X, T \mid r_t, t, \sigma(r_X, T)), \qquad (19.3)$$

where $B(r_X, T \mid r_t, t, \sigma)$ is the Black's caplet price with implied volatility σ (see Chapter 3). $\sigma(r_X, T)$ is the implied volatility surface. For $r_X \equiv r_X(T)$, the ATM exercise rate, $\sigma(r_X, T)$, $T > t$, is the term structure of volatility. For fixed T, as r_X varies, $\sigma(r_X, T)$ is the volatility smile.

The extended Vasicek model can calibrate to the term structure of volatility, but not the volatility smile. To calibrate to the full volatility surface one requires an implied model.

When calibrating an interest rate model—Longstaff and Schwartz, for instance, or BDFS—one may regard the model solely as a mechanism for interpolating between market data. Suppose a model has parameters θ and we have a set of market prices

$\hat{c}_k$, $k = 1, \ldots, N$. Write $c_k(\theta)$, $k = 1, \ldots, N$, for the model prices, conditional on the parameter set θ. To fit the model we find θ so that model prices match market prices,

$$\hat{\theta} = \arg \min_{\theta} D(\theta), \qquad (19.4)$$

where

$$D(\theta) = \sum_{k=1}^{N} (\hat{c}_k - c_k(\theta))^2, \qquad (19.5)$$

say. Normally $\hat{c}_k$ and $c_k(\hat{\theta})$ will differ systematically. An interest rate model determines a distinct family of prices; market prices need not correspond to any of these. Once a best fit set $\hat{\theta}$ is found other prices can be generated consistent with the set $\hat{c}_k$, $k = 1, \ldots, N$.

19.2 KEY RELATIONSHIPS

In this section we review some facts from option pricing. These relate option prices, implied volatilities, local volatilities, and the relevant PDEs. We start by looking at the equity case. This is simpler; in the equity case interest rates are often subsidiary to equity prices and they are often assumed to be constant. This makes relationships much more straightforward. The interest rate case is harder because discount factors are stochastic.

19.2.1 The Equity Case

Suppose we have a stock price S_t with a constant dividend yield q, and a constant interest rate r. Under the accumulator measure Q,

$$\frac{dS_t}{S_t} = (r - q)dt + \sigma(S_t, t)dz_t. \qquad (19.6)$$

$\sigma(S_t, t)$ is the local volatility of S_t. Let $C(X, T \mid S_t, t)$ be the value at time t of a European call with exercise price X, maturity time T, conditional on S_t and t. There are three key PDEs satisfied by C and its density, namely the Black–Scholes PDE:

$$\frac{1}{2}\sigma^2(S, t)S^2 \frac{\partial^2 C}{\partial S^2} + (r - q)S \frac{\partial C}{\partial S} + \frac{\partial C}{\partial t} = rC; \qquad (19.7)$$

the Fokker–Planck PDE:

$$\frac{\partial n^Q}{\partial T} + \frac{\partial}{\partial u}((r - q)un^Q) - \frac{1}{2}\frac{\partial^2}{\partial u^2}(\sigma^2(u, T)u^2 n^Q) = 0, \qquad (19.8)$$

where $n^Q(u, T \mid S, t)$ is the transition density function under Q; and the adjoint PDE:

$$\frac{\partial C}{\partial T} + qC + (r - q)X \frac{\partial C}{\partial X} - \frac{1}{2}\sigma^2(X, T)X^2 \frac{\partial^2 C}{\partial X^2} = 0. \qquad (19.9)$$

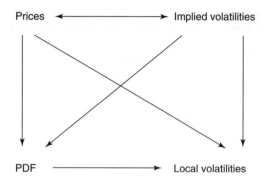

Figure 19.1   Relationships between functions

Prices, PDEs, local volatilities, probability density functions and implied volatilities determine one another. Figure 19.1 shows the relationships. Some directions are 'hard' and require regularisation techniques, described in Section 19.5.

The results in this section have been derived by, for example, Andersen (96) [16] and Andreasen (96) [25], amongst others.

Prices → *PDF*

From a set of prices, the probability density function is the normalised second derivative of C with respect to the exercise price,

$$n^Q(u, T; S, t) = e^{r(T-t)} \frac{\partial^2 C(X, T, S, t)}{\partial X^2}\bigg|_{X=u}. \tag{19.10}$$

This relationship is obtained by twice differentiating the call price, C, expressed as an expectation,

$$C(X, T; S, t) = e^{-r(T-t)} \int_X^\infty (u - X) n^Q(u, T; S, t) du, \tag{19.11}$$

with respect to the exercise price X.

Prices → *Local Volatilities*

Rearranging the adjoint PDE,

$$\sigma^2(X, t) = 2 \frac{\dfrac{\partial C}{\partial T} + qC + (r - q)X \dfrac{\partial C}{\partial X}}{X^2 \dfrac{\partial^2 C}{\partial X^2}}, \tag{19.12}$$

we obtain local volatilities from prices.

Implied Volatilities → Local Volatilities

From the Black–Scholes equation we find implied volatilities. The Black–Scholes equation is

$$C(X, T \mid S, t) = W(X, T \mid S, t, \sigma(X, T \mid S, t)), \tag{19.13}$$

where $\sigma(X, T \mid S, t)$ is the Black–Scholes implied volatility,

$$W(X, T \mid S, t, \sigma) = Se^{-q\tau}N(d_1) - Xe^{-r\tau}N(d_2), \tag{19.14}$$

with $\tau = T - t$ and

$$d_1 = \frac{1}{\sigma\sqrt{\tau}} \ln\left(\frac{Se^{-q\tau}}{Xe^{-r\tau}}\right) + \frac{1}{2}\sigma\sqrt{\tau}, \tag{19.15}$$

$$d_2 = d_1 - \sigma\sqrt{\tau}. \tag{19.16}$$

We have

$$\frac{\partial C}{\partial X} = \frac{\partial W}{\partial X} + \frac{\partial W}{\partial \sigma}\frac{\partial \sigma}{\partial X}, \tag{19.17}$$

but there are explicit formulae for the derivatives $\partial W/\partial X$ and $\partial W/\partial \sigma$ from the Black–Scholes equation. Substituting these into equation (19.12) we find

$$\sigma^2(u, T) = \frac{2}{X^2}\left[\frac{\dfrac{\sigma}{2\tau} + \dfrac{\partial\sigma}{\partial T} + (r-q)X\dfrac{\partial\sigma}{\partial X}}{\dfrac{1}{\sigma\tau X^2} + \dfrac{2d_1}{\sigma\sqrt{\tau}X}\dfrac{\partial\sigma}{\partial X} + \dfrac{d_1 d_2}{\sigma}\left(\dfrac{\partial\sigma}{\partial X}\right)^2 + \dfrac{\partial^2\sigma}{\partial X^2}}\right]. \tag{19.18}$$

(This result is described in Andersen (96) [16] and Andreasen (96) [25], *et cetera*.)

Implied Volatilities → PDF

By the previous method one shows

$$n^Q(u, T; S, t) = e^{r(T-t)}\frac{\partial^2 C}{\partial X^2}$$

$$= n(d_2)\left(\frac{1}{u\sigma\sqrt{\tau}} + \frac{2d_1}{\sigma}\frac{\partial\sigma}{\partial X} + u\sqrt{\tau}\frac{d_1 d_2}{\sigma}\left(\frac{\partial\sigma}{\partial X}\right)^2 + u\sqrt{\tau}\frac{\partial^2\sigma}{\partial X^2}\right).$$

$$\tag{19.19}$$

PDF → Local Volatilities

Integrating the Fokker-Planck PDE we obtain

$$\sigma^2(u, T) = \frac{2}{u^2}\left[\frac{\dfrac{\partial}{\partial T}\displaystyle\int_u^\infty\int_v^\infty n^Q(w, T)\mathrm{d}w\mathrm{d}v - (r-q)\int_u^\infty wn^Q(w, T)\mathrm{d}w}{n^Q(u, T)}\right], \tag{19.20}$$

(assuming reasonable regularity on n^Q and σ^2).

In principle, given a complete set of option prices, or a complete set of implied volatilities, we seem able to find local volatilities. In practice this does not work with real data. We need to be able to calculate second derivatives accurately. Any noise in the prices, perhaps due to bid–ask spreads or to non-synchronous prices, or gaps in the data, prevents us from doing this. There are also problems in the tails of the density function. There data are sparse and the second derivative is also very close to zero. Small errors in prices can give negative values for the density function. The inverse procedure is unstable; without regularisation, it does not work.

Another problem is that equations such as (19.19) are continuous-time formulae. Applied to a lattice or a grid, where there is only a discrete set of states, they give poor results. On a lattice or a grid it is necessary to find an exact discrete formula.

Example: Implied Volatilities → Local Volatilities

Figure 19.2 shows a plot of an implied volatility surface $\sigma(X, \tau)$,

$$\sigma(X, \tau) = a + b(X - S_t) + c(X - S_t)^2 + d\tau + e\tau^2 + f(X - S_t)\tau, \qquad (19.21)$$

for constants a, b, c, d, e and f, based on a quadratic fit to UK equity option implied volatility in November 1997. $S_t = 4770$ was the current value of the equity index. Figure 19.3 shows the recovered local volatility surface, based on equation (19.18) with numerical approximations to the derivatives.

In this case local volatilities have been successfully recovered. The curvature of the local volatility surface is much greater than that of the implied volatility surface. If a flat implied volatility surface is input, a flat local volatility surface is recovered.

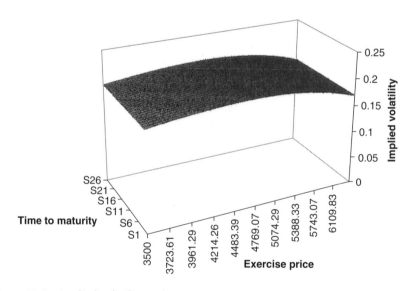

Figure 19.2   Implied volatility surface

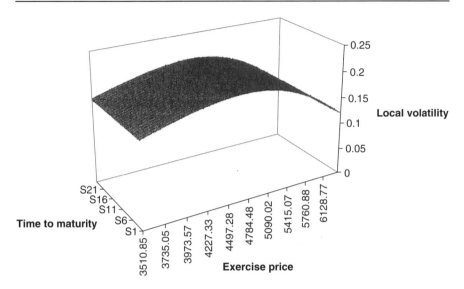

Figure 19.3   Imputed local volatility surface

Because there is a regular functional form for $\sigma(X, \tau)$, a procedure based on (19.18) works in this case. In general, if there is no functional form for $\sigma(X, \tau)$ and we are supplied only with option prices it is necessary to use numerical methods to find local volatilities, based on a discretised version of the backwards equation. We need to use regularisation methods to get numerical stability.

19.3   THE INTEREST RATE CASE

Suppose that the short rate is the sole state variable, and that

$$dr_t = \mu_t(r_t)dt + \sigma_t(r_t)dz_t^Q, \qquad (19.22)$$

under the accumulator measure Q. $\mu_t(r_t)$ and $\sigma_t(r_t)$ are the local drift and volatility, respectively.

Given $\mu_t(r_t)$ and $\sigma_t(r_t)$ we can compute the underlying probability densities, Arrow–Debreu security prices, caplet prices, *et cetera*. On the other hand, given caplet prices we can in principle back out Arrow–Debreu security prices, the underlying probability densities, and hence the local drifts and volatilities, $\mu_t(r_t)$ and $\sigma_t(r_t)$.

As in the equity case, deriving prices from the local drifts and volatilities is generally easy and stable. Deriving $\mu_t(r_t)$ and $\sigma_t(r_t)$ from prices is tricky and unstable. It is an 'inverse problem', that is, stable in one direction, unstable in the reverse direction. This is essentially because underlying densities are proportional to the second derivative $\partial^2 c(r_X, T)/\partial r_X^2$. Given $\partial^2 c(r_X, T)/\partial r_X^2$, integrating twice to find $c(r_X, T)$ is stable since small errors tend to average out. On the other hand, small perturbations in $c(r_X, T)$ give big changes in the second derivative $\partial^2 c(r_X, T)/\partial r_X^2$.

Let c_t be the value at time t of a derivative with payoff $H_T(r_T)$ at time $T > t$, so that H_T depends only on r_T. For a numeraire G_t, there exists an equivalent martingale measure Q^G such that

$$c_t = \mathbb{E}^{Q^G}\left[\frac{G_t}{G_T}H_T\right]. \tag{19.23}$$

We have

$$c_t = \int_{-\infty}^{\infty} \frac{G_t}{G_T}H_T n^{Q^G}(r_T, T \mid r_t, t)\mathrm{d}r_T, \tag{19.24}$$

where n^{Q^G} is the density under Q^G. We shall be interested in two particular numeraires: the accumulator account, $G_t = \exp\left(\int_0^t r_s \mathrm{d}s\right)$, with associated measure Q, and the T-maturity pure discount bond, $G_t = B_t(T)$, with measure Q^T. Each numeraire determines a different pair of PDEs.

19.3.1   The Backwards and Forwards Equations

Suppose the short rate process under Q, the accumulator account measure, is

$$\mathrm{d}r_t = \mu(r_t, t)\mathrm{d}t + \sigma(r_t, t)\mathrm{d}z_t^Q, \tag{19.25}$$

with transition density function $n^Q(r_T, T \mid r_t, t)$. In the interest rate case we obtain two key PDEs: the Kolmogorov backward equation,

$$\frac{1}{2}\sigma^2(r_t, t)\frac{\partial^2 c}{\partial r_t^2} + \mu(r_t, t)\frac{\partial c}{\partial r_t} + \frac{\partial c}{\partial t} = rc, \tag{19.26}$$

and the Fokker–Planck PDE, or forward equation,

$$\frac{\partial n^Q}{\partial T} + \frac{\partial}{\partial r_T}\left(\mu(r_T, T)n^Q\right) - \frac{1}{2}\frac{\partial^2}{\partial r_T^2}\left(\sigma^2(r_T, T)n^Q\right) = 0. \tag{19.27}$$

Under the T-forward measure we get different PDEs. Suppose the short rate process under the T-forward measure, Q^T, is

$$\mathrm{d}r_t = \mu^T(r_t, t)\mathrm{d}t + \sigma(r_t, t)\mathrm{d}z_t^T, \tag{19.28}$$

with transition density function $n^T(r_T, T \mid r_t, t)$, where the T-superscript indicates that the function is under the T-forward measure. Then

$$c(r_X, T \mid r_t, t) = B_t(T)\mathbb{E}^T[(r_T - r_X)_+]$$

$$= B_t(T)\int_{-\infty}^{\infty} (r_T - r_X)_+ n^T(r_T, T \mid r_t, t)\mathrm{d}r_T. \tag{19.29}$$

Differentiating twice with respect to r_X,

$$\left.\frac{\partial^2 c(r_X, T \mid r_t, t)}{\partial r_X^2}\right|_{r_X = r_T} = B_t(T)n^T(r_T, T \mid r_t, t). \tag{19.30}$$

This result is the same as the corresponding equity equation, but (19.30) is under Q^T, not Q, and the discount factor is explicitly the T-maturity pure discount bond price.

Under Q^T the Kolmogorov backward equation and the Fokker–Planck PDEs are just as before, but now drifts and densities are under Q^T rather than Q:

$$\frac{1}{2}\sigma^2(r_t, t)\frac{\partial^2 c}{\partial r_t^2} + \mu^T(r_t, t)\frac{\partial c}{\partial r_t} + \frac{\partial c}{\partial t} = 0, \tag{19.31}$$

$$\frac{\partial n^T}{\partial T} + \frac{\partial}{\partial r_T}(\mu^T(r_T, T)n^T) - \frac{1}{2}\frac{\partial^2}{\partial r_T^2}(\sigma^2(r_T, T)n^T) = 0. \tag{19.32}$$

19.3.2 Implied Pricing

Set $\theta(r_T, T \mid r_t, t)$ to be the value at time t of a security that pays off 1 in state (r_T, T) and 0 otherwise. This is the Arrow–Debreu density over states at time T. Let $\delta_{(r_T,T)}(r_t, t)$ be the Dirac delta function. We have (with slight abuse of notation)

$$\theta(r_T, T \mid r_t, t) = B_t(T)\mathbb{E}^T\left[\delta_{(r_T,T)}(r_t, t)\right] \tag{19.33}$$

$$= B_t(T)\int_{-\infty}^{\infty}\delta_{(r_T,T)}(r_t, t)n^T(r_T, T \mid r_t, t)dr_T \tag{19.34}$$

$$= B_t(T)n^T(r_T, T \mid r_t, t) \tag{19.35}$$

$$= \left.\frac{\partial^2 c(r_X, T \mid r_t, t)}{\partial r_X^2}\right|_{r_X=r_T}. \tag{19.36}$$

In the interest rate case, as in the equity case, θ can in principle be derived from option prices.

θ is a price, so it satisfies the backwards equation. We can use this as a basis for an implied pricing method. As in the equity case, numerical solutions will be required. The method we describe in Section 19.4 applies the backwards equation to Arrow–Debreu security prices θ derived (in principle) from caplet prices. It is an extension of the method applicable to equities. It has three distinct differences from the equity case.

1. The discount factor is state dependent.
2. The boundary conditions for the PDE can be simplified.
3. Both local drifts and volatilities need to be extracted from the market data, not just volatilities.

To model the tails of the implied density, canonical tails are used to extrapolate for missing data.

19.4 THE IMPLIED PRICING METHOD

This section is based on Kuan and Webber (98) [344] who describe a grid-based implied pricing method. It is closely related to Andersen (96) [16], extending Andersen's equity-based implied pricing method to interest rates.

Suppose that we know option prices on a grid (r_i, t_j), with maturity times t_j, $j = 0, \ldots, M + 1$, and short rate values r_i, $i = 0, \ldots, N + 1$. The initial yield curve is

$$P_j = B_t(t_j) = e^{-R_j t_j}, \tag{19.37}$$

for initial spot rates R_j. Write

$$P_{i,j} = e^{-r_i(t_{j+1} - t_j)} \tag{19.38}$$

for the time Δt_j discount factor at node (r_i, t_j) on the grid. Initial call values on the grid are $c(r_i, t_j) = c_{i,j|0}$, $i = 0, \ldots, N + 1$, $j = 0, \ldots, M + 1$. Write $\theta_{i,j|0}$, $i = 0, \ldots, N + 1$, $j = 0, \ldots, M + 1$, for Arrow–Debreu prices at time 0; $\theta_{i,j|0}$ pays off 1 if state (r_i, t_j) is reached, 0 otherwise. Then on the gird, since it exhausts the available states,

$$\sum_{i=0}^{N+1} \theta_{i,j|0} = P_j, \qquad\qquad j = 0, \ldots, M + 1,$$

$$c_{i,j|0} = \sum_{k=i+1}^{N+1} \theta_{k,j|0}(r_k - r_i), \quad i = 1, \ldots, N, j = 0, \ldots, M + 1. \tag{19.39}$$

For these conditions to be satisfied we must have

$$c_{N+1,j|0} = 0, \tag{19.40}$$

$$c_{0,j|0} = \sum_{i=0}^{N+1} \theta_{i,j|0} r_i - r_0 P_j, \quad j = 0, \ldots, M + 1, \tag{19.41}$$

so that

$$\theta_{i,j|0} = \frac{(r_i - r_{i-1})c_{i+1,j|0} - 2(r_{i+1} - r_{i-1})c_{i,j|0} + (r_{i+1} - r_i)c_{i-1,j|0}}{(r_{i+1} - r_i)(r_i - r_{i-1})}, \tag{19.42}$$

for $i = 1, \ldots, N$, $j = 0, \ldots, M + 1$ (see Andersen). (19.40) and (19.41) should be regarded as boundary conditions, necessary since we are pricing on a finite grid instead of the entire real line.

Also at the boundaries we have

$$\theta_{N+1,j|0} = \frac{c_{N,j|0}}{r_{N+1} - r_N}, \tag{19.43}$$

$$\theta_{0,j|0} = \frac{c_{0,j|0} - c_{1,j|0}}{r_1 - r_0}. \tag{19.44}$$

Arrow–Debreu Prices on the Grid

Suppose that the short rate process under the accumulator measure Q is

$$dr_t = \mu^Q(r_t, t)dt + \sigma(r_t, t)dz_t^Q, \tag{19.45}$$

and we have a security with payoff H_T at time T. Under Q the price H_t of the security at time t is

$$H_t = \mathbb{E}^Q \left[\exp \left(- \int_t^T r_s ds \right) H_T \right]. \tag{19.46}$$

Applying Feynman–Kac we get the PDE

$$\frac{1}{2} v(r,t) \frac{\partial^2 H}{\partial r^2} + b(r,t) \frac{\partial H}{\partial r} + \frac{\partial H}{\partial t} = rH, \tag{19.47}$$

where

$$v(r,t) = \sigma^2(r,t), \tag{19.48}$$

$$b(r,t) = \mu^Q(r,t), \tag{19.49}$$

with the appropriate boundary conditions.

We can solve for H_t on the grid. Suppose that there is a constant grid spacing,

$$r_{i+1} = r_i + \Delta_r, \quad i = 0, \ldots, N, \tag{19.50}$$

$$t_{j+1} = t_j + \Delta_t, \quad j = 0, \ldots, M. \tag{19.51}$$

We discretise the PDE (19.47). At interior grid points we use standard Crank–Nicolson forward and central difference schemes,

$$\frac{\partial H}{\partial t} \approx \frac{H(r_i, t_{j+1}) - H(r_i, t_j)}{\Delta_t}, \tag{19.52}$$

$$\frac{\partial H}{\partial x} \approx (1 - \Theta) \frac{H(r_{i+1}, t_j) - H(r_{i-1}, t_j)}{2\Delta_r} + \Theta \frac{H(r_{i+1}, t_{j+1}) - H(r_{i-1}, t_{j+1})}{2\Delta_r}, \tag{19.53}$$

$$\frac{\partial^2 H}{\partial x^2} \approx (1 - \Theta) \frac{H(r_{i+1}, t_j) - 2H(r_i, t_j) + H(r_{i-1}, t_j)}{\Delta_r^2}$$
$$+ \Theta \frac{H(r_{i+1}, t_{j+1}) - 2H(r_i, t_{j+1}) + H(r_{i-1}, t_{j+1})}{\Delta_r^2}, \tag{19.54}$$

for $\Theta = \frac{1}{2}$.

At the upper and lower boundaries we use implicit boundary conditions (Vetzal (98) [534], and Chapter 12). At the lower boundary we use

$$\frac{\partial H}{\partial r} \approx \frac{-H(r_2) + 4H(r_1) - 3H(r_0)}{2\Delta_r}, \tag{19.55}$$

$$\frac{\partial^2 H}{\partial r^2} \approx \frac{H(r_2) - 2H(r_1) + H(r_0)}{(\Delta_r)^2}, \tag{19.56}$$

and at the upper boundary we use

$$\frac{\partial H}{\partial r} \approx \frac{H(r_{N-1}) - 4H(r_N) + 3H(r_{N+1})}{2\Delta_r}, \tag{19.57}$$

$$\frac{\partial^2 H}{\partial r^2} \approx \frac{H(r_{N-1}) - 2H(r_N) + H(r_{N+1})}{(\Delta_r)^2}, \tag{19.58}$$

instead of the interior scheme. This is valid if $|\mu(r, t)| \to \infty$ as $r \to \pm\infty$ and $\sigma(r, t)$ does not increase as fast as $|\mu(r, t)|$. We assume that this is the case.

The system can now be put into matrix form. Let M_j be the matrix

$$M_j = \begin{pmatrix} \bar{l}_{0,j} & \bar{c}_{0,j} & \bar{u}_{0,j} & 0 & \cdots & & \cdots & 0 \\ l_{1,j} & c_{1,j} & u_{1,j} & 0 & \cdots & & & \vdots \\ 0 & \ddots & \ddots & \ddots & \ddots & & & \\ \vdots & \ddots & & & & & & \\ & & & & & \ddots & & \vdots \\ & & \ddots & \ddots & \ddots & \ddots & & 0 \\ \vdots & & \cdots & 0 & l_{N,j} & c_{N,j} & u_{N,j} \\ 0 & \cdots & & \cdots & 0 & \underline{l}_{N+1,j} & \underline{c}_{N+1,j} & \underline{u}_{N+1,j} \end{pmatrix}, \tag{19.59}$$

where

$$\alpha = \frac{\Delta_t}{(\Delta_r)^2}, \tag{19.60}$$

$$c_{i,j} = -\alpha v_{i,j}, \tag{19.61}$$

$$u_{i,j} = \frac{\alpha}{2}(v_{i,j} + \Delta_r b_{i,j}), \tag{19.62}$$

$$l_{i,j} = \frac{\alpha}{2}(v_{i,j} - \Delta_r b_{i,j}) \tag{19.63}$$

$$\bar{l}_{0,j} = \frac{\alpha}{2}(v_{0,j} - 3\Delta_r b_{0,j}), \tag{19.64}$$

$$\bar{c}_{0,j} = -\alpha(v_{0,j} - 2\Delta_r b_{0,j}), \tag{19.65}$$

$$\bar{u}_{0,j} = \frac{\alpha}{2}(v_{0,j} - \Delta_r b_{0,j}), \tag{19.66}$$

$$\underline{l}_{N+1,j} = \frac{\alpha}{2}(v_{N+1,j} + \Delta_r b_{N+1,j}), \tag{19.67}$$

$$\underline{c}_{N+1,j} = -\alpha(v_{N+1,j} + 2\Delta_r b_{N+1,j}), \tag{19.68}$$

$$\underline{u}_{N+1,j} = \frac{\alpha}{2}(v_{N+1,j} + 3\Delta_r b_{N+1,j}). \tag{19.69}$$

Set

$$H_j = \begin{pmatrix} H_{0,j} \\ H_{1,j} \\ \vdots \\ H_{N+1} \end{pmatrix}. \tag{19.70}$$

For a matrix Y and a vector y define the product $Y \circ y$,

$$\{Y \circ y\}_{i,j} = Y_{i,j} y_j. \tag{19.71}$$

Substituting out discrete approximations into the PDE and rearranging we obtain the matrix equation

$$(I \circ p_j - (1 - \Theta)M_j)H_j = (\Theta M_j + I)H_{j+1}, \qquad (19.72)$$

where $p_j = (p_{0,j}, \ldots, p_{N+1,j})'$ for $p_{i,j} = 1 + r_i\Delta_t$. This defines the evolution of H_j on the grid.

If v and b were known, then starting from $H_{M+1} \equiv H_T$ we could evolve backwards using the known values of p_j and M_j to find H_j, $j < M + 1$.

Conversely, given H_j, $j = 0, \ldots, M + 1$, the task is to back out the parameters of M_j. M_j is not quite tri-diagonal, but it is easily reduced to tri-diagonal form by eliminating $\bar{u}_{0,j}$ and $\underline{l}_{N+1,j}$.

We apply (19.72) to Arrow–Debreu securities. Define $\theta_{k,l|i,j}$ to be the value in state (i, j) of an Arrow–Debreu security that pays 1 in state (k, l), $l \geq j$. Set

$$\theta_{k,j+1|j} = \begin{pmatrix} \theta_{k,j+1|0,j} \\ \theta_{k,j+1|1,j} \\ \vdots \\ \theta_{k,j+1|N+1,j} \end{pmatrix}, \qquad (19.73)$$

$$\theta_{j+1|j} = \begin{pmatrix} \theta_{1,j+1|1,j} & \theta_{2,j+1|1,j} & \cdots & \theta_{N+1,j+1|1,j} \\ \theta_{1,j+1|2,j} & \theta_{2,j+1|2,j} & \cdots & \theta_{N+1,j+1|2,j} \\ \vdots & \vdots & \ddots & \vdots \\ \theta_{1,j+1|N+1,j} & \theta_{2,j+1|N+1,j} & \cdots & \theta_{N+1,j+1|N+1,j} \end{pmatrix}. \qquad (19.74)$$

Note that $\theta_{j+1|j+1} = I$. Then applying (19.72) to $\theta_{j+1|j}$ we have

$$(I \circ p_j - (1 - \Theta)M_j)\theta_{j+1|j} = \Theta M_j + I. \qquad (19.75)$$

Re-arranging this we have

$$\theta_{j+1|j} = -\frac{\Theta}{1 - \Theta}I + (I \circ p_j - (1 - \Theta)M_j)^{-1}I \circ \left(\frac{\Theta}{1 - \Theta}p_j + 1\right), \qquad (19.76)$$

where, like Andersen, Kuan and Webber assume that $I \circ p_j - (1 - \Theta)M_j$ is invertible.

We now use a recurrence relationship for Arrow–Debreu prices. To get a payoff of 1 in some state i at time t_{j+1}, we can buy a quantity $\theta_{i,j+1|k,j}$ of each security $\theta_{k,j|0}$ for time t_j. This means that

$$(\theta_{j+1|0})^T = (\theta_{j|0})^T \theta_{j+1|j}. \qquad (19.77)$$

Applying $(\theta_{j|0})^T$ to both sides of (19.76) we find

$$(\theta_{j+1|0})^T = -\frac{\Theta}{1 - \Theta}(\theta_{j|0})^T + (\theta_{j|0})^T(I \circ p_j - (1 - \Theta)M_j)^{-1}I \circ \left(\frac{\Theta}{1 - \Theta}p_j + 1\right). \qquad (19.78)$$

Re-arrange (19.78) to get

$$M_j^T \varphi_j = \frac{1}{1 - \Theta}(I \circ p_j)\varphi_j - \frac{1}{1 - \Theta}\theta_{j|0}, \qquad (19.79)$$

where q_j and φ_j are

$$q_j = \{q_{i,j}\}, \quad q_{i,j} = \left(\frac{\Theta}{1-\Theta}p_{i,j} + 1\right)^{-1}, \tag{19.80}$$

$$\varphi_j = (I \circ q_j)((1-\Theta)\theta_{j+1|0} + \Theta\theta_{j|0}). \tag{19.81}$$

If $\theta_{j|0}$, $j = 1, \ldots, M+1$, are known, then both φ_j and $(1/(1-\Theta))(I \circ p_j)\varphi_j - (1/(1-\Theta))\theta_{j|0}$ are known. We can now solve for M_j.

Set

$$v_j = \begin{pmatrix} v_{0,j} \\ v_{1,j} \\ \vdots \\ v_{N+1,j} \end{pmatrix}, \qquad b_j = \begin{pmatrix} b_{0,j} \\ b_{1,j} \\ \vdots \\ b_{N+1,j} \end{pmatrix}, \tag{19.82}$$

to be the vectors of local volatilities and drifts at time t_j. Define

$$A_j = \frac{\alpha}{2} \begin{pmatrix} 1 & 1 & 0 & \cdots & & & \cdots & 0 \\ -2 & -2 & 1 & \ddots & & & & \vdots \\ 1 & 1 & -2 & 1 & & & & \\ 0 & 0 & 1 & -2 & 1 & & & \\ \vdots & & \ddots & & & \ddots & & \vdots \\ & & & 1 & -2 & 1 & 0 & 0 \\ & & & 1 & -2 & 1 & 1 \\ \vdots & & & \ddots & 1 & -2 & -2 \\ 0 & \cdots & & & \cdots & 0 & 1 & 1 \end{pmatrix} \tag{19.83}$$

and

$$B_j = \frac{\alpha}{2}\Delta_r \begin{pmatrix} -3 & -1 & 0 & \cdots & & & \cdots & 0 \\ 4 & 0 & -1 & \ddots & & & & \vdots \\ -1 & 1 & 0 & -1 & & & & \\ 0 & 0 & 1 & 0 & -1 & & & \\ \vdots & & \ddots & & & \ddots & & \vdots \\ & & & 1 & 0 & -1 & 0 & 0 \\ & & & 1 & 0 & -1 & 1 \\ \vdots & & & \ddots & 1 & 0 & -4 \\ 0 & \cdots & & & \cdots & 0 & 1 & 3 \end{pmatrix}. \tag{19.84}$$

M_j can be decomposed in terms of A_j and B_j. In fact we have immediately

$$M_j^T = A_j \circ v_j + B_j \circ b_j. \tag{19.85}$$

Now substitute for M_j in (19.79). Note that

$$M_j^T \varphi_j = (A_j \circ v_j + B_j \circ b_j)\varphi_j = (A_j \circ \varphi_j)v_j + (B_j \circ \varphi_j)b_j, \tag{19.86}$$

so we obtain

$$(A_j \circ \varphi_j)v_j + (B_j \circ \varphi_j)b_j = \frac{1}{1-\Theta}(I \circ p_j)\varphi_j - \theta_{j|0}. \tag{19.87}$$

The values of $A_j \circ \varphi_j$, $B_j \circ \varphi_j$ and $(1/(1 - \Theta))(I \circ p_j)\varphi_j - \theta_{j|0}$ are known, so (19.87) is a system of $N + 2$ equations in $2(N + 2)$ unknowns. To solve we need an additional $N + 2$ equations.

One way of obtaining a second set of equations is by doubling the time step. Set $\underline{\Delta}_t = 2\Delta_t$ and define

$$\underline{\theta}_{i,j|0} = \theta_{i,j|0}, \tag{19.88}$$

$$\underline{\theta}_{i,j+1|0} = \theta_{i,j+2|0}. \tag{19.89}$$

Now repeat the procedure described above, using underlined variables instead of the un-underlined so that v_j and b_j are estimated over two time steps instead of one. We obtain

$$(\underline{A}_j \circ \underline{\varphi}_j)v_j + (\underline{B}_j \circ \underline{\varphi}_j)b_j = \frac{1}{1 - \Theta}(I \circ \underline{p}_j)\underline{\varphi}_j - \underline{\theta}_{j|0}, \tag{19.90}$$

where $\underline{A}_j$, $\underline{B}_j$, $\underline{\varphi}_j$ and $\underline{p}_j$ are found over two time steps. This gives a second set of $N + 2$ equations. $A_j \circ \varphi_j$, $B_j \circ \varphi_j$, $\underline{A}_j \circ \underline{\varphi}_j$ and $\underline{B}_j \circ \underline{\varphi}_j$ are almost tri-diagonal, so it might appear that the system can be solved using standard methods.

In principle, then, it seems possible to back out local volatilities and drifts from initial values of Arrow–Debreu securities, conditional on having a complete set of option prices on the grid. This turns out to be very difficult to implement.

When $\Theta = 1$ the derivation of (19.87) might appear to fail. In fact, cancellations occur and we obtain a result related to Jamshidian's forward induction method.

Set $\Theta = 1$ in equation (19.75). Simplifications occur in the procedure described above and instead of (19.78) we obtain

$$\theta_{j+1|0} = (M_j + I)^T (I \circ p_j)(\theta_{j|0})^T. \tag{19.91}$$

Writing this out in full we have

$$\theta_{i,j+1|0} = \sum_k \theta_{k,j|0}(1 + r_k \Delta_t)q_{k,i}, \tag{19.92}$$

where $q_{k,i} = (M_j + I)_{i,k}$ and the summation is over all nodes (k, j) such that $q_{k,i}$ is non-zero. This is simply the forward induction scheme of Jamshidian (91) [309]. It can be verified that the $q_{k,i}$ correspond exactly to the first-order approximation of the standard Hull and White probabilities, as described by Vetzal (98) [534].

Equity Illustration Continued

We illustrate the numerical method with an equity application incorporating the implied boundary condition. We find that even in this case there is evidence of numerical instability, and in this benchmark case local volatilities are not exactly recovered by the discrete approximation.

We use the implied volatility surface shown in (19.2). We saw earlier that we can recover local volatilities directly. We can also compute Arrow–Debreu prices explicitly. This enables us to illustrate the effectiveness of the method in a benchmark case. Using the implied volatilities we directly compute option prices, and from these compute Arrow–Debreu prices on the grid from (19.42). Figure 19.4 shows Arrow–Debreu prices found in this way. The density is more compact at small times to maturity, spreading out as time to maturity increases.

Although qualitatively correct, errors have been introduced during the numerical procedure. Figure 19.5 shows the difference between the density in Figure 19.4 and

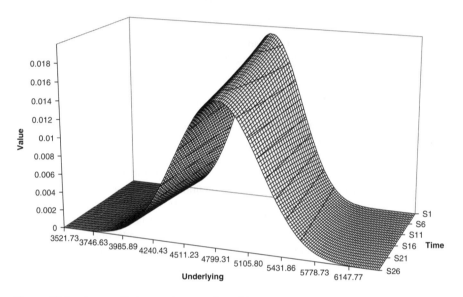

Figure 19.4 Arrow–Debreu prices on the grid

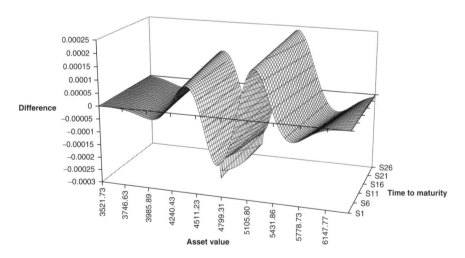

Figure 19.5 Errors in the Arrow–Debreu prices on the grid

the directly computed density. There are two types of error: a longer wavelength error, and a spike at around $S = 4800$. This leads to errors in the computed local drifts and volatilities.

Local drifts and volatilities, computed on the grid, are shown in Figures 19.6 and 19.7. Figure 19.7 should be compared with Figure 19.3, the exact local volatility function found earlier. The errors in the local volatilities found from the grid are shown in Figure 19.8.

The errors are significant as one moves away from the money. Also at around $S = 4800$ there is an error spike.

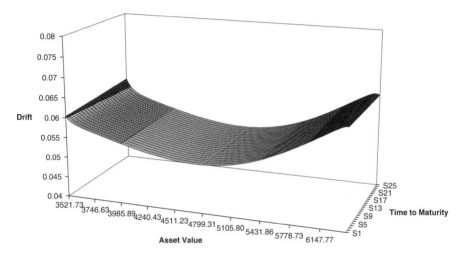

Figure 19.6   Local drifts, computed on the grid

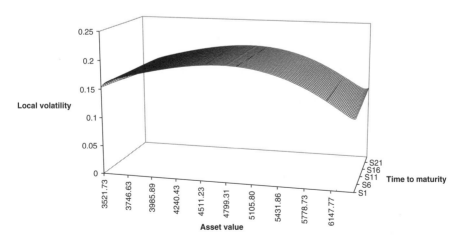

Figure 19.7   Local volatilities, computed on the grid

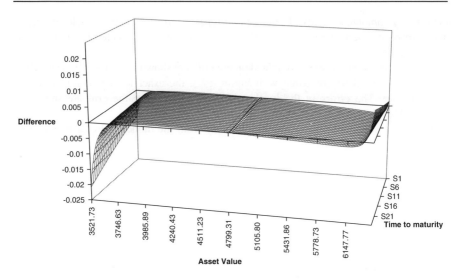

Figure 19.8   Errors in the local volatilities

This benchmark illustration was based on having a full grid of option prices or implied volatilities. In practice one needs to interpolate between a comparatively sparse data set and to extrapolate into the tails away from the money.

The procedure is not stable near the extremes. The PDF is virtually (and in practical terms, actually) zero at the extremes. Taking the second derivatives is not robust and trinomial inversion is not stable.

The way around the problem is to employ various types of regularisation.

19.5   REGULARISATION FUNCTIONS

We have seen that although the method described in Section 19.4 can theoretically back out implied densities, in practice it is unstable. There are two sets of problems.

The first is the regularisation issue concerned with numerical instabilities in going from a function to its second derivative.

The second set of problems concerns the range over which data are available. In the equity and FX markets it may be possible to find call or put prices for deep in-the-money or out-of-the-money options. In the interest rate markets one is unlikely to be able to find reliable prices for caps or swaptions far into or out of the money. This means that the range of exercise prices at which one has prices may be quite restricted, and constitutes only a limited subset of the range over which the pricing density is significantly non-zero. In such a situation one may decide that an implied pricing method is an inappropriate pricing tool. However, as we see in Section 19.6, by making assumptions about the tail behaviour of the short rate process it is possible to extend the implied pricing method outside the range for which observations are available.

The first set of problems can be addressed using standard techniques. These methods, a review of their use in the literature, and some applications to equity and FX examples, are discussed in Levin (98) [350]. Another review is the article by Cont (98) [140]. Jackwerth and Rubinstein (96) [307] also compare different regularisation schemes.

19.5.1 A Regularisation Technique

Given Arrow–Debreu security prices one can in principle back out v_j and b_j, $j = 1, \ldots, M - 1$. Since this does not work, v_j and b_j are instead chosen to optimise a criterion that smooths out irregularities in the data. Set

$$v = (v_0, \ldots, v_{M+1}), \tag{19.93}$$

$$b = (b_0, \ldots, b_{M+1}). \tag{19.94}$$

v and b are matrices of local volatilities and drifts. Suppose observed caplet prices are $\hat{c}(r_k, T_k)$, $k = 1, \ldots, K$. This need not be a complete set with one price for every point on the grid. Define

$$D(v, b) = \sum_{k=1}^{K} (\hat{c}(r_k, T_k) - c(r_k, T_k))^2, \tag{19.95}$$

where $c(r_k, T_k)$ are model prices. D is the squared error between market prices and model prices, called the discrepancy function.

One criterion might be to choose (v, b) to minimise $D(v, b)$. Unfortunately this is of no use; we can always find many pairs (v, b) for which $D = 0$. Instead we define an auxiliary regularisation function. Set

$$(v, b) = \arg \min_{v, b \in \mathcal{F}} \{D(v, b) + \alpha \Omega(v, b)\}, \tag{19.96}$$

where Ω is the regularisation function and α is a regularisation parameter that determines the relative importance of D and Ω. $\mathcal{F}$ is a function space; for instance, $\mathcal{F}$ could be a space of splines. The choice of Ω is critical. One choice, adapted from the equity case, is

$$\Omega_1(v, b) = \omega_1 \int ||\nabla v|| \, \mathrm{d}F + \omega_2 \int ||\nabla b|| \, \mathrm{d}F, \tag{19.97}$$

where $\omega = (\omega_1, \omega_2)$ is a constant weighting vector, ∇ is the gradient operator, $|| \cdot ||$ is a norm on $\mathcal{F}$, and F is a measure over (r_X, T)-space. Ω_1 attempts to make the (v, b) surface as flat as possible. This is not suitable for the interest rate case. If r_t is mean reverting, b will not be flat but sloping. Other possible regularisation criteria are mentioned below.

Equation (19.96) attempts to match prices as closely as possible while requiring v and b to be as 'regular' as possible, according to Ω. α determines whether it is more important to match to prices or to be regular.

Using a regularisation function solves the instability problem. We can now recursively generate Arrow–Debreu security prices, and hence caplet prices, using (19.96), optimising to find (v, b). The optimisation is now well-posed and stable. Our problem now becomes that of deciding upon the form of Ω that best reflects the market properties of (v, b).

19.5.2 Examples of Regularisation Functions

Several regularisation functions Ω have been suggested for use in implied pricing. Most applications have been in the equity market. In this case only the local volatility function $\sigma(S)$ needs to be recovered. Of course one can simply apply the functions listed below to both v and b.

- Lagnado and Osher (97) [347]: A 'flatness' criterion,

$$\Omega_2(\sigma) = \int |\nabla\sigma(S)|^2 dS. \tag{19.98}$$

- Adams and Van Deventer (94) [6]: A 'curvature' criterion,

$$\Omega_3(\sigma) = \int |\nabla^2\sigma(S)|^2 dS. \tag{19.99}$$

- Rubinstein (94) [462], Jackwerth and Rubinstein (96) [307]: The maximum entropy principle,

$$\Omega_4(\sigma) = \int \sigma(S) \ln \frac{\sigma(S)}{\tilde{\sigma}(S)} dS, \tag{19.100}$$

  for some reference function $\tilde{\sigma}(S)$.

Maximum entropy regularisation has been discussed in a number of papers, including Stutzer (96) [509], Avellaneda (97) [31] and Avellaneda et al. (96) [32]. Levin suggests that the reference function, which serves as an approximation to the local volatility surface, could be chosen to be either a constant equal to an estimated historical volatility, or else a Black–Scholes implied volatility surface.

The Adams and Van Deventer curvature criterion seems suitable for the interest rate case.

The basic criterion (19.96) can be modified in several ways. Rubinstein (94) [462] and Jackwerth and Rubinstein (96) [307] note that prices can be regarded as being observed with a known error, δ, due to a bid–ask spread. There is no point in trying to reduce the discrepancy to less than the magnitude of the observation error. We should instead estimate (v, b) by the optimisation

$$(v, b, \alpha) = \arg \min_{v,b \in \mathcal{F}, \alpha > 0} \{f(v, b) \mid D(v, b) \leq \delta\}, \tag{19.101}$$

for some discrepancy tolerance parameter δ, where

$$f(v, b) = \Omega(v, b), \tag{19.102}$$

as usual. Using (19.101) we get smoother results than using (19.96) since we no longer require prices to be matched as closely.

Note that if v and b have functional forms specified by some interest rate model, depending on a parameter set θ, then the model can be calibrated by solving

$$\theta = \arg\min_{\theta}\{f(v(\theta), b(\theta)) \mid D(v(\theta), b(\theta)) \le \delta\}, \qquad (19.103)$$

or a similar modification of one of the alternative criteria. It is not unusual in practice to set

$$\theta = \arg\min_{\theta} D(v(\theta), b(\theta)). \qquad (19.104)$$

The functional form of the coefficients of the interest rate model itself already implicitly provides a degree of smoothing.

The criteria described here should be compared with those mentioned in Chapter 15 where the problem was fit to the yield curve. The Adams and Van Deventer criterion was first met there.

19.5.3 Alternative Approaches to Interpolation

The scheme discussed in the previous section effectively interpolates directly on the local drift and volatilities b and v. Instead it is possible to interpolate on other objects. Figure 19.9 schematically compares interpolation at different levels of a model. Given

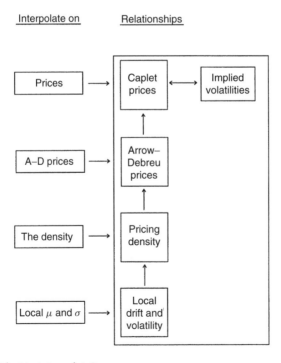

Figure 19.9 What to interpolate?

an object lower down the scale, it is easy to work upwards. Working down the scale is hard. By choosing to interpolate on local drifts and volatilities one can easily derive all other aspects of the interest rate model. The cost one pays is having to derive prices numerically.

It is possible to interpolate elsewhere on the scale. There seems to be little point in interpolating directly on prices. Although one may get good prices for instruments identical in form to those one is interpolating between, it will not in general be possible to price other categories of instrument.

In this section we focus on interpolating the pricing density. Various approximations to the density function have been tried. Perturbed normal densities are a popular choice.

We could also interpolate on Arrow–Debreu security prices. This is a valid technique, but we shall see that it is a special case of approximating to a density.

If we interpolate on a density we have to specify the measure the density is from. For instance, under the T-forward measure we have

$$c(r_X, T \mid r_t, t) = B_t(T)\mathbb{E}^T[(r_T - r_X)_+] \tag{19.105}$$

$$= B_t(T) \int_{-\infty}^{\infty} (r_T - r_X)_+ n^T(r_T, T \mid r_t, t) dr_T. \tag{19.106}$$

Under the objective measure we have the Arrow–Debreu density, $\theta(r_T, T \mid r_t, t)$,

$$c(r_X, T \mid r_t, t) = \int_{-\infty}^{\infty} (r_T - r_X)_+ \theta(r_T, T \mid r_t, t) dr_T. \tag{19.107}$$

Suppose that there is a numeraire G_t whose associated measure has a density n^G which is either normal or log-normal. Then

$$c(r_X, T \mid r_t, t) = \int_{-\infty}^{\infty} (r_T - r_X)_+ \frac{G_t}{G_T} n^G(r_T, T \mid r_t, t) dr_T, \tag{19.108}$$

where n^G is (log-)normal. Set $n^K = G_t/G_T$. n^K measures the extent by which the Arrow–Debreu density θ is perturbed away from (log-)normality. If there are grounds for supposing that θ is close to being (log-)normal it may be sensible to try to estimate n^K directly.

Interpolation methods in the literature include splines applied to the density n^Q (Mayhew (95) [384], (96) [385], Rubinstein (94) [462], Longstaff (95) [362]), or to the implied volatility surface (Andersen (96) [16]). Ait-Sahalia and Lo (95) [10] use a kernel estimator of the n^Q. Shimko (93) [491] and Malz (97) [378] approximated the implied volatility smile by a quadratic polynomial.

The kernel approximation method was used by Rubinstein (98) [463], who employed an Edgeworth expansion of the Arrow–Debreu density $\theta(S_T, T \mid S_t, t)$ (in the equity case) about a log-normal density to match the third and fourth moments of the underlying density.[1] Corrado and Su (97a) [142], (97b) [143] used a Gram–Charlier expansion.[2]

---

[1] Jarrow and Rudd (82) [317] introduced the Edgeworth expansion as an approximation method in option pricing.

[2] This is supposed to be more robust for the implied pricing problem (Rubinstein (98) [463]).

Abken *et al.* (96) [2] and Madan and Milne (94) [373] used a truncated Hermite polynomial expansion of $\theta(S_T, T \mid S_t, t)$, reporting that a fourth-order approximation gave good results. An expansion of this sort has also been used by Ait-Sahalia in a slightly different context.

A popular approach has been to fix upon a functional form for the underlying density, hoping that the form chosen will be sufficiently flexible to match the pricing density. Some of the functional forms used in the literature for this purpose include a Bessel density (Longstaff (95) [363]), a mixture of log-normals (Bahra (96) [44], Melick and Thomas (97) [390]), a bivariate normal distribution (Soderlind and Svensson (96) [498]), a Burr type III density (Sherrick *et al.* (96) [490]), and student and stable distributions (Blattberg and Gonedes (74) [76]). See also Bookstaber and McDonald (87) [81].

19.5.4 Perturbed Normal Densities

We describe Edgeworth and Gram–Charlier expansions, and Hermite polynomial expansions, as approximations to a density function. The advantage of these methods is that they enable higher moments, such as skewness and kurtosis, to be fitted quite easily.

The Edgeworth Expansion

Suppose that a density p has cumulants c_i, $i = 1, \ldots$, and moments μ_i, $i = 1, \ldots$ Cumulants and moments are related. For instance, $c_2 = \mu_2, c_3 = \mu_3, c_4 = \mu_4 - 3(\mu_2)^2$, *et cetera*. We can relate two densities by comparing their cumulants.

One performs a series expansion. Suppose we have a reference density p with an 'easy' functional form, and another density q with specified cumulants. These are treated as parameters to be fitted to market data. The Edgeworth expansion (Jarrow and Rudd (82) [317]) expresses q as a perturbation of p,

$$q = p + \frac{c_2(p) - c_2(q)}{2!} \frac{\partial^2 p}{\partial x^2} - \frac{c_3(p) - c_3(q)}{3!} \frac{\partial^3 p}{\partial x^3}$$
$$+ \frac{c_4(p) - c_4(q) + 3(c_2(p) - c_2(q))^2}{4!} \frac{\partial^4 p}{\partial x^4} + \varepsilon. \tag{19.109}$$

The expansion can be truncated. If we truncate to fourth order, then q is determined by three parameters, $c_2(q)$, $c_3(q)$ and $c_4(q)$. If the cumulants and the functional form of the reference density p are known (as they are if p is normal or log-normal) then we obtain an approximation to q. For instance, when $p \equiv n$ is normal we have

$$q(x) = n(x) \left(1 + \mu_3(x^3 - 3x) \right.$$
$$+ \frac{1}{4!}(\mu_4 - 3)(x^4 - 6x^2 + 3)$$
$$\left. + \frac{1}{5!}\frac{5}{3}(\mu_3)^2(x^5 - 10x^3 + 15x) + \cdots \right). \tag{19.110}$$

The Gram–Charlier expansion truncates the series (19.109) to third order instead of fourth order.

Hermite Polynomial Expansion

Hermite polynomials are an orthogonal basis for a particular function space with an inner product determined by the normal density function. This makes them a natural choice for expanding out the perturbing factor $n^K = G_t/G_T$.

Suppose we have

$$c(r_X, T \mid r_t, t) = \int (r_T - r_X)_+ \frac{G_t}{G_T} n^G(r_T, T \mid r_t, t) dr_T, \qquad (19.111)$$

where n^G is a normal density. In a suitable space of functions we can define an inner product $\langle f, g \rangle$ between two functions $f(x)$ and $g(x)$ as

$$\langle f, g \rangle = \int f(x)g(x)n(x)dx, \qquad (19.112)$$

where $n(x)$ is a normal density. We can apply this to the case where $f(x) = (x - r_X)_+$ and $g(x) = G_t/G_T$. Hermite polynomials are an orthogonal basis with respect to this inner product. The first five Hermite polynomials are

$$h_0(x) = 1, \qquad (19.113)$$

$$h_1(x) = x, \qquad (19.114)$$

$$h_2(x) = \frac{1}{\sqrt{2}}(x^2 - 1), \qquad (19.115)$$

$$h_3(x) = \frac{1}{\sqrt{6}}(x^3 - 3x), \qquad (19.116)$$

$$h_4(x) = \frac{1}{\sqrt{24}}(x^4 - 6x^2 + 3), \, et \, cetera. \qquad (19.117)$$

We can expand out the T-forward density $n^T(x) = \theta(x)/B_t(T) = (1/B_t(T))g(x)n(x)$ in this basis, where $g(x) = \Sigma_{i=0}^{\infty} b_i h_i(x)$. Including just the terms up to $i = 4$ we obtain (Abken et al. (96a) [1] (96b) [2]):

$$n^T(x) = \frac{1}{B_t(T)} g(x)n(x) \qquad (19.118)$$

$$= \frac{1}{B_t(T)} n(x) \left[b_0 - \frac{b_2}{\sqrt{2}} + \frac{3b_4}{\sqrt{24}} + \left(b_1 - \frac{3b_3}{\sqrt{6}} \right) x \right. $$
$$\left. + \left(\frac{b_2}{\sqrt{2}} - \frac{6b_4}{\sqrt{24}} \right) x^2 + \frac{b_3}{\sqrt{6}} x^3 + \frac{b_4}{\sqrt{24}} x^4 + \ldots \right]. \qquad (19.119)$$

It is now straightforward to back out the parameters b_i, $i = 0, \ldots, 4$, by calibrating to option prices. Once we have found $n^T(x)$, and hence $\theta(x) = B_t(T)n^T(x)$, we can price anything, consistent with the options we calibrated to.

Of course, even if we know the density this is not the same as knowing the underlying process. To find the local drifts and volatilities it is still necessary to implicitly solve a PDE. However, it is quite feasible to price using the density, without knowing the underlying process. This is true implied pricing. One feels slightly uneasy with this; after all, one would like to explain where the density comes from, but it does not make the procedure invalid.

19.6 PATCHING TAILS ONTO PRICING DENSITIES

We have seen that the tails of an implied pricing method pose particular problems. There may be missing data; we may have 'reliable' data only in a limited range of exercise rates or prices. Kuan and Webber (98) [344] proposed a tail method that extrapolates into the tails so as to sidestep, if not to solve, this type of problem.

Suppose that in some range of exercises rates, $[r_a, r_b]$, $0 < a < b < N + 1$, we have a set of caplet prices for every maturity time and every exercise price in the range, but we have no prices at grid points outside that range. From these prices we can in principle derive Arrow–Debreu security prices $\theta_{i,j|0}$, $i \in [a, b]$, and hence discrete densities for the same range. By imposing tails belonging to a certain canonical three-parameter family of densities, Kuan and Webber extrapolate the density across the entire grid $[r_0, r_{N+1}]$, and hence obtain extrapolated Arrow–Debreu security prices and caplet prices. The family of tail densities is canonical in the sense that, in the extremes, the tails of any continuous density resemble those of one of the members of this family.

This is a very natural procedure. In the absence of other information, one may suppose that the tails die away in a uniform fashion, according to the canonical family of distributions. The three parameters will be chosen so that the tails have the correct probability mass, and that both caplet prices and Arrow–Debreu security prices are matched at the boundary of the known region. In other contexts it is possible that other assumptions might be appropriate. For instance, Shimko (93) [491] and Andersen (96) [16] assume that in the tails volatility—local or Black–Scholes implied—is constant. This may be appropriate for equities, but for interest rates, where it may be plausible to assume that the distribution is bounded (Chapter 6), it may be inappropriate.

The choice of this particular extrapolation method has consequences for the values of caplets in the tails, and for the inferred values of local drifts and volatilities. Kuan and Webber argued that this choice of extrapolation method is no worse than others which could be devised, and has the advantages of fitting to known market data and at the same time being asymptotically correct. That is, if the upper boundary r_b of the known region $[r_a, r_b]$ were to increase, then in the limit the tailing procedure would yield the correct tails of the underlying distribution.

GPD tails will be pasted onto the density functions. There are three parameters for each tail. These are chosen so that on each boundary of $[r_a, r_b]$ we match

- the probability mass in the tail,
- the Arrow–Debreu security price,
- the caplet price.

The general Pareto distribution (GPD) with tail parameter τ and location and scale parameters μ and σ is non-zero on an interval $[\mu, r_{max})$,

$$N(r \mid \mu, \sigma, \tau) = \begin{cases} 1 - \left(1 + \tau \dfrac{r - \mu}{\sigma}\right)^{-1/\tau}, & r \in [\mu, r_{max}), \\ 1, & r > r_{max}, \\ 0, & r < \mu, \end{cases} \qquad (19.120)$$

where

$$r_{max} = \begin{cases} \infty, & \tau > 0, \\ \mu - \sigma/\tau, & \tau < 0. \end{cases}$$

($\tau = 0$ is treated as a limiting value, as in Chapter 6.) The general Pareto density is

$$n(r \mid \mu, \sigma, \tau) = \begin{cases} \dfrac{1}{\sigma}\left(1 + \tau \dfrac{r - \mu}{\sigma}\right)^{-(\tau+1)/\tau}, & r \in [\mu, r_{max}), \\ 0, & r \notin [\mu, r_{max}). \end{cases} \qquad (19.121)$$

19.6.1 Pasting on the Tails

We consider only the upper tail. The lower tail is handled analogously. We consider options maturing at time t_j. At the upper boundary r_b we know the caplet price, $c(r_b, t_j)$, the Arrow–Debreu security price,

$$\theta_{b,j|0} = \left. \frac{\partial^2 c(r_X, t_j \mid r_t, t)}{\partial r_X^2} \right|_{r_X = r_b}, \qquad (19.122)$$

and the tail probability mass,

$$1 - \left. \frac{\partial c(r_X, t_j \mid r_t, t)}{\partial r_X} \right|_{r_X = r_b}. \qquad (19.123)$$

If the state space were continuous the parameters (μ, σ, τ) for a general Pareto density $n^j(r \mid \mu, \sigma, \tau)$ would need to satisfy the relationships

$$B_t(t_j) \int_{r_b}^{\infty} n^j(r) dr = 1 - \left. \frac{\partial c(r_X, t_j \mid r_t, t)}{\partial r_X} \right|_{r_X = r_b}, \qquad (19.124)$$

$$B_t(t_j) n_j(r_b) = \left. \frac{\partial^2 c(r_X, t_j \mid r_t, t)}{\partial r_X^2} \right|_{r_X = r_b}, \qquad (19.125)$$

$$B_t(t_j) \int_{r_b}^{\infty} n^j(r)(r - r_b) dr = c(r_b, t_j). \qquad (19.126)$$

On a grid the state space is discrete. We assign a probability mass $n_{i,j} = n^j(r_i \mid \tau, \mu, \sigma)$ to the grid point (r_i, t_j), for $i > b$, and find parameters (μ, σ, τ) for a general Pareto density $n^j(r \mid \mu, \sigma, \tau)$ such that

$$B_t(t_j) \sum_{i=b+1}^{N+1} n_{i,j} = 1 - \left. \frac{\partial c(r_X, t_j \mid r_t, t)}{\partial r_X} \right|_{r_X = r_b}, \qquad (19.127)$$

$$B_t(t_j)n_{b,j} = \left.\frac{\partial^2 c(r_X, t_j \mid r_t, t)}{\partial r_X^2}\right|_{r_X = r_b}, \tag{19.128}$$

$$B_t(t_j) \sum_{i=b+1}^{N+1} n_{i,j}(r_i - r_b) = c(r_b, t_j). \tag{19.129}$$

Several points arise. First, bond prices $B_t(t_j)$ are recovered, so that the procedure matches the current term structure. Second, the procedure as described is carried out one maturity at a time. This is unsatisfactory; one would like to regularise across maturities. The method can be extended to do this, but we do not describe this here. Third, as a computational point, if $\tau < 0$ the grid can be restricted to the range $[r_0, r_{max}]$, since the density has zero mass for $r > r_{max}$.

It may happen that we can observe some data in the tails. Now, instead of exactly matching the option price at level r_b, we can choose parameters to minimise a discrepancy between model prices and observed prices. For instance, suppose at maturity time t_j we can see K prices $\hat{c}(r_k, t_j)$, $k = 1, \ldots, K$, where $r_k > r_b$. Set

$$D = \sum_{k=1}^{K} (\hat{c}(r_k, t_j) - c(r_k, t_j))^2, \tag{19.130}$$

where

$$c(r_k, t_j) = B_t(t_j) \sum_{i=k+1}^{N+1} n_{i,j}(r_i - r_k) \tag{19.131}$$

is the model price on the grid. Now we can choose (μ, σ, τ) to match the probability mass and Arrow–Debreu security price, and to minimise D.

Conclusion

Where practicable one wants to employ some form of implied pricing. Whenever one calibrates to a term structure of rates or volatilities one is implying pricing in some sense. Calibrating to a volatility smile is harder, but possible.

The main problems in the interest rate world are (a) extrapolating from insufficient data in the tails and (b) the numerical instabilities encountered in backing out implied densities and local drifts and volatilities. Nevertheless, by pasting on tail densities and using appropriate regularisation techniques to reduce instabilities, it is possible to price using implied methods.

Afterword

Interest rate modelling is a vital and growing area of research in financial mathematics. A successful model, with a successful implementation, allows derivatives to be valued and hedged, increasing the confidence with which instruments may be bought and sold. Advances in modelling techniques enable increased financial liquidity, as more subtle and complex risks can be hedged with confidence. Risk managers who wish to understand how portfolio values may vary in the future will be able to put limits on these values with greater confidence as model sophistication increases.

The future of interest rate modelling looks bright. While recent reaction to market upsets has been to scale back on exotic and illiquid instruments, the need to fully understand interest rate movements and introduce solid risk management procedures has correspondingly grown. As the global market becomes more and more connected, it is increasingly realised that not to hedge is in fact to speculate. While over-bold market participants may crash and burn, ignorant ones will without doubt lose their shirts. In the arms race that is the financial market, no institution can be without its basic weaponry. Many financial disasters of recent times would have been avoided if all parties concerned had a good understanding of deal valuation, and applied it.

There are several promising directions for the future; we expect to see rapid development of models and of implementation techniques. The development of interest rate modelling has been facilitated by the parallel increase and availability of computing power. Models have been able to become more complex, to better represent what is found in the market. A wider range of instruments is now cheaply and readily available. We expect this trend to continue.

On the theoretical side we expect to see developments in market models that might allow different categories of instrument to be consistently priced. Factor approaches to HJM/BGM models may develop. Increasing use may be made of random field models. With increasing liquidity and availability of instruments, techniques to enable model-free pricing and hedging—finding hedges and values directly from existing market prices—may begin to emerge. In another direction, models may be found that incorporate economic dynamics in a sensible way; perhaps including the explicit modelling of the monetary authorities' reaction functions.

More generally we may see explanations, and numerically implementable models, of differential credit risk, market micro-structure including the bid-ask spread, the early exercise behaviour in the market of American and Bermudan instruments, and the explicit modelling of market risk premia. We may see practical models of the exact shape and behaviour of the components of yield curve movements and their relation to market expectations and events.

On the implementation side we are sure to see continued development of numerical valuation methods. As computing power increases finite difference methods are likely to see greater use for valuing factor models. Theoretical and numerical advances may allow Monte Carlo methods to be applied routinely to American and Bermudan options. Lattice methods, particularly non-recombining lattices, seem likely to be increasingly used.

And what of model feedback? At the start of this book we noted the existence of trading models. If a proprietary trading model consistently generated abnormal returns, the behaviour of the market would fundamentally change if the model was (a) correct and (b) published. There is feedback of another sort already apparent in the market. Valuation models implicitly assume that the value of the underlying determine the value of the derivative, and not the other way around. However there are many instances where the existence of derivatives, and the strategies used to hedge them, might conceivably influence the underlying market; one thinks of the effects in the FX markets of hedging strategies for barrier options. In the bond market there are institutional reasons why there is likely to be excess demand for bonds of particular maturities. If there is only a certain amount of liquidity in the market, what determines where it goes? Perhaps we shall see the development of viable valuation models that incorporate these effects.

Will models popular today have the same far-reaching consequences as the Black–Scholes model did over two decades ago? Perhaps they will, but it seems unlikely that the last word has been said in the discourse of interest rate modelling.

Notation

a.a.	Almost always.
a.e.	Almost everywhere.
a.s.	Almost surely.
A	The generator of an Itō process.
$\arg\max_\theta f(\theta)$	The value of θ that maximises f.
$\arg\min_\theta f(\theta)$	The value of θ that minimises f.
$B_t(T)$	The price at time t of a pure discount bond maturing at time T with value 1. Also written $P_t(T)$ or $P(t, T)$ or $\delta(T - t)$.
$\mathbb{C}$	The complex numbers.
C^+	The positive valued continuous functions on $\mathbb{R}$.
corr	The correlation function.
cov	The covariance function.
Δf	An increment in the value of f.
$\delta(t)$	The t-maturity discount factor.
dz_t	An infinitesimal increment to a Wiener process.
$\mathbb{E}_t$	The expectation operator, conditional on $\mathcal{F}_t$.
$\mathbb{E}^x$	The expectation operator, conditional on $X_0 = x$.
$f(t)$, *et cetera*	A deterministic function of time.
$f(t \mid \theta)$	A function f depending on a parameter set θ.
$f_s(t, T)$	The forward rate at time s for the period $[t, T]$.
$f_t(T)$	The instantaneous forward rate at time t for time T.
F_T or F^T or Q^T	The T-forward measure.
$\mathbb{F}^\infty$	The ∞-forward measure.
$\mathcal{F}$	A filtration. Sometimes, a σ-algebra.
$\mathcal{F}_t$	The event set for time t, a σ-algebra.
i	The square root of -1.
i.i.d.	Independent, identically distributed.
$I_A(x)$	The indicator function with value 1 if $x \in A$, zero otherwise. Also written $I_{x \in A}$.
$\mu_t(T)$ or $\mu(t, T)$	The drift at time t of the spot rate maturing at time T.
$\mathbb{N}$	The natural numbers.
$N(d)$	The normal distribution function.

$N(0, 1)$	The standard normal distribution, with mean 0 and variance 1.
$n(\mu, \sigma^2)$	The normal density function, with mean μ and variance σ^2.
$O(\varepsilon)$	Order ε.
ρ	Usually, the correlation coefficent.
$P, \mathbb{P}$	A pricing measure, often the EMM.
$\Pr(A)$	The probability of the event A.
$\emptyset$	The empty set.
$Q, \mathbb{Q}$	A measure, often the objective probability measure.
$\mathbb{Q}$	The rational numbers.
$\text{Re}(z)$	The real part of $z \in \mathbb{C}$.
$r_t(T)$	Spot rate at time t maturing at time T.
r_t	The time t instantaneous short rate.
$\mathbb{R}^n$	The n-dimensional real vector space.
$\mathbb{R}^+$	The non-negative reals.
$\sigma_t(T)$ or $\sigma(t, T)$	The volatility at time t of the spot rate maturing at time T.
S	A state space.
S^{n-1}	The sphere in n dimensions.
S_t	Usually, a stock price at time t.
T	A maturity time.
t	Current time.
τ	Time to maturity.
$\mathbb{T}^*$	The terminal pricing measure.
$\mathbb{T}^\infty$	The ∞-forward measure.
$tr(M)$	The trace of the matrix M.
$U[a, b]$	The uniform distribution over the range $[a, b]$.
var	The variance function.
$z_t, \tilde{z}_t, w_t,$ et cetera	Wiener processes.
$\mathbb{Z}$	The integers.
$(\Omega, \mathcal{F}, \mathbb{Q})$	A probability space.
Ω	The sample space.
ω	A sample point.
A' or A^T	The transpose of A.
f'	The derivative of f with respect to its argument.
$x \in A$	x is an element of the set A.
$x \sim N$	x is distributed according to N.
$A \subseteq \Omega$	A is a subset of the set Ω.
$[a, b]$	The interval between a and b, including both a and b.
(a, b)	The open interval between a and b, containing neither a nor b.
dP/dQ	The Radon–Nikodým derivative.
$r_t \mid r_s$	The distribution of r_t conditional on r_s.
$(a)_+$	The maximum of a and 0.
$a \wedge b$	The minimum of a and b.
$a \vee b$	The maximum of a and b.

Glossary of Mathematical, Market and Model Terms

This glossary contains terms not defined in the text. If a term cannot be found in the glossary it may be present in the index.

a.a.: Almost Always. An event of probability one.

Absolute diffusion process: A process with a constant volatility but proportional drift.

Activation function: A function at a node of an ANN that is affine in its arguments.

Adapted process: A stochastic process X_t such that at each moment of time t and for each half-open interval, $(a, b]$, the set

$$A = \{\omega \in \Omega \mid X_t(\omega) \in (a, b]\} \in \mathcal{F}_t \tag{1}$$

is an event, and so can be assigned a probability.

Adaptive expectations: Expectations based on past and current values of state variables in the model.

Adjoint PDE: The PDE, relating derivatives of call prices with respect to strike, obtained from the Kolmogorov forward equation by substituting the density function with the second derivative of the call price with respect to strike.

Admissible control: In an optimisation problem, the set of functions, called controls, that the agent is permitted to choose between to optimise the criteria function. Examples are adapted controls, Markov controls, and deterministic controls.

a.e.: Almost Everywhere. An event of probability one.

Affine: f is an affine function of X if $f(X) = a + bX$.

Agio: A fee or cost to exchange money over and above a nominal exchange rate.

American option: An option which may be exercised at any time during its life.

Annual coupon rate: The sum of coupon payments per $100 nominal over one year.

AR process: Autoregressive process. A discrete time process whose evolution depends on its owns lags, and an innovation. For example, $X_t = aX_{t-1} + \varepsilon_t$.

Arbitrage: The ability to make a positive return from a zero investment with non-zero probability, with a zero probability of a negative return.

Arc: A line joining two points, specifically between two nodes in a lattice or ANN.

ARCH: Autoregressive Conditional Heteroscedasticity. An ARMA process where the variance h_t of the innovation series is itself an AR process in the square of the innovation that is, $h_t = a_0 + a_1 \varepsilon_{t-1}^2$, for instance.

ARMA processes: Autoregressive Moving Average process. A process with both AR and MA components, for example $X_t = aX_{t-1} + b\varepsilon_{t-1} + \varepsilon_t$.

a.s.: Almost Surely. An event of probability one.

ATM: At The Money. A call or put option whose strike is close to the current value of the underlying.

Attainable payoff: A payoff that can be replicated using an admissible hedging strategy.

Attractor: The smallest subset $A \subseteq U$, where U is a fixed open set in the state space of a dynamical system, such that all trajectories starting off in U end up in A, and where in addition at least one trajectory starting in A is dense in A.

Augmented natural filtration: The filtration $\mathcal{F}_t$ generated by (i) the smallest filtration for which some process X_t is adapted, $\mathcal{F}_t^X$, and (ii) all the sets of measure zero contained in events in $\mathcal{F}_t^X$.

Autoregression: The presence of non-zero correlation between observations of a stochastic process at time t and those at time $t - k$, for some fixed interval, k.

Banach space: A normed vector space in which limits exist for all Cauchy sequences with respect to the norm.

Basis functions: A set of basis elements in a vector space $V \subseteq C$, a space of functions.

Beltrami equations: For a two-dimensional second-order PDE, the equations satisfied by derivatives of the functions determining a change of variables under which the cross term vanishes and the remaining second-order terms have unit coefficient.

Bermudan instruments: A financial instrument that contains an option which may be exercised at one of several previously agreed points in time. It is called 'Bermudan' because it is half way between a 'European' instrument which may only be exercised at a single date, and an 'American' instrument which may be exercised at any point between inception and maturity.

Bessel density: The PDF

$$f(x \mid \alpha, \beta, \gamma) = \frac{|1 - \gamma^2|^{(2\alpha+1)/2}|x|^\alpha}{2^\alpha \beta^{\alpha+1} \sqrt{\pi}\, \Gamma\left(\dfrac{2\alpha+1}{2}\right)} e^{-(\gamma/\beta)x} K_\alpha\left(\left|\frac{x}{\beta}\right|\right), \qquad (2)$$

where $K_\alpha(z)$ is the modified Bessel function of order α.

Bessel function: A complex solution w of the differential equations

$$z^2 \frac{d^2 w}{dz^2} + z \frac{dw}{dz} + (z^2 - v^2)w = 0, \quad v \in \mathbb{R} \text{ (general order)},$$

(3)

$$z^2 \frac{d^2 w}{dz^2} + 2z \frac{dw}{dz} + (z^2 - n(n+1))w = 0, \quad n \in \mathbb{Z} \text{ (fractional order)}.$$

See Abramowitz and Stegun.

Bid–offer spread: The difference in price between the levels at which a bank will buy and sell the same instrument.

Bimetallic system: A monetary system based upon the simultaneous monetarisation of gold and silver.

Bimetallic ratio: The exchange rate between gold and silver when each is monetarised.

Binomial lattice: A lattice method in which the branching at every node is of order two.

Bivariate normal density: The density function $f(x, y)$ of the standard bivariate normal distribution,

$$f(x, y) = \frac{1}{2\pi \sqrt{1 - \rho^2}} \exp \left(-\frac{1}{2} \frac{x^2 - 2\rho xy + y^2}{1 - \rho^2} \right),$$

(4)

where ρ is the correlation between x and y.

Black's formula: A valuation formula of the form

$$c(S, X) = f(S)N(d) - g(X)N(d - \sigma),$$

(5)

for some functions f and g, where N is derived from the integral of a probability density function.

Bond option: An option where the underlying asset is a bond.

Boundary: In a finite difference method, the boundary of a grid upon which a PDE is solved using discrete approximations to the underlying state variables and their derivatives; The boundary of a domain upon which a stochastic process is defined.

Boundary conditions: Conditions satisfied by a differential equation on the boundary of its domain of definition; Conditions satisfied on the boundary of a grid acting as a discrete approximation to the solution of a differential equation; Conditions supplied at the boundary of the domain of definition of a stochastic process.

Bounded variation: See Finite variation.

Brownian motion: See Wiener process.

Bubble: A solution to an asset valuation equation in which the asset price increases (decreases) at a rate that is intuitively too fast; A solution that increases to infinity instead of remaining bounded; A market phenomenon in which a large movement (often an increase) in an asset value occurs that appears to be unrelated to fundamentals.

Burr type III density: The PDF

$$f(x \mid \alpha, \gamma, \tau) = \frac{\alpha\gamma\tau^{\alpha}x^{\alpha\gamma-1}}{(\tau^{\alpha} + x^{\alpha})^{\gamma+1}}, \quad x \geq 0, \quad \alpha, \gamma, \tau > 0, \tag{6}$$

with distribution function $F(x) = (1 + (\tau/x)^{\alpha})^{-\gamma}$.

Bushy tree: A non-recombining tree or lattice.

Business cycle: A change in economic activity over a period of time; A cyclical pattern of economic activity over a period of several years.

χ^2 **distribution:** The distribution with density

$$f(x \mid v) = \frac{1}{2^{v/2}\Gamma\left(\dfrac{v}{2}\right)}x^{v/2-1}e^{-x/2}, \quad x > 0. \tag{7}$$

Càdlàg process: A stochastic process continuous from the right, and with well-defined limits from the left. Also called an RCLL process (right continuous, left limits).

Callable: A callable instrument contains an option for the instrument to be bought back ('called') by its writer at some time in the future, at a price agreed at the inception of the deal.

Cap: An interest rate product which effectively imposes, for an agreed period of time, an upper level on the interest rate paid on a floating rate loan. On specified coupon dates it pays the difference between a reference market rate and the strike rate of the cap, if the market rate is higher than the strike. A cap is composed of one or more caplets. For example, one could purchase a one-year cap on the three-month rate, composed of three caplets (normally the cap does not include the caplet for the first reset date for which the cashflows are already known at inception).

Caplet: An instrument with payoff $\tau P \max(L_{t_i} - L_X, 0)$ at time t_{i+1} where L_X is a strike rate, L_{t_i} is a market rate observed at time t_i of tenor $\tau = t_{i+1} - t_i$, and P is a notional principal. A cap for a single interest payment.

Caption: An option where the underlying asset is a cap.

Chaos: A property of a dynamical system in which a small perturbation in an initial value results in a future evolution that deviates exponentially from what it was before.

Compact set: A set is compact with respect to a particular topology if all its covering sets have a finite sub-cover; In $\mathbb{R}^n$ with the usual topology, a set that is closed and bounded.

Compact support: A function has compact support if it is non-zero only within a compact set.

Compensated process: For a finite variation process P_t there may exist a predictable finite variation process v_t such that $P_t - v_t$ is a martingale. $P_t - v_t$ is the compensated process.

Complete market: A market in which all payoffs (in some class) can be constructed.

Conditional expectation: An expectation conditional upon particular values of underlying state variables; An expectation conditional upon information known at some particular time.

Confluent hypergeometric function: Solutions to Kummer's equation

$$z\frac{d^2w}{dz^2} + (b - z)\frac{dw}{dz} - aw = 0. \tag{8}$$

See Kummer's equation.

Constrained OLS regression: A modification of an OLS regression that chooses the regression coefficients so that additional constraints are satisfied.

Consumption process: The stochastic process modelling total consumption in an economy.

Continuous compounding: A continuously compounded interest rate is one where interest is calculated by taking an exponential of the rate times time. \$1 invested in a PDB with τ years to maturity with an annualised continuously compounded interest rate r_τ matures with a value of \$$e^{r_\tau \tau}$.

Convection dominated: A second-order PDE in which the coefficient of the first derivative essentially determines the behaviour of the PDE at large values of the underlying variable.

Convertible money: Bank notes that can (theoretically) be redeemed in specie.

Coordinate patch: A set of local coordinates on a manifold. For $x \in M$ a point on a manifold, with $x \in U$ an open set containing x, it is a diffeomorphism $\phi : U \to A \subseteq \mathbb{R}^n$.

Coupon bond: A bond making regular non-zero interim payments prior to maturity, usually of a pre-determined size.

Covering space: For two connected and locally connected topological spaces A and B, A is a covering space for B if there is a continuous map $\phi : A \to B$ such that for all $x \in B$ there is an open set $x \in U \subseteq B$ such that each component of $\phi^{-1}(U)$ is homeomorphic to U under ϕ.

Data reduction: A technique that reduces the effective dimensionality of a data set, making it easier to analyse.

Debasement: The process of fraudulently substituting specie in coinage with base metals, while keeping the face value unchanged, to purloin the precious metal.

DGP: Data Generating Process. The stochastic process that has generated a set of data.

Dirac delta function: The distribution $\delta(x)$ such that

$$\int_{-\infty}^{\infty} \delta(x - y)f(x)dx = f(y) \tag{9}$$

for functions f.

Discount curve: The set of discount factors for all times to maturity.

Discount factor: A factor which, when multiplying a cashflow, gives the present value of the cashflow.

Discount function: A functional form for the discount curve.

Discount rate: For a time to maturity t, the spot rate r corresponding to a discount factor $\delta(t)$, $r = -(1/t)\ln\delta(t)$; An official rate acting as a floor to the values of short-term interest rates.

Discrete compounding: A discretely compounded interest rate r is one where interest is calculated by taking a power of one plus a fraction of r. \$1 invested in a PDB with an annualised discretely compounded interest rate of r_τ, compounded n times a year, with $\tau = k/n$ years to maturity (where for simplicity k is an integer), matures with a value of \$$(1 + r_\tau/n)^k$.

Discretisation: Approximating a continuous function $f : A \to B$ by one in which the domain is a discrete subset of A; Approximating a continuous process $X : \mathbb{R}^+ \times \mathcal{S} \to \mathbb{R}^n$, $(t, s) \mapsto X(t, s) = X_t(s)$, defined for times $t \in \mathbb{R}^+$ and states $s \in \mathcal{S}$, by a process defined on a discrete subset of either $\mathbb{R}^+$ or $\mathcal{S}$ or both; Approximating a differential equation by taking discrete approximations to the derivatives it contains.

Discretisation error: Error introduced in a discrete approximation to a continuous system simply because the system is no longer continuous.

Double mean reverting model: A model in which a key state variable has a process that mean reverts to a level that is itself a process reverting towards some deterministic level.

Drift: The finite variation component of a stochastic process; The coefficient of the dt term in an SDE.

Dual linear programme: For an LP problem to find, for instance,

$$\min_{x} cx \quad \text{such that} \quad Ax \geq b \quad \text{and} \quad x \geq 0, \tag{10}$$

the dual LP is the LP that finds

$$\max_{\lambda} \lambda b \quad \text{such that} \quad \lambda A \leq c \quad \text{and} \quad \lambda \geq 0. \tag{11}$$

If a finite solution exists to either the LP or its dual, a finite solution exists to the other, and they are equal.

Edgeworth expansion: An asymptotic expansion of a probability density in terms of the normal density and its derivatives. Often expressed as a Hermite polynomial expansion since the Hermite polynomial He_m has a representation

$$He_m = (-1)^m \frac{n^{(m)}(x)}{n(x)}, \tag{12}$$

where $n^{(m)}(x)$ is the mth derivative of the normal density $n(x)$.

E-GARCH: Exponential General Autoregressive Conditional Heteroscedasticity. A modification of the GARCH method to allow $\text{sign}(\varepsilon_t)$ to effect the evolution of the variance h_t of ε_t.

Eigenvalue: The multiple by which an eigenvector is mapped onto itself under the action of a linear operator.

Eigenvector: An element in a vector space mapped onto a scalar multiple of itself by the action of a linear operator.

EMM: Efficient method of moments. A version of the general method of moments where moments are estimated by a simulation method.

EMM: Equivalent martingale measure. The measure under which, with respect to some numeraire, all relative processes are martingales; The EMM with respect to the accumulator numeraire.

ERM: Exchange rate mechanism. An agreement that existed between major European countries to regulate exchange rates between their currencies so that they stayed within certain percentage bands of one another.

Expectations formation: The process of, or a model for, the way economic agents form expectations for future values of economic parameters.

Explosion time: A time at which the value of a stochastic process becomes unbounded.

Exponential Bernoulli distribution: The distribution function of a random variable whose density is

$$
f(x) = \begin{cases} \dfrac{\psi}{\beta} e^{-x/\beta}, & x \geq 0, \\[2mm] \dfrac{1-\psi}{\beta} e^{-|x|/\beta}, & x < 0, \end{cases} \tag{13}
$$

for a parameter $\psi \in (0, 1)$.

Extreme value distributions: The canonical distributions of the extreme value of a set of samples drawn from some density function.

European option: An option which may be exercised at a single point in time called the exercise date or maturity date.

Event: An element of a σ-algebra $\mathcal{F}$; A measurable set; A set of paths to which a probability can be assigned.

∞-Forward measure: The measure given by $\lim_{T\to\infty} Q^T$, should this exist, where Q^T is the T-forward measure.

Factor model: An interest rate model defined using (a finite number of) state variables. Often there will be only a small number of state variables.

Fiat money: Money with no intrinsic value, which retains its purchasing power through official sanction.

Fibre: The elements of a covering space mapped onto a single point in the base space, especially when each fibre is topologically identical.

Filtration: A set $\{\mathcal{F}_t\}_{0 \leq t \leq T_{\max}}$ of σ-algebras such that $\mathcal{F}_{t_1} \subseteq \mathcal{F}_{t_2}$ for $t_1 \leq t_2$, representing the increase in information available by observing a stochastic system through time.

Finite variation process: A process X_t is of finite variation if

$$\sup_\tau \sum_{i=1}^n |X_{t_i}(\omega) - X_{t_{i-1}}(\omega)| < \infty \tag{14}$$

over all partitions $\tau = \{0 = t_0 < \cdots < t_n = T\}$ of $[0, T]$, for almost all sample points $\omega \in \Omega$, and for every interval $[0, T]$.

Fixed length swap: In an American swaption contract, an underlying swap that lasts for a fixed length of time from the exercise date.

Fixed maturity swaps: In an American swaption contract, an underlying swap that expires at a fixed maturity time, irrespective of the exercise date.

Fixed rate debt: A loan where successive coupon payments are calculated from an interest rate set at the start of the loan and fixed at this level for the duration of the loan.

Floating rate debt: A loan whose effective interest rate varies from coupon payment to coupon payment depending on the value of a reference market rate.

Floor: An interest rate product which effectively imposes, for an agreed period of time, a lower level to the interest rate paid on a floating rate loan. On specified coupon dates it pays the difference between a reference market rate and the strike rate of the floor, if the market rate is lower than the strike. See cap.

Floorlet: A floor for a single interest payment. See caplet.

Forward rate: An interest rate agreed now on a bond that is to be bought at some future time.

FRA: Forward rate agreement. Essentially, a money market contract that delivers, at a future time, borrowing at the forward rate determined in the FRA contract.

Forward start swap: A swap contract in which the time the cashflows in the first exchange are determined, and the date they are exchanged, takes place at a later date than in a standard swap.

Fourier transformation: The Fourier transformation Ff of a function $f : \mathbb{R}^n \to \mathbb{R}$ is defined by

$$(Ff)(z) = (2\pi)^{-(n/2)} \int_{\mathbb{R}^n} f(x)e^{-ix.z} dx. \tag{15}$$

Free boundary: A boundary whose location is determined by an optimality condition, and not directly by a deterministic function; The early exercise boundary of an American option.

Fubini's lemma: A result giving conditions under which the order of integration may be reversed in an expression involving probability integrals; Conditions under which $\int_A (\int_B f \, dP) dQ = \int_B (\int_A f \, dQ) dP$, defined in the appropriate spaces; Conditions under which $(\partial/\partial x)(\int_B f \, dP) = \int_B (\partial f/\partial x) dP + g(\partial B)$.

Full rank: The rank of a linear map is the dimension of its image space. A linear map has full rank if its kernel (the vector subspace it maps to zero) has dimension zero; A square matrix of full rank is invertible.

Futures contract: A contract to deliver an asset in the future at a price that gives the contract a current value of zero. The contract is marked to market, being replaced by a new contract each day at the new futures price. The difference in price from day to day is credited (debited) from a margin account.

Futures option: An option on a futures contract, itself marked to market.

Gamma function: The function $\Gamma(z) = \int_0^\infty t^{z-1} e^{-t} dt$. It has the properties that $\Gamma(z+1) = z\Gamma(z)$ and $\Gamma(2) = 1$.

Gamma variate: A random variable possessing a gamma density function,

$$f(x) = \frac{1}{\Gamma(p)} x^{p-1} e^{-x}, \quad x > 0. \tag{16}$$

GARCH process: An ARMA process in which the variance h_t of the innovation series is itself an ARMA process in the square of the innovation, $h_t = a_0 + a_1 \varepsilon_{t-1}^2 + b_1 h_{t-1}$, for instance.

Gaussian process: A process X_t is Gaussian if the joint density of $(X_{t_1}, \ldots, X_{t_n})$, for any n and times $t_1, \ldots, t_n$, is multivariate normal; A process whose volatility function depends only on time t and is not a function of any state variables of the model.

General cross validation criterion: A criterion to select the smoothing parameter in a smoothing spline approximation to a curve by minimising a weighted sum of errors at each data point when the fit is performed with each data point in turn dropped from the data set. See Dierckx.

GNP: Gross National Product.

Gold standard: A monetary system based upon the monetarisation of gold.

Gram–Charlier expansion: An expansion of a probability density function as the product of a normal density and a sum of the density's first three moments with polynomial coefficients.

Green's function: A solution to a PDE when the boundary condition is expressed as a Dirac delta function.

Hedge ratios: Otherwise known as the 'Greeks'. The delta (rate of change in value with respect to the underlying rate), gamma (rate of change in delta with respect to the underlying rate), vega (rate of change in value with respect to the volatility of the underlying rate), theta (rate of change in value with time) and rho (rate of change in value with respect to the interest rate).

Hedging: The act of constructing and maintaining a portfolio whose value exactly matches (theoretically) the value of some other portfolio. The matched portfolio may correspond to an option position that has been shorted.

Hermite polynomial expansion: An asymptotic expansion of a probability density function as the product of a normal density and a sequence of Hermite polynomials.

Hermite polynomials: A set of polynomials $He_n(x) = (-1)^n f(x)$ satisfying (and defined by) the orthogonality condition

$$\int_{-\infty}^{\infty} \exp\left(-\frac{x^2}{2}\right) f_n(x) f_m(x) \mathrm{d}x = \delta_{n,m} \sqrt{2\pi}\, n!$$ (17)

where $\delta_{n,m}$ is the Kronecker delta. In fact

$$He_n(x) = n! \sum_{m=0}^{[n/2]} (-1)^m \frac{1}{m! 2^m (n-2m)!} x^{n-2m}.$$ (18)

Heteroscedasticity: The property of a time series whose innovations have a volatility that changes through time.

Hidden variable: An unobservable state variable.

Hilbert space: A vector space (often infinite dimensional) with an inner product complete with respect to the induced metric.

Hitting time: The first time that a stochastic process hits a boundary.

HJB equation: Hamilton Jacobi Bellman equation. A necessary condition satisfied by an optimal control in an optimisation problem, which may enable an optimal control to be identified, if it exists.

Homoscedasticity: The property of a discrete time series whose innovations have a volatility that is constant over time.

Hopscotch method: A finite difference method for two-dimensional PDEs, involving a mixture of implicit and explicit steps at alternate points on the grid, that uses no tridiagonal inversions.

Hypercube: The unit hypercube $[0, 1] \times \cdots \times [0, 1] \subset \mathbb{R}^n$.

Hyperinflation: A situation where the inflation rate is determined by monetary factors that totally dominate the real economy; Persistent very high levels of inflation; An inflation rate of at least 50% per month (Cagan).

Identity: The identity function mapping objects in its domain to themselves; The identity matrix has ones down the leading diagonal, zeros elsewhere; An equivalence in the values of two functions that is valid over the entire range of definition of both functions.

i.i.d.: Independent, Identically Distributed.

Imbedding: A diffeomorphism from a manifold into $\mathbb{R}^n$, for some n.

Imbedding dimension: The dimension n of the imbedding space $\mathbb{R}^n$ of an imbedding.

Inconvertible money: (Paper) money that cannot be converted into specie.

Infemum, inf: Least upper bound.

Inflation: A situation where prices and incomes increase together at approximately the same rate, in conjunction with an increase in the money supply.

Information matrix: For the log-likelihood function $L(\theta)$ evaluated for parameter values θ, the information matrix is

$$I(\theta) = -\lim_{n\to\infty} \mathbb{E}\left[\frac{1}{n}\frac{\partial^2 L(\theta)}{\partial\theta\partial\theta'}\right]. \tag{19}$$

Asymptotically, the variance of the log-likelihood estimates $\hat{\theta}$ of the parameter values is $(1/n)I^{-1}\left(\hat{\theta}\right)$. See Campbell, Lo and MacKinlay.

Inner product: A symmetric bilinear map from a vector space to the field over which the vector space is defined.

Innovation: A random component in the evolution of a state variable in discrete time, often standard normal i.i.d.

Inverse problem: When there is an invertible operator H mapping a function f onto a function $g = H(f)$, the numerical computation of H may be straightforward, but that of H^{-1} may be highly unstable. The problem of robustly calculating H^{-1} is called the inverse problem. For instance, if H is an integral operator, H^{-1} may involve differentials whose evaluation is very sensitive to small perturbations in g.

Inverse transform method: A method of obtaining random variates from a distribution function $N(x)$ by first finding uniform variates $u \sim U[0, 1]$ and then transforming by N^{-1}.

Invertible: A function or operator possessing an inverse; A square matrix with a non-zero determinant.

Itō diffusion: A stochastic process X_t that can be expressed in the form $dX_t = \mu(X_t, t)dt + \sigma(X_t, t)dz_t$. It has continuous sample paths and is Markov.

Kitagawa algorithm: A non-linear filtering method based upon a numerical approximation to the underlying density function.

Klein bottle: The set $[0, 1] \times S^1 \backslash \sim$ under the equivalence $\{1\} \times \{a\} \sim \{0\} \times \{-a\}$ (endowed with the structure of a manifold).

Kummer's equation: The complex differential equation

$$z\frac{d^2w}{dz^2} + (b - z)\frac{dw}{dz} - aw = 0. \tag{20}$$

Solutions are Kummer functions $M(a, b, z)$ and functions

$$U(a, b, z) = \frac{\pi}{\sin \pi b}\left\{\frac{M(a, b, z)}{\Gamma(1 + a - b)\Gamma(b)} - z^{1-b}\frac{M(1 + a - b, 2 - b, z)}{\Gamma(a)\Gamma(2 - b)}\right\}. \tag{21}$$

See Abramowitz and Stegun.

Kummer functions: The function

$$M(a, b, z) = 1 + \sum_{n=1}^{\infty} \frac{(a + n - 1)!}{(a - 1)!}\frac{(b - 1)!}{(b + n - 1)!}\frac{z^n}{n!}, \tag{22}$$

a solution to Kummer's equation.

Kurtosis: The fourth moment of a random variable, divided by the square of its variance, $\mathbb{E}[(X - \mu)^4]/\sigma^4$.

Lag operator: The operator L giving the previous value of a discrete process, $L(X_t) = X_{t-1}$.

Lagrange multipliers: A constrained optimisation technique in which additional terms, multiples of the constraints, are introduced into the objective function. The multiple, a parameter to be estimated in the optimisation, is the Lagrange multiplier.

Leptokurtic: A distribution with a kurtosis greater than three. Leptokurtic distributions have longer, fatter tails than the normal distribution.

Lipschitz: A function $f : \mathbb{R}^n \to \mathbb{R}$ is Lipschitz if

$$|f(x) - f(y)| \le K \cdot |x - y|, \tag{23}$$

for some constant K and for all $x, y \in \mathbb{R}^n$; A diffusion process $X_t \in \mathbb{R}^n$ with SDE $dX_t = \mu(X_t, t)dt + \sigma(t, X_t)dz_t$, where $z_t \in \mathbb{R}^n$ is an n-dimensional Wiener process, is Lipschitz if

$$|\mu(x, t) - \mu(y, t)| + |\sigma(x, t) - \sigma(y, t)| \le K \cdot |x - y|, \tag{24}$$

for some constant K and for all $x, y \in \mathbb{R}^n$, $t \in [0, T]$.

Liquidity premium: See term premium.

Locally Lipschitz: If there exists a sequence of open sets A_i such that $A_i \subseteq A_{i+1}$ and $\bigcup A_i = \mathbb{R}^n$ such that a function $f : \mathbb{R}^n \to \mathbb{R}$ is Lipschitz on each A_i, then f is locally Lipschitz.

Log-normal density: The density function of a log-normal process.

Log-normal process: A process whose log is conditionally normal, for example geometric Brownian motion; A process S_t whose volatility is proportional to S_t.

Lombard rate: Formerly, an official rate controlled by the German monetary authorities acting as a ceiling on the values of short-term money market rates; Any official rate acting as a ceiling on short-term money market rates.

Lookback: An option whose exercise price is a function of a maximum or minimum value of a state variable since inception.

Lorenz system: A particular three-factor deterministic system exhibiting chaotic behaviour. The three variables X_t, Y_t and Z_t satisfy the system

$$\frac{dX_t}{dt} = \alpha(Y_t - X_t), \quad \frac{dY_t}{dt} = \delta X_t - Z_t X_t - Y_t, \quad \frac{dZ_t}{dt} = X_t Y_t - \gamma Z_t. \tag{25}$$

LP: Linear programme. An optimisation problem where both the objective function and the constraint set are linear. For instance, the problem of finding

$$\min_x cx \quad \text{and} \quad \widehat{x} = \arg\min_x cx \quad \text{such that} \quad Ax \ge b \quad \text{and} \quad x \ge 0, \tag{26}$$

where $b, c \in \mathbb{R}^n$, A is an $n \times n$ matrix and $x \in \mathbb{R}^n$ is a vector of unknowns.

LP method: A method to obtain an optimal solution to a linear programming problem.

Lucas framework: An economic paradigm in which prices adjust to demand, but in which consumption is exogenous.

MA process: A moving average process. A discrete time process whose evolution depends on an innovation and its lags, for example $X_t = a\varepsilon_{t-1} + \varepsilon_t$.

Manifolds: A topological space M in which each point $x \in M$ lies within an open set diffeomorphic to some open set in $\mathbb{R}^n$. A manifold with boundary can be defined similarly.

Mark space: The space in which the random variable specifying the outcome at each point in a marked point process takes values.

Marked point process: A sequence of pairs $(T_n, X_n)_{n=1,\ldots,\infty}$ where T_n is an increasing process and X_n is a sequence of random variables taking values in a mark space E. T_n can be regarded as the times at which successive events occur and X_n is the value of an outcome at time T_n. For instance, T_n might be the time that a jump occurs in a stochastic process and $X_n \in \mathbb{R} \equiv E$ the value of the process after the jump.

Market price of risk: The amount by which the risk-adjusted drift of a state variable is less than its drift under the objective measure, as a multiple of its volatility. In this context the risk-adjusted drift is usually given with respect to the measure associated with the accumulator numeraire.

Markov process: A stochastic process X_t is a Markov process if for all measurable functions f and $t \le T$,

$$\mathbb{E}_t[f(X_T)] = \mathbb{E}[f(X_T) \mid X_t]; \qquad (27)$$

A stochastic process whose future evolution depends only on its current value and not on its past values.

Maximum entropy principle: A regularisation technique that attempts to minimise pricing errors while simultaneously maximising the entropy of the fitted function. For a function $p(x)$ defined on $[0, \infty]$ the entropy is

$$e = -\int_0^\infty p(x) \ln p(x) \mathrm{d}x. \qquad (28)$$

Mean reverting process: A process with a stationary density; A process possessing a mean reversion level.

Measure: A function determining the probabilities of events occurring in some sample space.

Measure valued process, measure valued function: A process or function taking values in a space of measures.

Measurable: A measurable set; A function $f : A \to B$ mapping between two probability spaces A and B is measurable if the inverse image of each measurable set in B is a measurable set in A.

Measurable set: An event; a subset of Ω that is an element of a σ-algebra $\mathcal{F}$.

Mixture of log-normals: A random variable that is a linear combination of other random variables, each of which is log-normally distributed.

Mobius strip: The set $[0, 1] \times (0, 1)\backslash \sim$ under the equivalence relation $\{1\} \times \{a\} \sim \{0\} \times \{1 - a\}$ (endowed with the structure of a manifold).

Modified Bessel function: A complex solution w of the differential equations

$$z^2 \frac{d^2 w}{dz^2} + z \frac{dw}{dz} - (z^2 + v^2)w = 0, \quad v \in \mathbb{R}. \tag{29}$$

Solutions are of two types, denoted by $I_{\pm v}(z)$ and $K_v(z)$. See Abramowitz and Stegun.

Musiela parameterisation: A parameterisation where time to maturity is used instead of time of maturity, particularly in HJM and BGM models.

Nominal interest rate: A market interest rate; An interest rate denominated in money values (rather than consumption values).

Non-central χ^2 distribution: The distribution with density

$$f(x|v, \lambda) = \sum_{j=0}^{\infty} e^{-\lambda/2} \frac{\lambda^j}{2^j j!} \frac{1}{2^{v/2+j} \Gamma \left(\frac{v}{2} + j \right)} x^{v/2+j-1} e^{-x/2}, \tag{30}$$

for $x > 0$. λ is the non-centrality parameter.

Non-negative definite matrix: A matrix M such that $x'Mx \geq 0$ for all vectors x.

Norm: A function from a vector space to $\mathbb{R}^+$ consistently assigning a length to each vector.

Normed vector space: A vector space possessing a norm.

Null hypothesis: An hypothesis to be rejected by a statistical test.

ODE: Ordinary differential equation. A differential equation involving only one independent variable.

Official corridor: An allowed range for a short-term market rate, with a ceiling and floor determined by official interest rates.

Official rate: A rate set by a monetary authority, often acting as a ceiling or floor on short-term market rates, which may be used to signal to the market the policy stance of the monetary authority.

Official rate model: An interest rate model that explicitly models official rates and rate-setting behaviour.

OLS regression: Ordinary least squares regression. A method that, for instance, from a set of pairs of observations $(x_i, y_i)_{i=1,\ldots,n}$, determines a regression line, $y_i = a + bx_i + \varepsilon_i$, by choosing a and b to minimise the variance of the Gaussian error term ε_i.

Ornstein–Uhlenbeck process: A process of the form $dX_t = \alpha(\theta - X_t)dt + \sigma dz_t, \alpha > 0$.

OTC: Over the counter. A derivative product which has a certain degree of tailoring and is designed for a particular counterparty. A specialised product rather than a wholesale one of which many are sold.

Par coupon rate: The coupon rate on a coupon bond at which the market price of the bond is equal to its face value.

Parabolic cylinder functions: Solutions of the differential equation

$$\frac{d^2 w}{dz^2} + (az^2 + bz + c)w = 0. \tag{31}$$

These are of the form $U(a, z)$ and $V(a, z)$ where

$$U(a, z) = \cos \pi \left(\frac{1}{2}a + \frac{1}{4} \right) Y_1 - \sin \pi \left(\frac{1}{2}a + \frac{1}{4} \right) Y_2, \tag{32}$$

$$V(a, z) = \frac{1}{\Gamma \left(\frac{1}{2} - a \right)} \left\{ \sin \pi \left(\frac{1}{2}a + \frac{1}{4} \right) Y_1 + \cos \pi \left(\frac{1}{2}a + \frac{1}{4} \right) Y_2 \right\}, \tag{33}$$

and where

$$Y_1 = \frac{1}{\sqrt{\pi}} \frac{\Gamma \left(\frac{1}{4} - \frac{1}{2}a \right)}{2^{\frac{1}{2}a + \frac{1}{4}}} y_1, \quad Y_2 = \frac{1}{\sqrt{\pi}} \frac{\Gamma \left(\frac{3}{4} - \frac{1}{2}a \right)}{2^{\frac{1}{2}a - \frac{1}{4}}} y_2, \tag{34}$$

and

$$y_1 = e^{-\frac{1}{4}z^2} M \left(\frac{1}{2}a + \frac{1}{4}, \frac{1}{2}, \frac{1}{2}z^2 \right), \quad y_2 = z e^{-\frac{1}{4}z^2} M \left(\frac{1}{2}a + \frac{3}{4}, \frac{3}{2}, \frac{1}{2}z^2 \right). \tag{35}$$

See Abramowitz and Stegun.

Parabolic partial differential equation: The linear second-order PDE

$$a\frac{\partial^2 w}{\partial x^2} + 2b\frac{\partial^2 w}{\partial x \partial y} + c\frac{\partial^2 w}{\partial y^2} + d\frac{\partial w}{\partial x} + e\frac{\partial w}{\partial y} + fw = g \tag{36}$$

is parabolic if $ac - b^2$ is everywhere identically zero.

Path-dependent model: A model in which one or more of the state variables have non-Markov processes.

Path-dependent option: An option whose payoff at the exercise date depends on values of the state variable at times prior to exercise.

PDB: Pure discount bond. A bond with a single cashflow, conventionally of 1, at maturity.

PDDE: Partial differential difference equation. A system of PDEs $Df = Af$ satisfied by a vector valued function $f \in \mathbb{R}^n$, where D is an $n \times n$ diagonal matrix of differential operators and A is an $n \times n$ matrix of coefficients.

PDE: Partial differential equation. A differential equation with more than one independent variable.

PDF: Probability density function.

Platykurtic distribution: A distribution with a kurtosis less than three. Platykurtic distributions have shorter, thinner tails than the normal distribution.

Position taking: Constructing a zero-cost portfolio that acquires positive value if some expected event takes place in the market. If the event does not occur, the portfolio is likely to acquire negative value.

Positive definite matrix: A matrix M such that $x'Mx > 0$ for all vectors $x \neq 0$.

Potential: A supermartingale bounded below by zero whose future expected values also tend to zero.

Pratt–Arrow risk aversion: A measure of risk aversion, π, based upon the wealth equivalent of an incremental risky gamble with zero expected value and variance σ^2. The measure is $\pi(\sigma, w) = -\frac{1}{2}\sigma^2[u''(w)/u'(w)]$, where $u(w)$ is the agent's utility function, a function of wealth, w.

Predictable process: An adapted process measurable with respect to $\mathcal{F}_{t-}$.

Predictor–corrector simulation: A simulation technique in which an initial approximation to a simulated future value is used to provide an improved simulated future value.

Preferred habitual model: An explanation of the term structure based on the premise that different types of participant in the market prefer to hold long or short bonds at different maturities.

Price kernel: A random variable $\pi(t, T)$ with the property that the current market value of an asset v_t is equal to the expected value (under some measure) of the future value v_T of the asset multiplied by the price kernel, $v_t = \mathbb{E}_t[v_T\pi(t, T)]$. Intuitively, $\pi(t, T)$ represents the value today of a payoff in a future (path dependent) state.

Price kernel model: An interest rate model based upon explicitly modelling the price kernel.

Puttable: A puttable instrument contains an option for the instrument to be sold ('put') to the counterparty at some time in the future.

Radon–Nikodým derivative: The scale factor converting some measure to an equivalent measure.

Rational expectations: The premise that economic agents use the actual expected future value $X^*_{t,T} = \mathbb{E}_t[X_T]$ of economic values and state variables as their forecasts of these future values.

Reaction function: A functional form for the values of economic and financial variables when these variables are assumed to be controlled by the monetary authorities. For instance, if the monetary authorities control the short rate r, and are assumed to base their decisions upon a set of economic observables θ, the reaction function will specify r as a function of θ.

Real rate: An interest rate in consumption denominated terms; The nominal interest rate less the expected inflation rate.

Recombining tree: A tree or lattice in which number of nodes at each step grows as a polynomial function of the number of time steps; A lattice in which the number of nodes grows as a linear function of the number of time steps.

Rectilinear: A product of intervals.

Redemption yield: The yield to maturity of a coupon bond; The spot interest rate, the same for each maturity, at which the market value of a coupon bond equals the present value of its cashflows.

Replicating strategy: An algorithm specifying the contents of a hedge portfolio that exactly hedges the cashflows to another portfolio or to a derivative.

Representative agent model: A framework in which all economic agents are, or can be supposed to be, identical, so that only the characteristics of a representative agent need be considered.

Reversion level: A zero of the drift function of a stochastic process S_t at which the derivative of the drift with respect to S_t has negative sign.

Rho: The partial derivative of the value of a financial instrument with respect to a key interest rate.

Riccati equation: The differential equation

$$\frac{\mathrm{d}w}{\mathrm{d}z} + f(z)w^2 + g(z)w + h(z) = 0; \tag{37}$$

Also the matrix equation of similar form.

Richardson extrapolation: A technique to increase the accuracy of a numerical method by extrapolating from values achieved at several coarse grid sizes to estimate a value at a finer grid size.

Riemannian state space: A state space, assumed to be a manifold, consistently given an inner product on each tangent space, endowing the manifold with a metric enabling distances to be measured on it.

σ-algebra: A set of subsets of a sample space Ω closed under countable unions and intersections, and taking complements; The minimal properties required before probabilities can be assigned consistently to a set of events.

σ-field: See σ-algebra.

SACF: Sample autocorrelation function.

Seigniorage: The fees levied from the operation of a mint; The additional funding achievable through a relaxation in the money supply.

Silver standard: A monetary system based upon the monetarisation of silver.

SOR: Successive over-relaxation. A numerical solution method for PDEs that attempts to find a solution x to the matrix equation $Ax = b$, where A and b are derived from the discretised PDE, by iteratively finding approximations $x^{(r)}$ to x. At each stage $x^{(r+1)}$ is derived from $x^{(r)}$ by 'overshooting' the obvious next value.

Specie: An underlying monetarised commodity, such as gold or silver.

Sphere: The set S^{n-1} of points in $\mathbb{R}^n$ of distance 1 from the origin.

State price deflator: When a pricing measure P has a density, the state price deflator δ^P represents the present value of a payoff of 1 in each future state, so the current market value v_t of an asset is

$$v_t = \int_\Omega v_T(\omega)\delta^P(\omega)d\omega. \tag{38}$$

If the density of P is f^P, $dP = f^P(\omega)d\omega$, then $\delta^P(\omega) = \pi(t, T)f^P(\omega)$ where $\pi(t, T)$ is the price kernel.

State space: The space in which the state variables of a model take their values.

State variable: A set of variables whose values uniquely determine the state of a system.

Stationary density: The unconditional density function of a stochastic process, if it exists; A density satisfying the Kolmogorov forward equation without the time derivative, if a solution exists.

Stationary increments: If the process $Y_{t,\tau} = X_{t+\tau} - X_t$ is independent of t, then X_t has stationary increments.

Stationary process: A process X_t is stationary if the joint density of $(X_{t_1+\tau}, \ldots, X_{t_n+\tau})$ is identical to the joint density of $(X_{t_1}, \ldots, X_{t_n})$, for any τ, n, and times $t_1, \ldots, t_n$.

SDE: Stochastic differential equation. A differential equation of the form, for instance, $dX_t = \mu dt + \sigma dz_t$. A solution to an SDE represents X_t as a function of z_t (or its path). For instance, when μ and σ are constants a solution to the SDE above is $X_t = X_0 + \mu t + \sigma z_t$.

Stochastic process: A stochastic process is a set $\{X_t\}_{t\geq 0}$ of measurable functions from one probability space A to another, B, indexed by time t. (Usually extra structure is imposed onto the joint distribution function of the $\{X_t\}_{t\geq 0}$.)

Stochastic volatility: A model in which a volatility parameter is itself a stochastic process.

Strike price, strike rate: A parameter in a payoff function often determining the location of a kink or discontinuity in the payoff function; The exercise value X in the call (put) payoff function $\max(S_T - X, 0)$ ($\max(X - S_T, 0)$).

Subordinated diffusion: For a Markov diffusion process X_t and an increasing process T_t, with $T_0 = 0$, the process $Y_t(\omega) = X_{T_t(\omega)}(\omega)$ is a subordinated diffusion. A time changed Brownian motion is a subordinated diffusion process.

Submartingale: A stochastic process whose expected future values are equal to or greater than its current value, at all times.

Successor set: In a lattice, the set of nodes that a particular node can branch to in a single step.

Supermartingale: A stochastic process whose expected future values are equal to or less than its current value, at all times.

Super-replication: A portfolio whose value always exceeds that of another portfolio which it is supposed to hedge.

Supremum, sup: Greatest lower bound.

Swap: A financial instrument where one stream of cashflows are exchanged for another. The swap contract specifies how the size and timing of the cashflows are to be calculated. They may be in different currencies, or in the same currency but referenced to different underlying rates, or one set may be fixed while the other is floating and referenced to an underlying market rate.

Swaption: An option on a swap.

Tails: The region of the probability density function at extreme values of the underlying variable; A region of a state space over which a probability density has asymptotically zero values.

Tail distribution: A canonical asymptotic distribution of a tail of a density function.

Tail parameters: The parameters determining a canonical tail distribution.

Tangent space: The vector space of tangents to a point p on a manifold (spanned by the set $\{\partial/\partial x_i\}_{i=1,\ldots,n}$ of local differential operators at p).

Tenor: The interval between cashflows for a financial instrument, determined by the day count convention for the instrument.

Tenor structure: The set of dates when cashflows occur for a particular set of financial instruments, for example the dates upon which cashflows to a swap are made.

Term premium: The amount by which a current forward rate exceeds an expected future spot rate (usually under the objective measure).

Term structure: A set of spot rates for all times to maturity.

Term structure of volatility: Implied volatility for ATM options for all times to maturity; A volatility function parameterised by time to maturity.

_T_-forward measure: The measure under which relative prices with respect to the numeraire given by the T-maturity pure discount bond are martingales.

Theta: The partial derivative of the value of a financial instrument with respect to time.

Torus: The set $S^1 \times S^1$ (endowed with the structure on a manifold).

Tridiagonal matrix: A matrix whose only non-zero entries occur in the leading diagonal, the diagonal immediately above it, and the diagonal immediately below.

Tridiagonal system: A matrix equation whose solution involves, at most, inverting tridiagonal matrices.

Trinomial lattice: A lattice with order three branching at every node.

Truncation error: The error introduced by truncating the binary representation of a number to a fixed number of decimal places.

t-statistics: A measure of the confidence with which a normal variable is estimated in, for instance, a regression.

Uniform random numbers: Random numbers in the unit interval $[0, 1]$ whose probability density function is identically 1 over the whole interval.

Unit root: An ARMA process $\phi(L)X_t = \theta(L)\varepsilon_t$, where $\phi(L)$ and $\theta(L)$ are polynomials in the lag operator L, has a unit root if any of the roots of the polynomial equation $\phi(x) = 0$ lie strictly within the unit circle. If $\phi(x)$ has a unit root, the operator $\phi(L)$ is not invertible and the process for X_t does not possess an MA(∞) representation, and the process for X_t is not stationary.

Utility function: A function of consumption, time and wealth (for instance) that an economic agent is presumed to be attempting to maximise when making consumption and investment decisions.

Value process: The stochastic process followed by the value of some asset or portfolio.

VaR: Value at Risk. A measure of the possible loss in the value of a portfolio when events of specified levels of likelihood occur.

Vega: The derivative of an asset price with respect to a variable determining the size of a volatility.

Volatility: The coefficient of the $\mathrm{d}z_t$ term in an SDE; A volatility parameter in a Black's formula.

Weakly stationary: A process X_t is weakly stationary if $\mathbb{E}[X_t] = \mu$ is constant for all t, and $\mathbb{E}[(X_t - \mu)(X_{t+\tau} - \mu)] = f(\tau) < \infty$ for all t and τ.

Wiener process: A stochastic process whose conditional densities for some future time T, conditional on its value z_t at time t, are normally distributed with mean z_t and variance $T - t$.

Yield curve: See term structure. A set of spot rates for all maturities.

Zero coupon bonds: See pure discount bonds. A bond with a single, terminal, cashflow.

Zero valued instrument: An instrument whose value is zero, for example a swap an inception.

References

[1] P. Abken, D. B. Madan, and S. Ramamurtie. Estimation of Risk-Neutral and Statistical Densities by Hermite Polynomial Approximation: With an Application to Eurodollar Futures Options. *Working Paper, Federal Reserve Bank of Atlanta*, 96-5:1–41, 1996.

[2] P. Abken, D. B. Madan, and S. Ramamurtie. Pricing S&P 500 Index Options Using a Hilbert Space Basis. *Working Paper, Federal Reserve Board of Atlanta*, 96-21:1–41, 1996.

[3] M. Abramowitz and I. A. Stegun. *Handbook of Mathematical Functions*. Dover, 1965.

[4] P. Acworth, M. Broadie, and P. Glasserman. A Comparison of Some Monte Carlo and Quasi Monte Carlo Techniques for Option Pricing. *In Monte Carlo and Quasi Monte Carlo Methods*, Springer-Verlag, eds H. Niederreiter, P. Hellekalek, G. Larcher and P. Zinterhof, pages 1–17, 1997.

[5] D. Adams. *The Restaurant at the End of the Universe*. Pan, 1980.

[6] K. J. Adams and D. R. Van Deventer. Fitting Yield Curves and Forward Rate Curves with Maximum Smoothness. *Journal of Fixed Income*, 4:52–62, 1994.

[7] C. M. Ahn and H. E. Thompson. Jump-Diffusion Processes and the Term Structure of Interest Rates. *Journal of Finance*, 431:155–174, 1988.

[8] Y. Ait-Sahalia. Nonparametric Pricing of Interest Rate Derivative Securities. *Econometrica*, 64:527–560, 1996.

[9] Y. Ait-Sahalia. Testing Continuous-Time Models of the Spot Interest Rate. *Review of Financial Studies*, 9:385–426, 1996.

[10] Y. Ait-Sahalia and A. W. Lo. Nonparametric Estimation of State-Price Densities Implicit in Financial Asset Prices. *Working Paper, National Bureau of Economic Research*, 5351, 1995.

[11] S. R. Aiyagari, N. Wallace, and R. Wright. Coexistence of Money and Interest-bearing Securities. *Journal of Monetary Economics*, 37:397–419, 1996.

[12] V. Akgiray, G. G. Booth, and B. Seifert. Distribution properties of Latin American Black Market Exchange Rate. *Journal of International Money and Finance*, 7/1:37–48, 1988.

[13] G. S. Alogoskoufis and R. Smith. The Phillips Curve, The Persistence of Inflation, and the Lucas Critique: Evidence from Exchange-Rate Regimes. *American Economic Review*, 81:1254–1275, 1991.

[14]   K. I. Amin and A. J. Morton. Implied Volatility Functions in Arbitrage-Free Term Structure Models. *Journal of Financial Economics*, 35:141–180, 1994.

[15]   K. I. Amin and V. K. Ng. Inferring Future Volatility from the Information in Implied Volatility in Eurodollar Options: A New Approach. *Review of Financial Studies*, 10:333–367, 1997.

[16]   L. B. G. Andersen. Five Essays on the Pricing of Contingent Claims. *PhD Thesis*, Aarhus Business School, 1996.

[17]   L. B. G. Andersen. A Simple Approach to the Pricing of Bermudan Swaptions in the Multi-Factor Libor Market Model. *Working Paper, General Re Financial Products*, pages 1–26, 1999.

[18]   L. B. G. Andersen and J. Andreasen. Volatility Skews and Extensions of the Libor Market Model. *Working Paper, General Re Financial Products*, pages 1–39, 1998.

[19]   T. G. Andersen and J. Lund. Stochastic Volatility and Mean Drift in the Short Rate Diffusion: Sources of Steepness, Level and Curvature in the Yield Curve. *Working Paper, Northwestern University*, 214:1–28, 1996.

[20]   T. G. Andersen and J. Lund. Stochastic Volatility in the Short Term Interest Rate Diffusion with Implications for the Yield Curve. *Working Paper, Northwestern University*, pages 1–26, 1996.

[21]   T. G. Andersen and J. Lund. The Short Rate Diffusion Revisited: An Investigation Guided by the Efficient Method of Moments. *Working Paper, Northwestern University*, 215:1–28, 1996.

[22]   T. G. Andersen and J. Lund. Estimating Continuous-Time Stochastic Volatility Models of the Short-Term Interest Rate. *Journal of Econometrics*, 77:343–377, 1997.

[23]   N. Anderson, F. Breedon, M. Deacon, A. Derry, and M. Murphy. *Estimating and Interpreting the Yield Curve*. Wiley, 1996.

[24]   I. Andrade and A. Clare. Is the UK Treasury Bill Rate a Good Proxy for Expected Inflation in the United Kingdom. *Economics Letters*, 45:335–341, 1994.

[25]   J. Andreasen. Essays on Contingent Claim Pricing. *PhD Thesis, Aarhus University*, 1996.

[26]   D. W. K. Andrews. Heteroskedasticity and Autocorrelation Consistent Covariance Matrix Estimation. *Econometrica*, 59:817–858, 1991.

[27]   P. Artzner and F. Delbaen. Term Structure of Interest Rates: The Martingale Approach. *Advances in Applied Mathematics*, 10:95–129, 1989.

[28]   M. Attari. Discontinuous Interest Rate Processes: An Equilibrium Model for Bond Option Prices. *Working Paper, University of Iowa*, pages 1–32, 1996.

[29]   K. T. Au and D. C. Thurston. Exchange Options on Bonds. *Working Paper, University of New South Wales*, 63:1–8, 1994.

[30]   K. T. Au and D. C. Thurston. Markovian Term Structure Movements. *Working Paper, University of New South Wales*, 61:1–13, 1994.

[31]   M. Avellaneda. Minimum-Entropy Calibration on Asset Pricing Models. *Working Paper, Courant Institute, NYU*, pages 1–24, 1997.

[32] M. Avellaneda, C. Friedman, R. Holmes, and D. Samperi. Calibrating Volatility Surfaces Via Relative-Entropy Minimization. *Working Paper, Courant Institute, NYU* pages 1–38, 1996.

[33] M. Baadsgaard, J. N. Nielsen, H. Madsen, and M. Preisel. Samplng Techniques in Stochastic Differential Equations. *Working Paper, The Technical University of Denmark*, 1996.

[34] Y. Baba, D. F. Hendry, and R. M. Starr. The Demand for M1 in the U.S.A. 1960–1988. *Review of Economic Studies*, 59:25–61, 1992.

[35] S. H. Babbs. Interest Rate Models. *PhD thesis, Imperial College*, 1989.

[36] S. H. Babbs. Generalised Vasicek Models of the Term Structure. *In Applied Stochastic Models of Data Analysis*, 6th Annual Symposium Proceedings, J. Janssen and C. H. Skiadas, eds, vol 1, pages 49–62, 1993.

[37] S. H. Babbs. Rational Bounds. *Working Paper, First National Bank of Chicago*, pages 1–8, 1997.

[38] S. H. Babbs and K. B. Nowman. Econometric Analysis of a Continuous Time Multi-Factor Generalized Vasicek Term Structure Model: International Evidence. *Working Paper, FNBC*, pages 1–31, 1997.

[39] S. H. Babbs and K. B. Nowman. Kalman Filtering of Generalized Vasicek Term Structure Models. *Journal of Financial and Quantitative Analysis*, pages 115–130, 1999.

[40] S. H. Babbs and N. J. Webber. A Theory of the Term Structure with an Official Short Rate. *Working Paper, FORC 94/49, University of Warwick*, 1994.

[41] S. H. Babbs and N. J. Webber. Term structure modelling under alternative official regimes. *Working Paper, FORC 95/61, University of Warwick*, 1995.

[42] K. Back and S. R. Pliska. On the Fundamental Theorem of Asset Pricing with an Infinite State Space. *Journal of Mathematical Economics*, 20:1–18, 1991.

[43] D. K. Backus and S. E. Zin. Reverse Engineering the Yield Curve. *Working Paper, NBER 4676*, 1–32, 1994.

[44] B. Bahra. Probability Distributions of Future Asset Prices Implied by Option Prices. *Bank of England Quarterly Bulletin*, pages 299–311, 1996.

[45] G. S. Bakshi and Z. Chen. Inflation, Asset Prices, and the Term Structure of Interest Rates in Monetary Economics. *Review of Financial Studies*, 9:241–275, 1996.

[46] G. S. Bakshi and Z. Chen. An Alternative Valuation Model for Contingent Claims. *Journal of Financial Economics*, 44:123–165, 1997.

[47] P. Balduzzi, G. Bertola, and S. Foresi. A Model of Target Changes and the Term Structure of Interest Rates. *Journal of Monetary Economics*, 39:223–249, 1996.

[48] P. Balduzzi, S. R. Das, S. Foresi, and R. Sundaram. A Simple Approach to Three Factor Affine Term Structure Models. *Journal of Fixed Income*, 6:43–53, 1996.

[49] P. Balduzzi, S. R. Das, S. Foresi, and R. Sundaram. Stochastic Mean Models of the Term Structure of Interest Rates. *Working Paper, New York University*, pages 1–35, 1996.

[50] P. Balduzzi, S. Foresi, and D. J. Hait. Price Barriers and the Dynamics of Asset Prices in Equilibrium. *Journal of Financial and Quantitative Analysis*, 32:137–159, 1997.

[51] C. A. Ball and W. N. Torous. Unit Roots and the Estimation of Interest Rate Dynamics. *Journal of Empirical Finance*, 3:215–238, 1996.

[52] R. Banz and M. Miller. Prices for State-Contingent Claims: Some Estimates and Applications. *Journal of Business*, 51:653–672, 1978.

[53] S. Barle and N. Cakici. Growing a Smiling Tree. *Risk*, 8/10:76–80, 1995.

[54] R. B. Barsky and J. B. de Long. Forecasting Pre-World War I Inflation: The Fisher Effect and the Gold Standard. *Quarterly Journal of Economics*, 106:815–836, 1991.

[55] M. Baxter and A. Rennie. *Financial Calculus*. Cambridge University Press, 1996.

[56] J. Baz and S. R. Das. Analytical Approximations of the Term Structure for Jump–Diffusion Processes: A Numerical Analysis. *Journal of Fixed Income*, June:78–86, 1996.

[57] D. R. Beaglehole and M. S. Tenney. General Solutions of some Interest Rate-Contingent Claim Pricing Equations. *Journal of Fixed Income*, pages 69–83, 1991.

[58] D. R. Beaglehole and M. S. Tenney. Corrections and Additions to 'A Non-linear Equilibrium Model of the Term Structure of Interest Rates'. *Journal of Financial Economics*, 32:345–354, 1992.

[59] B. Bekdache and C. F. Baum. Comparing Alternative Models of the Term Structure of Interest Rates. *Working Paper, Boston College*, 271:1–41, 1994.

[60] H. Beladi, M. A. S. Choudhary, and A. K. Parai. Rational and Adaptive Expectations in the Present Value Model of Hyperinflation. *Review of Economics and Statistics*, 75:511–514, 1993.

[61] M. T. Belongia and J. A. Chalfant. Alternative Measures of Money as Indicators of Inflation: A Survey and Some New Evidence. *Federal Reserve Bank of St. Louise, Review*, 72/6:20–33, 1990.

[62] E. Berndt, B. Hall, R. Hall, and J. Hausman. Estimation and Inference in Nonlinear Structural Models. *Annals of Economic and Social Measurement*, 3:653–665, 1974.

[63] C. M. Bishop. *Neutral Networks for Pattern Recognition*. Clarendon Press, Oxford, 1995.

[64] T. Bjork. On the Term Structure of Discontinuous Interest Rates. *Working Paper, Royal Institute of Technology, Stockholm*, pages 1–44, n.d.

[65] T. Bjork. Interest Rate Theory—CIME Lectures 1996. *Working Paper, Stockholm School of Economics*, pages 1–90, 1996.

[66] T. Bjork. *Arbitrage Theory in Continuous Time*. Oxford University Press, 1998.

[67] T. Bjork and B. J. Christensen. Interest Rate Dynamics and Consistent Forward Rate Curves. *Working Paper, University of Aarhus*, pages 1–38, 1997.

[68] T. Bjork and B. J. Christensen. Interest Rate Dynamics and Consistent Forward Rate Curves. *Working Paper, CAF, University of Aarhus*, pages 1–31, 1999.

[69] T. Bjork, Y. Kabanov, and W. Runggaldier. Bond Markets where Prices are Driven by a General Marked Point Process. *Working Paper, Stockholm School of Economics*, pages 1–63, 1995.

[70] T. Bjork, Y. Kabanov, and W. Runggaldier. Bond Market Structure in the Presence of Marked Point Processes. *Mathematical Finance*, 7:211–239, 1997.

[71] T. Bjork, G. D. Masi, Y. Kabanov, and W. Runggaldier. Towards a General Theory of bond markets. *Working Paper, Stockholm School of Economics*, pages 1–33, 1996.

[72] F. Black. Interest Rates as Options. *Journal of Finance*, 50:1371–1376, 1995.

[73] F. Black, E. Derman, and W. Toy. A One-Factor Model of Interest Rates and its Application to Treasury Bond Options. *Financial Analysts Journal*, Jan-Feb:33–39, 1990.

[74] F. Black and P. Karasinski. Bond and Option Pricing When Short Rates are Lognormal. *Financial Analysts Journal*, July-Aug:52–59, 1991.

[75] O. J. Blanchard and S. Fischer. *Lectures on Macroeconomics*. MIT Press, 1989.

[76] R. Blattberg and N. Gonedes. A Comparison of the Stable and Student Distributions as Statistical Models for Stock Prices. *Journal of Business*, 47:244–280, 1974.

[77] R. R. Bliss. Testing Term Structure Estimation Methods. *Working Paper, Federal Reserve Bank of Atlanta, 96-12*, pages 1–30, 1996.

[78] R. R. Bliss and P. Ritchken. Empirical Tests of Two State-Variable HJM Models. *Working Paper, Federal Reserve Bank of Atlanta, 95-13*, pages 1–22, 1995.

[79] R. R. Bliss and D. C. Smith. The Elasticity of Interest Rate Volatility: Chan, Karolyi, Longstaff and Sanders Revisited. *Working Paper, Bank of England*, pages 1–25, 1998.

[80] T. Bollerslev. Generalised Autoregressive Conditional Heteroskedasticity. *Journal of Econometrics*, 31:307–327, 1986.

[81] R. M. Bookstaber and J. B. McDonald. A General Distribution for Describing Security Price Returns. *Journal of Business*, 60:401–424, 1987.

[82] J. Boudoukh and M. Richardson. Stock Returns and Inflation: A Long-Horizon Perspective. *American Economic Review*, 83:1346–1355, 1993.

[83] J. Boudoukh, M. Richardson, R. Stanton, and R. F. Whitelaw. The Stochastic Behavior of Interest Rates: Implications from a Multifactor, Nonlinear Continuous-Time Model. *Working Paper, Stern School of Business, New York University*, pages 1–45, 1998.

[84] P. P. Boyle. A Lattice Framework for Option Pricing with Two State Variables. *Journal of Financial and Quantitative Analysis*, 23:1–12, 1988.

[85] P. P. Boyle, M. Broadie, and P. Glasserman. Monte Carlo Methods for Security Pricing. *Journal of Economic Dynamics and Control*, 21:1267–1321, 1997.

[86] P. P. Boyle, J. Evnine, and S. Gibbs. Numerical Evaluation of Multivariate Contingent Claims. *Review of Financial Studies*, 2:241–250, 1989.

[87] P. P. Boyle and K. S. Tan. Quasi-Monte Carlo Methods. *Working Paper, University of Waterloo*, pages 1–23, 1997.

[88]   A. Brace, D. Gatarek, and M. Musiela. The Market Model of Interest Rate Dynamics. *Mathematical Finance*, 7:127–155, 1997.

[89]   M. W. Brandt and P. Santa-Clara. Simulated Likelihood Estimation of Multivariate Diffusions with an Application to Interest Rates and Exchange Rates with Stochastic Volatility. *Working Paper, The Wharton School, University of Pennsylvania*, 1999.

[90]   P. Bratley and L. F. Bennett. Algorithm 659 Implementing Sobol's Quasi-random Sequence Generator. *Working Paper, University of Montreal*, pages 88–100, 1988.

[91]   D. T. Breeden and R. Litzenberger. Prices of State-Contingent Claims Implicit in Option Prices. *Journal of Business*, 51:621–651, 1978.

[92]   M. J. Brennan and E. S. Schwartz. Finite Difference Methods and Jump Processes Arising in the Pricing of Contingent Claims: A Synthesis. *Journal of Financial and Quantitative Analysis*, 13:461–474, 1978.

[93]   M. J. Brennan and E. S. Schwartz. A Continuous Time Approach to the Pricing of Bonds. *Journal of Banking and Finance*, 3:133–155, 1979.

[94]   M. J. Brennan and E. S. Schwartz. Analyzing Convertible Bonds. *Journal of Financial and Quantitative Analysis*, 15-4:907–929, 1980.

[95]   M. J. Brennan and E. S. Schwartz. Alternative Methods for Valuing Debt Options. *Finance*, 4:119–137, 1983.

[96]   R. J. Brenner, R. H. Harjes, and K. F. Kroner. Another Look at Models of the Short-Term Interest Rate. *Journal of Financial and Quantitative Analysis*, 31-1:85–107, 1996.

[97]   R. J. Brenner and R. A. Jarrow. A Simple Formula for Options on Discount Bonds. *Advances in Futures and Options Research*, 6:45–51, 1993.

[98]   M. Broadie and J. Detemple. American Option Valuation: New Bounds, Approximations, and a Comparison of Existing Methods. *Review of Financial Studies*, 9:1211–1250, 1996.

[99]   M. Broadie and J. Detemple. Recent Advances in Numerical Methods for Pricing Derivative Securities. *In Numerical Methods in Finance*, eds Rogers and Talay, Cambridge University Press, pages 43–66, 1997.

[100] M. Broadie and P. Glasserman. Simulation for Option Pricing and Risk Management. *In Handbook of Risk Management*, ed. C. O. Alexander, Wiley, pages 1–20, 1997.

[101] R. Brotherton-Ratcliffe. Monto Carlo Motoring. *Risk*, 7–12, 1994.

[102] J. P. Broussard and G. G. Booth. The Behavior of Extreme Values in Germany's Stock Index Futures: An Application to Intra-daily Margin Setting. *European Journal of Operational Research*, 104:393–402, 1998.

[103] S. J. Brown and P. H. Dybvig. The Empirical Implications of the Cox, Ingersoll, Ross Theory of the Term Structure of Interest Rates. *Journal of Finance*, 41:617–632, 1986.

[104] R. H. Brown and S. M. Schaefer. Interest Rate Volatility and the Shape of the Term Structure. *Philosophical Transactions of the Royal Society of London A*, 347:563–576, 1994.

[105]   R. H. Brown and S. M. Schaefer. The Term Structure of Real Interest Rates and the Cox, Ingersoll and Ross Model. *Journal of Financial Economics*, 35:2–42, 1994.

[106]   L. Broze, O. Scaillet, and J-M. Zakoian. Testing for Continuous-Time Models of the Short-Term Interest Rate. *Working Paper, CEME*, 9313:1–28, 1993.

[107]   W. Buhler, M. Uhrig, U. Walter, and T. Weber. An Empirical Comparison of Alternative Models for Valuing Interest Rate Options. *Working Paper, University of Mannheim, WP 95-11*, pages 1–38, 1995.

[108]   J. B. Bullard. Samuelson's Model of Money with n-Period Lifetimes. *Federal Reserve Bank of St. Louise, Review*, 74/3:67–82, 1992.

[109]   J. B. Bullard. Measures of Money and the Quantity Theory. *Federal Reserve Bank of St. Louise, Review*, 76/1:19–30, 1994.

[110]   P. Cagan. International Evidence on the Cyclical Behavior of Inflation. In *The Monetary Dynamics of Hyperinflation in Studies in the Quantity Theory of Money*, ed. Friedman, University of Chicago Press, pages 205–212, 1956.

[111]   G. A. Calvo and C. A. Vegh. Disinflation and Interest-Bearing Money. *Economic Journal*, 106:1546–1563, 1996.

[112]   R. Cameron. *A Concise Economic History of the World*. Oxford University Press, 1989.

[113]   J. Y. Campbell, A. W. Lo, and C. MacKinlay. *The Econometrics of Financial Markets*, Princeton University Press, 1997.

[114]   J. Y. Campbell and R. J. Shiller. Yield Spreads and Interest Rate Movements: A Bird's Eye View. *Review of Economic Studies*, 58:495–514, 1991.

[115]   F. Canova and J. Marrinan. Reconciling the Term Structure of Interest Rates with the Consumption-Based ICAP Model. *Journal of Economic Dynamics and Control*, 20:709–750, 1996.

[116]   F. Capie. *Major Inflations in History*. Edward Elgar, 1991.

[117]   W. T. Carleton and I. A. Cooper. Estimation and Uses of the Term Structure of Interest Rates. *Journal of Finance*, 31:1067–1083, 1976.

[118]   P. Carr and G. Yang. Simulating Bermudan Interest Rate Derivatives. *Working Paper, Morgan Stanley*, pages 1–25, 1997.

[119]   P. Carr and G. Yang. Simulating American Bond Options in an HJM Framework. *Working Paper, Morgan Stanley*, 1–22, 1998.

[120]   A. P. Carverhill. When is the Short Rate Markovian? *Mathematical Finance*, 4:305–312, 1994.

[121]   A. P. Carverhill and K. Pang. Efficient and Flexible Bond Option Valuation in the Heath, Jarrow and Morton Framework. *Journal of Fixed Income*, pages 70–77, 1995.

[122]   A. P. Carverhill and C. Strickland. Money Market Term Structure Dynamics and Volatility Expectations. *FORC Options Conference, University of Warwick*, 1992.

[123]   D. R. Chambers, W. T. Carleton, and D. W. Waldman. A New Approach to Estimation of the Term Structure of Interest Rates. *Journal of Financial and Quantitative Analysis*, 19:233–252, 1984.

[124]   K. C. Chan, G. A. Karolyi, F. A. Longstaff, and A. B. Sanders. The Volatility of Short Term Interest Rates: An Empirical Comparison of Alternative Models of the Term Structure of Interest Rates. *Journal of Finance*, 47:1209–1227, 1992.

[125]   L. Chen. A Three-Factor Model of the Term Structure of Interest Rates. *Working Paper, Federal Reserve Board*, pages 1–39, 1995.

[126]   L. Chen. Interest Rate Dynamics, Derivatives Pricing, and Risk Management. Springer, LN in Economics and Mathematical Systems, 1996.

[127]   R-R. Chen and L. Scott. Pricing Interest Rate Options in a Two-Factor Cox–Ingersoll–Ross Model of the Term Structure. *Review of Financial Studies*, 5:613–636, 1992.

[128]   R-R. Chen and L. Scott. Maximum Likelihood Estimation for a Multifactor Equilibrium Model of the Term Structure of Interest Rates. *Journal of Fixed Income*, 3:14–31, 1993.

[129]   R-R. Chen and T. T. Yang. An Integrated Model for the Term and Volatility Structures of Interest Rates. *Working Paper, Rutgers University*, pages 1–35, 1996.

[130]   J. F. Chown. *A History of Money from AD 800*. Routledge, 1996.

[131]   M. Chu. The Random Yield Curve and Interest Rate Options. *Working Paper, Imperial College*, pages 1–23, 1996.

[132]   S. J. Clark. The Effects of Government Expenditure on the Term Structure of Interest Rates: A Comment. *Journal of Money, Credit, and Banking*, 17:397–400, 1985.

[133]   L. Clewlow. Finite Difference Techniques for One and Two Dimension Option Valuation Problems. *Working Paper, FORC preprint 90/10, University of Warwick*, 1990.

[134]   L. Clewlow and A. P. Carverhill. On the Simulation of Contingent Claims. *Journal of Derivatives*, 2:66–74, 1994.

[135]   L. Clewlow and A. P. Carverhill. On the Simulation of Contingent Claims. *Working Paper, FORC Preprint 95/56 University of Warwick*, 1995.

[136]   L. Clewlow and C. Strickland. Monte Carlo Valuation of Interest Rate Derivatives Under Stochastic Volatility. *Journal of Fixed Income*, 7:35–45, 1997.

[137]   L. Clewlow and C. Strickland. *Implementing Derivative Models*. Wiley, 1998.

[138]   T. G. Conley, L. P. Hansen, E. G. J. Luttmer, and J. A. Scheinkman. Short-Term Interest Rates as Subordinated Diffusions. *Review of Financial Studies*, 10:525–577, 1997.

[139]   G. M. Constantinides. A Theory of the Nominal Term Structure of Interest Rates. *Review of Financial Studies*, 5:531–552, 1992.

[140]   R. Cont. Beyond Implied Volatility: Extracting Information from Option Prices. *Econophysics: An Emerging Science*, eds, Kertesz and Kondor, Dordrecht, Kluwer, pages 1–26, 1998.

[141]   T. Cook and T. Hahn. Interest Rate Expectations and the Slope of the Money Market Yield Curve. *Federal Reserve Bank of Richmond Economic Review*, 76/5:3–26, 1990.

[142] C. J. Corrado and T. Su. Implied Volatility Skews and Stock Index Skewness and Kurtosis Implied by S&P 500 Index Option Prices. *Journal of Derivatives*, 4/4:8–19, 1997.

[143] C. J. Corrado and T. Su. Implied Volatility Skews and Stock Return Skewness and Kurtosis Implied by Stock Option Prices. *European Journal of Finance*, 3:73–85, 1997.

[144] G. Courtadon. A More Accurate Finite Difference Approximation for the Valuation of Options. *Journal of Financial and Quantitative Analysis*, 17:697–703, 1982.

[145] G. Courtadon. The Pricing of Options on Default Free Bonds. *Journal of Financial and Quantitative Analysis*, 17:75–100, 1982.

[146] S. Coutant, E. Jondeau, and M. Rockinger. Reading Interest Rate and Bond Futures Options' Smiles. *Working Paper, HEC*, pages 1–28, 1998.

[147] J. C. Cox, J. E. Ingersoll, and S. A. Ross. An Intertemporal General Equilibrium Model of Asset Prices. *Econometrica*, 53:363–384, 1985.

[148] J. C. Cox, J. E. Ingersoll, and S. A. Ross. A Theory of the Term Structure of Interest Rates. *Econometrica*, 53:385–407, 1985.

[149] J. C. Cox, S. A. Ross, and M. Rubinstein. Option Pricing: A Simplified Approach. *Journal of Financial Economics*, 7:229–264, 1979.

[150] A. Cukierman, S. Edwards, and G. Tabellini. Seigniorage and Political Instability, *American Economic Review*, 82:537–555, 1992.

[151] K. Cuthbertson. The Expectations Hypothesis of the Term Structure: The UK Interbank Market. *Economic Journal*, 106:578–592, 1996.

[152] H. Cutler, S. Davies, and M. Schmidt. The Demand for Nominal and Real Money Balances in a Large Macroeconomic System. *Southern Economic Journal*, 63:947–961, 1997.

[153] M. Dahlquist and L. E. O. Svensson. Estimating the Term Structure of Interest Rates for Monetary Policy Analysis. *Scandinavian Journal of Economics*, 98:163–183, 1996.

[154] Q. Dai and K. J. Singleton. Specification Analysis of Affine Term Structure Models. *Working Paper*, 1998.

[155] S. R. Das. A Direct Discrete-Time Approach to Poisson–Gaussian Bond Option Pricing in the Heath–Jarrow–Morton Model. *Working Paper, Harvard Business School*, pages 1–44, 1997.

[156] S. R. Das. Poisson–Gaussian Processes and the Bond Markets. *Working Paper, Harvard University*, pages 1–45, 1997.

[157] S. R. Das and S. Foresi. Exact Solutions for Bond and Option Prices with Systematic Jump Risk. *Review of Derivatives Research*, 1:1–24, 1996.

[158] R. Davidson and J. G. MacKinnon. *Estimation and Inference in Econometrics*. Oxford University Press, 1993.

[159] G. Davies. *A History of Money*. University of Wales Press, 1994.

[160] G. K. Davis and G. M. Pecquet. Interest Rates in the Civil War South. *Journal of Economic History*, 50:133–148, 1990.

[161] C. de Boor. *A Practical Guide to Splines*. Springer-Verlag, 1978.

[162] F. de Jong and P. Santa-Clara. The Dynamics of the Forward Interest Rate Curve: A Formulation with State Variables. *Journal of Financial and Quantitative Analysis*, 34:131–157, 1999.

[163] A. L. Dekker and L. de Hann. On the Estimation of the Extreme Value Index and Large Quantile Estimation. *Annals of Statistics*, 17:1795–1832, 1989.

[164] F. Delbaen. Consols in the CIR Model. *Mathematical Finance*, 3:125–134, 1993.

[165] R. Demmel. The Term Structure of Real Interest Rates and the Structural Impact of Fiscal Policy. *Working Paper, University of Saarland*, pages 1–40, 1998.

[166] E. Derman and I. Kani. Riding on a Smile. *Risk*, 7/2:32–37, 1994.

[167] E. Derman, I. Kani, and N. Chriss. Implied Trinomial Trees of the Volatility Smile. *Journal of Derivatives*, 3:7–22, 1996.

[168] P. Dierckx. *Curve and Surface Fitting with Splines*, Oxford Science Publications, 1995.

[169] H. Dillen. A Model of the Term Structure of Interest Rates in an Open Economy with Regime Shifts. *Journal of International Money and Finance*, 16:795–819, 1997.

[170] M. U. Dothan. On the Term Strucure of Interest Rates. *Journal of Financial Economics*, 6:59–69, 1978.

[171] M. U. Dothan. *Prices in Financial Markets*, Oxford University Press, 1990.

[172] M. Dotsey and C. Otrok. M2 and Monetary Policy: A Critical Review of the Recent Debate. *Federal Reserve Bank of Richmond Economic Quarterly*, 80/1:41–59, 1994.

[173] J. Douglas and J. E. Gunn. A General Formulation of Alternating Direction Methods. *Numerische Mathematik*, 6:428–453, 1964.

[174] J. Douglas and H. H. Rachford. On the Numerical Solution of Heat Conduction Problems in Two and Three Variables. *Transactions of the American Mathematical Society*, 82:421, 1956.

[175] L. Drake. Relative Prices in the UK Personal Sector Money Demand Function. *Economic Journal*, 106:1209–1226, 1996.

[176] J-C. Duan. A Unified Theory of Option Pricing Under Stochastic Volatility—From GARCH to Diffusion. *Working Paper, Hong Kong University of Science and Technology*, pages 1–15, 1996.

[177] J-C. Duan. Term Structure and Bond Pricing under GARCH. *Working Paper, Hong Kong University of Science and Technology*, 1–14, 1996.

[178] J-C. Duan. Augmented GARCH P,Q Process and its Diffusion Limit. *Journal of Econometrics*, 79:97–127, 1997.

[179] J-C. Duan and J-G. Simonato. Empirical Martingale Simulation for Asset Prices. *Working Paper, McGill University*, pages 1–17, 1995.

[180] J-C. Duan and J-G. Simonato. Estimating and Testing Exponential–Affine Term Structure Models by Kalman Filter. *Working Paper, McGill University*, pages 1–29, 1995.

[181] D. Duffie. *Dynamic Asset Pricing Theory*. Princeton University Press, 1992.

[182] D. Duffie and R. Kan. Multi-factor Term Structure Models. *Philosophical Transactions of the Royal Society of London A*, 347:577–586, 1994.

[183] D. Duffie and R. Kan. A Yield-Factor Model of Interest Rates. *Mathematical Finance*, 6:379–406, 1996.

[184] D. Duffie, J. Ma and J. Yong. Black's Consol Rate Conjecture. *Annals of Applied Probability*, 5:356–382, 1995.

[185] D. Duffie and J. Pan. An Overview of Value at Risk. *Journal of Derivatives*, 4/3:7–49, 1997.

[186] D. Duffie, J. Pan, and K. J. Singleton. Transform Analysis and Option Pricing for Affine Jump–Diffusions. *Working Paper, Stanford University*, pages 1–45, 1998.

[187] D. Duffie, M. Schoder, and C. Skiadas. A Term Structure Model with Preferences for the Timing Resolution of Uncertainty. *Economic Theory*, 9:3–22, 1997.

[188] D. Duffie and K. J. Singleton. Simulated Moments Estimation of Markov Models of Asset Prices. *Econometrica*, 61:929–952, 1993.

[189] D. Duffie and K. J. Singleton. An Econometric Model of the Term Structure of Interest Rate Swap Yields. *Working Paper, Stanford University*, pages 1–21, 1995.

[190] D. Duffie and K. J. Singleton. An Econometric Model of the Term Structure of Interest Rate Swap Yields. *Journal of Finance*, 52-4:1287–1321, 1997.

[191] B. Dupire. Pricing With a Smile. *Risk*, 7/1:18–20, 1994.

[192] B. Dupire and A. Savine. Dimension Reduction and other ways of Speeding Monte Carlo Simulation. *In Risk Handbook*, Risk Publications, pages 51–63, 1998.

[193] P. H. Dybvig. Bond and Bond Option Pricing Based on the Current Term Structure. *Working Paper, Washington University*, pages 1–21, 1989.

[194] P. H. Dybvig, J. E. Ingersoll, and S. A. Ross. Long Forward and Zero-Coupon Rates Can Never Fall. *Journal of Business*, 69:1–25, 1996.

[195] W. R. Easterly, P. Mauro, and K. Schmidt-Hebbel. Money Demand and Seigniorage-Maximising Inflation. *Journal of Money, Credit, and Banking*, 27:583–603, 1995.

[196] R. O. Edmister and D. B. Madan. Informational Content in Interest Rate Term Structures. *Review of Economics and Statistics*, 75:695–699, 1993.

[197] P. L. Edsparr. The Swedish Interest Rate Process—Estimation of the Cox, Ingersoll, and Ross Model. *Working Paper, Stockholm School of Economics*, 38:1–14, 1992.

[198] B. Eichengreen and I. W. McLean. The Supply of Gold under the Pre-1914 Gold Standard. *Economic History Review*, 47:288–309, 1994.

[199] P. Einzig. *Primitive Money*. Pergamon Press, 1966.

[200] L. El-Jahel, H. Lindberg, and W. Perraudin. Interest Rate Distributions, Yield Curve Modelling and Monetary Policy. *In Mathematics of Derivative Securities*, eds Dempster and Pliska, Cambridge University Press, pages 1–35, 1997.

[201] N. El-Karoui, A. Frachot, and H. Geman. A Note on the Behavior of Long Zero Coupon Rates in a No Arbitrage Framework. *Working Paper, CALFP*, 1996.

[202]   N. El-Karoui, R. Myneni, and R. Viswanathan. Arbitrage Pricing and Hedging of Interest Rate Claims with State Variables: II Applications. *Working Paper, University of Paris*, pages 1–19, 1992.

[203]   N. El-Karoui, R. Myneni, and R. Viswanathan. Arbitrage Pricing and Hedging of Interest Rate Claims with State Variables: Theory. *Working Paper, University of Paris*, pages 1–19, 1992.

[204]   S. Eller, A. R. Gallant, and J. Theiler. Detecting Nonlinearity and Chaos in Epidemic Data. *In Epidemic Models: Their Structure and Relation to Data*, ed. D. Mollison, Cambridge University Press, pages 54–78, 1995.

[205]   R. J. Elliott, P. Fischer, and E. Platen. Filtering and Parameter Estimation for a Mean Reverting Interest Rate Model. *Working Paper*, pages 1–20, 1997.

[206]   W. Enders. *Applied Econometric Time Series*, Wiley, 1995.

[207]   R. F. Engle. Autoregressive Conditional Heteroskedasticity with Estimates of the Variance of UK Inflation. *Econometrica*, 50:987–1008, 1982.

[208]   R. F. Engle and V. K. Ng. Time-Varying Volatility and the Dynamic Behavior of the Term Structure. *Journal of Money, Credit, and Banking*, 25:336–349, 1993.

[209]   T. Engsted. Cointegration and Cagan's Model of Hyperinflation Under Rational Expectations. *Journal of Money, Credit, and Banking*, 25:350–360, 1993.

[210]   T. Engsted. Does the Long Term Interest Rate Predict Future Inflation? A Multi-Country Analysis. *Working Paper, Aarhus University*, 1–17, 1993.

[211]   G. W. Evans and G. Ramey. Expectation Calculation and Macroeconomic Dynamics. *American Economic Review*, 82:207–224, 1992.

[212]   D. Feldman. European Options on Bond Futures: A Closed Form Solution. *Journal of Futures Markets*, 13:325–333, 1993.

[213]   M. Feldstein and J. H. Stock. Measuring Money Growth When Financial markets are Changing. *Journal of Monetary Economics*, 37:3–27, 1996.

[214]   N. Ferguson. Constraints and Room for Manoeuvre in the German Inflation of the Early 1920s. *Economic History Review*, 49:635–666, 1996.

[215]   R. Ferguson and S. Raymar. A Comparative Analysis of Several Popular Term Structure Estimation Models. *Journal of Fixed Income*, March:17–33, 1998.

[216]   S. Figlewski and B. Gao. The Adaptive Mesh Model: A New Approach to Efficient Option Pricing. *Journal of Financial Economics*, 53:313–351, 1999.

[217]   D. H. Fischer. *The Great Wave*. Oxford University Press, 1996.

[218]   I. Fisher. *The Rate of Interest*. Macmillan, 1907.

[219]   H. A. L. Fisher. *A History of Europe*. Eyre and Spottiswoode, 1935.

[220]   M. Fisher, D. Nychka, and D. Zervos. Fitting the Term Structure of Interest Rates with Smoothing Splines. *Working Paper, Federal Reserve Bank Finance and Economics Discussion paper, 95-1*, 1995.

[221]   B. Flesaker. Arbitrage Free Pricing of Interest Rate Futures and Forwards Contracts. *Journal of Futures Markets*, 13:77–91, 1993.

[222]   B. Flesaker. Testing the Heath–Jarrow–Morton/Ho–Lee Model of Interest Rate Contingent Claims Pricing. *Journal of Financial and Quantitative Analysis*, 28:483–495, 1993.

[223] B. Flesaker and L. P. Hughston. Positive Interest: Foreign Exchange. *Working Paper, Bear Stearns*, pages 1–26, 1996.

[224] B. Flesaker and L. P. Hughston. Positive Interest. *Risk*, 9/1:46–49, 1996.

[225] B. Flury. *Common Principal Components and Related Multivariate Models.* Wiley Series in Probability and Mathematical Statistics, 1988.

[226] G. Fong and O. Vasicek. Interest Rate Volatility as a Stochastic Factor. *Working Paper, Gifford Fong Associates*, 1991.

[227] P. A. Forsyth, K. R. Vetzal, and R. Zvan. A Finite Element Approach to the Pricing of Discrete Lookbacks with Stochastic Volatility. *Working Paper, University of Waterloo*, pages 1–20, 1997.

[228] A. Frachot, D. Janci, and V. Lacoste. Factor Analysis of the Term Structure: A Probabilistic Approach. *Working Paper, Banque de France*, NER No. 21:1–42, 1992.

[229] J. A. Frankel and C. S. Lown. An Indicator of Future Inflation Extracted from the Steepness of the Interest Rate Yield Curve along its Entire Length. *Quarterly Journal of Economics*, 109:517–530, 1994.

[230] B. M. Friedman and K. N. Kuttner. Money, Income, Prices, and Interest Rates. *American Economic Review*, 82:472–492, 1992.

[231] M. Friedman and A. J. Schwartz. *A Monetary History of the United States, 1868–1960.* Princeton University Press, 1963.

[232] J. C. Fuhrer. Monetary Policy Shifts and Long-Term Interest Rates. *Quarterly Journal of Economics*, 111:1183–1209, 1996.

[233] J. C. Fuhrer and B. F. Madigan. Monetary Policy when Interest Rates are Bounded at Zero. *Review of Economics and Statistics*, 79:573–585, 1997.

[234] J. C. Fuhrer and G. R. Moore. Forward-Looking Behavior and the Stability of a Conventional Monetary Policy Rule. *Journal of Money, Credit, and Banking*, 27:1060–1070, 1995.

[235] J. C. Fuhrer and G. R. Moore. Monetary Policy Trade-Offs and the Correlation Between Nominal Interest Rates and Real Output. *American Economic Review*, 85:219–239, 1995.

[236] K. Fukao and R. Benabou. History Versus Expectations: A Comment. *Quarterly Journal of Economics*, 108:535–542, 1993.

[237] J. Gali. How Well Does the IS–LM Model Fit Postwar U.S. Data? *Quarterly Journal of Economics*, 107:709–738, 1992.

[238] A. R. Gallant and J. R. Long. Estimating Stochastic Differential Equations Efficiently by Minimum Chi-Squared. *Biometrika*, 84:125–141, 1997.

[239] A. R. Gallant and G. Tauchen. Specification Analysis of Continuous Time Models in Finance. *Working Paper, Dept of Economics, University of North Carolina*, 1995.

[240] A. R. Gallant and G. Tauchen. Which Moments to Match? *Econometric Theory*, 12:657–681, 1996.

[241] S. K. Gandhi and P. Hunt. Numerical Option Pricing using Conditioned Diffusions. *Mathematics of Derivative Securities*, eds. M. A. H. Dempster and S. R. Pliska, pages 457–472, CUP, 1997.

[242] J. R. Garrett. Monetary Policy and Expectations: Market-Control Techniques and the Bank of England, 1925–1931. *Journal of Economic History*, 55:612–636, 1995.

[243] H. Geman. The Importance of the Forward Neutral Probability in a Stochastic Approach to Interest Rates. *Working Paper, ESSEC*, 1989.

[244] H. Geman, N. El-Karoui, and J. C. Rochet. Changes of Numeraire, Changes of Probability Measure and Pricing Option. *Journal of Applied Probability*, 32:443–458, 1995.

[245] S. Gerlach and F. Smets. The Term Structure of Euro-Rates: Some Evidence in Support of the Expectations Hypothesis. *Journal of International Money and Finance*, 16:305–321, 1997.

[246] J. A. Gherity. Interest-Bearing Currency: Evidence from the Civil War Experience, A Note. *Journal of Money, Credit, and Banking*, 25:125–131, 1993.

[247] M. R. Gibbons and K. Ramaswamy. A Test of the Cox, Ingersoll, and Ross Model of the Term Structure. *Review of Financial Studies*, 6:619–658, 1993.

[248] R. A. J. Gibson, A. B. Sim, and D. C. Thurston. Empirical Comparisons of One-Factor Heath–Jarrow–Morton Term Structure Models. *Working Paper, University of New South Wales*, 79:1–19, 1995.

[249] P. Glasserman and X. Zhao. Arbitrage-free Discretisation of Lognormal Forward Libor and Swap Rate Models. *Working Paper, Columbia Business School*, pages 1–33, 1998.

[250] D. H. Goldenberg. A Unified Method for Pricing Options on Diffusion Processes. *Journal of Financial Economics*, 29:3–34, 1991.

[251] D. Goldman, D. Heath, G. Kentwell, and E. Platen. Valuation of Two-Factor Term Structure Models. *Advances in Futures and Options Research*, 8:263–291, 1995.

[252] R. Goldstein. The Term Structure of Interest Rates as a Random Field. *Working Paper, Fisher College of Business, Ohio State University*, pages 1–28, 1997.

[253] R. Goldstein and P. Keirstead. On the Term Structure of Interest Rates in the Presence of Reflecting and Absorbing Barriers. *Working Paper, The Ohio State University*, 1997.

[254] J. A. Goldstone. Monetary Versus Velocity Interpretations of the 'Price Revolution': A Comment. *Journal of Economic History*, 51:176–181, 1991.

[255] J. A. Goldstone. The Causes of Long Waves in Early Modern Economic History. *Research in Economic History*, 6S:51–92, 1991.

[256] M. Goodfriend. Interest Rate Policy and the Inflation Scare Problem: 1979–1992. *Federal Reserve Bank of Richmond Economic Quarterly*, 79/1:1–24, 1993.

[257] C. Gourieroux and A. Monfort. *Simulation Based Econometric Methods*. Oxford University Press, 1996.

[258] C. Gourieroux and O. Scaillet. Estimation of the Term Structure from Bond Data. *Working Paper, CREST, no. 9415*, 1994.

[259] A. R. Gourlay. Hopscotch: A Fast Second-order Partial Differential Equation Solver. *Journal of the Institute of Mathematics and its Applications*, 6:375–391, 1970.

[260] A. R. Gourlay and S. McKee. The Construction of Hopscotch Methods of Parabolic and Elliptic Equations in Two Space Dimensions with a Mixed Derivative. *Journal of Computational and Applied Mathematics*, 3-3:201–206, 1977.

[261] E. L. Grinols and S. J. Turnovsky. Risk, the Financial Market, and Macroeconomic Equilibrium. *Journal of Economic Dynamics and Control*, 17:1–36, 1993.

[262] N. Groenewald, G. O'Rourke, and S. Thomas. Stock Returns and Inflation: A Macro Analysis. *Applied Financial Economics*, 7:127–136, 1997.

[263] A. Hadi and R. Ling. Some Cautionary Notes on the Use of PC Regression. *American Statisticians Association*, 52:15–19, 1998.

[264] R. W. Hafer and A. M. Kutan. More Evidence on the Money–Output Relationship. *Economic Inquiry*, 35:45–58, 1997.

[265] J. J. Hallman, R. D. Porter, and D. H. Small. Is the Price Level Tied to the M2 Monetary Aggregate in the Long Run? *American Economic Review*, 81:841–858, 1991.

[266] J. Hamilton. *Time Series Analysis*. Princeton University Press, 1994.

[267] L. P. Hansen. Large Sample Properties of Generalized Method of Moments Estimators. *Econometrica*, 50:1029–1055, 1982.

[268] L. P. Hansen and J. A. Scheinkman. Back to the Future: Generating Moment Implications for Continuous-Time Markov Processes. *Econometrica*, 63:767–804, 1995.

[269] J. M. Harrison and D. M. Kreps. Martingales and Arbitrage in Multiperiod Securities Markets. *Journal of Economic Theory*, 20:381–408, 1979.

[270] J. M. Harrison and S. R. Pliska. Martingales and Stochastic Integrals in the Theory of Continuous Trading. *Stochastic Processes and their Applications*, 11:215–260, 1981.

[271] J. M. Harrison and S. R. Pliska. A Stochastic Calculus Model of Continuous Trading: Complete Markets. *Stochastic Processes and their Applications*, 15:313–316, 1983.

[272] A. C. Harvey. *Forecasting, Structural Time Series Models and Kalman Filtering*. Cambridge University Press, 1989.

[273] S. Haykin. *Neural Networks*. Prentice Hall International. 1994.

[274] D. Heath, R. A. Jarrow, and A. J. Morton. Contingent Claim Valuation with a Random Evolution of Interest Rates. *Review of Futures Markets*, 9:55–76, 1990.

[275] D. Heath, R. A. Jarrow, and A. J. Morton. Bond Pricing and the Term Structure of Interest Rates: A New Methodology for Contingent Claims Valuation. *Econometrica*, 60:77–105, 1992.

[276] D. Heath, R. A. Jarrow, A. J. Morton, and M. Spindel. Easier Done than Said. *Risk*, 5:77–80, 1992.

[277] F. M. Heichelheim. *An Ancient Economic History*, A. W. Sijthoffs Uitgevers- maatschappij N.V., 1958.

[278] J. Hertz, A. Krogh, and R. G. Palmer. *Introduction to the Theory of Neural Computation, Santa Fe Institute Studies in the Sciences of Complexity*. Addison Wesley, 1991.

[279] S. L. Heston. Testing Continuous Time Models of the Term Structure of Interest Rates. *Working Paper, Carnegie Mellon University*, pages 1–27, 1988.

[280] T. S. Y. Ho and S-B. Lee. Term Structure Movements and Pricing Interest Rate Contingent Claims. *Journal of Finance*, 41:1011–1029, 1986.

[281] T. S. Ho, R. C. Stapleton, and M. G. Subrahmanyam. The Valuation of American Options in Stochastic Interest Rate Economies. *Working Paper, FORC, University of Warwick*, pages 1–35, 1991.

[282] J. D. Hoffman. *Numerical Methods for Engineers and Scientists*. McGraw-Hill, 1993.

[283] M. Hogan. Problems in Certain Two-Factor Term Structure Models. *Annals of Applied Probability*, 3:576–581, 1993.

[284] M. Hogan and K. Weintraub. The Log-normal Interest Rate Model and Eurodollar Futures. *Working Paper, Citibank, New York*, 1993.

[285] S. Homer and R. Sylla. *A History of Interest Rates*. Rutgers, 1991.

[286] P. Honore. Five Essays on Financial Econometrics in Continuous-Time Models. *PhD Thesis, Aarhus School of Business*, 1998.

[287] P. Howitt. Interest Rate and Nonconvergence to Rational Expectations. *Journal of Political Economy*, 100:776–800, 1992.

[288] L. P. Hughston. Stochastic Differential Geometry, Financial Modelling, and Arbitrage-Free Pricing. *Working Paper, Merrill Lynch*, 1–22, 1994.

[289] R. Huisman, K. G. Koedijk, C. J. M. Kool, and F. Palm. The Fat-Tailedness of FX Returns. *Working Paper, Limburg Institution, Maastricht University*, pages 1–31, 1998.

[290] J. C. Hull. *Options, Futures and Other Derivative Securities*. Prentice-Hall, 1999.

[291] J. C. Hull and A. D. White. The Use of the Control Variate Technique in Option Pricing. *Journal of Financial and Quantitative Analysis*, 23:237–251, 1988.

[292] J. C. Hull and A. D. White. Pricing Interest Rate Derivative Securities. *Review of Financial Studies*, 3-4:573–592, 1990.

[293] J. C. Hull and A. D. White. Valuing Derivative Securities Using the Explicit Finite Difference Method. *Journal of Financial and Quantitative Analysis*, 25:87–100, 1990.

[294] J. C. Hull and A. D. White. Bond Option Pricing Based on a Model for the Evolution of Bond Prices. *Advances in Futures and Options Research*, 6:1–13, 1993.

[295] J. C. Hull and A. D. White. One-Factor Interest-Rate Models and The Valuation of Interest-Rate Derivative Securities. *Journal of Financial and Quantitative Analysis*, 28:235–254, 1993.

[296] J. C. Hull and A. D. White. Numerical Procedures for Implementing Term Structure II: Two-factor Models. *Journal of Derivatives*, Winter:37–48, 1994.

[297] J. C. Hull and A. D. White. Numerical Procedures for Implementing Term Structure Models I: Single-factor Models. *Journal of Derivatives*, Fall:7–16, 1994.

[298] J. C. Hull and A. D. White. Using Hull–White Interest Rate Trees. *Journal of Derivatives*, pages 26–36, 1996.

[299] T. M. Humphrey. The Early History of the Real/Nominal Interest Rate Relationship. *Federal Reserve Bank of Richmond Economic Review*, 69/3:2–10, 1983.

[300] P. Hunt and J. Kennedy. Implied Interest Rate Pricing Models. *Finance and Stochastics*, 2:275–293, 1998.

[301] P. Hunt and J. Kennedy. Dynamic Term Structure Models. *Working Paper*, 1999.

[302] D. Husemoller. *Fibre Bundles*. Springer-Verlag, 1985.

[303] International Swap Dealers Association. 1991 ISDA Definitions. *1998 Supplement*, 1998.

[304] P. N. Ireland. Money and Growth: An Alternative Approach. *American Economic Review*, 84:47–65, 1994.

[305] P. N. Ireland. Long-Term Interest Rates and Inflation: A Fisherian Approach. *Federal Reserve Bank of Richmond Economic Quarterly*, 82/1:21–35, 1996.

[306] J. C. Jackwerth. Generalized Binomial Trees. *Journal of Derivatives*, 5:7–17, 1997.

[307] J. C. Jackwerth and M. Rubinstein. Recovering Probability Distributions from Option Prices. *Journal of Finance*, 51:1611–1632, 1996.

[308] F. Jamshidian. An Exact Bond Option Formula. *Journal of Finance*, 44:205–209, 1989.

[309] F. Jamshidian. Forward Induction and Construction of Yield Curve Diffusion Models. *Journal of Fixed Income*, 1:62–74, 1991.

[310] F. Jamshidian. A Simple Class of Square Root Interest Rate Models. *Applied Mathematical Finance*, 2:61–72, 1995.

[311] F. Jamshidian. Bond, Futures and Option Valuation in the Quadratic Interest Rate Model. *Applied Mathematical Finance*, 3:93–115, 1996.

[312] F. Jamshidian. Libor and Swap Market Models and Measures II. *Working paper, Sakura Global Capital*, pages 1–32, 1996.

[313] F. Jamshidian. Libor and Swap Market Models and Measures. *Finance and Stochastics*, 1:290–330, 1997.

[314] F. Jamshidian. Libor Market Model with Semimartingales. *Working Paper, NetAnalytic Limited*, pages 1–28, 1999.

[315] R. A. Jarrow. A Comparison of the Cox, Ingersoll, Ross and Heath, Jarrow, Morton Models of the Term Structure. *Working Paper, Cornell University*, pages 1–9, 1988.

[316] R. A. Jarrow and D. B. Madan. Option Pricing Using the Term Structure of Interest Rates to Hedge Systematic Discontinuities in Asset Returns. *Working Paper, Cornell University*, pages 1–47, 1991.

[317] R. A. Jarrow and A. Rudd. Approximate Option Valuation for Arbitrary Stochastic Processes. *Journal of Financial Economics*, 10:347–369, 1982.

[318] R. A. Jarrow and S. M. Turnbull. *Derivative Securities*. South-western, 1996.

[319] A. Jeffrey. Construction of a Single Factor Heath-Jarrow-Morton Term Structure Model. *Working Paper, University of New South Wales*. 67(94):1–34, 1994.

[320] A. Jeffrey. Single Factor Heath–Jarrow–Morton Term Structure Models based on Markov Spot Interest Rate Dynamics. *Journal of Financial and Quantitative Analysis*, 30:619–642, 1995.

[321] N. Jegadeesh and G. G. Pennacchi. The Behaviour of Interest Rates Implied by the Term Structure of Eurodollar Futures. *Journal of Money, Credit and Banking*, 28:426–446, 1996.

[322] X.-Q. Jiang and G. Kitagawa. A Time Varying Coefficient Vector AR Modeling of Nonstationary Covariance Time Series. *Signal Processing*, 33:315–331, 1992.

[323] Y. Jin and P. Glasserman. Equilibrium Positive Interest Rates. *Working Paper, Columbia Business School*, 1999.

[324] I. Jolliffe. *Principal Components Analysis*. Springer Series in Statistics, 1986.

[325] S. R. H. Jones. Devaluation and the Balance of Payments in Eleventh-Century England: An Exercise in Dark Age Economics. *Economic History Review*, 44:594–607, 1991.

[326] S. R. H. Jones. Transaction Costs, Institutional Change, and the Emergence of a Market Economy in Later Anglo-Saxon England. *Economic History Review*, 46:658–678, 1993.

[327] C. Joy, P. P. Boyle, and K. S. Tan. Quasi-Monte Carlo Methods in Numerical Finance. *Working Paper, University of Waterloo*, pages 1–34, 1994.

[328] B. Kamrad and P. Ritchken. Multinomial Approximating Models for Options with k State Variables. *Management Science*, 17:37–60, 1991.

[329] I. Karatzas and S. E. Shreve. *Brownian Motion and Stochastic Calculus*. Springer-Verlag, Graduate Texts in Mathematics 113, 1991.

[330] S. Karlin and H. M. Taylor. *A Second Course in Stochastic Processes*. Academic Press, 1981.

[331] D. P. Kennedy. The Term Structure of Interest Rates as a Gaussian Random Field. *Mathematical Finance*, 4:247–258, 1994.

[332] D. P. Kennedy. Characterizing and Filtering Gaussian Models of the Term Structure of Interest Rates. *Mathematical Finance*, 7:107–118, 1997.

[333] W. Kerr and R. G. King. Limits on Interest Rate Rules in the IS Model. *Federal Reserve Bank of Richmond Economic Quarterly*, 82/2:47–75, 1996.

[334] C. P. Kindleberger. The Economic Crisis of 1619 to 1623. *Journal of Economic History*, 51:149–175, 1991.

[335] G. Kitagawa. Non-Gaussian State-Space Modeling of Nonstationary Time Series. *Journal of the American Statistical Association*. 82-400:1032–1063, 1987.

[336] P. E. Kloeden and E. Platen. *Numerical Solution of Stochastic Differential Equations*. Springer, Applications of Mathematics, Stochastic Modelling and Applied Probability, 23, 1995.

[337] J. T. Klovland. Pitfalls in the Estimation of the Yield on British Consols, 1850-1914. *Journal of Economic History*, 54:164–187, 1994.

[338] P. J. Knez, R. Litterman, and J. A. Scheinkman. Explorations into Factors Explaining Money Market Returns. *Journal of Finance*, 49:1861–1882, 1994.

[339] K. G. Koedijk and C. J. M. Kool. Tail Estimates of East European Exchange Rates. *Journal of Business and Economic Statistics*, 10:83–96, 1992.

[340] K. G. Koedijk, M. M. A. Schafgans, and C. G. de Vries. The Tail Index of Exchange Rate Returns. *Journal of International Economics*, 29:93–108, 1990.

[341] P. Kofman and C. G. de Vries. Potato Futures Returns: A Tail Investigation. *Review of Futures Markets*, 8:244–258, 1989.

[342] P. Krugman. History Versus Expectations. *Quarterly Journal of Economics*, 106:651–667, 1991.

[343] C. H. Kuan and N. J. Webber. The Term Structure of Interest Rates and Economic Fundamentals: The Mexican Peso Crisis. *Working Paper, University of Warwick*, pages 1–16, 1997.

[344] C. H. Kuan and N. J. Webber. Valuing Interest Rate Derivatives Consistent with a Volatility Smile. *Working Paper, University of Warwick*, pages 1–30, 1998.

[345] P. Kugler. The Term Structure of Interest Rates and Regime Shifts: Some Empirical Evidence. *Economics Letters*, 50:121–126, 1996.

[346] O. Kurbanmuradov, K. Sabelfeld, and J. Schoenmakers. Lognormal Random Field Approximations to Libor Market Models. *Working Paper, Weierstrasse Institute, Berlin*, pages 1–16, 1999.

[347] R. Lagnado and S. Osher. A Technique for Calibrating Derivative Security Pricing Models: Numerical Solution of an Inverse Problem. *Journal of Computational Finance*, 1:13–25, 1997.

[348] R. Lagnado and S. Osher. Reconciling Differences. *Risk*, 10/4:79–83, 1997.

[349] T. C. Langetieg. A Multivariate Model of the Term Structure. *Journal of Finance*, 35:71–91, 1980.

[350] A. Levin. Recovering Implied Volatility and Distribution from American Futures Option Prices Using the Regularization Method. *Working Paper, Bank of Montreal*, pages 1–36, 1998.

[351] A. Li, P. Ritchken, and L. Sankarasubramanian. Lattice Methods for Pricing American Interest Rate Claims. *Journal of Finance*, 50:719–737, 1995.

[352] A. Li, P. Ritchken, and L. Sankarasubramanian. Lattice Works. *Risk*, 8, 1995.

[353] O. Linton, E. Mammen, J. Nielsen and C. Tanggaard. Estimating Yield Curves by Kernel Smoothing Methods. *Working Paper, Aarhus School of Business*, pages 1–43, 1998.

[354] R. Litterman and J. A. Scheinkman. Common Factors Affecting Bond Returns. *Working Paper, Goldman Sachs*, pages 1–16, 1988.

[355] R. Litterman and J. A. Scheinkman. Common Factors Affecting Bond Returns. *Journal of Fixed Income*, 1:54–61, 1991.

[356] A. W. Lo. Statistical Tests of Contingent Claims Asset Pricing Models. *Journal of Financial Economics*, 17:143–173, 1986.

[357] A. W. Lo. Maximum Likelihood Estimation of Generalized Ito Processes with Discretely Sampled Data. *Econometric Theory*, 4:231–247, 1988.

[358] F. M. Longin. The Asymptotic Distribution of Extreme Stock Market Returns. *Journal of Business*, 69:383–408, 1996.

[359] F. A. Longstaff. A Nonlinear Equilibrium Model of the Term Structure of Interest Rates. *Journal of Financial Economics*. 23:195–224, 1989.

[360] F. A. Longstaff. The Valuation of Options on Yields. *Journal of Financial Economics*, 26:97–121, 1990.

[361] F. A. Longstaff. Multiple Equilibria and Term Structure Models. *Journal of Financial Economics*, 32:333–344, 1992.

[362] F. A. Longstaff. Option Pricing and the Martingale Restriction. *Review of Financial Studies*, 8:1091–1124, 1995.

[363] F. A. Longstaff. Stochastic Volatility and Option Valuation: A Pricing Density Approach. *Working Paper, Anderson Graduate School of Management UCLA*, pages 1–27, 1995.

[364] F. A. Longstaff, P. Santa-Clara, and E. S. Schwartz. Throwing Away a Billion Dollars: The Cost of Suboptimal Exercise Strategies in the Swaptions Market. *Working Paper, Anderson Graduate School of Management UCLA*, pages 1–15, 1999.

[365] F. A. Longstaff and E. S. Schwartz. Interest Rate Volatility and the Term Structure: A Two-Factor General Equilibrium Model. *Journal of Finance*, 47:1259–1282, 1992.

[366] F. A. Longstaff and E. S. Schwartz. Valuing American Options by Simulation: A Simple Least Squares Aproach. *Working Paper, Anderson School, UCLA*, pages 1–29, 1998.

[367] R. E. Lucas. Asset Prices in an Exchange Economy. *Econometrica*, 46:1426–1446, 1978.

[368] R. E. Lucas. Liquidity and Interest Rates. *Journal of Economic Theory*, 50:237–264, 1990.

[369] F. T. Lui. Cagan's Hypothesis and the First Nationwide Inflation of Paper Money in World History. *Journal of Political Economy*, 91:1067–1074, 1983.

[370] J. Lund. Econometric Analysis of Continuous Time Arbitrage Free Models of the Term Structure of Interest Rates. *Working Paper, University of Aarhus*, 1997.

[371] J. Lund. Non Linear Kalman Filtering Techniques for Term Structure Models. *Working Paper, University of Aarhus*, pages 1–34, 1997.

[372] R. MacDonald and P. Macmillan. On the Expectations View of the Term Structure, Term Premia and the Survey-based Expectations. *Economic Journal*, 104:1070–1086, 1994.

[373] D. B. Madan and F. Milne. Contingent Claims Valued and Hedged by Pricing and Investing in a Basis. *Mathematical Finance*, 4:223–245, 1994.

[374] D. B. Madan, F. Milne, and H. Shefrin. The Multinomial Option Pricing Model and its Brownian and Poisson Limits. *Review of Financial Studies*, 4:251–266, 1989.

[375] G. S. Maddala. *Introduction to Econometrics*. Maxwell Macmillan, 1989.

[376] Y. Maghsoodi. Solution of the Extended CIR Term Structure and Bond Option Valuation. *Mathematical Finance*, 6:89–109, 1996.

[377] S. Makridakis, S. C. Wheelwright, and V. E. McGee. *Forecasting; Methods and Applications*. Wiley, 1983.

[378] A. Malz. Estimating the Probability Distribution of the Future Exchange Rate from Option Prices. *Journal of Derivatives*, 5:18–36, 1997.

[379] G. I. Marchuk. Splitting and Alternating Direction Methods. *In Handbook of Numerical Analysis*, vol. I, eds P. G. Ciarlet and J. L. Lions, North-Holland, pages 197–462, 1990.

[380] G. I. Marchuk and V. Shaidurov. *Difference Methods and Their Extrapolations*. Springer-Verlag, 1983.

[381] G. Marsaglia, A. Zaman, and J. Marsaglia. Rapid Evaluation of the Inverse of the Normal Distribution Function. *Statistics and Probability Letters*, 19:259–266, 1994.

[382] T. A. Marsh and E. R. Rosenfeld. Stochastic Processes for Interest Rates and Equilibrium Bond Prices. *Journal of Finance*, 38:635–647, 1983.

[383] N. J. Mayhew. Population, Money Supply, and the Velocity of Circulation in England, 1300–1700. *Economic History Review*, 48:238–257, 1995.

[384] S. Mayhew. On Estimating the Risk-Neutral Probability Distribution Implied by Option Prices. *Working Paper, Haas School of Business, UC Berkeley*, pages 1–16, 1995.

[385] S. Mayhew. Calculating Implied Parameters from Option Prices. *Working Paper, Haas School of Business, UC Berkeley*, pages 1–23, 1996.

[386] L. A. McCarthy and N. J. Webber. An Icosahedral Lattice Method for Three-Factor Models. *Working Paper, University of Warwick*, pages 1–45, 1999.

[387] J. H. McCulloch. Measuring the Term Structure of Interest Rates. *Journal of Business*, 44:19–31, 1971.

[388] J. H. McCulloch. The Tax Adjusted Yield Curve. *Journal of Finance*, 30:811–830, 1975.

[389] B. McKiernan. The Importance of Monetary Shocks: Evidence from Pre-Federal Reserve Data. *Economics Letters*, 45:69–71, 1994.

[390] W. R. Melick and C. P. Thomas. Recovering an Asset's Implied PDF from Option Prices: An Application to Crude Oil during the Gulf Crisis. *Journal of Financial and Quantitative Analysis*, 32:91–115, 1997.

[391] A. Melino and S. M. Turnbull. The Pricing of Foreign Currency Options. *Canadian Journal of Economics*, 24:251–281, 1991.

[392] F. Mercurio and J. M. Moraleda. A Family of Humped Volatility Structures. *Working Paper, Erasmus University, Rotterdam*, pages 1–23, 1996.

[393] R. C. Merton. Optimum Consumption and Portfolio Rules in a Continuous-time Model. *Journal of Economic theory*, 3:373–413, 1971.

[394] P. Mikkelsen. Pricing Interest Rate and Foreign Exchange Derivatives in a Consistent Libor Market. *Working Paper, Aarhus School of Business*, pages 1–37, 1999.

[395] M. H. Miller and L. Zhang. Hyperinflation and Stabilisation: Cagan Revisited. *Economic Journal*, 107:441–454, 1997.

[396] T. C. Mills. *Time Series Techniques for Economists*. Cambridge University Press, 1990.

[397] K. R. Miltersen. Pricing of Interest Rate Contingent Claims: Implementing the Simulation Approach. *Working Paper, Odense University*, pages 1–35, 1992.

[398] K. R. Miltersen. Pricing of Interest Rate Contingent Claims: Implementing a Simulation Approach. *Working Paper, Odense University*, pages 1–26, 1999.

[399] K. R. Miltersen, K. Sandmann, and D. Sondermann. Closed Form Solutions for Term Structure Derivatives with Log-normal Interest Rates. *Journal of Finance*, 52:409–430, 1997.

[400]   F. S. Mishkin. Is the Fisher Effect for Real? A Reexamination of the Relationship Between Inflation and Interest Rates. *Journal of Monetary Economics*, 30:195–215, 1992.

[401]   A. R. Mitchell and D. F. Griffiths. *The Finite Difference Method in Partial Differential Equations*. Wiley, 1980.

[402]   B. Moro. The Full Monte. *Risk*, 8:57–58, 1995.

[403]   A. J. Morton. Arbitrage and Martingales. *Working Paper, Cornell*, 1988.

[404]   K. W. Morton and D. F. Mayers. *Numerical Solution of Partial Differential Equations*. Cambridge Unversity Press, 1994.

[405]   A. Motomura. The Best and Worst of Currencies: Seigniorage and Currency Policy in Spain, 1597–1650. *Journal of Economic History*, 54:104–127, 1994.

[406]   M. Musiela. Nominal Annual Rates and Lognormal Volatility Structure. *Working Paper, University of New South Wales*, pages 1–8, 1994.

[407]   M. Musiela and M. Rutkowski. Continuous-time Term Structure Models: Forward Measure Approach. *Finance and Stochastics*, 1:261–291, 1997.

[408]   M. Musiela and M. Rutkowski. *Martingale Methods in Financial Modelling*. Springer, Applications of Mathematics, 36, 1997.

[409]   D. B. Nelson. ARCH Models as Diffusion Approximations. *Journal of Econometrics*, 45, 1990.

[410]   D. B. Nelson and K. Ramaswamy. Simple Binomial Processes as Diffusion Approximations in Financial Models. *Review of Financial Studies*, 3:393–430, 1990.

[411]   J. Nelson and S. M. Schaefer. The Dynamics of the Term Structure and Alternative Portfolio Immunization Strategies. *Innovations in Bond Portfolio Management: Duration Analysis and Immunization*, JAI Press, 41:61–101, 1983.

[412]   C. R. Nelson and A. F. Siegel. Parsimonious Modelling of Yield Curves. *Journal of Business*, 60:473–489, 1985.

[413]   M. J. M. Neumann. Seigniorage in the United States: How Much Does the U. S. Government Make from Money Production? *Federal Reserve Bank of St Louise, Review*, 74/2:29–40, 1992.

[414]   W. K. Newey and K. D. West. A Simple, Positive, Semi-definite, Heteroskedasticity and Autocorrelation Consistent Covariance Matrix. *Econometrica*, 55:703–708, 1987.

[415]   J. P. Nicolini. Ruling Out Speculative Hyperinflations: The Role of The Government. *Journal of Economic Dynamics and Control*, 20:791–809, 1996.

[416]   H. Niederreiter. *Random Number Generation and Quasi-Monte Carlo Methods, CBMS-NSF 63*, SIAM, 1992.

[417]   L. T. Nielsen and J. Saa-Requejo. Exchange Rates and Term Structure Dynamics and the Pricing of Derivative Securities. *Working Paper, INSEAD*, 1993.

[418]   S. C. Norrbin and K. L. Reffett. Trade Credit in a Monetary Economy. *Journal of Monetary Economics*, 35:413–430, 1995.

[419]   K. B. Nowman. Continuous Time Short Rate Interest Rate Models. *Working Paper, First National Bank of Chicago*, pages 1–20, 1997.

[420] K. B. Nowman. Gaussian Estimation of Single-Factor Continuous Time Models of the Term Structure of Interest Rates. *Journal of Finance*, 52-4:1695–1706, 1997.

[421] J. Nunes. Interest Rate Derivatives in a Duffie and Kan Model with Stochastic Volatility: Application of Green's Functions. *Working Paper, University of Warwick*, pages 1–46, 1998.

[422] J. Nunes and N. J. Webber. Low Dimensional Dynamics and the Stability of HJM Term Structure Models. *Working Paper, University of Warwick*, pages 1–27, 1997.

[423] M. Obstfeld and K. Rogoff. *Foundations of International Macroeconomics*. MIT Press, 1996.

[424] B. Øksendal. *Stochastic Differential Equations*. Springer-Verlag, 1995.

[425] K. Pang. Calibration of Kennedy and Multi-factor Gaussian HJM to Caps and Swaption Prices. *Working Paper, FORC 96/71, University of Warwick*, pages 1–50, 1996.

[426] K. Pang and S. Hodges. Non-negative Affine Yield Models of the Term Structure. *Working Paper, FORC 95/62, University of Warwick*, 1995.

[427] A. Papageorgiou and J. Traub. Beating Monte Carlo. *Risk*, 9:63–65, 1996.

[428] S. K. Park and K. W. Miller. *Communications of the ACM*, 31:1192–1201, 1988.

[429] S. H. Paskov. New Methodologies for Valuing Derivatives. *Working Paper, Columbia University*, pages 1–45, 1996.

[430] S. H. Paskov and J. Traub. Faster Valuation of Financial Derivatives. *Journal of Portfolio Management*, pages 113–120, 1995.

[431] D. W. Peaceman and H. H. Rachford. The Numerical Solution of Parabolic and Elliptic Differential Equations. *Journal of the Society of Industrial and Applied Mathematics*, 3:28–41, 1955.

[432] N. Pearson and T-S. Sun. An Empirical Examination of the Cox, Ingersoll and Ross Model of the Term Structure of Interest Rates using the Method of Maximum Likelihood. *Journal of Finance*, 54:929–959, 1994.

[433] A. R. Pedersen. A New Approach to Maximum Likelihood Estimation for Stochastic Differential Equations Based on Discrete Observations. *Scandinavian Journal of Statistics*, 22:55–71, 1995.

[434] M. B. Pedersen. Calibrating Libor Market Models. *Working Paper, SimCorp A/S, Copenhagen*, pages 1–26, 1998.

[435] M. B. Pedersen. Bermudan Swaptions in the Libor Market Model. *Working Paper, SimCorp A/S, Copenhagen*, pages 1–26, 1999.

[436] A. Pelsser. Efficient Methods for Valuing and Managing Interest Rate and Other Derivative Securities. *PhD Thesis, Erasmus University, Rotterdam*, 1996.

[437] G. G. Pennacchi. Identifying the Dynamics of Real Interest rates and Inflation: Evidence Using Survey Data. *Review of Financial Studies*, 4:53–86, 1991.

[438] E. H. Phelps Brown and S. V. Hopkins. Seven Centuries of the Prices of Consumables, Compared with Builders' Wages. *Economica*, 23:297–314, 1956.

[439] K. Phylaktis and M. P. Taylor. Money Demand, the Cagan Model and the Inflation Tax: Some Latin American Evidence. *Review of Economics and Statistics*, 75:32–37, 1993.

[440] I. Platten. Non Linear General Equilibrium Models of the Term Structure: Comments and Two-factor Generalization. *Working Paper, University of Notre Dame*, 1994.

[441] W. Press, S. Teukolsky, W. Vetterling, and B. Flannery. *Numerical Recipes in C*. Cambridge University Press, 1992.

[442] E. F. Prisman. A Unified Approach to Term Structure Estimation: A Methodology for Estimating the Term Structure in a Market with Frictions. *Journal of Financial and Quantitative Analysis*, 25:127–142, 1990.

[443] M. Pritsker. Nonparametric Density Estimation and Tests of Continuous Time Interest Rate Models. *The Review of Financial Studies*, 11, 1998.

[444] P. Protter. *Stochastic Integration and Differential Equations*. Springer-Verlag, 1990.

[445] S. Quinn. Gold, Silver, and the Glorious Revolution: Arbitrage Between Bills of Exchange and Bullion. *Economic History Review*, 49:473–490, 1996.

[446] S. Rady. Option Pricing in the Presence of Natural Boundaries and a Quadratic Diffusion Term with a Quadratic Diffusion Term. *Working Paper, LSE Financial Markets, WP 226*, pages 1–20, 1995.

[447] S. Rady. Option Pricing with a Quadratic Diffusion Term. *Finance and Stochastics*, 1:331–344, 1997.

[448] R. Rebonato. *Interest Rate Option Models*. 2nd edition, Wiley, 1998.

[449] A. Redish. The Evolution of the Gold Standard in England. *Journal of Economic History*, 50:789–805, 1991.

[450] A. Redish. The Persistence of Bimetallism in Nineteenth-Century France. *Economic History Review*, 48:717–736, 1995.

[451] J. Rhee. Interest Rate Models. *PhD thesis, University of Warwick*, 1999.

[452] S. F. Richard. An Arbitrage Model of the Term Structure of Interest Rates. *Journal of Financial Economics*, 6:33–57, 1978.

[453] P. Ritchken and L. Sankarasubramanian. On Markovian Representations of the Term Structure. *Working Paper, Federal Reserve Bank of Cleveland*, 9214:1–23, 1992.

[454] P. Ritchken and L. Sankarasubramanian. Volatility Structures of Forward Rates and the Dynamics of the Term Structure. *Mathematical Finance*, 5:55–72, 1995.

[455] J. A. Ritter. The Transition from Barter to Fiat Money. *American Economic Review*, 85:134–149, 1995.

[456] D. Robertson. Term Structure Forecasts of Inflation. *Economic Journal*, 102:1083–1093, 1992.

[457] L. C. G. Rogers. Which Model for the Term Structure of Interest Rates Should One Use? *Proceedings of the IMA Workshop on Mathematical Finance*, eds Duffie and Shreve: Springer-Verlag, pages 93–116, 1995.

[458] L. C. G. Rogers. The Potential Approach to the Term Structure of Interest Rates and Foreign Exchange Rates. *Mathematical Finance*, 7:157–176, 1997.

[459] L. C. G. Rogers and D. Williams. *Diffusions, Markov Processes and Martingales:* Vol. 2, *Ito Calculus.* Wiley, 1987.

[460] L. C. G. Rogers and O. Zane. Fitting Potential Models to Interest Rate and Foreign Exchange Data. In *Vasicek and Beyond*, Risk Publications, pages 328–342, 1998.

[461] H. L. Royden. *Real Analysis.* Macmillan, 1988.

[462] M. Rubinstein. Implied Binomial Trees. *Journal of Finance*, 49:771–818, 1994.

[463] M. Rubinstein. Edgeworth Binomial Trees. *Journal of Derivatives*, pages 20–27, 1998.

[464] G. D. Rudebusch. Federal Reserve Interest Rate Targeting, Rational Expectations, and the Term Structure. *Journal of Monetary Economics*, 35:245–274, 1995.

[465] S. Russell. The U. S. Currency System: A Historical Perspective. *Federal Reserve Bank of St. Louise, Review*, 73/5:34–61, 1991.

[466] M. Rutkowski. A Note on the Flesaker–Hughston Model of the Term Structure of Interest Rates. *Applied Mathematical Finance*, 4:151–163, 1997.

[467] M. Rutkowski. Spot, Forward, and Futures Libor Rates. *Working Paper, Institute of Mathematics, Warszawa*, pages 1–23, 1997.

[468] T. H. Rydberg. Existence of Unique Equivalent Martingale Measures in a Markovian Setting. *Working Paper, University of Aarhus*, pages 1–13, 1998.

[469] M. K. Salemi and T. J. Sargent. The Demand for Money During Hyperinflation Under Rational Expectations: II. *International Economic Review*, 20:741–758, 1979.

[470] K. Sandmann and D. Sondermann. A Term Structure Model and the Pricing of Interest Rate Derivatives. *Working Paper, University of Bonn*, pages 1–32, 1991.

[471] K. Sandmann and D. Sondermann. On the Stability of Lognormal Interest Rate Models. *Working Paper, University of Bonn*, B-263, 1994.

[472] P. Santa-Clara. Simulated Likelihood Estimation of Diffusion with an Application to the Short Term Interest Rate. *Working Paper, Anderson School of Management, UCLA*, 1995.

[473] T. J. Sargent. The Demand for Money During Hyperinflation Under Rational Expectations: I. *International Economic Review*, 18:59–82, 1977.

[474] T. J. Sargent and N. Wallace. Rational Expectations and the Dynamics of Hyperinflation. *International Economic Review*, 14:328–981, 1973.

[475] T. J. Sargent and N. Wallace. Rational Expectations, the Optimal Monetary Instrument, and the Optimal Money Supply Rule.*Journal of Political Economy*, 83:241–254, 1975.

[476] S. M. Schaefer. Measuring a Tax-Specific Term Structure of Interest Rates in the Market for British Government Securities. *The Economic Journal*, 91:415–438, 1981.

[477] S. M. Schaefer. Tax Induced Clientele Effects in the Market for British Government Securities. *Journal of Financial Economics*, 10:121–159, 1982.

[478]   S. M. Schaefer and E. S. Schwartz. A Two Factor Model of the Term Structure: An Approximate Analytical Solution. *Journal of Financial and Quantitative Analysis*, 19:413–424, 1984.

[479]   W. M. Schmidt. On a General Class of One-factor Models for the Term Structure of Interest Rates. *Finance and Stochastics*, 1:3–24, 1997.

[480]   N. Schnadt and J. Whittaker. Inflation-Proof Currency? The Feasibility of Variable Commodity Standards. *Journal of Money, Credit, and Banking*, 25:214–221, 1993.

[481]   A. J. Schwartz. Secular Price Change in Historical Perspective. *Journal of Money, Credit, and Banking*, 5:243–278, 1973.

[482]   D. W. Scott. *Multivariate Density Estimation: Theory, Practice and Visualization*, Wiley, 1992.

[483]   L. Scott. The Valuation of Interest Rate Derivatives in a Multifactor Term Structure Model with Deterministic Components. *Working Paper, University of Georgia*, pages 1–28, 1995.

[484]   L. Scott. Simulating a Multi-Factor Term Structure Model Over Relatively Long Discrete Time Periods. *Working Paper, Morgan Stanley*, pages 1–24, 1996.

[485]   M. J. P. Selby and C. Strickland. Computing the Fong and Vasicek Pure Discount Bond Price Formula. *Working Paper, FORC Preprint 93/42, University of Warwick*, 1993.

[486]   G. Selgin. On Ensuring the Acceptability of a New Fiat Money. *Journal of Money, Credit, and Banking*, 26:808–826, 1994.

[487]   G. S. Shea. Pitfalls in Smoothing Interest Rate Term Structure Data: Equilibrium Models and Spline Approximations. *Journal of Financial and Quantitative Analysis*, 19:253–269, 1984.

[488]   G. S. Shea. Interest Rate Term Structure Estimation with Exponential Splines: A Note. *Journal of Finance*, 40:319–325, 1985.

[489]   N. Shephard. Statistical Aspects of ARCH and Stochastic Volatility. *In Time Series Models in Econometrics, Finance and other fields*, eds Cox, Hinkley and Barndorff-Nielsen, pages 1–67, Chapman & Hall, 1996.

[490]   B. J. Sherrick, P. Garcia, and V. Tirupattur. Recovering Probabilistic Information from Option Markets: Tests of Distributional Assumptions. *Journal of Futures Markets*, 16:545–560, 1996.

[491]   D. C. Shimko. Bounds of Probability. *Risk*, 6/4:33–36, 1993.

[492]   H. Shirakawa. Interest Rate Option Pricing with Poisson–Gaussian Forward Rate Curve Processes. *Mathematical Finance*, 1:77–94, 1991.

[493]   A. F. Siegel and C. R. Nelson. Long Term Behaviour of Yield Curves. *Journal of Financial and Quantitative Analysis*, 23:105–110, 1988.

[494]   P. L. Siklos. Hyperinflations: Their Origins, Development and Termination. *Journal of Economic Surveys*, 4:225–248, 1990.

[495]   B. W. Silverman. *Density Estimation for Statistics and Data Analysis*, Chapman & Hall, 1986.

[496]   G. D. Smith. *Numerical Solution of Partial Differential Equations: Finite Difference Methods*, Oxford University Press, 1985.

[497] R. T. Smith. The Cyclical Behavior of Prices. *Journal of Money, Credit, and Banking*, 24:413–430, 1992.

[498] P. Soderlind and L. E. O. Svensson. New Techniques to Extract Market Expectations from Financial Instruments. *Working Paper, Stockholm University 1556*, 1996.

[499] M. Sola and J. Driffill. Testing the Term Structure of Interest Rates Using a Stationary Vector Autoregression with Regime Switching. *Journal of Economic Dynamics and Control*, pages 601–628, 1994.

[500] D. Sommer. Pricing and Hedging Contingent Claims in Term Structure Models with Exogenous Issuing of New Bonds. *Working Paper, University of Bonn*, 1996.

[501] C. Sørensen. Option Pricing in a Gaussian Two-Factor Model of the Term Strucure of Interest Rates. *Working Paper, Copenhagen Business School, WP-94-4*, 1994.

[502] R. Stanton. A Nonparametric Model of Term Structure Dynamics and the Market Price of Interest Rate Risk. *Journal of Finance*, 52, 1997.

[503] J. M. Steeley. Common Factors Affecting Gilt-Edged Securities. *Working Paper*, n.d.

[504] J. M. Steeley. Modelling the Dynamics of the Gilt-Edged Term Structure. *Working Paper, University of Warwick*, 1989.

[505] J. M. Steeley. Modelling the Dynamics of the Term Structure of Interest Rates. *The Economic and Social Review*, 21:337–361, 1990.

[506] J. M. Steeley. Estimating the Gilt-Edged Term Structure: Basis Splines and Confidence Intervals. *Journal of Business Finance and Accounting*, 18:513–530, 1991.

[507] R. M. Stulz. Interest Rates and Monetary Policy Uncertainty. *Journal of Monetary Economics*, 17:331–347, 1986.

[508] F. A. Sturzenegger. Hyperinflation with Currency Substitution: Introducing an Indexed Currency. *Journal of Money, Credit, and Banking*, 26:377–395, 1994.

[509] M. Stutzer. A Simple Nonparametric Approach to Derivative Security Valuation. *Journal of Finance*, 51:1633–1652, 1996.

[510] N. Sussman. Debasements, Royal Revenues, and Inflation in France During the Hundred Years' War, 1415–1422. *Journal of Economic History*, 53, 1993.

[511] L. E. O. Svensson. Estimating and Interpreting Forward Interest Rates: Sweden 1992–94. *Working paper, International Monetary Fund, 114*, 1994.

[512] E. W. Tallman. Inflation: How Long Has This Been Going On?. *Federal Reserve Bank of Atlanta Economic Review*, 78/6, 1993.

[513] E. W. Tallman. Inflation and Inflation Forecasting: An Introduction. *Federal Reserve Bank of Atlanta Economic Review*, 80/1:13–27, 1995.

[514] Y. Tang and J. Lange. Non-exploding Bushy Tree Technique and its Applications to the Multi-factor Interest Rate Market Model. *Working Paper, Rubicon Financial Systems*, pages 1–16, 1999.

[515] C. Tanggaard. Kernel Smoothing of Discount Functions. *Working Paper, Aarhus School of Business*, 21:1–10, 1992.

[516] C. Tanggaard. Nonparametric Smoothing of Yield Curves. *Working Paper, Aarhus School of Business, D 95-1*, 1995.

[517] H. Tanizaki and R. S. Mariano. Prediction, Filtering and Smoothing in Non-Linear and Non-Normal Cases Using Monte Carlo Integration. *Econometric Inference using Simulation Techniques*, 1995.

[518] M. P. Taylor. The Hyperinflation Model of Money Demand Revisited. *Journal of Money, Credit, and Banking*, 23:327–351, 1991.

[519] M. P. Taylor. Modelling the Yield Curve. *Economic Journal*, 102:524–537, 1992.

[520] M. P. Taylor. Modeling the Demand for U. K. Broad Money 1871-1913. *Review of Economics and Statistics*, 75:112–117, 1993.

[521] C. F. Thies. Interest Rates and Expected Inflation, 1831–1914: A Rational Expectations Approach. *Southern Economic Journal*, 51, 1985.

[522] J. Tice. Interest Rate Models. *PhD Thesis, University of Warwick*, 1998.

[523] J. Tice and N. J. Webber. A Non-Linear Model of the Term Structure of Interest Rates. *Mathematical Finance*, 7, 1997.

[524] M. Toma. Interest Rate Controls: The United States in the 1940s. *Journal of Economic History*, 52:631–650, 1992.

[525] A. H. Tsoi, H. Yang, and S-N. Yeung. European Option Pricing When the Riskfree Interest Rate Follows a Jump Process. *Working Paper, Hong Kong University of Science and Technology*, 1998.

[526] S. J. Turnovsky. *Methods of Macroeconomic Dynamics*. MIT Press, 1995.

[527] S. J. Turnovsky and M. H. Miller. The Effects of Government Expenditure on the Term Structure of Interest Rates. *Journal of Money, Credit, and Banking*, 16:16–33, 1984.

[528] M. Uhrig and U. Walter. A New Numerical Approach for Fitting the Initial Yield Curve. *Working Paper, University of Mannheim*, 1995.

[529] O. Vasicek. An Equilibrium Characterization of the Term Structure. *Journal of Financial Economics*, 5:177–188, 1977.

[530] O. Vasicek and G. Fong. Term Structure Modelling Using Exponential Splines. *Journal of Finance*, 37:339–348, 1982.

[531] A. Velasco. Real Interest rates and Government Debt During Stabilization. *Journal of Money, Credit, and Banking*, 25:259–272, 1993.

[532] M. Verhaegen and P. Van Dooren. Numerical Aspects of Different Kalman Filter Implementations. *IEEE Transactions on Automatic Control, AC*, 31, 1986.

[533] K. R. Vetzal. Stochastic Volatility Movements in Short Term Interest Rates, and Bond Option Values. *Journal of Banking and Finance*, 21:169–196, 1997.

[534] K. R. Vetzal. An Improved Finite Difference Approach to Fitting the Initial Term Structure. *Journal of Fixed Income*, March:62–81, 1998.

[535] R. von Glahn. Myth and Reality of China's Seventeenth-Century Monetary Crisis. *Journal of Economic History*, 56:429–454, 1996.

[536] D. F. Waggoner. Spline Methods for Extracting Interest Rate Curves from Coupon Bond Prices. *Working Paper, Federal Reserve Bank of Atlanta, 97-10*, 1997.

[537] M. P. Wand and M. C. Jones. *Kernel Smoothing*. Monographs on Statistics and Applied Probability 60, Chapman & Hall. 1995.

[538] N. J. Webber. The Consistency of Financial Models of Interest Rates with Evidence from Economic History, *Working Paper, University of Warwick*, 1997.

[539] D. Williams. *Probability with Martingales*. Cambridge University Press, 1991.

[540] J. Williams. *Money, A History*. ed J. Williams, British Museum Press, 1997.

[541] P. Wilmott. *Derivatives*. Wiley, 1999.

[542] P. Wilmott, S. Howison, and J. Dewynne. *The Mathematics of Financial Derivatives*, Cambridge, 1995.

[543] T. Wilson. Debunking the Myths. *Risk*, 7:67–73, 1994.

[544] J. Wiseman. The Exponential Yield Curve Model. *European Fixed Income Research, Technical Specification, JP Morgan*, 1994.

[545] J. Wolf. *Spaces of Constant Curvature*. Publish or Perish, 1984.

[546] C. C. Zheng. An Arbitrage-free SAINTS Model of Interest Rates. *Working Paper, First National Bank of Chicago*, 1993.

[547] R. Zvan, P. A. Forsyth and K. R. Vetzal. A General Finite Element Approach for PDE Option Pricing Models, *Working Paper, University of Waterloo*, pages 1–26, 1997.

Author Index

Subject Index